D. Justiniani Institutionum libri quatuor. = The four books of Justinian's Institutions, translated into English, with notes, by George Harris, LL.D.

Emperor of the East Justinian

D. Justiniani Institutionum libri quatuor. = The four books of Justinian's Institutions, translated into English, with notes, by George Harris, LL.D.
Justinian, Emperor of the East
ESTCID: N008181
Reproduction from British Library
In Latin and English; the final eleven pages of text, with the drop-head title 'Nov. CXVIII', also contain Greek. Each book has separate pagination.
London : printed for C. Bathurst and E. Withers, 1756.
xv,[1],73,[1];121,[1];100;92;11,[5]p.,plate ; 4°

Gale ECCO Print Editions

Relive history with *Eighteenth Century Collections Online*, now available in print for the independent historian and collector. This series includes the most significant English-language and foreign-language works printed in Great Britain during the eighteenth century, and is organized in seven different subject areas including literature and language; medicine, science, and technology; and religion and philosophy. The collection also includes thousands of important works from the Americas.

The eighteenth century has been called "The Age of Enlightenment." It was a period of rapid advance in print culture and publishing, in world exploration, and in the rapid growth of science and technology – all of which had a profound impact on the political and cultural landscape. At the end of the century the American Revolution, French Revolution and Industrial Revolution, perhaps three of the most significant events in modern history, set in motion developments that eventually dominated world political, economic, and social life.

In a groundbreaking effort, Gale initiated a revolution of its own: digitization of epic proportions to preserve these invaluable works in the largest online archive of its kind. Contributions from major world libraries constitute over 175,000 original printed works. Scanned images of the actual pages, rather than transcriptions, recreate the works ***as they first appeared.***

Now for the first time, these high-quality digital scans of original works are available via print-on-demand, making them readily accessible to libraries, students, independent scholars, and readers of all ages.

For our initial release we have created seven robust collections to form one the world's most comprehensive catalogs of 18th century works.

Initial Gale ECCO Print Editions collections include:

History and Geography
Rich in titles on English life and social history, this collection spans the world as it was known to eighteenth-century historians and explorers. Titles include a wealth of travel accounts and diaries, histories of nations from throughout the world, and maps and charts of a world that was still being discovered. Students of the War of American Independence will find fascinating accounts from the British side of conflict.

Social Science

Delve into what it was like to live during the eighteenth century by reading the first-hand accounts of everyday people, including city dwellers and farmers, businessmen and bankers, artisans and merchants, artists and their patrons, politicians and their constituents. Original texts make the American, French, and Industrial revolutions vividly contemporary.

Medicine, Science and Technology

Medical theory and practice of the 1700s developed rapidly, as is evidenced by the extensive collection, which includes descriptions of diseases, their conditions, and treatments. Books on science and technology, agriculture, military technology, natural philosophy, even cookbooks, are all contained here.

Literature and Language

Western literary study flows out of eighteenth-century works by Alexander Pope, Daniel Defoe, Henry Fielding, Frances Burney, Denis Diderot, Johann Gottfried Herder, Johann Wolfgang von Goethe, and others. Experience the birth of the modern novel, or compare the development of language using dictionaries and grammar discourses.

Religion and Philosophy

The Age of Enlightenment profoundly enriched religious and philosophical understanding and continues to influence present-day thinking. Works collected here include masterpieces by David Hume, Immanuel Kant, and Jean-Jacques Rousseau, as well as religious sermons and moral debates on the issues of the day, such as the slave trade. The Age of Reason saw conflict between Protestantism and Catholicism transformed into one between faith and logic -- a debate that continues in the twenty-first century.

Law and Reference

This collection reveals the history of English common law and Empire law in a vastly changing world of British expansion. Dominating the legal field is the *Commentaries of the Law of England* by Sir William Blackstone, which first appeared in 1765. Reference works such as almanacs and catalogues continue to educate us by revealing the day-to-day workings of society.

Fine Arts

The eighteenth-century fascination with Greek and Roman antiquity followed the systematic excavation of the ruins at Pompeii and Herculaneum in southern Italy; and after 1750 a neoclassical style dominated all artistic fields. The titles here trace developments in mostly English-language works on painting, sculpture, architecture, music, theater, and other disciplines. Instructional works on musical instruments, catalogs of art objects, comic operas, and more are also included.

D. JUSTINIANI INSTITUTIONUM LIBRI QUATUOR.

THE

FOUR BOOKS OF JUSTINIAN'S INSTITUTIONS,

Tranſlated into ENGLISH,

With NOTES,

BY

GEORGE HARRIS, LL. D.

LONDON,

Printed for C. BATHURST and E. WITHERS, in Fleet-Street.

MDCCLVI.

TO

THE RIGHT HONORABLE

Sir GEORGE LEE, Knt, LL. D.

Official Principal of the Arches Court of *Canterbury*;
Maſter, Keeper or Commiſſary of the Prerogative Court of *Canterbury*;
Dean or Commiſſary of the Deaneries of the Arches, *London*, *Shoreham*, and *Croydon*;
Treaſurer to her Royal Highneſs the Princeſs Dowager of WALES;
And one of his Majeſty's moſt honorable PRIVY COUNCIL.

SIR,

HAVING endeavored to give the true meaning of the original in the following verſion of *Juſtinian's* Inſtitutions, I venture, SIR,

to

to beg your protection of this work, declaring, that I aſk it not from any imagination, that the engliſh part is worthy of your patronage; but ſolely from a reliance upon your known diſpoſition to incourage every attempt, which carries an appearance of being uſeful. For I have not the vanity to think, that the tranſlation is perfect, or that the notes, altho' chiefly collected from authors of character, may not appear in ſome places redundant, and in others defective; and yet I affect not to ſay, but that I have uſed my utmoſt diligence: but, when the ſuggeſtions of friends and a greater experience ſhall have informed me of my miſtakes, it ſhall then be my endeavor to correct what is wrong and add what is wanting. And, as I have the honor to attend thoſe courts, in which you ſo eminently preſide, I may hope to avail myſelf of the many opportunities of inſtruction, which muſt continually offer themſelves;

ſelves; during my attendence upon a judge, who, whileſt he is diſtinguiſhed by genius and revered for impartiality, is remarkable for a ſuperior ſkill in the law, and the quickeſt as well as the cleareſt diſcernment in the moſt intricate points of evidence.

Theſe, SIR, are the qualifications, with which you adminiſter juſtice, and gain the daily admiration of the moſt experienced in the law. But the benefits, confered by you, are not confined to individuals; your conduct as a Lord Commiſſioner of the Admiralty, and the ſatisfaction it gave the public, are ſufficiently known. But the Senate, and that high board, his Majeſty's Privy Council, (to which your merits and your virtues, which I may juſtly call Hereditary, have moſt deſervedly ſummoned you,) afford a much larger ſcope for the exertion of great talents: nor

is

is Britain more indebted to you for aſſiſtence in her domeſtic councils, than in her foreign negotiations. Even * Pruſſia, by having made no public reply, has confeſſed the force of thoſe arguments, in which you had ſo large a ſhare; and I have the ſatisfaction to add, that the people in general know the worth of their Advocate and have a due ſenſe of his ſervices; which they attribute, with one common voice, to his knowledge as a Civilian, to his experience as a Senator, to his abilities as a Stateſman; but, above all, to his integrity in every ſtation, as a man of the ſtricteſt honor.

* See the Report, dated 18 Jan 1753, which was ſent in anſwer to Monſieur Michell's memorial, called *an Expoſition of the motives, which have determined the King of* Pruſſia *to lay an attachment upon the capital funds, which his* Pruſſian *Majeſty had promiſed to reimburſe to the ſubjects of Great* Britain, *in virtue of the Peace-treaties of* Breſlau *and* Dreſden; *and to procure to his ſubjects an indemnity for the loſſes, which they have ſuſtained by the depredations and violences of the* Engliſh *privateers.*

That

That you may therefore, Sir, long continue to adorn and ſupport that profeſſion, of which you are in every reſpect the chief; — that you may long enjoy thoſe honors, which your merit has obtained; — and that you may have health to execute the higheſt offices, which the future neceſſities of the ſtate may oblige you to accept;

are the ſincere and fervent wiſhes

of Your moſt obedient

and devoted ſervant,

Doctors Commons,
Feb. 25, 1756.

Geo. Harris.

ADVERTISEMENT.

THIS *translation of the* Institutions *of the civil law into* English *is principally intended, as an introduction to* Vinny's *Edition, and is published on a presumption, that most young persons are best acquainted with their own language; and that the Elements of a science can never be made too easy to the learner.*

As to the few notes, which are added to this version, they are chiefly relative to the law of England: *but the translator thinks it incumbent upon him to declare, that he does not print them from any opinion of his ability for such an undertaking, but merely thro' an humble hope, that, imperfect as they are, they may raise the curiosity of the young reader to search more deeply, and excite him to unite the study of the laws of his own country, (of which every* Englishman *ought to have a general knowledge,) with the study of the civil law, which is universally allowed to be the Master-work of human policy.*

A

BRIEF ACCOUNT

OF

The riſe and progreſs of the ROMAN LAW.

THE *Roman* ſtate was at firſt governed ſolely by the authority of *Romulus*; but, when the people were increaſed, he divided them into thirty *Curiæ*, which he conſtantly aſſembled for the confirmation of his laws: and this practice of conſulting the people was afterwards followed by the *Roman* kings, all whoſe laws were collected by *Sextus Papirius*, and called *Jus Papirianum*, from the name of their compiler. But, after the expulſion of *Tarquin* and the eſtabliſhment of the republic, the greateſt part of thoſe Regal laws ſoon became obſolete, and thoſe, which ſtill remained in force, related chiefly to the prieſthood. It thus happened, that the *Romans* for many years labored under great incertainty in reſpect to law in general, for, from the commencement of the conſular ſtate to the time of eſtabliſhing the XII tables, they were not governed by any regular ſyſtem. But at length, the people growing uneaſy at the arbitrary power of their magiſtrates, it was reſolved, after much oppoſition from the patricians, that ſome certain rule of government ſhould be fixed upon: and, to effect this purpoſe, a decemvirate was firſt appointed, compoſed ſolely of ſenators, who, partly from the laws of *Greece* and partly from their

Curiæ] vid *Pomponium*, ff 1 t. 2. *De origine juris*

Jus Papirianum] "Is liber appellatur "*jus civile Papirianum*, non quia *Papirius* "de ſuo quicquam adjecit, ſed quod leges "ſine ordine latas in unum compoſuit" vid ff 1 t. 2. l 2 This body of law is not now extant, nor any part of it, except a ſhort extract of 8 or 10 lines, which may be read in the 3d book of *Macrobius's Saturnalia*. cap 11

From the comm[illegible] of the conſular ſtate] The conſular ſtate was eſtabliſhed in the year U C 245, and the laws of the 12 tables were not perfected, till the year 304.

own laws ſtill ſubſiſting, framed x tables, which, in the year of *Rome* 303, were ſubmitted to the inſpection of the people, and highly approved of. Theſe however were ſtill thought to be deficient, and therefore in the year following, when a new decemvirate was appointed, which conſiſted of ſeven patricians and three plebeians, they added two tables to the former ten: and now the whole was regarded but as one body of law, and intituled, by way of eminence, the *twelve tables* But, altho' theſe new collected laws were moſt deſervedly in the higheſt eſteem, yet their number was ſoon found inſufficient to extend to all matters of controverſy, their conciſeneſs was often the occaſion of obſcurity, and their extraordinary ſeverity called aloud for mitigation. It therefore became a conſequence, that the twelve tables continually received ſome explanation, addition, or

Were ſubmitted to the inſpection of the people] "Tum legibus condendis opera "dabatur, ingentique hominum expectatio"ne propoſitis decem tabulis, populum ad "concionem advocaverunt et, quod bo"num, fauſtum, felixque reipublicæ, ipſis, "liberiſque eorum eſſet, ire et legere leges "propoſitas juſſere ſe, quantum decem "hominum ingeniis provideri potuerit, omni"bus, ſummis infimiſque, jura æquaſſe plus "pollere multorum ingenia conſiliaque "Verſarent in animis ſecum unamquamque "rem, agitarent deinde ſermonibus, atque "in medium, quid in quaque re plus, mi"nuſve eſſet, conferrent Fas leges habi"turum populum Romanum, quas conſen"ſus omnium non juſſiſſe latas magis, quam "tuliſſe, videri poſſet" *Liv* l 3 cap 33, 34.

And their extraordinary ſeverity] One of the laws, here hinted at, is the following, AST, SI PLURES ERUNT REI, TERTIIS NUNDINIS PARTIS SECANTO, SI PLUS MINUSVE SECUERINT, SE FRAUDE ESTO, SI VOLENT UIS TIBERIM PEREGRE VENUNDANTO *Grav op.* p 284 i e "If a debtor is inſolvent to ſeveral creditors, "let his body be *cut* in pieces on the third "market day It may be cut into more or "fewer pieces with impunity or, if his "creditors conſent to it, let him be ſold to "foreigners beyond the *Tyber*" *Hook's Roman hiſt* vol 1 p 316

Such is the ſenſe, in which this law has been generally underſtood by both antients and moderns But it has lately received quite a new conſtruction, very much to the honor of antient *Rome*, from two authors, not leſs diſtinguiſhed for their abilities in literature than their knowledge in the civil law, who from many authorities interpret the word *ſecanto*, as implying ſimply a diviſion, and the word *partis*, as denoting the parts of the debtor's eſtate, and not the parts of his body, ſo that they underſtand the expreſſion *partis ſecanto*, not as a direction, that the body of an inſolvent debtor ſhall be cut into pieces, but as if it meant. that his eſtate and ſervices ſhould be divided among his creditors in proportion to their reſpective claims vid. *Fyrkerſhoeck's* works, vol 1 obſ. 1 and Dr *Taylor's* commentary, *De inope debitore diſſecando*

But the reader is left to frame his own judgment of this interpretation, when he has read the apology for this law, which *Aulus Gellius* has given us in the perſon of *Cæcilius*, and alſo the opinion of *Tertullian*, who was a lawyer by profeſſion "Nihil profecto [fays *Cæcilius*] "immitius, nihil immanius, "niſi, ut re ipſa apparet, eo conſilio tanta "immanitas pœnæ denunciata eſt, ne ad "eam unquam perveniretur *addici* namque "nunc et *vinciri* multos videmus; *diſſectum* "eſſe antiquitus neminem, equidem neque "legi neque audivi" *Aulus Gell.* lib 20 cap 1 *Grav.* lib. 7 cap 72.

And *Tertullian* writes as follows "Sed "et, judicatos in partes ſecari a creditoribus, "leges erant, conſenſu tamen publico *cru*"*delitas* poſtea eraſa eſt" *Apologet* cap. 4.

alteration,

alteration, by virtue of a new *law*, a senatorial *decree*, or a *plebiscite*. And here it will be proper to observe, how they differ: a *plebiscite* was an ordinance of the plebeians or commonalty, which had the force of a law, without the authority of the senate; and a *senatus-consultum*, or senatorial decree, was an order made by the senators assembled for that purpose; but to constitute a *law*, properly so called, it was necessary, that it should first be proposed by some magistrate of the senate, and afterward be confirmed by the people in general. Recourse was also had to the interpretation and decisions of the learned, which were so universally approved of, that, altho' they were unwriten, they became a new species of law, and were called *Auctoritas Prudentum* and *Jus civile*. It must here be observed, that soon after the establishment of the twelve tables, the learned of that time composed certain solemn forms, called *Actions of law*, by which the process of all courts and several other acts, as adoption, emancipation, *&c.* were regulated. These forms were for above a century kept secret from the public, being in the hands only of the priests and magistrates; but about the year U. C. 448 they were collected and published by one *Flavius*, a scribe, and, from him, called the *Flavian law*, for which acceptable present the people in general shewed many instances of their gratitude. But, as this collection was soon found to be defective, another was afterwards published by *Sextus Ælius*, who made a large addition of many new forms, which passed under the title of *Jus Ælianum*, from the name of the compiler.

Solemn forms] "Civile jus, repositum "in penetralibus pontificum, Cn. Flavius evulgavit, fastosque circa forum in "albo proposuit, ut, quando lege agi posset, "sciretur." *Liv.* lib. 9 cap. 46. "Ve-"teres, [illegible] scientiæ [illegible] ob "[illegible] augendæ potentiæ suæ ca-"sa, [illegible] partem suam noluerunt, &c." *Ci*[illegible] lib. 1 c. 6. "Jus civile per "[illegible] inter sacra [illegible] deorum "[illegible] immortalium abditum, solisque "pontificibus notum." *Val. Max.* l. 2 c. 5. [illegible] t. 2 *de orig. juris.* *Liv.* lib. 9 sub fin. *Val. Max.* lib. 2 cap. 5. [illegible] lib. 6 c. 9.

Tully, in his oration [illegible], is remarkably severe upon these forms, and treats both them and their authors with that just contempt, which they most certainly deserve. "[illegible] "[illegible] Res [illegible] "[illegible] "[illegible], &c." *Pro Murena*, cap. [illegible] *L*[illegible] lib. 6. ep. 1 [illegible] lib. 1. [illegible] p. 4.

The *Flavian law*] "Postea, cum Ap-"pius Claudius proposuisset, et ad formam "redegisset, has actiones, Cneus Flavius "scriba ejus, libertini filius, surreptum li-"brum populo tradidit, et adeo gratum fuit "id munus populo, ut Tribunus plebis fieret "Senator, et Ædilis curulis, *&c.*" ff. 1

But, notwithstanding this, the use of [illegible] continued [illegible] till the reign of *Constantius* [illegible], who, to his great honour, put an end to these subtilties. His rescript to *Marcellinus* is in these words: "[illegible] aucupatione syl-"labarum insidiantes, cunctorum actibus "radicitus amputentur." Cod. 2. t. 58

 In

In proceſs of time there alſo aroſe another ſpecies of law, called the *Prætorian Edicts*, which, altho' they ordinarily expired with the annual office of the Prætor, who enacted them, and extended no farther than his juriſdiction, were yet of great force and authority: and many of them were ſo truly valuable for their juſtice and equity, that they have been perpetuated as *laws*.

Theſe were the ſeveral principal parts of the *Roman* law, during the free ſtate of the commonwealth, but, after the re-eſtabliſhment of monarchy in the perſon of *Auguſtus*, the law received two additional parts, the imperial *conſtitutions* and the *anſwers* of the lawyers

The conſtitutions ſoon became numerous, but were not framed into a body, till the reign of *Conſtantine* the great; when *Gregorius* and *Hermogenes*, both lawyers of eminence, collected in two codes the conſtitutions of the pagan emperors, from the reign of *Adrian* to that of *Diocleſian* incluſive. but theſe collections were not made by virtue of any public authority, and are not now extant.

Another code was afterwards publiſhed by order of the emperor *Theodoſius* the younger, which contained the conſtitutions of all the chriſtian emperors, down to his own time; and this was generally received both in the eaſtern and weſtern empires.

But theſe three codes were ſtill far from being perfect, for the conſtitutions, contained in them, were often found to be contradictory, and they wanted, but too plainly, that regulation, which they afterwards underwent through the care of *Juſtinian*, who in the year of Chriſt 528 ordered the compilation of a new Code, which was performed and publiſhed the year following by *Tribonian* and others; the three former codes being ſuppreſſed by the expreſs ordinance of the emperor. When

Gregorius and *Hermogenes*] vid *Gothofred* prolegom ad Cod *Theodoſianum*, cap 1 et *Heinecc* hiſt jur civ. lib 1 cap 5 ſect 363, &c

By the expreſs ordinance] "Hunc igitur "codicem in æternum valiturum judicio tui "culminis intimare perſpeximus, ut ſciant "omnes tam litigatores quam diſertiſſimi ad-"vocati, nullatenus eis licere de cætero con-"ſtitutiones ex veteribus tribus codicibus, vel "ex iis, quæ novellæ conſtitutiones ad præ-"ſens tempus vocabantur, in cognitionali-"bus recitare certaminibus, ſed ſolum, ei-"dem noſtro codici inſertis, conſtitutionibus "neceſſe eſt uti falſi crimini ſubdendis his, "qui contra hoc facere auſi fuerint, &c." *De Juſtinianeo codice confirmando.*

this work was thus expeditiouſly finiſhed, the emperor next extended his care to the Roman law in general, in order to render it both conciſe and perfect. The anſwers and other writings of the antient lawyers had long ſince acquired the full force of a *law*, and were now ſo numerous as to conſiſt of near two thouſand volumes; from which, by command of *Juſtinian*, the beſt and moſt equitable opinions were choſen; and, being firſt corrected, where correction was neceſſary, were afterwards divided into fifty books, called *Digeſts* or *Pandects*: and, that they might be the more firmly eſtabliſhed, the emperor not only prohibited the uſe of all other law-books, but alſo forbad, that any comment ſhould be writen upon theſe his new digeſted laws, or that any tranſcript ſhould be made of them with abbreviations. But, during the time of compiling the *Digeſts*, it was thought expedient by *Juſtinian*, for the benefit of ſtudents, that an abridgment ſhould be made of the whole Roman law; which work was ſoon performed in obedience to his order, and confirmed with the *Digeſts*, under the Title of *Inſtitutions*

Near two thouſand volumes.] "Poſtea "vero, maximum opus aggredientes, ipſa "vetuſtatis ſtudioſiſſima opera, jam pæne "confuſa et diſſoluta, eidem viro excelſo "(Triboniano) permiſimus tam colligere "quam certo moderamine tradere. Sed, "cum omnia percontabamur, a præfato viro "excelſo ſuggeſtum, duo pene millia libro-"rum eſſe conſcripta, quæ neceſſe eſſet "omnia et legere et perſcrutari: quod cœ-"leſti fulgore, et ſummæ trinitatis favore, "confectum eſt, ſecundum noſtra mandata, "quæ ab initio ad memoratum virum excel-"ſum fecimus, et in quinquaginta libros "omne, quod utiliſſimum erat, collectum "eſt, et omnes ambiguitates deciſæ, nullo "ſeditioſo relicto, nomenque libris impo-"ſuimus *Digeſtorum* ſeu *Pandectarum*." Cod. 1. t. 17. l. 2. *de vet. jur. enucl.*

Prohibited the uſe of all other law-books.] "Has itaque leges et adorate et obſervate, "omnibus antiquioribus quieſcentibus, ne-"moque veſtrum audeat vel comparare eas "prioribus, vel, ſi quid diſſonans in utro-"que eſt, requirere, quia omne, quod hic "poſitum eſt, hoc unicum et ſolum obſer-"vari cenſemus, nec in judicio nec in alio "certamine, ubi leges neceſſariæ ſunt, ex "aliis libris, niſi ab inſtitutionibus, noſtriſque "digeſtis, et conſtitutionibus a nobis com-"poſitis, aliquid vel recitare vel oſtendere "conetur, niſi temerator velit falſitatis cri-"mini ſubjectus una cum judice, qui eorum "audientiam patiatur, pœnis graviſſimis la-"borare." Cod. 1. t. 17. l. 2. ſec. 19. "Hoc autem tempeſtivum nobis videtur "et in præſenti ſancire, ut nemo neque "eorum, qui in præſenti juris peritiam ha-"bent, neque, qui poſtea fuerint, audeat "*commentarios* his legibus adnectere, niſi ve-"lit eas in Græcam vocem transformare "ſub eodem ordine eademque conſequen-"tia, ſub qua et voce Romana poſitæ ſunt, "hoc quod Græci κατὰ πόδα dicunt, &c." Cod. 1. t. 17. l. 2. § 21.

With abbreviations.] "Eandem autem "pœnam falſitatis conſtituimus et adverſus "eos, qui in poſterum leges noſtras, per "ſiglorum obſcuritates, auſi fuerint conſcri-"bere: omnia enim, id eſt, et nomina pru-"dentum, et titulos, et librorum numeros, "per conſequentias literarum volumus, non "per ſigla, manifeſtari." Cod. 1. t. 17. l. 2. § 22.

Confirmed with the *Digeſts*.] "Leges "autem noſtras, quæ in his codicibus, id "eſt, inſtitutionum ſeu elementorum et di-

The

The emperor afterwards, upon mature deliberation, suppressed the first edition of his Code, and published a second, which he intituled *Codex repetitæ prælectionis*, having omitted several useless laws, and inserted others, which were judged serviceable to the state.

The *Justinian*-law now consisted of three parts, the *Institutions*, the *Digest*, and the *second Code*. But the emperor, after the publication of the *second Code*, continued from time to time to enact diverse new constitutions or *Novels*, and also several *Edicts*, all which were collected after his decease, and became a fourth part of the law.

The 13 *Edicts* of *Justinian* and most of the *Novels* were originally conceived in the *Greek* Tongue, and so great was the decline of the *Roman* language at *Constantinople* within forty years after the death of this emperor, that his laws in general were not otherways intelligible to the major part of the people, than by the assistence of a *Greek* version: but, notwithstanding this disadvantage, they still subsisted intire, till the publication of the *Basilica*, by which the East was governed, til the dissolution of the empire.

" gestorum, posuimus, suum obtinere robur " ex tertio nostro felicissimo sanc imus con- " [illegible] præsentis duodecimæ indictionis, " ter [illegible] calendas januarias, in omne ævum " valiturum [illegible]." Cod 1. t 17 l 2. § 23

Suppressed the first edition of his code] " Nemini [illegible] rum concedimus, vel " ex decisionibus nostris, vel ex aliis con- " stitutionibus, quas antea fecimus, vel ex " prima Justinianei codicis editione, aliquid " recitare [illegible] renovato cod. [illegible] " [illegible] omnibus [illegible] et ju- " dicis et [illegible] cujus scrip- " turam [illegible] institu- " [illegible] et digestorum [illegible] " dubietate [illegible]." *Le Brun* " [illegible] sect 5

Basilica] " Versionibus juris Justinianei " Græcis, et novellis eadem [illegible] " in [illegible] donec, de " eo in compendium [illegible] " cogitare [illegible] imperatores Byzanti- " ni Ex his primus Basilius Macedo anno " 878 [illegible] quod con " stabit [illegible] Deinde Leo, " [illegible], patri Basilio succedens, collectionem " illam paternam perfecit, eamque sub titulo " [illegible] promulgavit, anno Christi " 886. Denique subsecutus Leonem Con- " stantinus, cognomento Porphyrogeneta, " paternum opus sub [illegible] revocavit, et " [illegible] publicavit sub initium " seculi decimi. Et hi quidem sunt libri " [illegible], ex Græca institutionum, " pandectarum, codicis, versione, Justinia- " [illegible] novellis et edictis tredecim, nec non ex " jurisconsultorum quorundam orientalium " [illegible] patribus " [illegible] ut multa " [illegible] " recesserint, multas etiam leges in com- " pendium contractas, multas denique ex " [illegible] principum legibus et consti- " tutionibus [illegible] Opus " illud in sexaginta libros divisum, præter " pauca, quæ [illegible] integra reperiri po- " tuerunt, cum glossis græce et latine edi- " tum est a *Car. Annib. Fabrotto*, Paris " 1647 [illegible] vol vii " vid *Heineccii hist.* [illegible] l 1 sect 405

The dissolution of the empire] *Constantinople* was taken by the *Turks*, and a period was put to the eastern empire in the year of Christ, 1453.

The laws publiſhed by *Juſtinian* were ſtill leſs ſucceſsful in the Weſt; where, even in the life-time of the emperor, they were not received univerſally; and, after the *Lombard* invaſion, they became ſo totally neglected, that both the *Code* and the *Pandects* were loſt, till the 12th Century, when it is ſaid, that the Pandects were accidently recovered at *Amalphi*, and the Code at *Ravenna*. But, as if fortune would make an attonement for her former ſeverity, they have ſince been the ſtudy of the wiſeſt men, and revered, as law, by the politeſt nations.

After the *Lombard* invaſion] The *Lombards* entered *Italy* under *Alboinus* about the year of Chriſt 568, in the reign of *Juſtin* the ſecond, ſucceſſor to *Juſtinian*.

At *Amalphi*] " Eo tempore (anno Dom 1130) " injuſtis perturbatiſque comitiis lacerarat eccleſiam falſus pontifex *Petrus* " *Leonis*, *Anacletus* ſecundus nuncupatus ab " ſua factione, cujus dux erat *Rogerius* Apuliæ ac Siciliæ comes, Regis nomine a falſo pontifice donatus Adverſus *Anacletum* creatus rite ac ſolenniter fuerat *Innocentius* ſecundus, cui favebat imperator " *Lotharius Saxo*, ſumma virtute atque prudentia princeps, quo bellum gerente adverſus *Rogerium*, *Amalphi*, urbe Salerno " proxima, (quam perperam aliqui locant in " *Apulia*, *Melphiam* cum *Amalphi* confundentes,) inopinato reperti fuerunt Digeſtorum libri, quos *Piſani*, qui claſſe *Lotharium* contra *Rogerium* adjuverant, præmio bene navatæ operæ ſibi exorarunt. " Piſis vero poſt longam obſidionem a *Capono* militiæ duce ſtrenuo expugnatis, " tranſlati fuere *Florentiam* ubi, pro Auguſta Mediceæ domus magnificentia, in " muſeo magni ducis conſervantur. Hinc " promiſcua Piſanarum et Florentinarum " apud ſcriptores pandectarum appellatio. " Iiſdem temporibus repertum *Ravennæ* fuit " conſtitutionum imperialium volumen, " quod *codex* appellatur indeque cæteros libros juris, imo et digeſtorum aliud exemplar in lucem aliqui rediiſſe putant nec " mirum, cum ea urbs longo tempore Romanis legibus vixerit, et orientali Romanorum imperio diu obtemperavit Novellæ vero conſtitutiones etiam antea per " Italiam vagabantur, utque mea fert opinio, multi juris civilis libri, poſtquam inceſſit homines cupido recipiendi Romani " juris, agniti potius fuere, quam reperti " nam, et aliquot ante *Lotharium* annis, jus " civile Juſtiniani commemoravit *Ivo* Carnotenſis, et libros pandectarum, cum antea, " ſi occurrerent, forſan ſocordia et oblivione " prætermitterentur " vid *Gravin de orig jur civ*. lib 1 cap 140. et *Hein hiſt jur. civ* lib 1. ſect 412

PROOEMIUM

DE

Confirmatione Institutionum.

In nomine Domini nostri JESU CHRISTI.

Imperator, Cæsar* FLAVIUS JUSTINIANUS, *Alemanicus, Gotthicus, Francicus, Germanicus, Anticus, Alanicus, Vandalicus, Africanus, Pius, Felix, Inclytus, Victor ac Triumphator, semper Augustus,* cupidæ legum juventuti *S. D.

De usu armorum et legum.

IMPERATORIAM majestatem non solum armis decoratam, sed etiam legibus oportet esse armatam, ut utrumque tempus et bellorum et pacis recte possit gubernari. et princeps Romanus non solum in hostilibus prælus victor existat, sed etiam per legitimos tramites calumniantium iniquitates expellat. et fiat tam juris religiosissimus, quam, victis hostibus, triumphator magnificus

The imperial dignity should be supported by arms, and guarded by laws, that the people, in time of peace as well as war, may be secured from dangers and rightly governed: for a Roman Emperor ought not only to be victorious over his enemies in the field, but should also take every legal course to clear the state from all those members, whose crafts and iniquities are subversive of the law. Be it the care therefore of him, upon whom government devolves, to be renowned for a most religious observance of law and justice, as well as for his triumphs.

De bellis et legibus Justiniani.

§ I. Quorum utramque viam cum summis vigiliis, summaque providentia, annuente Deo, perfecimus. Et bellicos quidem sudores nostros bar-

barica

baricæ gentes, ſub juga noſtra redactæ, cognoſcunt: et tam Africa, quam aliæ innumeratæ provinciæ, poſt tanta temporum ſpatia, noſtris victoriis a cœleſti numine præſtitis, iterum ditioni Romanæ noſtroque additæ imperio, proteſtantur. Omnes vero populi legibus tam a nobis promulgatis, quam compoſitis, reguntur.

§ 1. *By our inceſſant labors, and the aſſiſtence of divine providence, we have acquired the double fame of a lawgiver and a conqueror, for the barbarian nations have proved us in battle and ſubmitted to our yoke; even* Africa *and many other provinces, after ſo long an interval, are again added to the* Roman *empire: and yet this vaſt people, and our whole dominions, are governed either by laws enacted by ourſelves; or laws, which, tho' framed by others, have by our ſovereign authority been better regulated.*

Poſt tanta temporum ſpatia] *Africa* had then been 95 years in the poſſeſſion of the *Vandals*. *Cod.* 1 *t.* 27 *l.* 1 *de off. PP. Af.*

De compoſitione Codicis et Pandectarum.

§ II. Et cum ſacratiſſimas conſtitutiones, antea confuſas, in luculentam ereximus conſonantiam, tunc noſtram extendimus curam ad immenſa veteris prudentiæ volumina, et opus deſperatum, quaſi per medium profundum euntes, cœleſti favore jam adimplevimus.

§ 2. *When we had ranged the imperial conſtitutions in a regular order, and made thoſe, which were before confuſed and contradictory, to agree perfectly with each other, we then extended our care to the numerous volumes of the antient law, and have now completed, thro' the favor of heaven, a work, which exceeded even our hope, and was attended with the greateſt difficulties.*

De tempore, auctoritatibus, fine et utilitate compoſitionis Inſtitutionum.

§ III. Cumque hoc, Deo propitio, peractum eſt, Triboniano, viro magnifico, magiſtro, et exquæſtore ſacri palatii noſtri, et exconſule, nec non Theophilo et Dorotheo, viris illuſtribus, anteceſſoribus, (quorum omnium ſolertiam, et legum ſcientiam, et circa noſtras juſſiones fidem, jam ex multis rerum argumentis accepimus,) convocatis, mandavimus ſpecialiter, ut ipſi noſtra auctoritate, noſtriſque ſuaſionibus, Inſtitutiones componerent, ut liceat vobis prima legum cunabula non ab antiquis fabulis diſcere, ſed ab imperiali ſplendore appetere: et tam aures, quam animi veſtri, nihil inutile, nihilque perperam poſitum, ſed quod in ipſis rerum obtinet argumentis, accipiant. Et quod priore tempore vix poſt quatriennium prioribus contingebat, ut tunc conſtitutiones imperatorias legerent, hoc vos a primordio ingrediamini, digni tanto honore, tantaque reperti felicitate, ut et initium vobis, et finis legum eruditionis, a voce principali procedat.

§ 3. *As ſoon as this our undertaking was accompliſhed, we ſummoned* Tribonian, *our chancellor, with* Theophilus *and* Dorotheus, *men of known learning and tried fidelity, whom we injoined by our authority to compoſe the following Inſtitutions, to the intent, that the rudiments of law might be more effectually learned, by the ſole*

means

means of our imperial authority; and that your minds for the future should not be burdened with obsolete and unprofitable doctrines, but instructed only in those laws, which are allowed of and practised. And, whereas it was formerly necessary, that all students should go thro' a course of study, at least for the space of four years, preparatory to their reading the constitutions, they may now, (having been thought worthy of our princely care, to which they are indebted for the beginning and end of their studies,) apply themselves immediately to the imperial ordinances.

Nec non Theophilo] There is great reason to think, that the *Theophilus*, here mentioned, is the same *Theophilus*, who wrote the Greek paraphrase upon the Institutions. *vid. Heinec. Hist. Jur. lib* 1. *sect* 402.

Divisio Institutionum.

§ IV. Igitur post libros quinquaginta Digestorum, seu Pandectarum, (in quibus omne jus antiquum collectum est, quod per eundem virum excelsum Tribonianum, nec non cæteros viros illustres et facundissimos, confecimus,) in quatuor libros easdem Institutiones partiri jussimus, ut sint totius legitimæ scientiæ prima elementa.

§ 4. *When therefore, by the assistence of* Tribonian *and other illustrious persons, we had digested the whole antient law into fifty books, called* Digests *or* Pandects, *it was our pleasure, that the Institutions should be divided into four books, which might serve as the first elements, introductory to the science of the law.*

Quid in Institutionibus contineatur.

§ V. In quibus breviter expositum est, et quod antea obtinebat, et quod postea, desuetudine inumbratum, imperiali remedio illuminatum est

§ 5 *And, in these, we have briefly set forth the old laws, which formerly obtained, and those also, which for a time have lain dormant, but are now revived by our princely care*

Ex quibus libris compositæ sunt Institutiones, atque earum recognitio, et confirmatio.

§ VI Quas ex omnibus antiquorum Institutionibus, et præcipue ex commentariis Caii nostri, tam institutionum, quam rerum quotidianarum, aliisque multis commentariis compositas, cum tres viri prudentes prædicti nobis obtulerunt, et legimus, et recognovimus, et plenissimum nostrarum constitutionum robur eis accommodavimus.

§ 6. *The four books of our Institutions were compiled by* Tribonian, Theophilus, *and* Dorotheus, *from all the institutions of the antient law, but chiefly from the commentaries, institutions, and other writings of* Caius *And, as soon as these our Institutions were finished and presented to us, we read and diligently examined their contents, and, in testimony of our approbation, we have now given them a* constitutional *authority*

Adhortatio ad studium juris.

§ VII Summa itaque ope, et alacri studio, has leges nostras accipite et vosmetipsos sic eruditos ostendite, ut spes vos pulcherrima foveat, toto legitimo opere perfecto, posse etiam nostram rempublicam, in partibus ejus vobis credendis, gubernari.

D. CP. XI. Kalend. Decemb. *D.* JUSTINIANO *PP. A. III. COS.*

§ 7. *Receive therefore our laws, and so profit by them, that, when the course of your studies is completely finished, you may with reason expect to bear a part in the government, and be inabled to exercise those offices, which are committed to your charge.*

Given at *Constantinople* on the eleventh day before the calends of *december*, in the third consulate of the emperor JUSTINIAN, always august.

XI. Kalendas *decemb*] i. e on the 21st day of *november*, in the year of CHRIST, 533.

INSTI-

INSTITUTIONUM, SEU ELEMENTORUM, D. *JUSTINIANI* LIBER PRIMUS.

TITULUS PRIMUS.

De JUSTITIA et JURE.

D. 1. T. 1.

Definitio justitiæ.

JUSTITIA est constans et perpetua voluntas jus suum cuique tribuendi.

Justice is the constant and perpetual desire of giving to every man that, which is due to him.

Definitio jurisprudentiæ.

§ I Jurisprudentia est divinarum atque humanarum rerum notitia, justi atque injusti scientia.

§ 1. Jurisprudence is the knowledge of things divine and human, and the exact discernment of what is just and unjust.

De juris methodo.

§ II. His igitur generaliter cognitis, et incipientibus nobis exponere jura populi Romani, ita videntur posse tradi commodissime, si primo levi ac simplici via, post deinde diligentissima atque exactissima interpretatione, singula tradantur, alioqui, si statim ab initio rudem adhuc et infirmum animum studiosi multitudine ac varietate rerum oneraverimus, duorum alterum, aut desertorem studiorum efficiemus, aut cum magno labore, sæpe etiam cum diffidentia, (quæ plerumque juvenes avertit,) serius ad id perducemus.

perducemus, ad quod, leviore via ductus, ſine magno labore et ſine ulla diffidentia, maturius perduci potuiſſet.

§ 2. These definitions being premiſed, we ſhall now proceed. But it ſeems right to begin our Inſtitutions in the moſt plain and ſimple manner, altho' afterwards we intend to treat every particular with the utmoſt exactneſs: for, if at firſt we overload the mind of the ſtudent with a variety of things, we may cauſe him either wholly to abandon his ſtudies, or bring him late, thro' a ſeries of labors, to that knowledge, which he might otherwiſe have attained with eaſe and expedition

Juris præcepta.

§ III. Juris præcepta ſunt: honeſte vivere, alterum non lædere, ſuum cuique tribuere.

§ 3. The precepts of the law are theſe: to live honeſtly, not to hurt any man, and to give to every one that, which is his due.

De jure publico et privato.

§ IV. Hujus ſtudii duæ ſunt poſitiones, publicum et privatum. Publicum jus eſt, quod ad ſtatum rei Romanæ ſpectat. Privatum eſt, quod ad ſingulorum utilitatem pertinet Dicendum eſt igitur de jure privato, quod tripartitum eſt: collectum enim eſt ex naturalibus præceptis, aut gentium, aut civilibus.

§ 4. The law is divided into public and private. Public law regards the ſtate of the commonwealth but private law, of which we ſhall here treat, concerns the intereſt of individuals, and is tripartite, being collected from natural precepts, from the law of nations, and from the civil law of any particular city or ſtate.

TITULUS SECUNDUS.

De Jure naturali, gentium, et civili.

De jure naturali.

JUS naturale eſt, quod natura omnia animalia docuit: nam jus iſtud non humani generis proprium eſt, ſed omnium animalium, quæ in cœlo, quæ in terra, quæ in mari, naſcuntur. Hinc deſcendit maris atque fœminæ conjunctio, quam nos matrimonium appellamus Hinc liberorum procreatio, hinc educatio. Videmus enim, cætera quoque animalia iſtius juris peritia cenſeri.

The law of nature is not a law to man only, but likewiſe to all other animals, whether they are produced on the earth, in the air, or in the waters From hence proceeds the conjunction of male and female, which we among our own ſpecies ſtyle matrimony, from hence ariſes the procreation of children, and our care in bringing them up. We perceive alſo, that the reſt of the animal creation are regarded, as having a knowledge of this law, by which they are actuated

Cenſeri]

Censeri] Id est, æstimationi sive admirationi nobis esse, ut *Budæus* exponit [vid *Roberti Stephani* Thesaur et *Basilii Fabri* Thesaur. verb. *Censeor*] Sed *Theophilus* hunc locum ita vertit ἐφαμεν γαρ ὁ μονον ἀνθρωπυς, ἀλλα και τα λοιπα ζωα ἐν τοις τιμωσι τελον τον νομον αναγεγραμμενα. Quasi hic dictum sit, non hominem modo, sed cætera quoque animalia adscribi et referri sive recenseri inter ea, quæ naturæ legem observant, ejusque motu impelluntur *Mynsinger*

Distinctio juris gentium, et civilis, a definitione et etymologia.

§ I Jus autem civile a jure gentium distinguitur, quod omnes populi, qui legibus et moribus reguntur, partim suo proprio, partim communi omnium hominum, jure utuntur: nam, quod quisque populus sibi jus constituit, id ipsius proprium civitatis est, vocaturque jus civile, quasi jus proprium ipsius civitatis. Quod vero naturalis ratio inter omnes homines constituit, id apud omnes gentes peræque custoditur, vocaturque jus gentium, quasi quo jure omnes gentes utantur. Et populus itaque Romanus partim suo proprio, partim communi omnium hominum, jure utitur. Quæ singula, qualia sint, suis locis proponemus.

§ 1 *Civil law is distinguished from the law of nations, because every community uses partly its own particular laws, and partly the general laws, which are common to all mankind The law, which a people enacts for the government of itself, is called the civil law of that people But that law, which natural reason appoints for all mankind, is called the law of nations, because all nations make use of it. The people of* Rome *are governed partly by their own laws, and partly by the laws, which are common to all men But we propose to treat separately of these laws in their proper places.*

Ab appellatione et effectibus.

§ II. Sed jus quidem civile ex unaquaque civitate appellatur, veluti Atheniensium nam, si quis velit Solonis vel Draconis leges appellare jus civile Atheniensium, non erraverit. Sic enim et jus, quo Romanus populus utitur, jus civile Romanorum appellamus, vel jus Quiritium, quo Quirites utuntur Romani enim a Romulo, Quirites a Quirino, appellantur Sed, quoties non addimus nomen cujus sit civitatis, nostrum jus significamus: sicuti cum poetam dicimus, nec addimus nomen, subauditur apud Græcos egregius Homerus, apud nos Virgilius. Jus autem gentium omni humano generi commune est: nam, usu exigente et humanis necessitatibus, gentes humanæ jura quædam sibi constituerunt · bella etenim orta sunt, et captivitates secutæ, et servitutes, quæ sunt naturali juri contrariæ: jure enim naturali omnes homines ab initio liberi nascebantur Et ex hoc jure gentium omnes pene contractus introducti sunt, ut emptio et venditio, locatio et conductio, societas, depositum, mutuum, et alii innumerabiles.

§ 2 *All* civil *laws take their denomination from that city, in which they are established it would therefore not be erroneous to call the laws of* Solon *or* Draco *the civil laws of* Athens *And thus the law, which the* Roman *people make use of, is stiled the civil law of the* Romans, *or of the* Quirites, *for the* Romans *are also called* Quirites *from* Quirinus. *Whenever we mention the words* civil law, *without addition, we emphatically denote our own law; thus the* Greeks, *when they say* the poet, *mean* Homer, *and the* Romans Virgil. *The law of nations is common to mankind in general: and all nations have framed laws thro' human necessity, for wars arose, and the consequences were captivity and servitude, both which are contrary to the law of nature; for by that law all men are free. But almost all contracts were at first introduced by the law of nations; as for instance, buying, selling, letting, hireing, society, a deposit, a* mutuum, *and others, without number.*

Mutuum] The word *mutuum* denotes a contract, by which one man gives to another a thing, which consists in weight (as bullion) in number (as money) in measure (as wine) upon condition, that the donée shall return another thing of the same quantity, nature and value, upon demand This contract is not without its convenience, for lending without interest is in many cases a more useful charity, than an absolute gift vid *lib* 3 *Instit t.* 15

Divisio juris in scriptum et non scriptum; et subdivisio juris scripti.

§ III. Constat autem jus nostrum, quo utimur, aut scripto, aut sine scripto: ut apud Græcos των νομων ὁι μεν ἐγγραφοι, ὁι δε ἀγραφοι. Scriptum autem jus est lex, plebiscitum, senatus-consultum, principum placita, magistratuum edicta, responsa prudentum.

§ 3 *The* Roman *law is divided, like the* Grecian, *into written and unwritten. The written is sixfold, and comprehends the laws, the plebiscites, the decrees of the senate, the constitutions of princes, the edicts of magistrates, and the answers of the sages of the law.*

Constat autem] The laws of *England* are also divided into written, and unwritten The written laws consist of the statutes, which in their original formation are reduced into writing, and confirmed by the king, lords, and commons The unwritten laws include the common law, and all particular customs, they are called unwritten, because they had not their origin in writing, and have acquired their binding force by a long and immemorial usage But it must be observed, that the common law, altho' it was not originally conceived in writing, and is therefore properly defined to be *lex non scripta*, has nevertheless all it's monuments and memorials in writing, by which it is transfered with certainty from one age to another, and without which it would soon lose all kind of authority See *Hale's Hist of the Law*, cap 2

De lege et plebiscito.

§ IV. Lex est, quod populus Romanus, senatorio magistratu interrogante, (veluti consule,) constituebat Plebiscitum est, quod plebs, plebeio magistratu interrogante, (veluti tribuno,) constituebat. Plebs autem a populo eo differt, quo species a genere; nam appellatione populi universi cives significantur, connumeratis etiam patriciis et senatoribus. Plebis autem appellatione, sine patriciis et senatoribus, cæteri cives significantur. Sed et plebiscita, lege Hortensia lata, non minus valere, quam leges, cœperunt.

§ 4. *A law is what the* Roman *people enact at the request of a senatorial magistrate, as for instance, at the request of a consul A plebiscite is what the commonalty enact, when requested by a plebeian magistrate, as by a tribune. The word commonalty differs from people, as a species from it's genus, for all the citizens, including patricians and senators, are comprehended under the term people The term commonalty includes all the citizens, except patricians and senators The plebiscites, by the* Hortensian *law, began to have the same force, as the laws themselves*

Lege Hortensia lata] The law *Hortensia* was made by *Hortensius*, the dictator, in the year *U C* 467. But it appears to have been only decreed in confirmation of the law *Horatia*, which was enacted in the 304th year of *Rome*, when *Horatius* and *Valerius* were consuls.

De senatus-consulto.

§ V. Senatus-consultum est, quod senatus jubet atque constituit: nam, cum auctus esset populus Romanus in eum modum, ut difficile esset in unum eum convocari legis sanciendæ causa, æquum visum est, senatum vice populi consuli.

§ 5. *A senatorial decree is what the senate commands and appoints: for, when the people of* Rome *were increased to a degree, which made it difficult for them to assemble for the enacting of laws, it seemed but right, that the senate should be consulted instead of the whole body of the people.*

Cum auctus esset populus.] The *senatus-consulta* obtained the force of laws under the emperor *Tiberius*, who, pretending that the body of the people was too numerous to be assembled in one place, referred the whole legislative power of the commonalty to the senate

De constitutione.

§ VI. Sed et quod principi placuit, legis habet vigorem: cum lege regia, quæ de ejus imperio lata est, populus ei, et in eum, omne imperium suum et potestatem concedat. Quodcunque ergo imperator per epistolam constituit, vel cognoscens decrevit, vel edicto præcepit, legem esse constat. Hæc sunt, quæ constitutiones appellantur. Plane ex his quædam sunt personales, quæ nec ad exemplum trahuntur, quoniam non hoc princeps vult: nam quod alicui ob meritum indulsit, vel si quam pœnam irrogavit, vel si cui sine exemplo subvenit, personam non transgreditur. Aliæ autem, cum generales sint, omnes procul-dubio tenent.

§ 6. *The constitution of the prince hath also the force of a law; for the people by a law, called* lex regia, *make a concession to him of their whole power. Therefore whatever the emperor ordains by rescript, decree, or edict, it is a law. These acts are called constitutions. Of these, some are personal, and are not to be drawn into precedent; for, if the prince hath indulged any particular man upon account of his merit, or inflicted any extraordinary punishment on a criminal, or granted him some unprecedented indulgence, these acts extend not to others in the like circumstances. But other constitutions are general, and undoubtedly bind all people.*

Lege regia] There has been much controversy concerning this law; vid *Grav de Rom imp lib sing c* 24. *et Hopp in inst.* 1 *h t.* But the following seems at least to be a probable conjecture The senate and people conferred various honors upon *Augustus* at different times in the year of *Rome* 724, they made him tribune for life; in 727, they exempted him from the coercion of the laws, in 731, he was created perpetual consul, and, in the year 735, a power was given him either of amending or making whatever laws he thought proper. These and other decrees, made in favor of *Augustus*, were afterwards generally renewed at the commencement of the reign of every new emperor, as appears plainly from *Tacitus*, *tum senatus omnia principibus solita Vespasiano decrevit.* Tacit *hist* 11 3 Thus, in time, all the several decrees of the senate, by being frequently renewed together, became as it were one law, and were called *lex imperii*, or *regia*, and they probably gained this title in imitation of the antient *lex regia*, by which the first *Romans* conferred the supreme power upon *Romulus* in the infancy of their state *Liv lib* 34. c. 6. *Elementa jur per Robert Eden*, pag 17.

De jure honorario.

§ VII. Prætorum quoque edicta non modicam obtinent juris auctoritatem. Hoc etiam jus honorarium solemus appellare: quod, qui honores gerunt, (id est, magistratus,) auctoritatem huic juri dederunt. Proponebant et ædiles curules edictum de quibusdam causis; quod et ipsum juris honorarii portio est.

§ 7. *The edicts of the prætors are also of great authority. These edicts are called the honorary law, because those, who bear honors in the state, have given them their sanction. The curule ædiles also, upon certain occasions, published their edicts, which became a part of the* jus honorarium.

De responsis prudentum.

§ VIII. Responsa prudentum sunt sententiæ et opiniones eorum, quibus permissum erat de jure respondere: nam antiquitus constitutum erat, ut essent, qui jura publicè interpretarentur, quibus à Cæsare jus respondendi datum est, qui juris-consulti appellabantur: quorum omnium sententiæ et opiniones eam auctoritatem tenebant, ut judici recedere à responsis eorum non liceret, ut est constitutum.

§ 8. *The answers of the lawyers are the opinions of those, who were authorised to give their answers concerning matters of law. For antiently there were persons, who publicly interpreted the law, and to these the emperors gave a licence for that purpose. They were called* juris-consulti, *and their opinions obtained so great an authority, that it was not in the power of a judge to recede from them.*

Responsa prudentum] All those, whose particular application and abilities had rendered them learned in the law, undertook to give answers to all questions, which were proposed to them But these answers were of no weight in the time of the republic, nor even under *Augustus*, who impowered the lawyers to give their opinions by a general commission, which yet did not procure them any great authority *ff* 1. *t.* 2 *de orig jur* But their opinions afterwards grew into considerable credit in the reign of *Tiberius*, who prohibited any person from presuming to give an opinion in matters of law, without a special licence But still the answers of the lawyers had not the force of laws, for *Tiberius*, in his licences, laid not any injunction upon his judges to regard these answers. It is therefore highly probable, that the answers of the lawyers were first considered as law, under *Valentinian the third*, because he confirmed the writings of *Gaius*, *Ulpian*, *Paul*, *Papinian*, and others nominally, and forbad the judges to swerve from the opinions of these lawyers in points of law. And, because many inconveniences arose from the various opinions, which even these lawyers gave upon the same question, the emperor ordained, that the judges should be governed by a majority, and that, in case of an equality, they should follow the opinion of those, to whom *Papinian* adhered *Ubi diversæ sententiæ proferuntur, potius numerus vincat auctorum vel, si numerus æqualis sit, ejus partis præcedat auctoritas, in qua excellentis ingenii vir* Papinianus *emineat* Cod 1. *Theod.* t 4. l. un *De responsis prudentum.*

De jure non scripto.

§ IX. Sine scripto jus venit, quod usus approbavit; nam diuturni mores, consensu utentium comprobati, legem imitantur.

§ 9. *The unwritten law is that, which usage has approved: for all customs, which are established by the consent of those, who use them, obtain the force of a law.*

Ratio

Ratio superioris divisionis.

§ X. Et non ineleganter in duas species jus civile distributum esse videtur; nam origo ejus ab institutis duarum civitatum, Athenarum scilicet et Lacedæmoniorum, fluxisse videtur. In his enim civitatibus ita agi solitum erat, ut Lacedæmonii quidem ea, quæ pro legibus observabant, memoriæ mandarent: Athenienses vero ea, quæ in legibus scripta comprehendissent, custodirent.

§ 10. *The division of the law, into written and unwritten, seems to have taken rise from the peculiar customs of the* Athenians *and* Lacedemonians. *For the* Lacedemonians *trusted chiefly to memory, for the preservation of their laws, but the laws of the* Athenians *were committed to writing.*

Divisio juris in immutabile et mutabile.

§ XI. Sed naturalia quidem jura, quæ apud omnes gentes peræque observantur, divina quadam providentia constituta, semper firma atque immutabilia permanent. Ea vero, quæ ipsa sibi quæque civitas constituit, sæpe mutari solent, vel tacito consensu populi, vel alia postea lege lata.

§ 11. *The laws of nature, which are observed by all nations, inasmuch as they are the appointment of divine providence, remain constantly fixed and immutable But those laws, which every city has enacted for the government of itself, suffer frequent changes, either by tacit consent, or by some subsequent law, repealing a former.*

De objectis juris.

§ XII. Omne autem jus, quo utimur, vel ad personas pertinet, vel ad res, vel ad actiones. Et prius de personis videamus: nam parum est jus nôsse, si personæ, quarum causa constitutum est, ignorentur.

§ 12. *The laws, which we make use of, have relation either to persons, things, or actions. We must therefore first treat of persons, for it would be to little purpose to aim at knowledge in the law, while we are ignorant of persons, on whose sole account the law was constituted.*

TITULUS TERTIUS.

De Jure Personarum.

D. 1. T. 5.

Prima divisio personarum.

SUMMA itaque divisio de jure personarum hæc est: quod omnes homines aut liberi sunt, aut servi.

The first general division of persons, in respect to their rights, is into freemen and slaves.

Homines aut liberi sunt, aut servi] Tenure in villenage was formerly a common tenure in *England*, and those, who held by it, were called villeins, from the word *villa*, a farm. They were obliged to perform the most servile offices, and their condition did not differ from that of slaves; for both they and their children were the absolute property of their lords, who might lease them out to others for years, or for life, or make an absolute sale of them.

Of villeins there were two sorts, *viz.* villeins *regardant* to a manor, and villeins *in gross*.

Villeins *regardant*, or *glebæ adscriptitii*, were bound to their lord as members, belonging and annexed to the manor, of which their lord was the owner. Villeins *in gross* were such, who were not appendent to any manor, or lands, but belonged solely to the person of their lord, and his heirs. And note, a villein might become a villein *in gross* by prescription, by being granted away, or by confession.

Tenures in villenage were wholly taken away by a statute in the 12th Year of *Charles the second*, by which all tenures were turned into free and common socage: but it is observable, that long before this act, in which no notice is taken of villeins *in gross*, there were very few villeins in *England*, for the last case concerning villenage to be found in any of the law books is that of *Crouche* in the 10th year of Q. *Elizabeth*. *Dyer* 266 *b pl* 11.

And it is remarkable, that Sir *Thomas Smith*, who was one of the principal secretaries of state, first to King *Edward the sixth*, and afterwards to Q. *Elizabeth*, writes thus in his republic, "that "he never knew of any villeins *in gross* in his "time, and that villeins appendent to manors "were but very few in number: that, since *England* has received the christian religion, men "began to be affected in their consciences at "holding their brethren in servitude, and "that upon this scruple in process of time the "holy fathers, monks, and friars, so burdened "the minds of those, whom they confessed, "that temporal men were glad to manumit all "their villeins."

But he adds—"That the holy fathers them-"selves did not manumit their own slaves, and "that the bishops behaved like the other eccle-"siastics, but at last some bishops infranchised "their villeins for money, and others on account "of popular outcry, and that at length the mo-"nasteries, falling into lay hands, were the oc-"casion, that almost all the villeins in the king-"dom are now manumitted." *Smith's republic*, *cap* 10.

But it must not here be omitted, that even now, upon a presumption of necessity, the *English* permit slavery in the plantations, and this may lead the reader to inquire, whether a *Negro*, brought into *England*, where slaves are certainly not necessary, shall still continue to be a slave, and be recoverable at law, if he quits the service of his master? As to this question, it seems to be a settled point, that an action of trover will not lie for a *Negro*, because the owner has not an absolute property in his *Negro*, so as to kill him, as he could an ox. *Salk.* 666. *Smith* v *Gould.* Lord *Raymond*, 1274. And there has been some doubt as to an action of trespass, but the more prevalent and better opinion is, that a special action of trespass, *per quod servitium amisit*, will lie in favor of a master; so that, if property in a *Negro* can be fully proved, he will not be able to maintain his liberty by baptism, or residence in *England*.

But how much more noble and inlarged is the opinion of *Montesquiou*, in his *Esprit des loix*, who denies, with great force of argument, that slavery can any where be necessary, and indeavours to convince us by a fine irony, that it can never be justified.

"The most laborious works (says that great "author) may be performed by freemen, and "my reason for thinking so is, that before chris-"tianity had abolished civil slavery in *Europe*, the "working of mines was thought to be too hard "a labor for any, except slaves or criminals: "yet freemen are now employed in these very "works, and are known to live happily, as in "the mines of *Hartz* in lower *Saxony*, and in "those of *Hungary*. In short, no labor is so "heavy, but it may be proportioned to the "strength of the workman, and the violent fa-"tigues, which slaves are made to undergo, may "be greatly eased by commodious machines, "invented by art, and skillfully applied. The "*Turkish* mines in the bannat of *Temeswar*, tho' "richer than those of *Hungary*, yet produced "not so much, and for this plain reason, that "the invention of the *Turks* extended no far-"ther, than the strength of their slaves. I know "not whether this article is dictated by my un-"derstanding, or my heart, but I am induced to "think, that there is not a climate upon earth, "where the most laborious services might not "be performed by freemen.

"And were I to vindicate our right to make "slaves of *Negroes*, these should be my arguments.

"The *Europeans*, having exterminated the *Ame-*"*ricans*, were forced to make slaves of the *Afri-*"*cans*, to clear such vast Tracts of land.

"Sugar would be too dear, if the plants, which "produce it, were not cultivated by slaves.

"They are so black from head to foot, and "so very flat nosed, that it is impossible to pity "them.

"It is incredible, that God, who is a wise "Being, should place a soul, and especially a "good soul, in so black a body.

"It

"It is also a manifest proof of their want of "common sense, that they prefer a glass neck-"lace to one made of gold, which is a metal of "such great consequence among all polite na-"tions.

"And, in fine, it is impossible to suppose those "creatures to be men; for, in supposing them "such, we must begin to suspect, that we our-"selves are not christians." *Book* 15 *cap* 5 8.

Definitio libertatis.

§ I. Et libertas quidem (ex qua etiam liberi vocantur) est naturalis facultas ejus, quod cuique facere libet, nisi quid vi aut jure prohibetur.

§ 1. *Liberty, or freedom, from which we are denominated free, is that natural power, which we have of acting, as we please, if not hindered by force, or restrained by the law.*

Definitio servitutis.

§ II. Servitus autem est constitutio juris gentium, qua quis dominio alieno contra naturam subjicitur.

§ 2. *Slavery is that, by which one man is made subject to another, according to the law of nations, tho' contrary to natural right.*

Servi et mancipii etymologia.

§ III. Servi autem ex eo appellati sunt, quod imperatores captivos vendere, ac per hoc servare, nec occidere solent; qui etiam mancipia dicti sunt, eo, quod ab hostibus manu capiantur.

§ 3 *Slaves are denominated* servi, *from the verb* servare, *to preserve · for it is the practice of our generals to sell their captives, being accustomed to preserve, and not to destroy them. Slaves are also called* mancipia (a manu capere) *in that they are taken by the hand of the enemy.*

Imperatores captivos] At this day, prisoners, taken in war between christian princes, are not sold, or even forced to work, but remain, 'till they are either exchanged or ransomed Prisoners are also treated with the same lenity by mahometan princes, when they are at war among themselves *Molloy de jure mar.* 419

Nec occidere solent] vid *Esprit des loix* lib 15 cap 2.

Quibus modis servi constituuntur.

§ IV. Servi autem aut nascuntur, aut fiunt Nascuntur ex ancillis nostris · fiunt aut jure gentium, id est, ex captivitate, aut jure civili, cum liber homo, major viginti annis, ad pretium participandum sese venundari passus est.

§ 4 *Slaves are either born such, or become so. They are born slaves, when they are the children of bond-women . and they become slaves, either by the law of nations, that is, by captivity; or by the civil law, which happens, when a free person, above the age of twenty, suffers himself to be sold, for the sake of sharing the price given for him.*

Nascuntur ex ancillis] "Eodem jure ex an-"cillis nati servi sunt, quo sata cedunt solo, "mater enim solo comparatur, vis patris sato" *Cujacius*

Cum liber homo] Altho' absolute slavery is now disused in *Europe* (except when it is inflicted upon criminals, as a punishment, or upon *Turks*, when they are prisoners in *Roman* catholic countries) yet a species of servitude is allowed among us, which is justifiable thus an apprentice is bound for a certain time, and for particular purposes, and men of full age may also, by contract, bind themselves for a maintenance either for years, or for life. But such a con-

contract, made by the ancestor, is merely personal, and can by no means oblige his posterity. It must be added, that a person, bound to another for a term, does not labor under any civil incapacity, but is intituled to all the legal privileges of other men, and, in this, his condition is widely different from that of an absolute slave.

De liberorum et servorum divisione.

§ V. In servorum conditione nulla est differentia, in liberis autem multæ: aut enim sunt ingenui, aut libertini.

§ 5. *In the condition of slaves there is no diversity; but among those, who are free, there are many: thus some are* ingenui, *others* libertini

In liberis autem] Persons in *Great Britain* are distinguished after the following manner.

The nobility, strictly taken, is what makes up the Peerage of *Great Britain*, and consists of lords spiritual and temporal, who have a seat and vote in parliament, and are divided into five ranks or degrees, *viz* duke, marquis, earl, viscount, and baron All, who are not peers of the kingdom, come under the general name of commoners, who may be distinguished into two classes . the first comprehends the gentry of all denominations, whether baronets, knights, esquires, or gentlemen. Baronets and knights are made by creation. The honor of baronet is hereditary, and descends to the male issue That of a knight-batchelor is only personal, and dies with the person, upon whom the honor is conferred The titles of esquire, and gentleman, are acquired either by birth, by profession, or by certain offices, which distinguish those, who have served them, and their descendents Under the other class may be comprehended the yeomanry, or freeholders, who have lands or tenements of their own to the value of at least forty shillings a year; and all citizens, tradesmen, and day laborers *Strahan's Domat vol* 1. *p* 23

TITULUS QUARTUS.

De Ingenuis.

C. vii. T. 14.

De ingenui definitione.

INgenuus est is, qui statim, ut natus est, liber est; sive ex duobus ingenuis matrimonio editus est, sive ex libertinis duobus, sive ex altero libertino, et altero ingenuo. Sed et si quis ex matre nascitur libera, patre vero servo, ingenuus nihilominus nascitur: quemadmodum, qui ex matre libera et incerto patre natus est: quoniam vulgo conceptus est. Sufficit autem, liberam fuisse matrem eo tempore, quo nascitur, licet ancilla conceperit. et, e contrario, si libera conceperit, deinde ancilla facta pariat, placuit eum, qui nascitur, liberum nasci: quia non debet calamitas matris ei nocere, qui in ventre est. Ex his illud quæsitum est, si ancilla prægnans manumissa sit, deinde ancilla postea facta pepererit, liberum an servum pariat? Et Martianus probat, liberum nasci: sufficit enim ei, qui in utero est, liberam matrem vel medio tempore habuisse, ut liber nascatur; quod et verum est.

The term ingenuous *denotes a person, who is free at the instant of his birth, by being born in matrimony of parents, who are both* ingenuous, *or both* libertines, *or of parents, who differ in condition, the one being* ingenuous, *and the other a* libertine. *But*

But when the mother is free, altho' the father is a slave, or even unknown, the child is ingenuous: *and when the mother is free at the time of the birth of her infant, altho' she was a bond-woman when she conceived it, yet such infant will be* ingenuous. *Also if a woman, who was free at the time of conception, is afterwards reduced to slavery and delivered of a child, her issue is, notwithstanding this, free born; for the misfortune of the mother ought by no means to prejudice her infant. It has been a question, whether the child of a woman, who is made free during pregnancy, but becomes bond before delivery, would be free born?* Martianus *proves, that the child of such woman would be free. for, in his opinion, it is sufficient, if the mother hath been free at any time between conception and delivery; and this opinion is strictly true.*

Ex matre libera] It is a general maxim in the civil law, "that a child, born in lawful "wedlock, shall follow the condition of his fa-"ther" *Cum legitimæ nuptiæ factæ sunt* [says *Celsus*] *liberi patrem sequuntur* ff 1 5 19

But, where there is no lawful marriage, the children then follow the condition of their mother, and this happens, according to the *Roman* law, not only when slaves intermarry, but even when a free-man marries a bond-woman, for all such marriages are only called *contubernia* it therefore follows *a fortiori*, that, if a freeman debauches a bondwoman, their issue will be bond *Liberi ex coitu meretricio susrepti, qui vulgo quæsiti dicuntur, matris conditionem sequuntur, quia pater eorum ignoratur, quod idem est ac si patrem non haberent Liberi ex contubernio, sive inter servos, sive inter alterum liberum, alterum servum, in eadem conditione sunt, quia jus civile ad eos non pertinet* vid gloss et DD at l 19 ff 1 t 5.

But the rule of the law of *England* is still more general; for the maxim is, "that the children "shall never follow the condition of their mo-"ther, but always that of their father" *Lex Angliæ* [says *Fortescue*] *nunquam matris, sed semper patris, conditionem imitari partum judicat* Fortesc. de laud ll Angl

So that, if a villein in *England* had taken a free-woman to wife, their issue would have been villeins, and, if a niese had been married to a free man, their children would have been free *Litt ten lib 2 sect 187*

But the illegitimate issue of a villein and a free-woman, or of a villein and a niese, would have been free, altho' their issue in lawful matrimony would have been bond For, inasmuch as a bastard is not permitted by the law of *England* to follow the condition of his mother, and can not follow the condition of his father, who is unknown to the law, he is therefore feigned to be *nullius filius*, and, in favor of liberty, is presumed to have been born free.

De erronea ingenui manumissione.

§ I. Cum autem ingenuus aliquis natus sit, non officit ei, in servitute fuisse, et postea manumissum esse: sæpissime enim constitutum est, natalibus non officere manumissionem

§ 1. *When any man is by birth* ingenuous, *it will not injure him to have been in servitude, and to have been afterwards manumitted · for there are diverse constitutions, by which it is enacted, that manumission shall not prejudice free birth*

Sæpissime enim] For, if manumission was permitted to operate, the person manumitted must become a *libertine*, which would be injurious to a man, who was free by birth, and manumitted thro' ignorance and mistake *Cod* 7. *t* 16 *l* 21

TITULUS QUINTUS.

De Libertinis.

Definitio et origo libertinorum et manumissionis.

LIBERTINI sunt, qui ex justa servitute manumissi sunt. Manumissio autem est *de manu datio*: nam quamdiu aliquis in servitute est, ma-

manui et potestati suppositus est: et manumissus liberatur a domini potestate: quæ res a jure gentium originem sumpsit; utpote cum jure naturali omnes liberi nascerentur; nec esset nota manumissio, cum servitus esset incognita. Sed, postquam jure gentium servitus ingenuitatem invasit, secutum est beneficium manumissionis: et, cum uno communi nomine omnes homines appellarentur, jure gentium tria hominum genera esse cœperunt, liberi, et his contrarium, servi, et tertium genus, libertini, qui desierant esse servi.

Libertines, or free men, are those, who have been manumitted from just servitude. Manumission implies the giving of liberty; for whoever is in servitude, is subject to the hand and power of another; but whoever is manumitted, is free from both.

Manumission took its rise from the law of nations; for all men by the law of nature are born in freedom; nor was manumission heared of, whilest servitude was unknown. But, when servitude, under sanction of the law of nations, invaded liberty, the benefit of manumission became then a consequence. For all men at first were denominated by one common appellation, 'till, by the law of nations, they began to be divided into three classes, viz. *into* liberi, *or those, who are born free; into* servi, *or those, who are in slavery, and into* libertini, *who are those, who have ceased to be slaves, by having freedom conferred upon them.*

Quibus modis manumittatur.

§ I Multis autem modis manumissio procedit: aut enim ex sacris constitutionibus in sacrosanctis ecclesiis, aut vindicta, aut inter amicos, aut per epistolam, aut per testamentum, aut per aliam quamlibet ultimam voluntatem. Sed et aliis multis modis libertas servo competere potest, qui tam ex veteribus, quam ex nostris constitutionibus, introducti sunt.

§ 1. *Manumission is effected by various ways; either in the face of the church, according to the imperial constitutions, or by the* vindicta, *or in the presence of friends, or by letter, or by testament, or by any other last will. Liberty may also be properly conferred upon a slave by diverse other methods, some of which were introduced by the constitutions of former emperors, and others by our own.*

Multis autem modis] Liberty could antiently be conferred, but three ways viz by *testament*, by the *census*, and by the *vindicta* or lictor's rod And this is evident from the following passage in *Tully* *Si neque censu, neque vindicta, neque testamento liber factus est, non est liber*. In top

A man was said to be *liber censu*, when his name was inserted in the censor's roll with the approbation of his master at the public *census* But the method of acquiring liberty by the *vindicta* was more solemn and formal For it was necessary, that the master, placing his hand upon the head of the slave, should say in the presence of the prætor, *hunc hominem liberum esse volo*, to which the prætor always replied, *dico eum liberum esse more Quiritum* Then the lictor, or serjeant, receiving the *vindicta*, or rod, from the prætor, struck the new freed-man several blows with it upon the head, face, and back, after which his name was registered in the roll of freed-men, and his head being close shaved, a cap was given him, as a token of liberty

The various other forms of manumitting, introduced by the imperial constitutions, are almost all of a public nature, and even manumission *among friends*, or *by letter*, could not be effected without the presence of five witnesses *Cod 7 t 6 de lat lib toll*

With respect to villeins in *England*, it appears from the following law, enacted by *William the first*, in what manner they were antiently infranchised *Si quis velit servum suum liberum facere, tradat eum vice comiti per manum dextram in pleno comitatu, quietum illum clamare debet a jugo servitutis suæ per manumissionem, et ostendat ei liberas vias et portas, et tradat illi libera arma, scilicet, lanceam et gladium, deinde liber homo efficitur* "If "any person is willing to infranchise his slave, "let him, with his right hand, deliver the slave to "to the sheriff in a full county, proclaim him "exempt from the bond of servitude by manu- "mission, shew him open gates and ways, and "deliver him free arms, to wit, a lance, and a "sword, after which he commences a free- "man"

Another law, made by king *Henry the first*, gives a still farther light into this matter *Qui servum suum liberat in ecclesia, vel mercato, vel comitatu, vel hundredo coram testibus, et palam faciat, et liberas illi vias et portas conscribat apertas, et lanceam, et gladium, vel quæ liberorum arma sunt in manibus ei ponat.* vid *ll* Anglo Saxonicas, *&c.* Wilkins editore

But these ceremonies were disused in *England* by the more modern practice, and freedom was often conferred by grants, of which the following is a precedent, from whence the reader may collect, what interest the lord had in his villein, by observing how great an interest is released

To all to whom these presents shall come, &c T L *lord of the manor of* D *sendeth greeting.* Whereas A B *otherwise called our native, son of* C B. *otherwise called* C B *our native, belonging and appendent to our manor of* D *in the county of* E *was begotten in villenage, and for such a one was commonly called, held, had, and reputed openly, publickly, and privately,* Know ye, *that I the said* T L *for diverse good and lawful causes me thereunto moving, for me and my heirs for ever, have manumitted, released, and from the yoke of servitude and villenage discharged, and, by these my* letters patent, *do manumit, free, and discharge the said* A B *with all his sequels begotten, or to be begotten, with all his goods and chattels, lands and tenements by him already bought, or hereafter to be bought whatsoever* Know ye *also, that I the said* T L *have remised, and released, and for me, my heirs,* &c *have quiet clamed, and by this my present writing do remit, release, and quiet clame the said* A B *and his heirs, and all his sequels, from all, and all manner of actions real, and personal, suits, quarrels,* &c. *which against the said* A B *or any of the heirs of his sequels, or any of them, I have, or had, or which I, or my heirs hereafter, might have by reason of the said servitude aforesaid, or for any other cause whatsoever, from the beginning of the world unto the day of making these presents* *So that neither I the said* T L *nor my heirs, nor any other by and for us, or in our names, any action, right, title, clame, interest, or demand of villenage or servitude, by the king's writ, or by any other means whatsoever against the said* A B *or his sequels begotten, or to be begotten, or against the goods, chattels, lands and tenements purchased, or hereafter to be purchased, from henceforth may exact, clame, or challenge, at any time hereafter, but that we be wholly and for ever thereof debarred by these presents* And I *the said* T L *and my heirs, the said* A B *with all his sequel. begotten, or to be begotten, free-men, against all men, will warrant for ever by these presents* *In witness,* &c *vid* the complete clerk, reprinted in 1676

Per aliam quamlibet] By the words *per aliam quamlibet ultimam voluntatem,* are meant donations *mortis causa,* and codicils

Aliis multis modis] Many of which are enumerated in Cod. 7 t 6 *De latina libertate tollenda*

Ubi et quando manumitti potest.

§ II. Servi vero a dominis semper manumitti solent, adeo ut vel in transitu manumittantur, veluti cum prætor, aut præses, aut proconsul, in balneum, vel in theatrum eunt.

§ 2. *Slaves may be manumitted by their masters at any time, even whilest the prætor, the governor of a province, or the proconsul is going to the baths, or to the theater*

Veluti cum prætor.] For infranchisement is an act of voluntary, and not of contentious, jurisdiction, so that time and place are not material See *Cod* 3 *t* 12 *ll* 2, 8

Omnes proconsules statim, quam urbem egressi fuerint, habent jurisdictionem, sed non contentiosam, sed voluntariam, ut ecce manumitti apud eos possunt tam liberi quam servi, et adoptiones fieri ff 1 t. 16 *l.* 2.

De libertinorum divisione sublata.

§ III. Libertinorum autem status tripertitus antea fuerat: nam qui manumittebantur, modo majorem et justam libertatem consequebantur, et fiebant cives Romani: modo minorem, et Latini ex lege Junia Norbana fiebant: modo inferiorem, et fiebant ex lege Ælia Sentia Dedititii: sed quoniam Dedititiorum quidem pessima conditio jam ex multis tempo-

ribus

ribus in desuetudinem abierat; Latinorum vero nomen non frequentabatur; ideoque nostra pietas, omnia augere et in meliorem statum reducere desiderans, duabus constitutionibus hoc emendavit, et in pristinum statum reduxit: quia et a primis urbis Romæ cunabulis una atque simplex libertas competebat, id est, eadem, quam habebat manumissor; nisi quod, scilicet, libertinus sit, qui manumittitur, licet manumissor ingenuus sit. Et Dedititios quidem per constitutionem nostram expulimus, quam promulgavimus inter nostras decisiones; per quas, suggerente nobis Triboniano viro excelso quæstore nostro, antiqui juris altercationes placavimus. Latinos autem Junianos, et omnem, quæ circa eos fuerat, observantiam, alia constitutione, per ejusdem quæstoris suggestionem, correximus, quæ inter imperiales radiat sanctiones. Et omnes libertos (nullo, nec ætatis manumissi, nec domini manumittentis, nec in manumissionis modo, discrimine habito, sicuti antea observabatur) civitate Romana decoravimus, multis modis additis, per quos possit libertas servis cum civitate Romana, quæ sola est in præsenti, præstari.

§ 3. *The* libertini *were formerly distinguished by a threefold division. Those, who were manumitted, sometimes obtained what was called the greater liberty, and thus became* Roman *citizens; sometimes they obtained only the lesser liberty, and became* Latins, *according to the law* Junia Norbana, *and sometimes they obtained only the inferior liberty, and became* Dedititii, *by the law* Ælia Sentia. *But, the condition of the* Dedititii *differing but little from slavery, the inferior liberty has been long since disused, neither has the name of* Latins *been frequent. It therefore being our ardent desire to extend our bounty, and to reduce all things into a better state, we have amended our laws by two constitutions, and re-established the antient usage, for antiently liberty was simple and undivided, that is, it was conferred upon the slave, as his manumittor possessed it, admitting this single difference, that the person manumitted became only a* libertine, *altho' his manumittor was* ingenuous.

We have intirely abolished the name of Dedititii *by a constitution published among our decisions, by which, at the instance of* Tribonian, *our quæstor, we have suppressed all disputes concerning the antient law. We have also, at the suggestion of the same illustrious person, altered the condition of the* Latins, *and corrected the laws, which related to them, by another constitution, which eminently distinguishes itself among the imperial sanctions. And we have made all the freed men in general citizens of* Rome, *regarding neither the age of the person manumitted, nor of the manumittor, nor any of the forms of manumission, as they were antiently observed. We have also introduced many new methods, by which slaves may become* Roman *citizens, and the liberty of becoming such is that alone, which can now be conferred.*

Latini ex lege Junia Norbana.] The law *Junia Norbana* was made *Anno U. C.* 771, in the consulship of *Junius Silanus* and *Norbanus Balbus*. It was enacted by this law, that all slaves, who were infranchised otherwise than by testament, the *census*, or the *vindicta*, should not become *Roman* citizens, but have such privileges only, which the *Latins* enjoyed before the *Italian*, or social war. The condition of those, who obtained this lesser liberty, is thus described by *Justinian*. *ut liberi vitam suam peragebant, attamen sub ultimo spiritu simul animam atque libertatem amittebant, et quasi servorum, ita bona eorum, jure quodammodo peculii, ex lege Junia Norbana manumissores detinebant.* Inst. 3. t. 8. But it must be observed, that they were not prohibited from enjoying the freedom of *Rome*, if properly conferred.

Ex lege Ælia Sentia Dedititii.] By the law *Ælia Sentia*, which was enacted in the reign of *Augustus*, and in the consulate of *Ælius* and *Sentius*, all slaves, who had been condemned, as criminals,

nals, and afterwards obtained manumiſſion thro' the indulgence of their maſters, could only acquire the inferior liberty, and were termed *Dedititii*, becauſe their condition was equalled with that of conquered revolters, whom the *Romans*, in reproach, called *Dedititii*, *Quia ſe ſuaque omnia dediderunt*

These inferior freed-men were diſtinguiſhed from the *Latins* by many incapacities peculiar to themſelves, the moſt remarkable of which was, that they were for ever debarred from becoming citizens of *Rome* But theſe diſtinctions were deſtroyed by the conſtitutions of *Juſtinian*. vid Cod. 7. t. 5 l 1. t 6. l 1.

TITULUS SEXTUS.

Qui et ex quibus cauſis manumittere non poſſunt.

D. xl. T. 9. C. vii. T. 11.

Prius caput legis Æliæ Sentiæ, de manumittente in fraudem creditorum.

NON tamen cuicumque volenti manumittere licet: nam is, qui in fraudem creditorum manumittit, nihil agit: quia lex Ælia Sentia impedit libertatem

It is not in the power of every maſter to manumit at will: for whoever manumits with intent to defraud his creditors, may be ſaid to commit a nullity, the law Ælia Sentia *impeding all liberty thus granted.*

De ſervo inſtituto cum libertate.

§ I. Licet autem domino, qui ſolvendo non eſt, in teſtamento ſervum ſuum cum libertate hæredem inſtituere, ut liber fiat, hæreſque ei ſolus et neceſſarius, ſi modo ei nemo alius, ex eo teſtamento, hæres extiterit: aut quia nemo hæres ſcriptus ſit, aut quia is, qui ſcriptus eſt, qualibet ex cauſa hæres ei non extiterit Idque eadem lege Ælia Sentia proviſum eſt, et recte. Valde enim proſpiciendum erat, ut egentes homines, quibus alius hæres extiturus non eſſet, vel ſervum ſuum neceſſarium hæredem haberent, qui ſatisfacturus eſſet creditoribus: aut, hoc eo non faciente, creditores res hæreditarias ſervi nomine vendant, ne injuria defunctus afficiatur.

§ I. *A maſter, who is inſolvent, may appoint a ſlave to be his heir with liberty, that thus the ſlave may obtain his freedom, and become the only and neceſſary heir of the teſtator, on ſuppoſition that no other perſon is alſo heir by the ſame teſtament; and this may happen, either becauſe no other perſon was inſtituted heir, or becauſe the perſon, ſo inſtituted, is unwilling to act, as ſuch This privilege of maſters was for wiſe and juſt reaſons eſtabliſhed by the above named law* Ælia Sentia *: for it claimed a ſpecial proviſion, that indigent men, to whom no man would be a voluntary heir, might have a ſlave for a neceſſary heir to ſatisfy creditors; or otherwiſe, that the creditors*

creditors themselves should make sale of the hereditary effects of the master in the name of the slave, lest the deceased should suffer ignominy.

Ne injuria] "Hoc est, ignominia; quamvis "enim edicto prætoris de infamibus non note- "tur, oneratur tamen existimatio ejus, et facti "infamiam non effugit is, cujus bona auctioni "et hastæ publice subjiciuntur; cujus rei locu- "pletem testem habemus *Ciceronem* pro *Quintio*, "cap 15 vid. *Vinn.*

De servo instituto sine libertate.

§ II. Idemque juris est, etsi sine libertate servus hæres institutus est: quod nostra constitutio non solum in domino, qui solvendo non est, sed generaliter constituit, nova humanitatis ratione: ut ex ipsa scriptura institutionis etiam libertas ei competere videatur: cum non sit verisimile, eum, quem hæredem sibi elegit, si prætermiserit libertatis dationem, servum remanere voluisse, et neminem sibi hæredem fore.

§ 2. *A slave also becomes free by being instituted an heir, altho' no mention was made of liberty in the testament for our imperial constitution regards not only masters, who are insolvent, but, by a new act of our humanity, it extends generally; so that the very institution of an heir implies the conferring of liberty. For it is highly improbable, that a testator, altho' he hath omitted to mention liberty in his testament, would be willing, that the person, whom he hath instituted, should remain in servitude, since a testator would thus defeat his own purpose, and be destitute of an heir.*

Quod nostra constitutio] See *Cod* 6. *t.* 27 *l* 5 De necessariis hæredibus instituendis.

Quid sit in fraudem creditorum manumittere.

§. III. In fraudem autem creditorum manumittere videtur, qui vel jam eo tempore, quo manumittit, solvendo non est; vel qui, datis libertatibus, desiturus est solvendo esse. Prævaluisse tamen videtur, nisi animum quoque fraudandi manumissor habuerit, non impediri libertatem, quamvis bona ejus creditoribus non sufficiant · sæpe enim de facultatibus suis amplius, quam in his est, sperant homines. Itaque tunc intelligimus impediri libertatem, cum utroque modo fraudantur creditores, id est, et consilio manumittentis, et ipsa re, eo quod bona ejus non sunt suffectura creditoribus.

§ 3 *A man may be said to manumit in order to defraud creditors, if he is insolvent at the time when he manumits, or if he becomes insolvent by manumitting It is however the prevailing opinion, that liberty, when granted, is not impeached, unless the manumittor had an intent to defraud, altho' his goods are insufficient for the payment of his creditors; for men frequently imagine themselves to be in better circumstances, than they really are We therefore understand liberty to be then only impeded, when creditors are doubly defrauded; that is, both by the intention of the manumittor, and in reality.*

Alterum caput legis Æliæ Sentiæ de minore viginti annis.

§ IV Eadem lege Ælia Sentia, domino minori viginti annis non aliter manumittere permittitur, quam si vindicta apud consilium, justa causa manumissionis approbata, fuerint manumissi.

§ 4. *By the before-named law* Ælia Sentia, *a master, under the age of twenty years, can not manumit, unless a just cause is assigned, which must be approved of by a council, appointed for that purpose, at whose command liberty is conferred by the* vindicta.

Non aliter] This prohibition was in favor of minors, " ne, servorum suorum delinimentis " decepti, minores rebus suis spoliarentur, præ- " terea lex providere voluit, ne temere, et sine " certo animi judicio, servi libertate et civitate " donarentur " *ff* 40 *t.* 2 *l* 4 *et passim.*

Apud concilium] This council at *Rome* consisted of the prætor, five senators, and five *equites* or knights In the provinces it consisted of the proconsul, and twenty *recuperatores*, i e magistrates of municipal towns, who were called *recuperatores, quia jus suum per eos quisque recuperabat* Calvin.

Quæ sunt justæ causæ manumissionis.

§ V. Justæ autem causæ manumissionis sunt veluti si quis patrem aut matrem, filium filiamve, aut fratres, sororesve naturales, aut pædagogum, aut nutricem, aut educatorem, aut alumnum alumnamve, aut collectaneum manumittat: aut servum, procuratoris habendi gratia, aut ancillam, matrimonii habendi causa : dum tamen intra sex menses in uxorem ducatur, nisi justa causa impediat : et servus, qui manumittitur, procuratoris habendi gratia, non minor decem et septem annis manumittatur

§ 5. *A minor is deemed to assign a just reason for manumission, when he alleges any of the following,* viz *that the person to be manumitted is his father or mother, his son or daughter, his brother or sister, his preceptor, his nurse, his foster child, or his foster brother , or when he alleges, that he would manumit his slave, in order to constitute him his proctor , or his bond woman, with an intent to marry her, on condition, that the marriage is performed within six months. But a slave, who is to be constituted a proctor, can not be manumitted for that purpose, if he is under seventeen*

Justæ autem] vid *ff* 40 *t* 2 *l* 9, 10, &c

De causa semel probata.

§ VI Semel autem causa approbata, sive vera sit, sive falsa, non retractatur

§ 6. *A reason, which has once been admitted in favor of liberty, whether true or false, can not afterwards be disallowed*

Abrogatio posterioris capitis legis Æliæ Sentiæ.

§ VII Cum ergo certus modus manumittendi minoribus viginti annis dominis per legem Æliam Sentiam constitutus esset, eveniebat, ut qui quatuordecim annos expleverat, licet testamentum facere, et in eo sibi hæredem instituere, legataque relinquere, posset, tamen, si adhuc minor esset viginti annis, libertatem servo dare non posset, quod non erat ferendum : nam, cui totorum suorum bonorum in testamento dispositio data erat, quare non similiter ei, quemadmodum alias res, ita et de servis suis in ultima voluntate disponere, quemadmodum voluerit, permittimus, ut et libertatem eis possit præstare? Sed cum libertas inæstimabilis res sit, et propter hoc

hoc ante vigesimum ætatis annum antiquitas libertatem servo dare prohibebat; ideo nos, mediam quodammodo viam eligentes, non aliter minori viginti annis libertatem in testamento dare servo suo concedimus, nisi septemdecimum annum impleverit, et octodecimum attigerit. Cum enim antiquitas hujusmodi ætati et pro aliis postulare concesserit, cur non etiam sui judicii stabilitas ita eos adjuvare credatur, ut ad libertatem dandam servis suis possint pervenire?

§ 7. *When certain bounds were prescribed by the law* Ælia Sentia *to all under twenty, with regard to manumission, it was observed, that any person, who was fourteen complete, might make a testament, institute an heir, and bequeath legacies, and yet that no person, under twenty, could confer liberty; which was not longer to be tolerated. For can any just cause be assigned, why a man, permitted to dispose of all his effects by testament, should be debarred from infranchising his slaves? But, liberty being of inestimable value, and our antient laws prohibiting any person to make a grant of it, who is under twenty years of age, We therefore make choice of a middle way, and permit all, who are in their eighteenth year, to confer liberty by testament For since, by all former practice, persons at eighteen were permitted to plead for their clients, there is no reason, why the same stability of judgment, which qualifies them to assist others, should not be of advantage to themselves, by inabling them to infranchise their own slaves.*

TITULUS SEPTIMUS.

De lege Fusia Caninia tollenda.

C. vii. T. 3.

LEGE Fusia Caninia, certus modus constitutus erat in servis testamento manumittendis; quam, quasi libertates impedientem et quodammodo invidam, tollendam esse censuimus: cum satis fuerat inhumanum, vivos quidem licentiam habere totam suam familiam libertate donare, nisi alia causa impediat libertatem; morientibus autem hujusmodi licentiam adimere.

By the law Fusia Caninia, *all masters were restrained from manumitting more, than a certain number, by testament, but we have thought proper to abrogate this law, as odious and destructive of liberty, judging it inhuman, that persons in health should have power to manumit a whole family, if no just cause impedes the manumission, and that those, who are dying, should be prohibited from doing the same thing by testament.*

TITU-

TITULUS OCTAVUS.

De his, qui sui vel alieni juris sunt.

D. 1. T. 6.

Altera divisio personarum.

SEQUITUR de jure personarum alia divisio; nam quædam personæ sui juris sunt, quædam alieno juri subjectæ. Rursus earum, quæ alieno juri subjectæ sunt, aliæ sunt in potestate parentum, aliæ in potestate dominorum. Videamus itaque de his, quæ alieno juri subjectæ sunt; nam si cognoverimus, quænam istæ personæ sunt, simul intelligemus, quæ sui juris sunt; ac prius inspiciamus de his, quæ in potestate dominorum sunt.

We now proceed to another division of persons, for some are independent, and some are subject to the power of others. Of those, who are subject to others, some are in the power of parents, others in the power of their masters Let us then inquire, what persons are in subjection to others, for when we apprehend, who these persons are, we shall at the same time discover those, who are independent. Our first inquiry shall be concerning those, who are in the power of masters.

De jure gentium in servos.

§ I. In potestate itaque dominorum sunt servi, quæ quidem potestas juris gentium est, nam apud omnes peræque gentes animadvertere possumus, dominis in servos vitæ necisque potestatem fuisse: et, quodcunque per servum acquiritur, id domino acquiri.

§ I *All slaves are in the power of their masters, which power is derived from the law of nations for it is equally observable among all nations, that masters have always had the power of life and death over their slaves, and that whatsoever is acquired by the slave is acquired for the master*

Vitæ necisque potestatem] This power was abridged by the law *Cornelia de sicariis*, an U C 673, and by the law *Petronia de servis*, in 813 It was afterwards intirely taken away by the emperor *Adrian*, who enacted, "that slaves "should not suffer death, unless upon con-"viction of some capital crime before a ma-"gistrate"

De jure civium Romanorum in servos.

§ II. Sed hoc tempore nullis hominibus, qui sub imperio nostro sunt, licet, sine causâ legibus cognita, in servos suos supra modum sævire. Nam, ex constitutione divi Antonini, qui sine causa servum suum occiderit, non minus puniri jubetur, quam si alienum servum occiderit Sed et major asperitas dominorum, ejusdem principis constitutione, coercetur: nam Antoninus, consultus a quibusdam præsidibus provinciarum de his servis, qui ad ædem sacram vel statuam principum confugiunt, præcipit, ut, si intolerabilis videatur sævitia dominorum, cogantur servos suos bonis conditio-

nibus

nibus vendere, ut pretium dominis daretur; et recte: expedit enim reipublicæ, ne sua re quis male utatur. Cujus rescripti, ad Ælium Martianum missi, verba sunt hæc. *Dominorum quidem potestatem in servos illibatam esse oportet, nec cuiquam hominum jus suum detrahi. Sed et dominorum interest, ne auxilium contra sævitiam, vel famem, vel intolerabilem injuriam, denegetur iis, qui juste deprecantur. Ideoque cognosce de querelis eorum, qui ex familia Julii Sabini ad sacram statuam confugerunt, et, si vel durius habitos, quam æquum est, vel infami injuria affectos esse, cognoveris, venire jube, ita ut in potestatem domini non revertantur. Quod si meæ constitutioni fraudem fecerit, sciat, me hoc admissum adversus se severius executurum.*

§ 2. *All persons, under our imperial government, are now prohibited to inflict any extraordinary punishment upon their slaves, without a legal cause. For, by a constitution of* Antoninus, *it is enacted, that whoever kills his own slave without a just cause, is not to be punished with less rigor, than if he had killed a slave, who was the property of another. The too great severity of masters is also restrained by another constitution, made by the same prince: for* Antoninus, *being consulted by certain governors of provinces concerning those slaves, who took sanctuary either in temples, or at the statues of the emperors,* Ordained, *that, if the severity of masters should appear at any time excessive, they might be compelled to make sale of their slaves upon equitable terms, so that the full worth of such slaves might be given to their masters. And this constitution seems just and reasonable, inasmuch as it is a maxim, expedient for the commonwealth, "that no one should be permitted to misuse even his own property." The rescript of this emperor, sent to* Ælius Martianus, *is conceived in the following words* —The power of masters over their slaves ought by no means to be wrongfully diminished, neither ought any man to be deprived of his just right. But it is for the interest of all masters, that relief against cruelties, the denial of sustenance, or any other insufferable injury, should not be refused to those, who justly implore it. Therefore take cognisance of all complaints, made by those of the family of *Julius Sabinus*, whose slaves took sanctuary at the sacred statue, and, if you are made sensible of their having been more hardly treated than they ought, or of their having suffered any great injury, order them to be forthwith sold, and in such a manner, that they may never more be made subject to their former master. And, if *Julius Sabinus* indeavours by any fraud to evade our constitution, be it known to him, that such his offence shall be punished with the utmost rigor.

Ad sacram statuam] It was antiently the policy of almost all kingdoms to allow of sanctuaries or places of refuge, and they are said to have been permitted in *England*, almost as soon as christianity was received In the 8th year of *Henry the eighth*, the following points (which will give the reader some idea of the power of sanctuaries) were affirmed and resolved in the case of *Savage*,—To wit, that in *England* the pope without the king could not make a sanctuary. —that sanctuaries must commence with a grant from the king, and then be confirmed by the pope, but that, if they began by a bull from the pope, it would be insufficient, altho' they were afterwards confirmed by the king — that the general words *ambitus, præcinctus, clausura*, in such grants, whether papal or regal, did only include the church, cloyster, dormitory, and church-yard, but extended not to gardens, barns, stables, and the like — that sanctuary *de jure commun* was only for 40 days (which was a privilege belonging to all parochial churches and church-yards) and that sanctuary for life, or as long as the person pleased (which was a usual privilege of religious houses) depended upon special grants; and that those grants, together with custom and usage thereupon, were to *be well proved*, or otherwise declared null and void, being

being more than the common law allowed *Keilwey*, p. 188. Bp *Gib Cod* p 1188

Note, "that sanctuary was never of any farther protection in a civil action, than to save the body from execution—and, if sanctuary was granted in general words, it reached not to high treason; but, it seems agreed, that, in such case, it extended to murder and all felonies, SACRILEGE EXCEPTED" *Hawk pl of the crown, lib 2 cap.* 32

But sanctuaries lost much of their power in the reigns of *Henry the eighth* and *Edw the sixth*, and by the statute of the 21st of *James the first*, they were intirely taken away

By 27 *Hen* 8 *cap* 19 it was enacted, "that whereas sanctuaries have been a great incouragement to murder, rapes, robberies, &c. every sanctuary-person shall wear a badge openly upon their upper garment, and, being found without it, shall lose the privilege of sanctuary

And by 32 *Hen* 8 *cap* 12. it was ordained, "that all sanctuaries (except churches, church-yards, cathedral churches, hospitals, and churches collegiate, and all chapels dedicated and used as parish churches, and the sanctuaries to them belonging, and the places hereafter to be declared places of privilege) shall be utterly extinguished That *Wells*, *Westminster*, *Manchester*, *Northhampton*, *Norwich*, *York*, *Darby* and *Lanceston*, shall from henceforth be allowed to be places of privilege for term of life.

"That no privilege of any sanctuary shall for the future extend to persons guilty of willful murder, ravishment, burglary, robberies upon the highway, robberies of churches or chapels, burning of houses or barns, or to any of the abettors of the aforesaid offenders —That any persons taking sanctuary, and not guilty of any of the said offences, may abjure to any of the said privileged places"—Here note, that before the 22d of *Hen* 8 *c* 19. any persons taking sanctuary in places, which did not give privilege for life, were obliged to abjure the realm within 40 days, in the following tenor—*Hoc audite justitiarii (vel o vos coronatores) quod exibo è regno Angliæ, et illuc iterum non reverter, nisi de licentia domini regis, vel hæredum suorum, sic me Deus adjuvet* Brac de corona lib 3 cap 16

But, by that statute, it was declared, "that, whereas the strength of the realm hath been much diminished by mariners, and many able and expert persons in archery, taking sanctuary and abjuring the realm, offenders, who take sanctuary for the future, shall, instead of quitting the realm, be confined to some one sanctuary during life"

By 32 *Hen* 8 *cap* 20 it was farther ordained, "that all liberties belonging to religious houses shall be enjoyed by lay-possessors, except sanctuaries, churches and church-yards" —This contributed much to lessen the number of sanctuaries

But by 21 *James* 1 *cap* 28 which is now in force, it is finally enacted, "that no sanctuary, or privilege of sanctuary, shall be hereafter admitted or allowed in any case whatever" See also Dr *Middleton's Letter from Rome, in quarto*, pag 113

Sed et major asperitas] In *England* the lord might rob, beat, and chastise his villein at will, but was not allowed to maim him, for then the villein might have had an appeal of *maihem* against his lord Le seigneur poit rob, nauter et chastiser son villein a son volunt · salve que il ne poit lui maim, car donques il avera appel de maihem envers lui. Termes de la Ley.

TITULUS NONUS.

De Patria Potestate.

C. viii. T. 47.

Summa tituli.

IN potestate nostra sunt liberi nostri, quos ex justis nuptiis procreavimus.

The children, whom we have begotten in lawful wedlock, are under our power.

In potestate nostra] The citizens of *Rome* had antiently the power of life and death, over their children This despotic authority was established by *Romulus*, and afterwards confirmed by an express law in the twelve tables — *Endo liberis justis jus vitæ, necis, venundandique potestas patri esto.* But, as the *Romans* grew politer in their manners, this law of course became obsolete, and was restrained

ſtrained by the opinions of lawyers, and diverſe imperial conſtitutions, many years before the reign of *Juſtinian*

Inauditum filium pater occidere non poteſt, ſed accuſare eum apud præfectum præſidemve provinciæ debet. Ulp de adulteris.

Si filius tuus in poteſtate tua eſt, res acquiſitas tibi alienare non potuit; quem, ſi pietatem patri debitam non agnoſcit, caſtigare jure patriæ poteſtatis non prohiberis acriore remedio uſurus ſi in pari contumacia perſeveraverit; eumque præſidi provinciæ oblaturus, dicturo ſententiam, quam tu quoque dici volueris. Cod. 8 t. 47

Definitio nuptiarum.

§ I. Nuptiæ autem, ſive matrimonium, eſt viri et mulieris conjunctio, individuam vitæ conſuetudinem continens.

§ 1. *Matrimony is a ſocial contract between a man and woman, obliging them to an inſeparable cohabitation during life.*

Qui habent in poteſtate.

§ II. Jus autem poteſtatis, quod in liberos habemus, proprium eſt civium Romanorum; nulli enim alii ſunt homines, qui talem in liberos habeant poteſtatem, qualem nos habemus.

§ 2. *The power, which we have over our children, is peculiar to the citizens of* Rome, *for there is no other people, who have the ſame power over their children, which we have over ours*

Talem in liberos] The power of parents, among the *Romans*, was at this time very deſpotic, altho' it did not extend abſolutely over the lives of their children, as heretofore.

Qui ſunt in poteſtate.

§ III. Qui igitur ex te et uxore tua naſcitur, in tua poteſtate eſt. Item qui ex filio tuo et uxore ejus naſcitur, id eſt, nepos tuus et neptis, æque in tua ſunt poteſtate; et pronepos, et proneptis, et deinceps cæteri. Qui autem ex filia tua naſcuntur, in poteſtate tua non ſunt; ſed in patris eorum.

§ 3. *The iſſue of yourſelf and your legal wife are immediately under your own power. Alſo the iſſue of a ſon and ſon's wife, that is, either grand ſons or granddaughters by them, are equally in your power, and the ſame may be ſaid of great-grand children, &c But children born of a daughter will not be in your power, but in the power of their own father, or father's father, &c*

TITU-

TITULUS DECIMUS.

De Nuptiis.

D. xxiii. T. 2. C. v. T. 4. Nov. 74.

Qui possunt nuptias contrahere.

JUSTAS autem nuptias inter se cives Romani contrahunt, qui secundum præcepta legum coeunt, masculi quidem puberes, fœminæ autem viri potentes; sive patres familiarum sint, sive filii familiarum, dum tamen, si filii familiarum sint, consensum habeant parentum, quorum in potestate sunt: nam, hoc fieri debere, et civilis et naturalis ratio suadet, in tantum, ut jussus parentis præcedere debeat. Unde quæsitum est, an furiosi filia nubere, aut furiosi filius uxorem ducere, possit? Cumque super filio variabatur, nostra processit decisio, qua permissum est ad exemplum filiæ furiosi, filium quoque furiosi posse, et sine patris interventu, matrimonium sibi copulare, secundum datum ex nostra constitutione modum.

The citizens of Rome *contract valid matrimony, when they follow the precepts of the law, the males, when they arrive at puberty, and the females, when they attain to a marriageable age. The males, whether they are* patres familiarum, *fathers of a family, or* filii familiarum, *the sons of a family; but, if they are the sons of a family, they must first obtain the consent of the parents, under whose power they are. For reason, both natural and civil, convinces us, that the consent of parents should precede marriage. And from hence it became a question, whether the son of a madman could contract matrimony? But, the opinions of lawyers being various, we published our decision, by which the son, as well as the daughter of a madman, is permitted to marry without the intervention of his father, provided always, that the rules, set forth in our constitution, are observed.*

Inter se cives Romani] The words *cives Romani*, or *Roman* citizens, comprehend all free-men in subjection to the empire

In orbe Romano qui sunt, ex constitutione imperatoris Antonini cives Romani effecti sunt De statu hominum, *ff* 1 *t* 5 *l* 17 *Nov* 78 *cap* 5

Masculi quidem puberes.] *Puberty* is esteemed by the law of *England*, as well as by the civil law, to commence in males at fourteen complete, and in females at twelve But in *England* persons may legally enter into matrimony before puberty and a female, when she has completed her ninth year, is intituled to dower, altho her husband at his death was but seven, or even four years of age *Co Litt p* 31 *a* 33 *a.* 40 *a* But, when there is a marriage before puberty, the woman may dissent from it, at twelve or after, and the man at fourteene or after, and there needs no new marriage, if they so agree, but disagree they can not before the said ages, and then they may disagree, and marie againe to others without any divorce · and, if they once after give consent, they can never disagree after. If a man of the age of fourteene marie a woman of the age of ten, at her age of twelve, he may as well disagree as she may, tho' he were of the age of consent; because in contracts of matrimony either both must be bound, or equal election of disagreement given to both, and so, e converso, if the woman be of the age of consent, and the man under. Co Litt p. 78 b. 79 a

But, in contracts *De futuro*, the law is totally different For a contract *de futuro* is of no force, if both the parties are under the age of twenty-one, but, if one of the parties is twenty one complete, the contract will b binding to that party *Holt v Ward Trin* 5 *G* 2

Sive patres familiarum] Among the *Romans*, all, who were *suæ potestatis*, or independent, altho' unmarried, or even not arrived at puberty, ty, were denominated according to their sex, either *patres familiarum*, or *matres familiarum*. For, in these appellations, it was not intended, that the person only should be demonstrated, but also the right.

Civium Romanorum quidam sunt patres familiarum, quædam matres familiarum. Patres familiarum sunt, qui sunt suæ potestatis, sive puberes, sive impuberes sim.a modo matres familiarum ff. 1. t 6 l 4

Pater familias appellatur, qui in domo dominium habet recteque hoc nomine appellatur, quamvis filium non habeat Non enim solam personam ejus, sed et jus, demonstramus ff 50. t 16 l 195 de verb signif.

Consensum habeant parentum] The law of *England* requires the consent of parents, or guardians, to the marriage of their children, or wards, who are under the age of 21 years. *See the* canons *of* 1603 canon 62, 63, 100, 101, *&c.*

But the penalty in consequence of the marriage of a minor without the consent of his parents, or guardians, was chiefly levelled at the minister, who was liable to be suspended for three years, for altho' the consent of parents or guardians was required, previous to the marriage of minors, yet if the marriage had been celebrated by a priest without such consent, it was always held to be valid and binding, and from hence some bad men among the clergy took occasion to do much mischief, by marrying all, who offered themselves, whose numbers daily increased, by the strictness of the ecclesiastical officers in granting licences, and the obedience of the clergy in general to the canons of the church.

It was therefore thought necessary, in the reign of king *William the third*, to enact, "that "every parson, who shall marry any person "without banns or licence, or shall knowingly "permit any other minister to marry any persons in any church or chapel to such parson "belonging, shall forfeit 100 pounds, one moiety to his majesty, and the other to the informer And that every man so married shall "forfeit 10 pounds, and that every sexton or "parish clerk assisting shall forfeit 5 pounds" 7 *and* 8 *William* 3 *cap* 5

And, in the 10th year of Q *Anne*, it was farther enacted by statute, "that if a parson, vicar or "curate, is in prison, and the goaler shall "knowingly permit such clergyman to celebrate marriage before publication of banns, or "licence obtained, he shall forfeit 100 pounds" 10 *Ann. cap.* 19 *Sect* 176.

But these laws, strict as they may appear, were yet found, by experience, to be ineffectual: for those of the clergy, who were capable of offending, had seldom any sort of preferment, so that suspension to them could be little or no punishment; and, when the statutes were inforced, it generally happened, that the prosecutor was the greatest sufferer, thro' the poverty of the party prosecuted, so that the insufficiency of all these laws to effect the good purposes, for which they were intended, rendered it absolutely necessary to make a law, which, if I may be allowed the expression, should execute itself

This law is the statute of the 26th of K. *George the second*, by which it is ordained, in imitation of the *Roman* law (and not in contradiction to any divine precept, *see* Milton's *Tetrachordon*) "that all marriages celebrated, without banns "or licence first had, shall be null and void, to "all intents and purposes · and that the clergyman, who shall be proved to have solemnized "any such marriage, shall be transported to some "of his Majesty's plantations in *America* for 14 "years" 26 *Geo* 2

For particulars the reader is referred to the act at large, which tends in general to settle property, and wipe disgrace from the nation

Cumque super filio] As the children of a daughter are not under the power of her father, the consent of the father is, by the civil law, not so essential, but that it may be dispensed with upon extraordinary occasions, altho' regularly the precedent consent of the father, even of an emancipated daughter under the age of twenty-five years, was as necessary to confirm the marriage, as the consent of the father of the intended husband *v* C 5 *t* 4 *ll* 18, 20

Secundum datum] The rules, set forth in the constitution, are, that at *Rome* the curators of the father must give the portion with the approbation of the præfect of the city, and that, in the provinces, the portion must be given with the approbation of the governors. C 1 t 4. l 28

Quæ uxores duci possunt vel non. De cognatis, ac primum de parentibus et liberis.

§ I. Ergo non omnes nobis uxores ducere licet: nam a quarundam nuptiis abstinendum est. inter eas enim personas, quæ parentum liberorumve locum inter se obtinent, contrahi nuptiæ non possunt, veluti inter patrem et filiam, vel avum et neptem, vel matrem et filium, vel aviam et nepotem, et usque in infinitum: et, si tales personæ inter se coierint, nefarias atque incestas nuptias contraxisse dicuntur. Et hæc adeo vera sunt, ut ut, quamvis per adoptionem parentum liberorumve loco sibi esse cœperint, non possunt inter se matrimonio jungi; in tantum, ut etiam, dissoluta adoptione, idem juris maneat. Itaque eam, quæ tibi per adoptionem filia vel neptis esse cœperit, non poteris uxorem ducere, quamvis eam emancipaveris.

§ 1. We are not permitted to marry all women without distinction; for there are some, with whom marriage is forbidden. For matrimony must not be contracted between parents and their children, as between a father and daughter, a grandfather and his grand daughter, a mother and her son, a grand-mother and her grand-son; and the same prohibition extends with respect to all ascendents and descendents in a right line in infinitum. *And, if such persons cohabit together, they are said to have contracted a criminal and incestuous marriage; which is undoubtedly true, inasmuch as those, who only hold the place of parents and children by adoption, can by no means marry, and the same law remains in force, even after the adoption is dissolved. Whoever therefore hath once been either your adopted daughter or grand-daughter, the same cannot afterwards be taken by you to wife, altho' she hath been emancipated.*

De fratribus et sororibus.

§ II. Inter eas quoque personas, quæ ex transverso gradu cognationis junguntur, est quædam similis observatio, sed non tanta. Sane enim inter fratrem sororemque nuptiæ prohibitæ sunt, sive ab eodem patre eademque matre nati fuerint, sive ab altero eorum. Sed, si qua per adoptionem soror tibi esse cœperit, quamdiu quidem constat adoptio, sane inter te et eam nuptiæ consistere non possunt, cum vero per emancipationem adoptio sit dissoluta, poteris eam uxorem ducere: sed et si tu emancipatus fueris, nihil est impedimento nuptiis. Et ideo constat, si quis generum adoptare velit, debere eum antea filiam suam emancipare: et, si quis velit nurum adoptare, debere eum antea filium suum emancipare.

§ 2. Matrimony is also prohibited between collaterals, but the prohibition is not of so great an extent, as that which relates to parents and their children. A brother and sister are forbidden to marry, whether they are the children of the same father and mother, or of either. And, if any person becomes your sister by adoption, as long as such adoption subsists, a marriage contracted between her and you can not be valid. But, when the adoption is destroyed by emancipation, she may then be taken to wife. Also if you yourself are emancipated, there will not then remain any impediment, altho' your sister by adoption is not so. From hence it appears, that if a man would adopt his son-in-law, he should first emancipate his daughter, and that, whoever would adopt his daughter in law, should previously emancipate his son.

Inter eas quoque personas] Marriage in *England* is forbidden only between such persons, who are prohibited to marry by the *levitical law*, which is adjudged, in the collateral lines, to extend no farther than the third degree. But the prohibition is equally binding, whether the persons are related by affinity, or consanguinity. The levitical computation of degrees is the same as the computation in the civil law, by which there are counted as many degrees, as there are persons, the common stock not being reckoned. This was also the antient manner of computing by the canon law, according to some authors, who suppose, that pope *Alexander the second*, perceiving dispensations to be greatly lucrative to the church, and being at the same time conscious, that it had universally obtained, that persons might marry in the fourth degree, began a new

new computation, according to which the canonists have since reckoned all degrees, *in the equal transversal lines*, from the common stock on one side only: and, in *the unequal transversal lines*, according to the distance of that person, who is remotest from the common stock. *Decret part 2 caus 35 q 5*

It is evident from this alteration in, or revival of, the canon law, that not only first cousins, but also second, and third cousins, were prohibited from matrimony, nor is it less evident, that so extensive a prohibition must have caused frequent dispensations

But it was enacted by statute, in the reign of *Henry the eighth, that no prohibition* (God's law except) *shall impeach any marriage without the levitical degrees* 32 Hen 8 cap 38

The intention of this statute was to restore the levitical computation, which has since been followed by the judges in all their resolutions It has therefore been frequently resolved, that marriage with a sister's daughter is incestuous, because such marriage is in the *third degree* · that matrimony with a wife's sister's daughter is also incestuous, because it is likewise in the *third degree*. 5 *Mod*. 448 And that marriage with the relict or widow of a great uncle is not incestuous, because such person is in the *fourth degree Harrison* v *Burwel, Vaughan*, 206

Filium emancipare] For otherwise the marriage would be dissolved, inasmuch as it is contrary to law, that brothers and sisters should intermarry *Theoph*.

De fratris et sororis filia vel nepte.

§ III. Fratris vero vel sororis filiam uxorem ducere non licet: sed nec neptem fratris vel sororis quis ducere potest, quamvis quarto gradu sint: cujus enim filiam ducere non licet, neque ejus neptem permittitur. Ejus vero mulieris, quam pater tuus adoptavit, filiam non videris prohiberi uxorem ducere: quia neque naturali, neque civili, jure tibi conjungitur.

§ 3. *It is unlawful to marry the daughter of a brother, or a sister; neither is it lawful to marry the grand-daughter of a brother, or sister, altho' they are in the fourth degree. For when we are prohibited to take the daughter of any person in marriage, we are also prohibited to take his grand-daughter. But it appears not, that there is any impediment against the marriage of a son with the daughter of her, whom his father hath adopted, for they bear not to each other any relation either natural or civil.*

De consobrinis.

§ IV. Duorum autem fratrum, vel sororum liberi, vel fratris et sororis, conjungi possunt.

§ 4 *The children of two brothers, or two sisters, or of a brother and sister, may legally be joined together in matrimony*

De amita, matertera, amita magna, matertera magna.

§ V. Item amitam, licet adoptivam, ducere uxorem non licet. Item nec materteram: quia parentum loco habentur. Qua ratione verum est, magnam quoque amitam, et materteram magnam, prohiberi uxorem ducere.

§ 5 *A man is not permitted to marry his aunt on the father's side, altho' she is only so by adoption, neither can a man marry his aunt on the mother's side; because they are both esteemed to be the representatives of parents. And for the same reason no person can contract matrimony with his great-aunt, either on his father's, or his mother's side.*

Magnam quoque amitam] By the law of *England* it is otherwise, for upon a prohibition for proceeding against a person in the ecclesiastical court, who had married the widow of his great-uncle, it was determined by all the judges, that such marriage, being in the fourth degree, was not forbidden by the levitical law, and was therefore allowable. *Vaugh*. 206. 2 *Ven*. 9

De

De affinibus, et primum de privigna et nuru.

§ VI. Affinitatis quoque veneratione a quarundam nuptiis abſtinere neceſſe eſt: ut ecce privignam aut nurum ducere non licet: quia utræque filiæ loco ſunt. Quod ita ſcilicet accipi debet, ſi fuit nurus aut privigna tua. Nam, ſi adhuc nurus tua eſt, id eſt, ſi adhuc nupta eſt filio tuo, alia ratione uxorem eam ducere non poteris: quia eadem duobus nupta eſſe non poteſt. Item ſi adhuc privigna tua eſt, id eſt, ſi mater ejus tibi nupta eſt, ideo eam uxorem ducere non poteris, quia duas uxores eodem tempore habere non licet.

§ 6. *We are under a neceſſity of abſtaining from certain marriages, thro' a veneration for affinity; for it is unlawful to marry a wife's daughter, or a ſon's wife, in that both are in the place of daughters. And this rule muſt be underſtood to relate not only to thoſe, who actually are, but alſo to thoſe, who have been, our daughters in-law at any time. For marriage with a ſon's wife, whileſt ſhe continues to be his wife, is prohibited on another account, viz. becauſe the ſame woman can not, at one and the ſame time, be the wife of two. And the marriage of a man with his wife's daughter, whileſt her mother continues to be his wife, is alſo prohibited, becauſe it is unlawful for one man to have two wives at the ſame time.*

De ſocru et noverca.

§ VII. Socrum quoque et novercam prohibitum eſt uxorem ducere: quia matris loco ſunt: quod et ipſum, diſſoluta demum adfinitate, procedit: alioquin, ſi adhuc noverca eſt, id eſt, ſi adhuc patri tuo nupta eſt, communi jure impeditur tibi nubere, quia eadem duobus nupta eſſe non poteſt. Item ſi adhuc ſocrus eſt, id eſt, ſi adhuc filia ejus tibi nupta eſt, ideo impediuntur tibi nuptiæ, quia duas uxores habere non potes.

§ 7. *A man is forbidden to marry his wife's mother, and his father's wife, becauſe they both hold the place of mothers: and this injunction muſt be obſerved, altho' the affinity is diſſolved: for, omitting our veneration for affinity, a father's wife, whileſt ſhe continues to be ſo, is prohibited to marry, becauſe no woman can have two husbands at the ſame time. A man is alſo reſtrained from matrimony with his wife's mother, her daughter continuing to be his wife, becauſe it is againſt the law to have two wives.*

De comprivignis.

§ VIII. Mariti tamen filius ex alia uxore, et uxoris filia ex alio marito, vel contra, matrimonium recte contrahunt; licet habeant fratrem ſororemve ex matrimonio poſtea contracto natos.

§ 8. *The ſon of a husband by a former wife, and the daughter of a wife by a former husband, and,* e contra, *the daughter of an husband by a former wife and the ſon of a wife by a former husband may lawfully contract matrimony, even tho' a brother, or ſiſter, is born of ſuch ſecond marriage between their reſpective parents.*

De quaſi privigna, quaſi nuru, et quaſi noverca.

§ IX. Si uxor tua poſt divortium ex alio filiam procreavit, hæc non eſt quidem privigna tua: ſed Julianus ab hujuſmodi nuptiis abſtineri debere

ait.

ait: nam constat, nec sponsam filii nurum esse, nec patris sponsam novercam esse. rectius tamen et jure facturos eos, qui ab hujusmodi nuptiis abstinuerint

§ 9 *If a wife, after divorce, brings forth a daughter by a second husband, such daughter is not to be reckoned a daughter-in law to the first husband It is nevertheless the opinion of* Julian, *that we ought to abstain from such nuptials. It is also evident, that the* espoused *wife of a son is not a daughter-in-law to his father; and that the* espoused *wife of a father, is not a step mother to his son. Yet those, who abstain from such nuptials, demean themselves rightly*

Si uxor tua post divortium] It will be sufficient in this place to observe, that divorces with us are either *a mensa et thoro*, or, *a vinculo matrimonii* A divorce, *a mensa et thoro*, separates only from bed and board, but does not bastardize the children, who were begotten before such divorce, and persons so divorced may afterwards live together, if they mutually consent But a divorce, *a vinculo matrimonii*, intirely dissolves the bond of matrimony *ab initio*, so that the issue is bastardized, and the parties divorced at liberty to marry But, if either of the persons dies before the sentence of divorce is pronounced, the sentence ought not to be pronounced afterwards, and therefore the issue is esteemed legitimate For a marriage even within the levitical degrees is voidable only, and not void, until sentence is given *Vaugh.* 208 220

The causes of divorce *a vinculo matrimonii* are now three only, consanguinity, affinity, and impotence, for, by the late act of the 26th of *Geo the second*, precontract has ceased to be of this number, and all divorces for other causes than these three, which are precedent to matrimony, are only *a mensa et thoro*, from bed and board for a divorce on account of cruelty does not dissolve a marriage, but is only allowed for the safety of the woman against ill usage and even in a cause of adultery the sentence of an ecclesiastical court has no other effect than to separate the parties without affecting the bond of matrimony but, in cases of adultery in the woman, it is common to obtain an act of parliament for the absolute dissolution of the marriage

Among the *Romans* the bond of matrimony was frequently dissolved upon the most trivial pretences, and sometimes even the mutual consent of parties was alone sufficient, as in the case of *Cato* and *Martia*, related by *Plutarch*, " for when *Hortensius* earnestly desired *Martia*, " *Cato* did not deny the request of his friend, " but said, that *Philip* the father of *Martia* " ought also to be consulted *Philip* therefore, " being sent for, came, and, finding they were " all agreed, gave his daughter *Martia* to *Hortensius* in the presence of *Cato*, who himself " assisted at the marriage "

The reader may observe from this extract, that *Cato* did not lend his wife, but absolutely parted from her, which was allowable. See *Kennet's antiq* p 332. in which this matter is fully discussed, and the assertions of *Tertullian* are confuted

But the emperor *Justinian* prohibited all dissolutions of marriage, which were merely voluntary, unless it could be made evident, that chastity was the motive.

Quia vero ex consensu aliqui usque ad præsens alterna matrimonia solvebant, hoc de cætero fieri nullo sinimus modo, nisi forte quidam castitatis concupiscentia hoc fecerint Nov 17 cap 10

The emperor also limited the causes of divorce, and ordained, in favor of children, that they should not be prejudiced by the separation of their parents

Nati filii nullo modo lædantur ex separatione nuptiarum, sed ad parentum hereditatem vocentur, &c Nov 117 cap 7, 8

De servili cognatione.

§ X. Illud certum est, serviles quoque cognationes impedimento nuptiis esse, si forte pater et filia, aut frater et soror, manumissi fuerint.

§ 10. *It is not to be doubted, but that servile cognation is an impediment to matrimony, as when a father and daughter, or a brother and sister, are manumitted*

Impedimento nuptiis] Altho' the relation of father and daughter, brother and sister, &c produced no evil effect among slaves, whilest they continued so, yet it became a bar to matrimony after their infranchisement — *Semper enim in contrahendis matrimoniis naturale jus et pudor inspicitur* — And persons so nearly related, as father and daughter, brother and sister, &c even in a state of slavery, were not permitted to cohabit together in *contubernio* Vinn.

De reliquis prohibitionibus.

§ XI. Sunt et aliæ personæ, quæ propter diversas rationes nuptias contrahere prohibentur, quas in libris digestorum seu pandectarum, ex jure veteri collectarum, enumerari permisimus.

§ 11. *There are, besides these already mentioned, many other persons, who, for diverse reasons, are prohibited to marry with each other; all whom we have caused to be enumerated in the digests, collected from the old law.*

Sunt et aliæ personæ] Senators were prohibited to marry with libertines, tutors and curators with their wards, &c. *ff* 23 *t* 2. *ll.* 16 42 44 57 66 *de ritu nupt*

De pœnis injustarum nuptiarum.

§ XII. Si adversus ea, quæ diximus, aliqui coierint, nec vir, nec uxor, nec nuptiæ, nec matrimonium, nec dos intelligitur. Itaque ii, qui ex eo coitu nascuntur, in potestate patris non sunt: sed tales sunt (quantum ad patriam potestatem pertinet) quales sunt ii, quos mater vulgo concepit. Nam nec hi patrem habere intelliguntur, cum et iis pater incertus sit; unde solent *spurii* appellari παρα την σποραν, et ἀπατορες, quasi sine patre filii. Sequitur ergo, ut, dissoluto tali coitu, nec dotis, nec donationis exactioni locus sit. Qui autem prohibitas nuptias contrahunt, et alias pœnas patiuntur, quæ sacris constitutionibus continentur.

§ 12. *If any persons presume to cohabit together in contempt of the rules, which we have here laid down, they shall not be deemed husband and wife, neither shall their marriage, or any portion given on account of such marriage, be valid And the children, born in such cohabitation, shall not be under the power of their father. For, in respect to paternal power, they resemble the children of a common woman, who are looked upon as not having a father, because it is incertain, who he is They are therefore called in Latin* spurii, *and in Greek* ἀπάτορες; i e. *without a father and from hence it follows, that, after the dissolution of any such marriage, no portion, or gift,* propter nuptias, *can legally be claimed But those, who contract such prohibited matrimony, must undergo the farther punishments set forth in our constitutions.*

Constitutionibus] *Cod* 5 *t* 5 *ll* 4 6 *cum auth sequente,* quæ multam irrogat pecuniariam, infamiam, et cum infamia pœnam stupri *Vinn*

De legitimatione.

§ XIII. Aliquando autem evenit, ut liberi, qui statim, ut nati sunt, in potestate parentum non sunt, postea redigantur in potestatem patris: qualis est is, qui dum naturalis fuerat, postea curiæ datus, potestati patris subjicitur: nec non is, qui, a muliere libera procreatus, cujus matrimonium minime legibus interdictum fuerat, sed ad quam pater consuetudinem habuerat, postea, ex nostra constitutione dotalibus instrumentis compositis, in potestate patris efficitur. Quod et aliis liberis, qui ex eodem matrimonio fuerint procreati, similiter nostra constitutio præbuit.

§ 13. *It sometimes happens, that the children, who at the time of their birth were not under the power of their parents, are reduced under it afterwards. Thus a natu-*

 ral

ral son, who is made a Decurion, becomes subject to his father's power. And he also, who is born of a free-woman, with whom marriage is not prohibited, will likewise become subject to the power of his father, as soon as the marriage instruments are drawn, as our constitution directs, which allows the same benefits to those, who are born before marriage, as to those, who are born subsequent to it

Curia datus] The *Decurions* were so called, because the *curia*, or *senate*, of the colonies, was supposed to consist of a tenth part of the people "*Decuriones quidem dictos aiunt ex eo, quod initio, cum coloniæ deducerentur, decima pars eorum, qui ducerentur, consilii publici gratia conscribi solita sit* ff 50 t 16 *l* 239 § 5

Nec non is] By a constitution or canon, made in the time of pope *Alexander the third*, it was enacted, "that children, born before the solemnization of matrimony, might nevertheless become legitimate by the subsequent marriage of their parents" And, in consequence of this canon, all the bishops of *England*, in the reign of *Henry the third*, petitioned the lords, "that they would consent, that all such, who were born before matrimony, should be legitimate, as well as those, who were born after matrimony, in respect to hereditary succession; inasmuch as the church accepteth all such as legitimate"

But all the earls and barons with one voice answered, "that they would not change the laws of *England*, which hitherto had been used and approved" *Rogaverunt omnes episcopi magnates, ut consentirent, quod nati ante matrimonium essent legitimi, sicut illi, qui nati sunt post matrimonium, quantum ad successionem hereditariam, quia ecclesia tales habet pro legitimis. Et omnes comites et barones una voce responderunt, quod nolunt leges Angliæ mutare, quæ huc usque usitatæ sunt et approbatæ* Stat Merton 20 Henr 3. Co Litt. 245 a 2 Co inst 97

Ex nostra constitutione] *C* 5 *t*. 27 *l* 10 De naturalibus liberis.

TITULUS UNDECIMUS.

De Adoptionibus.

D. 1. T. 7. C. viii. T. 48.

Continuatio.

NON solum autem naturales liberi, secundum ea, quæ diximus, in potestate nostra sunt, verum etiam ii, quos adoptamus.

It appears from what has been already said, that all natural children are subject to paternal power. We must now add, that not only natural children are subject to it, but those also, whom we adopt.

Naturales liberi] The word *natural* is here used for *legitimate*.

Divisio adoptionis.

§ I. Adoptio autem duobus modis fit, aut principali rescripto, aut imperio magistratus. Imperatoris auctoritate adoptare quis potest eos, easve, qui, quæve, sui juris sunt, quæ species adoptionis dicitur *arrogatio*. Imperio magistratus adoptamus eos easve, qui quæve in potestate parentum sunt; sive primum gradum liberorum obtineant, qualis est filius, filia, sive inferiorem, qualis est nepos, neptis, pronepos, proneptis

§ 1 *Adoption is made two ways, either by a rescript from the emperor, or by the authority of the magistrate The imperial rescript impowers us to adopt persons of*

either

either ſex, who are ſui juris ; i. e. *independent and not under the power of parents, and this ſpecies of adoption is called* arrogation. *But it is by the authority of the magiſtrate, that we adopt perſons actually under the power of their parents, whether they are in the firſt degree, as ſons and daughters, or in an inferior degree, as grand-children, or great grand children.*

Adoptio autem] It is certain, that adoption was never practiſed in *England.* Sir *Edward Coke* writes thus concerning it. We remember not that we have read in any book of the legitimation or adoption of an heir, but only in Bracton, and that to no little purpoſe. But the ſureſt adoption is to make good aſſurance of the land by learned advice. The paſſage, referred to in *Bracton,* is in theſe words *Legitimentur etiam quandoque, quaſi per adoptionem, et de conſenſu et voluntate parentum, ut ſi uxor alicujus de alio conceperit, quam de viro ſuo, et, licet de hoc conſtiterit in veritate, ſi vir ipſum in domo ſua ſuſceperit et advocaverit et nutrierit ut filium, erit hæres et legitimus, vel ſi expreſſe non advocaverit, dum tamen illum non amoverit, ſive vir omnino ignoraverit, vel ſciverit, vel dubitaverit, talis legitimus ut hæres judicabitur, eo quod naſcitur de uxore, dum tamen præſumi poſſit, quod potuit ipſum generaſſe.* Bract lib 2 cap 29

Qui poſſunt adoptare filium-familias, vel non.

§ II. Sed hodie, ex noſtra conſtitutione, cum filius-familias à patre naturali extraneæ perſonæ in adoptionem datur, jura patris naturalis minime diſſolvuntur; nec quicquam ad patrem adoptivum tranſit, nec in poteſtate ejus eſt · licet ab inteſtato jura ſucceſſionis ei à nobis tributa ſint. Si vero pater naturalis non extraneo, ſed avo filii ſui materno, vel ſi ipſe pater naturalis fuerit emancipatus, etiam avo vel proavo ſimili modo paterno vel materno filium ſuum dederit in adoptionem, in hoc caſu, quia concurrunt in unam perſonam et naturalia et adoptionis jura, manet ſtabile jus patris adoptivi, et naturali vinculo copulatum, et legitimo adoptionis modo conſtitutum, ut et in familia et in poteſtate hujuſmodi patris adoptivi ſit.

§ 2 *But now, by our conſtitution, when the ſon of a family is given in adoption by his natural father to a ſtranger, the right of paternal power in the natural father is not diſſolved, neither does any thing paſs to the adoptive father, neither is the adopted ſon in his power, altho' ſuch ſon is by us allowed to have the right of ſucceſſion to his adoptive father, if he dies inteſtate. But if a natural father ſhould give his ſon in adoption, not to a ſtranger, but to the maternal grandfather of ſuch ſon, or if a natural father, who hath been emancipated, ſhould give his ſon, begotten after emancipation, to his paternal or maternal grandfather, or great grandfather, in this caſe, the rights of nature and adoption concurring, the power of the adoptive father is eſtabliſhed both by natural ties and legal adoption, ſo that the adopted ſon would be both in the family, and under the power of his adoptive father.*

Ex noſtra conſtitutione] *Cod* 8 *t* 47 *l pen De adoptionibus* Before this conſtitution, agnation was diſſolved by adoption, which frequently proved an injury, inſtead of a benefit, to thoſe, who were adopted.

Non extraneo] *Extraneam autem perſonam intelligit* Juſtinianus *omnem, quæ extra lineam parentum ſit unde qui a patruo aut avunculo adoptati ſunt, perinde habere debent, ac ſi a quovis extraneo adoptati forent* Vinn h t.

De arrogatione impuberis.

§ III. Cum autem impubes per principale reſcriptum arrogatur, cauſa cognita, adrogatio fieri permittitur: et exquiritur cauſa arrogationis, an honeſta ſit, expediatque pupillo? et cum quibuſdam conditionibus arrogatio fit; id est, ut caveat arrogator personæ publicæ, si intra pubertatem pupillus decesserit, restituturum se bona illis, qui, si adoptio facta non esset, ad successionem ejus venturi essent. Item non aliter emancipare eum potest arrogator, nisi, causa cognita, dignus emancipatione fuerit; et tunc sua bona ei reddat. Sed, et si decedens pater eum exhæredaverit, vel vivus sine justa causa emancipaverit, jubetur quartam partem ei bonorum suorum relinquere; videlicet, præter bona, quæ ad patrem adoptivum transtulit, et quorum commodum ei postea acquisivit.

§ 3. *When any person, not arrived at puberty, is arrogated by the imperial rescript, the cause is first inquired into, that it may be known, whether the arrogation is justly founded, and expedient for the pupil. For such arrogation is always made on certain conditions, and the arrogator is obliged to give caution before a public notary, thereby binding himself, if his pupil should die within the age of puberty, to restore all the goods and effects of such pupil to those, who would have succeeded him, if no arrogation had been made. The arrogator is also prohibited to emancipate, unless he has given legal proof, that his arrogated son deserves emancipation; and even then he is bound to make full restitution of all things belonging to such son. Also if a father, upon his death-bed, hath disinherited his arrogated son, or when in health hath emancipated him, without a just cause, then the father is commanded to leave the fourth part of all his goods to his son, besides what such son brought to him at the time of arrogation, and acquired for him afterwards.*

Bonorum] With us the word *goods* does not comprehend those things, which are in the nature of freehold, or parcel of it, but denotes only chattels. But in the civil law the word *bona* has a greater latitude, and generally comprehends a man's whole estate, of whatsoever it consists

De ætate adoptantis et adoptati.

§ IV. Minorem natu majorem non posse adoptare placet: adoptio enim naturam imitatur, et pro monstro est, ut major sit filius, quam pater. Debet itaque is, qui sibi filium per adoptionem aut arrogationem facit, plena pubertate [id est, decem et octo annis] præcedere.

§ 4. *A junior is not permitted to adopt a senior, for adoption imitates nature; and it seems unnatural, that a son should be older than his father. He therefore, who would either adopt or arrogate, should be a senior to his adopted or arrogated son by full puberty, that is, by eighteen years.*

De adoptione in locum nepotis vel neptis, vel deinceps.

§ V. Licet autem et in locum nepotis vel neptis, pronepotis vel proneptis, vel deinceps, adoptare, quamvis filium quis non habeat.

§ 5. *It is lawful to adopt a person either as a grand-son or grand-daughter, great grand-son or great grand-daughter, or in a more distant degree, altho' the adopter hath no son.*

De adoptione filii alieni in locum nepotis, et contra.

§ VI. Et tam filium alienum quis in locum nepotis adoptare potest, quam nepotem in locum filii.

§ 6.

§ 6. *A man may adopt the son of another as his grand-son, and the grand-son of another as his son.*

De adoptione in locum nepotis.

§ VII. Sed si quis nepotis loco adoptet, vel quasi ex filio, quem habet jam adoptatum, vel quasi ex illo, quem naturalem in sua potestate habet, eo casu et filius consentire debet, ne ei invito suus hæres agnascatur. Sed, ex contrario, si avus ex filio nepotem det in adoptionem, non est necesse, filium consentire.

§ 7. *If any man, who has already either a natural or an adopted son, is desirous to adopt another, as his grand-son, the consent of his son, whether natural or adopted, ought in this case to be first obtained, lest a* suus hæres, *or proper heir, should be intruded upon him. But, on the contrary, if a grand-father is willing to give his grand-son in adoption, the consent of the son is not necessary.*

Qui dari possunt in adoptionem.

§ VIII. In plurimis autem causis adsimilatur is, qui adoptatus vel arrogatus est, ei, qui ex legitimo matrimonio natus est, et ideo, si quis per imperatorem, vel apud prætorem, vel præsidem provinciæ, non extraneum adoptaverit, potest eundem in adoptionem alii dare.

§ 8 *He, who is either adopted or arrogated, bears similitude in many things to a son born in lawful matrimony, and therefore, whoever is adopted either by rescript, or before a prætor, or before the governor of a province, the same, if he is not a stranger, may be given in adoption to another.*

Non extraneum adoptaverit] No person can give another in adoption, who is not under his power, and it appears by the second paragraph of this title, that, if *Titius* should adopt a stranger, the stranger would not be subject to *Titius*, but still remain under the power of his natural father, and it therefore follows, that *Titius* could not give such stranger in adoption to another

Si is, qui generare non potest, adoptet.

§ IX. Sed et illud utriusque adoptionis commune est, quod et ii, qui generare non possunt, quales sunt spadones, adoptare possunt: castrati autem non possunt.

§ 9 *It is observed as a common rule both in adoption, and arrogation, that such, who are impotent [whom we denominate* Spadones] *may adopt children; but that those, who are castrated, can not adopt.*

Quales sunt Spadones] Those, who were denominated *Spadones* might also marry, as well as adopt, as there was a possibility of their becoming potent And by marriage they were intituled to have an action *pro dote* ff 23. t 3 *l* 39 *de jure dotium* The emperor *Leo*, in his novels, permitted even castrated persons to adopt *Leon Nov* 26

Si fœmina adoptet.

§ X. Fœminæ quoque arrogare non possunt, quia nec naturales liberos in sua potestate habent: sed, ex indulgentia principis, ad solatium liberorum amissorum adoptare possunt.

§ 10.

§ 10. *Women are also prohibited to adopt; for the law does not permit them to have even their own children under their power: but, when death hath deprived them of their children, they may, by the indulgence of the prince, adopt others, as a comfort and recompence for their loss.*

Sed ex indulgentia] ff 5 t 2. *l* 29. *de inofficioso testamento*

De liberis arrogatis.

§ XI. Illud proprium est adoptionis illius, quæ per sacrum oraculum fit, quod is, qui liberos in potestate habet, si se adrogandum dederit, non solum ipse potestati arrogatoris subjicitur, sed etiam liberi ejus fiunt in ejusdem potestate, tanquam nepotes. Sic etenim divus Augustus non ante Tiberium adoptavit, quam is Germanicum adoptasset; ut protinus, arrogatione facta, inciperet Germanicus Augusti nepos esse.

§ 11. *It is peculiar to that kind of adoption, which is made by rescript, that if a person, having children under his power, should give himself in arrogation, both he, as a Son, and his children, as grand-children, would become subject to the power of the arrogator. It was for this reason, that* Augustus *did not adopt* Tiberius, *'till* Tiberius *had adopted* Germanicus, *so that* Tiberius *became the son and* Germanicus *the Grandson of* Augustus, *at the same instant, by arrogation.*

Hoc proprium est] For in common adoptions, made before a magistrate, no other person can pass under the power of the adoptor, than the single person, whom he adopts, and the reason of this difference between adoption and arrogation is plain ' *Nam in adoptionem dantur filii-" familiarum, quorum liberi sunt in potestate alte-" rius, nempe ejus, qui in adoptionem dat ideoque " etiam in illius potestate remanent Arrogantur au-" tem patres-familiarum, qui cum ipsi liberos suos in " potestatem habeant, nihil mirum, si secum etiam " illos, in familiam et potestatem alienam, transfe-" rant* " Vinn *h l*

Augustus non ante] *vid* Tac 4 *annal cap.* 57 & Suetonium *in* Tib. *cap.* 15.

De servo adoptato, vel filio nominato, a domino.

§ XII. Apud Catonem bene scriptum refert antiquitas, servos, si a domino adoptati sint, ex hoc ipso posse liberari. Unde et nos eruditi, in nostra constitutione, etiam eum servum, quem dominus, actis intervenientibus, filium suum nominaverit, liberum esse constituimus: licet hoc ad jus filii accipiendum non sufficiat.

§ 12. *The following answer of* Cato *was approved of by the antient lawyers, viz. that slaves, adopted by their masters, obtain freedom by the adoption. And, from hence instructed, we have enacted by our constitution, that a slave, whom any master nominates to be his son, in the presence of a magistrate, becomes free by such nomination, altho' it does not convey to him any filial right.*

In nostra constitutione.] *C* 7. *t* 6 *p.* 10. *de latina libertate tollenda*

TITU-

TITULUS DUODECIMUS.

Quibus modis jus patriæ poteſtatis ſolvitur.

D. 1. T. 7. Nov. 81.

Scopus et nexus. De morte.

VIdeamus nunc, quibus modis ii, qui alieno juri ſunt ſubjecti, eo jure liberentur. Et quidem, quemadmodum liberentur ſervi a poteſtate dominorum, ex iis intelligere poſſumus, quæ de ſervis manumittendis ſuperius expoſuimus. Hi vero, qui in poteſtate parentis ſunt, mortuo eo, ſui juris fiunt. Sed hoc diſtinctionem recipit: nam, mortuo patre, ſane omnimodo filii, filiæve, ſui juris efficiuntur: mortuo vero avo, non omnino nepotes, nepteſve, ſui juris fiunt: ſed ita, ſi poſt mortem avi in poteſtatem patris ſui recaſuri non ſunt. Itaque, ſi, moriente avo, pater eorum vivit, et in poteſtate patris ſui eſt, tunc poſt obitum avi in poteſtate patris ſui fiunt. Si vero is, quo tempore avus moritur, aut jam mortuus eſt, aut, per emancipationem, exiit de poteſtate patris, tunc ii, qui in poteſtatem ejus cadere non poſſunt, ſui juris fiunt.

Let us now inquire how thoſe, who are in ſubjection to others, can be freed from that ſubjection. The means, by which ſlaves obtain their liberty, may be fully underſtood by what we have already ſaid in treating of manumiſſion. But thoſe, who are under the power of a parent, become independent at his death; yet this rule admits of a diſtinction. When a father dies his ſons and daughters are, without doubt, independent, but by the death of a grand-father his grand-children do not become independent, unleſs it happens, that there is an impoſſibility of their ever falling under the power of their father. Therefore, if their father is alive at the death of their grand-father and they are 'till then under his power, the grand-children, in this caſe, become ſubject to the power of their father. But, if their father is either dead or emancipated before the death of their grand-father, they then cannot fall under the power of their father, and therefore become independent.

De deportatione.

§ I. Cum autem is, qui ob aliquod maleficium in inſulam deportatur, civitatem amittit: ſequitur, ut qui eo modo ex numero civium Romanorum tollitur, perinde, quaſi eo mortuo, deſinant liberi in poteſtate ejus eſſe. Pari ratione et ſi is, qui in poteſtate parentis ſit, in inſulam deportatus fuerit, deſinit eſſe in poteſtate parentis. Sed, ſi ex indulgentia principis reſtituti fuerint per omnia, priſtinum ſtatum recipiunt.

§ 1. *If a man, upon conviction of ſome crime, is deported into an iſland, he loſes the rights of a* Roman *citizen, and it follows, that the children of ſuch a perſon ceaſe to be under his power, as if he was naturally dead. And, by a* [illegible]

[illegible]

soning, if a son is deported, he ceases to be under the power of his father. But if, by the indulgence of the prince, a criminal is wholly restored, he regains instantly his former condition.

Deportatur] Deportation denotes a perpetual banishment, and is so called, because the criminal is as it were carried from the rights, which he had in his native country; for by this punishment, he lost the birth-right of a citizen, his paternal power, his estate, and his right of succession.

De relegatione.

§ II. Relegati autem patres in insulam in potestate liberos retinent, et liberi relegati in potestate parentum remanent.

§ 2. *A Father, who is relegated, retains his paternal power; and a son, who is relegated, still remains under the power of his father.*

Relegati] Relegation imports either a perpetual or temporary banishment But a sentence of relegation did not necessarily deprive a man of the rights of a citizen; and in general it was a much milder punishment, than deportation *Myrsinger*

De servitute pœnæ.

§ III. Pœnæ servus effectus filios in potestate habere desinit. Servi autem pœnæ efficiuntur, qui in metallum damnantur, et qui bestiis subjiciuntur.

§ 3. *When a man is judicially pronounced to be the slave of punishment, he loses his paternal jurisdiction. The slaves of punishment are those, who are condemned to the mines, or sentenced to be destroyed by wild beasts.*

Servi autem pœnæ] The slaves of punishment are so called, because they have no other master, than the labor or punishment to which they are condemned. *Vinn* h t.

De dignitate.

§ IV. Filius-familias, si militaverit, vel si senator, vel consul factus fuerit, remanet in potestate patris: militia enim, vel consularis dignitas, de patris potestate filium non liberat. Sed, ex constitutione nostra, summa patriciatus dignitas illico, imperialibus codicillis præstitis, filium a patria potestate liberat. Quis enim patiatur, patrem quidem posse, per emancipationis modum, potestatis suæ nexibus filium liberare: imperatoriam autem celsitudinem non valere eum, quem patrem sibi elegit, ab aliena eximere potestate?

§ 4. *If the son of a family becomes a soldier, a senator, or a consul, he still remains under the power of his father, from which neither the army, the senate, nor consular dignity can emancipate him. But it is enacted by our constitution, that the patrician dignity, conferred by our special diploma, shall free every son from all paternal subjection For it is absurd to think, that a parent may emancipate his son, and that the power of an emperor should not be sufficient to make any person independent, whom he hath chosen to be a father of the commonwealth, or, in other words, a senator.*

Constitutione nostra] *Cod* 12 *t* 3 *l* 5 *De consulibus*

Patriciatus dignitas] During the republic the title of patricians was conferred on those only, who were the descendents of those senators, whom *Romulus* had created And *Livy* testifies, that in his time the children of every antient senatorial family were nominated patricians

Patricii

Patricii eorum senatorum progenies erant, quos Romulus crearat. hac tamen ætate, antiquissimæ cujusque senatoriæ familiæ liberi patricii appellantur But, after the translation of the seat of the empire to *Constantinople*, those only were called patricians (*quasi patres communis reipublicæ*) who, having been curule magistrates, were chosen by the emperors to be councillors of state.

De captivitate et postliminio.

§ V. Si ab hostibus captus fuerit parens, quamvis servus hostium fiat, tamen pendet jus liberorum, propter jus postliminii: quia hi, qui ab hostibus capti sunt, si reversi fuerint, omnia pristina jura recipiunt: idcirco reversus etiam liberos habebit in potestate: quia postliminium fingit eum, qui captus est, in civitate semper fuisse. Si vero ibi decesserit, exinde, ex quo captus est pater, filius sui juris fuisse videtur. Ipse quoque filius, nepósve, si ab hostibus captus fuerit, similiter dicimus, propter jus postliminii, jus quoque potestatis parentis in suspenso esse Dictum autem est postliminium à *limine* et *post*. Unde eum, qui ab hostibus captus est, et in fines nostros postea pervenit, postliminio reversum recte dicimus. Nam limina sicut in domo finem quendam faciunt, sic et imperii finem esse limen veteres voluerunt. Hinc et limen dictum est, quasi finis quidam et terminus. Ab eo postliminium dictum est, quia ad idem limen revertebatur, quod amiserat Sed et, qui captus victis hostibus recuperatur, postliminio redisse existimatur.

§ 5. *If a parent is taken prisoner by the enemy, altho' he thus becomes a slave, yet he loses not his paternal power, which remains in suspense by reason of a privilege granted to all prisoners; namely, the right of return. For captives, when they obtain their liberty, are repossessed of all their former rights, in which paternal power of course must be included. and, at their return, they are supposed, by a fiction of law, never to have been absent. If a prisoner dies in captivity, his son is deemed to have become independent, not from the time of the death of his father, but from the commencement of his captivity Also, if a son, or grand-son, becomes a prisoner, the power of the parent is said, for the reason before assigned, to be only in suspense. The term* postliminium *is derived from* post *and* limen *We therefore aptly use the expression* reversus postliminio, *when a person, who was a captive, returns within our own confines.*

De emancipatione, item de modis et effectibus ejusdem.

§ VI. Præterea emancipatione quoque desinunt liberi in potestate parentum esse. Sed emancipatio antea quidem vel per antiquam legis observationem procedebat, quæ per imaginarias venditiones et intercedentes manumissiones celebrabatur, vel ex imperiali rescripto. Nostra autem providentia etiam hoc in melius per constitutionem reformavit; ut, fictione pristina explosa, recta via ad competentes judices, vel magistratus, parentes intrent, et filios suos vel filias, vel nepotes vel neptes, ac deinceps, a sua manu dimittant. Et tunc, ex edicto prætoris in bonis ejusmodi filii vel filiæ, vel nepotis vel neptis, qui quæve à parente manumissus vel manumissa fuerit, eadem jura præstantur parenti, quæ tribuuntur patrono in bonis liberti. Et

præterea, si imbubes sit filius, vel filia, vel cæteri, ipse parens ex manumissione tutelam ejus nanscíscitur.

§ 6. *Children also cease to be under the power of their parents by emancipation Emancipation was effected according to our antient law, either by imaginary sales and intervening manumissions, or by the imperial rescript; but it has been our care to reform these ceremonies by an express constitution, so that parents may now have immediate recourse to the proper judge or magistrate, and emancipate their children, grand children,* &c. *of both sexes. And also, by a prætorian edict, the parent is allowed to have the same right in the goods of those, whom he emancipates, as a patron has in the goods of his freed-man. And farther, if the children emancipated are within the age of puberty, the parent, by whom they were emancipated, obtains the right of wardship or tutelage, by the emancipation.*

Emancipatio antea quidem] It was enacted by a law of the twelve tables, "that a son was "not free from paternal power, 'till he had been "thrice sold by his father" *Si pater filium ter venumdaut, filius a patre liber esto* Thus the condition of a son was worse than that of a slave. But, altho' this law soon lost it's force, yet the formal part of it was retained, and three sales were still thought requisite to effect the emancipation of a son, altho' they were but imaginary There was therefore always a feigned contract, made between the father and a person, whom he could confide in, called *pater fiduciarius*, who after every sale restored the son into the hands of his father The emperor *Anastasius* was the first, who dispensed with these fiduciary sales by his rescript, but *Justinian* entirely abolished them, having ordained, "that all parents might emancipate their children without the observance of such vain ceremonies." *Cum inspeximus in emancipationibus vanam observationem custodiri, et venditiones in liberas personas figuratas, &c quorum nullus rationabilis invenitur exitus, &c.* C. 8. t. 49. *l.* 6.

Si alii emancipentur, alii retineantur in potestate.

§ VII. Admonendi autem sumus, liberum arbitrium esse ei, qui filium, et ex eo nepotem vel neptem, in potestate habet, filium quidem de potestate dimittere, nepotem vero vel neptem retinere: et, è converso, filium quidem in potestate retinere, nepotem vero vel neptem manumittere: vel omnes sui juris efficere. Eadem et de pronepote et pronepte dicta esse intelliguntur.

§ 7. *A parent having a son under his power, and by that son a grandson or grand-daughter, may emancipate his son, and yet retain his grandson or grand-daughter in subjection He may also manumit his grandson or grand-daughter, and still retain his son under his power, or, if he is so disposed, he may make them all independent. And the same may be said of a great-grandson, or a great-grand daughter.*

De adoptione.

§ VIII. Sed et si pater filium, quem in potestate habet, avo, vel proavo naturali, secundum nostras constitutiones super his habitas, in adoptionem dederit, id est, si hoc ipsum actis intervenientibus apud competentem judicem manifestaverit, præsente eo, qui adoptatur, et non contradicente, nec non eo præsente, qui adoptat, solvitur quidem jus potestatis patris naturalis; transit autem in hujusmodi parentem adoptivum, in cujus persona et adoptionem esse plenissimam antea diximus.

§ 8. *If a father gives his son in adoption to the natural grand father or great-grand-father of such son, strictly adhering to the rules laid down in our constitutions*

for

for that purpose enacted, which injoin the parent to make his intention manifest before a competent judge, in the presence of the person to be adopted, in no wise contradicting, and also in the presence of the adoptor, then does the right of paternal power pass wholly from the natural father to the adoptive, in whose person, as we have before observed, adoption has it's fullest extent.

Secundum nostras constitutiones.] *C* 8 *t* 48 *ll* 10. 11. *De adoptionibus.*

De nepote nato post filium emancipatum.

§ IX. Illud scire oportet, quod si nurus tua ex filio tuo conceperit, et filium tuum emancipaveris, vel in adoptionem dederis, prægnante nuru tua, nihilominus, quod ex ea nascitur, in potestate tua nascitur Quod si post emancipationem vel adoptionem conceptus fuerit, patris sui emancipati, vel avi adoptivi, potestati subjicitur.

§ 9 *It is necessary to be known, that, if a son's wife hath conceived, and you afterwards emancipate that son or give him in adoption, his wife being pregnant, the child, which she brings forth, will, notwithstanding this, be born under your paternal authority But, if the conception is subsequent to the emancipation or adoption, the child so conceived becomes subject, at his birth, either to his emancipated father, or his adoptive grand father.*

Patris sui emancipati, vel avi adoptivi] In *England*, if a man hath a wife, and dieth, and within a very short time after the wife marrieth again, and within nine months hath a child, so as it may be the child of the one, or of the other, some have said, that in this case the child may chuse his father, quia filiatio non potest probari For avoiding of which question, and other inconveniences, this was the law before the conquest: Sit omnis vidua sine marito duodecem mensibus, et, si maritaverit, perdat dotem *Co Litt* 8 a *ll. Anglo-Sax* Wilkins, *Ed* 109 122 144

By the civil law a second marriage, in man or woman, is condemned, tho' not absolutely forbidden But a widow is prohibited to marry, *infra annum luctus*, under severe penalties

Si qua ex fœminis, perdito marito, infra anni spatium alteri festinaverit nubere (parvum enim tempus post decem menses servandum adjicimus, tamen id ipsum exiguum putemus) probrosis inusta notis, honestiori, nobilisque personæ decore et jure privetur atque omnia, quæ de prioris mariti bonis, vel jure sponsalium, vel judicio defuncti conjugis, consecuta fuerat, amittat Imppp Gratianus, Valentinianus, et Theodosius AAA Eutropio P P *Cod* 5 *t* 9

An parentes cogi possunt liberos suos de potestate dimittere?

§ X. Et quidem neque naturales liberi, neque adoptivi, ullo pene modo possunt cogere parentes de potestate sua eos dimittere.

§ 10 *Children, either natural or adopted, can rarely compel their parents by any method to dismiss them from subjection*

Ullo pene modo.] It is true in general, that parents could not be obliged to emancipate their children, and that their children could not be compelled to be emancipated But these rules were not without exception for a son might have compelled his father to emancipate him on various accounts, but particularly for cruelty *Divus Trajanus filium, quem pater malè contra pietatem adficiebat, coegit emancipare* D 37 t 12 *l* 5 D 35. t 1 *l* 50 Cod 1 t 4. *l* 12 D 1 t 7 *l* 32

And a father might also have forced his son to be emancipated in all cases, which would have justified him in disinheriting such son *vid Bart in l* 132. *D* 45 *t* 1 *Mynf h.t*

TITULUS DECIMUS-TERTIUS.

De tutelis.

D. xxvi. T. 1. Nov. 72.

De personis sui juris.

TRanseamus nunc ad aliam divisionem personarum. Nam ex his personis, quæ in potestate non sunt, quædam vel in tutela sunt, vel in curatione, quædam neutro jure tenentur. Videamus ergo de his, quæ in tutela vel curatione sunt: ita enim intelligemus cæteras personas, quæ neutro jure tenentur. Ac prius dispiciamus de his, qui in tutela sunt.

Let us now proceed to another division of persons. Of those, who are not in the power of their parents, some are under tutelage, some under curation, and some under neither. Let us then inquire what persons are under tutelage and curation, for thus we shall come to the knowledge of those, who are not subject to either. We will first treat of such persons, who are under tutelage.

In tutela vel curatione] By the law of *England* the term guardianship denotes either the tutelage or the curation of minors, and of guardianship there are three kinds, by *common law*, by *statute*, and by *particular custom* First, By *common law* there were formerly four species of guardians; but guardianship in chivalry having been taken away by 12 *Car* 2, there now remain but three, *viz.* guardianship by *nature*, by *nurture*, and in *socage* 3 *Co rep* 37 *b*

Secondly, by *statute*, for by 4 and 5 *Ph* and *M. cap* 8 a father, or mother, after the father's death, without assignation, are guardians of women-children And by 12 *Car* 2 " A father under " age, or of full age, by deed in his life-time, " or by will, in presence of two witnesses, may " dispose the custody of his child under twenty-" one years of age, and not married at the time " of his death, whether then born, or *in ventre* " *sa mere*, during his non-age, to any in posses-" sion or remainder, other than to Popish re-" cusants which persons may maintain any " action of trespass against wrongful takers-" away, and detainers of such child, and reco-" ver damages for the child's use, and may " take into their custody his lands and perso-" nal estate, according to such disposition, and " bring actions, as guardian in socage might " do.

Before this act, a tenent in socage, of age, might have disposed of his lands by deed, or last will, in trust for his heir, but not the custody of his heir, for the law gave that to the next of kin, to whom the land could not descend. *Vaugh.* 178

And 3dly, By *particular custom*, as in *London*, where the tuition of orphans unmarried, who are the children of freemen, belongs by custom to the city. *Co. Litt.* 88 *b.*

Tutelæ definitio.

§ I. Est autem tutela (ut *Servius* definivit) vis ac potestas in capite libero, ad tuendum eum, qui per ætatem se defendere nequit, jure civili data ac permissa.

§ 1 *Tutelage, as* Servius *has defined it, is an authority and power, given and permitted by the civil law, and exercised over such independent persons, who are unable, by reason of their age, to protect themselves.*

De

Definitio et etymologia tutoris.

§ II. Tutores autem ſunt, qui eam vim ac poteſtatem habent; exque ipſa re nomen acceperunt. Itaque appellantur tutores, quaſi tuitores atque defenſores, ſicut æditui dicuntur, qui ædes tuentur.

§ 2. *Tutors are those, who have the authority and power before mentioned, and they take their name from the nature of their office. For they are called tutors,* quaſi tuitores; *as those, who have the care of the sacred buildings, are called* æditui, quod ædes tueantur.

Quibus teſtamento tutor datur: et primum, de liberis in poteſtate.

§ III. Permiſſum eſt itaque parentibus liberis impuberibus, quos in poteſtate habent, teſtamento tutores dare. Et hoc in filios filiaſque procedit omnimodo: nepotibus vero neptibuſque ita demum parentes poſſunt teſtamento tutores dare, ſi poſt mortem eorum in poteſtatem patris ſui non ſunt recaſuri. Itaque, ſi filius tuus mortis tuæ tempore in poteſtate tua ſit, nepotes ex eo non poterunt ex teſtamento tuo tutores habere, quamvis in poteſtate tua fuerint. ſcilicet, quia, mortuo te, in poteſtatem patris ſui recaſuri ſunt.

§ 3. *Parents are permitted to assign tutors by testament to such of their children, who are not arrived at puberty, and are under their power. And this privilege of parents extends without exception over sons and daughters. But grand-fathers can only give tutors to their grand-children, when it is impossible, that such grand-children should ever fall under the power of their father, after the death of their grand-father. And therefore, if your son is in your power at the time of your death, your grand-children by that son can not receive tutors by your testament, altho' they were actually in your power, because at your decease they will become subject to their father*

Tutores dare] Becauſe after puberty curators only can be appointed.

De poſthumis.

§ IV. Cum autem in compluribus aliis cauſis poſthumi pro jam natis habeantur, et in hac cauſa placuit non minus poſthumis, quam jam natis, tutores dari poſſe; ſi modo in ea cauſa ſint, ut, ſi vivis parentibus naſcerentur, ſui hæredes et in poteſtate eorum fierent.

§ 4 *As posthumous children are in many cases reputed to have been born before the death of their fathers; therefore tutors may be given by the testament of a parent as well to a posthumous child, as to a child already born, if such posthumous child, had he been born in the life-time of his father, would have been his proper heir and under his power.*

De emancipatis.

§ V. Sed et, ſi emancipato filio tutor à patre datus fuerit teſtamento, confirmandus eſt ex ſententia præſidis omnimodo, id eſt, ſine inquiſitione.

§ 5

§ 5. *But, if a father gives a tutor by testament to his emancipated son, such tutor must be confirmed by the sentence of the governor of the province without inquisition.*

Sine inquisitione.] Τουτεστιν, οὐκ ἐπιζητησας, ποτερον εὐπορος ᾖ, ἠ των δυναμενων τα του νεου διοικειν πραγματα, αρκουσης αὐτῳ, προς τελειωτατην τουτων παραστασιν, της του τελευτησαντος μαρτυριας. That is, without inquiring, whether the person appointed to be a tutor is in good circumstances, or whether he is otherwise qualified to conduct the affairs of his pupil: for, in relation to these points, the sole testimony of the deceased gives a perfect satisfaction. *Theoph. h. t.*

TITULUS DECIMUS-QUARTUS.

Qui testamento tutores dari possunt.

D. xxvi. T. 2. C. v. T. 28.

Qui tutores dari possunt.

DARI autem tutor potest testamento non solum pater-familias, sed etiam filius-familias.

Not only the father of a family may be appointed by testament to be a tutor, but also the son of a family

De servo.

§ I. Sed et servus proprius testamento cum libertate recte tutor dari potest: sed sciendum est, et sine libertate tutorem datum tacite libertatem directam accepisse videri; et per hoc recte tutorem esse. Plane si per errorem, quasi liber, tutor datus sit, aliud dicendum est. Servus autem alienus *pure* inutiliter testamento datur tutor: sed ita, *cum liber erit*, utiliter datur. Proprius autem servus inutiliter eo modo tutor datur.

§ 1. *A man may by testament assign his own slave to be a tutor with liberty. But note, that, if a master by testament appoints his slave to be a tutor without mentioning liberty, such slave seems tacitly to have received immediate liberty, and is thus legally inabled to commence a tutor: yet, if a testator thro' error, imagining his slave to be a free person, by testament appoints him, as such, to be a tutor, the appointment will not avail. Also the absolute appointment of another man's slave to be a tutor is altogether ineffectual: but, if the appointment is upon condition, that the person appointed obtains his freedom, then it is made profitably: but, if a man by testament appoints his own slave to be a tutor,* when he shall obtain his liberty, *the appointment will be void*

De furioso et minore viginti-quinque annis.

§ II. Furiosus, vel minor viginti-quinque annis, tutor testamento datus, tutor tunc erit, cum compos mentis, aut major viginti-quinque annis, fuerit factus.

§ 2

§ 2. *If a madman, or a minor, is by testament appointed to be a tutor, the one shall begin to act, when he becomes of sound mind, and the other, when he has completed his twenty-fifth year.*

Furiosus vel minor] The same law is also observed in *England*, in respect to madmen and minors. But it must be noted, that with us the minority of all persons determines at the age of twenty-one years complete *Co. Litt* 78 *b.*

Quibus modis tutores dantur.

§ III. Ad certum tempus, vel ex certo tempore, vel sub conditione, vel ante hæredis institutionem, posse dari tutorem non dubitatur.

§ 3. *It is not doubted, but that a testamentary tutor may be given either to a certain time, or* from *a certain time, or conditionally, or before the institution of an heir.*

Ad certum tempus] *e g* Let *Titius* be my son's tutor 'till the calends of *December*

Ex certo tempore] *e g* Let *Titius* commence to be my son's tutor after the expiration of two years.

Sub conditione] *e g* Let *Titius* take upon him the tutelage of my son, if the ship *Argo* returns from *Asia*

Ante hæredis institutionem] *e g* Let *Titius* be tutor to my son, and let *Titius* also be my heir.

It must here be observed, that the civil law calls him heir, who succeeds to the whole estate of another, whether it is real or personal

But, by the law of *England*, he only is heir, who succeeds to a real estate of inheritance by the act of God, and by right of blood *Co Litt*. 237 *b*. And he, who succeeds to personal estate, or goods, is in law called an executor, if he succeeds by the appointment of the deceased in his last will, or administrator, if he succeeds by the appointment of the ordinary.

Cui dantur.

§ IV. Certæ autem rei, vel causæ, tutor dari non potest: quia personæ, non causæ vel rei, tutor datur.

§ 4. *A tutor cannot be assigned to any particular thing, or upon any certain account, but can only be given to persons.*

De tutore dato filiabus, vel filiis, vel liberis, vel nepotibus.

§ V. Si quis filiabus suis, vel filiis, tutores dederit, etiam posthumæ vel posthumo dedisse videtur: quia, filii vel filiæ appellatione, et posthumus et posthuma continentur. Quod si nepotes sint, an appellatione filiorum et ipsis tutores dati sint? Dicendum est, ut et ipsis quoque dati videantur, si modo liberos dixerit: cæterum, si filios, non continebuntur. Aliter enim filii, aliter nepotes appellantur. Plane, si posthumis dederit, tam filii posthumi, quam cæteri liberi, continebuntur.

§ 5. *If a man by testament nominates a tutor for his sons or his daughters, the same person seems also to be appointed tutor to his posthumous issue; because, under the appellation of son or daughter, a posthumous child is comprehended But, should it be questioned, whether grand-children are denoted by the word sons, and can receive tutors by that denomination, we answer, that under the general term,* children, *grand-children are undoubtedly included, but that the word sons does not comprehend them for the word son, and grandson, widely differ in their signification But, if a testator assigns a tutor to his descendents, it is evident, that not only his posthumous sons are comprehended, but all his other children.*

TITU-

TITULUS DECIMUS-QUINTUS.

De legitima agnatorum tutela.

D. xxvi. T. 4. C. v. T. 30.

Summa.

QUIBUS autem testamento tutor datus non est, his, ex lege duodecim tabularum, agnati sunt tutores, qui vocantur legitimi.

The Agnati *are, by the law of the twelve tables, appointed to be tutors to those, to whom no testamentary tutor was given; and these tutors are called legitime.*

Quibus autem] By a law in the twelve tables, if a man died intestate and had no children, the *agnati* were called to the legitime inheritance But, if the intestate had a child, the *agnati* were then called to the legitime tutelage. For it was the opinion of the *Romans*, that as the next heir to the pupil was most interested in the estate, he was therefore the most proper person to take care of it But *Solon* was of a very different opinion *Lege autem* Solonis (says *Laertius) tutela non deferebatur* agnatis, *nisi remotioribus, contraria habita ratione, quod fere quisque conatus eum, quem proximus hæres insequitur, expungere* Vinn And our own law goes still farther, for he, who is guardian in socage, must be the next of blood, who can never inherit for example, if the lands of a minor descended to him from his mother, then the wardship belongs to the uncle on the side of the father, but, if the lands of a minor descended from his father, then the uncle on the mother's side must be guardian in socage And the same rule ought also to be observed for the common benefit of all minors, whose inheritances do not lie in tenure. *Co Litt* 87 *b*

Qui vocantur legitimi] These tutors are called legitime, because tutelage, when there is no testamentary tutor, devolves upon the *agnati* merely by the act of the law, without the intervention of any magistrate *Quippe legitimos tutores nemo dat* ff. 26. t. 4 *l*. 5.

Qui sunt agnati.

§ I. Sunt autem agnati cognati, per virilis sexus cognationem conjuncti, quasi à patre cognati: veluti frater ex eodem patre natus, fratris filius, neposve ex eo: item patruus et patrui filius, neposve ex eo. At, qui per fœminini sexus personas cognatione junguntur, agnati non sunt, sed alias naturali jure cognati. Itaque amitæ tuæ filius non est tibi agnatus, sed cognatus: et invicem tu illi eodem jure conjungeris · quia, qui ex ea nascuntur, patris, non matris, familiam sequuntur.

§ I Agnati *are those, who are collaterally related to us by males, as a brother by the same father, or the son of a brother, or by him a grandson; also a father's brother, or the son of such brother, or by him a grandson. But those, who are related to us by a female, are not said to be* agnate, *but* cognate, *bearing only a natural relation to us. Thus the son of a father's sister is not related to you by* agnation, *but by* cognation, *and you are related to him in the same manner, that is, by cognation; for the children of a father's sister follow the family of their father, and not that of their mother.*

Sunt autem agnati] The distinction, between the *agnati* and *cognati*, is intirely taken away by *Justinian* Nov. 118 cap 4, 5

Quis

Quis dicatur inteſtatus.

§ II. Quod autem lex duodecim tabularum ab inteſtato vocat ad tutelam agnatos, non hanc habet ſignificationem, ſi omnino non fecerit teſtamentum is, qui poterat tutores dare; ſed ſi, quantum ad tutelam pertinet, inteſtatus deceſſerit: quod tunc quoque accidere intelligitur, cum is, qui datus eſt tutor, vivo teſtatore deceſſerit.

§ 2. *The law of the twelve tables, in calling the* agnati *to tutelage in caſe of inteſtacy, relates not ſolely to perſons altogether inteſtate, in whoſe power it was to have appointed a tutor, but extends alſo to thoſe, who are inteſtate only in reſpect to tutelage; and this may happen, if a tutor, nominated by teſtament, ſhould die in the life-time of the teſtator.*

Quibus modis agnatio, vel cognatio, finitur.

§ III. Sed agnationis quidem jus omnibus modis capitis diminutione plerumque perimitur: nam agnatio juris civilis nomen eſt, cognationis vero jus non omnibus modis commutatur: quia civilis ratio civilia quidem jura corrumpere poteſt, naturalia vero non utique.

§ 3 *The right of agnation is taken away by almoſt every diminution, or change of ſtate; for agnation is but a name given by the civil law. But the right of cognation is not thus altered, for altho' civil policy may extinguiſh civil rights, yet over our natural rights it has no ſuch power.*

TITULUS DECIMUS-SEXTUS.

De capitis diminutione.

D. iv. T. 5.

Definitio et diviſio.

EST autem capitis diminutio prioris ſtatus mutatio: eaque tribus modis accidit. Nam aut maxima eſt capitis diminutio, aut minor, (quam quidam mediam vocant) aut minima.

Diminution is the change of a man's former condition, which is effected three ways, according to the threefold diviſion of diminution into the greater, the leſs, and the leaſt.

De maxima capitis diminutione.

§ I. Maxima capitis diminutio eſt, cum aliquis ſimul et civitatem et libertatem amittit, quod accidit his, qui ſervi pœnæ efficiuntur atrocitate ſententiæ: vel libertis, ut ingratis erga patronos condemnatis; vel his, qui ſe ad pretium participandum venundari paſſi ſunt.

§ 1. *The greater diminution is, when a man loses both the right of a citizen and his liberty, which is the case of those, who by the rigor of their sentence are pronounced to be the slaves of punishment.— And of freedmen, who are condemned to slavery for ingratitude to their patrons.— And of all such, who suffer themselves to be sold, in order to become sharers of the price.*

Vel libertis ut ingratis] In *England*, if a villein was once manumitted, altho' he afterwards became ingrateful in the highest degree, yet the manumission remained good 1 *Inst* 137 *b*. *Libertinum ingratum leges civiles in pristinam redigunt servitutem, sed leges Angliæ semel manumissum semper liberum judicant gratum et ingratum*. Fort de laud *ll Angliæ*, cap. 46.

Ingratis] The emperor *Claudius* first inflicted this punishment upon libertines or freed-men *Ingratos libertinos* (says *Suetonius*) *et de quibus patroni quererentur, revocavit in servitutem*.

And *Constantine* afterwards promulged a law to the same effect.

Imp Constant *ad* Maximum

Si manumissus ingratus circa patronum suum extiterit, et, quadam jactantia vel contumacia, cervicem adversus eum erexit, a patrono rursus sub imperium ditionemque mittatur Cod. 6. t. 7. *l*. 2 ann. Dom 319

But thus far the *Romans* only copied from the *Athenians*, who permitted a patron to bring an action called ἀποστασίου against such freed-persons, who had been remiss in their duty, and to reduce them to their pristin state of bondage, if the charge was proved. *Archæologia Græc* vol. 1. p 153

And, in the year 367, the emperors *Valentinian*, *Valens*, and *Gratian*, enacted, "that children, who had behaved ungratefully after emancipation, should forfeit their liberty by being reduced under the power of their parents.

Imppp Valentin. Valens, *et* Gratianus, A A A

Filios (et filias, cæterosque liberos) contumaces, qui parentes, vel acerbitate convitii, vel cujuscunque atrocis injuriæ dolore, pulsassent, leges emancipatione rescissa damno libertatis immeritæ multari voluerunt Cod 7. t. 50 . un

But the emperor *Justinian* was not content, that the law against ingratitude should take place in regard only to freedmen and emancipated children, but extended it to the case of donations to all his subjects in general.

Imp Justinianus A. Juliano, *PP*

"Generaliter sancimus, omnes donationes, lege confectas, firmas illibatasque manere, si non donationis acceptor ingratus circa donatorem inveniatur, ita ut injurias atroces in eum effundat, vel manus impias inferat, vel jacturæ molem ex insidiis suis ingerat, quæ non levem censum substantiæ donatoris imponat, vel vitæ periculum aliquod ei intulerit; vel quasdam conventiones, sive in scriptis donationi impositas, sive sine scriptis habitas, quas donationis acceptor spospondit, minime implere voluerit. Ex his enim tantummodo causis, si fuerint in judicium dilucidis argumentis cognitionaliter approbatæ, etiam donationes in eos factas everti concedimus, ne sit cuiquam licentia, et alienas res capere, et frugalitatem irridere donatoris, et ipsum iterum donatorem suasque res perdere, et præfatis malis ab ingrato donationis acceptore affici. Hoc tamen usque ad primas personas tantummodo stare censemus, nulla licentia concedenda donatoris successoribus hujusmodi querimoniarum primordium instituere Etenim si ipse, qui hoc passus est, tacuerit, silentium ejus maneat semper, et non a posteritate ejus suscitari concedatur, vel adversus eum, qui ingratus esse dicitur, vel adversus ejus successores." C 8. *t*. 56. *l*. 10

De media.

§ II. Minor, sive media, capitis diminutio est, cum civitas quidem amittitur, libertas vero retinetur, quod accidit ei, cui aqua et igni interdictum fuerit, vel ei, qui in insulam deportatus est.

§ 2 *The less or mesne diminution is, when a man loses the rights of a citizen, but retains his liberty; which happens to him, who is forbidden the use of fire and water, or to him who is deported into an island.*

De minima.

§ III. Minima capitis diminutio est, cum civitas retinetur et libertas, sed status hominis commutatur: quod accidit his, qui cum sui juris fuerint,

rint, cœperunt alieno juri subjecti esse; vel contra, veluti si filius-familias à patre emancipatus fuerit, est capite diminutus.

§ 3. *The least diminution is then said to have been suffered, when the condition of a man is changed without the forfeiture either of his civil rights, or his liberty: as when he, who is independent, becomes subject by adoption: or when the son of a family hath been emancipated by his father.*

De servo manumisso.

§ IV. Servus autem manumissus capite non minuitur: quia nullum caput habuit.

§ 4. *The manumission of a slave works not any change of state in him, because he had, before manumission, no state or civil capacity.*

De mutatione dignitatis.

§ V. Quibus autem dignitas magis quam status permutatur, capite non minuuntur, et ideo, à senatu motos capite non minui, constat.

§ 5. *Those, whose dignity is rather changed than their state, are not said to have suffered diminution; and therefore it appears, that they, who are removed from the senatorial dignity, do not suffer diminution*

Interpretatio § ult. sup. tit. prox.

§ VI. Quod autem dictum est, manere cognationis jus etiam post capitis diminutionem, hoc ita est, si minima capitis diminutio interveniat: manet enim cognatio. Nam, si maxima capitis diminutio interveniat, jus quoque cognationis perit, ut puta servitute alicujus cognati; et ne quidem, si manumissus fuerit, recipit cognationem. Sed et, si in insulam quis deportatus sit, cognatio solvitur.

§ 6. *What has already been said in a section of the preceding title, to wit, that the right of cognation remains after diminution, relates only to the least diminution. For, by the greater diminution, as for instance, by servitude, the right of cognation is wholly destroyed, even so as not to be recovered by manumission The right of cognation is also lost by the less or mesne diminution, as by deportation into an island.*

Ad quos agnatos tutela pertinet.

§ VII. Cum autem ad agnatos tutela pertineat, non simul ad omnes pertinet, sed ad eos tantum, qui proximiore gradu sunt. vel si plures ejusdem gradus sunt, ad omnes pertinet; veluti si plures fratres sunt, qui unum gradum obtinent, pariter ad tutelam vocantur.

§ 7. *Altho' the right of tutelage belongs to the* agnati, *yet it belongs not to all the* agnati *in common, but to those only, who are in the nearest degree. But, if there are many in the same degree, the tutelage belongs to all of them, however numerous For example, if there are several brothers, they are all called equally to tutelage.*

TITULUS DECIMUS-SEPTIMUS.

De legitima patronorum tutela.

D. xxvi. T. 4. C. v. T. 30.

Ratio, ob quam patronorum tutela dicitur legitima.

EX eadem lege duodecim tabularum, libertorum et libertarum tutela ad patronos liberosque eorum pertinet, quæ et ipsa legitima tutela vocatur; non quia nominatim in ea lege de hac tutela caveatur; sed quia perinde accepta est per interpretationem, ac si verbis legis introducta esset. Eo enim ipso, quod hæreditates libertorum libertarumque, si intestati decessissent, jusserat lex ad patronos liberosve eorum pertinere, crediderunt veteres, voluisse legem, etiam tutelas ad eos pertinere; cum et agnatos, quos ad hæreditatem lex vocat, eosdem et tutores esse jusserit; quia plerumque ubi successionis est emolumentum, ibi et tutelæ onus esse debet. Ideo autem diximus *plerumque*, quia si fœmina impubes manumittatur, ipsa ad hereditatem vocatur, cum alius sit tutor.

By the same law of the twelve tables, the tutelage of freed-men, and freed-women, is adjudged to belong to their patrons, and to the children of such patrons: and this tutelage is called legitime, altho' it exists not nominally in the law; but it is as firmly established by interpretation, as if it had been introduced by express words. For inasmuch as the law commands, that patrons and their children shall succeed to the inheritance of their freed-men or freed-women, who die intestate, it was the opinion of the antient lawyers, that tutelage also by implication should belong to patrons and their children And the law, which calls the agnati *to the inheritance, commands them to be tutors, because the advantage of succession ought to be attended in most cases with the burden of tutelage. We have said, in* most cases, *because when any person, not arrived at puberty, is manumitted by a female, such female is called to the inheritance, but not to the tutelage.*

Cum alius sit tutor] The tutelage of a child, by the civil law, could not regularly be committed to a woman

Fœminæ tutores dari non possunt, quia id munus masculorum est ff 26 t 1 *l.* 18. *de tutelis*

But the mother or grandmother was allowed by constitution to execute this office upon condition, that she bound herself solemnly not to contract a second marriage. *Cod* 5 *t* 35 *l* 2 *Nov.* 118 *cap* 5

But in *England* women, as well as men, are equally permitted to become Guardians.

TITULUS DECIMUS-OCTAVUS.

De legitima parentum tutela.

EXEMPLO patronorum recepta eſt et alia tutela, quæ et ipſa legitima vocatur; nam, ſi quis filium aut filiam, nepotem aut neptem ex filio, et deinceps, impuberes emancipaverit, legitimus eorum tutor erit.

In ſimilitude of the tutelage of patrons, another kind of tutelage is received, which is alſo called legitime; for if any parent emancipates a ſon or a daughter, or a grandſon or a grand-daughter, the iſſue of that ſon, or any others deſcended from him by males in a right line and not arrived at puberty, then ſhall ſuch parent be their legitime tutor.

TITULUS DECIMUS-NONUS.

De fiduciaria tutela.

Filii-familias a patre manumiſſi pater tutor eſt legitimus; eo vero defuncto, frater tutor fiduciarius exiſtit.

EST et alia tutela, quæ fiduciaria appellatur: nam, ſi parens filium vel filiam, nepotem vel neptem, vel deinceps, impuberes manumiſerit, legitimam nanciſcitur eorum tutelam. Quo defuncto, ſi liberi ejus virilis ſexus exiſtant, fiduciarii tutores filiorum ſuorum, vel fratris, vel ſororis, vel cæterorum, efficiuntur. Atqui, patrono legitimo tutore mortuo, liberi quoque ejus legitimi ſunt tutores, quoniam filius quidem defuncti, ſi non eſſet à vivo patre emancipatus, poſt obitum ejus ſui juris efficeretur, nec in fratrum poteſtatem recideret, ideoque nec in tutelam. Libertus autem, ſi ſervus manſiſſet, utique eodem jure apud liberos domini poſt mortem ejus futurus eſſet. Ita tamen hi ad tutelam vocantur, ſi perfectæ ſint ætatis: quod noſtra conſtitutio in omnibus tutelis et curationibus obſervari generaliter præcepit.

There is another kind of tutelage called fiduciary, for, if a parent manumits a ſon or a daughter, a grandſon or a grand-daughter, or any other of his children, not arrived to puberty, he is then their legitime tutor: but, at his death, his male children of age become the fiduciary tutors of their own ſons, or of a brother, a ſiſter, or of any other children emancipated by the deceaſed. But, when a patron, who is a legitime tutor, dies, his children alſo become legitime tutors. The reaſon of which difference is this: a ſon, altho' he was never emancipated, becomes independent at the death of his father, and therefore, as he falls not under the power of his brothers, it follows, that he can not be under their legitime tutelage. But the condition of a ſlave is not altered at the death of his maſter, for he then becomes a ſlave to the children of the deceaſed.

deceased. It must here be noted, that the persons above mentioned can not be called to tutelage, unless they are of full age; and our constitution hath in general commanded this rule to be observed in all tutelages and curations.

Si perfectæ sint ætatis] No man is said, by the civil law, to be *perfectæ ætatis*, until the twenty-fifth year of his age is completed. *Si quis absolute dixerit perfectæ ætatis, illam tantummodo ætatem intellectam esse videri volumus, quæ et viginti-quinque annorum curriculis completur.* Cod. 5. t. 45. *l.* ult.

TITULUS VIGESIMUS.

De Attiliano tutore, et eo, qui ex lege Julia et Titia dabatur.

D. xxvi. T. 5. C. v. T. 34 et 36.

Jus antiquum, si nullus sit tutor.

SI cui nullus omnino tutor fuerat, ei dabatur, in urbe quidem à prætore urbano et majore parte tribunorum plebis, tutor ex lege Attilia: in provinciis vero à præsidibus provinciarum ex lege Julia et Titia.

By virtue of the law Attilia, *the prætor of the city, with a majority of the tribunes, had authority to assign tutors to all such, who otherwise were not intituled to tutors: but, in the provinces, tutors were appointed by the respective governors of each province, in consequence of the law* Julia *and* Titia.

Ex lege Attilia] The law *Attilia* was a Plebiscite, made in the year *U. C.* 444, by *Lucius Attilius* and *Caius Martius*, tribunes of the people. *Muretus.*

But of the law *Julia-Titia* there is no certain account *Vinny* speaks thus of it *unica hæc lex fuit, ut lex* Julia *et* Papia, *sed quando, aut a quibus lata sit, parum constat.*

Si spes sit futuri tutoris testamentarii.

§ I. Sed etsi in testamento tutor sub conditione, aut ex die certo datus fuerat, quamdiu conditio aut dies pendebat, ex iisdem legibus tutor alius interim dari poterat. Item si pure datus fuerat, quamdiu ex testamento nemo hæres existebat, tamdiu ex iisdem legibus tutor petendus erat, qui desinebat esse tutor, si conditio extiterat, aut dies venerat, aut hæres extiterat.

§ 1. *If a tutor had been given by testament conditionally, or from a certain day, another tutor might have been assigned by virtue of the above named laws, whilest the condition depended, or 'till the day came. Also if a tutor had been given simply,* i. e. *upon no condition, yet as long as the testamentary heir deferred taking upon him the inheritance, another tutor might have been appointed during the interval. But the office of such tutor ceased, when the cause ceased, for which he was appointed; as when the event of the condition happened, the day came, or the inheritance was entered upon.*

Sed

Sed si in testamento.] With us also guardians may be appointed either *from* a certain time, or *conditionally*. and, in either of these cases, the guardianship is committed, and the committee administers, 'till the term, for which he was assigned, is expired, or 'till the condition is fulfilled. *Swin.* 215.

Si tutor ab hostibus sit captus.

§ II. Ab hostibus quoque tutore capto, ex his legibus tutor petebatur; qui desinebat esse tutor, si is, qui captus erat, in civitatem reversus fuerat. Nam reversus recipiebat tutelam jure postliminii.

§ 2. *By the* Attilian *and* Julio-titian *laws, if a tutor was taken by the enemy, another tutor was immediately requested, whose office ceased of course, when the first tutor returned from captivity; for he then resumed the tutelage by his right of return.*

Quando et cur desierint ex dictis legibus tutores dari.

§ III. Sed ex his legibus tutores pupillis desierunt dari, posteaquam primo consules pupillis utriusque sexus tutores ex inquisitione dare cœperunt, deinde prætores ex constitutionibus. Nam supradictis legibus neque de cautione à tutoribus exigenda, rem pupillis salvam fore, neque de compellendis tutoribus ad tutelæ administrationem, quicquam cavebatur.

§ 3 *The* Attilian *and* Julio-titian *laws, concerning the appointment of tutors, were first disused, when the consuls began to give tutors to pupils of either sex with inquisition; and the prætors were afterwards invested with the same authority by the imperial constitutions. For, by the above mentioned laws, no caution was required from the tutors for the security of their pupils, neither were these tutors compelled to act.*

Jus novum.

§ IV. Sed hoc jure utimur, ut Romæ quidem præfectus urbi, vel prætor secundum suam jurisdictionem, in provinciis autem præsides ex inquisitione tutores crearent, vel magistratus jussu præsidum, si non sint magnæ pupilli facultates.

§ 4. *But, by the later usage, at* Rome *the præfect of the city, or the prætor according to his jurisdiction, and, in the provinces, the governors [each in his respective province] may assign tutors, after an inquiry into their morals and circumstances. and an inferior magistrate, at the command of a governor, may also appoint tutors, if the possessions of the pupil are not large.*

Sed hoc jure] In *England*, if a minor has no tutor, and is possessed only of goods and chattels, then the ordinary may commit the tuition of such minor to the next of kin, who demands it 2 *Lev* 162 217 *Swin Part*. 3. *Sec*. 9. But, according to the usage of court christian, if the child is past seven years of age, it must be at his own request and nomination, that the judge appoints him a tutor; but, if the child is under the age of seven years, then the ordinary may proceed *ex officio*. Strahan

And, in the court of chancery, a guardian can not be otherwise appointed, than by bringing the infant into court, or his praying a commission to have a guardian assigned him. *Abr. of Cases in Eq.* 260

Jus novissimum.

§ V. Nos autem, per constitutionem nostram hujusmodi difficultates hominum resecantes, nec expectata jussione præsidum, disposuimus, si facultates

cultates pupilli vel adulti usque ad quingentos solidos valeant, defensores civitatum una cum ejusdem civitatis religiosissimo antistite, vel alias personas publicas, id est, magistratus, vel juridicum Alexandrinæ civitatis, tutores vel curatores creare: legitima cautela secundum ejusdem constitutionis normam præstanda, videlicet eorum periculo, qui eam accipiunt.

§ 5. *But we, for the ease of our subjects, have ordained by our constitution, that the judge of* Alexandria *and the magistrates of every city, together with the chief ecclesiastic, may give tutors or curators to pupils or adults, whose fortunes do not exceed five hundred* aurei, *without waiting for the command of the governor, to whose province they belong. But all such magistrates must, at their peril, take from every tutor, so appointed, the caution required by our constitution.*

Nos autem per constitutionem] *Cod.* 1. *t.* 4. *l.* 30. De episcopali audientia.

Ratio tutelæ.

§ VI. Impuberes autem in tutela esse, naturali juri conveniens est, ut is, qui perfectæ ætatis non sit, alterius tutela regatur.

§ 6. *It is agreeable to the law of nature, that all such, who are not arrived at puberty, should be put under tutelage, to the intent that all, who are not adults, may be under the government of proper persons.*

De tutelæ ratione reddenda.

§ VII. Cum ergo pupillorum pupillarumque tutores negotia gerant, post pubertatem tutelæ judicio rationem reddunt.

§ 7. *Tutors therefore, since they have the administration of the affairs of their pupils, may be compelled to render an account, by an action of tutelage, when their pupils arrive at puberty.*

Cum ergo] By the civil law an action of tutelage can not be instituted, 'till the tutelage is expired *Nisi finita tutela sit, tutelæ agi non potest.* ff 27. t 3 *l.* 4. *De tut et rat. distrab.* &c. But in *England* an infant may, by *prochein amy*, oblige his guardian to account. 1 *Ver.* 342.

TITULUS VIGESIMUS-PRIMUS.

De auctoritate tutorum.

D. xxvi. T. 8. C. v. T. 59.

In quibus causis auctoritas sit necessaria.

AUCTORITAS autem tutoris in quibusdam causis necessaria pupillis est, in quibusdam non est necessaria: ut ecce, si quid dare sibi stipulentur, non est necessaria tutoris auctoritas; quod si aliis promittant pupilli, necessaria est tutoris auctoritas. Namque placuit, meliorem quidem con-

conditionem licere iis facere etiam sine tutoris auctoritate: deteriorem vero non aliter, quam cum tutoris auctoritate. Unde in his causis, ex quibus obligationes mutuæ nascuntur, ut in emptionibus, venditionibus, locationibus, conductionibus, mandatis, depositis, si tutoris auctoritas non interveniat, ipsi quidem, qui cum his contrahunt, obligantur: at invicem pupilli non obligantur.

The authority or confirmation of a tutor is in some cases necessary, and in others not necessary. When a man stipulates to make a gift to a pupil, the authority of the tutor is not requisite; but, if a pupil enters into a contract, there is a necessity for the tutor's authority, for it is an established rule, that pupils may better their condition, but not impair it, without the authority of their tutors. And therefore in all cases, where there are mutual obligations, as in buying, selling, letting, hiring, mandates, deposites, &c. *he, who contracts with a pupil, is bound by the contract, but the pupil is not bound, unless the tutor hath authorized it.*

In quibusdam necessaria, in quibusdam non necessaria] A minor, by the laws of *England*, may bind himself without the authority of a guardian, either by bond or promise, to pay for those things, which are suitable to his degree, and necessary.

Namque placuit.] In *England*, if the act of the guardian is prejudicial to the minor, it is in most cases voidable, and when it is not voidable, the guardian may be obliged to indemnify his pupil. Thus, if an infant appears by guardian, and suffers a recovery, the recovery is not voidable, but the guardian is answerable, if his pupil sustains damage Also if a guardian faint-pleads, or mispleads in an action, to the injury of his pupil, the pupil will be bound, but he may afterwards have an action against his guardian. 1 *mod* 48, 49

Unde in his causis] The same law obtains also in *England* thus a lease, made to an infant, is not void of itself, but voidable only at his election 2 *Cro* 320.

Exceptio.

§ I. Neque tamen hæreditatem adire, neque bonorum possessionem petere, neque hæreditatem ex fidei-commisso suscipere, aliter possunt, nisi tutoris actoritate, (quamvis illis lucrosa sit) ne ullum damnum habeant.

§ 1. *But no pupil, without the authority of his tutor, can enter upon an inheritance, or take upon him the possession of goods, or an inheritance in trust, for, altho' there may be a probability of profit, there is a possibility of damage.*

Quomodo auctoritas interponi debet.

§ II. Tutor autem statim in ipso negotio præsens debet auctor fieri, si hoc pupillo prodesse existimaverit Post tempus vero, vel per epistolam, aut per nuntium, interposita auctoritas nihil agit.

§ 2. *If a tutor would authorise any act, which he esteems advantageous to his pupil, such tutor ought to be present at the negotiation For the authority of a tutor can have no effect, when given by letter, by messenger, or after a contract is finished.*

Quo casu interponi non potest.

§ III. Si inter tutorem pupillumque judicio agendum sit; quia ipse tutor in rem suam auctor esse non potest, non prætorius tutor (ut olim) constituitur, sed curator in locum ejus datur, quo curatore interveniente, judicium peragitur, et, eo peracto, curator esse desinit.

§ 3. *When a suit is to be commenced between a tutor and his pupil, inasmuch as the tutor can not exercise his authority, as such, against himself, a curator, and not a prætorian tutor, (as it was formerly the custom) is appointed, by whose intervention the suit is carried on, and, when it is determined, the curatorship ceases.*

Si inter tutorem] In *England*, according to the present practice, the *prochein amy*, or next friend of the minor, supplies the place of the *curator*, mentioned in the text. For *prochein amy* was first appointed by *W* 1 *cap* 47 in case of necessity, where the infant was to sue his guardian, or where the guardian would not sue for him. 2 *Cro* 640.

TITULUS VIGESIMUS-SECUNDUS.

Quibus modis tutela finitur.

C. v. T. 60.

De pubertate.

PUPILLI, pupillæque, cum puberes esse cœperint, à tutela liberantur. Pubertatem autem veteres quidem non solum ex annis, sed etiam ex habitu corporis, in masculis æstimari volebant. Nostra autem majestas, dignum esse castitate nostrorum temporum existimans, bene putavit, quod in fœminis etiam antiquis impudicum esse visum est, id est, inspectionem habitudinis corporis, hoc etiam in masculos extendere. Et ideo, nostra sancta constitutione promulgata, pubertatem in masculis post decimum quartum annum completum illico initium accipere disposuimus: antiquitatis normam in fœminis bene positam in suo ordine relinquentes, ut post duodecim annos completos viri potentes esse credantur.

Pupils, both male and female, are freed from tutelage, when they arrive at puberty. The antients judged of puberty in males, not by years only, but also by the habit of their bodies. But our imperial majesty, regarding the purity of the present times, hath esteemed the inspection of males to be an immodest practice, and hath thought it proper, that the same decency, which was ever observed in respect to females, should be also observed in respect to males. And therefore, by our sacred constitution, we have enacted, that puberty in males should be reputed to commence immediately after the completion of their fourteenth year. But, in relation to females, we leave that wholesom and antient rule of law unaltered, by which they are esteemed marriageable after the twelfth year of their age is completed.

Et ideo nostra sancta constitutione] *vid* Cod 5 t 60 l ult *Quando tutores vel curatores esse desinant* "Indecoram observationem in examinanda marium pubertate resecantes, &c

De capitis diminutione pupilli.

§ I. Item finitur tutela, si arrogati sint adhuc impuberes, vel deportati: item si in servitutem pupillus redigatur, vel si ab hostibus captus fuerit.

§. 1.

§ 1. *Tutelage is determined before puberty, if the pupil is either arrogated or suffers deportation; and it also determines, if he is reduced to slavery, or becomes a captive.*

Ab hostibus captus.] Quia nemo in tutela esse potest, nisi qui sit sui juris. *ff.* 26 *t.* 1. *l* 14.

De conditionis eventu.

§ II. Sed, etsi usque ad certam conditionem datus sit tutor testamento, æque evenit, ut desinat esse tutor existente conditione.

§ 2. *But, if a testamentary tutor is given upon a certain condition, after that condition is fulfilled, the tutelage ceases.*

De morte.

§ III. Simili modo finitur tutela morte pupillorum vel tutorum.

§ 3. *Tutelage is also determined either by the death of the tutor, or by the death of the pupil.*

De capitis diminutione.

§ IV. Sed et capitis diminutione tutoris, per quam libertas vel civitas amittitur, omnis tutela perit. Minima autem capitis diminutione tutoris, veluti si se arrogandum dederit, legitima tantum perit: cæteræ non pereunt. Sed pupilli et pupillæ capitis diminutio, licet minima sit, omnes tutelas tollit.

§ 4. *When a tutor suffers the greater diminution of state, by which he at once loses his liberty and the privileges of a citizen, every kind of tutelage is then extinguished. But, if the least diminution is only suffered, as when a tutor gives himself in arrogation, then no species of tutelage is extinguished, except the legitime. But every diminution of state in pupils takes away all tutelage.*

De tempore.

§ V. Præterea, qui ad certum tempus testamento dantur tutores, finito eo, deponunt tutelam.

§ 5. *Those, who are by testament made tutors for a term only, are, at the expiration of such term, discharged from the tutelage.*

De remotione et excusatione.

§ VI. Desinunt etiam tutores esse, qui vel removentur à tutela ob id, quod suspecti visi sunt; vel qui ex justa causa se excusant, et onus administrandæ tutelæ deponunt, secundum ea, quæ inferius proponemus.

§ 6. *They also cease to be tutors, who are either removed from their office upon suspicion, or excuse and exempt themselves from the burden of tutelage for just reasons, of which we shall treat hereafter.*

TITULUS VIGESIMUS-TERTIUS.

De curatoribus.

D. xxvii. T. 10. C. v. T. 70.

De adultis.

MASCULI quidem puberes, et fœminæ viri potentes, usque ad vicesimum quintum annum completum curatores accipiunt; quia licet puberes sint, adhuc tamen ejus ætatis sunt, ut sua negotia tueri non possint.

Males arrived at puberty, and females marriageable, do neverthelesss receive curators, 'till they have compleated their twenty-fifth year: for, altho' they have attained to puberty, they are not as yet of an age to take a proper care of their own affairs.

Masculi quidem puberes] By the civil law, males at the age of twenty years complete, and females at eighteen, having given a sufficient proof, by five or more witnesses, of their prudence and morality, may obtain a licence from the emperor, inabling them to administer their own affairs under proper restrictions. For minors are not permitted by this licence to alien, or even to mortgage their immoveable possessions, but must always obtain a special decree for such purposes *Cod 2. t. 45. l. 1, 2, 3. de his qui ven. æt. impetraverunt.*

A quibus dentur curatores.

§ I. Dantur autem curatores ab eisdem magistratibus, à quibus et tutores. Sed curator testamento non datur; datus tamen confirmatur decreto prætoris vel præsidis.

§ 1. *Curators are appointed by the same magistrates, who appoint tutors. A curator can not be absolutely given by testament, but a tutor, named in a testament, may be confirmed such, either by a prætor or the governor of a province.*

Testamento non datur] A curator can not be given by testament, because a curator, by virtue of his office, has the care of the minor's estate and a father can not dispose of the goods of his son, who is arrived at puberty, for at that age he hath a right to make a will ff 28 t 6. l 2 But the magistrates generally appoint him to be curator, whom the father hath recommended, tho' not always ff 26 t 1. l 39 § 1

Quibus dentur.

§ II. Item inviti adolescentes curatores non accipiunt, præterquam in litem, curator enim et ad certam causam dari potest.

§ 2 *No adults can be obliged to receive curators, unless* ad litem; *for a curator may be appointed to any special purpose, or to the management of any particular affair.*

Item inviti adolescentes] *Rævardus* and others have accused *Tribonian*, as guilty of an error, in saying, that minors, after fourteen, could not be obliged to receive curators —— And, in support of their accusation, they allege the opinion of *Ulpian*, whose words are these —— *Hodie in hanc usque ætatem adolescentes curatorum auxilio reguntur, nec ante rei suæ administratio eis committi debebit, quamvis bene rem suam gerentibus* ff 4. t 4 l 1 —— But it must be observed, that, with

with regard to minors after puberty, the *Roman* law has freqently been altered. By the law *Laetoria, ann. urb con.* 550. such minors only, who behaved ill, were obliged to receive curators after proof had been made of their ill behavior. But afterwards it was enacted, by a constitution of *Marcus Antoninus*, *Ut omnes adulti curatores acciperent, non redditis causis* · which must mean, that adults might be *obliged* to receive curators, altho' nothing could be alleged against their conduct . for it is certain, that adults might voluntarily receive curators, even before the law *Laetoria* And, when *Ulpian* wrote, the constitution of *Marcus Antoninus* was as yet unrepealed; but afterwards, in the latter part of the reign of *Antoninus Caracalla*, it appears from *Cod.* 5. *t* 31 *l.* 1 that the *Roman* law was again altered, and that curators could not be given, but to such minors as were willing to receive them, unless *ad litem*

And, in this, the law of *England* may be said to agree in general with the civil law: for, with us, guardianship regularly determines, when the minor has completed his fourteenth year, except, when there is a guardian by nature, or when the father of a minor has specially appointed a guardian either by deed, or will, to continue for a longer time. And therefore a minor, after fourteen, being of course freed from custody, is at liberty, if willing, to put himself a second time under guardianship, until he is of full age But, if a minor, being an adult, does not consent to receive a new guardian, then no court would appoint a guardian, unless *ad litem*

But, if a testator nominates a guardian, 'till his son arrives at full age, then the son, altho' above fourteen, is compelled to receive the guardian, who is thus expressly appointed for a certain time, but if no certain time is mentioned, there is then no guardianship, if the minor is an adult. *Vaugh* 185

De furiosis et prodigis.

§ III. Furiosi quoque, et prodigi, licet majores viginti quinque annis sint, tamen in curatione sunt agnatorum, ex lege duodecim tabularum. Sed solent Romae praefectus urbi vel praetores, et in provinciis praesides, ex inquisitione eis curatores dare.

§ 3. *By a law of the twelve tables, all madmen and prodigals, altho' of full age, must nevertheless be under the curation of their* agnati. *But, if there are no* agnati, *or if such, who do exist, are unqualified, then curators are appointed, at* Rome, *by the praefect of the city, or the praetor, and in the* provinces, *by the governors, after the requisite inquiry.*

Sed solent] The text in this place is undoubtedly deficient, and *Theophilus*, whose authority is followed in the *English*, has thus supplied, what seems to have been omitted 'Ηνικα μη ὑπεςι ἀδελφος, ἠ ὑπων, ἀνεπιτηδειος ἐςι προς διοικησιν. h. t

De mente captis, surdis, &c.

§ IV. Sed et mente captis, et surdis, et mutis, et illis, qui perpetuo morbo laborant, (quia rebus suis superesse non possunt) curatores dandi sunt.

§ 4. *Those, who are deprived of their intellects, or deaf, or mute, or subject to any continual disorder, inasmuch as they are unable to take a proper care of their own affairs, must be placed under curators.*

Sed et mente captis] With us all persons *non mentis compotes* are reputed to labor under either idiocy or lunacy, and the king, by law, is their general guardian. Idiocy is a fatuity, or madness, *a nativitate*, and this excuses the party, as to his acts, but intitules the king, during the life of the idiot, to the profits of his estate, both real and personal, without rendering an account.

Lunacy is an adventitious madness or fatuity, either *permanent*, or with *intervals*, and equally excuseth with idiocy, as to all acts done, during the phrenzy But the king, in case of lunacy, acts as a guardian and trustee for the lunatic, and is therefore accountable to him, if he regains his understanding, or to his representatives, if it happens otherwise 4 *Co rep* 125 *Bacon's abr.* 80. *vol* 3.

De pupillis.

§ V. Interdum autem et pupilli curatores accipiunt; ut puta, si legitimus tutor non sit idoneus: quoniam habenti tutorem tutor dari non potest. Item, si testamento datus tutor, vel à prætore aut præside, idoneus non sit ad administrationem, nec tamen fraudulenter negotia administret, solet ei curator adjungi. Item loco tutorum, qui non in perpetuum, sed ad tempus à tutela excusantur, solent curatores dari.

§ 5 Sometimes even pupils receive curators; for instance, when the legal tutor is unqualified: for a tutor must not be given to him, who already has a tutor. Also, if a testamentary tutor, or a tutor given by a prætor *or the governor of a province, appears to be afterwards incapable of executing his trust, it is usual, altho' he is guilty of no fraud, to appoint a curator to be joined with him. It is also usual to assign curators in the place of such tutors, who are not wholly excused, but excused for a time only.*

De constituendo actore.

§ VI. Quod si tutor vel adversa valetudine, vel alia necessitate, impediatur, quo minus negotia pupilli administrare possit, et pupillus vel absit, vel infans sit, quem velit actorem, periculo ipsius tutoris, prætor, vel qui provinciæ præerit, decreto constituet.

§ 6. If a tutor, by illness or any other necessary impediment, should be hindered from the personal execution of his office, and his pupil should be absent, or an infant, then the prætor or the governor of the province shall decree any person, whom the tutor approves of, to be the pupil's agent, for whose conduct the tutor must be answerable.

TITULUS VIGESIMUS-QUARTUS.

De satisdatione tutorum, vel curatorum.

D. xxvii. T. 7. C. v. T. 57.

Qui satisdare cogantur.

NE tamen pupillorum, pupillarumve, et eorum, qui quæve in curatione sunt, negotia à curatoribus tutoribusve consumantur vel diminuantur, curet prætor, ut et tutores et curatores eo nomine satisdent. Sed hoc non est perpetuum, nam tutores testamento dati satisdare non coguntur: quia fides eorum et diligentia ab ipso testatore approbata est. Item ex inquisitione tutores vel curatores dati satisdatione non onerantur, quia idonei electi sunt.

It is a branch of the prætor's office to see, that tutors and curators give a sufficient caution for the safety and indemnification of their pupils. But this is not always neces-

necessary; for a testamentary tutor is not compelled to give caution, inasmuch as his fidelity and diligence seem sufficiently approved of by the testator. Also all tutors, and curators, appointed to be such, after inquiry, are supposed in every respect to be qualified, and are therefore not obliged to give security.

Quatenus satisdatio in iis, qui satisdare non compelluntur, locum habere possit.

§ I. Sed, si ex testamento vel inquisitione duo pluresve dati fuerint, potest unus offerre satisdationem de indemnitate pupilli vel adolescentis, et contutori suo vel concuratori præferri, ut solus administret; vel ut contutor aut concurator satis offerens præponatur ei, ut et ipse solus administret. Itaque per se non potest petere satisdationem à contutore vel concuratore; sed offerre debet, ut electionem det concuratori vel concuratori suo, utrum velit satis accipere, an satisdare. Quod si nemo eorum satis offerat, siquidem adscriptum fuerit à testatore, quis gerat, ille gerere debet; quod si non fuerit adscriptum, quem major pars elegerit, ipse gerere debet, ut edicto prætoris cavetur Sin autem ipsi tutores dissenserint circa eligendum eum vel eos, qui gerere debent, prætor partes suas interponere debet. Idem et in pluribus ex inquisitione datis comprobandum est, id est, ut major pars eligere possit, per quem administratio fiat

§ 1. *If two, or more, are appointed by testament or by a magistrate, after inquiry, to be tutors or curators, any one of them, by offering caution, may be preferred to the sole administration, or cause his co-tutor, or co-curator, to give caution, in order to be admitted himself to the administration. Thus it appears, that a man can not demand security from his co-tutor or co-curator, but that, by offering caution himself, he may compel his co-tutor, or co-curator, to give or receive caution But, when no security is offered, if the testator hath appointed any particular person to act, such person must be preferred; but, if no particular person is specified by the testator, then must the administration be committed to such person or persons, whom a majority of the tutors shall elect, according to the prætorian edict but, if they disagree in their choice, the prætor may interpose his authority The same rule is also to be observed, when many, either tutors or curators, are nominated by the magistrate,* viz. *that a majority of them may appoint one of their number, to whom the administration shall be committed.*

Edicto prætoris] Not extant

Qui ex administratione tutelæ vel curationis tenentur.

§ II. Sciendum autem est, non solum tutores vel curatores pupillis vel adultis, cæterisque personis, ex administratione rerum teneri . sed etiam in eos, qui satisdationem accipiunt, subsidiariam actionem esse, quæ ultimum eis præsidium possit afferre. Subsidiaria autem actio in eos datur, qui aut omnino a tutoribus vel curatoribus satisdari non curaverunt, aut non idoneè passi sunt caveri. Quæ quidem tam a prudentum responsis, quam ex constitutionibus imperialibus, etiam in hæredes eorum extenditur

§ 2

§ 2. *It is necessary to be known, that tutors and curators are not the only persons subject to an action, on account of the administration of the affairs of pupils, minors, and others under their protection. For a subsidiary action, which is the last remedy to be used, will also lie against a magistrate, either for intirely omitting to take sureties, or for taking such, who are insufficient. And this action, according to the answers of the lawyers as well as by the imperial constitutions, is extended even against the heir of any such magistrate.*

Sciendum] Various remedies are given to pupils and minors, who have received any damage by the male-administration or negligence of their tutors or curators

The personal actions, to which minors are intituled, against their tutors or curators, are called *Actiones tutelæ* and *negotiorum gestorum utiles* —— *Quicquid tutoris dolo vel lata culpa aut levi, seu curatoris, minores amiserint, vel, cum possent, non acquisierint hoc in tutelæ seu negotiorum gestorum utile judicium venire, non est incerti juris.* Cod 5 t 51 *l* 7

And the heirs of tutors and curators are also liable to the same actions *ob dolum et latam culpam* Cod 2 t 19. *l* 17

Pupils or minors may also sue the sureties of their tutors or curators, by an action arising from the stipulation entered into by such sureties. *D* 27 *t* 7 *ll* 3, 5 *Cod.* 5. *t* 57 *ll* 1, 2.

And lastly, as their dernier ressort, minors have a right to an action called *subsidiary*, against any magistrate, who hath neglected to do his duty, either by taking no security, or what was not sufficient *D* 27 *t* 8 *l* 1 § .6.

But the heirs of tutors, curators, sureties and magistrates, are only suable in cases of fraud in themselves, or in those, to whom they are heirs; but not merely on account of negligence. *D* 27 *t* 7. *l*. 4 *C* 5 *t* 75. *l* 2. *Claude Ferriere, h t.*

Constitutionibus] *Cod* 5. *t* 43. *l* 3

Si tutor vel curator cavere nolit.

§ III. Quibus constitutionibus et illud exprimitur, ut, nisi caveant tutores et curatores, pignoribus captis coerceantur.

§ 3. *And by the same constitutions it is expresly enacted, that all tutors and curators, who refuse to give caution, may be compelled to it.*

Qui dicta actione non tenentur.

§ IV. Neque autem præfectus urbi, neque prætor, neque præses provinciæ, neque quisquam alius, cui tutores dandi jus est, hac actione tenebitur: sed hi tantummodo, qui satisdationem exigere solent.

§ 4. *Neither the præfect of the city, nor the prætor, nor the governor of a province, nor any other, who has power to assign tutors, shall be subject to a subsidiary action. but those magistrates only are liable to it, who exact the caution.*

Exigere solent.] The exaction of caution was the business of the inferior magistrates, of the *scribes* at Rome, and of the *duumviri* in the provinces. *Cod.* 5 *t* 75 *l. ult.* *D* 27. *t* 8 *l* 1 *D* 15 *t* 1 *l* 1

TITU-

TITULUS VIGESIMUS-QUINTUS.

De excuſationibus tutorum vel curatorum.

D.xxvii.T.1. C.v.T.62.

De numero liberorum.

EXCUSANTUR autem tutores et curatores variis ex cauſis; plerumque tamen propter liberos, ſive in poteſtate ſint, ſive emancipati. Si enim tres liberos ſuperſtites Romæ quis habeat, vel in Italia quatuor, vel in provinciis quinque, à tutela vel cura poteſt excuſari, exemplo cæterorum munerum; nam et tutelam et curam placuit publicum munus eſſe. Sed adoptivi liberi non proſunt; in adoptionem autem dati naturali patri proſunt. Item nepotes ex filio proſunt, ut in locum patris ſui ſuccedant; ex filia non proſunt. Filii autem ſuperſtites tantum ad tutelæ vel curæ muneris excuſationem proſunt: defuncti autem non proſunt. Sed, ſi in bello amiſſi ſunt, quæſitum eſt, an proſint? Et conſtat, eos ſolos prodeſſe, qui in acie amittuntur. Hi enim, qui pro republica ceciderunt, in perpetuum per gloriam vivere intelliguntur.

Perſons, who are nominated to be either tutors or curators, may, upon diverſe accounts, excuſe themſelves; but the moſt general plea offered is that of having children, whether they are ſubject, or emancipated. For at Rome, *if a man has three children living, in* Italy *four, and in the* provinces *five, he may therefore be excuſed from tutelage and curation, as well as from other employments of a public nature, for both tutelage and curation are eſteemed public offices. But adopted children will not avail the adoptor; they will nevertheleſs excuſe their natural father, who gave them in adoption. Alſo grand-children by a ſon, when they ſucceed in the place of their father, will excuſe their grand father, yet grand-children by a daughter will not excuſe him. But thoſe children only, who are* living, *can excuſe from tutelage and curation: for the deceaſed are of no ſervice. And ſhould it now be demanded, whether a parent can avail himſelf of thoſe ſons, whom war has deſtroyed? It muſt be anſwered,——that he can avail himſelf of thoſe only, who have periſhed in battle: for thoſe, who have fallen for the republic, are eſteemed to live for ever, in the immortality of their fame.*

Excuſantur autem] The laws of *England* are ſilent concerning the excuſes of guardians, becauſe no man can be compelled to take the office of guardianſhip. *De excuſatione tutorum vel curatorum, leges noſtræ nihil loquuntur, quia nemini invito hoc munus imponunt* Cow Inſt t 25

Qui in acie amittuntur] *Acies* is here oppoſed to *bellum,* in conformity to the following opinion of *Ulpian* —— *Bello amiſſi ad tutelæ excuſationem proſunt — Quæſitum eſt autem, qui ſint iſti utrum hi, qui in acie ſint interempti, an vero omnes omnino, qui per cauſam belli parentibus ſunt abrepti, in obſidione forte? Melius igitur probabitur, eos ſolos, qui in acie amittuntur, prodeſſe debere, cujuſcunque ſexus, vel ætatis ſint hi enim pro republica ceciderunt* ff 27 t 1 l 18. de excuſationibus.

De administratione rei fiscalis.

§ I. Item divus Marcus in semestribus rescripsit, eum, qui res fisci administrat, à tutela et cura, quamdiu administrat, excusari posse.

§ 1. *The emperor* Marcus *declared by rescript from his* Semestrial *council, that whoever is ingaged in the administration of affairs relating to the treasury, may be excused from tutelage and curation, whilest he is so imployed.*

In Semestribus] The *Semestre concilium* was a privy council, composed of a certain number of senators, who were chosen by lot, and were changed every six months. This council was first appointed by *Augustus Cæsar*, that he might diminish the power of the senate and increase his own. *Sibique instituit consilia sortiri semestria, cum quibus de negotiis ad frequentem senatum referendis ante tractaret.* Suet. in Aug. c. 35. Dion. lib. 53. ff. 27. t. 1. *l.* 41. Cod. 5. t. 62. *ll.* 10, 25.

De absentia reipublicæ causa.

§ II. Item, qui reipublicæ causa absunt, à tutela vel cura excusantur. Sed et, si fuerint tutores vel curatores dati, deinde reipublicæ causa abesse cœperint, à tutela vel cura excusantur, quatenus reipublicæ causa absunt: et interea curator loco eorum datur; qui, si reversi fuerint, recipiunt onus tutelæ: nam nec anni habent vacationem, ut Papinianus libro quinto responsorum scripsit: nam hoc spatium habent ad novas tutelas vocati.

§ 2. *Those, who are absent on the affairs of the republic, are exempted from tutelage and curation. And if such, who are already assigned to be either tutors or curators, should afterwards be absent on the business of the republic, their absence is dispensed with, whilest they continue in the public service; and curators must be appointed in their place, but, when such tutors return, they must again take upon them the burden of tutelage. And they are not intituled (as* Papinian *asserts in the fifth book of his answers) to the privilege of a year's vacation: for that term is allowed to those only, who are called, at their return, to a new tutelage.*

De potestate.

§ III. Et, qui potestatem aliquam habent, se excusare possunt, ut divus Marcus rescripsit: sed susceptam tutelam deserere non possunt.

§ 3. *By a rescript of the emperor* Marcus, *all superior magistrates may, as such, excuse themselves. But they can not desert a tutelage, when once they have undertaken it.*

Qui potestatem] "Non nunquam, κατ' ἐξοχήν, soli magistratus majores imperium et potestatem habere dicuntur, minores sine imperio et potestate esse: atque in excellentiori hoc significatu verbum *potestatis* hic accipiendum est." *Vinn. h. l.* "Majores esse dicuntur, qui majora habent auspicia, ut consules, prætores, et censores, minores, qui minora. Secundò majores dicuntur, qui lictorem et viatorem habent, quos nec ædiles, nec quæstores habuerunt." *Eden. elem.*

De lite cum pupillo vel adulto.

§ IV. Item propter litem, quam cum pupillo vel adulto tutor vel curator habet, excusari non potest: nisi forte de omnibus bonis vel hæreditate controversia sit.

§ 4.

§ 4. *No man can excuse himself from taking the office of a tutor or curator, by alleging a law-suit with the pupil or minor, unless the suit is for all the goods, or the whole inheritance of such pupil or minor.*

Propter litem] This law is now useless; for, by the 72d Novel of *Justinian*, the debtors or creditors of minors are prohibited to be their tutors or curators.

De tribus tutelæ et curæ oneribus.

§ V. Item tria onera tutelæ non affectatæ, vel curæ, præstant vacationem, quamdiu administrantur: ut tamen plurium pupillorum tutela vel cura eorundem bonorum, veluti fratrum, pro una computetur.

§ 5. *Three tutelages or curatorships, which are not acquired merely for advantage, will exempt a man from the burden of a fourth. But the tutelage or curation of three or more brothers is reckoned but as one.*

De paupertate.

§ VI. Sed et propter paupertatem excusationem tribui, tam divi fratres, quam per se divus Marcus rescripsit, si quis imparem se oneri injuncto possit docere.

§ 6. *The divine brothers have declared by their rescript, and the emperor* Marcus *by his separate rescript, that poverty is a sufficient excuse, when it can be proved to be such, which must render a man incapable of the burden imposed upon him.*

Divi fratres] The emperors were called *divi* or divine, because they were always considered, in every respect, as gods, after the ceremony of their *apotheosis* had been performed. *vid Herod lib* 3. As to the emperors here meant by the words *divi fratres*, the commentators are not agreed in ascertaining, who they were, but *Vinny* supposes them to have been *Marcus Aurelius* the philosopher, and *Ælius Verus*, the sons of *Antoninus Pius*.

De adversa valetudine.

§ VII. Item propter adversam valetudinem, propter quam ne suis quidem negotiis interesse potest, excusatio locum habet.

§ 7. *Illness also, if it is so great as to hinder a man from transacting his own business, is a sufficient excuse.*

De imperitia literarum.

§ VIII. Similiter eos, qui literas nesciunt, esse excusandos, Divus Pius rescripsit; quamvis et imperiti literarum possint ad administrationem negotiorum sufficere.

§ 8 *By the rescript of the emperor* Antoninus Pius, *illiterate persons are to be excused, altho' in some cases an illiterate man may not be incapable of the administration.*

De inimicitia patris.

§ IX. Item si propter inimicitias aliquem testamento tutorem pater dederit, hoc ipsum præstat ei excusationem; sicut per contrarium non excusantur, qui, se tutelam administraturos, patri pupillorum promiserant.

§ 9. *If a father thro' enmity appoints any particular person, by testament, to be tutor to his children, the motive of such an appointment will afford a sufficient excuse. But he, who by promise hath ingaged himself to a testator, is not to be excused from the office of tutelage.*

De ignorantia testatoris.

§ X. Non esse autem admittendam excusationem ejus, qui hoc solo utitur, quod ignotus patri pupillorum sit, Divi fratres rescripserunt.

§ 10. *The divine brothers have enacted by their rescript, that the pretence of being unknown to the father of a pupil, is not to be admitted solely, as a sufficient excuse.*

De inimicitiis cum patre pupilli vel adulti.

§ XI. Inimicitiæ, quas quis cum patre pupillorum vel adultorum exercuit, si capitales fuerunt, nec reconciliatio intervenit, a tutela vel cura solent excusare.

§ 11. *An enmity, against the father of a pupil or adult, will sufficiently excuse any man, either from tutelage or curatorship, if no reconciliation hath intervened.*

Si capitales.] By a capital enmity is understood such an hatred, which might arise from a public accusation, affecting the life, liberty, and good name of the party accused. *ff* 38 *l* 14. *ff*. 50 *l* 103 *de verb. sign.* But even such an accusation could not excuse a testamentary tutor, inasmuch as the appointment would imply the testator's forgiveness, unless it appeared, that he acted upon another motive, and intended only to lay a burden upon the person, whom he had nominated. *Hein. Vinn.*

De status controversia a patre pupilli illata.

§ XII. Item is, qui status controversiam a pupillorum patre passus est, excusatur a tutela.

§ 12. *Also he, whose condition hath been controverted at the instance of the father of the pupil, is upon that account excused from the tutelage.*

De ætate.

§ XIII. Item major septuaginta annis a tutela et cura se potest excusare. Minores autem viginti quinque annis olim quidem excusabantur: nostra autem constitutione prohibentur ad tutelam vel curam adspirare: adeo ut nec excusatione opus sit. Qua constitutione cavetur; ut nec pupillus ad legitimam tutelam vocetur, nec adultus: cum sit incivile, eos, qui alieno auxilio in rebus suis administrandis egere noscuntur, et ab aliis reguntur, aliorum tutelam vel curam subire

§ 13. *Any person, who is above seventy years of age, may be excused both from tutelage and curation. Also minors, as such, were formerly excusable, but, by our constitution, they are now prohibited from aspiring to these trusts; and of course all excuses are become unnecessary. It is also enacted by the same constitution, that neither pupils, nor adults, shall be called even to a legitime tutelage. For it is absurd, that persons, who are themselves under governors, and known to want assistence in the administration of their own affairs, should notwithstanding this be admitted, either as tutors or curators, to have the management of the affairs of others.*

De

De militia.

§ XIV. Idem in milite observandum est, ut nec volens ad tutelæ onus admittatur.

§ 14 *And we must also observe, that no military person, altho' willing, can be admitted to become a tutor or curator.*

Idem et in milite] *Militiæ armatæ muneribus occupatus, neque si legitimus sit, neque si ex testamento datus fuerit, nec alio modo, etsi voluerit, tutor vel curator fieri potest; sed, si errore ductus res administraverit, negotiorum gestorum actione conventur.* Cod. 5. t. 33. l 4 Cod 6. t. 36. l 8

De grammaticis, rhetoribus, et medicis.

§ XV. Item Romæ grammatici, rhetores, et medici, et qui in patria sua has artes exercent, et intra numerum sunt, à tutela et cura habent vacationem.

§ 15. *Both at* Rome *and in the* provinces, *all grammarians, teachers of rhetoric, and physicians, who exercise their professions within their own country, and are within the number authorized, are exempted from tutelage and curation.*

De tempore et modo proponendi excusationes.

§ XVI. Qui autem se vult excusare, si plures habeat excusationes, et de quibusdam non probaverit, aliis uti, intra tempora constituta, non prohibetur. Qui autem excusare se volunt, non appellant, sed intra quinquaginta dies continuos, ex quo cognoverint se tutores vel curatores datos, se excusare debent, cujuscunque generis sint, id est, qualitercunque dati fuerint tutores, si intra centesimum lapidem sint ab eo loco, ubi tutores dati sunt. Si vero ultra centesimum lapidem habitant, dinumeratione facta viginti millium diurnorum, et amplius triginta dierum; qui tamen, ut Scævola dicebat, sic debent computari, ne minus sint, quam quinquaginta dies.

§ 16. *He, who can allege many excuses, and hath failed in his proof of those, which he hath already given, is not prohibited from assigning others within the time prescribed. But tutors and curators of whatever kind, whether legal, testamentary, or dative, (if they are willing to excuse themselves) ought not to prefer an appeal merely on account of their appointment, but they should first exhibit their excuses before the proper magistrate: and this they ought to do within fifty days after they are certified of their nomination, on supposition, that they are within an hundred miles from the place, where they were nominated But, if they are at the distance of more than an hundred miles, they are allowed a day for every twenty miles, and thirty days besides, which, taken together, ought never, according to* Scævola, *to make a less number of days than* 50

Non appellant] They ought not to appeal from the appointment, but from the sentence, by which their excuses are rejected. *Non a datione sed a sententia, qua excusatio non fuit admissa si quis enim tutor datus fuerit, vel testamento, vel a quo alio, qui jus dandi habet, non oportet eum provocare, hoc enim divus* Marcus Aurelius *effecit, sed intra tempora præstituta excusationem allegandam habet, et, si fuerit pulsa, tunc demum appellare debebit, cæterum ante frustra appellatur* ff 49 t 4 l 1.

De

De excusatione pro parte patrimonii.

§ XVII. Datus autem tutor ad universum patrimonium datus esse creditur.

§ 17. *When a tutor is appointed, he is reputed to have the care of the whole patrimony of his pupil.*

De tutelæ gestione.

§ XVIII. Qui tutelam alicujus gessit, invitus curator ejusdem fieri non compellitur: in tantum, ut licet pater-familias, qui testamento tutorem dedit, adjecerit, se eundem curatorem dare, tamen invitum eum curam suscipere non cogendum, divi Severus et Antoninus rescripserunt.

§ 18. *He, who hath been the tutor of a minor, can not be compelled to become his curator And, by the rescript of the emperors* Severus *and* Antoninus, *altho' the father of a family should, by testament, appoint any person to be first the tutor of his children, and afterwards their curator, if the person so appointed is unwilling to take upon him the curation, he is by no means compellable.*

De marito.

§ XIX. Iidem rescripserunt, uxoris suæ curatorem datum excusare se posse, licet se immisceat.

§ 19. *The same emperors have likewise, by their rescript, enacted, that an husband may excuse himself from being a curator to his wife, even after he hath begun to act.*

De falsis allegationibus.

§ XX. Si quis autem falsis allegationibus excusationem tutelæ meruerit, non est liberatus onere tutelæ.

§ 20. *If any man should, by false allegations, have appeared to merit a dismission from the office of tutelage, he is not therefore freed from the burden of this office.*

TITULUS VIGESIMUS-SEXTUS.

De suspectis tutoribus vel curatoribus.

D. xxvi. T. 10. C. v. T. 43.

Unde suspecti crimen descendat.

SCIENDUM est, suspecti crimen ex lege duodecim tabularum descendere.

The accusation of a suspected tutor, or curator, is derived from the law of the twelve tables.

Suspecti crimen] *Crimen* here signifies an accusation, and is so interpreted by *Theophilus* in his paraphrase 'Ειπω μεν δε τα περι της κατηγοριας. It is also frequently used by *Tully* and the best commentators, in the same sense · *tria sunt quantum existimare possum, quæ obstant, hoc tempore, sexto* Roscio, *crimen adversariorum, et audacia, et potentia* Pro *Rosc Amer.*

Qui

Qui de hoc crimine cognoscunt.

§ I. Datum autem est jus removendi tutores suspectos Romæ prætori, et in provinciis præsidibus earum, et legato proconsulis.

§ 1. *At* Rome *the power of removing suspected tutors belongs to the prætor, and in the* provinces *to the governors, or to the* legate *of a proconsul.*

Qui suspecti fieri possunt.

§ II. Ostendimus, qui possunt de suspecto cognoscere: nunc videamus, qui suspecti fieri possint. Et possunt quidem omnes tutores fieri suspecti, sive sint testamentarii, sive non sint, sed alterius generis tutores. Quare, etsi legitimus fuerit tutor, accusari poterit. Quid si patronus? Adhuc idem erit dicendum: dummodo meminerimus, famæ patroni parcendum esse, licet ut suspectus remotus fuerit.

§ 2. *We have already shewed, what magistrates may take cognizance of suspected persons let us now therefore inquire, what persons may become suspected. And indeed all tutors may become so, whether they are testamentary, or of any other denomination. For even a legitime tutor may be accused, neither is a* patron *less subject to an accusation, but we must remember, that, as such, his reputation must be spared, altho' he is removed from his trust, as a suspected person.*

Et possunt quidem omnes] Guardians at *common law* may be removed, or compelled to give security, if there appears any danger of their abusing either the person, or the estate of the minor. *Stile* 456. *Hard.* 96. 3 *Chan. rep* 58 1 *Sid.* 424. 3 *Salk* 177

But there is no instance of the removal of a *statute guardian*, yet terms have frequently been imposed, so as effectually to prevent such guardian from doing any act to the prejudice of a minor But *quære*, whether causes may not arise, for which a statute or testamentary guardian may totally be removed, notwithstanding the statute, as if he become mad, lunatic, &c. for a guardianship is not assignable, neither can it go to executors, or administrators, being a personal trust. *Vaugh* 180 *Cases in eq abr.* 261.

Famæ patroni parcendum] When an action is brought against a suspected patron or parent, it must be an action *in factum*, and no mention must be made of fraud *sed ex quibus causis actio in* alios *famosa datur, ex iisdem adversus* illos *in factum datur, omissa doli mentione.* ff. 4. t. 3 *l* 11. De dolo malo.

Qui possunt suspectos postulare.

§ III. Consequens est, ut videamus, qui possint suspectos postulare. Et sciendum est, quasi publicam esse hanc accusationem, hoc est, omnibus patere. Quinimo mulieres admittuntur ex rescripto divorum Severi et Antonini, sed hæ solæ, quæ, pietatis necessitudine ductæ, ad hoc procedunt: ut puta mater, nutrix quoque et avia: potest et soror. Sed et si qua alia mulier fuerit; quam prætor propensa pietate intellexerit sexus verecundiam non egredientem, sed pietate productam, non sustinere injuriam pupillorum, admittet eam ad accusationem.

§ 3 *It now remains, as a consequence, that we inquire, by whom suspected persons may be accused. It must therefore be known, that an accusation of this sort is of a public nature, and open to all. For, by a rescript of the emperors* Severus *and* Antoninus, *even women are admitted to be accusers, yet such only, who are induced to it by their duty, or by their relation to the minor thus a mother, a nurse, or a grandmother, may become accusers, and also a sister. But the prætor can at discretion admit*

mit any woman, who acting with a becoming modesty, but impatient of wrongs offered to pupils, appears to have no other motive, than to relieve the injured.

An pubes vel impubes.

§ IV. Impuberes non possunt tutores suos suspectos postulare: puberes autem curatores suos ex consilio necessariorum suspectos possunt arguere: et ita Divi Severus et Antoninus rescripserunt.

§ 4. *No pupil can bring an accusation of suspicion against his tutor: but adults, by the rescript of* Severus *and* Antoninus, *are permitted, when they act by advice of persons related to them, to accuse their curators.*

Qui dicatur suspectus.

§ V. Suspectus autem est, qui non ex fide tutelam gerit, licet solvendo sit, ut Julianus quoque scripsit. Sed, et anteaquam incipiat tutelam gerere tutor, posse eum quasi suspectum removeri, idem Julianus scripsit: et secundum eum constitutum est.

§ 5 *Any tutor, who does not faithfully execute his trust, let his circumstances be ever so sufficient to answer damages, may, according to* Julian, *be pronounced suspected. And it is also the opinion of the same* Julian, *(which opinion is adhered to in our constitutions) that a tutor may be removed from his office, as suspected, even before he has begun to execute it.*

Constitutum est] *Cod.* 5. *t.* 43. *l.* 23.

De effectu remotionis.

§ VI. Suspectus autem remotus, siquidem ob dolum, famosus est: si ob culpam, non æque.

§ 6. *When any person is removed upon* suspicion, *if it is of* fraud, *he is stigmatized with infamy, but, if of* neglect *only, he does not become infamous.*

De effectu accusationis.

§ VII. Si quis autem suspectus postulatur, quoad cognitio finiatur, interdicitur ei administratio, ut Papiniano visum est.

§ 7. *If any tutor is accused upon suspicion, his administration, according to* Papinian, *is suspended, whilest the accusation is under cognisance.*

Quibus modis cognitio finitur.

§ VIII. Sed, si suspecti cognitio suscepta fuerit, posteaque tutor vel curator decesserit, extinguitur suspecti cognitio.

§ 8 *If a suspected tutor or curator should die, pending the accusation, then the cognisance of it is extinguished*

Si tutor copiam sui non faciat.

§ IX. Si quis tutor copiam sui non faciat, ut alimenta pupillo decernantur, cavetur epistola divorum Severi et Antonini, ut in possessionem bono-

bonorum ejus pupillus mittatur; et quæ mora deteriora futura ſunt, dato curatore, diſtrahi jubentur. Ergo ut ſuſpectus removeri poterit, qui non præſtat alimenta.

§ 9. *If a tutor fails to appear, with an intent to defer the appointment of an allowance for the maintenance of his pupil, it is provided by the conſtitution of* Severus *and* Antoninus, *that the pupil ſhall be put into the poſſeſſion of his tutor's effects; and that, a curator being appointed, thoſe things, which will be impaired by delay, may be immediately put to ſale. And therefore any tutor, who, by abſenting himſelf, impedes the grant of an allowance to his pupil, may be removed, as ſuſpected.*

Si neget alimenta decerni poſſe, vel tutelam redemerit.

§ X. Sed ſi quis præſens negat propter inopiam alimenta poſſe decerni, ſi hoc per mendacium dicat, remittendum eum eſſe ad præfectum urbi puniendum placuit: ſicut ille remittitur, qui, data pecunia, miniſterium tutelæ acquiſierit, vel redemerit.

§ 10. *But, if a tutor makes a perſonal appearance, and falſely avers, that the effects of his pupil are inſufficient for an allowance, ſuch tutor ſhall be remitted to the præfect of the city, and puniſhed by him in the ſame manner, as he, who hath acquired a tutelage by bribery.*

De liberto fraudulenter adminiſtrante.

§ XI. Libertus quoque, ſi fraudulenter tutelam filiorum vel nepotum patroni geſſiſſe probetur, ad præfectum urbi remittitur puniendus.

§ 11 *Alſo a freed-man, who is proved to have fraudulently adminiſtered the tutelage of the ſon, or grandſon of his patron, muſt be remitted to the præfect to be condignly puniſhed.*

Si ſuſpectus ſatis offerat; et quis dicatur ſuſpectus.

§ XII. Noviſſime autem ſciendum eſt, eos, qui fraudulenter tutelam adminiſtrant, etiamſi ſatis offerant, removendos eſſe à tutela, quia ſatiſdatio tutoris propoſitum malevolum non mutat, ſed diutius graſſandi in re familiari facultatem præſtat. Suſpectum etiam eum putamus, qui moribus talis eſt, ut ſuſpectus ſit. Enimvero tutor vel curator, quamvis pauper ſit, fidelis tamen et diligens, removendus non eſt, quaſi ſuſpectus.

§ 12 *It is laſtly to be obſerved, that they, who unfaithfully adminiſter their truſt, muſt be immediately removed from it, altho' they tender a ſufficient caution For the act of giving caution alters not the malevolent purpoſe of the tutor, but procures him a longer time for the continuance of his depredations We alſo deem every man ſuſpected, whoſe immoralities give cauſe for it but a tutor or curator, who, altho' poor, is yet faithful and diligent, can by no means be removed, as a ſuſpected perſon, merely on account of poverty*

FINIS LIBRI PRIMI.

DIVI JUSTINIANI INSTITUTIONUM LIBER SECUNDUS.

TITULUS PRIMUS.

De rerum diviſione, et acquirendo earum dominio.

D. 1. T. 8. C. xli. T. 1.

Continuatio et duplex rerum diviſio.

SUPERIORE libro de jure perſonarum expoſuimus, modo videamus de rebus; quæ vel in noſtro patrimonio, vel extra patrimonium noſtrum, habentur. Quædam enim naturali jure communia ſunt omnium, quædam publica, quædam univerſitatis, quædam nullius, pleiaque ſingulorum, quæ ex variis cauſis cuique acquiruntur, ſicut ex ſubjectis apparebit.

We have already treated of perſons in the foregoing book; let us now therefore inquire concerning things, which may be divided into thoſe, which can, and thoſe, which can not, come within our patrimony and be acquired, for ſome things are in common among mankind in general,— ſome are public,— ſome univerſal,— and ſome are ſuch, to which no man can have a right But moſt things are the private property of individuals, by whom they are variouſly acquired, as will appear hereafter.

De aëre, aqua profluente, mari, littore, &c.

§ I. Et quidem naturali jure communia ſunt omnium hæc, aer, aqua profluens, mare, et per hoc littora maris Nemo igitur ad littus maris accedere prohibetur; dum tamen à villis et monumentis et ædificiis abſtineat: quia non ſunt juris gentium, ſicut eſt mare.

§ 1. *Thoſe things, which are given to mankind in common by the law of nature, are the air, running water, the ſea, and conſequently the ſhores of the ſea: no man therefore is prohibited from approaching any part of the ſea ſhore, whileſt he abſtains*

from

from committing acts of violence in destroying farms, monuments, edifices, &c. which are not in common, as the sea is.

De fluminibus et portubus.

§ II. Flumina autem omnia, et portus, publica ſunt. Ideoque jus piſcandi omnibus commune eſt in portu fluminibuſque.

§ 2. *All rivers and ports are public; and therefore the right of fiſhing in a port, or in rivers, is in common.*

Definitio littoris.

§ III. Eſt autem littus maris, quatenus hybernus fluctus maximus excurrit.

§ 3. *All that tract of land, over which the greateſt winter flood extends itſelf, is the ſea-ſhore.*

De uſu et proprietate riparum.

§ IV. Riparum quoque uſus publicus eſt jure gentium, ſicut ipſius fluminis. Itaque naves ad eas appellere, funes arboribus ibi natis religare, onus aliquod in his reponere, cuilibet liberum eſt, ſicut per ipſum flumen navigare: ſed proprietas earum illorum eſt, quorum prædiis hærent: qua de cauſa arbores quoque in eiſdem natæ eorundem ſunt.

§ 4 *By the law of nations the uſe of the banks of rivers is alſo public, as the rivers themſelves are, and therefore all perſons have the ſame liberty to land their veſſels, to unload them, and to faſten ropes to trees upon the banks of a river, as they have to navigate upon the river itſelf. But, notwithſtanding this, the banks of a river are the property of thoſe, who poſſeſs the land, adjoining to ſuch banks; and therefore the trees, which grow upon them, are alſo the property of the ſame perſons.*

De uſu et proprietate littorum.

§ V. Littorum quoque uſus publicus eſt et juris gentium, ſicut et ipſius maris: et ob id cuilibet liberum eſt caſam ibi ponere, in quam ſe recipiat, ſicut retia ſiccare, et ex mari deducere. Proprietas autem eorum poteſt intelligi nullius eſſe; ſed ejuſdem juris eſſe, cujus et mare, et, quæ ſubjacet mari, terra vel arena.

§ 5. *The uſe of the ſea ſhore is alſo public and common by the law of nations, as is the uſe of the ſea, and therefore any perſon is permitted to erect a cottage upon it, for his habitation, in which he may dry his nets, and preſerve them from the water; for the ſhores are not underſtood to be a property in any man, but are compared to the ſea itſelf, and to the ſand or ground, which is under the ſea.*

De rebus univerſitatis.

§ VI. Univerſitatis ſunt, non ſingulorum, quæ in civitatibus ſunt, theatra, ſtadia, et his ſimilia, et ſi qua alia ſunt communia civitatum.

§ 6. *Theaters, ground appropriated for a race or public exerciſes, and things of the like nature, which belong to a whole city, are univerſal, and not the property of any particular perſon.*

De

De rebus nullius.

§ VII. Nullius autem ſunt res ſacræ, et religioſæ, et ſanctæ: quod enim divini juris eſt, id nullius in bonis eſt.

§ 7. *Things ſacred, religious, and holy, cannot be veſted in any perſon, as his own: for that, which is of divine right, is* nullius in bonis, *and can be no man's property.*

De rebus ſacris.

§ VIII. Sacræ res ſunt, quæ rite per pontifices Deo conſecratæ ſunt; veluti ædes ſacræ, et donaria, quæ rite ad miniſterium Dei dedicata ſunt; quæ etiam per noſtram conſtitutionem alienari et obligari prohibuimus, excepta cauſa redemptionis captivorum. Si quis autem auctoritate ſua quaſi ſacrum ſibi conſtituerit, ſacrum non eſt, ſed profanum. Locus autem, in quo ædes ſacræ ſunt ædificatæ, etiam, diruto ædificio, ſacer adhuc manet, ut et Papianus ſcripſit.

§ 8. *Thoſe things, which have been conſecrated by the pontiffs in due form, are eſteemed ſacred; ſuch are churches, chapels, and alſo all moveable things, if they have been properly dedicated to the ſervice of God: and we have forbidden by our conſtitution, that theſe things ſhould be either aliened or obligated, unleſs for the redemption of captives. But, if a man ſhould conſecrate a building merely by his own authority, it would not be rendered ſacred by ſuch a conſecration; but the very ground, upon which a ſacred edifice hath once been erected, will, according to* Papinian, *continue to be ſacred, altho' the edifice is deſtroyed.*

Per noſtram conſtitutionem.] *Cod.* 1. *t.* 2. *l.* 22. *de ſacro-ſanctis eccleſiis.*

De religioſis.

§ IX. Religioſum locum unuſquiſque ſua voluntate facit, dum mortuum infert in locum ſuum. In communem autem locum purum, invito ſocio, inferre non licet: in commune vero ſepulchrum etiam, invitis cæteris, licet inferre. Item, ſi alienus uſusfructus eſt, proprietarium placet, niſi conſentiente uſufructuario, locum religioſum non facere. In alienum locum, conſentiente domino, licet inferre; et, licet poſtea ratum non habuerit, quam illatus eſt mortuus, tamen locus religioſus fit.

§ 9. *Any man may at his will render any place, which belongs ſolely to himſelf, religious, by making it the repoſitory of a dead body; yet, when two are joint poſſeſſors of a place or ſpot of ground, not before uſed for ſuch a purpoſe, it is not in the power of the one, without the conſent of the other, to cauſe it to become religious. But, when there is a ſepulcher in common among many, it is in the power of any one joint-poſſeſſor to make uſe of it, altho' the reſt ſhould diſſent. And, when there is a proprietor, and an uſufructuary, of the ſame place, the proprietor, without the conſent of the uſufructuary, can not render it religious. But it is lawful to lay the body of a dead perſon in a place, belonging to any man, who has given his conſent to it; and, altho' he ſhould diſſent after the burial, yet the place becomes religious.*

De rebus sanctis.

§ X. Sanctæ quoque res, veluti muri et portæ civitatis, quodammodo divini juris sunt; et ideo nullius in bonis sunt. Ideo autem muros sanctos dicimus, quia pœna capitis constituta est in eos, qui aliquid in muros deliquerint. Ideo et legum eas partes, quibus pœnas constituimus adversus eos, qui contra leges fecerint, sanctiones vocamus.

§ 10. *Holy things also, as the walls and gates of a city, are in some degree of divine right, and therefore the property of no man. The walls of a city are esteemed* sancti *or holy, inasmuch as any offence against them is always punished capitally; and therefore all those parts of the laws, by which punishments are inflicted upon transgressors, we generally term* sanctions.

De rebus singulorum.

XI. Singulorum autem hominum multis modis res fiunt: quarundam enim rerum dominium nanciscimur jure naturali, quod sicut diximus, appellatur jus gentium: quarundam vero jure civili. Commodius est itaque à vetustiore jure incipere. Palam est autem, vetustius esse jus naturale, quod cum ipso genere humano rerum natura prodidit. Civilia autem jura tunc esse cœperunt, cum et civitates condi, et magistratus creari, et leges scribi, cœperunt.

§ 11 *There are various means, by which things become the property of private persons. Of some things we obtain dominion and property by the law of nature, which (as we have already observed) is also called the law of nations: and we acquire a property in other things by the civil law. But it will be most convenient to begin from the more antient law: and that the law, which nature established at the birth of mankind, is the most antient, appears evident. for civil laws could then only commence to exist, when cities began to be built, magistrates to be created, and laws to be written.*

De occupatione ferarum.

§ XII. Feræ igitur bestiæ, et volucres, et pisces, et omnia animalia, quæ mari cœlo et terra nascuntur, simul atque ab aliquo capta fuerint, jure gentium statim illius esse incipiunt: quod enim ante nullius est, id naturali ratione occupanti conceditur: nec interest, feras bestias et volucres utrum in suo fundo quis capiat, an in alieno. Plane, qui alienum fundum ingreditur venandi aut aucupandi gratia, potest à domino, si is præviderit, prohiberi ne ingrediatur. Quicquid autem eorum ceperis, eo usque tuum esse intelligitur, donec tua custodia coercetur. Cum vero tuam evaserit custodiam, et in libertatem naturalem sese receperit, tuum esse desinit, et rursus occupantis fit. Naturalem autem libertatem recipere intelligitur, cum vel oculos tuos effugerit, vel ita sit in conspectu tuo, ut difficilis sit ejus persecutio.

§ 12 *Wild beasts, birds, fish, and all the animals, which are bred either in the sea, the air, or upon the earth, do, as soon as they are taken, become instantly,*

by

by the law of nations, the property of the captor: for it is agreeable to natural reason, that those things, which have no owner, should become the property of the first occupant: and it is not material, whether they then are taken by a man upon his own ground, or upon the ground of another: but yet it is certain, that whoever hath entered into the ground of another for the sake of hunting or fowling, might have been prohibited from entering by the proprietor of the ground, if he had foreseen the intent. But, tho' wild beasts, or fowl, when taken, are esteemed to be the property of the captor, whilest they continue in his custody; yet, when they have once escaped and recovered their natural liberty, the right of the captor ceases, and they become the property of the first, who seizes them. And they are understood to have recovered their natural liberty, if they have run or flown out of sight; and even if they are not out of sight, when it so happens that they can not without difficulty be persued and retaken.

De vulneratione.

§ XIII. Illud quæsitum est, an si fera bestia ita vulnerata sit, ut capi possit, statim tua esse intelligatur. Et quibusdam placuit, statim esse tuam, et, eousque tuam videri, donec eam persequaris. quod si desieris persequi, desinere tuam esse, et rursus fieri occupantis. alii vero putaverunt, non aliter tuam esse, quam si eam ceperis. Sed posteriorem sententiam nos confirmamus, quod multa accidere soleant, ut eam non capias.

§ 13. *It hath been a question, whether a wild beast is understood to belong to him, by whom it hath been so wounded, that it may easily be taken. And, in the opinion of some, it belongs to such person, as long as he persues it; but, if he quits the persuit, they say it ceases to be his, and again becomes the right of the first* occupant. *But others have thought, that the property in a wild beast can not otherwise be obtained, than by actually taking it. And we confirm this latter opinion, because many accidents frequently happen, which prevent the capture.*

De apibus.

§ XIV. Apium quoque fera natura est. Itaque apes, quæ in arbore tua consederint, antequam à te alveo includantur, non magis tuæ intelliguntur esse, quam volucres, quæ in arbore tua nidum fecerint: ideoque, si alius eas incluserit, is earum dominus erit. Favos quoque, si quos effecerint, eximere quilibet potest. Plane integra re, si prævideris ingredientem fundum tuum, poteris eum jure prohibere, ne ingrediatur. Examen quoque, quod ex alveo tuo evolaverit, eousque intelligitur esse tuum, donec in conspectu tuo est, nec difficilis persecutio ejus est, alioquin occupantis fit.

§ 14. *Bees also are wild by nature, and therefore, altho' they swarm upon a tree, which is yours, they are not reputed, until they are hived by you, to be more your property, than the birds, which have nests there: and therefore, if any other person shall inclose them in a hive, he thus becomes their proprietor. Then honeycombs also become the property of him, who takes them: but, if you observe any person entering into your ground, with that intent, you may justly hinder him. A swarm, which hath flown from your hive, is still reputed to continue yours, as long as it remains in sight, and may easily be persued, but, in any other case, it will become the property of the* occupant.

De

De pavonibus et columbis, et cæteris animalibus mansuefactis.

§ XV. Pavonum quoque et columbarum fera natura est; nec ad rem pertinet, quod ex consuetudine evolare et revolare solent: nam et apes idem faciunt, quarum constat feram esse naturam. Cervos quoque quidam ita mansuetos habent, ut in silvam ire et redire soleant, quorum et ipsorum feram esse naturam nemo negat. In iis autem animalibus, quæ ex consuetudine abire et redire solent, talis regula comprobata est; ut eousque tua esse intelligantur, donec animum revertendi habeant: nam, si revertendi animum habere desierint, etiam tua esse desinunt, et fiunt occupantium. Revertendi autem animum videntur desinere habere tunc, cum revertendi consuetudinem deseruerint.

§ 15 *Peacocks and Pidgeons are also naturally wild; nor is it any objection to say, that, after every flight, it is their custom to return: for bees do the same thing; and, that bees are naturally wild, is evident. Some have been known to have trained deer to be so tame, that they would go into, and return from the woods, at regular periods. and yet no man denies, but that deer are wild by nature But, with respect to these animals, which go and return customarily, the rule to be observed is, that they are understood to be yours, as long as they appear to retain an inclination to return: but, if this inclination ceases, that they cease to be yours; and will again become the property of him, who takes them. And these animals seem then to cease to have an inclination to return, when they disuse the custom of returning.*

De gallinis et anseribus.

§ XVI. Gallinarum autem et anserum non est fera natura: idque ex eo possumus intelligere, quod aliæ sunt gallinæ, quas feras vocamus: item alii sunt anseres, quos feros appellamus. Ideoque, si anseres tui, aut gallinæ tuæ, aliquo modo turbati turbatæve evolaverint, licet conspectum tuum effugerint, quocumque tamen loco sint, tui tuæve esse intelliguntur. et, qui lucrandi animo ea animalia detinet, furtum committere intelligitur.

§ 16. *But geese, and fowls, are not wild by nature, and this we are induced to observe, because there is a species of fowls, and a species of geese, which in contradistinction we term wild. and therefore, if the geese, or fowls of Titius, being disturbed and frightened, should take flight, they are nevertheless reckoned to belong to him, in whatever place they are found, altho' he shall have lost sight of them: and whoever detains such animals, with a lucrative view, is understood to commit a theft.*

De occupatione in bello.

§ XVII. Item ea, quæ ex hostibus capimus, jure gentium statim nostra fiunt: adeo quidem, ut et liberi homines in servitutem nostram deducantur: qui tamen, si evaserint nostram potestatem, et ad suos reversi fuerint, pristinum statum recipiunt.

§. 17.

§ 17. *All those things, which we take from our enemies in war, become instantly our own by the law of nations: so that free-men may be brought into a state of servitude by capture: but, if they afterwards escape, and shall have returned to their own people, they then obtain again their former state.*

De occupatione eorum, quæ in littore inveniuntur.

§ XVIII. Item lapilli, et gemmæ, et cætera, quæ in littore maris inveniuntur, jure naturali statim inventoris fiunt.

§ 18. *Pretious stones, pearls, and other things, which are found upon the sea-shore, become instantly, by the law of nations, the property of the finder.*

De fœtu animalium.

§ XIX. Item ea, quæ ex animalibus dominio tuo subjectis nata sunt, eodem jure tibi acquiruntur.

§ 19. *The product of those animals, of which we are the owners and masters, is, by the same law, esteemed to be our own.*

De alluvione.

§ XX. Præterea, quod per alluvionem agro tuo flumen adjecit, jure gentium tibi acquiritur Est autem alluvio incrementum latens. Per alluvionem autem id videtur adjici, quod ita paulatim adjicitur, ut intelligi non possit, quantum quoque temporis momento adjiciatur.

§ 20. *And farther— that ground, which a river hath added to your estate by alluvion, [i e. by an imperceptible increase] is properly acquired by you according to the law of nations. And that is said to be added by* alluvion, *which is added in a manner, which renders it impossible to judge, how much ground is added in the space of each moment of time.*

De vi fluminis.

§ XXI. Quod si vis fluminis de tuo prædio partem aliquam detraxerit, et vicini prædio attulerit, palam est, eam tuam permanere. Plane si longiore tempore fundo vicini tui hæserit, arboresque, quas secum traxerit, in eum fundum radices egerint; ex eo tempore videntur vicini fundo acquisitæ esse.

§ 21. *But, if the impetuosity of a river should sever any part of your estate, and adjoin it to that of your neighbour, it is certain, that such part wou'd still continue yours, but if it should remain, for a long time joined to the estate of your neighbour, and the trees, which accompanied it, shall have taken root, in his ground, such trees seem, from the time of their taking root, to be gained and acquired to his estate.*

De insula.

§ XXII. Insula, quæ in mari nata est (quod raro accidit) occupantis fit nullius enim esse creditur. At insula in flumine nata (quod frequenter accidit) si quidem mediam partem fluminis tenet, communis est eorum, qui ab utraque parte fluminis prope ripam prædia possident, pro modo scilicet latitudinis cujusque prædii, quæ prope ripam sit. Quod si alteri proximior sit parti, eorum est tantum, qui ab ea parte prope ripam prædia possident. Quod si qua parte divisum sit flumen, deinde infra unitum, agrum alicujus in formam insulæ redegerit, ejusdem permanet is ager, cujus et fuerat.

§ 22. *When an island rises in the sea, (an event which rarely happens) the property of it is in the occupant; for the property, before occupation, is in no man. But, if an island rises in a river, (which frequently happens) and is placed exactly in the middle of it, such island shall be in common to them, who possess the lands near the banks on each side of the river, according to the proportion of the extent and latitude of each man's estate, adjoining to the banks. But, if the island is nearer to one side, than the other, it belongs to them only, who possess lands next to the banks on that side, to which the island is nearest. But, if a river divides itself and afterwards unites again, having reduced a tract of land into the form of an island, the land still continues to be the property of him, to whom it before appertained.*

De alveo.

XXIII. Quod si, naturali alveo in universum derelicto, ad aliam partem fluere cœperit; prior quidem alveus eorum est, qui prope ripam ejus prædia possident, pro modo scilicet latitudinis cujusque agri, quæ prope ripam sit: novus autem alveus ejus juris esse incipit, cujus et ipsum flumen est, id est, publici. Quod si post aliquod tempus ad priorem alveum reversum fuerit flumen, rursus novus alveus eorum esse incipit, qui prope ripam ejus prædia possident.

§ 23. *If a river, intirely forsaking its natural channel, hath begun to flow elsewhere, the first channel appertains to those, who possess the lands, close to the banks of it, in proportion to the breadth of each man's estate, next to such banks: and the new channel partakes of the nature of the river, and becomes public. And, if after some time the river shall return to its former channel, the new channel commences to be the property of those, who possess the lands, contiguous to the banks of it.*

De inundatione.

§ XXIV. Alia sane causa est, si cujus totus ager inundatus fuerit; neque enim inundatio fundi speciem commutat: et ob id, si recesserit aqua, palam est eum fundum ejus manere, cujus et fuit.

§ 24. *But it is otherwise in respect to lands, which are overflowed only; for an inundation alters not the face and nature of the earth; and therefore, when the waters have receded, it is apparent, that the property will be found still to remain in him, in whom it was vested before the inundation.*

De specificatione.

§ XXV. Cum ex aliena materia species aliqua facta sit ab aliquo, quæri solet, quis eorum naturali ratione dominus sit: utrum is, qui fecerit, an potius ille, qui materiæ dominus fuerit: ut ecce, si quis ex alienis uvis, aut

aut olivis, aut spicis, vinum, aut oleum, aut frumentum, fecerit: aut ex alieno auro, vel argento, vel ære, vas aliquod fecerit: vel ex alieno vino et melle mulsum miscuerit: vel ex medicamentis alienis emplastrum aut collyrium composuerit: vel ex aliena lana vestimentum fecerit: vel ex alienis tabulis navem, vel armarium, vel subsellia, fabricaverit. Et, post multam Sabinianorum et Proculianorum ambiguitatem, placuit media sententia existimantium, si ea species ad priorem et rudem materiam reduci possit, eum videri dominum esse, qui materiæ dominus fuerit: si non possit reduci, eum potius intelligi dominum, qui fecerit: ut ecce, vas conflatum potest ad rudem materiam æris, vel argenti, vel auri, reduci: vinum autem, vel oleum, aut frumentum, ad uvas, vel olivas, vel spicas, reverti non potest: ac ne mulsum quidem ad vinum et mel resolvi potest. Quod si partim ex sua materia, partim ex aliena, speciem aliquam fecerit quis; veluti ex suo vino et alieno melle mulsum miscuerit, aut ex suis et alienis medicamentis emplastrum aut collyrium; aut ex sua lana et aliena vestimentum fecerit; dubitandum non est, hoc casu eum esse dominum, qui fecerit: cum non solum operam suam dederit, sed et partem ejusdem materiæ præstiterit.

§ 25. *When a man hath made any* species, *or kind of work, with materials, belonging to another, it is often demanded, which of them ought, in natural reason, to be deemed the master of it,—— whether he, who made the* species; *or he, who was the undoubted owner of the materials? as, for instance, if any person should make wine, oil, or flower, from the grapes, olives, or corn of another,—— should cast a vessel out of gold, silver, or brass, belonging to another man,—— should make a liquor, called* mulse, *with the wine and honey of another,—— should compose a plaster or collyrium, with another man's medicines,—— should make a garment with another's wool,—— or should fabricate, with the timber of another, a bench, a ship, or an armory? —— And after much controversy, concerning this question, between the* Sabinians *and* Proculians, *the opinion of those, who kept a mean between the two parties, proved most satisfactory to us: and their opinion was this;—— that, if the* species *can be reduced to its former, rude materials, then the master of such materials is also to be reckoned the master of the new* species: *but, if the* species *can not be so reduced, then he, who made it, is understood to be the master of it for example; a vessel can easily be reduced to the rude mass of brass, silver, or gold of which it was made, but wine, oil, or flower, can not be converted into grapes, olives, or corn, neither can* mulse *be resolved and separated into wine and honey But, if a man makes any species, partly with his own materials, and partly with the materials of another as, for instance, if he should make* mulse *with his own wine, and another's honey; or a plaster, or eye water, partly with his own, and partly with another man's medicines, or should make a garment with an intermixture of his own wool with the wool of another,—— it is not to be doubted in all such cases, but that he, who made the* species, *is master of it, since he not only gave his labor, but furnished also a part of the materials.*

Sabinianorum et Proculianorum] The two sects of *Sabinians* and *Proculians* took their rise in the reign of *Augustus*, but were not distinguished by any particular appellation, till long afterwards. for the *Sabinians* obtained their name from *Sabinus*, who was a favorite of the emperor *Tiberius*, and the *Proculians* were so called from *Proculus*, who flourished under *V*[illegible] *pasian.* It is generally held, that *Atteius Capito*, who lived in the *Augustan* age, and was a person remarkable for his great attachment to precedents and old customs, was the chief of the *Sabinians*, and that *Antistius Labeo*, his cotemporary, who did not confine himself wholly to rules, but followed principally the dictates of reason and his own understanding, was the head of the *Proculian* sect. These sects continued in vogue to the reign of *Marcus Aurelius*, till which time the students of the law generally attached themselves to either the one, or the other. But the lawyers of that reign affected neither party in particular, for at different times they dispassionately approved the opinions of either sect, as they judged them more or less agreeable to justice and right reason and they generally indeavored by an equal temperature to avoid the absurdities, into which both parties, by reason of their great dislike and opposition to each other, had frequently fallen. *ff. 1 de origine juris. Hist du droit Romain, par* Claude Ferriere.

These lawyers (who from their conduct were denominated *Eriscundi*, from the old verb *erisce-re* to divide) are the persons, hinted at by *Justinian* in this paragraph, as observing a just mean between the two parties.

De accessione.

§ XXVI. Si tamen alienam purpuram vestimento suo quis intexuerit, licet pretiosior sit purpura, tamen accessionis vice cedit vestimento: et qui dominus fuit purpuræ, adversus eum, qui surripuit, habet furti actionem et condictionem, sive ipse sit, qui vestimentum fecit, sive alius. Nam extinctæ res licet vindicari non possint, condici tamen à furibus et quibusque aliis possessoribus possunt.

§ 26. *If any man shall have interwoven the purple of another into his own vestment, then the purple, altho' it may be more valuable, doth yield and appertain to the vestment by accession: and he, who was the owner of the purple, may have an action of theft, and a personal action, called a* condiction, *against the purloiner, nor is it of any consequence, whether the vestment was made by him, who committed the theft, or by another: for altho' things, which become, as it were, extinct by the change of their form, can not be recovered identically, yet a* condiction *may be brought for the recovery of the value of them, either against the thief, or against any other possessor.*

De confusione.

§ XXVII. Si duorum materiæ voluntate dominorum confusæ sint, totum id corpus, quod ex confusione fit, utriusque commune est: veluti si qui vina sua confuderint, aut massas argenti vel auri conflaverint. Sed, etsi diversæ materiæ sint, et ob id propria species facta sit, forte ex vino et melle mulsum, aut ex auro et argento electrum, idem juris est. Nam et hoc casu, communem esse speciem, non dubitatur. Quod si fortuito et non voluntate dominorum confusæ fuerint vel ejusdem generis materiæ, vel diversæ, idem juris esse placuit.

§ 27. *If the materials of two persons are incorporated together, then the whole mass, or composition, is common to both the proprietors: for instance, if two owners shall have intermixed their wines, or shall have melted together their gold or their silver. The same rule is also observed, if diverse substances are so incorporated, as to become one* species: *as when* mulse *is made with wine and honey, or when an* electrum *is composed by an intermixture of gold and silver in different proportions: for in these cases it is not doubted, but that the species becomes common. Neither is any other rule observed, when either homogeneous, or even different substances, are confounded and incorporated together fortuitously, without the consent of their proprietors.*

De

De commixtione.

§ XXVIII. Quod si frumentum Titii frumento tuo mistum fuerit, siquidem voluntate vestra, commune est; quia singula corpora, id est, singula grana, quæ cujusque propria fuerunt, consensu vestro communicata sunt. Quod si casu id mistum fuerit, vel Titius id miscuerit sine tua voluntate, non videtur commune esse: quia singula corpora in sua substantia durant. Sed nec magis istis casibus commune fit frumentum, quam grex intelligitur esse communis, si pecora Titii tuis pecoribus mista fuerint. Sed, si ab alterutro vestrum totum id frumentum retineatur, in rem quidem actio pro modo frumenti cujusque competit: arbitrio autem judicis continetur, ut ipse æstimet, quale cujusque frumentum fuerit.

§ 28. *If the corn of* Titius *hath been mixed with the corn of another by consent, then the whole is in common, because the single bodies, or grains, which were the private property of each, are, by the mutual consent, made common. But, if the intermixture was accidental, or if* Titius *made it without consent, it then seems, that the corn is not in common; because the single grains still remain ununited, and in their proper substance for corn, in such a case, is no more understood to be in common, than a flock would be, if the sheep of* Titius *should accidentally intermix with the sheep of another. But, if the whole quantity of corn should be retained by either of the parties, then an action* in rem *lies for the quantity of each man's corn: and it is the business and duty of the judge to make an exact estimate of the* quality *of the corn, belonging to each party.*

De his quæ solo cedunt. De ædificatione in suo solo ex aliena materia.

§ XXIX. Cum in suo solo aliquis ex aliena materia ædificaverit, ipse intelligitur dominus ædificii: quia omne, quod solo inædificatur, solo cedit. Nec tamen ideo is, qui materiæ dominus fuerat, desinit dominus ejus esse: sed tantisper neque vindicare eam potest, neque ad exhibendum de ea re agere, propter legem duodecim tabularum, qua cavetur, ne quis tignum alienum ædibus suis junctum eximere cogatur, sed duplum pro eo præstet, per actionem, quæ vocatur, *de tigno juncto.* Appellatione autem tigni omnis materia significatur, ex qua ædificia fiunt. Quod ideo provisum est, ne ædificia rescindi necesse sit. Quod si aliqua ex causa dirutum sit ædificium, poterit materiæ dominus, si non fuerit duplum jam consequutus, tunc eam vindicare, et ad exhibendum de ea re agere

§ 29 *When any man hath raised a building upon his own ground, he is understood to be the proprietor of such building, altho' the materials, used in it, were the property of another for every building is an accession to the ground, upon which it stands. But, notwithstanding this, he, who was the owner of the materials, does not cease to be the owner, yet he cannot demand his materials, or bring an action for the exhibition of them; for it is provided, by a law of the twelve tables, that a person, whose house is built with the materials of another, can not be compelled to restore those materials, but, by an action, intituled* de tigno juncto, *he may be obliged to pay*

pay double the value: and here note, that all the materials for building are comprehended under the general term tignum. *The above cited provision, in the law of the twelve tables, was made to prevent the demolition of buildings. But, if it happens, that, by any cause, a building should be dissevered, or pulled down, then the owner of the materials, if he hath not already obtained double the value of them, is not prohibited to claim his identical materials, and to bring his action* ad exhibendum.

De ædificatione ex sua materia in solo alieno.

§ XXX Ex diverso, si quis in alieno solo ex sua materia domum ædificaverit, illius fit domus, cujus et solum est. Sed hoc casu materiæ dominus proprietatem ejus amittit, quia voluntate ejus intelligitur esse alienata; utique si non ignorabat, se in alieno solo ædificare: et ideo, licet diruta sit domus, materiam tamen vindicare non potest. Certe illud constat, si, in possessione constituto ædificatore, soli dominus petat, domum suam esse, nec solvat pretium materiæ et mercedes fabrorum, posse eum per exceptionem doli mali repelli, utique si bonæ fidei possessor fuerit, qui ædificavit. Nam scienti, solum alienum esse, potest objici culpa, quod ædificaverit temere in eo solo, quod intelligebat alienum esse.

§ 30 *On the contrary, if a man shall have built an edifice with his own materials upon the ground of another, such edifice becomes the property of him, to whom the ground appertains: for, in this case, the owner of the materials loses his property, because he is understood to have made a voluntary alienation of it. and this is the law, if he was not ignorant, that he was building upon another's land and therefore, if the edifice should fall, or be pulled down, such person can even then have no claim to the materials. But it is apparent, if the proprietor of the ground, of which the builder was in confirmed possession, should plead, that the edifice is his; and refuse to pay the price of the materials and the wages of the workmen, that then such proprietor may be repelled by an* exception *of* fraud: *and this may assuredly be done, if the builder was the possessor of the ground* bona fide. *But it may be justly objected to any man, who understood, that the land appertained to another, "that "he hath built rashly upon that ground, which he knew to be the property of an-"other."*

De plantatione.

§ XXXI. Si Titius alienam plantam in solo suo posuerit, ipsius erit, et ex diverso, si Titius suam plantam in Mævii solo posuerit, Mævii planta erit: si modo utroque casu radices egerit: ante enim quam radices egerit, ejus permanet, cujus fuerat. Adeo autem ex eo tempore, quo radices egerit planta, proprietas ejus commutatur, ut, si vicini arbor ita terram Titii presserit, ut in ejus fundum radices egerit, Titii effici arborem dicamus: ratio enim non patitur, ut alterius arbor esse intelligatur, quam cujus in fundum radices egerit. Et ideo circa confinium arbor posita, si etiam in vicini fundum radices egerit, communis fit.

§ 31. *If* Titius *sets another man's plant in his own ground, the plant will become the property of* Titius *and, on the contrary, if* Titius *shall have set his own plant in* Mævius's *ground, the plant will appertain to* Mævius; *on supposition in either case,*

case, that it hath already taken root; for, until then, the property of the plant remains still in him, by whom it was planted. But from the instant, in which a plant hath taken root, the property of it is changed: so that, if the tree of a neighbour borders so closely upon the ground of Titius, *as to take root in it,* and be wholly nourished there, *we may affirm, that such tree is become the property of* Titius. *for reason doth not permit, that a tree should be deemed the property of any other, than of him, in whose ground it hath cast it's roots. And therefore, if a tree, planted near the bounds of the lands of one person, shall also extend it's roots into the lands of another, such tree will become common to both the land-proprietors.*

De satione.

§ XXXII. Qua ratione autem plantæ, quæ terræ coalescunt, solo cedunt, eadem ratione frumenta quoque, quæ sata sunt, solo cedere intelliguntur. Cæterum sicut is, qui in alieno solo ædificavit, si ab eo dominus petat ædificium, defendi potest per exceptionem doli mali, secundum ea, quæ diximus: ita ejusdem exceptionis auxilio tutus esse potest is, qui alienum fundum sua impensa bona fide conservit.

§ 32 *As all plants are esteemed to appertain to the soil, in which they have rooted, so every kind of grain is also understood to follow the property of that ground, in which it is sowed. But as he, who hath built upon the ground of another, may (according to what we have already said) be defended by an* exception *of* fraud, *if the proprietor of the ground should demand the edifice, so he, who at his own expense and* bona fide, *hath sowed in another man's land, may also be benefited by the help of this* exception.

De scriptura.

§ XXXIII. Literæ quoque, licet aureæ sint, perinde chartis membranisve cedunt, ac solo cedere solent ea, quæ inædificantur, aut inseruntur. Ideoque, si in chartis membranisve tuis carmen vel historiam vel orationem Titius scripserit, hujus corporis non Titius, sed tu dominus esse videris. Sed, si à Titio petas tuos libros, tuasve membranas, nec impensas scripturæ solvere paratus sis, poterit se Titius defendere per exceptionem doli mali, utique si earum chartarum membranarumve possessionem bona fide nactus est.

§ 33. *As whatever is built upon, or sowed in the ground, belongs to that ground by accession; so letters also, altho' written with gold, do appertain to the paper or parchment, upon which they are written. And therefore, if* Titius *shall have written a poem, an history, or an oration, upon the paper or parchment of* Seius, *then* Titius *will not be deemed the master of his own work, but the whole will be reputed to be* Seius's *property. But if* Seius *demands his books or parchments from* Titius, *and at the same time refuses to defray the expense of the writing, then* Titius *can defend himself by an* exception *of* fraud. *and this he may certainly do, if he was in possession of such papers and parchments* bona fide; *that is, honestly, and believing them to be his own.*

De pictura.

§ XXXIV. Si quis in aliena tabula pinxerit, quidam putant tabulam picturæ cedere: aliis videtur, picturam (qualiscunque sit) tabulæ cedere: sed nobis videtur melius esse, tabulam picturæ cedere: ridiculum est enim, picturam Apellis vel Parrhasii in accessionem vilissimæ tabulæ cedere. Unde si à domino tabulæ imaginem possidente is, qui pinxit, eam petat, nec solvat pretium tabulæ, poterit per exceptionem doli mali submoveri. At si is, qui pinxit, eam possideat, consequens est, ut utilis actio domino tabulæ adversus eum detur: quo casu, si non solvat impensam picturæ, poterit per exceptionem doli mali repelli. utique si bonæ fidei possessor fuerit ille, qui picturam imposuit. Illud enim palam est, quod sive is, qui pinxit, surripuit tabulas, sive alius, competit domino tabularum furti actio.

§ 34. *If any man shall have painted upon the tablet of another, some think, that the tablet should yield and accede to the picture but it is the opinion of others, that the picture (whatever the quality of it may be) should accede to the tablet. But it appears to us to be the better opinion, that the tablet should accede to the picture, for it seems ridiculous, that the painting of an* Apelles, *or a* Parrhasius, *should yield, as an accession, to a worthless tablet. But if he, who hath painted upon a tablet, demands it from the owner and possessor, and offers not the price of it, then such demandant may be defeated by an* exception *of* fraud: *but, if the painter is in possession of the picture, the owner of the tablet is intituled to an action called* utilis, *i. e.* beneficial, *in which case, if the owner of the tablet demands it, and does not tender the value of the picture, he may also be repelled by an* exception *of* fraud, *if he, who painted upon the tablet, was the possessor of it upon good faith. But, if he, who hath painted upon it, or any other, shall have taken away a tablet feloniously, it is evident, that the owner of it may prosecute such person by an action of theft.*

De fructibus bona fide perceptis.

§ XXXV. Si quis à non domino, quem dominum esse crediderit, bona fide fundum emerit, vel ex donatione, aliave qualibet justa causa, æque bona fide acceperit, naturali ratione placuit, fructus, quos percepit, ejus esse pro cultura et cura: et ideo, si postea dominus supervenerit, et fundum vindicet, de fructibus ab eo consumptis agere non potest. Ei vero, qui alienum fundum sciens possederit, non idem concessum est: itaque cum fundo etiam fructus, licet consumpti sint, cogitur restituere.

§ 35 *If any man shall have purchased lands from another, believing the seller to have been the true owner, when in fact he was not, or shall have obtained an estate* bona fide, *either by donation, or any other just means, it is agreeable to natural reason, that the fruits, which he shall have gathered, shall be reckoned to have become his own, on account of his care in the culture and tillage And therefore, if the true owner shall afterwards appear and claim his lands, he can have no action against the* bona fide *possessor, for those fruits and that product, which have been consumed. But this exemption from such an action is not granted to him, who knowingly keeps possession of another's estate, and therefore, when ever there is a* mala fides, *the possessor is compellable to restore all the mesne profits together with the land.*

De

De fructibus ab eo consumptis.] The law of England seems in general agreeable to this doctrine. vid 2d chan. cas. 144. Bac. abr account. Stat. of Glocester, 6 Edw. 1. cap. 1. 2. Co. inst. 284, &c.

A fructuario et colono perceptis.

§ XXXVI. Is vero, ad quem usus fructus fundi pertinet, non aliter fructuum dominus efficitur, quam si ipse eos perceperit. Et ideo licet maturis fructibus, nondum tamen perceptis, decesserit, ad hæredes ejus non pertinent, sed domino proprietatis acquiruntur. Eadem fere et de colono dicuntur.

§ 36. *He, to whom the usufruct of lands belongs, can gain no property in the fruits of such lands, until he hath actually gathered them; and therefore, if the usufructuary should die, whilest the fruits, altho' ripe, are yet ungathered, they could not be claimed by his heirs, but would be acquired by the proprietor of the lands; and the same may be said in general, in relation to farmers.*

Quæ sunt in fructu.

§ XXXVII. In pecudum fructu etiam fœtus est, sicuti lac, pilus, et lana: itaque agni, hædi, et vituli, et equuli, et suculi, statim naturali jure dominii fructuarii sunt. Partus vero ancillæ in fructu non est: itaque ad dominum proprietatis pertinet. Absurdum enim videbatur, hominem in fructu esse: cum omnes fructus rerum natura gratia hominis comparaverit.

§ 37. *In estimating the product of animals, we not only reckon milk, skins, and wool, but also their young; and therefore lambs, kids, calves, colts, and pigs, appertain by natural right to the usufructuary, but the offspring of a female slave is not to be included within this product; and can belong to him only, in whom the property of such female slave is vested: for it seemed absurd to think, that man, for whom nature hath framed all things, should be enumerated among the productions of the brute creation.*

De officio fructuarii.

§ XXXVIII. Sed, si gregis usumfructum quis habeat, in locum demortuorum capitum ex fœtu fructuarius submittere debet (ut et Juliano visum est) et in vinearum demortuarum vel arborum locum alias debet substituere. Recte enim colere, et quasi bonus paterfamilias uti, debet.

§ 38 *He, who hath the usufruct of a flock, ought, (according to the opinion of* Julian*) to preserve the original number of his sheep intire, by supplying the place of those, which die, out of the produce of the flock. And the duty of a usufructuary is the same in regard to other things, for he ought to supply the place of dead vines, or trees, by substituting others in their stead, and to act in every respect, like a good husbandman.*

De inventione thesauri.

§ XXXIX. Thesauros, quos quis in loco suo invenerit, divus Adrianus, naturalem æquitatem sequutus, ei concessit, qui eos invenerit. Idemque statuit, si quis in sacro aut religioso loco fortuito casu invenerit. At si quis in alieno loco, non data ad hoc opera, ſed fortuito invenerit, dimidium domino ſoli conceſſit, et dimidium inventori. Et convenienter, ſi quis in Cæſaris loco invenerit, dimidium inventoris, et dimidium eſſe Cæſaris, ſtatuit. Cui conveniens eſt, ut ſi quis in fiſcali loco vel publico vel civitatis invenerit, dimidium ipſius eſſe debeat, et dimidium fiſci, vel civitatis.

§ 39. *It hath been allowed by the emperor* Adrian, *in perſuance of natural equity, that any treaſure, which a man finds in his own lands, ſhall become the property of the finder, and that whatever is caſually found, in a ſacred or religious place, ſhall alſo become the property of him, who finds it. But, if a perſon, not making it his buſineſs to ſearch, ſhould fortuitouſly find a treaſure in the ground of another, the emperor hath granted the half of ſuch treaſure to the proprietor of the ſoil, and half to the finder He hath in like manner ordained, that, if any thing is found within the imperial demeſnes, half ſhall appertain to the finder and half to the emperor · and, ſimilar to this, if a man finds any valuable thing in a place or diſtrict belonging to the treaſury, the public, or the city, the ſame emperor hath decreed, that half ſhall appertain to the finder, and half to the treaſury, the public, or the city, to which the place or diſtrict belongs.*

Theſauros] Treaſures naturally belong to the finder, that is, to him, who moves them from the place where they are, and ſecures them, yet nothing forbids but that the laws and cuſtoms of any country may ordain otherwiſe. *Plato* was deſirous, that notice ſhould be given to the magiſtrates, and that the oracle ſhould be conſulted. and *Apollonius*, looking upon a treaſure found as a particular bleſſing from heaven, adjudged it to the *beſt man*. The *Hebrews* gave it to the owner of the ground where it was found, as may be gathered from *Chriſt*'s parable, *Matt* xiii 44 and, that the *Syrians* did the ſame, we may infer from a ſtory in *Philoſtratus*, lib vi. cap 16 The laws of the *Roman* emperors are very various upon this ſubject, as appears partly from their conſtitutions, and partly from the hiſtories of *Lampridius*, *Zonarus*, and *Cedrenus*. The *Germans* awarded treaſures found, and indeed all other ἀδέσποτα (i e things without an owner) to their prince; which is now grown ſo common, that it may paſs for the law of nations; for it is now obſerved in *Germany*, *France*, *Spain*, *Denmark*, and *England*; where treaſure-trove is underſtood to be any gold or ſilver, in coin, plate or bullion, which hath been of antient time hidden, and whereſoever it is found, if no perſon can prove it to be his property, it belongs to the king, or his grantee A concealment of treaſure-trove is now only puniſhed by fine and impriſonment, but it appears from *Glanvill* and *Bracton*, that *occultatio theſauri inventi frauduloſa* was formerly an offenſe puniſhable with death. 3 *Co. inſt* 132, 133 *Cuſtum de Norm cap* 18 *Grot. de jur. bell. et pac. l.* 2. *cap* 8 *ſect* 7

De traditione. I. *Regula ejuſque ratio.*

§ XL. Per traditionem quoque jure naturali res nobis acquiruntur: nihil enim tam conveniens eſt naturali æquitati, quam voluntatem domini, volentis rem ſuam in alium transferre, ratam haberi: et ideo, cujuſcunque generis ſit corporalis res, tradi poteſt, et à domino tradita alienatur: itaque ſtipendiaria quoque et tributaria prædia eodem modo alienantur Vocantur autem ſtipendiaria et tributaria prædia, quæ in provinciis ſunt: inter quæ nec non et Italica prædia, ex noſtra conſtitutione, nulla eſt differentia: ſed ſiquidem ex cauſa donationis, aut dotis, aut qualibet alia ex cauſa, tradantur, ſine dubio transferuntur.

§ 40 *Things are alſo acquired (according to the law of nature) by tradition or livery; for nothing is more conformable to natural equity, than to confirm the will of him, who is deſirous to transfer his property into the hands of another. and therefore*

cor-

corporeal things, of whatever kind they are, may be delivered; and, when delivered by the true owner, are absolutely aliened. Stipendiary *and* tributary *possessions (and those, which are situated in the provinces, are so called) may also be aliened in the same manner: for between these, and the* Italian *estates, we have now taken away all distinction, by our imperial ordinance: so that, on* account *of a donation, a marriage-portion, or any other just cause,* stipendiary *and* tributary *possessions may undoubtedly be transfered by livery.*

Ex nostra constitutione] *vid Cod* 7 *t* 31 *l. un.* de usucapione transformanda, et de sublata differentia rerum mancipi et nec mancipi. *ann Ch.* 531.

2. *Limitatio.*

§ XLI. Venditæ vero res et traditæ non aliter emptori acquiruntur, quam si is venditori pretium solverit, vel alio modo ei satisfecerit; veluti ex promissore aut pignore dato: quod quamquam cavetur lege duodecim tabularum, tamen recte dicitur et jure gentium, id est, jure naturali, id effici. Sed, si is, qui vendidit, fidem emptoris sequutus fuerit, dicendum est, statim rem emptoris fieri.

§ 41. *Things, altho' sold and delivered, are yet not acquired by the buyer, until he hath either paid the seller for them, or satisfied him in some other manner; as by a bondsman or pledge And, altho' this is so ordained by a law of the twelve tables, yet the same rule of justice is rightly said to arise from the law of nations, that is, from the law of nature. But, if the seller shall have given credit to the buyer, we must affirm, that the things will then become instantly the property of the latter.*

3. *Ampliatio.*

§ XLII. Nihil autem interest, utrum ipse dominus tradat alicui rem suam, an voluntate ejus alius, cui ejus rei possessio permissa sit. Qua ratione, si cui libera universorum negotiorum administratio permissa fuerit à domino, isque ex his negotiis rem vendiderit et tradiderit, faciet eam accipientis.

§ 42 *It makes no difference, whether the owner of a particular thing delivered it himself, or whether another, to whom the care and possession of it was intrusted, shall have delivered it with the owner's consent. And, for this reason, if the free and universal administration of all business is commited by a proprietor to any certain person, and the committée, by virtue of his commission, shall sell and deliver any goods, then will such goods become the property of the receiver.*

De quasi traditione. Si traditio ex alia causa præcesserit.

§ XLIII. Interdum etiam sine traditione nuda voluntas domini sufficit ad rem transferendam; veluti si rem, quam tibi aliquis commodaverit, aut locaverit, aut apud te deposuerit, postea aut vendiderit tibi, aut donaverit, aut dotis nomine dederit: quamvis enim ex ea causa tibi eam non tradiderit, eo tamen ipso, quod patitur tuam esse, statim tibi acquiritur proprietas, perinde ac si eo nomine tibi tradita fuisset.

§ 43. *In some cases, even without delivery, the mere consent of the proprietor is sufficient to transfer property: as, when it happens, that a person hath lent any thing to you, let it, or deposited it in your possession, and hath afterwards sold it to you, made a donation of it, or given it to you, as a marriage portion: for altho' he shall not have delivered it, for any of these last mentioned purposes, yet, as soon as it is by consent reputed to be yours, you have instantly acquired the property of it, and that as fully, as if it had actually been delivered to you, as a thing sold, a donation, or a marriage portion.*

Acquiritur proprietas] This is called *fictio brevis manus*, which takes place, when goods are put into the possession of some person by way of deposit or loan, and are afterwards given or sold to the same person, he being already the possessor. *ff.* 23. *t.* 3. *l.* 43.

De traditione clavium.

§ XLIV. Item, si quis merces in horreo depositas vendiderit, simul atque claves horrei tradiderit emptori, transfert proprietatem mercium ad emptorem.

§ 44. *Also if a person hath sold any species of merchandise, deposited in a storehouse, such person is understood to have transfered the property of his merchandise, as soon as he hath delivered the keys of the store-house to the buyer.*

De missilibus.

§ XLV. Hoc amplius, interdum et in incertam personam collata voluntas domini transfert rei proprietatem: ut ecce, prætores et consules, cum missilia jactant in vulgus, ignorant quid eorum quisque sit excepturus: et tamen, quia volunt, quod quisque acceperit, ejus esse, statim eum dominum efficiunt.

§ 45. *It also sometimes happens, that the property of a thing is transfered, by the master of it, to an incertain person: thus for instance, when the prætors and consuls cast their* missilia, *or liberalities, among the people, they know not what any particular man will receive, and yet, because it is their will and desire, that what every man then receives shall be his own, it therefore instantly becomes his property.*

De habitis pro derelicto.

§ XLVI. Qua ratione verius esse videtur, si rem pro derelicto à domino habitam occupaverit quis, statim eum dominum effici. Pro derelicto autem habetur, quod dominus ea mente abjecerit, ut id in numero rerum suarum esse nolit: ideoque statim dominus ejus esse desinit.

§ 46 *By a parity of reason it appears true, that a thing, which hath been made a* derelict *by the owner, will become the property of the first occupant. And whatever hath either been thrown away, or abandoned by the owner, to the intent, that it might never more be reckoned among his possessions, is properly accounted a* derelict *: and therefore ceases to be his property.*

Pro derelicto] What the *Romans* called a *derelict* the *English* lawyers call a *waife* and this was formerly looked upon as the natural right of the finder, but it now belongs to the prince A *waife*, strictly so called, is a personal or moveable chattel, which having been feloniously taken, and then forsaken thro' fear, has no owner to claim it, and therefore, if any such thing is found, it becomes either the property of the king, or of the lord, to whom the king hath granted

granted it; but it must be restored, if the true and proper owner claims it within a year and a day In the same manner, all beasts, which stray, are regarded as *derelicts*, and were by our antient writers included under the word *waives*; but they are now specified more particularly by the term *estrays*, which is rendered in *Latin Extraburæ*; because such cattle break forth and wander against the will of their owner; and, if they are not claimed within a year and a day, they escheat to the king or the lord of the manor, where they were taken, if they have been publicly proclaimed in the neighbouring markets *Cow*. inst. h. t. 5 *Co. rep*. 109. *Wood's* inst. 213

De jactis in mare levandæ navis causa. Item de his, quæ de rheda currente cadunt.

§ XLVII. Alia sane causa est earum rerum, quæ in tempestate levandæ navis causa ejiciuntur: hæ enim dominorum permanent: quia palam est, eas non eo animo ejici, quod quis eas habere nolit, sed quo magis cum ipsa navi maris periculum effugiat. Qua de causa, si quis eas fluctibus expulsas, vel etiam in ipso mari nactus, lucrandi animo abstulerit, furtum committit. Nec longe videntur discedere ab his, quæ de rheda currente, non intelligentibus dominis, cadunt.

§ 47. *But the law is otherwise in respect to those things, which are thrown overboard in a storm, for the sake of lightening a ship; for such things remain the property of the owners, inasmuch as it is evident, that they were not thrown away, through dislike, but that each person in the ship might avoid the dangers of the sea. And, upon this account, whoever hath, with a lucrative intention, taken away such goods, altho' found even upon the high sea, he is guilty of theft And, with these, those goods may be ranked, which have droped from a carriage in motion, without the knowledge of the owner*

Furtum committit] None of those goods, which are called *Jetsam*, (from being cast into the sea while the ship is in danger) or those called *Flotsam* (from floating after shipwreck) or those called *Ligan*, (that is, goods sunk in the sea, but tied to a buoy, that they may be found) are to be esteemed wreck, so long as they remain in the sea And by 3 *Edw* 1. *cap* 4 it is enacted—*that if a man, cat, or dog, escape alive out of the ship, whereby the owner of the goods may be known, neither the vessel, nor any thing therein, shall be adjudged wreck, but shall be restored to the owner, if he claims within a year and a day* A man, cat, or dog, are only put for examples, but all other living things are to be understood, and if the owner of the ship should die within the year and a day, his executors or administrators may make proof. 2. *Co inst* 167, 168 *Wood's inst*. 214 If the goods are taken away by wrong doers, the owner may have his action; and, if the wrong-doers are unknown, he may have a commission of oyer and terminer, to inquire what persons commited the trespass, and make restitution

---

TITULUS SECUNDUS.

De rebus corporalibus et incorporalibus.

Secunda rerum divisio.

QUÆDAM præterea res corporales sunt, quædam incorporales. Corporales hæ sunt, quæ sui natura tangi possunt, veluti fundus, homo, vestis, aurum, argentum, et denique aliæ res innumerabiles. Incorporales

porales autem sunt, quæ tangi non possunt: qualia sunt ea, quæ in jure consistunt, sicut hæreditas, ususfructus, usus, et obligationes, quoquo modo contractæ. Nec ad rem pertinet, quod in hæreditate res corporales continentur: nam et fructus, qui ex fundo percipiuntur, corporales sunt: et id, quod ex aliqua obligatione nobis debetur, plerumque corporale est, veluti fundus, homo, pecunia: nam ipsum jus hæreditatis, et ipsum jus utendi fruendi, et ipsum jus obligationis incorporale est. Eodem numero sunt et jura prædiorum urbanorum et rusticorum, quæ etiam servitutes vocantur.

Things may also be farther divided into corporeal *and* incorporeal. *Things* corporeal *are those, which may be touched; as, for example, lands, slaves, vestments, gold, silver, and others innumerable. Things* incorporeal *are those, which are not subject to the touch, but consist in rights and privileges; as inheritances, usufructs, uses, and all obligations, in what manner soever they are contracted: nor is it an objection of any consequence to urge, that things* corporeal *are contained in an inheritance. for fruits, gathered from the earth, are* corporeal; *and that also is generally* corporeal, *which is due to us upon an obligation; as a field, a slave, or money· but it must be observed, that we here mean only the* right *to an inheritance, the* right *of using and enjoying any particular thing, and the* right *of an obligation; all which* rights *are undoubtedly* incorporeal. *And to these may be added the* rights, *or rather qualities, of rural and city estates, which are also termed* services.

Rusticorum prædiorum jura] Predial or real services are the rights, which one estate owes to another And, as estates are either rural inheritances, as lands, barns, stables, &c. or city-inheritances, as houses for habitation, predial services are subdivided into *rusticas* et *urbanas*, rural and city-services. Personal services are those, which are due from a thing to a person. By some these are called mixed; and they are many and various, without any certain name, except three, which are termed, usufruct, use, and habitation. *Wood's imp. law p.* 145.

TITULUS TERTIUS.

De servitutibus rusticorum et urbanorum prædiorum.

D. viii. T. 1. et 2. C. iii. T. 34.

De servitutibus rusticis.

RUSTICORUM prædiorum jura sunt hæc: iter, actus, via, aquæductus Iter est jus eundi, ambulandi hominis, non etiam jumentum agendi vel vehiculum. Actus est jus agendi jumentum vel vehiculum. Itaque, qui habet iter, actum non habet: sed, qui actum habet, et iter habet, eoque uti potest etiam sine jumento. Via est jus eundi, et agendi, et ambulandi. nam iter et actum via in se continet. Aquæductus est jus aquæ ducendæ per fundum alienum.

The

The rights or services of rural estates are these; *a* path, *a* road, *an* highway, *and an* aqueduct *or free passage for water. A* path *denotes the right of passing and repassing on foot over another man's ground, but not of driving cattle or a carriage over it. A* road *implies the liberty of driving either cattle or carriages: and therefore he, who hath a* path, *hath not a* road *: but he, who hath a* road, *hath inclusively a* path; *for he may use such* road, *when he doth not drive cattle. An* highway *is a service, which imports the right of passing, driving cattle, &c. and includes in it both a* path *and a* road: *and an* aqueduct *is a service, by which one man may have the right of a free passage or conduit for water, through the grounds of another.*

De servitutibus urbanis.

§ I. Prædiorum urbanorum servitutes sunt hæ, quæ ædificiis inhærent; ideo urbanorum prædiorum dictæ, quoniam ædificia omnia urbana prædia appellamus, etsi in villa ædificata sunt. Item urbanorum prædiorum servitutes sunt hæ, ut vicinus onera vicini sustineat: ut in parietem ejus liceat vicino tignum immittere: ut stillicidium, vel flumen recipiat quis in ædes suas, vel in aream, vel in cloacam, vel non recipiat: et ne altius quis tollat ædes suas, ne luminibus vicini officiat.

§ 1. *The services of city-estates and inheritances are those, which appertain and adhere to buildings. and they are therefore called the services of city-estates, because we call all edifices city-estates, altho' they are built upon farms or in villages. It is required by city-services, that neighbours should bear the burdens of neighbours; and, by such services, one neighbour may be permitted to place a beam upon the wall of another,—— may be compelled to receive the droppings and currents from the gutter-pipes of another man's house, upon his own house, area, or sewer, or may be exempted from receiving them,—— or may be restrained from raising his house in height, lest he should darken the habitation of his neighbour.*

Etsi in villa.] In the *Roman* law all houses and buildings, whether in town or country, are called *prædia urbana* and all lands, whether meadows, arable lands, or vineyards, are denominated *prædia rustica.* *Urbana prædia omnia ædificia accipimus, non solum ea, quæ sunt in oppidis, sed etsi forte stabula vel alia meritoria in villis et in vicis, vel si prætoria voluptati tantum deservientia quia urbanum prædium non locus facit sed materia* ff 50 t 16 l 198

De reliquis servitutibus rusticis.

§ II. Inter rusticorum prædiorum servitutes quidam computari recte putant aquæ haustum, pecoris ad aquam appulsum, jus pascendi, calcis coquendæ, arenæ fodiendæ.

§ 2 *Some are with reason of opinion, that, among rural services, we ought to reckon those, by which we obtain the right of drawing water, watering and feeding cattle, making lime, digging sand,* &c. *in the ground of another.*

Quidam recte putant] These services are sometimes predial, and sometimes personal, according to the cause and reason of their constitution *Personales, si non in usum vicini prædii, sed personæ, constituantur prædiales, si vicino prædio inserviunt.* Hein

Qui servitutem debere vel acquirere possunt.

§ III. Ideo autem hæ servitutes prædiorum appellantur, quoniam sine prædiis consistere non possunt. Nemo enim potest servitutem acquirere urbani

bani vel rustici prædii, nisi qui habet prædium: nec quisquam debere, nisi qui prædium habet.

§ 3. *All these services are called the services of estates or inheritances; because they can not be constituted without an inheritance to support them; for no man can either owe, or acquire, a rural or city-service, if he possesses neither house nor lands.*

Quibus modis servitus constituitur.

§ IV. Si quis velit vicino aliquod jus constituere, pactionibus atque stipulationibus id efficere debet. Potest etiam quis testamento hæredem suum damnare, ne altius tollat ædes suas, ne luminibus vicini officiat; vel ut patiatur eum tignum in parietem suum immittere, stillicidiumve adversus eum habere, vel ut patiatur eum per fundum ire, agere, aquamve ex eo ducere.

§ 4. *When ever any one is willing to demise the right of a service to another, he may do it by contract and stipulation. A man may also by testament prohibit his heir from heightening his house, lest he should obstruct the view of his neighbour: or may oblige his heir to permit the rafter of another man's house to be laid upon his wall. or to receive upon his own house the droppings of anothers: or to suffer any person to walk, drive cattle, or draw water in his grounds.*

TITULUS QUARTUS.

De Usufructu.

D. vii. T. 1. C. iii. T. 33.

Definitio usufructus.

USUSFRUCTUS est jus alienis rebus utendi fruendi, salva rerum substantia. Est autem jus in corpore, quo sublato et ipsum tolli necesse est.

An usufruct *is the right of using and enjoying, without diminution, the things, which are the property of another. But altho' an* usufruct *is a right, and therefore incorporeal, yet, as it appertains always to a substance, it necessarily follows, that, if the substance perishes, the* usufruct *must cease.*

Quibus modis constituitur.

§ I. Ususfructus à proprietate separationem recipit, idque pluribus modis accidit: ut ecce, si quis usumfructum alicui legaverit: nam hæres nudam habet proprietatem, legatarius vero usumfructum. Et contra, si fundum legaverit deducto usufructu, legatarius nudam habet proprietatem, hæres vero usumfructum. Item alii usumfructum, alii deducto eo fundum legare potest. Sine testamento vero si quis velit usumfructum alii con-

constituere, pactionibus et stipulationibus id efficere debet. Ne tamen in universum inutiles essent proprietates, semper abscedente usufructu, placuit certis modis extingui usumfructum, et ad proprietatem reverti.

§ 1. *The* usufruct *of things is frequently separated from the property; and thi happens by various means: it happens, for instance, when the* usufruct *is bequeathed by testament: for the heir hath then only the nude property vested in him, whilest the legatèe possesses the* usufruct—— *or, on the contrary, it happens, when a testator hath bequeathed his lands without the* usufruct; *for then the legatary hath only the nude property, whilest the heir enjoys the profits: for the* usufruct *may be bequeathed to one man, and the lands, without the* usufruct, *to another. Yet, if any man would constitute an* usufruct *otherwise, than by testament, he must do it by paction and stipulation. But lest the property of lands should be rendered wholly unbeneficial by deducting the* usufruct *for ever, it was thought convenient, that the* usufruct *should by certain means become extinguished, and revert to the property.*

Ususfructus a proprietate] In the laws of *England* there is no mention of such usufructs, which were among the *Romans*, but they may undoubtedly be created among us by agreement or by testament An estate for life, for years, or at the will of the lord, *&c.* are almost of the same nature *Wood's imp law.* 149.

Quibus in rebus constituitur.

§ II. Constituitur autem ususfructus non tantum in fundo et ædibus, verum etiam in servis, et jumentis, et cæteris rebus: exceptis iis, quæ ipso usu consumuntur. Nam hæ res neque naturali ratione, neque civili, recipiunt usumfructum: quo in numero sunt vinum, oleum, frumentum, vestimenta: quibus proxima est pecunia numerata: namque ipso usu, assidua permutatione, quodammodo extinguitur. Sed utilitatis causa Senatus censuit, posse etiam earum rerum usumfructum constitui, ut tamen eo nomine hæredi utiliter caveatur. Itaque, si pecuniæ ususfructus legatus sit, ita datur legatario, ut ejus fiat, et legatarius satisdet hæredi de tanta pecunia restituenda, si morietur, aut capite minuetur. Cæteræ quoque res ita traduntur legatario, ut ejus fiant: sed æstimatis his satisdatur, ut, si moriatur aut capite minuatur, tanta pecunia restituatur, quanti hæ fuerint æstimatæ. Ergo Senatus non fecit quidem earum rerum usumfructum, (nec enim poterat) sed per cautionem quasi usumfructum constituit.

§ 2. *The* usufruct *not only of lands and houses is grantable, but also the* usufruct *of slaves, cattle, and other things, except those, of which the nature is such, that they may be consumed by using, for the* usufruct *of such things is neither grantable by civil policy, nor natural reason, and among these may be reckoned wine, oil, cloaths,* &c. *And money also is almost of the same nature: for by constant use, and the frequent change of owners, it in a manner becomes extinguished. But the senate, thro' a motive of public utility, hath ordained, that the* usufruct *of these things may be constituted, if a sufficient caution is given upon this account to the heir: and therefore, if the* usufruct *of money is bequeathed, the money is so given to the legatary, as to make it instantly his own but then the legatary, lest he should die, or suffer diminution, is obliged to give security to the heir for the repayment of a like sum Other things also, which are in their nature liable to consumption in using, when the* usufruct *of them is bequeathed, are so delivered to the legatary, as to become wholly his property;*

property; but in this case, after an exact valuation hath been made, caution must be given to the heir for the payment of a sum, equal to such valuation, either at the death of the legatary, or if it happens, that he should suffer diminution. It is not therefore to be understood, that the senate hath created an usufruct *of these things, which is impossible, but that the senate hath constituted a* quasi-usufruct *by means of a caution.*

Senatus censuit.] *vid. ff. 7. t. 5. ll. 1, 2. de usufructu earum rerum, quæ usu consumuntur.* Ulp.

Quibus modis finitur.

§ III. Finitur autem usufructus morte usufructuarii, et duabus capitis diminutionibus, maxima et media, & non utendo per modum et tempus; quæ omnia nostra statuit constitutio. Item finitur usufructus, si domino proprietatis ab usufructuario cedatur, (nam cedendo extraneo nihil agitur) vel ex contrario, si usufructuarius proprietatem rei acquisiverit: quæ res consolidatio appellatur. Eo amplius constat, si ædes incendio comsumptæ fuerint, vel etiam terræ motu, vel vitio suo corruerint, extingui usumfructum, et ne areæ quidem usumfructum deberi.

§ 3. *The* usufruct *of a thing determines by the death of the usufructuary, and by two of the three diminutions, namely, the greatest and the middle diminution, or change of state, and also by not being used, according to the manner, and during the time prescribed: all which things are set forth in our constitution. The* usufruct *of a thing also determines, if the usufructuary hath surrendered it to the lord of the property, but a cession of it to a stranger does not work a surrender to the proprietor: or, on the contrary, an* usufruct *determines, if the usufructuary hath acquired the property of it: and this is called consolidation. And it is certain, if an house hath been consumed by fire, or hath fallen by means of an earthquake, or thro' decay, that then the* usufruct *of such house is wholly destroyed, and that no* usufruct *of the area or ground of it can afterwards become due to the usufructuary.*

Statuit constitutio.] *vid. Cod. 3. t. 23. l. 16.*

Si finitus sit.

§ IV. Cum autem finitus fuerit totus usufructus, revertitur scilicet ad proprietatem, et, ex eo tempore, nudæ proprietatis dominus incipit plenam in re habere potestatem.

§ 4. *When the whole* usufruct *of a thing is determined, it then reverts to the property, and, from that instant of time, the owner of the nude property commences to have a full and intire power over the thing.*

TITULUS QUINTUS.

De usu et habitatione.

D. vii. T. 8. C. iii. T. 33.

Communia de usufructu et usu.

ISDEM illis modis, quibus ususfructus constituitur, etiam nudus usus constitui solet: iisdem illis modis finitur, quibus et ususfructus desinit.

The usufruct, *and the nude* use *of a thing, are both of them constituted, and both determined by the same means.*

Quid intersit inter usumfructum et usum fundi.

§ I. Minus autem juris est in usu quam in usufructu: nam is, qui fundi nudum habet usum, nihil ulterius habere intelligitur, quam ut oleribus, pomis, floribus, fœno, stramentis, et lignis, ad usum quotidianum utatur: inque eo fundo hactenus ei morari licet, ut neque domino fundi molestus sit, neque iis, per quos opera rustica fiunt, impedimento: nec ulli alii jus, quod habet, aut locare, aut vendere, aut gratis concedere, potest: cum is, qui usumfructum habet, possit hæc omnia facere.

§ 1. *There is less benefit and emolument in the* use *of a thing, than in the* usufruct *for he, who hath but simply the use of lands, is understood to have nothing more, than the liberty of using such a quantity of herbs, fruit, flowers, hay, straw, and wood, which may be sufficient to supply his daily exigences: and he is permited only to be commorant upon the land, on condition, that he neither becomes troublesome to the owner, nor impedes the workmen in their country-labors And an usuary, having but a mere use, can neither let, sell, or give away his right to another, altho' it is in the power of an usufructuary to convey his* usufruct, *either by lease, sale, or donation*

Minus autem] An *Use*, by the laws of *England*, is of as great an extent, as an usufruct by the *Roman* law And by 27 *H.* 8 *He, who hath the use of land, is deemed to have the land itself.* But as to such uses and rights of habitation, which were among the *Romans*, tho' our laws have not treated of them in any particular manner, yet they may certainly be granted and acquired by special covenants and agreements, as was said of usufruct. *Usus apud nos æque late extenditur, atque ususfructus apud authores juris civilis, sed non video, cur idem jus tam de usu, ut illi eum intelligunt, quam de habitatione, apud nos non teneat, quod olim inter* Romanos *tenebat.* Cowel, h t. Wood's imp. Law 151

Ædium usus.

§ II. Item is, qui ædium usum habet, hactenus jus habere intelligitur, ut ipse tantum inhabitet; nec hoc jus ad alium transferre potest. et vix receptum esse videtur, ut hospitem ei recipere liceat, et cum uxore liberisque suis, item libertis, nec non personis aliis liberis, quibus non minus,

quam

quam servis utitur, habitandi jus habeat. Et convenienter, si ad mulierem usus ædium pertineat, cum marito ei habitare liceat.

§ 2. *He, who hath but the mere use of an house, is understood to have a right in it so far only, as to inable him to inhabit it himself: for he hath no power to transfer this right to another; and it is hardly thought allowable, that he should receive a guest or a lodger. But the usuary, notwithstanding what has been said, hath a right to inhabit the house together with his wife, his children, and his freed men, and also with such other free persons, who are in the quality of servants. And, agreeably to this, if the use of an house appertains to a woman, she also hath the liberty of living in it with her husband, and her dependents.*

Nudum habet usum.] An usufruct is a right of enjoying all the fruits and revenues, which the estate, subject to it, is capable of producing, but an use consists only in a right to take out of the fruits of the ground what is necessary for the person, who has the use, or what is settled by his title, and the surplus belongs to the proprietor of the estate: thus those, who have the right of use in a forest or copice, can only take what is necessary for their use, or is regulated by their title. And he, who has the use of any other ground, can only take out of it what shall be necessary to supply the occasions he shall have for those kinds of fruits, which the grounds produce: or the use may even be restrained to certain kinds of fruits, or revenues, without extending it to others. Thus we see in the *Roman* law, that he, who had only the simple use of a piece of ground, had no share of the corn or oil, which grew in it, and that he, who had the use of a flock of sheep, was restrained only to make use of them for dunging his grounds, and had no share either in the wool or lambs: and even of the milk, it is said in some places, that the usuary could take but a very small portion, and in others, that he had no right to any of it. *ff. 7. t. 8. l. 12. Domat. lib. 1. t. 2. sect. 2.*

De servi vel jumenti usu.

§ III. Item is, ad quem servi usus pertinet, ipse tantum opera atque ministerio ejus uti potest: ad alium vero nullo modo jus suum transferre ei concessum est. Idem scilicet juris est et in jumento.

§ 3. *He also, who hath simply the use of a slave, can benefit* himself *only by the labor and service of such slave: for it is by no means in the power of the usuary to transfer his right over to another. And the same law prevails in regard to beasts of burden.*

De pecorum usu.

§ IV. Sed et, si pecorum vel ovium usus legatus sit, neque lacte, neque agnis, neque lana, utetur usuarius: quia ea in fructu sunt. Plane ad stercorandum agrum suum pecoribus uti potest.

§ 4. *If the use of cattle is left by testament, as, for example, the use of sheep, yet the usuary can neither use the milk, the lambs, nor the wool; for these of right belong to the* usufruct. *But the usuary may undoubtedly imploy the sheep, in soiling and improving his lands.*

De habitatione.

§ V. Sed, si cui habitatio legata, sive aliquo modo constituta sit, neque usus videtur, neque ususfructus, sed quasi proprium aliquod jus: quanquam habitationem habentibus, propter rerum utilitatem, secundum Marcelli sententiam nostra decisione promulgata, permisimus non solum in ea degere, sed etiam aliis locare.

§. 5.

§ 5. *An habitation, whether given by testament, or constituted by any other means, appears to be neither an* use, *nor an* usufruct, *but seems to be rather a* particular right. *And, for the public utility and in conformity to the opinion of* Marcellus, *we have permited by our decision, that he, who hath an habitation, may not only live in it, but also let it to another.*

Nostra decisione] Whoever hath a right of habitation in a house, or in a part of it, may assign over and let out his right to another, unless the instrument, from which he derives his title, bears some condition to the contrary and the right of habitation, as well as that of use, if simply given, continues during the life of him, who possesses it *Cod.* 3 *t.* 33 *l* 13. *de usufructu et habitatione. ff.* 7 *t* 8. *l.* 10 *sect* 3

Transitio.

§ VI. Hæc de servitutibus, et usufructu, et usu, et habitatione, dixisse sufficiat. De hæreditatibus autem et obligationibus suis locis proponemus. Exposuimus summatim, quibus modis jure gentium res acquiruntur: modo videamus, quibus modis legitimo et civili jure acquiruntur.

§ 6. *What we have already delivered, concerning real services, usufructs, uses, and habitations, may at this time be sufficient. Concerning inheritances, and obligations, we will treat in their proper places. We have already explained summarily by what means things are acquired, according to the law of nations; let us now therefore examine, by what means they are acquired according to the civil law.*

TITULUS SEXTUS.

De usucapionibus et longi temporis prescriptionibus.

D. xli. T. 3. C. vii. T. 31, et 33.

Præcipua usucapionis requisita. 1. *Bona fides.* 2. *Possessio per tempus definitum continuata.* 3. *Justus titulus.*

JURE civili constitutum fuerat, ut, qui bona fide ab eo, qui dominus non erat, cum crederet eum dominum esse, rem emerit, vel ex donatione, aliave quavis justa causa acceperit, is eam rem, si mobilis erat, anno ubique uno, si immobilis, biennio tantum in Italico solo, usucaperet: ne rerum dominia in incerto essent. Et cum hoc placitum erat putantibus antiquioribus, dominis sufficere ad inquirendas res suas præfata tempora, nobis melior sententia resedit, ne domini maturius suis rebus defraudentur neque certo loco beneficium hoc concludatur. Et ideo constitutionem super hoc promulgavimus, qua cautum est, ut res quidem mobiles per triennium, immobiles vero per longi temporis possessionem (id est, inter præsentes decennio, inter absentes viginti annis) usucapiantur. Et his modis, non

non ſolum in Italia, ſed etiam in omni terra, quæ noſtro imperio gubernatur, dominia rerum, juſta cauſa poſſeſſionis præcedente, acquirantur.

It was antiently decreed by the civil law, that he, who by means of purchaſe, donation, or any other juſt title, had obtained a thing from another, whom he thought to be the true owner of it, (altho' in reality he was not) and, if it was moveable, had poſſeſſed it bona fide *for the ſpace of one year, either in* Italy *or the provinces —— or, if it was immoveable, had poſſeſſed it for the term of two years within the limits of* Italy, *ſhould preſcribe to ſuch thing by uſe: and this was held to be law, leſt the dominion, or property of things, ſhould be uncertain. But altho' it was thought by the more antient legiſlators, that the above mentioned terms were of ſufficient length to inable every owner to ſearch after his different kinds of property, yet a better determination hath ſuggeſted itſelf to our thoughts, leſt the true owners ſhould be defrauded, or too haſtily excluded, by the circumſcription of time and place, from the benefit of recovering their juſt due: and we have therefore promulged our ordinance, by which it is provided, that things moveable may be preſcribed to after the expiration of three years, and that a poſſeſſion, during a long tract of time, will alſo found a preſcription to things immoveable: and note, that, by* a long tract of time, *we mean ten years, if the parties are preſent, (i.e. in the province) and twenty years, if either of them is abſent. By theſe means the property of things may be acquired; and this not only in* Italy, *but throughout our dominions in general, if the poſſeſſion was juſtly founded.*

Et ideo conſtitutionem] *Vid Cod 7 t 31 l un de uſucapione transformanda, et de ſublata differentia rerum mancipi et nec mancipi.* By the common law of *England* the time of preſcription is that time of which there is no memory of man, or *record,* to the contrary, for if there is any ſufficient proof of a record or writing to the contrary, altho' it exceeds the memory or proper knowledge of any man living, yet it is deemed to be within the memory of man: and this is the reaſon, that regularly a man can not preſcribe or allege a cuſtom againſt an act of parliament, becauſe it is the higheſt proof and matter of record in the law. *Co Litt* 115. But, altho' a preſcription is ſaid to be conſtituted by a portion of time, which exceeds the memory of man, yet this is not *always* true, for our laws admit a great variety of preſcriptions, which for the ſake of order may be divided into two ſorts, — into thoſe, which ſecure us from loſs and puniſhment, and into thoſe, which inable us to acquire a property.

The ſtatute of the 31ſt of *Eliz* cap 5. bars all popular actions on account of offenſes by a preſcription of two years, in the caſe of the king, and by a preſcription of one year, when there is an informer. Other penal ſtatutes allow different periods to preſcribe in —— as one year; (3 *H* 7 c 1. 31 *Eliz* c 4) —— ſix months, (5 *Eliz* c 5) —— three months, (1 *Edw* 6 c 1) —— one month, (23 *Eliz* c. 1) &c &c &c —— and, by the common law, if a man is acquitted upon an indictment of murder, he may after a year and a day plead preſcription againſt any appeal brought by the wife, or the next of kin to the party killed. *Natura brevium* 624 G —— Things immoveable alſo, whether corporeal or incorporeal, are variouſly preſcribed to. The moſt uſual preſcription is that, which is called emphatically *the longeſt*, and extends beyond the memory of man; for whoever will preſcribe againſt another in regard to the maintenance of a chaplain to celebrate divine ſervice, the repairs of a church, an annuity, or any ſervice in his fee, he muſt prove them to have been time out of mind, or he does nothing. But there are preſcriptions of a ſhorter time, as of 40 years in the caſe of predial tithes, by the 2d and 3d of *Ed* VI. — of five years for lands and tenements, when a fine hath been lawfully acknowledged with the due proclamations (4 *Hen* 7. c. 24) —— of three years, when lands and tenements gotten by forcible entry, have been ſo long held in quiet poſſeſſion, (8 *H*. 6. c. 9) —— of a year and a day for a villein to aſſert his liberty againſt his lord, if the villein has continued ſo long in antient demeſne or in any of the king's cities or towns without being claimed or moleſted —— of a year and a day for the confirmation of any deed made by one, who is in priſon, unleſs he, who made it, doth in the interim revoke it. —— Alſo of a year and a day, to hinder the entry of him, who, having omited to make continual claim, indeavours, after a deſcent caſt, to recover lands and tenements, of which he hath been unjuſtly diſſeized. *Co.* 1 *inſt page* 250 &c *of continual claim.* But preſcriptions do not take place in all things. No man can preſcribe, for example, to things not in commerce, nor to

thoſe

those, of which the king is properly the sole lord; nor to a custom, which is repugnant to reason or good manners. *Co. Litt lib.* 2d *sect.* 212 *of villenage*. And it is a known maxim, in the laws of *England*, "that no prescription in "lands maketh a right" *Doct* and *Stud. Dial.* 1. *cap.* 8. *Cowel's inst. h. t.* *Wood's inst.* 297, 298.

De his, quæ sunt extra commercium.

§ I. Sed aliquando, etiamsi maxime quis bona fide rem possederit, non tamen illi usucapio ullo tempore procedit: veluti si quis liberum hominem, vel rem sacram, vel religiosam, vel servum fugitivum, possideat.

§ 1. *But it is certain in some cases, that altho' there hath been a possession incontestable* bona fide, *yet no length of time will be sufficient to found a prescription: and this happens, when a man possesses, as his property, a free person, a thing sacred or religious, or a fugitive slave.*

De rebus furtivis, et vi possessis.

§ II. Furtivæ quoque res, et quæ vi possessæ sunt, nec, si prædicto longo tempore bona fide possessæ fuerint, usucapi possunt: nam furtivarum rerum lex duodecim tabularum, et lex Attilia, inhibent usucapionem; vi possessarum lex Julia et Plautia. Quod autem dictum est, furtivarum et vi possessarum rerum usucapionem per leges prohibitam esse, non eo pertinet, ut ne ipse fur, quive per vim possidet, usucapere possit, (nam his alia ratione usucapio non competit; quia scilicet mala fide possident) sed ne ullus alius, quamvis ab eis bona fide emerit, vel ex alia causa acceperit, usucapiendi jus habeat. Unde in rebus mobilibus non facile procedit, ut bonæ fidei possessoribus usucapio competat. Nam, qui sciens alienam rem vendiderit, vel ex alia causa tradiderit, furtum ejus committit. Sed tamen id aliquando aliter se habet. Nam, si hæres rem defuncto commodatam, aut locatam, vel apud eum depositam, existimans hæreditariam esse, bona fide accipienti vendiderit, aut donaverit, aut dotis nomine dederit, quin is, qui acceperit, usucapere possit, dubium non est: quippe cum ea res in furti vitium non ceciderit; cum utique hæres, qui bona fide tanquam suam alienaverit, furtum non committat. Item si is, ad quem ancillæ ususfructus pertinet, partum suum esse credens vendiderit, aut si donaverit, furtum non committit. Furtum enim, sine affectu furandi, non committitur. Aliis quoque modis accidere potest, ut quis, sine vitio furti, rem alienam ad aliquem transferat, et efficiat, ut à possessore usucapiatur. Quod autem ad eas res, quæ solo continentur, expedit, jus ita procedit, ut, si quis loci vacantis possessionem, propter absentiam aut negligentiam domini, aut quia sine successore decesserit, sine vi nancisatur, quamvis ipse mala fide possideat, (quia intelligit, se alienum fundum occupasse) tamen, si alii bona fide accipienti tradiderit, poterit ei longa possessione res acquiri, quia neque furtivum, neque vi possessum, acceperit. Abolita est enim quorundam veterum sententia, existimantium, etiam fundi locive furtum fieri. Et eorum utilitati, qui res soli possident, principalibus constitutionibus prospicitur, ne cui longa et indubitata possessio debeat auferri.

§ 2.

§ 2. *It is also equally certain, that no prescription can be founded to things moveable, which have been stolen; or to things immoveable, seized by violence, altho' such things have been possessed* bona fide, *during the length of time required by our constitution: for a prescription to things stolen is prohibited by a law of the twelve tables, and also by the law* Atilia; *and the laws* Julia *and* Plautia *forbid a prescription to things seized by violence. And it is not to be infered from these laws, that a thief, or disseizer only, is prohibited to take by prescription; (for such are prohibited for another reason, namely, because they are fraudulent and dishonest possessors;) but that all other persons are also disabled to prescribe to things stolen, or seized forcibly, altho' they shall have purchased such things* bona fide, *or otherwise received them upon a just account, and from hence it follows, that things moveable can not easily be prescribed to, even by honest possessors: for whoever hath either sold or delivered the goods of another knowingly, upon any consideration, he is guilty of theft. But this rule sometimes admits of exceptions; for in some cases a thing moveable may be prescribed to. thus, if an heir, thinking a particular thing to be hereditary, which in reality had only been lent, let to, or deposited with the deceased, shall have sold, given it, or otherwise disposed of it to another, who received it* bona fide, *it is not to be doubted but that the receiver may prescribe: for such thing can never be reputed* stolen, *inasmuch as it was honestly possessed from the beginning; and the heir, who hath aliened it, believing it to have been his own property, hath commited no theft. Also if he, who hath the usufruct of a female slave, either sells or gives away the child of such slave, believing it to be his own property, he does not commit theft, for theft can not be constituted without an intention to commit it. It may also happen, by various means, that one man may transfer the property of another without theft, and give a right of prescription to the possessor. And in regard to things immoveable the law ordains, that, if any man should take possession of an estate without force, by reason either of the absence, or negligence of the owner, or because he died without heirs, and (altho' he hath thus possessed the land dishonestly) shall have made livery of it to another, who took it* bona fide, *the land by long possession may be acquired by such taker, who can not be said to have received either a thing stolen, or possessed by violence for the opinion of those antient lawyers, who held, that lands and things immoveable, might be stolen, is now abolished: and it is therefore provided by the imperial constitutions, in favor of all such, who possess an immoveable property, that a long and undoubted possession ought not to be taken away.*

De vitio purgato.

§ III. Aliquando etiam furtiva, vel vi possessa, res usucapi potest; veluti si in domini potestatem reversa fuerit: tunc enim, vitio rei purgato, procedit ejus usucapio.

§ 3. *A prescription may sometimes be founded even to things which have been stolen, or possessed by violence; as for instance, when such things shall have fallen again under the power of their true owner; for they are then reputed to be purged from the contamination of theft or violence, and may afterwards be claimed by prescription.*

De re fiscali et bonis vacantibus.

§ IV. Res fisci nostri usucapi non potest: sed Papinianus scripsit, bonis vacantibus fisco nondum nuntiatis, bonæ fidei emptorem traditam sibi rem ex ex his bonis usucapere posse; et ita Divus Pius, et Divi Severus et Antoninus rescripserunt.

§ 4. *The things, which appertain to our treasury, can not be acquired by prescription. But, when things escheatable have not been certified to the treasury, it is held by* Papinian, *that a purchaser,* bona fide, *may prescribe to any of them after delivery. And not only the emperor* Pius, *but the emperors* Severus *and* Antoninus *have also issued their rescripts, conformable to this opinion.*

Regula generalis.

§ V. Novissime sciendum est, rem talem esse debere, ut in se non habeat vitium, ut à bonæ fidei emptore usucapi possit, vel qui ex alia justa causa possidet.

§ 5. *It is lastly to be observed, that, if any man shall purchase a particular thing* bona fide, *or obtain the possession of it by any other just title, he can by no means prescribe to it, unless the thing, in itself, is free from all manner of exception.*

De errore falsæ causæ.

§ VI. Error autem falsæ causæ usucapionem non parit; veluti si quis, cum non emerit, emisse se existimans, possideat, vel, cum ei donatum non fuerit, quasi ex donato possideat.

§ 6. *A mistake of the cause of possession shall not give rise to a prescription: as when he, who possesses a thing, imagines, that he hath purchased it, when he hath not purchased it; or that the thing was a gift, when in reality it was not given.*

De accessione possessionis.

§ VII. Diutina possessio, quæ prodesse cœperat defuncto, et hæredi et bonorum possessori continuatur, licet ipse sciat, prædium alienum esse. Quod si ille initium justum non habuit, hæredi et bonorum possessori, licet ignoranti, possessio non prodest. Quod nostra constitutio similiter et in usucapionibus observari constituit, ut tempora continuentur.

§ 7. *If a thing immoveable is possessed by any man* bona fide, *so that the possession is justly commenced, then the heir of that man, when deceased, or the possessor of his goods, may continue the possession, so as to raise a prescription, altho' he is conscious, that what he possesses is the property of another; but, if the possession was commenced from the beginning* mala fide, *or unjustly, then will the continuance of it avail neither the heir, nor the possessor of the goods, altho' he was ignorant of any male-feazance. And we have enacted by our imperial constitution, that the time of usucapion or prescription to things moveable shall be continued in the same manner from the deceased to his successor.*

Quod nostra constitutio.] *vid. Cod. 7. t. 31. l un. de usucapione transformanda.*

§ VIII. Inter venditorem quoque et emptorem conjungi tempora, divi Severus et Antoninus rescripserunt.

§ 8. *And, in regard to the computation of the years, necessary to raise a prescription, the emperors* Severus *and* Antoninus *have ordained by their rescript, that, between seller and buyer, the time of the continuance of the possession of the one shall be joined to the time of the continuance of the possession of the other.*

De his, qui à fisco, aut Imp. Augustæve domo, aliquid acceperunt.

§ IX. Edicto divi Marci cavetur, eum, qui à fisco rem alienam emit, si post venditionem quinquennium præterierit, posse dominum rei exceptione repellere. Constitutio autem divæ memoriæ Zenonis bene prospexit iis, qui à fisco per venditionem, aut donationem, vel alium titulum accipiunt aliquid; ut ipsi quidem securi statim fiant, et victores existant, sive experiantur, sive conveniantur: adversus autem sacratissimum ærarium usque ad quadriennium liceat iis intendere, qui pro dominio vel hypotheca earum rerum, quæ alienatæ sunt, putaverint, sibi quasdam competere actiones. Nostra autem divina constitutio, quam nuper promulgavimus, etiam de iis, qui à nostra vel venerabilis Augustæ domo aliquid acceperint, hæc statuit, quæ in fiscalibus alienationibus præfatæ Zenonianæ constitutionis continentur.

§ 9 *It is enacted by an edict of the emperor* Marcus, *that, when a thing is purchased from the treasury, the purchaser, after an uninterrupted possession of it for the space of five years, subsequent to the sale, may repel the true owner by an exception of prescription. But the emperor* Zeno, *of sacred memory, hath well provided by his constitution, that all those, who by sale, donation, or any other title, have received things either moveable, or immoveable, from the public treasury, may instantly be secured in their possession, and made certain of success, whether they are plaintiffs or defendents—— and that those, who think, that they are intituled to certain actions, either as proprietors or mortgagèes of the things aliened, may commence their suits against the treasury, at any time within the space of four years, but not afterwards. And, in our own sacred ordinance, which we have lately promulged in favor of those, who receive any thing, whether moveable or immoveable, from the private possessions either of our-self, or of the empress, our consort, we have made the same regulations, which are contained in the above mentioned constitution of the emperor* Zeno, *concerning fiscal alienations.*

Edicto divi Marci.] *vid. Cod.* 2. *t.* 37. *l.* 3.
Constitutio autem.] *vid. Cod.* 7. *t.* 37. *l.* 2.
Divina constitutio.] *vid. Cod.* 7. *t.* 36. *l.* 3.

TITU-

TITULUS SEPTIMUS.

De donationibus.

D. xxxix. T. 5. et 6. C. viii. T. 54. Nov. 162.

De donatione.

EST et aliud genus acquiſitionis, donatio. Donationum autem duo ſunt genera; mortis cauſa, et non mortis cauſa.

There is another way, by which property is acquired, namely, by donation; of which there are two kinds, the one mortis cauſa, *i. e. on account of death, the other* non mortis cauſa, *i. e. not on account of death; and this takes effect, during the life of the donor.*

De mortis cauſa donatione.

§ I. Mortis cauſa donatio eſt, quæ propter mortis fit ſuſpicionem; cum quis ita donat, ut, ſi quid humanitus ei contigiſſet, haberet is, qui accipit: ſin autem ſupervixiſſet is, qui donavit, reciperet: vel ſi eum donationis pœnituiſſet, aut prior deceſſerit is, cui donatum ſit. Hæ mortis cauſa donationes ad exemplum legatorum redactæ ſunt per omnia: nam, cum prudentibus ambiguum fuerat, utrum donationis, an legati inſtar eam obtinere oporteret, (et utriuſque cauſæ quædam habebat inſignia,) et alii ad aliud genus eam retrahebant, à nobis conſtitutum eſt, ut per omnia fere legatis connumeretur, et ſic procedat, quemadmodum noſtra conſtitutio eam formavit. Et in ſumma mortis cauſa donatio eſt, cum magis ſe quis velit habere, quam eum, cui donat, magiſque eum, cui donat, quam hæredem ſuum. Sic et apud Homerum Telemachus donat Piræo.

Πειραι, ου γαρ τ' ἰδμεν ὁπως ἐςαι ταδε ἐργα·
'Ει κεν ἐμε μνηςηρες ἀγηνορες, ἐν μεγαροισι
Λαθρῃ κτειναντες, πατρωια παντα δασωνται,
'Αυτον ἐχοντα σε βουλομ' ἐπαυρεμεν, ἠ τινα των δε.
Εἰ δε κ' ἐγω τουτοισι φονον καὶ κηρα φυτευσω,
Δη τοτε μοι χαιροντι φερειν προς δωματα χαιρων.

Hos verſus ſic vertere licebit.

Cum Piræ *homines lateant ſecreta futuri,*
Si me forte proci ſceleratis ad Styga mittant
Inſidiis, patriaſque velint erciſcere prædas;
Hæc ego præ reliquis multo tibi cedere malim:
Sin ego eos juſtis proſternam cladibus ultor,
Hæc mihi tu gaudens media inter gaudia reddas.

§ 1. A donation on account of death it that, which is made under an apprehension or suspicion of death: as when any thing is given upon condition, that, if the donor dies, the donèe shall possess it absolutely; or that the thing given shall be returned, if the donor should survive the danger, which he apprehends; or should repent, that he hath made the gift; or, if the donèe should die before the donor. Donations, mortis causa, *are now reduced, as far as possible, to the similitude of legacies: for, when it was much doubted by our lawyers, whether a donation* mortis causa *ought to be reputed as a gift, or as a legacy, inasmuch as, in some things, it partakes of the nature of both, we then* constituted *and* ordained, *that every such donation should be considered as a legacy; and be made in the manner, which our constitution directs. But, in brief, a donation,* mortis causa, *is then said to be made, when a man so gives, as to demonstrate, that he would rather possess the thing given himself, than that the donèe should possess it; and yet, at the same time, evinces, that he is more willing, that the donèe should possess it, than his own heir.*

The donation, which Telemachus *makes to* Piræus *in* Homer, *is of this species.*

He (when *Piræus* ask'd for slaves, to bring
The gifts and treasures of the *Spartan* king)
Thus thoughtful answer'd: —— those we shall not move,
Dark and unconscious of the will of *Jove.*
We know not yet the full event of all:
Stabb'd in his palace, if your prince must fall,
Us, and our house, if treason must o'erthrow,
Better a friend possess them than a foe.
But on my foes should vengeance heav'n decree,
Riches are welcome then, not else, to me.
'Till then, retain the gifts. ——————

POPE's *Odyss. lib* 17.

Quemadmodum nostra constitutio.] *vid. Cod.* 8. *t.* 57. *l.* 4.

De simplice inter vivos donatione.

§ II. Aliæ autem donationes sunt, quæ sine ulla mortis cogitatione fiunt, quas inter vivos appellamus, quæ non omnino comparantur legatis: quæ, si fuerint perfectæ, temere revocari non possunt. Perficiuntur autem, cum donator suam voluntatem scriptis aut sine scriptis manifestaverit. Et, ad exemplum venditionis, nostra constitutio eas etiam in se habere necessitatem traditionis voluit, ut, etiamsi non tradantur, habeant plenissimum et perfectum robur, et traditionis necessitas incumbat donatori. Et, cum retro principum dispositiones insinuari eas actis intervenientibus volebant, si majores fuerant ducentorum solidorum, constitutio nostra eam quantitatem usque ad quingentos solidos ampliavit, quam stare etiam sine insinuatione statuit: sed et quasdam donationes invenit, quæ penitus insinuationem fieri minime desiderant, sed in se plenissimam habent firmitatem. Alia insuper multa ad uberiorem exitum donationum invenimus, quæ omnia ex nostris constitutionibus, quas super his exposuimus, colligenda sunt. Sciendum est

eſt tamen, quod, etſi pleniſſimæ ſint donationes, ſi tamen ingrati exiſtant homines, in quos beneficium collatum eſt, donatoribus per noſtram conſtitutionem licentiam præſtitimus certis ex cauſis eas revocare; ne illi, qui ſuas res in alios contulerint, ab his quandam patiantur injuriam vel jacturam, ſecundum enumeratos in conſtitutione noſtra modos.

§ 2. *Donations, made without any thought or apprehenſion of death, we call donations* inter vivos; *and theſe admit of no compariſon with legacies: for, when once they are perfected, they can not afterwards be revoked without cauſe: and donations are then eſteemed perfect, when the donor hath declared and manifeſted his will either in writing or otherwiſe. And it is appointed by our conſtitution, that a donation* inter vivos *ſhall, in imitation of a ſale, neceſſarily inforce a delivery; for when things are given they become fully and perfectly veſted in the donèe, and it is incumbent upon the donor to deliver them: and altho' it is enacted by the conſtitutions of our predeceſſors, that donations, amounting to the value of two hundred* ſolidi, *ſhall be publicly and formally inrolled and regiſtered, we have yet thought it expedient to inlarge this ſum to five hundred* ſolidi *by our ordinance, by which we permit all donations of leſs value to be firm and binding without inſinuation or inrollment, and there are likewiſe ſome donations, which, altho' they exceed five hundred* ſolidi, *are yet of full force without inſinuation. We have alſo, for the inlargement of donations, enacted many other rules, all which may be collected by peruſing our conſtitutions, ſet forth for that purpoſe. It nevertheleſs remains to be obſerved, that, when a donation is fully and validly made, the donor may revoke it on account of ingratitude in the donée in ſome particular caſes: and this may be done, leſt he, who hath been liberal and kind to another, ſhould in any of the inſtances, enumerated in our conſtitution, ſuffer either injury or damage from him, upon whom a benefit was confered.*

Noſtra conſtitutio.] *vid. Cod.* 8. *t.* 54 *l.* 35.
Conſtitutio noſtra.] *vid. Cod.* 8 *t.* 54 *l.* 36.
Enumeratos in conſtitutione.] *vid. Cod.* 8. *t.* 56 *l.* 10.

De donatione ante nuptias vel propter nuptias.

§ III. Eſt et aliud genus inter vivos donationis, quod veteribus quidem prudentibus penitus erat incognitum, poſtea autem à junioribus Divis Principibus introductum eſt, quod ante nuptias vocabatur, et tacitam in ſe conditionem habebat, ut tunc ratum eſſet, cum matrimonium eſſet inſecutum. ideoque ante nuptias vocabatur, quod ante matrimonium efficiebatur: et nunquam poſt nuptias celebratas talis donatio procedebat. Sed primus quidem Divus Juſtinus pater noſter, cum augeri dotes et poſt nuptias fuerat permiſſum, ſi quid tale eveniret, et ante nuptias augeri donationem, et conſtante matrimonio, ſua conſtitutione permiſit. ſed tamen nomen inconveniens remanebat, cum ante nuptias quidem vocabatur, poſt nuptias autem tale accipiebat incrementum. Sed nos pleniſſimo fini tradere ſanctiones cupientes, et conſequentia nomina rebus eſſe ſtudentes, conſtituimus, ut tales donationes non augeantur tantum, ſed etiam conſtante matrimonio initium accipiant: et non ante nuptias, ſed propter nuptias, vocentur: et dotibus in hoc exæquentur, ut quemadmodum dotes conſtante matrimonio non ſolum augentur, ſed etiam fiunt, ita et iſtæ donationes,

quæ

quæ propter nuptias introductæ ſunt, non ſolum antecedant matrimonium, ſed eo etiam contracto augeantur et conſtituantur.

§ 3. *There is also another ſpecies of donations* inter vivos, *which was wholly unknown to the antient lawyers, being introduced by later emperors: this ſpecies of donations* inter vivos *was called* ante nuptias, *(i. e. before marriage) and contained in it the following tacit condition; namely, that it ſhould then take effect, when the marriage was performed; and theſe donations were properly called* ante nuptias, *becauſe they could never be conſtituted after the celebration of matrimony. But, inaſmuch as it was permitted by the antient law, that portions might be augmented after marriage, the emperor* Juſtin, *our father, hath enacted by his conſtitution, that donations called* ante nuptias *might alſo be augmented at any time, whileſt the matrimony ſubſiſted: and, as it was improper, that a donation ſhould be ſtill termed* ante nuptias, *when it had received an augmentation* poſt nuptias, *i. e. after matrimony, we therefore, being deſirous, that our ſanctions might become as perfect as poſſible, and that names ſhould be properly adapted to things, have ordained and conſtituted, that the above mentioned donations may be not only augmented, but may alſo receive their commencement at any time during matrimony, and that for the future they ſhall not be called donations* ante nuptias, *but donations* propter nuptias; *i. e. on account of marriage: and thus theſe donations are made equal with portions, for as portions may be augmented, and even made, when matrimony is ſubſiſting and perſons are actually married, ſo donations, which are introduced on account of matrimony, may now not only precede marriage, but be augmented, or even conſtituted, after the celebration of it.*

Sua conſtitutione] *vid. Cod.* 5. *t.* 3. *l.* 19.
Conſtituimus.] *vid. Cod* 5. *t.* 3. *l* 20. beginning thus—— *Sancimus, nomine prius emendato, ita rem corrigi, et non* ante nuptias donationem *eandem vocari, ſed* PROPTER NUPTIAS DONATIONEM.

De jure accreſcendi.

§ IV. Erat olim et alius modus civilis acquiſitionis per jus accreſcendi, quod eſt tale; ſi, communem ſervum habens aliquis cum Titio, ſolus libertatem ei impoſuerit, vel vindicta vel teſtamento, eo caſu pars ejus amittebatur, et ſocio accreſcebat. Sed cum peſſimum fuerat exemplo, et libertate ſervum defraudari, et ex eo humanioribus quidem dominis damnum inferri, ſeverioribus autem dominis lucrum accedere, hoc, quaſi invidia plenum, pro remedio per noſtram conſtitutionem mederi neceſſarium duximus. Et invenimus viam, per quam manumiſſor, et ſocius ejus, et qui libertatem accepit, noſtro beneficio fruantur, libertate cum effectu procedente, (cujus favore antiquos legum latores multa etiam contra communes regulas ſtatuiſſe manifeſtum eſt,) et eo, qui eam libertatem impoſuit, ſuæ liberalitatis ſtabilitate gaudente, et ſocio indemni conſervato, pretiumque ſervi ſecundum partem dominii, quod nos definivimus, accipiente.

§ 4 *There was formerly another manner of acquiring property by the civil law; namely by accretion, as for inſtance, if* Primus *had poſſeſſed a ſlave in common with* Titius, *and* Primus *had infranchiſed that ſlave, either by the* vindicta *or by teſtament, then would the ſhare of* Primus *in that ſlave be loſt and accrue to* Titius. *But, inaſmuch as it affords a bad example, that a man ſhould be defrauded of his liberty, and that thoſe maſters, who are moſt humane, ſhould ſuffer loſs, whileſt thoſe, who are*

are most severe, receive emolument, we have thought it necessary, that a proper remedy should be applied to this grievance; and we have found a method, by which the manumittor, his co-partener, and the freed person, may all partake of our beneficence: for we have decreed, (and it is manifest, that the antient legislators have often transgressed the strict rules of law in favor of liberty,) that freedom, altho' granted by one partener only, shall immediately take effect, so that the manumittor shall have reason to be pleased with the validity of his gift, if his co-partener is indemnified by receiving his share of the worth of the slave.

Quod nos definivimus.] *vid. Cod. 7. t. 7. l. 1. de communi servo manumisso.*

TITULUS OCTAVUS.

Quibus alienare licet, vel non licet.

De marito, qui, licet fundi dotalis dominus sit, alienare nequit.

ACCIDIT aliquando, ut, qui dominus rei sit, alienare non possit: et contra, qui dominus non sit, alienandæ rei potestatem habeat. Nam dotale prædium maritus, invita muliere, per legem Juliam prohibetur alienare; quamvis ipsius sit, dotis causa ei datum · quod nos, legem Juliam corrigentes, in meliorem statum deduximus. Cum enim lex in solis tantummodo rebus locum habebat, quæ Italicæ fuerant, et alienationes inhibebat, quæ invita muliere fiebant, hypothecas autem earum rerum etiam volente ea, utique remedium imposuimus, ut etiam in eas res, quæ in provinciali solo positæ sunt, interdicta sit alienatio vel obligatio, ut neutrum eorum neque consentientibus mulieribus procedat: ne sexus muliebris fragilitas in perniciem substantiæ earum convertatur.

It sometimes happens, that the proprietor of a thing can not alien it, and on the contrary that he, who is not the proprietor, may alien it · for example, by the law Julia *an husband is prohibited to make an alienation of lands, which came to him in right of his wife, unless his wife consents to the alienation; and yet every man is deemed the proprietor of whatever is given to him, as a marriage portion. But, in this respect, we have corrected the law* Julia, *and brought it into a better state: for, having observed, that this law regards only those immoveable possessions, which are situated within the precincts of* Italy; *and that, altho' it inhibits the husband to make a mortgage of such possessions, even with the consent of his wife, yet it permits him, with the consent of his wife, to make an alienation, we have therefore provided a remedy by our imperial authority; so that now no husband can either alien or mortgage, even with the consent of his wife, any immoveable possession, whether* provincial *or* Italian, *obtained with her, as a marriage portion; and we have been induced to make these regulations, lest the frailty of women should occasion the ruin of their fortunes.*

Remedium imposuimus] *vid. Cod. 5. t. 13 l. un.*

§ I.

De creditore, qui, licet non ſit dominus, tamen alienare pignus poteſt.

§ I. Contra autem creditor pignus, ex pactione, quamvis ejus ea res non ſit, alienare poteſt. Sed hoc forſitan ideo videtur fieri, quod voluntate debitoris intelligitur pignus alienari, qui ab initio contractus pactus eſt, ut liceret creditori pignus vendere, ſi pecunia non ſolvatur. Sed, ne creditores jus ſuum perſequi impedirentur, neque debitores temere ſuarum rerum dominium amittere viderentur, noſtra conſtitutione conſultum eſt, et certus modus impoſitus eſt, per quem pignorum diſtractio poſſit procedere; cujus tenore utrique parti creditorum et debitorum ſatis abundeque proviſum eſt.

§ 1. *But a creditor, by virtue of a compact, may ſell or alien a pledge, altho' it is not his own property; yet this ſeems to be allowable for no other reaſon, than becauſe the pledge is underſtood to be aliened by the conſent of the debtor, with whom it was covenanted from the commencement of the contract, that the creditor might be permited to ſell the pledge, if the money borrowed was not paid at the time ſtipulated. But, leſt creditors ſhould be impeded from proſecuting, what is juſtly due to them, and leſt debtors, on the contrary, ſhould loſe the property of their poſſeſſions too ſoon, we have in our ordinance, promulged for this purpoſe, inſtituted certain methods, by which the ſale of pledges may be warrantably made: and, thro' the whole tenor of our conſtitution, a ſufficient caution hath been taken in regard to both creditors and debtors.*

Conſtitutione conſultum eſt.] *vid. Cod.* 8. *t.* 34. *l* 3.

De pupillo, qui, licet dominus, non tamen ſine tutoris auctoritate alienare poteſt.

§ II. Nunc admonendi ſumus, neque pupillum, neque pupillam, ullam rem ſine tutoris auctoritate alienare poſſe. Ideoque, ſi mutuam pecuniam ſine tutoris auctoritate alicui dederit, non contrahit obligationem: quia pecuniam non facit accipientis: ideoque vindicari nummi poſſunt, ſicubi extant. Sed, ſi nummi, quos mutuo minor dederit, ab eo, qui accepit, bona fide conſumpti ſunt, condici poſſunt: ſi mala fide, ad exhibendum de his agi poteſt.

§ 2. *It muſt now be obſerved, that no pupil, whether male or female, hath power to alien any thing without the authority of a tutor: and therefore, if a pupil, without the authority of his tutor, ſhall lend money to any man, ſuch pupil contracts no obligation for he is incapable of veſting the property of his money in the borrower; and therefore the money may be claimed by* vindication, *(that is, by a real action,) if it exiſts intire and unſpent. But if money, lent by a minor, is conſumed by the borrower*, bona fide, *(i e. believing that the lendor was of full age) it may be recovered from ſuch borrower by condiction, that is, by a perſonal action. And, if ſuch money is conſumed by the borrower* mala fide, *an action* ad exhibendum *will lie againſt him.*

§ III.

De pupillo, qui, licet ſit dominus, tamen alienare non poteſt.

§ III. At ex contrario omnes res pupillo et pupillæ ſine tutoris auctoritate recte dari poſſunt: ideoque, ſi debitor pupillo ſolvat, neceſſaria eſt debitori tutoris auctoritas: alioqui non liberabitur. Sed hoc etiam evidentiſſima ratione ſtatutum eſt in conſtitutione, quam ad Cæſarienſes advocatos ex ſuggeſtione Triboniani, viri eminentiſſimi, quæſtoris ſacri palatii noſtri, promulgavimus: qua diſpoſitum eſt, ita licere tutori vel curatori debitorem pupillarem ſolvere, ut prius judicialis ſententia ſine omni damno celebrata hoc permittat: quo ſubſecuto, ſi et judex pronunciaverit, et debitor ſolverit, ſequatur hujuſmodi ſolutionem pleniſſima ſecuritas. Sin autem aliter, quam diſpoſuimus, ſolutio facta fuerit, pecuniam autem ſalvam habeat pupillus, aut ex ea locupletior ſit, et adhuc eandem pecuniæ ſummam petat, per exceptionem doli mali poterit ſubmoveri. Quod ſi male conſumpſerit, aut furto aut vi amiſerit, nihil proderit debitori doli mali exceptio, ſed nihilominus condemnabitur: quia temere ſine tutoris auctoritate, et non ſecundum noſtram diſpoſitionem, ſolverit Sed ex diverſo pupilli vel pupillæ ſolvere ſine tutoris auctoritate non poſſunt: quia id, quod ſolvunt, non fit accipientis: cum ſcilicet nullius rei alienatio eis ſine tutoris auctoritate conceſſa ſit.

§ 3. *But, on the contrary, the property of any thing may be transfered to pupils, whether male or female, without the authority of their tutors · yet, if a debtor makes a payment to a pupil, it is neceſſary, that the debtor ſhould be warranted by the authority of the pupil's tutor; otherwiſe he will not be acquited of the debt: and this, for a moſt evident reaſon, was ordained by a conſtitution, which we promulged to the advocates of* Cæſarea, *at the ſuggeſtion of that moſt eminent man* Tribonian, *the queſtor of our ſacred palace: and by this conſtitution it is enacted, that the debtor of a minor may lawfully pay any ſum to his tutor or curator, if a judicial decree, permitting the payment, is previouſly obtained without expenſe to the minor: for, when the payment of a debt is warranted by, and ſubſequent to, the decree of a judge, it is always attended with the fulleſt ſecurity. But, altho' money hath been paid to a pupil, otherwiſe than we have ordained, yet, if he ſhould afterwards require, that the money ſhould be paid him again, and demand it by action, he might be deprived of his plea by an* exception *of* fraud, *if it could be proved, that he had become richer by the increaſe of this money; or even, that he had preſerved it ſafely. But, if the pupil hath ſquandered and conſumed the money paid to him, or loſt it either by theft or violence, an exception of fraud will be of no benefit to the debtor, who will be compelled to make a ſecond payment, becauſe the firſt was made inconſiderately, without the authority of the tutor, and not according to our ordinance. Pupils are alſo incapacitated to pay money without the authority of their tutors; becauſe money, when paid by a pupil without ſuch authority, doth not become the property of him, to whom it is paid: for the alienation of no one thing is granted to a pupil without the authority of his tutor*

Statutum eſt in conſtitutione.] *vid. Cod* 5 *t* 37. *ll* 25, 27.

TITULUS NONUS.

Per quas perſonas cuique acquiritur.

C. iv. T. 27.

Summa.

ACQUIRITUR vobis non ſolum per voſmetipſos, ſed etiam per eos, quos in poteſtate habetis: item per ſervos, in quibus uſumfructum habetis: item per homines liberos, et per ſervos alienos, quos bona fide poſſidetis: de quibus ſingulis diligentius deſpiciamus.

Things may be acquired not only by ourſelves, but alſo by thoſe, who are under our power, and alſo by ſlaves, of whom we have the uſufruct only—— acquiſitions may alſo be made for us by free-men—— and even by ſlaves, whom we poſſeſs bona fide, *altho' they are the property of another. Let us therefore inquire diligently concerning all theſe perſons.*

De liberis in poteſtate.

§ I. Igitur liberi veſtri utriuſque ſexus, quos in poteſtate habetis, olim quidem quicquid ad eos pervenerat, (exceptis videlicet caſtrenſibus peculiis,) hoc parentibus ſuis acquirebant ſine ulla diſtinctione: et hoc ita parentum fiebat, ut etiam eſſet iis licentia quod per unum vel unam eorum acquiſitum eſſet, alii filio, vel extraneo donare, vel vendere, vel, quocumque modo voluerant, applicare: quod nobis inhumanum viſum eſt: et generali conſtitutione emiſſa, et liberis pepercimus, et parentibus honorem debitum reſervavimus: ſancitum etenim à nobis eſt, ut, ſi quid ex re patris ei obveniat, hoc ſecundum antiquam obſervationem totum parenti acquiratur. Quæ enim invidia eſt, quod ex patris occaſione profectum eſt, hoc ad eum reverti? Quod autem ex alia cauſa ſibi filiusfamilias acquiſivit, hujus uſumfructum patri quidem acquirat, dominium autem apud eum remaneat: ne, quod ei ſuis laboribus vel proſpera fortuna acceſſerit, hoc in alium perveniens, luctoſum ei procedat.

§ 1. *It was antiently the law, that whatever eſtate came to children, whether male or female, who were under the power of their parents, it was acquired for the parents of ſuch children without any diminution, if we except the* peculium caſtrenſe. *and theſe eſtates were ſo abſolutely veſted in the parents, that what was acquired by one child they might have given to another child, or to a ſtranger; or might have ſold it, or applied it in what manner, and to what purpoſe they thought proper. but this ſeemed to be inhuman, and we have therefore, by a general conſtitution, mitigated the rigor of the law in regard to children, and have, at the ſame time, maintained that honor, which is due to parents, having ordained, that, if any thing accrues to the ſon by means of the father's fortune, the* whole *ſhall be acquired for the father, according to antient practice. (for can it be unjuſt, that the wealth, which the ſon hath obtained, by by means of the father, should revert to him?) but that the dominion and property of whatever the son of a family hath acquired, by any other means, shall remain in the son; and that the father shall be intituled only to the usufruct of such acquisition. And this we have thought proper to decree, lest that, which hath accrued to a man from his labor or good fortune, should be unjustly transfered to another.*

Generali constitutione.] *vid Cod.* 6 *t* 61. *l.* 6

De emancipatione liberorum.

§ II. Hoc quoque à nobis dispositum est et in ea specie, ubi parens, emancipando liberos suos, ex rebus, quæ acquisitionem effugiebant, sibi tertiam partem retinere (si voluerat) licentiam ex anterioribus constitutionibus habebat, quasi pro pretio quodammodo emancipationis: et inhumanum quiddam accidebat, ut filius rerum suarum ex hac emancipatione dominio pro tertia parte defraudaretur: et, quod honoris ei ex emancipatione additum erat, quod sui juris effectus esset, hoc per rerum diminutionem decresceret. Ideoque statuimus, ut parens pro tertia parte dominii, quam retinere poterat, dimidiam non dominii rerum, sed ususfructus, retineat. Ita etenim res intactæ apud filium remanebunt, et pater ampliore summa fruetur, pro tertia, dimidia potiturus.

§ 2. *We have also regarded the interest of children in respect to emancipation: for a parent, when he emancipated his children, might, according to former constitutions, have taken to himself, if he was so inclined, the property of the third part of those things, which were excepted from paternal acquisition, retaining it as the price of emancipation. But it appeared to be inhuman, that the son should be thus defrauded of the third part of his property, and that the honor, which he had obtained by becoming independent, should be decreased by the diminution of his estate; and we have therefore decreed, that the parent instead of the third part of the property, which he formerly might have retained, shall now be intituled to an half-share, not of the property, but of the usufruct, so that the property will, for the future, remain intire in the son, and the father will enjoy a greater share; namely, half instead of a third part.*

Ex anterioribus constitutionibus.] *vid. ll.* 1, 2. Ideoque statuimus] *vid Cod.* 6. *t.* 61 *l.* 6 *Cod. Theod de maternis bonis.*

De servis nostris.

§ III. Item vobis acquiritur, quod servi vestri ex traditione nanciscuntur, sive quid stipulentur, sive ex donatione, vel ex legato, vel ex qualibet alia causa, acquirant. Hoc enim vobis et ignoantibus et invitis obvenit, ipse enim servus, qui in potestate alterius est, nihil suum habere potest. Sed, si hæres institutus sit, non alias, nisi vestro jussu, hæreditatem adire potest et, si vobis jubentibus adierit, vobis hæreditas acquiritur, perinde ac si vos ipsi hæredes instituti essetis. Et convenienter scilicet vobis legatum per eos acquiritur. Non solum autem proprietas per eos, quos in potestate habetis, vobis acquiritur, sed etiam possessio: cujuscunque enim rei possessionem adepti fuerint, id vos possidere videmini. Unde etiam per eos usucapio, vel longi temporis possessio, vobis accidit.

§ 3. *Whatever our slaves have at any time acquired, whether by delivery, stipulation, donation, bequest, or any other means, the same is reputed to be acquired by ourselves, and we thus acquire things, altho' we are ignorant of, or even averse to, the acquisition; for he, who is a slave, can have no property. And, if a slave is instituted an heir, he can not otherwise take upon himself the inheritance, than at the command of his master; but, if the slave is commanded to do this, the inheritance is as fully acquired by the master, as if he had been himself made the heir; and consequently a legacy, left to a slave, is acquired by his master. It is farther to be observed, that masters acquire by their slaves not only the property of things, but also the possession, for whatever is possessed by a slave, the same seems to be possessed by his master; who may therefore found a prescription to it by means of his slave.*

De fructuariis et bona fide possessis.

§ IV. De iis autem servis, in quibus tantummodo usumfructum habetis, ita placuit, ut, quicquid ex re vestra, vel ex operis suis, acquirunt, id vobis adjiciatur; quod vero extra eas causas consecuti sunt, id ad dominum proprietatis pertineat. Itaque, si is servus hæres institutus sit, legatumve quid ei, aut donatum fuerit, non usufructuario sed domino proprietatis acquiritur.

§ 4 *In regard to those slaves, of whom the possessor has the usufruct only, it is an established rule, that whatever they acquire by means of his goods, or by their own work and labor, it appertains to their usufructuary master. But whatever is obtained by a slave, otherwise than by those means, it belongs to him, who hath the property of the slave and therefore, if a slave is instituted an heir, or hath received a legacy, or a gift, the inheritance, legacy, or gift, will not be acquired for the usufructuary master, but for the proprietor.*

Continuatio.

§ V. Idem placet et de eo, qui à vobis bona fide possidetur, sive is liber sit, sive alienus servus: quod enim placuit de usufructuario, idem placet et de bonæ fidei possessore. Itaque, quod extra istas duas causas acquiritur, id vel ad ipsum pertinet, si liber est, vel ad dominum, si servus est. Sed bonæ fidei possessor, cum usuceperit servum, (quia eo modo dominus fit,) ex omnibus causis per eum sibi acquirere potest. Fructuarius vero usucapere non potest: primum quia non possidet, sed habet jus utendi, fruendi: deinde, quia scit, servum alienum esse. Non solum autem proprietas per eos servos, in quibus usumfrumctum habetis, vel quos bona fide possidetis, aut per liberam personam, quæ bona fide vobis servit, vobis acquiritur, sed etiam possessio. Loquimur autem in utriusque persona secundum distinctionem, quam proxime exposuimus, id est, si quam possessionem ex re vestra, vel ex suis operis, adepti fuerint.

§ 5. *The same rule is observed in regard to him, who is possessed as a slave* bona fide, *whether he is a free man, or the slave of another: for the law concerning an usufructuary master prevails equally in relation to a* bona fide *possessor, and therefore whatever is acquired otherwise, than by the two causes abovementioned, it either belongs to the person possessed, if he is free, or to the proprietor, if the person possessed is the slave of another. But a* bona fide *possessor, who hath gained a slave by* usucapion *or prescription, (inasmuch as he thus becomes the absolute proprietor,) can acquire by virtue of such slave, by all manner of ways. But an usufructuary master can not prescribe; first, because he can never be strictly said to possess, having only the power of using: and farther, because he knows, that the slave belongs to another We nevertheless may acquire not only property, but also possession, by means of the slaves, whom we possess* bona fide, *or of whom we have only the usufruct; and even by means of a free person, of whom we have a* bona fide *possession. But, in saying this, we adhere to the distinction, which we have before explained, and speak of those things only, of which a slave may acquire the possession, either by means of the goods of his master, or by his own industry.*

De reliquis personis.

§ VI. Ex his itaque apparet, per liberos homines, quos neque vestro juri subjectos habetis, neque bona fide possidetis, item per alienos servos, in quibus neque usumfructum habetis, neque possessionem justam, nulla ex causa vobis acquiri posse. Et hoc est, quod dicitur, per extraneam personam nihil acquiri posse; excepto eo, quod per liberam personam (veluti per procuratorem) placet non solum scientibus, sed et ignorantibus, vobis acquiri possessionem, secundum Divi Severi constitutionem; et per hanc possessionem etiam dominium, si dominus fuerit, qui tradidit; vel usucapionem aut longi temporis præscriptionem, si dominus non sit.

§ 6. *It is apparent from what has been said; that we can by no means make acquisitions by free persons, who are not under our subjection nor possessed by us* bona fide. *neither can we acquire property by another's slave, of whom we have neither the usufruct, nor the just possession. And this is meant, when it is said, that nothing can be acquired by means of a stranger; which we must understand with an exception; for it hath been determined according to the constitution of the emperor* Severus, *that possession may be acquired for us by a free person, as for instance by a proctor, not only with, but even without our knowledge, and, by this possession, the property may be gained, if the delivery was made by the proprietor; and an usucapion or prescription may be acquired, altho' the delivery was made by one, who was not the proprietor.*

Divi Severi constitutionem] *vid Cod 7. t. 32. l 1.*

Transitio.

§ VII. Hactenus tantisper admonuisse sufficiat, quemadmodum singulæ res vobis acquirantur: nam legatorum jus, quo et ipso singulæ res vobis acquiruntur, item fideicommissorum, ubi singulæ res vobis relinquuntur, opportunius inferiore loco referemus. Videamus itaque nunc, quibus modis per universitatem res vobis acquirantur. Si cui ergo hæredes facti sitis, sive cujus bonorum possessionem petieritis, vel si quem adrogaveritis, vel si cujus bona, libertatum conservandarum causa, vobis addicta fuerint, ejus res omnes ad vos transeunt. Ac prius de hæreditatibus dispiciamus, quarum duplex conditio est; nam vel ex testamento, vel ab intestato, ad

vos

vos pertinent. Et prius eſt, ut de his deſpiciamus, quæ ex teſtamento vobis obveniunt; qua in re neceſſarium eſt initium de teſtamentis ordinandis exponere.

§ 7. *The obſervations, which we have already made, concerning the acquiſition of particular things, may ſuffice for the preſent; for we ſhall treat more opportunely hereafter in another place of the rights of legacies and truſts. We will now proceed to ſhew, how things may be acquired* per univerſitatem, *that is, wholly and in groſs by one ſingle acquiſition: for example; if* Titius *is nominated an heir, or ſeeks the poſſeſſion of the goods of another, or arrogates any one as his ſon, or if goods are adjudged to him for the ſake of preſerving the liberty of ſlaves, in all theſe caſes, the intire inheritance paſſes to* Titius. *Let us now therefore inquire into inheritances, which are of a twofold nature; for they proceed either from a teſtacy, or an inteſtacy. We will firſt treat of thoſe, which come to us by teſtament; and, in doing this, it will be neceſſary to begin by explaining the manner of making teſtaments.*

TITULUS DECIMUS.

De teſtamentis ordinandis.

D. xxviii. T. 1. C. vi. T. 23. Nov. 66. 119.

Etymologia.

TESTAMENTUM ex eo appellatur, quod teſtatio mentis ſit.

A teſtament is ſo called from the latin word teſtatio; *becauſe it bears witneſs or teſtimony to the determination of the mind.*

Teſtamentum ex eo] The writers on the civil law give various definitions of a teſtament *Modeſtinus* calls it *voluntatis noſtræ juſta ſententia de eo, quod quis poſt mortem ſuam fieri velit* —— *Ulpian* defines it to be *mentis noſtræ juſta conteſtatio, in id ſolemniter facta, ut poſt mortem noſtram valeat* —— But others, with a greater degree of exactneſs, define a teſtament "to be the appointment of an executor or teſtamentary heir, made according to the formalities, preſcribed by law *Domat. lib* 1. *t.* 1. *ſect.* 1" For in reality the conſtitution of an heir, or an executor, is the eſſence of a teſtament, and that, which diſtinguiſhes it from a codicil, or donation *mortis cauſa* *Quinque verbis poteſt quis facere teſtamentum, ut dicat,* LUCIUS TITIUS MIHI HÆRES ESTO. *ff* 28 *t* 5 *l.* 1. *Swin. p.* 3, 4, 5.

De antiquis modis teſtandi civilibus.

§ I. Sed, ut nihil antiquitatis penitus ignoretur, ſciendum eſt, olim quidem duo genera teſtamentorum in uſu fuiſſe; quorum altero in pace et otio utebantur, quod calatis comitiis appellabant; altero, cum in prælium exituri eſſent, quod procinctum dicebatur. Acceſſit deinde tertium genus teſtamentorum, quod dicebatur per æs et libram, ſcilicet quod per emancipationem, id eſt, imaginariam quandam venditionem agebatur, quinque teſtibus et libripende, civibus Romanis puberibus, præſentibus, et eo, qui familiæ emptor dicebatur. Sed illa quidem priora duo genera teſtamentorum ex veteribus temporibus in deſuetudinem abierunt: quod

vero

vero per æs et libram fiebat, licet diutius permanſerit, attamen partim et hoc in uſu eſſe deſiit.

§ 1. *But, leſt the antient uſage ſhould be forgotten, it is neceſſary to obſerve, that two kinds of teſtaments were formerly in uſe; the one was practiced in times of peace, and named* calatis comitiis, *becauſe it was made in a full aſſembly of the people; and the other was uſed when the people were going forth to battel, and was ſtiled* procinctum teſtamentum. *But a third ſpecies was afterwards added, which was called* per æs et libram, *becauſe it was effected by emancipation, which was an alienation, made by an imaginary ſale in the preſence of five witneſſes, and the* libripens *or ballance-holder, all citizens of* Rome, *above the age of fourteen; and alſo in the preſence of him, who was called the* emptor familiæ *or purchaſer. The two former kinds of teſtaments have been diſuſed for many ages; and that, which was made* per æs et libram, *altho' it continued longer in practice, hath now ceaſed in part to be obſerved.*

Per æs et libram] *Cujacius* is of opinion, that this ſpecies of teſtaments was abrogated by *Conſtantine* Cod 6. t. 23 l 15.

Attamen partim] It is ſaid to have ceaſed *in part* only, becauſe the ſame number of witneſſes were ſtill neceſſary, for tho' the civil law required but five, yet the ballance-holder and the purchaſer in reality made ſeven; and it was to ſupply the place of theſe, that the prætorian law added two witneſſes to the number requiſite by the civil law; ſo that in effect both the civil and the prætorian law required the preſence of the ſame number of perſons

De antiqua teſtandi ratione prætoria.

§ II. Sed prædicta quidem nomina teſtamentorum ad jus civile referebantur: poſtea vero ex edicto prætoris forma alia faciendorum teſtamentorum introducta eſt Jure etenim honorario nulla mancipatio deſiderabatur, ſed ſeptem teſtium ſigna ſufficiebant: cum jure civili ſigna teſtium non eſſent neceſſaria.

§ 2 *The three kinds of teſtaments before mentioned all took their riſe from the civil law; but afterwards another ſpecies was introduced by the edict of the prætor; for, by the* honorary *or* prætorian *edict, the ſignature of ſeven witneſſes was decreed ſufficient to eſtabliſh a will without any emancipation or imaginary ſale, but this ſignature of witneſſes was not required by the civil law.*

De conjunctione juris civilis et prætorii.

§ III. Sed, cum paulatim, tam ex uſu hominum quam ex conſtitutionum emendationibus, cœpit in unam conſonantiam jus civile et prætorium jungi, conſtitutum eſt, ut, uno eodemque tempore, quod jus civile quodammodo exigebat, ſeptem teſtibus adhibitis, et ſubſcriptione teſtium, quod ex conſtitutionibus inventum eſt, et ex edicto prætoris, ſignacula teſtamentis imponerentur: ita ut hoc jus tripertitum eſſe videatur: et teſtes quidem, eorumque præſentia, uno contextu, teſtamenti celebrandi gratia, à jure civili deſcendant: ſubſcriptiones autem teſtatoris et teſtium ex ſacrarum conſtitutionum obſervatione adhibeantur: ſignacula autem et teſtium numerus ex edicto prætoris.

§ 3.

§ 3. *When the civil and prætorian laws began to be blended together partly by usage, and partly by the emendation, made by the imperial constitutions, it became an established rule, that all testaments should be made at one and the same time according to the civil law; that they should be sealed by seven witnesses according to the prætorian law, and that they should also be subscribed by the witnesses, in obedience to the constitutions. Thus the law concerning testaments seems to be tripartite. for the civil law inforces the necessity of having witnesses to make a testament valid, who must all be present at one and the same time without interval; the sacred constitutions ordain, that every testament must be subscribed by the testator and the witnesses, and the prætorian edict requires sealing, and fixes the number of witnesses.*

Quod ex constitutionibus] The subscription of witnesses was in use from the time of the first emperors, as appears from *Ulpian* D. 28. t 1. *l*, 22 But the subscription of the testator was introduced by the following constitution of *Theodosius* *Hac consultissima lege sancimus, licere per scripturam conficientibus testamentum, si nullum scire volunt ea, quæ in eo scripta sunt, consignatam, vel ligatam, vel tantum clausam involutamque proferre scripturam, vel ipsius testatoris, vel cujuslibet alterius manu conscriptam, eamque rogatis testibus septem numero, civibus Romanis, puberibus, omnibus simul offerre signandam et subscribendam. dum tamen testibus præsentibus testator suum esse testamentum dixerit, quod offertur, eique ipse coram testibus sua manu in reliqua parte testamenti subscripserit, quo facto, et testibus uno eodemque die ac tempore subscribentibus et consignantibus, testamentum valere nec ideo infirmari, quod testes nesciant, quæ in eo scripta sunt testamento. Quod si literas testator ignoret, vel subscribere nequeat, octavo subscriptore pro eo adhibito, eadem servari decernimus,* &c &c. &c Dat id. Septemb Theodosio A. et Festo Coss 439.—— Cod 6 t. 23. *l* 21

Ex edicto prætoris] In *England* it is not necessary, that the witnesses to a will should affix their seals to it, for, if they subscribe their names, as witnesses, it is sufficient And, when a testament disposes only of personal estate, we follow the canon law, which never requires more than two witnesses with the minister of the parish, and in some cases only two witnesses, *quoniam scriptum est, in ore duorum vel trium testium stat omne verbum.* Decret. *Greg.* IX. lib. 3. t 26 *ll* 10, 11 —— Nor are even two witnesses necessarily required by the law of *England*, if there are circumstances to supply the want of them. *Cowel's inst lib* 2. *t.* 10. *sect.* 2 ———— And this practice in *England* is not wholly without a precedent, even among the *Romans* —— for the emperors *Theodosius* and *Valentinian*, by a novel constitution, allowed every holograph testament to be of full force tho' made without witnesses. *Si holographa manu testamenta condantur, testes necessarios non putamus. Scripto enim taliter sufficiet hæredi, asserere etiam sine testibus fidem rerum, dummodo reliqua congruere demonstret, quæ in testamentis debere servari tam veterum principum quam nostræ præcipiunt sanctiones, ut in hæreditariorum corporum possessionem probata scripturæ veritate mittatur. Cum tamen testium præsentiam testator elegerit, legitimum numerum semper oportebit adhiberi.* Novel. *Theod.* lib. 2. tit. 4. In *England* lands and tenements in general are not devisable by the common law of the realm; they have however been made devisable by the 32d of *Hen.* the 8th. And, by a statute of the 29th of *Charles* the *second*, it is enacted, "that "all devises of lands, devisable either by the "statute of wills, or by this statute, or by custom, shall be in writing, signed by the party "devising, or by some other in his presence and "by his express direction, and shall be attested "and subscribed, in the presence of the devisor, "by three or four credible witnesses, or else "they shall be void.

Solemnitas addita à Justiniano.

§ IV. Sed his omnibus à nostra constitutione propter testamentorum sinceritatem, ut nulla fraus adhibeatur, hoc additum est, ut, per manus testatoris vel testium, nomen hæredis exprimatur, et omnia secundum illius constitutionis tenorem procedent.

§ 4. *To all these solemnities we have made an addition for the better security of testaments and the prevention of frauds, having enacted by our constitution, that the name of the heir shall be expressed, by the hand-writing either of the testator, or of the*

the witnesses; and that every thing shall be done in conformity to the tenor of our ordinance.

A nostra constitutione.] *vid. Cod.* 6. *t.* 23. *l.* 29. *Jubemus. Nov.* 119. *cap.* 9.

De annulis, quibus testamenta signantur.

§ V. Possunt autem omnes testes et uno annulo signare testamentum; (quid enim si septem annuli una sculptura fuerint?) secundum quod Papiniano visum est. Sed et alieno quoque annulo licet signare testamentum.

§ 5 *Every witness to a testament, according to* Papinian, *may use the same signet. for otherwise, what must be the consequence, if seven seals should happen all to bear the same device? It is therefore allowable to seal with the signet of another.*

Qui testes esse possunt.

§ VI. Testes autem adhiberi possunt ii, cum quibus testamenti factio est. Sed neque mulier, neque impubes, neque servus, neque furiosus, neque mutus, neque surdus, neque is, cui bonis interdictum est, neque ii, quos leges jubent improbos intestabilesque esse, possunt in numerum testium adhiberi.

§ 6. *Those persons are allowed to be good witnesses, who are themselves legally capable of taking by testament: but yet no woman, slave, or interdicted prodigal, no person under puberty, mad, mute, or deaf, nor any one, whom the laws have reprobated and rendered intestable, can be admited a witness to a testament.*

Sed neque mulier.] Women may be admited witnesses, by the civil law, in all matters, whether civil or criminal, when the nature of the case is such, that other evidence can not be obtained, but, when the choice of witnesses is altogether voluntary, as in making testaments, and doing many other acts, the civil law will not receive the testimony of a woman. *Domat lib.* 3. *t* 1. The *Romans* had also another reason for rejecting women as witnesses to wills, namely, because women were never suffered to be present at public assemblies, where all wills and testaments were formerly made. But to use the words of *Swinburn*, "whatsoever diverse do "write, that a woman is not without all exception, because of the inconstancy and frailty of "the feminine sex, whereby they may the sooner "be corrupted, yet I take it, that their testimony is so good, that a testament may be "proved by two women alone, being other-"wise without exception *Swin* of Testaments, "*part.* IV. *sect* 24" And, by the laws of *England* in general, women may be witnesses, sureties, guardians, &c. in all cases, as well as men.

De servo, qui liber existimabatur.

§ VII. Sed, cum aliquis ex testibus, testamenti quidem faciendi tempore, liber existimabatur, postea autem servus apparuit, tam Divus Adrianus Catoni quam postea Divi Severus et Antoninus rescripserunt, subvenire se ex sua liberalitate testamento, ut sic habeatur firmum, ac si, ut oportebat, factum esset; cum, eo tempore, quo testamentum signaretur, omnium consensu hic testis liberi loco fuerit, nec quisquam esset, qui status ei quæstionem moveret.

§ 7 *If a witness, at the time of attesting, was reputed to have been a free person, but afterwards appeared to have been a slave at that time, the emperor* Adrian *declared in his rescript to* Cato, *and afterwards the emperors* Severus *and* Antoninus *by their rescript decreed in a similar case, that they would aid such a defect in a testa-*

testament, and cause it to be accounted equally firm, as if it had been made, as it ought; if the witness, at the time of sealing, was, in the estimation of all men, taken to be a free person, no one having made a question of his condition.

Adrianus Catoni] *vid. Cod* 6 *t.* 23. *l* 1.

De pluribus testibus ex eadem domo.

§ VIII. Pater, nec non is, qui in potestate ejus est; item duo fratres, qui in ejusdem patris potestate sunt, utique testes in uno testamento fieri possunt: quia nihil nocet, ex una domo plures testes alieno negotio adhiberi.

§ 8. *A father and a son under his power, or two brothers, under the power of the same father, may be made witnesses to a testament: for nothing hinders, but that several persons may be admited witnesses, out of the same family, to a business, in which that family is not interested.*

De his, qui sunt in familia testatoris.

§ IX. In testibus autem non debet esse is, qui in potestate testatoris est. Sed, si filiusfamilias de castrensi peculio post missionem faciat testamentum, nec pater ejus recte adhibetur testis, nec is, qui in potestate ejusdem patris est. Reprobatum est enim in ea re domesticum testimonium.

§ 9. *No person can be a witness to a testament, who is under the power of the testator. And, if the son of a family gives away his military estate by testament after his dismission from the army, neither his father nor any one under the power of his father, can be admited a witness to it. For, in this case, the law does not allow of a domestic testimony.*

De hærede.

§ X. Sed neque hæres scriptus, neque is, qui in ejus potestate est, neque pater ejus, qui eum habet in potestate, neque fratres, qui in ejusdem patris potestate sunt, testes adhiberi possunt, quia hoc totum negotium, quod agitur testamenti ordinandi gratia, creditur hodie inter testatorem et hæredem agi. Licet autem totum jus tale conturbatum fuerat, et veteres quidem familiæ emptorem, et eos, qui per potestatem ei conjuncti fuerant, à testamentariis testimoniis repellebant: hæredi autem, et iis, qui per potestatem ei conjuncti fuerant, concedebant testimonia in testamentis præstare: licet ii, qui id permittebant, hoc jure minime abuti eos debere suadebant: tamen nos eandem observationem corrigentes, et quod ab illis suasum est, in legis necessitatem transferentes, ad imitationem pristini familiæ emptoris, merito nec hæredi, qui imaginem vetustissimi familiæ emptoris obtinet, neque aliis personis, quæ ei, (ut dictum est,) conjunctæ sunt, licentiam concedimus sibi quodammodo testimonia præstare. ideoque nec ejusmodi veteres constitutiones nostro codici inseri permisimus.

§ 10. *No heir can be admited a witneſs to that teſtament, by which he is appointed heir; neither can the teſtimony of any one be admited, who is in ſubjection to ſuch heir; nor the teſtimony of his father, to whom he is himſelf under ſubjection; nor the teſtimony of his brothers, if they are under the power of the ſame father: for this whole buſineſs, which is performed for the ſake of completing a teſtament, is now always tranſacted between the teſtator and the real or very heir. But formerly there was great confuſion; for altho' the antients would never admit the teſtimony of the* emptor familiæ, *or the ſuppoſed heir, nor of any one allied to him by ſubjection, yet they admited that of the real heir, and of thoſe, who were connected with him by ſubjection; and the only precaution taken was to exhort and perſuade thoſe perſons not to abuſe their privilege. But we have corrected this practice, preventing by the coercion of law that, which the antient lawyers indeavored to prevent by perſuaſion only: for we permit neither the real heir, who repreſents the* emptor familiæ *of the antients, nor any perſon allied to ſuch real heir, to be a witneſs to the teſtament, by which he was nominated. And it is for this reaſon, that we have not ſuffered the old conſtitutions to be inſerted in our code.*

De legatariis et fideicommiſſariis, et his, qui ſunt in eorum familia.

§ XI. Legatariis autem et fideicommiſſariis, quia non juris ſucceſſores ſunt, et aliis perſonis eis conjunctis, teſtimonium non denegamus: imo in quadam noſtra conſtitutione et hoc ſpecialiter eis conceſſimus. Et multo magis iis, qui in eorum poteſtate ſunt, vel qui eos habent in poteſtate, hujuſmodi licentiam damus.

§ 11. *But we refuſe not the teſtimony of legataries and truſtees, and of thoſe, who are allied to them, becauſe ſuch perſons are not univerſal heirs or ſucceſſors: and, by virtue of our conſtitution, we have even ſpecially granted to all legataries and truſtees the liberty of bearing teſtimony; and therefore we grant this permiſſion much more readily to thoſe, who are in ſubjection to them, and to thoſe, to whom they are ſubject.*

Legatariis autem.] Altho' it was a general rule in the *Roman* law, that no one ſhould be permited to bear teſtimony in his own cauſe, *Cod.* 4. *t.* 20. *l.* 10 yet legataries were allowed to give evidence upon this diſtinction, that they were particular, and not univerſal ſucceſſors, and that a teſtament would be valid without legataries. The difficulty alſo, which muſt frequently have occurred, in obtaining ſo great a number of witneſſes, as ſeven, might probably induce the *Romans* to be leſs ſtrict, as to the perſons, whom they admited upon this occaſion. *Qui teſtamento hæres inſtituitur*, ſays ULPIAN, *in eodem teſtamento teſtis eſſe non poteſt quod in legatario, et in eo, qui tutor ſcriptus eſt, contra habetur. Hi enim teſtes poſſunt adhiberi, ſi aliud eos nihil impediat.* ff. 28. t. 1. *l* 20. But by the practice of the eccleſiaſtical courts of this kingdom, which have the ſole cognizance of the validity of all wills as far as they relate to perſonal eſtate, no legatèe, who is a ſubſcribed witneſs to the will, by which he is benefited, can be admited to give his teſtimony *in foro contradictorio*, as to the validity of that will, 'till either the value of his legacy hath been paid to him, or he hath renounced it, and, in caſe of payment, the executor of the ſuppoſed will muſt releaſe all title to any future claim upon ſuch ſuppoſed legatèe, who might otherwiſe be obliged to refund, if the will ſhould be ſet aſide, and a releaſe in this caſe is always made, to the intent, that the legatèe may have no ſhadow of intereſt at the time of making his depoſition. *Swinb.* 397. The ſame practice alſo prevailed at common law in regard to witneſſes, who were benefited under wills, diſpoſing of real eſtate And, if a legatee, who was a witneſs to a will, had refuſed either to renounce his legacy, or to be paid a ſum of money in lieu of it, he could not have been compelled by law, to diveſt himſelf of his intereſt, and, whileſt his intereſt continued, his teſtimony was uſeleſs and this was determined in the caſe of *Anſtey* verſ *Dowſing*, in eaſter-term, 19 *Geo* 2. the brief ſtate of which caſe was, as follows

" *James Thompson*, Esq. made his will, by which " he disposed of his real estate, and gave to one " *John Hailes* and his wife 10£ each for mourn- " ing, and an annuity of 20£. to *Eliz Hailes*, " the wife of *John*. This will of *James Thomp-* " *son* was regularly attested, as the statute di- " rects, by three witnesses, of which number " the above-named *John Hailes* was one, and " he refused to be paid 20£ in lieu of his " wife's legacy and his own The cause was " thrice argued at bar, and the judges of the " King's-bench were unanimously of opinion, " that a right to devise lands is not a com- " mon-law right, but depends upon powers, " given by statutes, the particulars of which are, " that a will of lands must be in writing, sign- " ed and attested by three credible witnesses in " the presence of the devisor that these were " checks to prevent men from being imposed up- " on, and certainly meant, that the witnesses " to a will, (who are required to be credible) " should not be persons, who are intituled to " any benefit under that will; and that there- " fore *John Hailes* was not a good witness." *Repts of Sir* John Strange, *p* 1254 — But this very singular case, and the unanimous opinions of the judges upon the meaning and intent of the statute of the 29th of *Charles the second*, called the statute of frauds, gave rise to the following act of parliament, made in the 25th year of *Geo the second* by which it is enacted; " that if any " person shall attest the execution of any will " or codicil, which shall be made after the " 24th of *June*, 1752, to whom any beneficial " devise, legacy, estate, interest, gift, or ap- " pointment, of or affecting any real or personal " estate (charges on lands, tenements, or heredi- " taments for payment of debts excepted) shall " be thereby given, &c the devise shall, so far " only as concerns such person, or any claim- " ing under him be void, and he shall be ad- " mitted a witness to the execution of such will. 25 *Geo* 2d

In quadam nostra constitutione.] *Not extant.*

De materia, in qua testamenta scribuntur.

§ XII. Nihil autem interest, testamentum in tabulis, an chartis, membranisve, vel in alia materia fiat.

§ 12 *It is immaterial, whether a testament is written upon a tablet of wax, upon paper, parchment, or any other substance.*

De pluribus codicibus.

§ XIII. Sed et unum testamentum pluribus codicibus conficere quis potest, secundum obtinentem tamen observationem omnibus factis: quod interdum etiam necessarium est, veluti si quis navigaturus et secum ferre et domi relinquere judiciorum suorum contestationem velit: vel propter alias innumerabiles causas, quæ humanis necessitatibus imminent.

§ 13. *Any person may commit the same testament to diverse tablets, each of which will be an original, if the requisite forms are observed And this sometimes is necessary, as when a man, who is going a sea-voyage, is desirous to carry his will with him, and at the same time to leave a counter-part of it at home for his better security Innumerable other reasons for doing this may arise, according to the various necessities of mankind*

Propter alias innumerabiles] Some persons, for their better security, have deposited their own wills in the prerogative office of the archbishop of *Canterbury* and this is certainly a wise precaution, against either fraud or accidents

De testamento nuncupativo.

§ XIV. Sed hæc quidem de testamentis, quæ scriptis conficiuntur, sufficiunt. Si quis autem sine scriptis voluerit ordinare jure civili testamentum, septem testibus adhibitis, et sua voluntate coram eis nuncupata, sciat, hoc perfectissimum testamentum jure civili firmumque constitutum.

§. 14.

§ 14. *What we have already said concerning written testaments, is sufficient. But if any man is willing to dispose of his effects by a nuncupative testament; i e by a testament without writing, let him be assured, if, in the presence of seven witnesses, he declares his will by word of mouth, that such verbal declaration will be a complete and valid testament according to the civil law.*

Si quis sine scriptis] Nuncupative testaments are certainly the most antient, and the great formalities injoined by the civil law, in regard to wills, took their rise originally from that liberty, which the *Romans* always enjoyed of making testaments without writing, for, as it was necessary, that the remembrance of the testator's will should be preserved, it was but reasonable not to suffer so serious an act to be made but in the most solemn manner It was ordained by *Theodosius*, that there should be seven witnesses, citizens of *Rome*, called on purpose, and that they should be present during the whole time of making a nuncupative testament *Per nuncupationem, hoc est, sine scriptura, testamenta non alias valere sancimus, quam si septem testes simul uno eodemque tempore collecti testatoris voluntatem, ut testamentum sine scriptura facientis, audierint.* Cod 6. t. 23 *l* 21 sect. 2. In *England* it is enacted by 29 *Car* 2. *cap* 3. " that no nuncupative will shall be good, " where the estate bequeathed shall exceed the " the value of 30£, if it is not proved by the " oaths of three witnesses, who were present at " the making, nor unless it be proved, that the " testator, at the time of pronouncing the same, " did bid the persons present, or some of them, " bear witness, that such was his will, or to that " effect; nor unless such nuncupative will were " made in the time of the last sickness of the " deceased, or in the house of his habitation, " or where he hath been resident ten days next " before the making of such will, except where " such person was taken sick, being from his " own home, and died before his return. And " that, after six months passed, after the speaking of the pretended testamentary words, " no testimony shall be received to prove any " will nuncupative, except the testimony, or " the substance thereof, were commited to writing within six days, after the making of the " will." 29 *Car*. 2. *cap*. 3.

TITULUS UNDECIMUS.

De militari testamento.

D xxix. T. 1. C. vi. T. 21.

In militum testamentis solemnitates remissæ.

SUPRADICTA diligens observatio in ordinandis testamentis militibus, propter nimiam imperitiam eorum, constitutionibus principalibus remissa est. Nam, quamvis ii neque legitimum numerum testium adhibuerint, neque aliam testamentorum solemnitatem observaverint, recte nihilominus testantur, videlicet cum in expeditionibus occupati sunt. quod merito nostra constitutio introduxit. Quoquo enim modo voluntas ejus suprema inveniatur, sive scripta, sive sine scriptura, valet testamentum ex voluntate ejus. Illis autem temporibus, per quæ citra expeditionum necessitatem in aliis locis, vel suis ædibus, degunt, minime ad vindicandum tale privilegium adjuvantur. Sed testari quidem, etsi filii-familiarum sint, propter militiam conceduntur: jure tamen communi, eadem observatione et in eorum testamentis adhibenda, quam in testamentis paganorum proxime exposuimus.

The

The beforementioned strict observation of formalities, in the construction and formation of testaments, is dispensed with by the imperial constitutions, in regard to all military persons, on account of their unskilfulness in these matters. For, altho' they neither call the legal number of witnesses, nor observe any other solemnity, yet they may make a good testament, if they are actually upon service against an enemy. This was introduced by our own ordinance with good reason; and thus, in whatever manner the testament of a military person is conceived, whether in writing, or not in writing, it prevails according to his intention: but, when soldiers are not upon an expedition, and live in their own houses or elsewhere, they are by no means intituled to claim this privilege; but a soldier, who is upon actual service against an enemy, may make a testament, altho' he is the son of a family, and consequently under power; but, if a soldier is willing to make his will according the the common law, he must observe all the formalities, which are required of others, who are not soldiers, when they make their testaments

Quod nostra constitutio.] *vid Cod.* 6. *t.* 21 *l.* 17.

Rescriptum Divi Trajani.

§ I. Plane de testamentis militum Divus Trajanus Catilio Severo ita rescripsit. *Id privilegium, quod militantibus datum est, ut quoquo modo facta ab his testamenta rata sint, sic intelligi debet, ut utique prius constare debeat, testamentum factum esse: quod et sine scriptura, et à non militantibus quoque, fieri potest. Si ergo miles, de cujus bonis apud te quæritur, convocatis ad hoc hominibus, ut voluntatem suam testaretur, ita loquutus est, ut declararet quem vellet sibi hæredem esse, et cui libertatem tribueret; potest videri sine scripto hoc modo esse testatus, et voluntas ejus rata habenda est. Cæterum, si (ut plerumque sermonibus fieri solet) dixit alicui,* ego te hæredem facio, *aut,* bona mea tibi relinquo, *non oportet hoc pro testamento observari. Nec ullorum magis interest, quam ipsorum, quibus id privilegium datum est, ejusmodi exemplum non admitti. Alioqui non difficulter post mortem alicujus militis testes existerent, qui affirmarent, se audisse dicentem aliquem relinquere se bona, cui visum sit: et per hoc vera judicia subverterentur.*

§ 1. *The emperor* Trajan *wrote, as follows, in his rescript to* Catilius Severus *concerning military testaments* The privilege, which is given to military persons, that their testaments, in whatever manner made, shall be valid, must be understood with this proviso, that it ought first to be apparent, that a testament was made in some manner: and here observe, that a testament may be made without writing, even by a person, who is not in the army. And therefore, if it appears, that the soldier, concerning whose goods question is now made before you, did, in the presence of witnesses, purposely called, declare what person should be his heir, and upon what slave, or slaves, he would confer the benefit of liberty, he shall be reputed to have made his testament without writing, and his will shall be ratified. But, if it is only proved, that he said to somebody, as it often happens in discourse, *I appoint you my heir* — or — *I leave you all my estate*, such words do not amount to a testament. Nor are any persons more interested than the soldiery, that words so spoken should not amount to a will, for, if this was once

once allowed, witnesses might without difficulty be produced after the death of any military man, who would affirm, that they had heared him bequeath his estate, to whomever they please; and thus the true intentions of numbers would be defeated.

Trajanus Catilio.] *vid. ff.* 29. *t.* 1. *l.* 24.

De surdo et muto.

§ II. Quinimo et mutus et surdus miles testamentum facere potest.

§ 2. *A soldier, tho' mute and deaf, may yet make a testament.*

Mutus et surdus miles] This was a privilege peculiar to soldiers, 'till the reign of *Justinian*, who granted this liberty to all his subjects in general *Cod* 6. *t.* 22. *l* 10.

De militibus et veteranis.

§ III. Sed hactenus hoc illis à principalibus constitutionibus conceditur, quatenus militant et in castris tegunt. Post missionem vero veterani, vel extra castra alii, si faciant adhuc militantes testamentum, communi omnium civium Romanorum jure id facere debent. Et quod in castris fecerint testamentum non communi jure, sed quomodo voluerint, post missionem intra annum tantum valebit. Quid ergo si intra annum quis decesserit, conditio autem hæredi adscripta post annum extiterit? an quasi militis testamentum valeat? Et placet valere quasi militis.

§ 3. *The privilege of making testaments without the usual formalities was granted by the imperial constitutions to military men, to be enjoyed only during the time of actual service, and whilest they lived in their tents For, if veterans after dismission, or even soldiers, if not upon service against the enemy, would make their testaments, they must not omit the forms required to be observed in common by all the citizens of* Rome. *And, if a testament is made by a soldier, even in his tent upon an expedition, yet, if the solemnities of the law are not adhered to, such testament will continue valid only for one year after his dismission from the army. Suppose therefore, that a soldier should die testate within a year after his dismission, and the event of the condition, upon which his heir is instituted, should not happen, 'till after the expiration of the year, would the testament of such soldier be valid? We answer, that it would prevail as a military testament.*

De facto ante militiam testamento.

§ IV. Sed et, si quis ante militiam non jure fecit testamentum, et miles factus, et in expeditione degens, resignavit illud, et quædam adjecit sive detraxit, vel alias manifesta est militis voluntas hoc valere volentis, dicendum est, valere hoc testamentum, quasi ex nova militis voluntate.

§ 4. *If a man, before his enterance into the army, should make his testament without observing the requisite formalities, and afterwards, when he became a soldier, and was upon an expedition, should open his testament for the sake of adding to it, or of substracting something from it; or if he should cause it to appear manifestly by any other means, that he was willing that his testament should be valid, we pronounce, that it would be valid, by virtue of this new act, amounting to a republication of his will.*

§ V.

De milite arrogato vel emancipato.

§ V. Denique, et si in arrogationem datus fuerit miles, vel filius-familias emancipatus est, testamentum ejus quasi ex nova militis voluntate valet: nec videtur capitis diminutione irritum fieri.

§ 5. *If a soldier is given in arrogation, or, being the son of a family, is emancipated, his testament is nevertheless good, having the same effect, as if he had republished it by a new declaration: for it is by no means invalidated by his change of state.*

Capitis diminutione] From the military privileges it is observable, how far the *Romans* found it necessary to dispense with the strictness of their laws in many cases The canon law therefore, with good reason, hath reformed this nicety of circumstantials in regard to wills, and hath reduced the number of seven witnesses to three, (the parish priest being one,) and in some cases to two witnesses, returning again to the law of God and the law of nations, by which two witnesses are sufficient But in *England*, where there is not any use of solemn testaments, the soldiery stand in no need of testamentary privileges, for wills of personal estate are made with all liberty and freedom, according to the *jus gentium*, which requires but two witnesses, and it is certain and undoubted, " that, if a testament was written or " subscribed with the testator's own hand, the " testimony of witnesses is not at all necessary, " but the proof may be from several circumstances, as that the testator was heared to say, " that he had made his testament, or, if such " testament was found in the testator's custody, " among his other writings, and papers of consequence " *Swin. of test part* 1. *sect.* 10 — *part* 4 *sect.* 27. But, as it has been before observed, " all devises of *lands* in *England* must be " in *writing*, signed by the testator, or some " other in his presence, and by his direction, " and must be attested and subscribed in the " presence of the testator, by three witnesses at " least, or else such devises are utterly void." See 29 *Car.* 2. *cap* 3.

De peculio quasi castrensi.

§ VI. Sciendum tamen est, quod, cum ad exemplum castrensis peculii, tam anteriores leges quam principales constitutiones, quibusdam quasi castrensia dederant peculia, et horum quibusdam permissum fuerat etiam in potestate degentibus testari, nostra constitutio, id latius extendens, permiserit omnibus in hujusce modi peculiis testari quidem, sed jure communi. Cujus constitutionis tenore perspecto, licentia est nihil eorum, quæ ad præfatum jus pertinent, ignorare.

§ 6 *We must here make it known, that, since the antient laws, as well as the later constitutions, have, in imitation of the* peculia castrensia, *or military estates, given to some persons* peculia quasi castrensia, *or* quasi *military estates, and have indulged some of these in the liberty of making testaments, whilest they were under power, we therefore, extending this privilege still farther, have by our ordinance permited all persons, who possess these estates, to make their testaments, on condition, that they observe the common solemnities of the law. But whoever thoroughly inspects our constitution, will have an opportunity of informing himself of every point, which relates to the before-mentioned privilege.*

Cujus constitutionis.] *vid Cod* 3. *t.* 28. *l* 37.

TITU-

TITULUS DUODECIMUS.

Quibus non eſt permiſſum facere teſtamentum.

D. xxviii. T. 1. C. vi. T. 22.

De filio-familias.

NON tamen omnibus licet facere teſtamentum: ſtatim enim ii, qui alieno juri ſubjecti ſunt, teſtamenti faciendi jus non habent: adeo quidem ut, quamvis parentes eis permiſerint, nihilo magis jure teſtari poſſint: exceptis iis, quos antea enumeravimus, et præcipue militibus, qui in poteſtate parentum ſunt: quibus de eo, quod in caſtris acquiſiverunt, permiſſum eſt ex conſtitutionibus principum teſtamentum facere. Quod quidem jus ab initio tantum militantibus datum eſt, tam ex auctoritate DIVI Auguſti, quam Nervæ, nec non optimi imperatoris Trajani: poſtea vero ſubſcriptione Divi Hadriani etiam dimiſſis à militia, id eſt, veteranis, conceſſum eſt. Itaque, ſiquidem fecerint de caſtrenſi peculio teſtamentum, pertinebit hoc ad eum, quem hæredem reliquerunt: ſi vero inteſtati deceſſerint, nullis liberis vel fratribus ſuperſtitibus, ad parentes eorum jure communi pertinebit. Ex hoc intelligere poſſumus, quod in caſtris acquiſierit miles, qui in poteſtate patris eſt, neque ipſum patrem adimere poſſe, neque patris creditores id vendere, vel aliter inquietare, neque patre mortuo cum fratribus commune eſſe; ſed ſcilicet proprium eſſe ejus, qui id in caſtris acquiſierit: quanquam jure civili omnium, qui in poteſtate parentum ſunt, peculia perinde in bonis parentum computentur, ac ſervorum peculia in bonis dominorum numerantur: exceptis videlicet iis, quæ ex ſacris conſtitutionibus, et præcipue noſtris, propter diverſas cauſas non acquiruntur. Præter hos igitur, qui caſtrenſe peculium vel quaſi caſtrenſe habent, ſi quis alius filius-familias teſtamentum fecerit, inutile eſt; licet ſuæ poteſtatis factus deceſſerit.

The right of making a teſtament with effect is not granted to all perſons alike: for thoſe, who are under the power of others, have not this right: inſomuch that, altho' parents have given permiſſion, their children will not be the more inabled by it to make a teſtament legally valid, if we except ſuch, whom we have already mentioned, and principally thoſe, who, on account of their being in the army, have permiſſion by virtue of our conſtitutions to diſpoſe by teſtament of whatever they have acquired by military ſervice, altho' they are ſtill under the power of their parents. This permiſſion was at firſt granted by Auguſtus, Nerva, *and that excellent prince* Trajan, *to actual ſoldiers only, but afterwards it was extended by the emperor* Adrian *to the veterans, that is, to thoſe, who had received their diſmiſſion: and therefore, if the ſon of a family bequeaths his* caſtrenſian *or military eſtate, it will paſs to him, who is instituted the heir: but, if such son dies intestate without children or brothers, his estate will then pass of common right to his father, or other paternal ascendents. We may from hence infer, that whatever a soldier, altho' under power, hath acquired by military service, it can not be taken from him even by his father; and that the creditors of the father can neither sell it, or otherwise disturb the son in his possession. and that what is thus acquired is not liable to be shared in common with brothers, upon the demise of the father, but that it remains the sole property of him, who acquired it: altho' by the civil law the* peculia *or estates of those, who are under power, are reckoned among the wealth of their parents, in the same manner as the* peculium *of a slave is esteemed the property of his master. But those estates must be excepted, which by the constitutions of the emperors, and chiefly by our own, are prohibited for diverse reasons to be acquired for parents Upon the whole, if the son of a family, who is neither possessed of a military or* quasi-*military estate, makes a testament, it will not be valid, even altho' he had been emancipated, and became* sui juris *before his death.*

De impubere et furioso.

§ I. Præterea testamentum facere non possunt impuberes; quia nullum eorum animi judicium est. Item furiosi; quia mente carent. Nec ad rem pertinet, si impubes postea pubes, aut furiosus postea compos mentis factus fuerit, et decesserit. Furiosi autem, si per id tempus fecerint testamentum, quo furor eorum intermissus est, jure testati esse videntur: certe eo, quod ante furorem fecerint, testamento valente. Nam neque testamentum recte factum, neque ullum aliud negotium recte gestum, postea furor interveniens perimit.

§ 1. *A person, within the age of puberty, can by no means make a good testament, because he is not supposed to possess that judgment of mind, which is requisite and the same holds true of a madman, inasmuch as he is deprived of his senses. And the testament of a minor under puberty will not become valid, altho' he arrives at puberty before his death, neither will the testament of a madman become valid, altho' he afterwards regains his senses, and then dies But, if he makes his testament, during a lucid interval, he is a legal testator; since it is certain, that the testament, which a man hath made, before the malady of madness has seized upon him, is good: for a subsequent fit of phrenzy can neither destroy the force of a regular testament, nor the validity of any other transaction, in which the rules of the law have been punctually observed.*

Non possunt impuberes.] The rules of the civil law take place in *England*, in regard both to the capacity and incapacity of minors to make wills, as far as those wills relate only to personal estate so that, if a boy, not arrived at the age of *fourteen*, or a girl, not arrived at the age of *twelve*, makes a will of personal estate, it will not be good, altho' such boy, or girl, was *doli capax* at the time of making the will, and capable of discerning right from wrong neither will a testament, made by a male infant under *fourteen*, or a female under *twelve*, become good, without a republication, altho such infant should afterwards arrive at the proper age but it hath been allowed in the case of *Hide* and *Hide*, that a male infant of 14, and a female of 12, might make a will of personal estate, and it was said to have been so agreed by lord keeper *Wright*, in the case of *Sharpe* and *Sharpe*, in which the court followed the civil law of *Justinian*, which permits minors to consent to marriage at such their respective ages. *Gilbert's Reps page* 74.— *Swinb fol.* 74 But, in regard to a will of real estate, it was enacted in the reign of *Hen* 8. "that wills or testaments made "of any manors, lands, tenements, or other "hereditaments, by any woman covert, or per- "son within the age of one and twenty years, "ideot, or insane, shall not be good or effectual "in law." 34 *H.* 8. *cap.* 5. *sect.* 14.

And

And it hath been adjudged, that, if a minor under twenty-one makes his will, and devises his lands, and afterwards attains the full age of twenty-one years, but dies without making any new publication of his will, the will is void. 1 *Sid.* 162. *And.* 182 *Dyer.* 143. *Raym* 84

Furiosi autem] "Mad folks and lunatics, "during the time of their insanity, can not "make a testament nor dispose of any thing by "will, not even to pious uses. The reason is, "because they know not what they do, for, in "making a will, integrity and perfectness of "mind, and not health of body, is required "and thereupon arose that common clause "used in every testament, *sick in body, but* "*of perfect mind and memory.* It was there- "fore determined by the judges, in *Combe*'s case "in the *Star-chamber*, (*Moor* 759) that sane "memory for making a will is not at all times, "when the party can speak *yea* or *no*, or hath "life in him, nor when he can answer to any "thing with sense; but he ought to have judg- "ment to discern, and to be of perfect memo- "ry, otherwise the will is void And so strong "is this impediment of insanity, that, if the "testator makes his testament after this furor "hath overtaken him, and whilest it as yet pos- "sesses his mind, albeit the furor afterwards de- "parts, and the testator recovers his former "understanding, yet doth not the testament, "made during his former fit, recover any force "or strength thereby. Howbeit if these mad "or lunatic persons have clear and calm inter- "missions, then during the time of such their "freedom of mind, they may make their testa- "ments, so that neither the *furor* going before, "nor following the making of the testament, "doth hinder the same begun and finished in "the mean time" *Swinburn of test. part* 2. *sect* 3 *Cod.* 6. *t.* 22. *l.* 9.

De prodigo.

§ II. Item prodigus, cui bonorum suorum administratio interdicta est, testamentum facere non potest: sed id, quod ante fecerit, quam interdictio bonorum suorum ei fiat, ratum est.

§ 2. *A prodigal also, who is under an interdiction, and prohibited from having the management of his own affairs, can not make a testament : but, if he hath bequeathed his estate before interdiction, his testament will be valid.*

Item prodigus] The laws of *England* take no care of prodigals.

De surdo aut muto.

§ III. Item surdus et mutus non semper testamentum facere possunt. Utique autem de eo surdo loquimur, qui omnino non exaudit, non qui tarde exaudit. Nam et mutus is intelligitur, qui eloqui nihil potest, non qui tarde loquitur. Sæpe enim etiam literati homines variis casibus et audiendi et loquendi facultatem amittunt. Unde nostra constitutio etiam his subvenit, ut, certis casibus et modis, secundum normam ejus possint testari, aliaque facere, quæ eis permissa sunt. Sed, si quis post testamentum factum, adversa valetudine aut quolibet alio casu mutus aut surdus esse cœperit, ratum nihilominus manet ejus testamentum.

§ 3. *A man deaf and dumb is not always capable of making a testament but we would be understood to mean this of him, who is so deaf as to be unable to hear at all, and not of him, who is afflicted only with a thickness of hearing, and of him, who is so dumb, as to be totally deprived of utterance, and not of him, who only labors under a difficulty of speech for it often happens, that the most literate persons lose the faculty of hearing and speaking by various misfortunes, we have therefore published a constitution, which aids all such persons, so that in certain cases they may make testaments, if they observe the rules of our ordinance, and may do many other acts, which are there permited But, if any man, after making his testament, becomes either deaf or mute by reason of ill health or any other accident, his testament will notwithstanding this remain good.*

Unde nostra constitutio] *vid. Cod* 6. *t.* 22. *l.* 10.

De cæco.

§ IV. Cœcus autem non poteſt facere teſtamentum, niſi per obſervationem, quam lex Divi Juſtini patris noſtri introduxit.

§ 4. *A blind man is not allowed to have the power of making a teſtament, unleſs he obſerves thoſe rules, which the law of the emperor* Juſtin, *our father, has introduced.*

Cœcus autem.] "He, who is blind, may make "a nuncupative teſtament, by declaring his will "before a ſufficient number of witneſſes, but "he can not make his teſtament in writing, un-"leſs the ſame be read before witneſſes, and in "their preſence acknowledged by the teſtator "for his laſt will And therefore, if a writing "were delivered to the teſtator, and he, not hear-"ing the ſame read, acknowledged it for his "will, this would not be ſufficient, for it may "be, that, if he ſhould hear the ſame, he would "not own it." *Swin. part 2 ſect* 11.

De eo, qui eſt apud hoſtes.

§ V. Ejus, qui apud hoſtes eſt, teſtamentum, quod ibi fecit, non valet, quamvis redierit: ſed quod, dum in civitate fuerat, fecit, ſive redierit, valet jure poſtliminii, ſive illic deceſſerit, valet ex lege Cornelia.

§ 5. *The teſtament of him, who is in the hands of an enemy, is not valid, if it was made during his captivity; even altho' he lives to return But a teſtament, made by a man in the city, or before captivity, is good, either by virtue of the* jus poſtliminii, *if the priſoner returns, or by virtue of the law* Cornelia, *if he dies a captive.*

Ex lege Cornelia] "Quo tempore, aut quo auctore, lata ſit, non liquet. *Vinn*

TITULUS DECIMUS-TERTIUS.

De exhæredatione liberorum.

D. xxviii. T. 2. C. vi. T. 28, 29. Nov. 115.

Jus vetus de liberis in poteſtate.

NON tamen, ut omnino valeat teſtamentum, ſufficit hæc obſervatio, quam ſupra expoſuimus: ſed, qui filium in poteſtate habet, curare debet, ut eum hæredem inſtituat, vel exhæredem eum nominatim faciat. Alioqui, ſi eum ſilentio prætererit, inutiliter teſtabitur: adeo quidem ut, ſi vivo patre filius mortuus ſit, nemo hæres ex eo teſtamento exiſtere poſſit· quia ſcilicet ab initio non conſtiterit teſtamentum. Sed non ita de filiabus, et aliis per virilem ſexum deſcendentibus liberis utriuſque ſexus, antiquitati fuerat obſervatum· ſed, ſi non fuerant ſcripti hæredes ſcriptæve, vel exhæredati exhæredatæve, teſtamentum quidem non infirmabatur, jus tamen accreſcendi eis ad certam portionem præſtabatur Sed nec nominatim eas perſonas exhæredare parentibus neceſſe erat, ſed licebat inter cæteros

teros hoc facere. Nominatim autem quis exhæredari videtur, five ita exhæredetur, *Titius filius meus exhæres esto*; five ita, *filius meus exhæres esto*, non adjecto proprio nomine; scilicet, si alius filius non extet.

The solemnities of law, which we have before explained, are not alone sufficient to make a testament valid. For he, who has a son under his power, should take care either to institute him his heir, or to disinherit him nominally: for, if a father in his testament, pretermits or passes over his son in silence, the testament will have no effect. And even if the son dies, living the father, yet no one can take upon himself the heirship by virtue of that testament, inasmuch as it was null from the very beginning. But the antients did not observe this rule in regard to daughters and grand-children of either sex, tho' descended from the male line; for altho' these were neither instituted heirs, nor disinherited, yet the testament was not invalidated; because a right of accretion intituled them to a certain portion of the inheritance: parents were therefore not necessitated to disinherit these children nominally, but might do it inter cæteros. *A child is nominally disinherited, if the words of the will are,* let Titius my son be disinherited, *or even thus*—— let my son be disinherited, *without the addition of any proper name, on supposition, that the testator had no other son living.*

Sed qui filium.] "In *England* the liberty of a "testator is so large and ample, that altho' he "hath children of his own naturally and law-"fully begotten, yet, by the laws and customs "of this realm, he may appoint others to be his "heirs or executors, secretly omiting or open-"ly excluding his own children." *Swin part* 5. *sect.* 1

De posthumis.

§ I. Posthumi quoque liberi vel hæredes institui debent vel exhæredari. Et in eo par omnium conditio est, quod et filio posthumo, et quolibet ex cæteris liberis, five feminini sexus five masculini, præterito, valet quidem testamentum, sed postea, agnatione posthumi five posthumæ, rumpitur, et ea ratione totum infirmatur. Ideoque, si mulier, ex qua posthumus aut posthuma sperabatur, abortum fecerit, nihil impedimento est scriptis hæredibus ad hæreditatem adeundam. Sed fœminini quidem sexus personæ vel nominatim vel inter cæteros exhæredari solebant: dum tamen, si inter cæteros exhæredarentur, aliquid eis legaretur, ne viderentur præteritæ esse per oblivionem. Masculos vero posthumos, id est, filios et deinceps, placuit non aliter recte exhæredari, nisi nominatim exhæredarentur, hoc scilicet modo, *quicunque mihi filius genitus fuerit, exhæres esto.*

§ 1. *Also posthumous children should either be instituted heirs, or disinherited: and in this the condition of all children is equal but, if a posthumous son, or any posthumous descendent in the right line, whether male or female, is pretermited in a testament, such testament will nevertheless be valid at the time of making, but, by the subsequent birth of a child of either sex, it will be annulled And therefore, if a matron, from whom there is reason to expect a posthumous child, should miscarry, nothing can prevent the written heirs from entering upon the inheritance. But female posthumous children may be either nominally disinherited, or* inter cæteros *by a general clause. yet, if they are disinherited* inter cæteros, *something must be left them to shew, that they were not omitted tho' forgetfulness but male posthumous children,* i. e. *sons, and their descendants in the direct line, can not be disinherited otherwise, than nominally*

nominally in this form—— whatever son is hereafter born to me, I disinherit him.

Agnatione posthumi] The rights of posthumous children seem to be regulated by the rights of those, who are born in the life-time of their parents Thus the civil law permits the birth of a posthumous child to annul a testament; because it is by that law in the power of any child, who hath been either omited in his father's testament, or disinherited nominally without cause, to set that testament aside, and where preterition is a sufficient reason to destroy a will, at the instance of a child born in the life-time of his father, it would be extremely hard not to allow this reason at least an equal force in regard to a posthumous child But by the law of *England* the birth of a posthumous child does not affect the testament of the father in any degree, which is in appearance a very rigid doctrine but with us the testament of a parent can not be annulled on account of the preterition, or causeless disinherison of a child, born in his life-time; for the law permits every man to dispose of his own fortune, as he pleases. and therefore, if a posthumous child was allowed to annul a will, it must follow, that such child would have a greater right, than if he had been born in his father's life-time, namely, the right of annulling his father's will on account of preterition. And, if the law was to persue a middle way, and admit a posthumous child to take a share of the deceased's estate without annulling the whole testament, this would be in effect to make a new will for the deceased, and to remedy a less evil by the introduction of a greater, in countenancing a practice so very dangerous, and contrary to that established rule of law, which gives every man an uncontrouled power in the disposition of his own fortune. What has been here said is intended only in regard to wills of personal estate, for, in respect to wills of real estate, there are, besides the statute of frauds, many other reasons, which might be urged to evince, that the birth of a posthumous child can not be allowed to operate as a revocation

De quasi posthumis.

§ II. Posthumorum autem loco sunt et hi, qui in sui hæredis locum succedendo, quasi agnascendo, fiunt parentibus sui hæredes: ut ecce, si quis filium, et ex eo nepotem neptemve, in potestate habeat, quia filius gradu præcedit, is solus jura sui hæredis habet, quamvis nepos quoque et neptis ex eo in eadem potestate sint. Sed, si filius ejus vivo eo moriatur, aut qualibet alia ratione exeat de potestate ejus, incipit nepos neptisve in ejus locum succedere, et eo modo jura suorum hæredum quasi agnatione nanciscitur. Ne ergo eo modo rumpatur ejus testamentum, sicut ipsum filium vel hæredem instituere vel nominatim exhæredare debet, ne non jure faciat testamentum; ita et nepotem neptemve ex filio necesse est ei vel hæredem instituere vel exhæredare, ne forte eo vivo, filio mortuo, succedendo in locum ejus nepos, neptisve, quasi agnascendo, rumpat testamentum. Idque lege Julia Velleia provisum est: in qua similis exhæredationis modus ad similitudinem posthumorum demonstratur.

§ 2. *Those also are reckoned in the place of posthumous children, who, succeeding in the stead of proper heirs, become, by a* quasi-*birth, proper heirs to their parents. for example, if* Titius *has a son under his power, and by him a grandson, or grand-daughter, then would the son, because he is first in degree, have the sole right of a proper heir, altho' the grandson, or grand-daughter by that son, is under the same parental power. But, if the son of* Titius *should die in his father's life-time, or should by any other means cease to be under his father's power, the grandson or grand-daughter would succeed in his place, and would thus, by what may be called a* quasi-*birth, obtain the right of a proper heir. Therefore, as it behoves a testator for his own security, either to institute or disinherit his son, lest his testament should be deemed not legal, so it is equally necessary for him either to institute or disinherit*

inherit his grandson or grand-daughter by that son, lest, if his son should die in his (the testator's) life-time, his grandson or grand-daughter, succeeding to the place of his son, should make void his testament by a quasi-*agnation. And this has been introduced by the law* Julia Velleia, *in which is set forth a form of disinheriting* quasi-*posthumous children, similar to that of disinheriting posthumous children.*

Lege Julia Velleia.] *vid. ff* 28. *t.* 2. *l.* 29 Gallus *sic posse institui posthumos nepotes induxit, &c*

De emancipatis.

§ III. Emancipatos liberos jure civili neque hæredes instituere, neque exhæredare, necesse est: quia non sunt sui hæredes. Sed prætor omnes, tam fœminini sexus quam masculini, si hæredes non instituantur, exhæredari jubet; virilis sexus nominatim, fœminini vero inter cæteros: quia, si neque hæredes instituti fuerunt, neque ita (ut diximus) exhæredati, promittit eis prætor contra tabulas testamenti bonorum possessionem.

§ 3. *In regard to emancipated children, the* civil law *does not make it necessary, either to institute them heirs or to disinherit them in a testament; inasmuch as they are not* sui hæredes, *i e. proper heirs. But the prætor commands, that all children in general, whether male or female, if they are not instituted heirs, shall be disinherited; the males nominally; the females* inter cæteros: *for, if children have neither been instituted heirs, nor properly disinherited in the manner, which we have mentioned, the prætor gives them the possession of the goods, contrary to the disposition of the testament.*

De adoptivis.

§ IV. Adoptivi liberi, quamdiu sunt in potestate patris adoptivi, ejusdem juris habentur, cujus sunt justis nuptiis quæsiti: itaque hæredes instituendi vel exhæredandi sunt, secundum ea, quæ de naturalibus exposuimus. Emancipati vero à patre adoptivo neque juri civili, neque eo jure, quod ad edictum prætoris attinet, inter liberos connumerantur. Qua ratione accidit, ut ex diverso, quod ad naturalem parentem attinet, quamdiu quidem sunt in adoptiva familia, extraneorum numero habeantur, ut eos neque hæredes instituere, neque exhæredare, necesse sit: cum vero emancipati fuerint ab adoptivo patre, tunc incipiant in ea causa esse, in qua futuri essent, si à naturali patre emancipati fuissent.

§ 4. *Adopted children, as long as they continue under the power of their adoptive father, are intituled to the same rights, as children born in lawful matrimony: and therefore they must either be instituted heirs, or disinherited, according to the rules laid down in regard to natural and lawful children But it is neither enacted by the civil law, nor injoined by prætorian equity, that children, emancipated by an adoptive father, should be numbered among his natural children, so as to partake of their rights: whence it happens, that adopted children, as long as they continue in adoption, are reputed strangers to their natural parents, who are not necessitated either to institute them heirs, or to disinherit them but, when they are emancipated by their adoptive father, they are then in the same state, in which they would have been, if they had been emancipated by their natural father.*

§ V.

Jus novum.

§ V. Sed hæc quidem vetustas introducebat. Nostra vero constitutio, inter masculos et fœminas in hoc jure nihil interesse existimans, quia utraque persona in hominum procreatione simili naturæ officio fungitur, et lege antiqua duodecim tabularum omnes simpliciter ad successionem ab intestato vocabantur, quod et prætores postea sequuti esse videntur, ideo simplex ac simile jus, et in filiis et in filiabus et in cæteris descendentibus per virilem sexum personis, non solum jam natis, sed etiam posthumis, introduxit; ut omnes, sive sui sive emancipati sint, vel hæredes instituantur, vel nominatim exhæredentur: et eundem habeant effectum circa testamenta parentum suorum infirmanda, et hæreditatem auferendam, quem filii sui vel emancipati habent, sive jam nati sint, sive adhuc in utero constituti, postea nati sint. Circa adoptivos autem filios certam induximus divisionem, quæ in nostra constitutione, quam super adoptivis tulimus, continetur.

§ 5. *These were the rules, which the antient lawyers introduced. But we (not thinking, that any distinction can reasonably be made between the two sexes, inasmuch as they both contribute alike to the procreation of the species, and because, by the antient law of the twelve tables, all children, male as well as female, were equally called to the succession* ab intestato, *which law the prætors seem afterwards to have followed) have by our constitution introduced the same law in regard both to sons and daughters, and to all the other descendents in the male line, whether in being, or posthumous: so that all children, whether they are proper heirs or emancipated, must either be instituted heirs or nominally disinherited. And, in regard to adopted children, we have introduced certain regulations, which are contained in our constitution of adoptions.*

Nostra vero constitutio] *vid. Cod.* 6. *t.* 28. *l* 4.

In nostra constitutione.] *vid. Cod.* 8. *t.* 48. *l.* 10. *cum in adoptivis.*

De testamento militis.

§ VI. Sed, si in expeditione occupatus miles testamentum faciat, et liberos suos jam natos vel posthumos nominatim non exhæredaverit, sed silentio præterierit, non ignorans, an habeat liberos, silentium ejus pro exhæredatione nominatim facta valere, constitutionibus principum cautum est.

§ 6. *If a soldier makes his testament, whilest he is upon a military expedition, and neither nominally disinherits his children already born, nor his posthumous children, but passes them over in silence, altho' it is known to him, that he has such children, or that his wife was enseint, it is provided by the constitutions of the emperors, that such silence shall be of equal force with a nominal disherison.*

De testamento matris, aut avi materni.

§ VII. Mater vel avus maternus necesse non habent liberos suos aut hæredes instituere, aut exhæredare, sed possunt eos silentio omittere: nam silentium matris aut avi materni, et cæterorum per matrem ascendentium, tantum

tantum facit, quantum exhæredatio patris. Neque enim matri filium filiamve, neque avo materno nepotem neptemve ex filia, si eum eamve hæredem non instituat, exhæredare necesse est, sive de jure civili quæramus, sive de edicto prætoris, quo prætor præteritis liberis contra tabulas bonorum possessionem promittit: sed aliud eis adminiculum servatur, quod paulo post vobis manifestum fiet.

§ 7. *Neither a mother, nor a grandfather on the mother's side, is under any necessity of either instituting their children heirs, or of disinheriting them, but may pass them by in silence, for the silence of a mother, a maternal grandfather, and of all other ascendents on the mother's side, works the same effect, as an actual disinherison by a father. For a mother is not obliged to disinherit her children, if she does not think proper to institute them her heirs; neither is a maternal grandfather under a necessity either of instituting or disinheriting his grandson or grand-daughter by a daughter, inasmuch as this is not required either by the civil law, or the* edict *of the prætor, which gives the possession of goods* contra tabulas *(i e contrary to the disposition of the testament) to those children, who have been passed over in silence But children, in this case, are not without a remedy against the testament of their mother or maternal grandfather, which shall be shewed hereafter.*

TITULUS DECIMUS-QUARTUS.

De hæredibus instituendis.

D. xxviii. T. 5. C. vi. T. 24.

Qui possunt hæredes institui.

HÆREDES instituere permissum est tam liberos homines quam servos; et tam proprios, quam alienos. Proprios autem olim quidem secundum plurium sententias non aliter, quam cum libertate, recte instituere licebat: hodie vero etiam sine libertate ex nostra constitutione eos hæredes instituere permissum est. Quod non per innovationem induximus, sed quoniam æquius erat, et Atilicino placuisse Paulus suis libris, quos tam ad Masurium Sabinum quam ad Plautium scripsit, refert. Proprius autem servus etiam is intelligitur, in quo nudam proprietatem testator habet, alio usumfructum habente. Est tamen casus, in quo nec cum libertate utiliter servus à domina hæres instituitur, ut constitutione Divorum Severi et Antonini cavetur. Cujus verba hæc sunt: *servum, adulterio maculatum, non jure testamento manumissum ante sententiam ab ea muliere videri, quæ rea fuerat ejusdem criminis postulata, rationis est Quare sequitur, ut, in eundem à domina collata, hæredis institutio nullius momenti habeatur.* Alienus servus etiam is intelligitur, in quo usumfructum testator habet.

A man may appoint slaves, as well as freemen, to be his heirs by testament; and may nominate the slaves of another as well as his own: yet, according to the opinion of many, no master could formerly institute his own slaves to be his heirs, without giving them their liberty: but at present, by virtue of our constitution, masters may appoint their slaves to be their heirs, without making even any mention of liberty: and this we have introduced, not for the sake of innovation, but because it seemed most just; and because Paulus, *in his commentaries upon* Sabinus *and* Plautius, *affirms, that this was also the opinion of* Atilicinus. *Here note, that we call a slave* proprius servus, *if the testator had only a nude property in him, the usufruct being in another. But, in a constitution of the emperors* Severus *and* Antoninus, *there is a case, in which a slave was not permited to be instituted an heir by his owner, altho' his liberty was expresly given to him The words of the constitution are these——* It is consonant to right reason, that no slave, accused of adultery with his mistress, shall be allowed, before a sentence of acquital, to be made free by that mistress, who is alleged to be a partener in the crime. *It therefore follows, that, if a mistress institutes such a slave to be her heir, the institution is of no avail.—— The expression* alienus servus *(i e.* the slave of another,*) is also sometimes used to denote him, of whom the testator had the usufruct, tho' not the property.*

Ex nostra constitutione] *vid. Cod.* 6. *t.* 27. *l.* 5.

Si servus hæres institutus in eadem causa manserit, vel non.

§ I. Servus autem à domino suo hæres institutus, siquidem in eadem causa manserit, fit ex testamento liber, hæresque ei necessarius. Si vero à vivo testatore manumissus fuerit, suo arbitrio adire hæreditatem potest; quia non fit hæres necessarius, cum utrunque ex domini testamento non consequatur. Quod si alienatus fuerit, jussu novi domini adire hæreditatem debet, et ea ratione per eum dominus fit hæres: nam ipse alienatus neque liber, neque hæres, esse potest; etiamsi cum libertate hæres institutus fuerit: destitisse enim à libertatis datione videtur dominus, qui eum alienavit. Alienus quoque servus hæres institutus, si in eadem causa duraverit, jussu ejus domini adire hæreditatem debet. Si vero alienatus fuerit ab eo, aut vivo testatore, aut post mortem ejus, antequam adeat, debet jussu novi domini adire. At, si manumissus est vivo testatore, vel mortuo, antequam adeat, suo arbitrio adire potest hæreditatem.

§ 1. *When a slave hath been instituted by his master, and remains in the same state, he will obtain his freedom at the death of his master, by virtue of the testament, and become his necessary heir. But, if that slave is manumited in the life-time of his master, it is in his power either to accept or refuse the inheritance; for he will not become a necessary heir, as he can not be said to have obtained both his liberty and the inheritance, by virtue of the testament But, if such instituted heir should be aliened, he can not then enter upon the inheritance but at the command of his new master, who by means of his slave may become the heir of the testator. For a slave, who hath been aliened, can not afterwards obtain his liberty, or take an inheritance to his own use, by virtue of the testament of that master, who made the alienation, altho' his freedom was*

was expresly given by such testament; because a master, who has aliened his slave, seems to have departed from having any intention to infranchise him. And, when the slave of another is appointed an heir, but remains in the same condition, he can not take the inheritance, but by his master's order: and, if the slave is aliened in the life-time of the testator, or even after his death, at any time before he has actually taken the inheritance, he must then either accept, or refuse it, at the command of his new master. But, if the slave is infranchised, living the testator, or after his death, before he has accepted the heirship, he either may, or may not, enter upon the inheritance at his own option.

De servo hæreditario.

§ II. Servus etiam alienus post domini mortem recte hæres instituitur: quia et cum hæreditariis servis testamenti factio est. Nondum enim adita hæreditas personæ vicem sustinet non hæredis futuri, sed defuncti: cum etiam ejus, qui in utero est, servus recte hæres instituatur.

§ 2 *The slave of another may legally be instituted an heir, after the death of his master; for the slaves of an inheritance, not entered upon, are intituled to the* factio passiva testamenti, *i. e are capable of taking, tho' not of giving, by testament and the reason of this is, because an inheritance, which is open, and not as yet entered upon, is supposed to represent the person of the deceased, and not the person of the future heir: and thus the slave even of a child in the womb may be constituted an heir.*

De servo plurium.

§ III. Servus autem plurium, cum quibus testamenti factio est, ab extraneo institutus hæres, unicuique dominorum, cujus jussu adierit, pro portione dominii acquirit hæreditatem.

§ 3 *If the slave of many masters, who are all capable of taking by testament, is instituted an heir by a stranger, then that slave acquires a part of the inheritance for each master, who commanded him to take it, according to their several proportions of property.*

De numero hæredum.

§ IV. Et unum hominem, et plures, usque in infinitum, quot quis hæredes velit, facere licet.

§ 4. *A testator may appoint one heir, or as many heirs as he pleases* in infinitum.

De divisione hæreditatis.

§ V. Hæreditas plerumque dividitur in duodecim uncias; quæ assis appellatione continentur. Habent autem et hæ partes propria nomina ab uncia usque ad assem; ut puta hæc, sextans, quadrans, triens, quincunx, semis, septunx, bes, dodrans, dextans, deunx. Non autem utique semper duodecim uncias esse oportet: nam tot unciæ assem efficiunt, quot testator voluerit: et, si unum tantum quis ex semisse (verbi gratia) hæredem scripserit, totus as in semisse erit. Neque enim idem ex parte testatus, et ex parte intestatus, decedere potest, nisi sit miles, cujus sola volun-

tas

tas in testando spectatur. Et è contrario potest quis in quantascunque voluerit plurimas uncias suam hæreditatem dividere.

§ 5. *An inheritance is generally divided into twelve* unciæ, *that is, parts or ounces, all which are comprehended under one total, termed an* As: *and each of these parts, from the* uncia *to the* As, *has its peculiar name, viz.*

Sextans—— *a sixth part, or two ounces.*

Quadrans—— *a fourth, or three ounces.*

Triens—— *a third, or four ounces.*

Quincunx—— *five ounces.*

Semis—— *a moity, or six ounces.*

Septunx—— *seven ounces.*

Bes—— *two thirds, or 8 ounces*; quasi, bis triens.

Dodrans—— *nine ounces, or three fourths*; quasi, dempto quadrante, As.

Dextans—— *ten ounces*, quasi, dempto sextante, As.

Deunx—— *eleven ounces out of twelve*; quasi, demptâ unciâ, As.

But it is not necessary, that an As, *or* total, *should always be divided into twelve parts, for an* As *may consist of what parts the testator pleases, and, if a man names but one heir, and appoints him* ex semisse, i e. *the heir of six parts; yet the whole* As *will be included; for no man can die partly testate and partly intestate, except a soldier, whose intention is solely to be regarded And a testator may also divide his estate into as many parts, as he thinks convenient.*

Ex parte testatus, et ex parte intestatus] In *England*, if a man disposes of only the half of his personal estate by testament, he will nevertheless die intestate, as to the other half, which will be disposed of among his next of kin, as the statute of distributions directs.

De portionibus singulorum hæredum. Si testator assem non diviserit, aut partes in quorundam persona non ultra assem expresserit.

§ VI. Si plures instituantur hæredes, ita demum in hoc casu partium distributio necessaria est, si nolit testator, eos ex æquis partibus hæredes esse. Satis enim constat, nullis partibus nominatis, ex æquis partibus eos hæredes esse. Partibus autem in quorundam personis expressis, si quis alius sine parte nominatus erit, siquidem aliqua pars assi deerit, ex ea parte hæres fit. Et, si plures sine parte scripti sunt, omnes in eandem partem concurrunt. Si vero totus as completus sit, ii, qui nominatim expressas partes habent, in dimidiam partem vocantur, et ille, vel illi omnes, in alteram dimidiam. Nec interest, primus an medius, an novissimus, sine parte hæres scriptus sit: ea enim pars data intelligitur, quæ vacat.

§ 6 *When a testator hath instituted many heirs, it is incumbent upon him to make a division of his effects, if he does not intend, that all his heirs should share his inheritance in equal portions: for, if no distribution is made by the testator, it is evident, that all his heirs must be equal sharers But, if the shares of some of the nominated heirs in a testament should be expressed, and the share or shares of one or more should*

be

be omited, then he or they, whose share or shares had not been specified, would be intituled to the undisposed remainder of the inheritance. But, if a whole As, *or inheritance, is given among some of the nominated heirs, yet they, whose shares are mentioned, are intituled only to a moity; and he or they, whose shares are not mentioned, are called to the succession of the other moity. And, when a whole inheritance is not given away, it is immaterial whether an heir, whose share is not specified, holds the first, middle, or last place in the nomination: for, whatever place he holds in it, he is equally intituled to the part not bequeathed in the testament.*

In alteram dimidiam] " Semis illi, vel illis, " videatur testator, ex viginti quatuor unciis, " qui sine parte instituti sunt, dabitur, quasi " hæredes instituisse " *Theoph*

Si pars vacet, aut exuperet.

§ VII. Videamus, si pars aliqua vacet, nec tamen quisquam sine parte sit hæres institutus, quid juris sit, veluti si tres ex quartis partibus hæredes scripti sunt. Et constat, vacantem partem singulis tacite pro hæreditaria parte accedere, et perinde haberi, ac si ex tertiis partibus hæredes scripti essent: et ex diverso, si plures hæredes scripti in portionibus sint, tacite singulis decrescere; ut, si (verbi gratia) quatuor ex tertiis partibus hæredes scripti sint, perinde habeantur, ac si unusquisque ex quarta parte hæres scriptus fuisset.

§ 7. *Let us now inquire, what the law would direct, if a part of an inheritance should remain unbequeathed, and yet a certain portion of it should be given by testament to every nominated heir. as if three should be instituted, and a fourth given to each. It is clear in this case, that the undisposed part would vest in each of them in proportion to the share bequeathed to him, and that each would be reputed the written heir of a third And, on the contrary, if many are nominated heirs in certain portions, so as to exceed the* As, *then each heir must suffer a defalcation* pro ratâ —— *for example, if four are instituted and a third is given to each, then this disposition would work the same effect, as if each of the written heirs had been instituted to a fourth only.*

Si plures unciæ quam duodecim distributæ sunt.

§ VIII. Et, si plures unciæ, quam duodecim, distributæ sint, is, qui sine parte institutus est, quod dupondio deest, habebit. Idemque erit, si dupondius expletus sit. Quæ omnes partes ad assem postea revocantur, quamvis sint plurium unciarum.

§ 8. *If more parts or ounces, than twelve, are bequeathed, then he, who is instituted without any prescribed share, shall be intituled to what remains of a* dupondius, *that is, of twenty-four parts and, if more, than twenty-four parts, are bequeathed, then the heir, who is nominated without any determinate share, is intituled to the remainder of a* tripondius, *i e of thirty six parts or ounces. But all these parts are afterwards reduced to twelve.*

De modis instituendi.

§ IX. Hæres et pure et sub conditione institui potest: ex certo tempore, aut ad certum tempus, non potest: veluti, *post quinquennium, quam*

moriar;

moriar; vel, *ex calendis illis*; vel, *usque ad calendas illas hæres esto.* Denique diem adjectum haberi pro supervacuo placet, et perinde esse, ac si pure hæres institutus esset.

§ 9. *An heir may be constituted simply, or conditionally — but not* from *or* to *any certain period · as if a testator should say to* Titius, be thou my heir after five years *to be computed* from my death — *or* — from the calends of such a month — *or* — 'till the calends of such a month. *For time, thus added, is in law deemed superfluous, and such an institution takes place immediately, as if it was a simple appointment.*

Ad certum tempus non potest] Altho' by the civil law an heir can not be instituted either *from* a certain time or '*till* a certain time, *lest the deceased should seem to die partly testate and partly intestate*, yet, in *England*, an executor, who is *quasi-hæres*, may be appointed either *from* or *until* a certain time and the ordinary may commit the administration of the goods of the deceased to the next of kin in the mean time, during which time the act of the administrator is good, and can not afterwards be avoided by the executor. *Swin* 310.

De conditione impossibili.

§ X. Impossibilis conditio in institutionibus et legatis, nec non in fideicommissis et libertatibus, pro non scripta habetur.

§ 10. *An impossible condition in the institution of heirs, the disposition of legacies, the appointment of trusts, or the confering of liberty, is treated as unwritten or void.*

Impossibilis conditio.] "Altho' impossible " conditions, whether they are so by nature or " by law, do not hinder the effect of the disposition, being reputed as if they were not written or uttered, yet, if a testator supposes a " condition to be possible, which is in reality " impossible or illegal, then such condition is " not void, but will render the disposition void, " to which it is added as for instance, if the " testator makes *Titius* his executor, or gives " him an hundred pounds, if he marries his, " the testator's, daughter, supposing her to be " living, when she is dead in this case, the " condition is impossible; and yet *Titius* can " not become executor, or obtain the legacy; " because it is not probable, that the testator " would have made him executor, or given " him an hundred pounds, if he had known, " or believed, his daughter to have been dead. *Swinb. part* 4 *sect* 6.

De pluribus conditionibus.

§ XI. Si plures conditiones in institutionibus adscriptæ sunt, siquidem conjunctim, ut puta, *si illud et illud factum fuerit*, omnibus parendum est: si separatim, veluti, *si illud aut illud factum erit*, cuilibet conditioni obtemperare satis est.

§ 11 *If many conditions are jointly required in the institution of an heir; as thus,* if this thing *and* that thing be done, *then both must be complied with. But, if the conditions are placed separately and in the disjunctive, as thus,* if this, *or* that be done, *it will then be sufficient to obey either.*

De his, quos nunquam testator vidit.

§ XII Ii, quos nunquam testator vidit, hæredes institui possunt, veluti si fratris filios peregrinantes, ignorans qui essent, hæredes instituerit. Ignorantia enim testantis inutilem institutionem non facit.

§ 12.

§ 12. *A testator may appoint persons, whom he hath never seen, to be his heirs. He may, for example, institute his brother's sons, who are in a foreign country, altho' he does not know where they are; for the want of this knowledge in a testator will not vitiate the institution of an heir.*

TITULUS DECIMUS-QUINTUS.

De vulgari substitutione.

D. xxviii. T. 6. C. vi. T. 25 et 26.

De pluribus gradibus hæredum.

POTEST autem quis in testamento suo plures gradus hæredum facere; ut puta, *si ille hæres non erit, ille hæres esto.* Et deinceps, in quantum velit, testator substituere potest: ut novissimo loco in subsidium vel servum necessarium hæredem instituere possit.

A man by testament may appoint many degrees of heirs; as thus— if *Titius* will not be my heir, let *Seius* be my heir. *And he may proceed in such a substitution as far as he shall think proper; and lastly, in default of all others, he may constitute a slave to be his necessary heir.*

De numero hæredum in singulis gradibus.

§ I. Et plures in unius locum possunt substitui, vel unus in plurium, vel singuli in singulorum, vel invicem ipsi, qui hæredes instituti sunt.

§ 1. *A testator may substitute many in the place of one, or one in the place of many, or one in the place of each, or he may substitute even his instituted heirs reciprocally to one another.*

Plures in unius locum] This kind of substitution, which is called ordinary or vulgar, is of no small use in *England,* and we do therein, for the most part, follow the precepts and rules of the civil law for it is nothing else but the adding a condition, which we commonly call *tail* in the case of lands, namely, a limitation of heirs, to whom a testator intends, that his lands should descend *Strahan* on *Domat* vol 2 p. 221. *Cowel's* inst. tit 15.

Quam partem singuli substituti accipiant, si partes in substitutione expressæ non sint.

§ II. Et, si ex disparibus partibus hæredes scriptos invicem substituerit, et nullam mentionem partium in substitutione habuerit, eas videtur in substitutione partes dedisse, quas in institutione expressit: et ita Divus Pius rescripsit.

§ 2. *If a testator, having instituted several co-heirs in unequal portions, substitutes them reciprocally the one to the other, and makes no mention of their shares of the inheritance in the substitution, he seems to have given the same shares by the substitution, which he gave by the institution, and this is agreeable to the rescript of the emperor* Antoninus.

Et

Et ſi ex diſparibus.] For example, if a teſtator ſhould bequeath to *Primus* one twelfth of his eſtate — to *Secundus* eight twelfths, and to *Tertius* three twelfths, adding, that he ſubſtitutes them all, the one to another reciprocally — then if *Primus*, for inſtance, ſhould at the death of the teſtator refuſe to take his twelfth, it muſt be ſubdivided into eleven equal parts, of which eight muſt be given to *Secundus*, and three to *Tertius* Ferriere, *h. l.*

Ita Divus Pius.] *vid. Cod.* 6. *t.* 26. *l.* 1. *ff* 28. *t.* 6 l 24.

Si cohæredi ſubſtituto alius ſubſtituatur.

§ III. Sed, ſi inſtituto hæredi, cohærede ſubſtituto dato, alius ei ſubſtitutus fuerit, Divi Severus et Antoninus ſine diſtinctione reſcripſerunt, ad utramque partem ſubſtitutum admitti.

§ 3. *If a co-heir is ſubſtituted to an inſtituted heir, and a third perſon is ſubſtituted to that co-heir, the emperors,* Severus *and* Antoninus, *have by reſcript ordained, that ſuch ſubſtituted perſon ſhall be admited to the portions of both the coheirs without diſtinction.*

Cohærede ſubſtituto dato] *Syphax* gave ſix 12ths of his eſtate to *Titius*, and ſix to *Caius*, making them co-heirs, he then ſubſtituted *Titius* to *Caius* and *Sempronius* to *Titius* · but, *Titius* and *Caius* dying, or declining the inheritance, it became a queſtion, to what ſhare *Sempronius* ſhould be admited; and it was determined, that the emperor or treaſury ſhould take no ſhare of the deceaſed's effects in this caſe, but that *Sempronius* the ſubſtitute ſhould be admitted without diſtinction as well to the ſhare of *Caius* as to that of *Titius*. *Mynſinger*, *h l.* *ff* 28. *t* 6. *l* 27.

Si quis ſervo, qui liber exiſtimabatur, inſtituto ſubſtitutus fuerit.

§ IV. Si ſervum alienum quis patremfamilias arbitratus hæredem ſcripſerit, et, ſi hæres non eſſet, Mævium ei ſubſtituerit; iſque ſervus juſſu domini adierit hæreditatem, Mævius ſubſtitutus in partem admittitur. Illa enim verba, *ſi hæres non erit*, in eo quidem, quem alieno juri ſubjectum eſſe teſtator ſcit, ſic accipiuntur, *ſi neque ipſe hæres erit, neque alium hæredem effecerit:* in eo vero, quem patremfamilias arbitratur, illud ſignificant, *ſi hæreditatem ſibi, vel ei, cujus juri poſtea ſubjectus eſſe cæperit, non acquiſierit.* Idque Tiberius Cæſar in perſona Parthenii ſervi ſui conſtituit.

§ 4 *If a teſtator constitutes the ſlave of another to be his heir, ſuppoſing him to be free, and adds* — if he does not become my heir, I ſubſtitute *Mævius* in his place — *then, if that* ſlave *ſhould afterwards enter upon the inheritance at the command of his maſter,* Mævius, *the ſubſtitute, would be admited to a moity. For the words*, if he does not become my heir, *in regard to him, whom the teſtator knew to be under the dominion of another, are taken to mean,* if he will neither become my heir himſelf, nor cauſe another to be my heir. *but in regard to him, whom the teſtator ſuppoſed to be free, they imply this condition, viz.* if my heir will neither acquire the inheritance for himſelf, nor for him, to whoſe dominion he may afterwards become ſubject. *But it was determined by* Tiberius, *the emperor, in the caſe of his own ſlave* Parthenius, *that a ſubſtitute in ſuch a caſe ſhould be admited to a moity.*

Illa enim verba] *Servum tuum, ſui juris eſſe credens, inſtitui hæredem, et ſic adjeci* SI AUTEM HÆRES MIHI NON FIAT, MÆVIUS HÆRES ESTO *Poſt mortem meam tu juſſiſti ſervum tuum, quem inſtitueram, adire hæreditatem. Quærimus, an locus ſit ſubſtituti? Et dicimus ſubſtitutum accipere*

accipere ſemiſſem. Sed dicere quis poſſit, ſubſtitutum accipere totum, dixit enim teſtator, ILLE MIHI HÆRES ESTO, SI AUTEM NON FIAT, MÆVIUS ESTO *igitur hic, quoniam inſtitutus, qui ſervus eſt, hæres eſſe non poterat, ſubſtitutum oportet in totum aſſem vocari. Sed ad hoc dicendum eſt, verba illa,* SI HÆRES NON ERIT, *ſiquidem inſtitutus eſt alieni juris, atque hoc teſtator novit, ſic intelligere debemus, hoc eſt, ſi neque ipſe inſtitutus hæres fiat, neque alium hæredem faciat, hoc eſt, alii haud acquiſierit, ut ſic ſubſtitutio locum inveniat. Aſt in illo inſtituto, quem ſui eſſe juris teſtator credidit, dictio,* SI HÆRES NON ERIT, *hoc ſignificat, ſi hæreditatem ſibi, aut ei, cujus in poteſtate poſtea eſſe incipiet, non acquiſierit, ut ſubſtitutio locum capiat in univerſum. Hic autem, quoniam alieni juris jam erat, qui credebatur ſui eſſe juris, idcirco ſubſtitutus ſemiſſem accipit. Atque hoc Divus Pius reſcripſit in Parthenio ſervo ſuo. Parthenium enim imperatoris ſervum aliquis credens liberum eſſe, hæredem inſtituit, ſic ſubſtituens ac dicens:* SIN AUTEM PARTHENIUS MIHI HÆRES NON FIAT, MÆVIUS HÆRES ESTO. *Et facta tunc eſt conſtitutio, ut ſemis hæreditatis per Parthenium Cæſari acquireretur, in alterum vero ſemiſſem Mævius ſubſtitutus vocaretur.* Theoph.

TITULUS DECIMUS-SEXTUS.

De pupillari ſubſtitutione.

D. xxviii. T. 6. C. vi. T. 26.

Forma, effectus, origo, et ratio pupillaris ſubſtitutionis.

LIBERIS ſuis impuberibus, quos in poteſtate quis habet, non ſolum ita, ut ſupra diximus, ſubſtituere poteſt, id eſt, ut, ſi hæredes ei non extiterint, alius ſit ei hæres: ſed eo amplius, ut, ſi hæredes ei extiterint, et adhuc impuberes mortui fuerint, ſit eis aliquis hæres: veluti ſi quis dicat hoc modo: *Titius filius hæres mihi eſto; et, ſi filius mihi hæres non erit, ſive hæres erit, et prius moriatur, quam in ſuam tutelam venerit,* id eſt, antequam pubes factus ſit, *tunc Seius hæres eſto.* Quo caſu, ſiquidem non extiterit hæres filius, tunc ſubſtitutus patri fit hæres: ſi vero extiterit hæres filius, et ante pubertatem deceſſerit, ipſi filio fit hæres ſubſtitutus. Nam moribus inſtitutum eſt, ut, cum ejus ætatis filii ſint, in qua ipſi ſibi teſtamentum facere non poſſunt, parentes eis faciant.

A parent can ſubſtitute to his children, who are within puberty, and under his power, not only in the manner before-mentioned, which is thus --- if my children will not be my heirs, let ſome other perſon be my heir --- *but he may write* --- if my children actually become my heirs, but die within puberty, let another become their heir. *for example*, let *Titius*, my ſon, be my heir; and, if he either does not, or does, become my heir, and dies before he ceaſes to be under tutelage, [i. e. *before he arrives at the age of puberty*,] let *Seius* be my heir. *And, in this caſe, if the ſon does not enter upon the inheritance, the ſubſtitute becomes heir to the father; and, if the ſon takes the inheritance, and dies a pupil before the age of puberty, the substitute is then heir to the son. For custom has ordained, that parents may make wills for their children, when their children are not of age to make wills for themselves.*

De substitutione mente capti.

§ I. Qua ratione excitati, etiam constitutionem posuimus in nostro codice, qua prospectum est, ut, si qui mente captos habeant filios, vel nepotes, vel pronepotes, cujuscunque sexus vel gradus, liceat eis, etsi puberes sint, ad exemplum pupillaris substitutionis, certas personas substituere: sin autem resipuerint, eandem substitutionem infirmari sancimus: et hoc ad exemplum pupillaris substitutionis, quæ, postquam pupillus adoleverit, infirmatur.

§ 1. *Excited by humanity, and the reasonableness of the foregoing usage, we have inserted a constitution into our code, by which it is provided, that, if a man has children, grand-children, or great-grand-children, who are mad or disordered in their senses, he may make a substitution of certain persons to such children, in the manner of a pupillary substitution, altho' they are arrived at the age of full puberty. But we have decreed, that this species of substitution shall be void, as soon as they shall have recovered from their disorder; and this we have done in imitation of pupillary substitution, which ceases to be in force, when the minor attains to puberty.*

Infirmari sancimus] *vid Cod* 6. *t.* 26 *l* 9 *ff* 28 *t.* 6 *l* 93.

Proprium pupillaris substitutionis.

§ II. Igitur in pupillari substitutione secundum præfatum modum ordinata duo quodammodo sunt testamenta, alterum patris, alterum filii; tanquam si ipse filius sibi hæredem instituisset: aut certe unum testamentum est duarum causarum, id est, duarum hæreditatum.

§ 2 *In a pupillary substitution, made after the form before-mentioned, there are in a manner two testaments, the one of the father, the other of the son, as if the son had instituted an heir for himself: at least there is, in such a substitution, one testament containing a disposition of two inheritances.*

Alia forma substituendi pupillariter.

§ III. Sin autem quis ita formidolosus sit, ut timeat, ne filius suus pupillus adhuc ex eo, quod palam substitutum acceperit, post obitum ejus periculo insidiarum subjaceat, vulgarem quidem substitutionem palam facere, et in primis testamenti partibus ordinare, debet: illam autem substitutionem, per quam, si hæres extiterit pupillus et intra pubertatem decesserit, substitutus vocatur, separatim in inferioribus partibus scribere debet, eamque partem proprio lino propriaque cera consignare. et in priore parte testamenti cavere, ne inferiores tabulæ, vivo filio et adhuc impubere, aperiantur. Illud palam est, non ideo minus valere substitutionem impuberis filii, quod in iisdem tabulis scripta

ſcripta ſit, quibus ſibi quiſque hæredem inſtituiſſet; quamvis pupillo hoc periculoſum ſit.

§ 3. *If a teſtator is apprehenſive, leſt, at the time of his death, his ſon, being as yet a pupil, ſhould be liable to fraud and impoſition, if a ſubſtitute ſhould be publicly given to him, he ought to inſert a vulgar ſubſtitution in the firſt tablet of his teſtament; and to write that ſubſtitution, in which a ſubſtitute is named,* if his ſon ſhould die within puberty, *in the lower tablet, which ought to be ſeparately tied up and ſealed: and it alſo behoves the teſtator to inſert a clauſe in the firſt part of his teſtament, forbiding the lower part to be opened, whilſt his ſon is alive, and within the age of puberty. But, altho' it is certain, that a ſubſtitution to a ſon within puberty is not leſs valid, becauſe it is writen on the ſame tablet, in which the teſtator hath appointed him to be his heir, it is however unſafe and dangerous.*

Quibus ſubſtituitur.

§ IV. Non ſolum tamen hæredibus inſtitutis impuberibus liberis ita ſubſtituere parentes poſſunt, ut, ſi hæredes eis extiterint, et ante pubertatem mortui fuerint, ſit eis hæres is, quem ipſi voluerint; ſed etiam exhæredatis. Itaque eo caſu, ſi quid exhæredato pupillo ex hæreditatibus, legatiſve, aut donationibus, propinquorum atque amicorum acquiſitum fuerit, id omne ad ſubſtitutum pertinebit. Quæcunque diximus de ſubſtitutione impuberum liberorum, vel hæredum inſtitutorum, vel exhæredatorum, eadem etiam de poſthumis intelligimus.

Parents are not only allowed to give a ſubſtitute to their children within puberty, if ſuch children become their heirs, and die within puberty, but parents are alſo permited to give a ſubſtitute to their diſinherited children, and therefore, whatever a diſinherited child, within the age of puberty, may have acquired by inheritances, by legacies, or by the gift of relations and friends, the whole will become the property of the ſubſtitute. All, which we have hitherto ſaid concerning the ſubſtitution of pupils, whether they are inſtituted heirs, or diſinherited children, is underſtood to extend alſo to poſthumous children.

Pupillare teſtamentum ſequela paterni.

§ V. Liberis autem ſuis teſtamentum nemo facere poteſt, niſi et ſibi faciat, nam pupillare teſtamentum pars et ſequela eſt paterni teſtamenti: adeo ut, ſi patris teſtamentum non valeat, nec filii quidem valebit.

§ 5. *No parent can make a teſtament for his children, unleſs he hath made a teſtament for himſelf for the teſtament of a child within puberty is a part and conſequence of the teſtament of the parent, inſomuch that, if the teſtament of the father is not valid, the teſtament of the ſon will not take effect*

Quot liberis ſubſtituitur.

§ VI. Vel ſingulis autem liberis, vel ei, qui eorum noviſſimus impubes morietur, ſubſtitui poteſt. Singulis quidem, ſi neminem eorum inte-

intestatum decedere voluerit: novissimo, si jus legitimarum hæreditatum integrum inter eos custodiri velit.

§ 6. *A parent may make a pupillary substitution to each of his children, or to him, who shall die the last within puberty. He may substitute to each of his children, if he is unwilling, that any of them should die intestate; and he may substitute to the last, who shall die within puberty, if he is willing, that they should preserve among themselves the intire right of succession.*

De substitutione nominatim aut generaliter facta.

VII. Substituitur autem impuberi aut nominatim, veluti, Titius *hæres esto.* aut generaliter, ut, *Quisquis mihi hæres erit.* Quibus verbis vocantur ex substitutione, impubere mortuo filio, illi, qui et scripti sunt hæredes, et extiterunt, et pro qua parte hæredes facti sunt.

§ 7. *A substitution may be made to a child within puberty, either nominally; as for example* --- If my son becomes my heir, and dies a pupil, let TITIUS be my heir, --- *or generally thus* --- Whoever shall be my heir, let the same person be a substitute to my son, if he dies within puberty. *And, by these general words, all, who have been instituted, and have taken upon them the inheritance of the father, might be called, by virtue of the substitution, to the inheritance of the son, if he dies within puberty, each being intituled to a part of the son's inheritance, in proportion to the share, which he had in the father's.*

Quisquis mihi hæres erit] This general form must be understood to be of use, either when a parent hath appointed many to be his heirs with his son, or hath disinherited his son, and instituted others. But, for the better explanation of this section, it will be proper to set down the words of *Theophilus*, whose paraphrase of the text is a work of great authority, and will always be of infinite use in explaining the institutes "*Præ-" terea nominatim impuberi substituere possum, et di-" cere, si filius meus hæres mihi fuerit, et impubes de-" cesserit, Titius hæres esto. Possum et generaliter " substituere, verbi gratia, multos una cum filio " meo hæredes instituens, aut multis institutis hæredibus " filium exhæredavi. Possum generaliter ita sub-" stituere dicens, quisquis mihi patri hæres erit, " is et filio meo ante pubertatem morienti substitutus " esto. Per quæ verba, ex substitutione ad heredi-" tatem impuberis venient, qui et scripti sunt hæredes " et exstiterunt. Nam, si instituti hæreditatem ex " principali parte repudiaverint, ex pupillari sub-" stitutione nil capient, dividitur autem inter eos " pupilli hæreditas pro portione hæreditaria, i. e. pro " qua parte patri hæredes facti sunt."* Theoph. h. t.

Quemodo substitutio pupillaris finitur.

§ VIII. Masculo igitur usque ad quatuordecim annos substitui potest: fœminæ usque ad duodecim annos. Et, si hoc tempus excesserint, substitutio evanescit.

§ 8. *A pupillary substitution may be made to males, till they arrive at fourteen complete, and to females, till they have completed their twelfth year; and, when they exceed either of these ages, the substitution becomes extinct.*

Quibus pupillariter non substituitur.

§ IX. Extraneo vero vel filio puberi hæredi instituto ita substituere nemo potest, ut, si hæres extiterit, et intra aliquod tempus decesserit, alius ei sit hæres: sed hoc solum permissum est, ut eum per fideicommissum

miſſum teſtator obliget alii hæreditatem ejus vel totam vel pro parte reſtituere: quod jus quale ſit, ſuo loco trademus.

§ 9 *A pupillary ſubſtitution cannot be made with effect, either to a ſtranger, who is inſtituted, or even to a ſon, who is inſtituted, if his age excedes that of puberty. But a teſtator may oblige his heir to give to another either a part, or even the whole of the inheritance, by virtue of a* fidei-commiſſum, *or gift in truſt, which we will treat of in it's proper place.*

TITULUS DECIMUS-SEPTIMUS.

Quibus modis teſtamenta infirmantur.

D. xxviii. T. 3.

Quibus modis teſtamenta infirmentur.

TEſtamentum jure factum uſque eo valet, donec rumpatur, irritumve fiat.

A Teſtament, legally made, remains valid, until it is either broken, or rendered ineffectual.

Quando teſtamentum dicatur rumpi. Primum de adoptione.

§ I. Rumpitur autem teſtamentum, cum, in eodem ſtatu manente teſtatore, ipſius teſtamenti jus vitiatur. Si quis enim poſt factum teſtamentum adoptaverit ſibi filium per imperatorem eum, qui eſt ſui juris, aut per prætorem, ſecundum noſtram conſtitutionem, eum, qui in poteſtate parentis fuerit, teſtamentum ejus rumpitur quaſi agnatione ſui hæredis.

§ I. *A teſtament is ſaid to be broken, or revoked, when the force of it is deſtroyed, whilſt the teſtator ſtill remains in the ſame ſtate For, if a teſtator, after making his teſtament, ſhould arrogate an independent perſon, by licence from the emperor, or in the preſence of the prætor, ſhould adopt a child under the power of his natural parent, by virtue of our conſtitution, then that teſtament would be broken by this* quaſi *birth of a proper heir.*

Secundum noſtram conſtitutionem] 2 *Cod* t 48 *l* 10.

De

De posteriori testamento.

§ II. Posteriore quoque testamento, quod jure perfectum est, superius rumpitur: nec interest, extiterit aliquis hæres ex eo, an non. Hoc enim solum spectatur, an aliquo casu existere potuerit. Ideoque, si quis aut noluerit hæres esse, aut vivo testatore, aut post mortem ejus, antequam hæreditatem adiret, decesserit, aut conditione, sub qua hæres institutus est, defectus sit, in his casibus pater-familias intestatus moritur. Nam et prius testamentum non valet, ruptum à posteriore; et posterius æque nullas vires habet, cum ex eo nemo hæres extiterit.

§ 2. A former testament, altho' legally perfect, may be broken or revoked by a subsequent testament, nor is it material, whether the heir, nominated in the later testament, can or will take the heirship at the death of the testator; for the only thing regarded is, whether he might have been the heir: and therefore, if an instituted heir should refuse to take the heirship, or should die, living the testator, or after his death, and before he could enter upon the inheritance, or if he should die, before the the condition is accomplished, upon which he was instituted, then, in any of these cases, the testator would die intestate, for the first testament would be invalid, being broken or revoked by the second, and the second would be of as little force, for want of an heir.

De posteriore, in quo hæres certæ rei institutus.

§ III. Sed, si quis, priore testamento jure perfecto, posterius æque jure fecerit, etiamsi ex certis rebus in eo hæredem instituerit, superius tamen testamentum sublatum esse, Divi Severus et Antoninus Augusti rescripserunt: cujus constitutionis verba et hic inseri jussimus, cum aliud quoque præterea in ea constitutione expressum sit. *Imperatores Severus et Antoninus Augusti Cocceio Campano. Testamentum secundo loco factum, licet in eo certarum rerum hæres scriptus sit, perinde jure valere, ac si rerum mentio facta non esset: sed et teneri hæredem scriptum, ut contentus rebus sibi datis, aut suppleta quarta ex lege Falcidia, hæreditatem restituat his, qui in priore testamento scripti fuerant, propter inserta fidei-commissi verba, quibus ut valeret prius testamentum expressum est, dubitari non oportet.* Et ruptum quidem testamentum hoc modo efficitur.

§ 3. If a man, who has already made a testament legally perfect, should make a subsequent testament equally good, and institute an heir in it to some particular things only, the emperors Severus *and* Antoninus *have by rescript declared, that, in this case, the first will shall be broken or revoked, as a testament. But we have commanded the words of this constitution to be here inserted." The emperors* Severus *and* Antoninus *to* Cocceius Campanus. We determine, that a second testament, altho' the heir named in it is not universal, but instituted to particular things only, shall be as good in law, as if no mention had been made of particular things; yet it is not to be doubted, but that the writen heir shall be obliged to content himself either with the things given him, or with the fourth part, allowed by the *Falcidian* law, and shall be bound to restore the rest of the inheritance to

to the heirs instituted in the first testament, on account of the words, denoting a trust, inserted in the second testament, by which words it is expresly declared, that the first testament shall subsist. --- *And, in this manner, a testament may be said to be broken or cancelled.*

In ea constitutione] *vid ff* 36 *t.* 1 *l,* 29.
Ex lege Falcidia] *vid. titulum* 22 *hujus libri.*

De testamento irrito; et quibus modis fit irritum.

§ IV. Alio autem modo testamenta jure facta infirmantur; veluti cum is, qui fecit testamentum, capite diminutus sit: quod, quibus modis accidat, primo libro retulimus.

§ 4. *Testaments, legally made, are also invalidated, if the testator suffers diminution, that is, changes his condition. and, in the first book of our institutes, we have shewed by what means diminution, or a change of state, may happen.*

Cur dicatur irritum.

§ V. Hoc autem casu irrita fieri testamenta dicuntur; cum alioqui, et quæ rumpuntur, irrita fiant, et ea, quæ statim ab initio non jure fiunt, irrita sint. Sed et ea, quæ jure facta sunt, et postea per capitis diminutionem irrita fiunt, possumus nihilominus rupta dicere. Sed, quia sane commodius erat, singulas causas singulis appellationibus distingui, ideo quædam non jure facta dicuntur, quædam jure facta rumpi vel irrita fieri.

§ 5 *In the case of diminution, testaments are said to become* irrita, *i e ineffectual; altho' those, which are broken or revoked, and those, which from the beginning were not legal, do all equally become ineffectual* [*or* irrita] *in reality. We may also term those testaments broken, which are at first legally made, but are afterwards rendered ineffectual, by diminution, or change of state. But, as it is proper, that every particular defect should be distinguished by a particular appellation, those testaments, which are illegal, are termed* null, --- *those, which were at first legal, but afterwards lose their force, by some revocatory act of the testator, are said to be* rupta, *or broken; and those, since the making of which, the testator hath suffered a change of state, are said to be* irrita, *or ineffectual.*

Quibus modis convalescit.

§ VI. Non tamen per omnia inutilia sunt ea testamenta, quæ, ab initio jure facta, per capitis diminutionem irrita facta sunt: nam, si septem testium signis signata sunt, potest scriptus hæres, secundum tabulas testamenti, bonorum possessionem agnoscere; si modo defunctus et civis Romanus, et suæ potestatis, mortis tempore fuerit. Nam, si ideo irritum factum sit testamentum, quia civitatem vel etiam libertatem testator amisit, aut quia in adoptionem se dedit, et mortis tempore in adoptivi patris potestate sit, non potest scriptus hæres secundum tabulas bonorum possessionem petere.

§ 6 *But a testament, which was at first legally made, and hath afterwards been rendered void by diminution, is not always without effect; for the writen heir is intituled to the possession of the goods, by virtue of the testament, if it appears, that it was sealed by seven witnesses, and that the testator was a* Roman *citizen, and not under power, at the time of his death but, if a testament become void, because the testator had lost the right of a citizen, or his liberty, or had given himself in adoption, and at the time of his death, still continued under the power of his adoptive father, than the writen heir could not demand the possession of the goods, in consequence of the testament.*

De nuda voluntate.

§ VII. Ex eo autem solo non potest infirmari testamentum, quod postea testator id noluerit valere. usque adeo ut, si quis, post factum prius testamentum, posterius facere cœperit, et, aut mortalitate præventus, aut quia eum ejus rei pœnituit, id non perfecerit, Divi Pertinacis oratione cautum sit, ne alias tabulæ priores, jure factæ, irritæ fiant, nisi sequentes jure ordinatæ et perfectæ fuerint: nam imperfectum testamentum sine dubio nullum est.

§ 7 *A testament cannot be invalidated solely, because the testator was afterwards unwilling, that it should subsist, so that, if a man, after making one testament, should begin another, and by reason of death, or change of mind, should not proceed to perfect that testament, it is provided by the oration or ordinance of the emperor* Pertinax, *that the first testament shall not be revoked, unless the second is both legal and perfect, for an imperfect testament is undoubtedly null.*

Pertinacis oratione] The emperors were accustomed to speak orations in the senate, or send them to the senate in writing, and the decrees were afterwards drawn up according to the tenor of those speeches or orations *ff* 23 *t* 2 *l* 16 *Vinn.*

Si princeps litis causa, vel ob testamentum imperfectum, institutus fuerit.

§ VIII. Eadem oratione expressit, non admissurum se hæreditatem ejus qui litis causa principem reliquerit hæredem: neque tabulas non legitime factas, in quibus ipse ob eam causam hæres institutus erat, probaturum. neque ex nuda voce hæredis nomen admissurum: neque ex ulla scriptura, cui juris auctoritas desit, aliquid adepturum Secundum hoc Divi Severus et Antoninus sæpissime rescripserunt. *Licet enim,* inquiunt, *legibus soluti simus, attamen legibus vivimus.*

§ 8 *The emperor* Pertinax *hath declared by the same ordinance, that he would not take the inheritance of any testator, who left him his heir, because a law-suit was depending --- that he would never establish a will, deficient in point of form, if he was upon that account instituted the heir --- that he would by no means suffer himself to be nominated an heir by the mere word of mouth of a testator, and that he would never take any emolument by virtue of any writing whatever, not authorised by the strict rules of law. The emperors* Severus *and* Antoninus *have*

have alſo often iſſued reſcripts to the ſame purpoſe: " for altho', [ſay they,] we are " certainly not ſubject to the laws, yet we live in obedience to them.

Legibus vivimus] " Claudianus poeta, in " panegyr. v 307. de quarto conſulatu Hono- " rii, his verſibus principem hujus officii ſic " commonefacit.

" In commune jubes ſi quid, cenſeſve tenendum,
" Primus juſſa ſubi. tunc obſervantior æqui
" Fit populus, nec ferre negat, cum viderit ipſum
" Auctorem parere ſibi. Componitur orbis
" Regis ad exemplum, nec ſic inflectere ſenſus
" Humanos edicta valent, ut vita Regentis."

Vinn.

TITULUS DECIMUS-OCTAVUS.

De inofficioſo teſtamento.

D. v. T 2. C. iii. T. 28.

Ratio hujus querelæ.

QUIA plerumque parentes ſine cauſa liberos ſuos exhæredant vel omittunt, inductum eſt, ut de inofficioſo teſtamento agere poſſint liberi, qui queruntur, aut inique ſe exhæredatos, aut inique præteritos: hoc colore, quaſi non ſanæ mentis fuerint, cum teſtamentum ordinarent. Sed hoc dicitur, non quaſi vere furioſus ſit, ſed recte quidem teſtamentum fecerit, non autem ex officio pietatis. Nam, ſi vere furioſus ſit, nullum teſtamentum eſt.

Inaſmuch as parents often diſinherit their children without cauſe or omit to mention them in their teſtaments, it has therefore been introduced, as law, that children, who have been unjuſtly diſinherited or unjuſtly omited in the teſtaments of their parents, may complain, that ſuch teſtaments are inofficious, under color, that their parents were not of ſane mind, when they made them. but, in theſe caſes, it is not averred to be ſtrictly true, that the teſtator was really mad or diſordered in his ſenſes, but it is urged as a mere fiction only; for the teſtament is acknowledged to have been well made, and the only exception to it is, that the teſtament is not conſiſtent with the duty of a parent. For, if a teſtator was really not in his ſenſes at the time of making his teſtament, it is certainly null.

Quia plerumque parentes] The plaint, or action, in the caſe of an undutiful teſtament, which civilians call *teſtamentum inofficioſum*, is not in uſe in *England*, where, by the common law, all perſons, intituled to make a will, have ever had a free power of bequeathing their goods and chattels, in whatever manner they thought beſt, and it was only by the particular cuſtom of ſome places, that this power was reſtrained ſo that the writ called *breve de rationabili parte bonorum*, which the wife or children of the deceaſed had againſt the executors for the recovery of part of the goods, was not general throughout the kingdom, but peculiar to certain countries, where the cuſtom was, that, debts being paid, the remainder ſhould be divided into three equal parts, *viz* one to the wife, another to the children, and a third to attend the will of the teſtator *Cowel lib* 2 *t* 18

The cuſtom of reſerving a reaſonable part of the goods for the widows and children of teſtators is ſtill in force in the city of *London*, as to the widows and children of freemen, but in other parts of the kingdom, where this cuſtom did formerly prevail, it has been aboliſhed by act of parliament, ſee 4 and 5 *Will* and *Mary*, *cap* 6. The inhabitants of the province of *York* are alſo impowered to diſpoſe of their perſonal eſtates by their wills, notwithſtanding the cuſtom of that province, as to the reaſonable part claimed by widows and children; but the act excepts the cities of *York* and *Chester*; yet the same liberty was afterwards extended to the freemen of the city of *York*, by the statute of the 2d and 3d of Queen *Anne* And by the 7th and 8th of *William* the 3d, *cap* 38 the same custom was abolished in the principality of *Wales*. See Dr *Strahan's* notes on *Domat*, vol 2 p 109 — But, by the law of *Scotland*, a testator cannot by testament deprive his wife or children of their legitime or reasonable part *Stair's inst lib.* 3 *t* 8 *Mackenzie's inst lib* 3 *t* 9 *p* 251

Hoc colore] This pretext was made use of to avoid the appearance of impugning the testament of a man in his senses, contrary to the authority of the 12 tables, which give all persons, capable of making a will, a free and uncontroled power of bequeathing their effects just as they think proper. "*Verbis legis* 12 *tabularum* "*his*, uti legassit suæ rei, ita jus esto, *latissima* "*potestas tributa videtur, et hæredis instituendi, et* "*legata et libertates dandi, tutelas quoque con-* "*stituendi, sed id interpretatione coangustatum est.* "*&c. ff* 50 *t.* 16. *l* 120. de verb sign."

Qui de inofficioso agunt.

§ I. Non autem liberis tantum permissum est testamentum parentum inofficiosum accusare, verum etiam liberorum parentibus: soror autem et frater turpibus personis scriptis hæredibus ex sacris constitutionibus prælati sunt. Non ergo contra omnes hæredes agere possunt. Ultra fratres igitur et sorores cognati nullo modo aut agere possunt, aut agentes vincere.

§ 1. *Children are not the only persons allowed to complain, that testaments are inofficious, for parents are in like manner permited to make the same complaint Also the brothers and sisters of a testator are, by virtue of the imperial constitutions, prefered to infamous persons, if any such have been instituted by the deceased to be his heirs, but brothers and sisters are not therefore allowed to make a complaint against any heir, whom the testator shall have instituted. And collaterals, beyond brothers and sisters, can by no means complain of the undutifulness of a testament, if their right to complain is opposed; but if their right of complaining is not disputed and the testament is annulled, yet those only can be benefited, who are the nearest in succession upon the intestacy.*

Constitutionibus] *vid Cod* 3 *t* 28 *ll* 21 27.

Aut agentes vincere] *Si quis, ex iis personis quæ ad successionem ab intestato non admittuntur, de inofficioso egerit, [nemo eorum eum repellit,] et ipse obtinuerit, non ei prosit victoria, sed his, qui habent ab intestato successionem ff.* 5. *t* 2 *l* 6

Qui alio jure veniunt, de inofficioso non agunt.

§ II Tam autem naturales liberi, quam secundum nostræ constitutionis divisionem adoptati, ita demum de inofficioso testamento agere possunt, si nullo alio jure ad defuncti bona venire possint: nam, qui ad hæreditatem totam vel partem ejus alio jure veniunt, de inofficioso agere non possunt. Posthumi quoque, qui nullo alio jure venire possunt, de inofficioso agere possunt

§ 2 *Adopted children, according to the distinction taken in our constitution, are admitted, as well as natural children, to complain against a testament, as inofficious, if they can obtain the effects of the deceased no other way, but, if they can get the whole or a part of the inheritance by any other means, they then cannot bring a complaint of undutifulness against the testament Posthumous children also, who are unable to recover their inheritance by any other method, are allowed to bring this complaint.*

Secundum

Secundum nostræ constitutionis divisionem] *vid Cod* 8 *t* 48. *l.* 10

Si nullo alio jure] When a complaint against a testament, as inofficious, is well founded, it affects the character and memory of the deceased, who cannot be thought to have acted as became him this complaint therefore was regarded as an extraordinary remedy, and never allowed to be made, but by those, who had no other and thus emancipated children, who had been pretermited in the testament of their father could not complain of that testament as inofficious, because the *Prætorian* law gave them another remedy, to wit, the possession of the goods, contrary to the letter of the testament *vid. Vinn h. t.*

De eo, cui testator aliquid reliquit.

§ III. Sed hæc ita accipienda sunt, si nihil eis penitus a testatoribus testamento relictum est: quod nostra constitutio ad verecundiam naturæ introduxit. Sin vero quantacunque pars hæreditatis, vel res, eis fuerit relicta, de inofficioso querela quiescente, id, quod eis deest, usque ad quartam legitimæ partis repleatur, licet non fuerit adjectum, boni viri arbitratu debere eam compleri.

§ 3 *What we have hitherto said must be understood to take place only, when nothing has been left by the will of the deceased; [and this hath been introduced by our constitution out of reverence to parents and the ties of nature·] for, if any single thing, or the least part of an inheritance, hath been bequeathed to those, who have a right to a fourth part or legitime portion of the testator's estate, they are barred from bringing a querele or complaint against the testament, as undutiful, but are intituled by action to recover whatever sum is wanting to complete their legitime, altho' it was not added by the testator,* that their legitime portion should be completed according to the arbitration of some person of an approved character.

Constitutio ad verecundiam] *vid Cod* 3 *t* 28 *l* 30

Si tutor, cui nihil a patre relictum, pupilli nomine legatum acceperit.

§ IV. Si tutor nomine pupilli, cujus tutelam gerebat, ex testamento patris sui legatum acceperit, cum nihil erat ipsi tutori relictum a patre suo, nihilominus poterit nomine suo de inofficioso patris testamento agere

§ 4 *If a tutor should accept a legacy in the name of his pupil, in consequence of a bequest made in the testament of such tutor's father, who left nothing to his son, the tutor may nevertheless complain in his own name against the testament of his father, as undutiful*

Si de inofficioso nomine pupilli agens succubuerit.

§ V. Sed, si e contrario pupilli nomine, cui nihil relictum fuerat, de inofficioso egerit et superatus est, ipse tutor, quod sibi in testamento eodem relictum est, non amittit.

§ 5 *And, on the contrary, if a tutor should bring a complaint of undutifulness in the name of his pupil, against the testament of his pupil's father, who left nothing to his son, and this testament should be confirmed by sentence, yet the tutor would not af-*

terwards be barred, on account of this proceeding, from taking whatever was left him in that testament, which he controverted only for the benefit of his pupil and by virtue of his office.

De quarta legitimæ partis.

§ VI. Igitur quartam quis debet habere, ut de inofficioso agere non possit, sive jure hæreditario, sive jure legati vel fidei-commissi, vel si mortis causa ei quarta donata fuerit, vel inter vivos in iis tantummodo casibus, quorum mentionem nostra facit constitutio, vel aliis modis, qui in nostris constitutionibus continentur. Quod autem de quarta diximus, ita intelligendum est, ut, sive unus fuerit, sive plures, quibus agere de inofficioso testamento permittitur, una quarta eis dari possit, ut ea pro rata eis distribuatur, id est, pro virili portione quarta.

§ 6. *No person, who hath right, can be hindered from bringing a complaint of undutifulness, unless he hath in some manner received his fourth or legitime part, as by being appointed heir, by having a legacy, or by means of a trust for his use; or unless his legitime part hath been given him by donation* propter mortem, *or even* inter vivos, [*in those cases, of which our constitution makes mention,*] *or by any other means set forth in our ordinances. What we have said of the fourth or legitime is to be so understood, that, if there are more persons than one, who have a right to bring a plaint of undutifulness against a testament, yet one fourth will be sufficient, divided among them all in equal portions.*

Facit constitutio.] *vid. Cod.* 3. *t.* 28. *l.* 35.

TITULUS DECIMUS-NONUS.

De hæredum qualitate et differentia.

D. xxix. T. 11. C. vi. T. 31.

Divisio hæredum.

HÆREDES autem aut necessarii dicuntur, aut sui et necessarii, aut extranei.

Heirs are divided into three sorts, called proper; proper *and* necessary; *and* strangers

De hæredibus necessariis.

§ I. Necessarius hæres est servus hæres institutus: ideoque sic appellatur, quia, sive velit, sive nolit, omnino post mortem testatoris protinus liber

liber et necessarius hæres fit. Unde, qui facultates suas suspectas habent, solent servum suum primo aut secundo aut etiam ulteriore gradu hæredem instituere: ut, si creditoribus satis non fiat, potius ejus hæredis bona, quam ipsius testatoris, a creditoribus possideantur, vel distrahantur, vel inter eos dividantur. Pro hoc tamen incommodo illud ei commodum præstatur, ut ea, quæ post mortem patroni sui sibi acquisierit, ipsi reserventur. Et quamvis bona defuncti non sufficiant creditoribus, iterum tamen ex ea causa res ejus, quas sibi acquisierit, non væneunt.

§ 1. *A slave, instituted by his master, is a necessary heir; and he is so called, because at the death of the testator he becomes instantly free, and is compellable to take the heirship; he therefore, who suspects his circumstances, commonly institutes his slave to be his heir in the first, second, or some other place; so that, if he does not leave a sum equal to his debts, the goods, which are seized, sold, or divided among his creditors, may rather seem to be those of his heir, than his own But a slave, in recompense of this dishonor, is allowed to reserve to himself whatever he hath acquired after the death of his patron; for such acquisitions are not to be sold, altho' the goods of the deceased are ever so insufficient for the payment of his creditors.*

De suis hæredibus.

§ II. Sui autem et necessarii hæredes sunt, veluti filius filia, nepos neptisve ex filio, et deinceps cæteri liberi, qui in potestate morientis modo fuerint. Sed, ut nepos neptisve sui hæredes sint, non sufficit eum eamve in potestate avi mortis tempore fuisse: sed opus est, ut pater ejus vivo patre suo desierit suus hæres esse, aut morte interceptus, aut qualibet alia ratione liberatus a patria potestate: tunc enim nepos neptisve in locum patris sui succedit. Sed sui quidem hæredes ideo appellantur, quia domestici hæredes sunt, et vivo quoque patre quodammodo domini existimantur. Unde etiam, si quis intestatus moriatur, prima causa est in successione liberorum. Necessarii vero ideo dicuntur, quia omnino, sive velint, sive nolint, tam ab intestato quam ex testamento, ex lege duodecim tabularum hæredes fiunt. Sed his prætor permittit volentibus abstinere hæreditate, ut potius parentis quam ipsorum bona similiter a creditoribus possideantur.

§ 2. *Proper and necessary heirs are sons, daughters, grandsons or grand-daughters by a son or any other descendents in the direct line, who were in the power of the deceased at the time of his death. But, in order to constitute grandchildren proper or domestic heirs, it does not suffice, that they were in the power of their grandfather at the time of his decease, but it is requisite, that their father should have ceased to be a proper heir in the life-time of his father, by having been freed, either by death or some other means, from paternal authority, for then it is, that the grandson or grand daughter succeeds in the place of their father. And note, that heirs are called* sui *or proper, because they are domestic; and in the very life-time of their father are reputed masters or proprietors of the inheritance in a certain degree. Hence it is, that, if a man dies inteſtate, his children are prefered before all others to the ſucceſſion; and are called neceſſary heirs, becauſe, willing or unwilling, they become the heirs of their parent according to the law of the 12 tables, either by virtue of a teſtament or in conſequence of an inteſtacy. But, when children requeſt it, the prætor permits them to abſtain from the inheritance, that the effects of their parents, rather than their own, may be ſeized by the creditors*

De extraneis.

§ III Cæteri, qui teſtatoris juri ſubjecti non ſunt, extranei hæredes appellantur. Itaque liberi noſtri, qui in poteſtate noſtra non ſunt, hæredes a nobis inſtituti, extranei hæredes nobis videntur. Qua de cauſa et qui hæredes a matre inſtituuntur eodem numero ſunt. quia fœminæ in poteſtate liberos non habent. Servus quoque hæres a domino inſtitutus, et poſt ſactum teſtamentum ab eo manumiſſus, eodem numero habetur.

§ 3 *But all other heirs, not ſubject to the power of the teſtator at the time of his death, are called ſtrangers thus even children, who are not under the power of their father, but yet are conſtituted his heirs, are reckoned ſtrangers in a legal ſenſe: and, for the ſame reaſon, children, inſtituted heirs by their mother, are alſo reputed ſtrangers, for a woman is not allowed to have her children under her own power A ſlave alſo, whom his maſter hath inſtituted by teſtament and afterwards manumited, is numbered among thoſe heirs, who are called ſtrangers*

De teſtamenti factione.

§ IV. In extraneis hæredibus illud obſervatur, ut ſit cum eis teſtamenti factio, ſive hæredes ipſi inſtituantur, ſive ii, qui poteſtate eorum ſunt. Et id duobus temporibus inſpicitur: teſtamenti quidem facti tempore, ut conſtiterit inſtitutio: mortis vero teſtatoris, ut effectum habeat Hoc amplius, et, cum adit hæreditatem, eſſe debet cum eo teſtamenti factio, ſive pure ſive ſub conditione hæres inſtitutus ſit. Nam jus hæredis eo maxime tempore inſpiciendum eſt, quo acquirit hæreditatem Medio autem tempore, inter factum teſtamentum et mortem teſtatoris vel conditionem inſtitutionis exiſtentem, mutatio juris non nocet hæredi quia, ut diximus, tria tempora inſpici debent. Teſtamenti autem factionem non ſolum is habere videtur, qui teſtamentum facere poteſt: ſed etiam, qui ex alieno teſtamento vel ipſe capere poteſt vel alii acquirere, licet non poſſit facere teſtamentum. Et ideo furioſus, et mutus, et poſthumus, et infans, et filius-familias, et ſervus alienus, teſtamenti factionem habere dicuntur. Licet enim teſtamentum facere non poſſint attamen ex teſtamento vel ſibi vel alii acquirere poſſunt.

§ 4 *In regard to ſtrangers, it is requiſite, that they ſhould be capable of the faction of a teſtament, whether they are inſtituted heirs themſelves, or whether thoſe, under their power, are inſtituted. And this qualification is required at two ſeveral times*

times; —— *at the time of making the testament, that the institution may be valid; and at the time of the testator's death, that such institution may take effect. and farther, whether an heir is appointed simply or conditionally, yet he ought to be capable of the faction of a testament at the time of entering upon the inheritance, for his right is principally regarded at the time of acquiring the possession But, in the intermediate time, between the making of the testament and the death of the testator, or the completion of the condition of the institution, the heir will not be prejudiced by incapacity or change of state, because the three particular times, which we have mentioned, are the times to be regarded But a man, capable of giving his effects by testament, is not the only person, who is said to have* testamenti factionem; *for whoever is capable of taking for the benefit of himself, or of acquiring by testament for the benefit of another, is also understood to have the faction of a testament and therefore persons mad, mute, or posthumous, also infants, the sons of a family, or slaves not your own, may all be said to have the faction of a testament in it's passive signification. For, altho' such persons are incapable of making a testament, yet they are capable of acquiring by testament, either for themselves or others*

De jure deliberandi, et de beneficio inventarii.

§ V. Extraneis autem hæredibus deliberandi potestas est de adeunda hæreditate vel non adeunda. Sed, sive is, cui abstinendi potestas est, immiscuerit se bonis hæreditatis, sive extraneus, cui de adeunda hæreditate deliberare licet, adierit, postea relinquendæ hæreditatis facultatem non habet, nisi minor sit 25 annis: nam hujusmodi ætatis hominibus, sicut in cæteris omnibus causis, deceptis, ita et si temere damnosam hæreditatem susceperint, prætor succurrit. Sciendum est tamen, Divum Hadrianum etiam majori 25 annis veniam dedisse, cum post aditam hæreditatem grande æs alienum, quod aditæ hæreditatis tempore latebat, emersisset. Sed hoc quidem Divus Hadrianus cuidam speciali beneficio præstitit. Divus autem Gordianus postea militibus tantummodo hoc concessit. Sed nostra benevolentia commune omnibus subjectis imperio nostro hoc beneficium præstitit: et constitutionem tam æquissimam quam nobilissimam scripsit, cujus tenorem si observaverint homines, licet eis adire hæreditatem, et in tantum teneri, quantum valere bona hæreditatis contingit: ut ex hac causa neque deliberationis auxilium sit eis necessarium, nisi, omissa observatione nostræ constitutionis, et deliberandum existimaverint, et sese veteri gravamini aditionis supponere maluerint.

§ 5 *Strangers, who are appointed heirs, have the power of deliberating, whether they will, or will not, enter upon an inheritance But, if even a proper or domestic heir, who has the liberty of abstaining, should intermeddle, or, if a stranger, who is permitted to deliberate, should once take on inheritance, it will not afterwards be in his power to renounce it, unless he was under the age of 25 years: for the prætor, who in all other cases relieves minors, who have been deceived, affords them equal assistance, when they rashly take upon themselves an injurious inheritance And here it must be noted, that the emperor* Adrian *once gave permission to a major, or person of* [illegible] *full age, to relinquish an inheritance, when it appeared to be incumbered with a great debt, which had been concealed, till the heir had taken upon himself the administration. But this permission was granted as a very special instance of beneficence. The emperor* Gordian *afterwards promulged a constitution for the indemnification of heirs, yet confined the force of it to those only, who were of the soldiery. But our extended benevolence hath rendered this benefit common to all our subjects in general, having dictated a constitution both just and noble, which, if heirs will strictly observe, they may enter upon their inheritance, and not be made farther chargeable, than the value of the estate will extend; so that they are under no necessity of praying a time for deliberation, unless they omit to observe the tenor of our ordinance, chusing rather to deliberate and submit themselves to the danger attending the acceptance of an inheritance according to the antient law.*

Sed nostra benevolentia] The power of deliberating was obtained after the following manner —the heir, who was called to a succession, either by virtue of a testament or by a right to succeed *ab intestato*, made application to a magistrate for a time to deliberate, upon which a delay was always granted him of at least an hundred days, in which he might examine the circumstances of the deceased, and, by the antient law, the testator himself might have fixed a certain time, in which his appointed heir must either take the inheritance, or, by suffering that time to elapse, intirely exclude himself This appointment of a certain time was called *Cretion*, [from *crevi* a *cernere* to decree] and was afterwards forbidden by the emperors *Arcadius*, *Honorius*, and *Theodosius*, in these words " *Scrupulosam Cretionum solennitatem hac lege penitus amputari decernimus* Cod 6 t 30 l. 17 "

This power of deliberating was of no other use than to give the heir time to examine the affairs of the deceased, at the expiration of which, the heir was obliged either to accept the inheritance simply, or renounce it, without being at liberty to chuse any middle way, and from hence followed many inconveniences to legataries and creditors, as well as to heirs — The law however continued the same, and heirs were without remedy, except that given by the emperor *Gordian* to the soldiery, till the reign of *Justinian*, who established, in favor of heirs in general a liberty of accepting an inheritance with the benefit of an inventary, *i e* on condition, that they shall not be liable to actions beyond the value of the goods, of which an inventary ought to be made by a public officer; the effect of which is, that creditors, legataries, and other persons concerned, may have a just account of all the goods, and that the heir does not engage his own estate, but obliges himself only to be answerable for what is contained in the inventary, yet the benefit of an inventary has not abolished the use of deliberating *Cod* 6. *t*. 30. *l ult*. *Domat lib* 1. *t* 2. *part* 2

In *England* all executors and administrators are allowed the benefit of an inventary of course, and are supposed to accept the succession always under that benefit, so that, if they exhibit an inventary upon oath, they are no farther accountable than for what is contained in that inventary, unless the creditors or legatees can prove, that there are more goods belonging to the succession, than are set down in the inventary, in which case the executors or administrators will be obliged to charge themselves; but, if an executor will make no inventary, then every legatary may recover his whole legacy; for, in this case, the law presumes, that there are sufficient effects to pay all the legacies, and that the executor hath fraudulently substracted them, whereas, when an inventary is given, the executor is presumed not to have any more of the testator's goods in his possession, than were described in the inventary, if lawfully made *Swin*, part 3 sec 17 page 228

Et constitutionem tam æquissimam] *vid. Cod*, 6 *t* 30 *l* 22

De acquirenda vel omittenda hæreditate.

§ VI. Item extraneus hæres testamento institutus, aut ab intestato ad legitimam hæreditatem vocatus, potest aut pro hærede gerendo, aut etiam nuda voluntate suscipiendæ hæreditatis, hæres fieri. Pro hærede autem gerere quis videtur, si rebus hæreditariis tanquam hæres utatur, vel vendendo res hæreditarias, vel prædia colendo, locandove: et quo-

quoquo modo voluntatem ſuam declaret, vel re, vel verbo, de adeunda hæreditate: dummodo ſciat, eum, in cujus bonis pro hærede gerit, teſtatum inteſtatumve obiiſſe, et ſe ei hæredem eſſe. Pro hærede enim gerere eſt pro domino gerere. Veteres enim hæredes pro dominis appellabant. Sicut autem nuda voluntate extraneus hæres fit, ita contraria deſtinatione ſtatim ab hæreditate repellitur. Eum, qui ſurdus vel mutus natus vel poſtea factus eſt, nihil prohibet pro hærede gerere, et acquirere ſibi hæreditatem; ſi tamen intelligit, quod agit.

§ 6. *A ſtranger, who is inſtituted by teſtament, or called by law to take a ſucceſſion in caſe of an inteſtacy, may make himſelf accountable as heir, either by doing ſome act as ſuch; or by barely ſignifying his acceptance of the heirſhip And a man is deemed to act, as the heir of an inheritance, if he treats it as his own, by ſelling any part of it, by cultivating the ground, or by tilling it; or even if he declares his conſent to accept it in any manner, either by act or ſpeech; when he knows, at the ſame time, that the perſon, with whoſe eſtate he intermeddles, is dead teſtate or inteſtate, and that he himſelf is the heir. for to act as heir is to act as proprietor; and the antients frequently uſed the term heir, when they would denote the proprietor of an eſtate. But as a ſtranger may become an heir by a bare conſent only, ſo on the contrary, by a mere diſſent, he may bar himſelf from an inheritance. And nothing prevents, but that a perſon, who was born deaf and dumb, or became ſo by accident, may, by acting as heir, either acquire the advantages or bring upon himſelf the diſadvantages of an inheritance, if he was ſenſible of what he was doing, and that he was acting in the capacity of an heir.*

Item extraneus hæres] The law of *England* takes no notice of proper or domeſtic heirs, and therefore can make no diſtinction between *ſui hæredes* and *extranei*, but, in *England*, if an executor [who may be regarded as the heir of perſonal eſtate] once intermeddles with the eſtate of the teſtator, he ſhall not afterwards be permitted to renounce his executorſhip, and yet he is not liable *de bonis propriis* to pay more than he has received, unleſs in ſome particular caſes, as when he hath waſted the eſtate of the deceaſed, or acted otherwiſe improperly and diſhoneſtly — and even an executor *de ſon tort* ſhall in general be charged only to the amount of the goods wrongfully adminiſtered by him 1 Mod. 21, *Parten* v. *Baſeden* — S. mb [illegible]

TITULUS VIGESIMUS.

De legatis.

D. xxx. xxxi. xxxii. C. vi. T. 37.

Continuatio.

POST hæc videamus de legatis: quæ pars juris extra propositam quidem materiam videtur: nam loquimur de iis juris figuris, quibus per universitatem res nobis acquiruntur: sed, cum omnino de testamentis et de hæredibus, qui in testamento instituuntur, loquuti simus, non sine causa sequenti loco potest hæc juris materia tractari.

After what has been said, we will make some observations upon the doctrine of legacies; altho' a discussion of this part of the law may not seem exactly to fall in with the subject proposed; for we are treating only of those legal methods, by which things may be acquired universally: but, as we have already spoken at large of testaments and testamentary heirs, it is not without reason, that we intend to treat of legacies in the following paragraphs.

Definitio.

§ I. Legatum itaque est donatio quædam a defuncto relicta, ab hærede præstanda.

§ 1 *A legacy is a species of donation, which is left or ordered by the deceased; and, if possible, must be performed by his heir.*

De antiquis generibus legatorum sublatis.

§ II. Sed olim quidem erant legatorum genera quatuor: per vindicationem, per damnationem, sinendi modo, per præceptionem: et certa quædam verba cuique generi legatorum assignata erant, per quæ singula genera legatorum significabantur: sed ex constitutionibus Divorum principum solemnitas hujusmodi verborum sublata est. Nostra autem constitutio, quam cum magna fecimus lucubratione, defunctorum voluntates validiores esse cupientes, et non verbis sed voluntatibus eorum faventes, disposuit, ut omnibus una sit natura, et, quibuscunque verbis aliquid relictum sit, liceat legatariis id persequi, non solum per actiones personales, sed etiam per in rem et per hypothecariam. Cujus constitutionis perpensum modum ex ipsius tenore perfectissime accipere possibile est.

§ 2. *An-*

§ 2. *Antiently there were four kinds of legacies in use; namely* — per vindicationem — per damnationem — sinendi modo — *and* per præceptionem. *And to each of these was assigned a certain form of words, by which their different species were signified; but these fixed forms have been wholly taken away by the imperial ordinance of the later emperors,* Constantinus, Constantius, *and* Constans. *And we also, being desirous, that the wills of deceased persons might be corroborated, and that their intentions should be more regarded than their words, have with great care and study composed a constitution, which enacts, that the nature of all legacies shall be the same, and that legataries, by whatever words they are constituted, may sue for what is left them, not only by a personal, but by a real or hypothecary action. But the reader may most perfectly comprehend the well weighed matter of this constitution, by perusing the tenor of it.*

Sed ex constitutionibus.] *vid. Cod.* 6. *t.* 37. *l.* 21.
Nostra autem constitutio.] *vid. Cod.* 6. *t.* 43. *l.* 1.

Collatio legatorum et fidei-commissorum.

§ III. Sed non usque ad eam constitutionem standum esse existimavimus: cum enim antiquitatem invenimus legata quidem stricte concludentem, fidei-commissis autem, quæ ex voluntate magis descendebant defunctorum, pinguiorem naturam indulgentem, necessarium esse duximus, omnia legata fidei-commissis exæquare, ut nulla sit inter ea differentia, sed, quod deest legatis, hoc repleatur ex natura fidei-commissorum: et, si quid amplius est in legatis, per hoc crescat fidei-commissorum natura. Sed, ne in primis legum cunabulis permistim de his exponendo studiosis adolescentibus quandam introducamus difficultatem, operæ pretium esse duximus interim separatim prius de legatis et postea de fidei-commissis tractare; ut, natura utriusque juris cognita, facile possint permistionem eorum eruditi subtilioribus auribus accipere.

§ 3. *But we have judged it expedient, that our constitution should not rest here, but extend still farther: for, when we observed, that the antients confined legacies within very strict rules, and yet were extremely favorable to gifts in trust, it was thought necessary to make all legacies equal to gifts in trust, that no difference in effect should remain between them, so that whatever is deficient in the nature of legacies may be supplied by the nature of trusts, and whatever is abundant in the nature of legacies may become an accretion to the nature of trusts.——But, that we may not [illegible] and perplex the minds of young persons at their entrance upon the study of the law, by explaining these things promiscuously, we have esteemed it worth our pains to treat separately first of legacies and afterwards of trusts, that, the nature of each being known, the student, thus instructed, may more easily understand their [illegible] and intermixture.*

Necessarium esse duximus.] *vid. Cod.* 6. *t.* 43. *Communia de legatis, &c.*

De re legata. Et primum de re testatoris, hæredis, aliena, cujus non est commercium.

§ IV. Non solum autem testatoris vel hæredis res, sed etiam aliena legari potest, ita ut hæres cogatur redimere eam et præstare; vel, si eam non potest redimere, æstimationem ejus dare. Sed, si talis sit res, cujus commercium non est, vel adipisci non potest, nec æstimatio ejus debetur; veluti si quis campum martium, vel basilicas, vel templa, vel, quæ publico usui destinata sunt, legaverit: nam nullius momenti tale legatum est. Quod autem diximus, alienam rem posse legari, ita intelligendum est, si defunctus sciebat, alienam rem esse, non si ignorabat. Forsitan enim, si scivisset alienam rem esse, non legasset, et ita Divus Pius rescripsit. Et verius est, ipsum, qui agit, id est, legatarium, probare oportere, scivisse alienam rem legare defunctum, non hæredem probare oportere, ignorasse alienam: quia semper necessitas probandi incumbit illi, qui agit.

§ 4. *A testator may not only bequeath his own property, or that of his heir, but also the property of others, and, if the thing bequeathed belongs to another, the heir can be obliged either to purchase and deliver it, or to render the value of it, if it cannot be purchased. But, if the thing bequeathed is not in commerce, and what the law will not permit to be purchased, the heir in this case can never be obliged to pay the value of it to the legatary, as if a man should bequeath to another the* Campus Martius, *the palaces of the prince, the temples, or any of those things, which appertain to the public. for such legacies can be of no moment or efficacy. But, when we said, that a testator might bequeath the goods of another man, we would be understood to mean, that this can be done only, if the deceased knew, that what he bequeathed belonged to another, and not, if he was ignorant of it, since, if he had known it, he probably would not have left such a legacy. and to this purpose is the rescript of the emperor* Antoninus *And it is incumbent upon the party agent or legatary to bring proof, that the deceased knew, that what he left belonged to another, for the heir is by no means obliged to prove, that the deceased did not know it, because, by the general rule of law, the necessity of proving lies upon the complainant.*

De re pignorata

§ V. Sed et, si rem obligatam creditori aliquis legaverit, necesse habet hæres eam luere. Et in hoc quoque casu idem placet, quod in re aliena, ut ita demum luere necesse habeat hæres, si sciebat defunctus rem obligatam esse: et ita Divi Severus et Antoninus rescripserunt. Si tamen defunctus voluerit legatarium luere, et hoc expresserit, non debet hæres eam luere.

§ 5. *If a man bequeaths the thing, which he hath pledged to a creditor, the heir is under a necessity of redeeming it: but in this case, as in the former, concerning the goods of another, the heir cannot be obliged to redeem the thing bequeathed, unless the*

deceased

deceased knew, that it was pledged; and this the emperors Severus *and* Antoninus *have declared by their rescript But nevertheless, whenever it appears to have been the express will of the deceased, that the legatary should himself redeem the thing left to him, then the heir is free from the obligation of doing it.*

De re aliena post testamentum a legatario acquisita.

§ VI. Si res aliena legata fuerit, et ejus rei vivo testatore legatarius dominus factus fuerit, siquidem ex causa emptionis, ex testamento actione pretium consequi potest; si vero ex causa lucrativa, veluti ex donatione, vel ex alia simili causa, agere non potest. Nam traditum est, duas lucrativas causas in eundem hominem et eandem rem concurrere non posse. Hac ratione, si ex duobus testamentis eadem res eidem debeatur, interest, utrum rem, an æstimationem, ex testamento consecutus sit: nam, si rem habet, agere non potest; quia habet eam ex causa lucrativa: si æstimationem; agere potest.

§ 6. *If a thing bequeathed is the property of another, and the legatee becomes the proprietor of it in the life-time of the testator, it is necessary to be known by what means the legatee became the proprietor; for, if he bought it, he may nevertheless recover the price given, by an action in consequence of the testament; but, if he obtained it as a gift, or by any such lucrative title, no action will lie; for it is a maxim, that two lucrative causes can never concur in the same person and thing. And therefore, if the same specific thing is left by two testaments to one and the same person, the question will be, when the legatary sues in virtue of one of the testaments, whether he hath obtained the thing itself, or the value of it, by virtue of the other? for, if he is already possessed of the thing itself, the suit is at an end, because he hath received it on a lucrative account; but, if he hath obtained the value of it only from the heir of one of the testators, he may bring an action for the thing itself, against the heir of the other.*

Nam traditum est] When it is said, that two lucrative titles can never concur in the same person on account of the same thing, this must be understood in regard only to something certain and determinate, as a particular purse of money, an horse, a diamond, &c. for the maxim does not hold in general with respect to things, which consist in quantity, and may be numbered, weighed or measured — *Possunt enim duæ causæ lucrativæ in eandem personam et eandem quantitatem concurrere, quia quantitates [illegible] rerum naturam multiplicantur, licet enim ea [illegible] mea sæpius fieri non possit, eadem tamen quantitas possit, quia res eadem non videtur* Cujacius, [illegible] riere

De his, quæ non sunt in rerum natura.

§ VII. Ea quoque res, quæ in rerum natura non est, si modo futura est, recte legatur, veluti fructus, qui in illo fundo nati erunt, aut quod ex illa ancilla natum erit.

§ 7 *Things, which do not exist, may be rightly bequeathed, if there is but a possibility, that they may exist thus a man may devise the fruits, which shall grow on such a spot of ground, or the offspring, which shall be born of a particular slave.*

D.

De eadem re duobus legata.

§ VIII. Si eadem res duobus legata sit, sive conjunctim sive disjunctim, si ambo perveniant ad legatum, scinditur inter eos legatum: si alter deficiat, quia aut spreverit legatum, aut vivo testatore decesserit, vel alio quoquo modo defecerit, totum ad collegatarium pertinet. Conjunctim autem legatur, veluti si quis dicat, *Titio et Seio hominem Stichum do, lego:* disjunctim ita, *Titio hominem Stichum do, lego: Seio hominem Stichum do, lego.* Sed et, si expresserit *eundem hominem Stichum,* æque disjunctim legatum intelligitur.

§ 8. *When the same specific legacy is left to two persons either conjunctively or disjunctively, if they are both willing to accept it, it must be divided between them. But, if one of the legatees dies in the life-time of the testator, dislikes his legacy, or is by any means prevented from taking it, the whole vests in his co-legatee. A legacy thus worded is in the conjunctive* — I give and bequeath my slave STICHUS to TITIUS *and* SEIUS — *but a legacy, worded as follows, is in the disjunctive:* — I give and bequeath my slave STICHUS to TITIUS. I give and bequeath my slave STICHUS to SEIUS. *And, altho' the testator should add, that he gives the* same slave STICHUS to SEIUS, *yet the legacy would nevertheless be understood to be left in the disjunctive.*

Si legatarius proprietatem fundi alieni sibi legati emerit et usus fructus ad eum pervenerit.

§ IX. Si cui fundus alienus legatus sit, et emerit proprietatem deducto usufructu, et usufructus ad eum pervenerit, et postea ex testamento agat, recte eum agere et fundum petere Julianus ait: quia usufructus in petitione servitutis locum obtinet: sed officio judicis continetur, ut deducto usufructu jubeat æstimationem præstari.

§ 9. *If a man hath bequeathed the ground of another, and the legatary hath purchased the property of that ground without the usufruct, which hath also afterwards descended to him, it is said by* Julianus, *that the legatary may rightly bring an action by virtue of the testament, and demand the ground, because the usufruct is regarded as a service only. But it is the duty of a judge, in this case, to order the price of the property of the ground to be paid, the value of the usufruct being deducted.*

De re legatarii.

§ X. Sed, si rem legatarii quis ei legaverit, inutile est legatum: quia, quod proprium est ipsius, amplius ejus fieri non potest. Et, licet alienaverit eam, non debetur, nec ipsa res, nec æstimatio ejus.

§ 10. *If a man bequeaths to another what already belongs to him, the legacy is ineffectual, for that, which is already the property of a legatee, can by no means become more so. And, if the legatee should, after the bequest, alien the thing bequeathed, neither the thing itself, nor even the value of it, would become due to him from the heir of the testator.*

Siquis

Si quis rem suam, quasi non suam, legaverit.

§ XI. Si quis rem suam quasi alienam legaverit, valet legatum: nam plus valet quod in veritate est, quam quod in opinione. Sed et, si legatarii esse putavit, valere constat: quia exitum voluntas defuncti habere potest.

§ 11. *If a testator should bequeath what is his own, as if it was the property of another, the bequest would nevertheless be good; for truth is more prevalent than what is founded upon opinion only. But even suppose the testator to imagine, that what he bequeaths belongs already to the legatary, yet, if it does not, it is certain, that such a legacy would also be valid, because the will of the deceased can thus take effect.*

De alienatione et oppignoratione rei legatæ.

§ XII. Si rem suam legaverit testator, posteaque eam alienaverit, Celsus putat, si non adimendi animo vendidit, nihilominus deberi: idemque Divi Severus et Antoninus rescripserunt. Iidem rescripserunt, eum, qui post testamentum factum prædia, quæ legata erant, pignori dedit, ademisse legatum non videri: et ideo legatarium cum hærede ejus agere posse, ut prædia a creditore luantur. Si vero quis partem rei legatæ alienaverit, pars, quæ non est alienata, omnino debetur: pars autem alienata ita debetur, si non adimendi animo alienata sit.

§ 12. *But, if a testator bequeaths what is his own property, and afterwards aliens it, it is the opinion of* CELSUS, *that the thing bequeathed will nevertheless become due to the legatee, if the testator did not dispose of it, with an intention to oust him. The emperors* Severus *and* Antoninus *have published their rescript to this effect, and they have also signified by another rescript, that whoever has bequeathed a legacy, and hath afterwards pawned or mortgaged it, shall not be deemed to have retracted it, and that the legatee may therefore of course bring an action against the heir, and oblige him to redeem. And, if a testator shall have aliened but a part of the thing bequeathed, then all that part, which remains unaliened, is still due, and that, which is aliened, is only due, when it appears not to have been aliened by the testator with a design to retract the legacy.*

De liberatione legata.

§ XIII. Si quis debitori suo liberationem legaverit, legatum utile est: et neque ab ipso debitore, neque ab hærede ejus, potest hæres petere, neque ab alio, qui hæredis loco sit. Sed et potest a debitore conveniri, ut liberet eum. Potest etiam quis vel ad tempus jubere, ne hæres petat.

§ 13. *If a man by will bequeaths a discharge to his debtor, the bequest is effectual, and the heir can bring no suit against the debtor, or his heir, or any one, who represents him: but, on the contrary, the heir of the testator may be convened by the debtor, and obliged to give him his discharge. A man may also by testament command his heir not to sue a debtor, within a time limited.*

D.

De debito legato creditori.

§ XIV. Ex contrario si debitor creditori suo, quod debet, legaverit, inutile est legatum, si nihil plus est in legato, quam in debito: quia nihil amplius per legatum habet. Quod si in diem, vel sub conditione, debitum ei pure legaverit, utile est legatum propter repræsentationem. Quod si vivo testatore dies venerit, vel conditio extiterit, Papinianus scripsit utile esse nihilominus legatum, quia semel constitit: quod et verum est. Non enim placuit sententia existimantium, extinctum esse legatum, quia in eam causam pervenerit, a qua incipere non potest.

§ 14 *On the contrary, if a debtor bequeaths by testament to his creditor the money, which he owes him, this legacy is ineffectual, if the value of the legacy amounts but merely to the value of the debt, for thus the creditor can receive no benefit from the legacy. But, if a debtor bequeaths simply to his creditor a sum of money, which was to be paid at a day certain, or which he owed upon condition, the legacy will take effect on account of the representation,* i. e. *on account of the immediate payment, the legacy becoming due before the debt — But, according to* PAPINIAN, *if the day of payment should come, or the event of the condition happen in the life-time of the testator, the legacy would nevertheless be effectual, because it was once good, which is true. For we are by no means satisfied with the opinion of those, who imagine, that a legacy once good, may afterwards become extinct, by falling into a state, from which it could not have taken a legal commencement*

De dote uxori legata.

§ XV. Sed, si uxori maritus dotem legaverit, valet legatum: quia plenius est legatum, quam de dote actio. Sed, si, quam non accepit, dotem legaverit, Divi Severus et Antoninus rescripserunt, siquidem simpliciter legaverit, inutile esse legatum, si vero certa pecunia, vel certum corpus, aut instrumenta dotis in prælegando demonstrata sunt, valere legatum.

§ 15 *If a man gives back to his wife by legacy her marriage portion, the legacy is valid for such a legacy is more beneficial to her than the action, which she might maintain for the recovery of her portion But, if an husband bequeaths to his wife her marriage portion, and hath never actually received it, the emperors* Severus *and* Antoninus *have declared by their rescript, that, if it is left simply without any specification of a sum certain, the legacy is void, but that, if any certain sum, or thing is specified, or if the instruments, in which the exact value of the portion is mentioned, are referred to, the legacy is valid.*

De interitu et mutatione rei legatæ.

§ XVI. Si res legata sine facto hæredis perierit, legatario decedit. Et, si servus alienus legatus sine facto hæredis manumissus fuerit, non tenetur hæres. Si vero hæredis servus legatus sit, et ipse eum manumiserit, teneri eum, Julianus scripsit: nec interest, sciverit, an ignoraverit, a se eum legatum esse. Sed et, si alii donaverit servum, et is, cui donatus est, eum

eum

eum manumiſerit, tenetur hæres: quamvis ignoraverit, a ſe eum legatum eſſe.

§ 16. *If a thing bequeathed ſhould periſh before delivery, otherwiſe than by the act or fault of the heir, the loſs muſt fall upon the legatary. And, if the ſlave of another, who is bequeathed, ſhould be manumited, and the heir hath not been acceſſary to the manumiſſion, he can be ſubject to no action. But, if a teſtator bequeaths the ſlave of his heir, who afterwards manumits that ſlave, it is the opinion of* JULIAN, *that the heir is anſwerable: nor is at all material, whether he did or did not know of the legacy. And alſo, if the heir hath made a preſent of a ſlave bequeathed, and the donee hath manumited him, the heir is liable to an action, altho' he was ignorant of the bequeſt.*

De interitu quarundam ex pluribus rebus legatis.

§ XVII. Si quis ancillas cum ſuis natis legaverit, etiamſi ancillæ mortuæ fuerint, partus legato cedunt. Idem eſt et ſi ordinarii ſervi cum vicariis legati fuerint: quia, licet mortui ſint ordinarii, tamen vicarii legato cedunt. Sed, ſi ſervus fuerit cum peculio legatus, mortuo ſervo, vel manumiſſo, vel alienato, peculii legatum extinguitur. Idem eſt, ſi fundus inſtructus, vel cum inſtrumento, legatus fuerit: nam, fundo alienato, et inſtrumenti legatum extinguitur.

§ 17. *If a teſtator gives by legacy his female ſlaves and their offſpring, altho' the ſlaves die, yet their iſſue will become due to the legatary: and the ſame obtains, if ordinary ſlaves are bequeathed together with vicarial; for altho' the ordinary ſlaves die, yet the vicarial ſlaves will paſs by virtue of the bequeſt But, if a ſlave is bequeathed with his* peculium, *and afterwards dies, or is manumited, or aliened, the legacy of the* peculium *becomes extinct. And the conſequences will be the ſame, if a piece of ground is bequeathed with the inſtruments for improving it; for, if the teſtator aliens the ground, the legacy of the inſtruments of huſbandry is of courſe extinguiſhed.*

De grege legato.

§ XVIII. Si grex legatus fuerit, et poſtea ad unam ovem pervenerit, quod ſuperfuerit, vindicari poteſt. Grege autem legato etiam eas oves, quæ poſt teſtamentum factum gregi adjiciuntur, legato cedere Julianus ait. Eſt autem gregis unum corpus ex diſtantibus capitibus, ſicut ædium unum corpus eſt ex cohærentibus lapidibus.

§18 *If a flock is bequeathed, and afterwards reduced to a ſingle ſheep, that ſheep is claimable, and, if a flock receives an increaſe or addition, after it hath been diſpoſed of by teſtament, the increaſe or addition will alſo, according to* Julian, *become due to the legatary. For a flock is deemed one body, conſiſting of ſeparate members, as an houſe is reckoned one body, compoſed of materials, joined together and adhering*

De ædibus legatis.

§ XIX. Ædibus denique legatis, columnas et marmora, quæ post testamentum factum adjecta sunt, legato dicimus cedere.

§ 19 *And lastly, when an house is bequeathed, the marble or pillars, which are added after the bequest is made, will pass under the general legacy.*

De peculio.

§ XX. Si peculium legatum fuerit, sine dubio quicquid peculio accedit vel decedit, vivo testatore, legatarii lucro vel damno est. Quod si post mortem testatoris ante aditam hæreditatem aliquid servus acquisierit, Julianus ait, siquidem ipsi manumisso peculium legatum fuerit, omne, quod ante aditam hæreditatem acquisitum est, legatario cedere; quia hujusmodi legati dies ab adita hæreditate cedit: sed, si extraneo peculium legatum fuerit, non cedere ea legato, nisi ex rebus peculiaribus auctum fuerit peculium. Peculium autem, nisi legatum fuerit, manumisso non debetur: quamvis, si vivus manumiserit, sufficit, si non adimatur; et ita Divi Severus et Antoninus rescripserunt. Iidem rescripserunt, peculio legato non videri id relictum, ut petitionem habeat pecuniæ, quam in rationes dominicas impenderit. Iidem rescripserunt, peculium videri legatum, cum rationibus redditis liber esse jussus est, et ex eo reliqua inferre.

§ 20 *When the* peculium *of a slave is bequeathed, it is certain, that the increase or decrease of it, in the life of the testator, becomes the loss or gain of the legatary. And, if the* peculium *of a slave is left to him together with his liberty, and such slave makes an Acquisition to the* peculium, *subsequent to the death of the testator, and before the inheritance is entered upon, it is the opinion of* JULIAN, *that whatever is acquired within that period, will pass to him as the legatary, for such a legacy does not become due, but from the day of the acceptance of the inheritance. But it is the opinion of the same* JULIAN, *that, if the* peculium *of a slave is bequeathed to a stranger, an increase, acquired within the period above-mentioned, will not pass under the legacy, unless the acquisition was made, by means of something appertaining to the* peculium, *for the* peculium *of a slave does not belong to him, after he is manumited by testament, unless it is expresly given; altho', if a master in his life-time manumits his slave, his* peculium *will pass to him of course, if not excepted: and thus the emperors* SEVERUS *and* ANTONINUS *have decreed by their rescript. And the same emperors have also declared, that, when a* peculium *is bequeathed to a slave, it does not seem to be the intention of the testator, that such slave should have the power of demanding what he may have expended for the use of his master. And the same princes have farther declared, that a slave seems to be intituled to his* peculium, *if his liberty is left him, on condition, that he will bring in his accounts, and supply any deficiency out of the profits of his* peculium.

De

De rebus corporalibus et incorporalibus.

§ XXI. Tam autem corporales res legari possunt, quam incorporales: et ideo, quod defuncto debetur, potest alicui legari, ut actiones suas hæres legatario præstet; nisi exegerit vivus testator pecuniam: nam hoc casu legatum extinguitur. Sed et tale legatum valet; *damnas esto hæres meus domum illius reficere:* vel *illum ære alieno liberare.*

§ 21. *Things incorporeal may be bequeathed as well as things corporeal: and therefore a debt, due to the testator, may be left as a legacy, and the heir be obliged to transfer his right of action to the legatary; unless the testator in his life-time received the money due to him; for in this case the legacy would become extinct. A legacy is also good, if conceived in the terms following: —* I command my heir to rebuild the house of TITIUS: *or* to free him from his debts.

De legato generali.

§ XXII. Si generaliter servus, vel res alia, legetur, electio legatarii est, nisi aliud testator dixerit.

§ 22. *If a testator bequeaths a slave, or any particular thing generally, the power of election is in the legatary, unless the testator hath declared otherwise.*

De optione legata.

§ XXIII. Optionis legatum, id est, ubi testator ex servis suis vel aliis rebus optare legatarium jusserat, habebat olim in se conditionem: et ideo, nisi ipse legatarius vivus optasset, ad hæredem legatum non transmittebat. Sed ex constitutione nostra et hoc in meliorem statum reformatum est, et data est licentia hæredi legatarii optare servum, licet vivus legatarius hoc non fecerit. Et, diligentiore tractatu habito, et hoc in nostra constitutione additum est, sive plures legatarii extiterint, quibus optio relicta est, et dissentiant in corpore eligendo; sive unius legatarii plures hæredes sint, et inter se circa optandum dissentiant, alio aliud corpus eligere cupiente, ne pereat legatum, (quod plerique prudentum contra benevolentiam introducebant,) fortunam esse hujus optionis judicem, et sorte hoc esse dirimendum, ut, ad quem sors pervenerit, illius sententia in optione præcellat.

§ 23 *The legacy of an option is made, when a testator commands his legatary to chuse any slave, whom he likes, from among his slaves, or any one thing, which he best approves of, from any certain class of things, and such a legacy was formerly presumed to imply this condition, that, if the legatee in his life-time did not make his election, the legacy could not be transmitted to his heir. But, by virtue of our constitution, this presumption of law is now taken away, and the heir of the legatary is permitted to make his option, altho' the legatary in his life-time hath neglected to do it. And, upon a more diligent inspection, we have farther added to our constitution, that, if there are several legatories, to whom an option is left, and they differ in their choice, or if there are many heirs of one legatary, who are of divers sentiments, then* Fortune *might be the judge: for, lest the loss of the legacy should insue, (which loss the generality of the antient lawyers, contrary to all benevolence, would have permited,) we have decreed, that such dissentions between heirs, or legataries, should be decided by lot; so that the option of him, to whom the lot falls, shall be prefered.*

Sed ex constitutione] *vid. Cod.* 6. *t.* 43 *l. ult.*

Quibus legari potest.

§ XXIV. Legari autem illis solum potest, cum quibus testamenti factio est.

§ 24. *A legacy cannot be left but to those, who have the capacity of taking by testament.*

Jus antiquum de incertis personis.

§ XXV. Incertis vero personis neque legata neque fidei-commissa olim relinqui concessum erat. Nam nec miles quidem incertæ personæ poterat relinquere, ut Divus Hadrianus rescripsit. Incerta autem persona videbatur, quam incerta opinione animo suo testator subjiciebat, veluti, si quis ita dicat, *quicunque filio meo filiam suam in matrimonium dederit, ei hæres meus illum fundum dato.* Illud quoque, quod iis relinquebatur, qui *post testamentum scriptum primi consules designati essent,* æque incertæ personæ legari videbatur: et denique multæ aliæ hujusmodi species sunt. Libertas quoque incertæ personæ non videbatur posse dari, quia placebat nominatim servos liberari. Sub certa vero demonstratione, id est, ex certis personis, incertæ personæ recte legabatur: veluti, *ex cognatis meis, qui nunc sunt, si quis filiam meam uxorem duxerit, ei hæres meus illam rem dato.* Incertis autem personis legata vel fidei-commissa relicta, et per errorem soluta, repeti non posse, sacris constitutionibus cautum erat.

§ 25. *It was not formerly permitted, that either legacies, or gifts in trust, should be bequeathed to incertain persons, for even a soldier was prohibited to bequeath to incertain persons, as the emperor* Adrian *hath declared by his rescript. and an incertain person is reputed to be one, whom the testator hath figured only in his imagination, without any determinate knowledge of him as if a testator should thus express himself* — whoever shall give his daughter in marriage to my son, to that person let my heir deliver up such a piece of ground. *And, if a testator had made a bequest* to the first consuls designed after his testament was written, *this also would have been esteemed a bequest to incertain persons, and of the same kind there are divers other examples. Freedom likewise could not be confered upon an incertain person, for it was necessary, that all slaves should be nominally infranchised but a legacy might have been given to an incertain person under a certain demonstration, or, in other words, to an incertain person, if he was one of a number of persons certain; as for instance, if a testator should bequeath in the manner following* — I command Titius my heir to give such a particular thing to any one of my present collateral relations, who shall think proper to take my daughter in marriage.

Lit,

But, if a legacy or fiduciary gift had been paid to incertain persons by mistake, it was provided by the constitutions, that such persons were not compellable to refund.

Sacris constitutionibus.] These constitutions are not extant.

Jus antiquum de posthumo alieno.

XXVI. Posthumo quoque alieno inutiliter antea legabatur. Est autem alienus posthumus, qui natus inter suos hæredes testatori futurus non est: ideoque, ex emancipato filio conceptus nepos, extraneus erat posthumus avo.

§ 26 *Formerly a legacy could not have been profitably or legally given to a posthumous stranger, and a posthumous stranger is he, who, if he had been born before the death of the testator, could not have been numbered among his proper heirs. and of consequence a posthumous grandson, by an emancipated son, was a posthumous stranger in regard to his grandfather.*

Jus novum de personis incertis et posthumo alieno.

§ XXVII. Sed nec hujusmodi species penitus est sine justa emendatione relicta, cum in nostro codice constitutio posita sit, per quam et huic parti medemur, non solum in hæreditatibus, sed etiam in legatis et fidei-commissis: quod evidenter ex ipsius constitutionis lectione clarescit. Tutor autem nec per nostram constitutionem incertus dari debet: quia certo judicio debet quis pro tutela suæ posteritati cavere.

§ 27. *Such was the state of the antient law, which hath not been left without a proper emendation, for we have promulged a constitution, by which we have altered the law concerning incertain persons, not only in respect to inheritances, but in regard also to legacies and fiduciary bequests But this alteration will evidently appear from a perusal of the constitution itself, which nevertheless gives no authority to the nomination of an incertain tutor, for it is incumbent upon every parent to take care of his posterity in this respect, by a certain and determinate appointment*

Constitutio posita] not extant

De posthumo alieno hærede instituto.

§ XXVIII. Posthumus autem alienus hæres institui et ante poterat, et nunc potest: nisi in utero ejus sit, quæ jure nostro uxor esse non potest.

§ 28 *A posthumous stranger could formerly have been instituted and may now be appointed an heir, unless it appears, that he was conceived by a woman, who could not have been legally married to his father.*

Posthumus autem alienus] Tho' the antient civil law would not suffer a posthumous stranger to be an heir, or a legatary, yet the Prætorian law allowed a posthumous stranger to be an heir in effect, by giving him the possession *secundum tabulas*, *i. e.* according to the tenor of the testament and this is what is meant by saying, *that a posthumous stranger could antiently have been instituted*, but a posthumous stranger never had that power or capacity under the *civil law*, till it was given by *Justinian*'s constitution.

De

De errore in nomine legatarii.

XXIX. Siquidem in nomine, cognomine, prænomine, agnomine, legatarii testator erraverit, cum de persona constat, nihilominus valet legatum. Idemque in hæredibus servatur; et recte: nomina enim significandorum hominum gratia reperta sunt: qui si alio quolibet modo intelligantur, nihil interest.

§ 29. *Altho' a testator may happen to have mistaken the* nomen, cognomen, prænomen, *or* agnomen *of a legatary, yet, if his person is certain, the legacy is good. The same rule of law is also observed in regard to heirs, and with great reason: for the use of names is but to point out persons, and, if persons can be denoted by any other method, it will make no difference.*

Siquidem in nomine] *Charisius* the grammarian gives the following brief but clear account of the *Roman* names " Propria nomina in quatuor species dividuntur, prænomen, nomen, " cognomen, agnomen, ut Publius Cornelius " Scipio Africanus, prænomen est, quod nomini " præponitur, ut Publius; nomen, quod familiæ originem declarat, ut Cornelius, cognomen, quod nomini subjungitur, ut Scipio, " agnomen, quod extrinsecus adjici solet, ut " Africanus. *vid. Vinn* "

De falsa demonstratione.

XXX. Huic proxima est illa juris regula, falsa demonstratione legatum non perimi: veluti, si quis ita legaverit, *Stichum servum meum vernam do, lego* Licet enim non verna, sed emptus sit, si tamen de servo constat, utile est legatum. Et convenienter, si ita demonstraverit, *Stichum servum, quem a Seio emi*, sitque ab alio emptus, utile est legatum, si de servo constat.

§ 30 *The rule of law, which comes nearest to the foregoing, is, that a legacy is not rendered null by a false demonstration. suppose, for instance, that a bequest is thus worded:* —— I give and bequeath STICHUS my slave, who was born in my family · — *in this case, altho'* Stichus *was not born in the family of the testator, but bought, yet, if there is a certainty of his person, the legacy is valid. And if a testator should write as follows* —— I bequeath STICHUS my slave, whom I bought of SEIUS — *yet, altho' he was bought of another, the legacy would be good, if there was no doubt as to the identity of the person of* STICHUS.

De falsa causa adjecta.

XXXI. Longe magis legato falsa causa adjecta non nocet: veluti cum quis ita dixerit. *Titio, qui me absente negotia mea curavit, Stichum do, lego:* vel ita, *Titio, quia patrocinio ejus capitali crimine liberatus sum, Stichum do, lego.* Licet enim neque negotia testatoris unquam gesserit Titius, neque patrocinio ejus liberatus sit, legatum tamen valet. Sed, si conditionaliter enunciata fuerit causa, aliud juris est: veluti hoc modo, *Titio, si negotia mea curaverit, fundum meum do, lego.*

§ 31 A

§ 31. A fortiori *a legacy is not rendered the less valid, altho' a false reason is assigned for bequeathing it: as if a testator should thus express himself:* — I give my slave STICHUS to TITIUS, because he took care of my affairs in my absence: *or*, because I was acquited upon an accusation of a capital offense by his care and protection. *For, altho'* Titius *had never taken care of the affairs of the deceased, and altho' the testator was never acquited from any charge of a capital crime by means of* Titius, *the legacy will nevertheless be good. But if the bequest had been declared to be conditional, as for example, if the testator had expressed himself as follows* —— I give to TITIUS such a piece of ground, if it shall appear, that he hath taken a proper care of my affairs, *then the law would be different.*

De servo hæredis.

§ XXXII. An servo hæredis recte legemus, quæritur: et constat, pure inutiliter legari, nec quicquam proficere, si vivo testatore de potestate hæredis exierit; quia, quod inutile foret legatum, si statim post factum testamentum decessisset testator, hoc non debet ideo valere, quia diutius testator vixerit. Sub conditione vero recte legatur servo, ut requiramus, an, quo tempore dies legati cedit, in potestate hæredis non sit.

§ 32. *It hath been a question, whether a testator can legally give a legacy to the slave of his heir? and it is certain, that a legacy, purely and simply given to such a slave, can avail him nothing, altho' he should afterwards be freed from the power of the heir in the life-time of the testator; for a bequest, which would have been null, if the testator had expired immediately after he had made it, ought not to become valid, merely because the testator happened to enjoy a longer life. But a testator may give a conditional legacy to the slave of his instituted heir, and such legacy will be good, if the slave is not under the power of the heir, when the condition is fulfilled.*

Quæritur] If a testator gives a legacy to the slave of his heir without annexing any condition, such a legacy is void, for a bequest, made to the slave, is in effect made to the heir, and it would be highly absurd in a testator to command his heir to pay a legacy to himself. And altho' the slave of the heir should afterwards *cease to be under the power of his master* in the life-time of the testator, either by passing to another master, or by obtaining his freedom, yet this would give no force to the legacy, for it is laid down as a rule by *Cato*, *quod, si testamenti facti tempore decessit testator, inutile foret, id legatum, quandocunque decesserit, non valere.* ff. 34. t. 7. But, when legacies are conditional, this rule is not observed, for in such bequests nothing is regarded but the *event of the condition.*

De domino hæredis.

§ XXXIII. Ex diverso hærede instituto servo, quin domino recte etiam sine conditione legetur, non dubitatur. Nam, etsi statim post factum testamentum decesserit testator, non tamen apud eum, qui hæres sit, dies legati cedere intelligitur, cum hæreditas a legato separata sit, et possit per eum servum alius hæres effici, si prius, quam jussu domini adeat, in alterius potestatem translatus sit: vel manumissus ipse hæres efficitur: quibus casibus utile est legatum. Quod si in eadem causa permanserit, et jussu legatarii adierit, evanescit legatum.

§ 33. Cu

§ 33. *On the contrary it is not doubted, but that a slave may be appointed an heir, and that his then master may take even a simple legacy by the same testament: for, altho' the testator should die instantly after making his testament, yet the legacy is not understood to become immediately due from the slave, who is the heir; for the inheritance is here separate from the legacy, and another may become heir by means of the slave, if he should be transfered to a new master, before he hath entered upon the inheritance at the command of his master, who is the legatary; or the slave himself may become heir in his own right by manumission; and in these cases the legacy would be good. But, if the slave should remain in the same state, and enter upon the inheritance by order of his master, who is the legatary, the legacy would, as such, become extinct.*

De modo et ratione legandi. De ordine scripturæ.

§. XXXIV. Ante hæredis institutionem inutiliter antea legabatur; scilicet, quia testamenta vim ex institutione hæredis accipiunt, et ob id veluti caput atque fundamentum intelligitur totius testamenti hæredis institutio. Pari ratione nec libertas ante hæredis institutionem dari poterat. Sed, quia incivile esse putavimus, scripturæ ordinem quidem sequi, (quod et ipsi antiquitati vituperandum fuerat visum,) sperni autem testatoris voluntatem, per nostram constitutionem et hoc vitium emendavimus, ut liceat et ante hæredis institutionem et inter medias hæredis institutiones legatum relinquere, et multo magis libertatem, cujus usus favorabilior est.

§ 34. *A legacy could not formerly have been given with effect, till the heir was instituted; because a testament receives it's whole force and efficacy from the institution of the heir, which is understood to be the basis and foundation of it: and by a parity of reasoning it was also necessary, that the institution of an heir should always precede the grant of freedom in a testament. But we have thought it to be wrong and absurd, that a strict regard should be paid to the mere order of writing, in direct opposition to the express intention of a testator: and the antients themselves seem to have been of this opinion in general: we have therefore, by virtue of our constitution, amended the law in this point; so that a legacy may now be given, and,* a fortiori, *a grant of liberty, which is always favored, may be bequeathed, before the institution of an heir, where there is but one, and, either before or between the institutions of heirs, where there are several.*

De legato post mortem hæredis, vel legatarii.

§ XXXV. Post mortem quoque hæredis aut legatarii simili modo inutiliter legabatur: veluti, si quis ita dicat, *cum hæres meus mortuus fuerit, do, lego:* item *pridie quam hæres aut legatarius morietur.* Sed simili modo et hoc correximus, firmitatem hujusmodi legatis ad fidei-commissorum similitudinem præstantes; ne in hoc casu deterior causa legatorum, quam fidei-commissorum, inveniatur.

§ 35. *A bequest, made to take place after the death of an heir or legatary, was also ineffectual: for, if a testator had written,* when my heir is dead I give and bequeath

bequeath an hundred AUREI to Titius,—*or even thus*, I give and bequeath an hundred AUREI to be paid to Titius, on the day preceding the day of the death of my heir, — *or*, on the day preceding the day of the death of my legatary,—— *the legacies in any of these cases would have been void. But we have corrected the antient rule of law in this respect, by giving all such legacies the same validity, which is given to gifts in trust; lest trusts should be found to be more favored, than legacies.*

Correximus] *vid. Cod.* 8. *t.* 38. l 11.

Si pœnæ nomine relinquatur, adimatur, vel transferatur.

§ XXXVI. Pœnæ quoque nomine inutiliter antea legabatur, et adimebatur, vel transferebatur. Pœnæ autem nomine legari videtur, quod coercendi hæredis causa relinquitur, quo magis aliquid faciat, aut non faciat: veluti si quis ita scripserit; *hæres meus si filiam suam in matrimonium Titio collocaverit:* vel ex diverso, *si non collocaverit, dato decem aureos Seio:* aut si ita scripserit; *hæres meus si servum Stichum alienaverit:* vel ex diverso, *si non alienaverit, Titio decem aureos dato.* Et in tantum hæc regula observabatur, ut quam plurimis principalibus constitutionibus significaretur, nec principem agnoscere, quod ei pœnæ nomine legatum sit: nec ex militis quidem testamento talia legata valebant; quamvis aliæ militum voluntates in ordinandis testamentis valde observabantur: quinetiam nec libertates pœnæ nomine dari posse placebat: eo amplius, nec hæredem pœnæ nomine adjici posse, Sabinus existimabat: veluti si quis ita dicat, *Titius hæres esto: si Titius filiam suam in matrimonium Seio collocaverit, Seius quoque hæres esto.* Nihil enim intererat, qua ratione Titius coerceretur, utrum legati datione, an cohæredis adjectione. Sed hujusmodi scrupulositas nobis non placuit: et generaliter ea, quæ relinquuntur, licet pœnæ nomine fuerint relicta et adempta, vel in alium translata, nihil distare a cæteris legatis constituimus, vel in dando, vel in adimendo, vel in transferendo: exceptis videlicet iis, quæ impossibilia sunt, vel legibus interdicta, aut alias probrosa. Hujusmodi enim testamentorum dispositiones valere secta meorum temporum non patitur.

§ 36. *Also formerly, if a testator had given, revoked, or transfered a legacy* pœnæ nomine, *he would have acted ineffectually. and a legacy is reputed to be bequeathed* pœnæ nomine, [i e. *as a punishment or penalty,*] *when an heir is put under the necessity of doing or not doing something: as for instance, if a testator had thus writen;* —— if my heir gives his daughter in marriage to TITIUS ; *or*, if he does not give her in marriage to TITIUS, let him pay ten AUREI to SEIUS : *or thus :* —— if my heir shall alien my slave STICHUS ; *or, on the contrary*, if my heir shall not alien my slave STICHUS, let him pay ten AUREI to TITIUS. *And this rule was so far observed, that it was expresly ordained by many constitutions, that even the emperor could not receive a legacy, which was bequeathed* pœnæ nomine ; *nor could a penal legacy be valid, even when it had been bequeathed by the testament of a soldier; altho', in every other respect, the intention of a testator in a military testament was always scrupulously adhered to. And even freedom could not*

be

be bequeathed, nor, in the opinion of SABINUS, *could an heir be added in a testament*, sub pœnæ nomine: *for, if a testator had said*, let TITIUS be my heir, but if he gives his daughter in marriage to SEIUS, let SEIUS also be my heir, *the appointment of* SEIUS *would have been void; for the manner, in which an heir was laid under coertion, whether it was by the gift of a legacy, or by the addition of another heir, worked no alteration in the general rule of law. But this scrupulosity hath been by no means agreeable to us, and we have therefore ordained, that in general the doctrine of the law in regard to any thing left, revoked, or transfered, in punishment of an heir, should not differ from the rules of law observed in relation to other legacies, when the performance of the condition of obtaining them is neither impossible, prohibited by law, nor contrary to good manners: for the morality, religion, and justice, of the present times will not suffer such testamentary dispositions to take place.*

Constituimus.] *vid. Cod.* 6. *t* 41.

TITULUS VIGESIMUS-PRIMUS.

De ademptione legatorum et translatione.

D.xxxiv. T.4.

De ademptione.

ADemptio legatorum, sive eodem testamento adimantur, sive codicillis, firma est. Sed et, sive contrariis verbis fiat ademptio, veluti si quod ita quis legaverit, *do, lego*, ita adimatur, *non do, non lego:* sive non contrariis, sed aliis quibuscumque verbis.

A revocation of a legacy is valid, altho' it is inserted in the same testament or codicil, in which the legacy was given. And it is immaterial, whether the revocation is made in words contrary to the bequest; as when a testator gives a legacy in these terms, I give and bequeath to TITIUS, —— *and revokes it by adding*, — I do not give and bequeath to TITIUS · *or whether the revocation is made by any other form of words*

De translatione.

§ I. Transferri quoque legatum ab alio ad alium potest, veluti si quis ita dixerit, *hominem Stichum, quem Titio legavi, Seio do, lego:* sive in eodem testamento, sive codicillis, id fecerit: quo casu simul et Titio adimi videtur et Seio dari.

§ I *A legacy may also be transfered from one person to another; as thus* —— I give to SEIUS my slave STICHUS, whom I have bequeathed to TITIUS. *This may be done in the same testament or codicil, in which the legacy was first given; and thus a legacy may be taken tacitly and by implication from* TITIUS *and transfered to* SEIUS.

TITULUS

TITULUS VIGESIMUS-SECUNDUS.

De lege Falcidia.

D. xxxv. T. 2. C. vi. T. 50. Nov. 1.

Ratio et summa hujus legis.

SUPEREST, ut de lege Falcidia dispiciamus, qua modus novissime legatis impositus est. Cum enim olim lege duodecim tabularum libera erat legandi potestas, ut liceret vel totum patrimonium legatis erogare: quippe, cum ea lege ita cautum esset, *uti quisque legassit suæ rei, ita jus esto*, visum est hanc legandi licentiam coarctare; idque ipsorum testatorum gratia provisum est, ob id, quod plerumque intestati moriebantur, recusantibus scriptis hæredibus pro nullo aut minimo lucro hæreditates adire. Et, cum super hoc tam lex Furia quam lex Voconia latæ sunt, quarum neutra sufficiens ad rei consummationem videbatur, novissime lata est lex Falcidia, qua cavetur, ne plus legare liceat, quam dodrantem totorum bonorum: id est, ut, sive unus hæres institutus sit, sive plures, apud eum eosve pars quarta remaneat.

It remains to speak of the law Falcidia, *by which legacies have received their latest regulation. By the law of the* 12 *tables*, — uti quisque legassit suæ rei, ita jus esto, —— *a testator was permited to dispose of his whole patrimony in legacies: but it was thought proper to restrain this licence even for the benefit of testators themselves, because they frequently died intestate, their heirs refusing to enter upon an inheritance, from which they could receive no profit, or but very little. And this occasioned the introduction first of the law* Furia, *and afterwards of the law* Voconia: *but, when neither of these was found adequate to the purpose intended, the* Falcidian *law was at length enacted, which prohibits a testator to give more in legacies, than three fourths of all his effects; so that, whether there is one or more heirs, there must now remain to him, or them, an intire fourth part of the whole.*

Ut de lege Falcidia] This law was a *plebiscitum*, made by *Pub. Falcidius*, tribune of the people, in the reign of *Augustus, anno U. C.* 745.

Tam lex Furia, quam lex Voconia] The law *Furia* prohibited any testator to give more in legacies than one thousand *asses*, but notwithstanding this law a testator, who was worth only one thousand *asses*, might have bequeathed his whole estate, and left nothing for his heir. The law *Voconia* [made by *Voconius*, tribune of the people *ann. U. C.* 524] abrogated the law *Furia*, and ordained, that no one legatary should be intituled to more by virtue of his legacy, than would afterwards remain to the heir out of the effects of the testator, but this law also was in time found rather to multiply legataries, than benefit heirs, and was therefore abrogated by the law *Falcidia*.

De pluribus hæredibus.

§ I. Et, cum quæsitum esset, duobus hæredibus institutis (veluti Titio et Seio) si Titii pars aut tota exhausta sit legatis, quæ nominatim ab eo data sunt, aut supra modum onerata, a Seio vero aut nulla relicta sint legata, aut quæ partem ejus duntaxat in partem diminuant, an, quia is quartam partem totius hæreditatis, aut amplius habet, Titio nihil ex legatis, quæ ab eo relicta sunt, retinere liceat, ut quartam partem suæ partis salvam habeat? placuit posse retinere. Etenim in singulis hæredibus ratio legis Falcidiæ ponenda est.

§ 1. *When two heirs are instituted, for example,* TITIUS *and* SEIUS, *and* Titius's *moity of the inheritance is wholly exhausted, or overcharged by legacies, which he is expresly ordered to pay; and on the other side* Seius's *moity is either not incumbered, or is charged with legacies, which amount only to the half of his share; it hath in this case been a question, whether, altho'* Seius *hath a fourth or more of the whole inheritance, it may not nevertheless be lawful for* TITIUS *to make a stoppage out of the legacies, with which he is charged, so as to retain a fourth part of his own moity? and it hath been determined, that* Titius *may make such stoppage; for the reason and equity of the law* Falcidia *extends to each heir in particular.*

Quo tempore spectatur quantitas patrimonii, ad quam ratio legis Falcidiæ redigitur.

§ II. Quantitas autem patrimonii, ad quam ratio legis Falcidiæ redigitur, mortis tempore spectatur. Itaque, (verbi gratia) si is, qui centum aureorum patrimonium in bonis habeat, centum aureos legaverit, nihil legatariis prodest, si ante aditam hæreditatem per servos hæreditarios, aut ex partu ancillarum hæreditariarum, aut ex fœtu pecorum, tantum accesserit hæreditati, ut, centum aureis legatorum nomine erogatis, hæres quartam partem hæreditatis habiturus sit: sed necesse est, ut nihilominus quarta pars legatis detrahatur. Ex diverso, si septuaginta quinque legaverit, et ante aditam hæreditatem in tantum decreverint bona, (incendiis forte, aut naufragiis, aut morte servorum) ut non amplius quam septuaginta quinque aureorum substantia vel etiam minus relinquatur, solida legata debentur Nec ea res damnosa est hæredi, cui liberum est non adire hæreditatem: quæ res efficit, ut sit necesse legatariis, ne destituto testamento nihil consequantur, cum hærede in portione pacisci.

§ 2. *But the law* Falcidia *hath regard only to the quantity of the estate at the time of the death of the testator; and therefore, if he, who is worth but an hundred* aurei *at his decease, bequeaths them all in legacies, the legatees must suffer a defalcation, for they will receive no manner of advantage, altho' the inheritance, after the death of the testator and before it is entered upon, should so increase by the acquisitions of slaves, the children of female slaves, or the product of cattle, that, after a full payment of the* 100 aurei *in legacies, an intire fourth of the whole estate might remain*

remain to the heir; for, notwithstanding the increase of the testator's estate, subsequent to his death, a fourth part of the hundred aurei *would still be due to the heir, and the legacies would remain subject to a defalcation upon that account. But, on the contrary, if a testator hath bequeathed 75* aurei *in legacies, and was worth an hundred* aurei *at his death, then altho' it should happen, that, before the enterance of the heir, the estate should so decrease by fire, shipwreck, or the loss of slaves, that the whole value of it should not be more than 75* aurei, *and perhaps less, yet the legacies would still be due without defalcation: nor is this law prejudicial to an heir, who is always at his election either to refuse or accept an inheritance; but it obliges legataries to come to an agreement with him to take a part, lest they should lose the whole of their legacies by his desertion of the testament.*

Quæ detrahuntur ante Falcidiam.

§ III. Cum autem ratio legis Falcidiæ ponitur, ante deducitur æs alienum, item funeris impensa, et pretia servorum manumissorum: tunc demum in reliquo ita ratio habetur, ut ex eo quarta pars apud hæredem remaneat, tres vero partes inter legatarios distribuantur, pro rata scilicet portione ejus, quod cuique eorum legatum fuerit. Itaque, si fingamus, quadringentos aureos legatos esse, et patrimonii quantitatem, ex qua legata erogari oportet, quadringentorum esse, quarta pars singulis legatariis debet detrahi. Quod si trecentos quinquaginta legatos fingamus, octava debet detrahi. Quod si quingentos legaverit, initio quinta, deinde quarta, detrahi debet. Ante enim detrahendum est, quod extra bonorum quantitatem est, deinde quod ex bonis apud hæredem remanere oportet.

§ 3 *The* Falcidian *portion is not taken by the heir, till the debts, funeral expenses, and the price of the manumission of slaves, have all been previously deducted; and then the fourth part of the remainder appertains to the heir, and the other three parts are divided among the legataries in a ratable proportion: for example, let it be supposed, that* 400 aurei *have been bequeathed in legacies, and that the estate, from which these legacies are intended to issue, is worth but exactly that sum, it follows, that a fourth must be subtracted from the legacy of each legatary, but, if the testator gave in legacies no more than* 350 aurei, *and there remained after debts paid* 400, *then an eighth only ought to be deducted from each legacy. And, if a testator hath bequeathed* 500 aurei *in legacies, and there remain clear in the hands of the heir but* 400, *then a fifth must first be deducted from every legacy, and afterwards a fourth: for that, which exceeds the real value of the goods of the deceased, must first be subtracted, and then follows the deduction of what is due to the heir.*

TITULUS VIGESIMUS-TERTIUS.

De fidei-commissariis hæreditatibus.

D.xxxvi.T.1. C.vi.T.42. et 49. Nov. 39. 108.

Continuatio.

NUNC transeamus ad fidei-commissa. Sed prius est, ut de hæreditatibus fidei-commissariis videamus.

Let us now proceed to trusts; in treating of which we will first speak of fiduciary inheritances.

Origo fidei-commissorum.

§ I. Sciendum itaque est, omnia fidei-commissa primis temporibus infirma fuisse; quia nemo invitus cogebatur præstare id, de quo rogatus erat. Quibus enim non poterant hæreditatem vel legata relinquere, si relinquebant, fidei committebant eorum, qui capere ex testamento poterant. Et ideo fidei-commissa appellata sunt, quia nullo vinculo juris sed tantum pudore eorum, qui rogabantur, continebantur. Postea Divus Augustus primus semel iterumque gratia personarum motus, vel quia per ipsius salutem rogatus quis diceretur, aut ob insignem quorundam perfidiam, jussit consulibus auctoritatem suam interponere. Quod, quia justum videbatur et populare erat, paulatim conversum est in assiduam jurisdictionem; tantusque eorum favor factus est, ut paulatim etiam prætor proprius crearetur, qui de fidei-commissis jus diceret, quem fidei-commissarium appellabant.

§ I. *It must be observed, that in the first times all trusts were weak and precarious; for no man could be compelled to the performance of what he was only* requested *to perform And yet, when testators were desirous of giving an inheritance or legacy to persons, to whom they could directly bequeath neither, they then committed the inheritance or legacy in trust to those, who were capable of taking, and such commitments were called fiduciary, because the performance of the trust could not be inforced by the law, but depended solely upon the honor of the trustee. But the emperor* Augustus, *having been frequently moved with compassion on account of particular persons, and detesting the perjury and perfidiousness of trustees in general, commanded the consuls to interpose their authority, and this, being a just and popular command, gave them by degrees a continued jurisdiction, and in process of time trusts became so common, and were so highly favored, that a prætor was purposely appointed to give judgment in these cases, and was therefore called the commissary of trusts.*

De

De fidei-commisso hæredis scripti.

§ II. In primis igitur sciendum est, opus esse, ut aliquis recto jure testamento hæres instituatur, ejusque fidei committatur, ut eam hæreditatem alii restituat: alioqui inutile est testamentum, in quo nemo hæres instituitur. Cum igitur aliquis scripserit, *Lucius Titius hæres esto*, potest adjicere, *rogo te, Luci Titi, ut, cum primum poteris hæreditatem meam adire, eam Caio Seio reddas, restituas.* Potest autem quisque et de parte restituenda hæredem rogare: et liberum est vel pure, vel sub conditione, relinquere fidei-commissum, vel ex certo die.

§ 2. *We must here observe, that there is an absolute necessity of appointing an heir in direct terms to every testament, but he then may be requested to restore the inheritance to any other person; for without an heir a testament is ineffectual. And therefore, when a testator says* — let LUCIUS TITIUS be my heir — *he may add* — and I request you, LUCIUS TITIUS, that, as soon as you enter upon my inheritance, you would restore it to CAIUS SEIUS. *But a testator is at liberty to request his heir to restore a part of the inheritance only, and may make him a trustee upon condition, or from a day certain.*

Hæres instituatur.] The substantial and essential part of every testament is the appointment of an executor, for in *England*, if a man bequeaths ever so many legacies and appoints no executor, such a disposition may be called a codicil or a will, but not a testament, and therefore he, who made such a disposition, shall be deemed to have died without a testament, and the administration of his goods, with the will annexed, shall be commited to his widow or next of kin, as in the case of an intestate. *Swinb part* 4 *sect.* 2

Effectus restitutionis hæreditatis.

§ III. Restituta autem hæreditate, is quidem, qui restituit, nihilominus hæres permanet: is vero, qui recipit hæreditatem, aliquando hæredis aliquando legatarii loco habetur.

§ 3. *After an heir hath restored an inheritance in obedience to the trust reposed in him, he neverthelesss continues heir. But he, who hath received the inheritance from such fiduciary heir, is sometimes reputed to be in the place of the heir, and sometimes in the place of a legatary.*

De senatus-consulto Trebelliano.

§ IV. Et Neronis quidem temporibus, Trebellio Maximo et Annæo Seneca coss. senatus-consultum factum est, quo cautum est, ut, si hæreditas ex fidei-commissi causa restituta sit, omnes actiones, quæ jure civili hæredi et in hæredem competerent, ei et in eum darentur, cui ex fidei-commisso restituta esset hæreditas. Post quod senatus-consultum prætor utiles actiones ei et in eum, qui recepit hæreditatem, quasi hæredi et in hæredem, dare cœpit.

§ 4. *In the reign of* NERO *the emperor, when* TREBELLIUS MAXIMUS *and* ANNÆUS SENECA *were consuls, it was provided by a decree of the senate, that, if an inheritance was restored by reason of a trust, all actions, which by the civil law might be brought by or against the heir, should be given to and against him, to whom the*

the inheritance was reſtored. — And, after this decree, the prætor began to give equitable and beneficial actions to and againſt the receiver of an inheritance, as if he was the heir.

Utiles actiones] See the 4th book of the *inſtitutions*, title 6, law 16.

De ſenatus-conſulto Pegaſiano.

§ V. Sed, quia hæredes ſcripti, cum aut totam hæreditatem, aut pene totam, plerumque reſtituere rogabantur, adire hæreditatem ob nullum vel minimum lucrum recuſabant, atque ob id extinguebantur fidei-commiſſa, poſtea Veſpaſiani Auguſti temporibus, Pegaſo et Puſione conſulibus, ſenatus cenſuit, ut ei, qui rogatus eſſet hæreditatem reſtituere, perinde liceret quartam partem retinere, atque ex lege Falcidia ex legatis retinere conceditur. Ex ſingulis quoque rebus, quæ per fidei-commiſſum relinquuntur, eadem retentio permiſſa eſt. Poſt quod ſenatus-conſultum ipſe hæres onera hæreditaria ſuſtinebat: ille autem, qui ex fidei-commiſſo recipiebat partem hæreditatis, legatarii partiarii loco erat, id eſt, ejus legatarii, cui pars bonorum legabatur: quæ ſpecies legati *partitio* vocabatur, quia cum hærede legatarius partiebatur hæreditatem. Unde, quæ ſolebant ſtipulationes inter hæredem et partiarium legatarium interponi, eædem interponebantur inter eum, qui ex fidei-commiſſo recepit hæreditatem et hæredem, id eſt, ut lucrum et damnum hæreditarium pro rata parte inter eos commune eſſet.

§ 5 *But, when writen heirs were requeſted to reſtore the whole, or almoſt the whole, of an inheritance, they often refuſed to accept it, ſince they could receive but little or no emolument; and thus it happened, that truſts were frequently extinguiſhed. But afterwards in the conſulate of* Pegaſus *and* Pugio, *in the reign of the emperor* Veſpaſian, *the ſenate ordained by their decree, that an heir, who was requeſted to reſtore an inheritance, might retain a fourth, as in the caſe of legacies by the* Falcidian *law. And an heir is alſo allowed to make the ſame deduction from particular things, which are left to him in truſt for the benefit of another. For ſome time after this decree, the heir alone bore the burden of the inheritance,* [i. e. *all the charges and demands incident to it*;] *but afterwards, whoever had received a ſhare or part of an inheritance, by being benefited under a truſt, was regarded as having a partial legacy, and this ſpecies of legacy was called* partition, *becauſe the legatary took a part of the inheritance together with the heir, and hence it aroſe, that the ſame ſtipulations, which were formerly uſed between the heir and the legatary in part, were alſo interpoſed between the perſon benefited under the truſt and the heir or truſtee, to the intent, that the profit and loſs might be in common between them in due proportion.*

Poſt quod ſenatus-conſultum ipſe hæres] The beſt way to explain this ſection will be to tranſcribe a paſſage from the paraphraſe of *Theophilus*, as it is tranſlated by *Gul Otto Reitz*, to whom the literary world is much obliged, for his late moſt complete edition of *Theophilus* in *Greek* and *Latin*, to which is added a great variety of notes by the editor and others This edition conſiſts of two volumes in *4to*, and was publiſhed at the *Hague* in the year 1751

" Poſt hoc autem hæres ſolus ſubjacebat one-
" ribus hæreditatis, non vero fidei-commiſſarius.
" ſed denique placuit, fidei-commiſſarium vi-
" cem obtinere legatarii partiarii, id eſt, partem
" dimidiam accipientis Quondam enim quin-
" tum genus legati erat, dicebaturque *partitio*,
" et relinquebatur hoc modo *Titius mihi hæres*
" *eſto, et cum Seio hæreditatem dividito in dimidia*
" *portione* Porro igitur hujuſmodi inter eos
" ſtipulationes fiebant. Hæres legatarium ſic
" inter-

" rogabat; — *spondes, legatarie, si ego conventus* " *viginti aureos solvero, eorum mihi semissem dare?* " et dicebat, *spondeo*. Rursusque legatarius hæ- " redem sic interrogabat, — *spondes, si ab hære-* " *ditario debitore viginti aureos acceperis, semissem* " *mihi dare, i. e. decem?* et dicebat, *spondeo*: " atque hæc stipulatio vocabatur PARTIS ET " PRO PARTE. Ad exemplum igitur legatarii " partiarii stipulatio procedebat hæredem inter " et fidei-commissarium: et interrogabat hæres " fidei-commissarium sic, — *spondes, fidei-* " *commissarie, si quadraginta aureos poscar a* " *creditore hæreditario, dare mihi triginta?* et " hæres interrogabatur a fidei-commissario, " *spondes, hæres, si a debitore hæreditario qua-* " *draginta aureos acceperis, triginta mihi dare?* " et dicebat, *spondeo*. Atque hoc modo fidei- " commissarius universalis vicem obtinebat le- " gatarii: oportebatque commune esse pro rata, " fidei-commissarium inter et hæredem, lucrum " et damnum." *Theoph. h. t.*

Quibus casibus locus est senatus-consulto Trebelliano vel Pegasiano.

§ VI. Ergo, siquidem non plus quam dodrantem hæreditatis scriptus hæres rogatus sit restituere, tum ex Trebelliano senatus-consulto restituebatur hæreditas, et in utrumque actiones hæreditariæ pro parte rata dabantur: in hæredem quidem jure civili: in eum vero, qui recipiebat hæreditatem ex senatus-consulto Trebelliano, tanquam in hæredem. At, si plus quam dodrantem, vel etiam totam hæreditatem, restituere rogatus esset, locus erat Pegasiano senatus-consulto: et hæres, qui semel adierat hæreditatem, (si modo sua voluntate adierat,) sive retinuerat quartam partem, sive retinere noluerat, ipse universa onera sustinebat. Sed, quarta quidem retenta, quasi *partis* et *pro parte* stipulationes interponebantur, tanquam inter partiarium legatarium et hæredem: si vero totam hæreditatem restitueret, emptæ et venditæ hæreditatis stipulationes interponebantur. Sed, si recusabat scriptus hæres adire hæreditatem, ob id, quod diceret, eam sibi suspectam esse, quasi damnosam, cavebatur Pegasiano senatus-consulto, ut; desiderante eo, cui restituere rogatus esset, jussu prætoris adiret, et restitueret hæreditatem, perindeque ei et in eum, qui reciperet hæreditatem, actiones darentur, ac juris est ex Trebelliano senatus-consulto: quo casu nullis stipulationibus est opus: quia simul et huic, qui restituit, securitas datur, et actiones hæreditariæ ei et in eum transferuntur, qui recipit hæreditatem; utroque senatus-consulto in hac specie concurrente.

§ 6 *And therefore, if a written heir, or heir in trust, had not been requested to surrender more than three fourths of the inheritance, he was obliged to* [illegible] *of it, by virtue of the* Trebellian senatus-consultum; *and all actions, whether* [illegible] *of, or against, the inheritance, were brought, or* [illegible]*, against the heir and* fidei-commissary, *according to their respective shares; and this obtain*[illegible] *to the heir, by virtue of the civil law; and, in regard to the* fidei commissary, *by virtue of the* Trebellian *decree. But, if the written heir was requested by the testator to restore the whole inheritance, or more than three fourths, then the* Pegasian senatus-consultum *took place; for, if he had once taken upon himself the* [illegible]*, he was obliged to sustain all charges, and this, whether he did, or did not, retain the fourth, to which he was intituled. But, when an heir retained the fourth part, the stipulations, called* partis et pro parte, *were entered into,* [illegible] *in part and on* [illegible]*; and, when the heir did not retain a fourth,* [illegible] *called* emptæ et venditæ hæreditatis, *were interposed. But, if the writen heir, or heir in trust, refused to accept the inheritance on suspicion, that there would not be assets, and that the acceptance would be detrimental to him, it was provided by the* Pegasian *decree, that the prætor, at the instance of the* fidei-commissary *might compel such heir to take upon himself the inheritance, and then restore it; and that afterwards all actions should be brought by or against the* fidei-commissary *only; as it is ordained by the* Trebellian *decree. And in this case stipulations are not necessary; for the heir, who restores the inheritance, is made effectually secure, and all hereditary actions are transfered to and against him, by whom the inheritance is received, there being, in this instance, a concurrence of both decrees, the* Pegasian *and the* Trebellian.

Pegasiani in Trebellianum transfusio.

§ VII. Sed, quia stipulationes ex senatus-consulto Pegasiano descendentes et ipsi antiquitati displicuerunt, et quibusdam casibus captiosas eas homo excelsi ingenii Papinianus appellat, et nobis in legibus magis simplicitas, quam difficultas, placet, ideo omnibus nobis suggestis tam similitudinibus, quam differentiis utriusque senatus-consulti, placuit, exploso senatus-consulto Pegasiano, quod postea supervenit, omnem auctoritatem Trebelliano senatus-consulto præstare, ut ex eo fidei-commissariæ hæreditates restituantur: sive habeat hæres ex voluntate testatoris quartam, sive plus, sive minus, sive nihil penitus: ut tunc, quando vel nihil, vel minus quarta, apud eum remanet, liceat ei vel quartam, vel quod ei deest, ex nostra auctoritate retinere, vel repetere solutum, quasi ex Trebelliano senatus-consulto pro rata portione actionibus tam in hæredem, quam in fidei-commissarium, competentibus. Si vero totam hæreditatem sponte restituerit, omnes hæreditariæ actiones fidei-commissario, et adversus eum, competunt. Sed etiam id, quod præcipuum Pegasiani senatus-consulti fuerat, ut, quando recusaret hæres scriptus sibi datam hæreditatem adire, necessitas ei imponeretur totam hæreditatem volenti fidei-commissario restituere, et omnes ad eum, et contra eum, transferre actiones: et hoc transposuimus ad senatus-consultum Trebellianum, ut ex hoc solo necessitas hæredi imponatur, si, ipso nolente adire, fidei-commissarius desideret restitui sibi hæreditatem, nullo nec damno nec commodo apud hæredem remanente.

§ 7 *But, as the stipulations, which took their rise from the* Pegasian *decree, were displeasing even to the antients themselves, insomuch that* Papinian, *a man of a true sublime genius, does not scruple to call them captious in some cases, and, as simplicity is far more agreeable to us in all matters of law, than unnecessary difficulties, it hath therefore pleased us, upon comparing the agreement and disagreement of each decree, to abrogate the* Pegasian, *which was subsequent to the* Trebellian, *and to transfer a greater authority to the* Trebellian *decree, by which all* fidei-commissary *inheritances shall be restored for the future, whether the testator hath given by his will a fourth part of his estate to his writen heir, or more or less than a fourth, or even nothing, so that, whenever nothing is given to the heir, or less than a fourth part, he may be permited to retain a fourth, or as much as will complete the deficiency, by*

virtue

virtue of our authority, or even to demand a repayment of what he hath paid in his own wrong, all actions being divided between the heir and the fidei-commissary *in a just proportion according to the* Trebellian *decree. But, if the heir spontaneously restores the whole inheritance, all actions must be brought either by or against the* fidei-commissary. *And, whereas it was the principal effect of the power of the* Pegasian *decree, that, when a writen heir had refused to accept an inheritance, he might be constrained to take it, and restore it, at the instance of the* fidei-commissary, *to whom, and against whom, all actions passed, we have transfered that power to the* Trebellian *decree, so that this is now the only law, by which a fiduciary heir can be compelled to enter upon the inheritance, when the* fidei-commissary *is desirous, that it should be restored, and the heir, in this case, can neither receive profit, or suffer loss.*

Quam in fidei-commisiarium.] The term *cestui que trust*, used at present in our own law, seems in general to convey the meaning of the word *fidei-commissarius*, but yet not precisely; it was therefore thought most proper to anglicise it in the translation, as we have no single *English* word, adequate to the sense of it: for a *fidei-commissary*, in the *Roman* law, denotes a person, who has a beneficial interest in an estate, which for a time is committed to the faith or trust of another.

De quibus hæredibus et in quibus fidei-commissarius supra dicta locum habeant.

§ VIII. Nihil autem interest, utrum aliquis, ex asse hæres institutus, aut totam hæreditatem aut pro parte restituere rogatur, an, ex parte hæres institutus, aut totam eam partem, aut partem partis, restituere rogatur. Nam et hoc casu eadem observari præcipimus, quæ in totius hæreditatis restitutione diximus.

§ 8. *But it makes no difference, whether an heir, who is instituted to the whole of an inheritance, is requested by the testator to restore the whole or a part of it only;— or whether an heir, who is nominated but to a part of an inheritance, is requested to restore that intire part, or only a portion of it, for we have ordained, that the same rule of law shall be observed, whether an heir is requested to restore the whole or a part only of an inheritance.*

De eo, quod hæres voluntate testatoris deducit, præcipitve.

§ IX. Si quis, una aliqua re deducta sive præcepta, quæ quartam continet, (veluti fundo vel alia re,) rogatus sit restituere hæreditatem, simili modo ex Trebelliano senatus-consulto restitutio fiet, perinde ac si, quarta parte retenta, rogatus esset reliquam hæreditatem restituere. Sed illud interest, quod altero casu, id est, cum deducta sive præcepta aliqua re restituitur hæreditas, in solidum ex eo senatus consulto actiones transferuntur, et res, quæ remanet apud hæredem, sine ullo onere hæreditario apud eum remanet, quasi ex legato ei acquisita. altero vero casu, cum quarta parte retenta rogatus est hæres restituere hæreditatem, et restituit, scinduntur actiones, et pro dodrante quidem transferuntur ad fidei-commissarium, pro quadrante remanent apud hæredem. Quin etiam, licet una aliqua re deducta aut præcepta restituere aliquis hæreditatem rogatus sit, in qua maxima pars hæreditatis contineatur, æque in solidum transferuntur actiones. Et secum deliberare debet is, cui restituitur hæreditas, an expediat sibi restitui Eadem scilicet interveniunt, et si, duabus pluribusve rebus deductis præceptisve, restituere hæreditatem rogatus sit. Sed et, si certa summa deducta præceptave, quæ quartam vel etiam maximam partem hæreditatis continet, rogatus sit aliquis hæreditatem restituere, idem juris est. Quæ autem diximus de eo, qui ex asse institutus est, eadem transferimus et ad eum, qui ex parte hæres scriptus est.

§ 9 *If an heir is requested to give up an inheritance, after deducting some particular thing, amounting to a fourth, as a piece of ground,* &c. *he may be compelled to give it up by the* Trebellian *decree, in the same manner, as if he had been requested to restore the remainder of an inheritance, after reserving to himself a fourth. There is however this difference, that, in the one case, when an heir is requested to give up an inheritance, after deducting a particular thing, then all actions, passive as well as active, are transfered by virtue of the decree to the* fidei-commissary, *and what remains with the heir is free of all incumberance, as if acquired by legacy; and, in the other case, when an heir is requested in general terms to give up an inheritance, after retaining a fourth to himself, all actions are proportionably divided; those, which regard the three fourths of the estate, being transfered to the* fidei-commissary, *and those, which regard the single fourth, remaining for the benefit of the heir. And, even if an heir is requested to give up an inheritance, after making a deduction of some particular thing, which amounts to the value of the greatest part of it, all actions, both active and passive, are nevertheless transfered to the* fidei-commissary, *who ought therefore always well to consider, whether it will be expedient or not, that the inheritance should be given up to him. And the law is the same, whether an heir is requested to give up an inheritance after a deduction of two, or more, specific things — or of a certain sum of money, which exceeds in value the greatest part of the inheritance. Thus what we have said of an heir, who is instituted to the whole of an inheritance, is equally true of him, who is instituted only to a part.*

De fidei-commissis ab intestato relictis.

§ X. Præterea, intestatus quoque moriturus potest rogare eum, ad quem bona sua vel legitimo jure vel honorario pertinere intelligit, ut hæreditatem suam totam, partemve ejus, aut rem aliquam, veluti fundum, hominem, pecuniam, alicui restituat: cum alioqui legata nisi ex testamento non valeant.

§ 10 *And farther, even a man, who is willing to die intestate, may request the person, who he thinks will succeed him, either by the civil or prætorian law, to give up the whole inheritance, or a part of it, or any particular thing, as a piece of ground, a slave, a sum of money,* &c. *But this liberty is granted to intestates in regard to trusts only, for legacies are not valid, unless they are bequeathed by testament.*

Cum alioqui legata] It is strictly true, that legacies as such, are not valid, unless bequeathed by testament, but by virtue of *Justinian's* ordinance, [*Cod.* 6 *t.* 43] which puts legacies and gifts in trust upon an equality, whatever is bequeathed in a *codicil*, will be good, as a gift in trust, tho' not as a legacy

De

De fidei-commisso relicto a fidei-commissario.

§ XI. Eum quoque, cui aliquid restituitur, potest rogare, ut id rursus alii, aut totum, aut partem, vel etiam aliquid aliud, restituat.

§ 11. *A* fidei-commissary *may also himself be requested to pay over, or give up, to another, either the whole, or a part, of what he receives; or even to give some other thing in lieu of it.*

De probatione fidei-commissi.

§ XII. Et, quia prima fidei-commissorum cunabula a fide hæredum pendent, et tam nomen, quam substantiam, acceperunt, ideo D. Augustus ad necessitatem juris ea retraxit. Nuper et nos, eundem principem superare contendentes, ex facto, quod Tribonianus, vir excellentissimus, quæstor sacri palatii, suggessit, constitutionem fecimus, per quam disposuimus, si testator fidei hæredis sui commisit, ut vel hæreditatem vel speciale fidei-commissum restituat; et neque ex scriptura, neque ex quinque testium numero, qui in fidei-commissis legitimus esse noscitur, possit res manifestari, sed vel pauciores, vel nemo penitus testis intervenerit; tunc, sive pater hæredis, sive alius quicunque sit, qui fidem hæredis elegerit, et ab eo restitui aliquid voluerit, si hæres perfidia tentus adimplere fidem recusat, negando rem ita esse subsecutam, si fidei-commissarius ei jusjurandum detulerit, cum prius ipse de calumnia juraverit, necesse eum habere, vel jusjurandum subire, quod nihil tale a testatore audiverit, vel recusantem ad fidei-commissi vel universalis vel specialis solutionem coarctari, ne depereat ultima voluntas testatoris fidei hæredis commissa. Eadem observari censuimus, etsi a legatario vel fidei-commissario aliquid similiter relictum sit. Quod si is, a quo relictum dicitur, [postquam negaverit,] confiteatur quidem, aliquid a se relictum esse, sed ad legis subtilitatem recurrat, omnino solvere cogendus est

§ 12. *All fiduciary gifts or bequests depended formerly in a precarious manner upon the sole* faith *of the heir; from which they took as well their name as their essence, and the emperor* Augustus *was the first, who thought it proper to reduce them under a judicial cognisance But we have since indeavored to exceed that prince, and, at the instance of that most excellent man* Tribonian, *the questor of our palace, we have enacted by our constitution, that, if a testator hath trusted to the faith of his heir for the surrender of an inheritance, or any particular thing, and this trust cannot be made manifest by the depositions of five witnesses, (which is known to be the legal number in such cases,) there having been not so many, or perhaps no witnesses present, the heir at the same time perfidiously refusing to make any payment, and denying the whole transaction, then in this case the* fidei-commissary, *having previously taken the oath of calumny, may put the heir, altho' he is even the son of the testator, to his oath, and thus force him either to deny the trust upon oath, or comply with it, whether the trust is universal or particular, and this is allowed,* lest

lest the last will of a testator, commited to the faith of an heir, should be defeated. And we have thought it right, that the same remedy should be taken against a legatary, or even a fidei-commissary, *to whom a testator hath left any thing with a request to give it up. And, if any man, to whom something hath been left in trust to be given to another, should confess the trust,* [*after he hath denied it,*] *but indeavor at the same time to shelter himself under the subtility of the law, he may nevertheless be compelled to perform his duty.*

De calumnia juraverit] *vid Cod.* 6 *t* 42 *l* 32

TITULUS VIGESIMUS-QUARTUS.

De singulis rebus per fidei-commissum relictis.

Summa.

POTEST tamen quis etiam singulas res per fidei-commissum relinquere; veluti fundum, argentum, hominem, vestem, et pecuniam numeratam, et vel ipsum hæredem rogare, ut alicui restituat, vel legatarium, quamvis a legatario legari non possit.

A man may also leave particular things in trust; as a field, silver, cloaths, or a certain sum of money, — and may request either his heir to restore them, or even a legatary, altho' a legatary cannot be made chargeable with a legacy.

Quamvis a legatario] This was the antient law, but by *Justinian's* constitution [*Cod* 6 *t* 43] legacies, and gifts in trust, are allowed to come in aid of each other reciprocally, so that, to use the words of the ordinance, *omnia, quæ naturaliter insunt legatis, et fidei-commissis inhærere intelligantur, et contra quicquid fidei-committitur, hoc intelligatur esse legatum* — from which it follows, that a legatary may now be charged with the payment of a legacy

Quæ relinqui possunt.

§ I Potest autem non solum proprias res testator per fidei-commissum relinquere, sed et hæredis, aut legatarii, aut fidei-commissarii, aut cujuslibet alterius. Itaque et legatarius et fidei-commissarius non solum de ea re rogari potest, ut eam alicui restituat, quæ ei relicta sit, sed etiam de alia, sive ipsius, sive aliena sit. Hoc solum observandum est, ne plus quisquam rogetur alicui restituere, quam ipse ex testamento ceperit: nam, quod amplius est, inutiliter relinquitur. Cum autem aliena res per fidei-commissum relinquitur, necesse est ei, qui rogatus est, aut ipsam rem redimere et præstare, aut æstimationem ejus solvere.

§ 1. *A testator may leave not only his own property in trust, but also the property of his heir, of a legatary, of a* fidei-commissary, *or of any other so that a legatary or* fidei commissary *may not only be requested to give what hath been left to him, but what is his own, or even what is the property of another And the only caution necessary to be observed by the testator is, that no man be requested to give more,*

more, than he hath received by means of the testament; for the excess will be ineffectually bequeathed. And, when the property of another is left in trust, the person, requested to restore it, is obliged either to obtain from the proprietor the very thing bequeathed, or to pay the value of it.

De libertate.

§ II. Libertas quoque servo per fidei-commissum dari potest, ut hæres eum rogetur manumittere, vel legatarius, vel fidei-commissarius: nec interest, utrum de suo proprio servo testator roget, an de eo, qui ipsius hæredis, aut legatarii, vel etiam extranei sit. itaque et alienus servus redimi et manumitti debet. Quod si dominus eum non vendit, (si modo nihil ex judicio ejus, qui reliquit libertatem, perceperit,) non statim extinguitur fidei-commissaria libertas, sed differtur, quoad possit tempore procedente, ubicumque occasio servi redimendi fuerit, præstari libertas. Qui autem ex fidei-commissi causa manumittitur, non testatoris fit libertus, etiamsi testatoris servus sit, sed ejus, qui manumittit. At is, qui directo ex testamento liber esse jubetur, ipsius testatoris libertus fit; qui etiam Orcinus appellatur Nec alius ullus directo ex testamento libertatem habere potest, quam qui utroque tempore testatoris fuerit, et quo faceret testamentum, et quo moreretur. Directo autem libertas tunc dari videtur, cum non ab alio servum manumitti rogat, sed velut ex suo testamento libertatem ei competere vult.

§ 2. *Liberty may also be confered upon a slave by virtue of a trust, for an heir, a legatary, or a* fidei-commissary, *may be requested to manumit: nor does it make any difference, whether the testator requests the manumission of his own slave, of the slave of his heir, of the slave of a legatary, or of the slave of a stranger: and therefore, when a slave is not the testator's own property, he must be bought, if possible, and manumitted But, if the proprietor of the slave refuses to sell him, (which refusal the proprietor may justify, if he hath taken nothing under the will of the testator,) yet the fiduciary bequest is not extinguished, but defered only, till it can be conveniently performed. It is here to be observed, that he, who is manumitted in consequence of a trust, does not become the freedman of the testator, altho' he was the testator's own slave, but he becomes the freedman of the manumittor. but a slave, to whom liberty is directly given by testament, becomes the freedman of the testator, and is called* Orcinus, *and no one can obtain liberty directly by testament, unless he was the slave of the testator, not only at the time of the testator's death, but also at the time of the making of his testament And liberty is understood to be directly given, not when a testator requests, that his slave shall be made free by another, but when he commands, that the freedom of his slave shall commence instantly by virtue of his testament.*

De verbis fidei-commissorum.

§ III. Verba autem fidei-commissorum hæc maxime in usu habentur: *peto, rogo, volo, mando, fidei tuæ committo*: quæ perinde singula firma sunt, atque si omnia in unum congesta essent.

§ 3. The

§ 3. *The terms generally used in the commitment of trusts are the following:* — peto, rogo, volo, mando, fidei tuæ committo: — *any of which words, singly taken, is as firm and binding, as if all were joined together.*

TITULUS VIGESIMUS-QUINTUS.

De codicillis.

D. xxix. T. 7. C. vi. T. 36.

Codicillorum origo.

ANTE Augusti tempora constat, codicillorum jus in usu non fuisse: sed primus Lucius Lentulus, ex cujus persona etiam fidei-commissa esse cœperunt codicillos introduxit. Nam, cum decederet in Africa, scripsit codicillos testamento confirmatos, quibus ab Augusto petiit per fidei-commissum, ut faceret aliquid. Et, cum D. Augustus voluntatem ejus implesset, deinceps reliqui, ejus auctoritatem secuti, fidei-commissa præstabant: et filia Lentuli legata, quæ jure non debebat, solvit. Dicitur autem Augustus convocasse sapientes viros, interque eos Trebatium quoque, cujus tunc auctoritas maxima erat, et quæsisse, an posset recipi hoc, nec absonans a juris ratione codicillorum usus esset? et Trebatium suasisse Augusto, quod diceret, utilissimum et necessarium hoc civibus esse, propter magnas et longas peregrinationes, quæ apud veteres fuissent: ubi, si quis testamentum facere non posset, tamen codicillos posset. Post quæ tempora, cum et Labeo codicillos fecisset, jam nemini dubium erat, quin codicilli jure optimo admitterentur.

It is certain, that codicils were not in frequent use before the reign of Augustus: *for* Lucius Lentulus, *by whose means trusts became efficatious, was the first, who caused authority to be given to codicils. When he was dying in* Africa, *he wrote several codicils, which were confirmed by his testament, and in these he requested* Augustus *to perform some particular act in consequence of a trust: the emperor complied with the request, and many other persons afterwards, being influenced by the authority of the emperor's example, punctually performed trusts, which had been committed to their charge: and the daughter of* Lentulus *paid debts, which in strictness of law were not due. But it is reported, that* Augustus, *having convened upon this occasion the sages of the law, and also* Trebatius, *whose opinion was of the greatest authority, demanded, whether codicils could be admitted to be of force, and whether they were not repugnant to the very reason of the law?*

to which Trebatius *answered, that codicils were not only most convenient, but most necessary on account of the great and long voyages, which the* Romans *were frequently obliged to take, to the intent, that, where a man could not make a testament, he might bequeath his effects by codicil And afterwards, when* Labeo, *a lawyer of great eminence, disposed of his own property by codicil, it was no longer a doubt, but that codicils might be legally allowed.*

Codicillorum jus] The word *codicillus*, or codicil, is a diminutive from *codex*, a book, and denotes any unsolemn last will, in which no heir or executor is named " Codicilli dicti " sunt parvi codices, id est, tabellæ ex codi- " cibus aut ligno Itaque, quemadmodum " testamentum *codex* appellatur,

" *Codice sævo*

" Hæredes vetat esse suos, &c *Juv Sat* 10 " quia testamentum in codicibus tantum scri- " bebatur, sive tabulis grandioribus, ita vo- " luntas suprema, minus solemnis aut [illegible], " *codicilli*, et aliquando numero un[illegible] " *cillus*, propterea quod scribi [illegible] co- " dicillis, id est, tabulis bre[illegible]bus et [illegible]o- " ribus, ita factis, ut facile, quo [illegible] com- " modum esset, circumferri possent [illegible] " autem judice, *codicilli* apud veteres [illegible] e- " pistolæ, vel scriptura ad alios [illegible] " ergo codicilli plerumque p[illegible] " forma epistolarum, hinc et nomen retinu- " erunt " *Vinn*

Codicilli fieri possunt vel ante, vel post testamentum, imo etiam ab intestato.

§ I. Non tantum autem testamento facto potest quis codicillos facere, sed et intestatus quis decedens fidei-committere codicillis potest Sed, cum ante testamentum factum codicilli facti erant, Papinianus ait, non aliter vires habere, quam si speciali voluntate postea confirmentur Sed Divi Severus et Antoninus rescripserunt, ex iis codicillis, qui testamentum præcedunt, posse fidei-commissum peti, si appareat, eum, qui testamentum fecit, a voluntate, quam in codicillis expresserat, non recessisse.

§ 1. *Not only he, who hath already made his testament, is* [illegible] *a codicil, but even an intestate may commit a trust to others by* [illegible] *codicil is antecedent to a testament, the* [illegible], *according to* Papinian, [illegible] *wise take effect, than by being* [illegible] *by the subsequent test*[illegible] Severus *and* Antoninus [illegible] *declared, that* [illegible], *left in trust in a codicil preceding a testament,* [illegible] *be demanded by the* fidei-commissary, *if it appears, that the testator hath not* [illegible] *from the intention, which he at first* [illegible] *in his codicil*

Non tantum testamentum] " It is [illegible] of " all, [illegible]] " [illegible] " made [illegible] him, [illegible] " by him, [illegible] " the codicils [illegible] in- " testate, [illegible] " him, [illegible] " goods of the [illegible] " testament [illegible] a " codicil [illegible] by him who [illegible] " a regular [illegible] " made [illegible] " be [illegible] as part and parcel of the testa- " ment, and is to be performed [illegible] " testament, unless [illegible] the " testament, it [illegible] " testament, or to [illegible] " contained in the [illegible] [illegible] " Codicilli [illegible] " [illegible] " [illegible] " [illegible] " [illegible] " [illegible] " [illegible] " [illegible]mento [illegible]

"cunque tempore facti fuerint, ad testamentum pertinent, viresque ex eo capiunt, etiamsi in eo confirmati non sint, et infirmato testamento codicilli concidunt. Illud vero interest inter codicillos testamento nominatim confirmatos et non confirmatos, quod illis relicta etiam directo jure valent, veluti legata et libertates directo datæ, perindeque omnia habeantur, ac si in testamento scripta essent, excepta causa hæreditatis: at quæ codicillis non confirmatis relicta sunt, sive verbis directis sive precariis, debentur jure fidei-commissi. Sed non est, quod de his amplius dicamus; cum enim confusa nunc sit legatorum et fidei-commissorum natura, dubitandum non est, quin legata, codicillis etiam non confirmatis data directo, nunc valeant." *Vinn*

Codicillis hæreditas directo dari non potest.

§ II. Codicillis autem hæreditas neque dari, neque adimi, potest; ne confundatur jus testamentorum et codicillorum: et ideo nec exhæredatio scribi. Directo autem hæreditas codicillis neque dari neque adimi potest. nam per fidei-commissum hæreditas codicillis jure relinquitur. Nec conditionem hæredi instituto codicillis adjicere, neque substituere directo, quis potest.

§ 2. *But an inheritance can neither be given nor taken away by codicil, lest the different operations of testaments and codicils should be confounded and of course an heir can not be disinherited by codicil —— But, altho' an inheritance can neither be given nor taken away by codicil, in* direct *terms, yet it may be legally left from the heir in a codicil by means of a trust or* fidei-commissum. *But no man is allowed to impose a condition upon his heir by codicil, nor to substitute* directly.

Codicillis autem hæreditas] *Groenewegen*, in his book of abrogated laws, says, that the distinctions between testaments and codicils have now ceased to be observed almost every where *Eandem enim ordinationis solemnitatem requirunt, atque ita suprema Hollardiæ curia censuit, et confusis eorum nominibus hæredi institutionem ad substantiam testamenti necessariam esse negant pragmatici, hinc quoque codicillis hæreditatem directo dari et adimi, adeoque et exhæredationem scribi, moribus nostris nil vetat* Groenew de ll abr in Inst 2 t 21

In *England* the appointment of an executor makes the only difference between a testament and a codicil, and this difference is little more than nominal, for whatever may be done by the one, may be also done by the other, so that a condition may be imposed, an estate may be given, or an heir disinherited, as well by codicil as by testament, and even lands may be disposed of by a codicil, if it is signed by the deceased, and attested by three witnesses in his presence, tho' the deceased left no testament, (for a codicil, in it's true sense, denotes any testamentary schedule, and may stand singly, without relation to any other paper,) and, even where there is a testament, disposing of real estate, that testament may be altered or revoked by a codicil properly executed And, where personal estate only is bequeathed, the same degree of proof, (and it has already been said what degree of proof is sufficient,) will establish either a testament or a codicil, and the one may revoke or confirm the other, either wholly or in part, according to it's respective contents

De numero et solemnitate.

§ III. Codicillos autem etiam plures quis facere potest: et nullam solemnitatem ordinationis desiderant.

§ 3 *A man may make many codicils, and they require no solemnity*

Nullam solemnitatem] When it is said, that no solemnity is required in making a codicil, the compilers of the institutions must be understood to mean no extraordinary solemnity, as that of bringing seven witnesses to subscribe it, as in case of a testament for it is necessary by the civil law, that a codicil should be supported by five witnesses, [*Cod* 6 *t* 36 *l* 8] which is the

the ordinary number required to atteſt ſeveral other tranſactions [*Cod* 4 *t* 20 *l* 18] But, in *England*, there is in this reſpect no diſtinction between a teſtament and a codicil, for either may be ſupported by an equal number of witneſſes. —— two are regularly required to a teſtament, and the ſame number is alſo required to a codicil; but, if either a teſtament, or a codicil, contains a deviſe of a real eſtate, three witneſſes are indiſpenſably neceſſary by act of parliament. *vid* 29. *Car* 2 *cap*. 3

FINIS LIBRI SECUNDI.

DIVI JUSTINIANI INSTITUTIONUM LIBER TERTIUS.

TITULUS PRIMUS.

De hæreditatibus, quæ ab inteſtato deferuntur.

D. xxxviii. T. 16. C. vi. T. 55 et 58. Nov. 118.

Definitio inteſtati.

INTESTATUS decedit, qui aut omnino teſtamentum non fecit, aut non jure fecit; aut id, quod fecerat, ruptum irritumve factum eſt, aut ſi ex eo nemo hæres extiterit.

Every perſon is ſaid to die inteſtate, who hath either not made a teſtament; or, if he has made one, hath neglected to uſe the ſolemnities preſcribed by law. A man is alſo ſaid to die inteſtate, if his teſtament, altho' rightly made, is either cancelled or rendered void, or if no one will take upon himſelf the heirſhip by virtue of the teſtament.

Primus ordo ſuccedentium ab inteſtato.

§ I. Inteſtatorum autem hæreditates ex lege duodecim tabularum primum ad ſuos hæredes pertinent.

§ 1. *The inheritances of inteſtates, according to the law of the twelve tables, belong primarily to the* ſui hæredes, i. e. *to the proper or domeſtic heirs of ſuch inteſtates.*

Ex lege duodecim tabularum] This law of the 12 tables is not extant

Qui ſunt ſui hæredes.

§ II. Sui autem hæredes exiſtimantur, (ut ſupra diximus,) qui in poteſtate morientis fuerint; veluti filius filiave, nepos neptiſve ex filio, pronepos proneptiſve ex nepote, ex filio nato prognatus prognatave: nec in-

 tereſt

tereſt, utrum naturales ſint liberi, an adoptivi. Quibus connumerari neceſſe eſt etiam eos, qui ex legitimis quidem nuptiis vel matrimoniis non ſunt progeniti, curiis tamen civitatum dati, ſecundum Divalium conſtitutionum, quæ ſuper his poſita ſunt, tenorem, hæredum ſuorum jura nanciſcuntur: nec non eos, quos noſtræ amplexæ ſunt conſtitutiones, per quas juſſimus, ſi quis mulierem in ſuo contubernio copulaverit, non ab initio affectione maritali, eam tamen, cum qua poterat habere conjugium, et ex ea liberos ſuſtulerit, poſtea vero, affectione procedente, etiam nuptialia inſtrumenta cum ea fecerit, et filios vel filias habuerit, non ſolum eos liberos, qui poſt dotem editi ſunt, juſtos et in poteſtate patris eſſe; ſed etiam anteriores, qui et iis, qui poſtea nati ſunt, occaſionem legitimi nominis præſtiterunt. Quod obtinere cenſuimus, etſi non progeniti fuerint poſt dotale inſtrumentum confectum liberi, vel etiam nati ab hac luce fuerint ſubtracti. Ita demum tamen nepos neptiſve, pronepos proneptiſve, ſuorum hæredum numero ſunt, ſi præcedens perſona deſierit in poteſtate parentis eſſe, ſive morte id acciderit, ſive alia ratione, veluti emancipatione. Nam, ſi per id tempus, quo quis moritur, filius in poteſtate ejus ſit, nepos ex eo ſuus hæres eſſe non poteſt. idque et in cæteris liberorum perſonis dictum intelligimus. Poſthumi quoque, qui, ſi vivo patre nati eſſent, in poteſtate ejus futuri forent, ſui hæredes ſunt.

§ 2. *And, as we have obſerved before, thoſe are eſteemed* ſui hæredes *or proper heirs, who, at the time of the death of the deceaſed, were under his power: as a ſon or a daughter, a grandſon or a grand daughter by a ſon, a great-grandſon or great-grand-daughter by a grandſon of a ſon,* &c. —— *neither is it material, whether theſe children are natural or adopted. But, in the number of natural children, we muſt reckon thoſe, who, altho' they were not born in lawful wedlock, are nevertheleſs, according to the tenor of the imperial conſtitutions, intituled to the rights of proper heirs, by being admitted into the order of Decurions. We muſt alſo add thoſe perſons, who are comprized within our own conſtitutions, by which it is ordained, that, if any perſon, without intending matrimony, ſhall keep a woman, with whom he is not prohibited to marry, and have children by her, and ſhall afterwards, thro' the dictates of affection, marry that woman, and have other children by her, ſons or daughters, then not only theſe latter children, born after the celebration of marriage, ſhall be legitimate and in the power of their father, but alſo the former, who gave occaſion to the legitimacy of thoſe, who were born afterwards. And we have thought it expedient, that this law ſhall alſo obtain in regard to the children born before marriage, altho' the children, born ſubſequent to it, are dead, or even altho' there never were any children ſubſequent to the marriage. But a grandſon or grand-daughter, a great grandſon or great grand daughter, is not reckoned in the number of proper heirs, unleſs the perſon preceding them in degree hath ceaſed to be under paternal power, either by death or ſome other means, as by emancipation. for, if a ſon, when his father died, was under the power of his father, the grandſon can by no means be the proper or domeſtic heir of his grand-father, and, by a parity of reaſoning, this rule is underſtood to take place in relation to all deſcendents in the right line. But all poſthumous children, who would have been under the power of their father, if they had been born in his life-time, are eſteemed* ſui heredes, *or proper heirs.*

Naturales

Naturales sint] The word *natural* here signifies legitimate, in which sense it is always used, when opposed to the term *adopted*.

Divalium constitutionum] *vid. Cod.* 5 *t* 27. *ll.* 3, 4 *Nov.* 89. *cap.* 2

Nostræ amplexæ sunt constitutiones] *vid. Cod.* 5. *t.* 27 *ll.* 10, 11.

Quomodo sui hæredes fiunt.

§ III. Sui autem hæredes fiunt etiam ignorantes, et, licet furiosi sint, hæredes possunt existere: quia, quibus ex causis ignorantibus nobis acquiritur, ex his causis et furiosis acquiri potest. Et statim à morte parentis quasi continuatur dominium; et ideo nec tutoris auctoritate opus est pupillis, cum etiam ignorantibus acquiratur suis hæredibus hæreditas: nec curatoris assensu acquiritur furioso, sed ipso jure.

§ 3. *Persons may become* sui hæredes, *or proper heirs, without their knowledge, and even altho' they are disordered in their senses: for, as inheritances may be acquired without our knowledge, it is a consequence, that they may also be acquired by persons deprived of their understanding And here observe, that the dominion of an inheritance is continued in the heir from the very instant of the death of his ancestor, and that the authority of a Tutor is not necessary to enable a pupil to inherit, because inheritances may be acquired by proper heirs, without their knowledge: neither does a disordered person inherit by the assent of his curator, but by operation of law.*

A morte parentum.] Persons are said to be *sui hæredes*, or proper heirs, *quod non alienarum sed suarum, sive propriarum, quodammodo rerum hæredes esse videantur* i e because they seem to be the heirs of their own property, and not the heirs of another's for a proper heir is, in the life-time of his parent, the co-heir or partener with that parent in his possessions, so that a son, who is a proper heir, does not acquire a new property at the death of his father, but only possesses in a fuller manner what was before vested in him. *Vinny, h t.*

De filio, post mortem patris, ab hostibus reverso.

§ IV. Interdum autem, licet in potestate parentis mortis tempore suus hæres non fuerit, tamen suus hæres parenti efficitur: veluti si ab hostibus quis reversus fuerit post mortem patris sui: jus enim postliminii hoc facit.

§ 4. *But sometimes a child becomes a proper heir, altho' he was not under power, at the time of the death of his parent, as when a person returns from captivity after the death of his father: and this is effected by the* jus postliminii, *or right of return*

De memoria patris damnata ob crimen perduellionis.

§ V. Per contrarium autem hoc evenit, ut, licet quis in familia defuncti sit mortis tempore, tamen suus hæres non fiat, veluti si post mortem suam pater judicatus fuerit perduellionis reus, ac per hoc memoria ejus damnata fuerit. Suum enim hæredem habere non potest, cum fiscus ei succedat: sed potest dici, ipso quidem jure suum hæredem esse, sed desinere.

§ 5. *On the contrary, it may happen, that a child, who at the time of the death of his Parent, was under his power, shall not be his proper heir. as when a parent,*

A 2 *after*

after his decease, is adjudged to have been guilty of lese majesty, by which crime his memory is rendered infamous; for a criminal of this sort can have no proper heir, inasmuch as all his possessions are forfeited to the treasury. But a son, in this case, may strictly be said to have been *the proper heir of his father, and afterwards to have ceased to be so.*

De divisione hæreditatis inter suos hæredes.

§ VI. Cum filius filiave et ex altero filio nepos neptisve existunt, pariter ad hæreditatem avi vocantur, nec, qui gradu proximior est, ulteriorem excludit. Æquum enim esse videtur, nepotes neptesve in patris sui locum succedere. Pari ratione et si nepos neptisve sit ex filio, et ex nepote pronepos proneptisve, simul vocantur. Et, quia placuit, nepotes neptesve, item pronepotes proneptesve, in parentis sui locum succedere, conveniens esse visum est, non in capita, sed in stirpes, hæreditatem dividi; ut filius partem dimidiam hæreditatis habeat, et ex altero filio duo pluresve nepotes alteram dimidiam. Item, si ex duobus filiis nepotes neptesve existant, ex altero unus aut duo forte, ex altero tres aut quatuor, ad unum aut duos dimidia pars pertineat, ad tres vel quatuor altera dimidia.

§ 6. *When there is a son or a daughter, and a grandson or grand-daughter by another son, they are called equally to the inheritance of their parents, nor does the nearest exclude the more remote: for it appears just, that grandsons and grand daughters should succeed in the place of their father. And, by the same reasoning, if there is a grandson or grand daughter by a son, and a great grandson or great grand-daughter by a grandson, they ought all to be called to the inheritance. And, inasmuch as it hath been esteemed right, that grandsons and grand-daughters, great-grandsons and great grand daughters, should succeed in the place of their parent, it seemed convenient, that inheritances should not be divided into* capita, *but into* stirpes: *so that, where there is a son and grand-children by another son, the son possesses half the inheritance, and the grand-children, however numerous, are intituled only to the other half, as the representatives of their father. And in like manner, where there are grand-children by two sons, the one son leaving one or two children, and the other three or four, the inheritance must be equally divided, half belonging to the single grand child, or the two grand children by the one son, and half to the three or four grand children by the other son.*

Item ex duobus filiis] By the civil law, representation takes place *in infinitum* in the right line descending, and therefore it follows, according to that law, that, when any person dies, leaving grand-children by sons or daughters, who died in his life time, such grand children, tho' equal in degree and unequal in their number in regard to their respective stocks, will divide the estate of their grand father *per stirpes*, *i. e.* according to their stocks. For example, if *A* dies worth nine hundred *aurei*, and intestate, leaving only grand children by three sons, already dead, to wit, three grand-children by one son, five by another, and six by another, then each of these classes of grand-children would be intituled to a third, that is, to three hundred *aurei*, no regard being paid to that class, in which there were most persons. *In hoc casu,* (says *Vinnius*,) *maxime conspicua est vis repræsentationis; licet enim omnes hi pari gradu sint, ut proinde singuli jure succedere posse videantur, tamen postquam semel placuit, nepotes in locum patris sui demortui, aliave ratione exuti jure sui hæredis, succedere, non debuit hoc jus ex accidenti aliquo variari, puta ut soli nepotes ex diversis filiis et numero inæquales, seu pauciores cum pluribus ex hac vel illa stirpe concurrentes, in capita hæreditatem dividerent.* Cod. 6. t. 55. *l.* 2. *Quare sic in universum recte definiemus, descendentes ex masculis omnes, qui sunt directarum personarum, quantumvis ejusdem omnes gradus,*

dus, in ſtirpes, non in capita, ſuccedere. But, in *England,* altho' repreſentation may alſo be ſaid to extend *in infinitum* in the right line deſcending, yet this I apprehend muſt be underſtood to be in thoſe caſes only, where repreſentation is abſolutely *neceſſary* to prevent the excluſion of grand-children, great grand-children, &c For example therefore, if *Titius* dies leaving a ſon, and *D, E, F,* his grand children by another ſon, who died before *Titius,* then the ſurviving ſon would take one moity, and the grand-children *D, E, F,* would take the other, as the repreſentatives of their deceaſed father for in this caſe repreſentation would be *neceſſary*, becauſe, if repreſentation was not allowed, the grand-children of *Titius,* being in a more remote degree, than his ſon, would be totally excluded; which would be highly unjuſt But, if *Titius* dies, and leaves only grand children by two ſons, already dead, *e g* three grand-children by one ſon, and ſix by the other, then repreſentation would not only not be neceſſary, (as all perſons are in the ſame degree, ſo that none of them can be excluded,) but it would occaſion a very unequal diſtribution of the effects; namely, of only half the eſtate to ſix of the grand children, and of half to the other three, which does not ſeem agreeable either to the ſenſe, or even the words of the ſtatute. See 22, 23, *Car.2. cap.*10.

Quo tempore ſuitas ſpectatur.

§ VII. Cum autem quæritur, an quis ſuus hæres exiſtere poſſit, eo tempore quærendum eſt, quo certum eſt, aliquem ſine teſtamento deceſſiſſe: quod accidit et deſtituto teſtamento. Hac ratione, ſi filius exhæredatus fuerit et extraneus hæres inſtitutus, et, filio mortuo, poſtea certum fuerit, hæredem inſtitutum ex teſtamento non fieri hæredem, aut quia noluit eſſe hæres, aut quia non potuit, nepos avo ſuus hæres exiſtet: quia, quo tempore certum eſt, inteſtatum deceſſiſſe patrem-familias, ſolus invenitur nepos: et hoc certum eſt.

§ 7 *Whenever it is demanded, whether any perſon is a proper heir, we muſt inquire at what time it was certain, that the deceaſed died without a teſtament, and a man is ſaid to die without a teſtament, if his teſtament is relinquiſhed Thus if a ſon is diſinherited and a ſtranger is inſtituted heir, and, after the death of the ſon, it becomes certain, that the inſtituted heir was not in fact the heir, either becauſe he was unwilling, or unable, to accept the inheritance, in this caſe, the grand-ſon of the deceaſed becomes the proper heir of his grandfather. for at the time, when it was certain, that the deceaſed died inteſtate, there was no other heir, but the grandchild; and this is evident.*

De nato poſt mortem avi, vel adoptato à filio emancipato.

§ VIII. Et, licet poſt mortem avi natus ſit, tamen avo vivo conceptus, mortuo patre ejus, poſteaque deſerto avi teſtamento, ſuus hæres efficitur Plane, ſi et conceptus et natus fuerit poſt mortem avi, mortuo patre ſuo, deſertoque poſtea avi teſtamento, ſuus hæres avo non exiſtet, quia nullo jure cognationis patrem ſui patris attigit. ſed nec ille eſt inter liberos avi, quem filius emancipatus adoptavit Hi autem, cum non ſint ſui, (quantum ad hæreditatem,) liberi, neque bonorum poſſeſſionem petere poſſunt, quaſi proximi cognati Hæc de ſuis hæredibus.

§ 8 *And altho' a child is born after the death of his grandfather, yet, if he was conceived in the life time of his grandfather, he will, at the death of his father and after his grandfather's teſtament is deſerted by the inſtituted heir, become the proper heir of his grandfather But, if a child is both conceived and born after the death of his grandfather, ſuch child, altho' his father ſhould die and the teſtament of his grand-father*

father be deserted, could not become the proper heir of his grandfather; because he was never allied to his grandfather by any tye of cognation. Neither is he, whom an emancipated son hath adopted, to be reckoned in any respect among the children of his adoptive father's father. So that the adopted children of an emancipated son can neither become the proper heirs of their father's father in regard to the inheritance, nor demand the possession of goods, as next of kin. This is what we have thought it expedient to observe concerning proper heirs

Plane si et conceptus et natus.] "Sunt, qui "velint hunc nepotem, etsi ad hæreditatem avi "jure suo non veniat, posse nihilominus jure "paterno eam adipisci etenim certum est, libe- "ros parentum hæreditatem, quantumvis non ac- "quisitam, ad liberos suos transmittere. *Cod.* "6 *t* 51 *l.* 1. *sect* 5 *Cod.* 6. *t.* 52. *l* 1." "Filius porro in proposita facti specie, si adhuc "viveret, posset patris hæreditatem acquirere; "sic igitur ad filium suum posthumum, etsi post "avi mortem conceptum, hæreditatem ejus "transmittere posse putant *Pileus* nepoti huic, "per Novellam 118, succursum esse censet, ut "suo jure avo succedere possit, et hoc quidem "suadet æquitas, sed non favent satis perspicue "verba legum." *Doujatius.*

De liberis emancipatis.

§ IX. Emancipati autem liberi jure civili nihil juris habent: neque enim sui hæredes sunt, qui in potestate morientis esse desierunt, neque ullo alio jure per legem duodecim tabularum vocantur. Sed prætor, naturali æquitate motus, dat eis bonorum possessionem *unde liberi*, perinde ac si in potestate parentis tempore mortis fuissent, sive soli sint, sive cum suis hæredibus concurrant. Itaque, duobus liberis existentibus, emancipato uno, et eo, qui tempore mortis in potestate fuerit, sane quidem is, qui in potestate fuit, solus jure civili hæres est, et solus suus hæres: sed, cum emancipatus, beneficio prætoris, in partem admittitur, evenit, ut suus hæres pro parte hæres fiat.

§ 9. *Emancipated children by the civil law have no right to the inheritances of their parents: for those are not proper heirs, who have ceased to be under the power of their parent deceased, before his death, neither are they called to inherit by any other right according to the law of the twelve tables. But the prætor, induced by natural equity, grants them the possession of goods, by the edict beginning,* unde liberi, *as fully, as if they had been under power at the time of the death of their parent, and the prætor grants this, whether they are sole, or mixed with others, who are* proper heirs: *therefore, when there are two sons, the one emancipated, and the other under power at the time of his father's death, the latter, by the civil law, is alone the heir, and alone the proper heir but, when the emancipated son, by the indulgence of the prætor, is admitted to his share, then the proper heir becomes the heir only of his own moiety.*

Si emancipatus se dederit in adoptionem.

§ X. At hi, qui emancipati à parente in adoptionem se dederunt, non admittuntur ad bona naturalis patris quasi liberi, si modo, cum is moreretur, in adoptiva familia fuerint: nam vivo eo emancipati ab adoptivo patre perinde admittuntur ad bona naturalis patris, ac si emancipati ab ipso essent, nec unquam in adoptiva familia fuissent: et convenienter, quod ad adoptivum patrem pertinet, extraneorum loco esse incipiunt. Post mortem

vero

vero naturalis patris emancipati ab adoptivo patre, et, quantum ad hunc adoptivum patrem pertinet, æque extraneorum loco fiunt, et, quantum ad naturalis patris bona pertinet, nihilo magis liberorum gradum nanciſcuntur. Quod ideo ſic placuit, quia iniquum erat, eſſe in poteſtate patris adoptivi, ad quos bona naturalis patris pertineant, utrum ad liberos ejus, an ad agnatos.

§ 10 *But thoſe, who after emancipation have given themſelves in adoption, are not admitted, as children, to the poſſeſſion of the effects of their natural father, if, at the time of his death, they were in the adoptive family But, if in the life-time of their natural father they were emancipated by their adoptive father, they are then admitted by the prætor to take the goods of their natural father, as if they had been emancipated by him, and had never entered into the family of the adoptor · and conſequently, in regard to their adoptive father, they are looked upon as mere ſtrangers. But thoſe, who are emancipated by their adoptive father, after the death of their natural father, are nevertheleſs reputed ſtrangers to their adoptive father; and, in regard to the inheritance of their natural father, they are not at all the more intituled to reaſſume the rank of children. Theſe rules of law have been eſtabliſhed, inaſmuch as it was unjuſt, that it ſhould be in the power of an adoptor to determine at his pleaſure, to whom the inheritance of a natural father ſhould appertain, whether to his children, or to his* agnates.

Ad liberos, an ad agnatos] For the arrogator, by retaining under his power the emancipated ſon of the deceaſed, might make room for the *agnati* of the deceaſed, or, by emancipating his arrogated ſon, who was the natural ſon of the deceaſed, the arrogator might exclude the *agnati*, ſo that thus the right of inheritance would depend upon the will and pleaſure of a ſtranger, which the law would not permit.

Collatio filiorum naturalium et adoptivorum.

§ XI. Minus ergo juris habent adoptivi filii, quam naturales: namque naturales, emancipati beneficio prætoris, gradum liberorum retinent, licet jure civili perdant. Adoptivi vero emancipati et jure civili perdunt gradum liberorum, et à prætore non admittuntur: et recte. Naturalia enim jura civilis ratio perimere non poteſt, nec, quia deſinunt ſui hæredes eſſe, poſſunt deſinere filii filiæve, nepotes neptesve eſſe. Adoptivi vero emancipati extraneorum loco incipiunt eſſe: quia jus nomenque filii filiæve, quod per adoptionem conſecuti ſunt, alia civili ratione, id eſt, emancipatione, perdunt.

§ 11 *Adopted children have therefore fewer rights and privileges, than natural children: for natural children, even after emancipation, retain the rank of children by the indulgence of the prætor, altho' they loſe it by the civil law but adopted children, when emancipated, loſe the rank of children by the civil law, and are denied admittance into the rank of children by the prætor, and not without reaſon for civil policy can by no means deſtroy natural rights, and thus natural children cannot ceaſe to be ſons and daughters, grandſons and grand-daughters, altho' they may ceaſe to be proper heirs but adopted children, when emancipated, commence immediately ſtrangers, for the right and name of ſon or daughter, which were obtained by the civil right of adoption, may be deſtroyed by another civil right; namely, by emancipation.*

§ XII.

De bonorum poſſeſſione contra tabulas.

§ XII. Eadem hæc obſervantur et in ea bonorum poſſeſſione, quam contra tabulas teſtamenti parentis liberis præteritis, id eſt, neque hæredibus inſtitutis, neque, ut oportet, exhæredatis, prætor pollicetur. Nam eos quidem, qui in poteſtate mortis tempore fuerint, et emancipatos, vocat prætor ad eandem bonorum poſſeſſionem; eos vero, qui in adoptiva familia fuerint per hoc tempus, quo naturalis parens moreretur, repellit. Item adoptivos liberos, emancipatos ab adoptivo patre, ſicut nec ab inteſtato, ita longe minus contra tabulas teſtamenti, ad bona ejus admittit: quia deſinunt in numero liberorum ejus eſſe.

§ 12 *The ſame rules are obſerved in regard to that poſſeſſion of goods, which the prætor, contrary to the teſtament of the parent, grants to the children, who are not mentioned in the teſtament, that is, to ſuch, who are neither inſtituted heirs, nor properly diſinherited For the prætor calls thoſe, who were under power at the time of the death of their parents, and thoſe alſo, who are emancipated, to the ſame poſſeſſion of goods · but he repels thoſe, who were in an adoptive family at the time of the deceaſe of their natural parents. And, as the prætor admits not theſe adopted children, who have been emancipated by their adoptive father, to ſucceed him* ab inteſtato, *much leſs therefore does the prætor admit ſuch children to poſſeſs the goods of their adoptive father contrary to his teſtament; for, by virtue of the emancipation, they ceaſe to be in the number of his children.*

Unde cognati.

§ XIII. Admonendi tamen ſumus, eos, qui in aliena familia ſunt, quive poſt mortem naturalis parentis ab adoptivo patre emancipati fuerint, inteſtato parente naturali mortuo, licet ea parte edicti, qua liberi ad bonorum poſſeſſionem vocantur, non admittantur, alia tamen parte vocari, ſcilicet, qua cognati defuncti vocantur Ex qua ita admittuntur, ſi neque ſui hæredes liberi, neque emancipati obſtent, neque agnatus quidem ullus interveniat. Ante enim prætor liberos vocat, tam ſuos hæredes quam emancipatos, deinde legitimos hæredes, tertio proximos cognatos.

§ 13 *We muſt nevertheleſs obſerve, that, altho' thoſe, who were in an adoptive family, but have been emancipated by their adoptive father, after the deceaſe of their natural father, dying inteſtate, are not admited by that part of the edict, by which children are called to the poſſeſſion of goods, yet they are admited by another part, by which the* cognates *of the deceaſed are called to the poſſeſſion of his effects. But, by this laſt-named part of the edict, the* cognates *are only called, when there is no oppoſition from* proper heirs, *emancipated children, or* agnates · *for the prætor firſt calls the* proper heirs *with the emancipated children, then the* agnates, *and laſtly the neareſt* cognates

Emendatio juris antiqui. De adoptivis.

§ XIV. Sed ea omnia antiquitati placuerunt: aliquam autem emendationem à noſtra conſtitutione acceperunt, quam ſuper iis perſonis expoſuimus,

mus, quæ à patribus ſuis naturalibus in adoptionem aliis dantur: invenimus etenim nonnullos caſus, in quibus filii et naturalium ſucceſſionem propter adoptionem amittebant, et, adoptione facile per emancipationem ſoluta, ad neutrius patris ſucceſſionem vocabantur. Hoc, ſolito more, corrigentes, conſtitutionem ſcripſimus, per quam definimus, quando parens naturalis filium ſuum adoptandum alii dederit, integra omnia jura ita ſervari, atque ſi in patris naturalis poteſtate permanſiſſet, nec penitus adoptio fuiſſet ſubſecuta, niſi in hoc tantummodo caſu, ut poſſit ab inteſtato ad patris adoptivi venire ſucceſſionem. Teſtamento autem ab eo facto, neque jure civili, neque prætorio, ex hæreditate ejus aliquid perſequi poteſt, neque contra tabulas bonorum poſſeſſione agnita, neque inofficioſi querela inſtituta, cum nec neceſſitas patri adoptivo imponatur, vel hæredem eum inſtituere, vel exhæredem facere, utpote nullo vinculo naturali copulatum: neque ſi ex Sabiniano ſenatus-conſulto ex tribus maribus fuerit adoptatus: nam, et in ejuſmodi caſu, neque quarta ei ſervatur, neque ulla actio ad ejus perſecutionem ei competit. Noſtra autem conſtitutione exceptus eſt is, quem parens naturalis adoptandum ſuſceperit. Utroque enim jure, tam naturali quam legitimo, in hanc perſonam concurriente, priſtina jura tali adoptioni ſervamus, quemadmodum ſi pater-familias ſeſe dederit arrogandum: quæ ſpecialiter et ſingulatim ex præfatæ conſtitutionis tenore poſſunt colligi.

§ 14. *Theſe were the rules of law, which formerly obtained; but they have received ſome emendation from the conſtitution, which we promulged, relating to thoſe perſons, who are given in adoption by their natural parents: for we have found frequent inſtances of ſons, who by adoption have loſt their ſucceſſion to their natural parents, and who, by the eaſe with which adoption is diſſolved by emancipation, have alſo loſt the right of ſucceeding to their adoptive parents. We therefore, correcting as uſual whatever is amiſs, have enacted a conſtitution, by which it is decreed, that, when a natural father hath given his ſon in adoption, all the rights of ſuch ſon ſhall nevertheleſs be preſerved intire, in the ſame manner, as if he had ſtill remained under the power of his natural father, and there had been no adoption; except only, that the perſon adopted may ſucceed to his adoptor, if he dies inteſtate. And it is alſo enacted, that, if the adoptor makes a teſtament and omits the name of his adopted ſon, ſuch ſon can neither by the civil nor the prætorian law obtain any part of the inheritance, whether he demands the poſſeſſion of the effects* contra tabulas teſtamenti, *(contrary to the letter of the teſtament,) or prefers a complaint, alleging, that the teſtament is inofficious: for an adoptor is under no obligation either to inſtitute, or diſinherit, his adopted ſon, inaſmuch as there ſubſiſts not between them any natural tye or relation. And we have farther decreed, that no adopted perſon ſhall receive any benefit from the* Sabinian ſenatus-conſultum, *by being one of three ſons: for in this caſe he ſhall neither obtain the fourth part of his adoptive father's effects, nor be intituled to any action upon that account. But all thoſe, who are adopted by their natural parents,* i. e. *by a grand father or great-grand-father,*&c. *are excepted in our conſtitution: for, inaſmuch as ſuch perſons are united together by the concurrence both of natural and civil rights, we have thought proper to retain the old law in relation to thoſe adoptions; in the ſame man-*

ner, as when the father of a family hath given himself in arrogation. But all, which we have here observed, may be collected from the tenor of the above-mentioned constitution.

Constitutionem scripsimus] *vid. Cod* 8. *t.* 48. *l.* 10. *De adoptionibus.*

Ex Sabiniano senatus-consulto.] "Quo senatus consulto, quantum ex hoc loco conjicere "est, cautum fuit, ut, qui unum è tribus alte- "rius liberis manibus adoptasset, quartum par- "tem ei bonorum suorum relinquere cogeretur, "sicut ex constitutione *Antonini Pii* quarta "relinquenda est arrogato impuberi" *vid. Vinn.*

De descendentibus ex fœminis.

§ XV. Item vetustas, ex masculis progenitos plus diligens, solos nepotes vel neptes, qui quæve ex virili sexu descendunt, ad suorum vocabat successionem, et jure agnatorum eos anteponebat: nepotes autem, qui ex filiabus nati sunt, et pronepotes, qui ex neptibus, cognatorum loco connumerans, post agnatorum lineam eos vocabat, tam in avi vel proavi materni, quam in aviæ vel proaviæ, sive paternæ sive maternæ, successionem. Divi autem principes non passi sunt talem contra naturam injuriam sine competenti emendatione relinquere: sed, cum nepotis et pronepotis nomen commune sit utrisque, tam qui ex masculis, quam qui ex fœminis descendunt, ideo eundem gradum et ordinem successionis eis donaverunt. Sed, ut amplius aliquid sit eis, qui non solum naturæ, sed etiam veteris juris, suffragiis muniuntur, portionem nepotum vel neptum, vel deinceps, (de quibus supra diximus) paulo minuendam esse existimaverunt; ut minus tertia parte acciperent, quam mater eorum, vel avia, fuerat acceptura, vel pater eorum vel avus, paternus sive maternus, quando fœmina mortua sit, cujus de hæreditate agitur: iisque, licet soli sint, adeuntibus, agnatos minime vocabant. Et, quemadmodum lex duodecim tabularum, filio mortuo, nepotes vel neptes, pronepotes vel proneptes, in locum patris sui ad successionem avi sui vocat: ita et principalis dispositio in locum matris suæ vel aviæ eos, cum jam designata partis tertiæ diminutione, vocat. Sed nos, cum adhuc dubitatio maneret inter agnatos et memoratos nepotes, quartam partem substantiæ defuncti agnatis sibi vindicantibus ex cujusdam constitutionis auctoritate, memoratam quidem constitutionem à nostro codice segregavimus, neque inseri eam ex Theodosiano codice in eo concessimus. Nostra autem constitutione promulgata, toti juri ejus derogatum est: et sanximus, talibus nepotibus ex filia, vel pronepotibus ex nepte, vel deinceps superstitibus, adgnatos nullam partem mortui successionis sibi vindicare: ne hi, qui ex transversa linea veniunt, potiores his habeantur, qui recto jure descendunt. Quam constitutionem nostram obtinere secundum sui vigorem et tempora et nunc sancimus: ita tamen ut, quemadmodum inter filios et nepotes ex filio antiquitas statuit, non in capita, sed in stirpes, dividi hæreditatem, similiter nos, inter filios et nepotes ex filia, distributionem fieri jubeamus, vel inter omnes nepotes et neptes, et inter pronepotes vel proneptes, et alias deinceps personas; ut utraque progenies matris vel patris, aviæ vel avi, portionem sine ulla diminu-

tione

tione consequatur: ut, si forte unus vel duo ex una parte, ex altera tres aut quatuor, extent, unus aut duo dimidiam, alteri tres aut quatuor alteram dimidiam, hæreditatis habeant.

§ 15. *The antient law, shewing most favor to descendents from males, called those grand children only, who were so descended, to the succession as proper heirs, and prefered them by the right of agnation: for the old law, reputing the grand-children born of daughters, and the great-grand-children born of grand-daughters, to be* cognates, *prohibited such children from succeeding to their grand-father and great-grand-father, maternal or paternal, 'till after the line of* agnati *was exhausted. But the emperors* Valentinian, Theodosius, *and* Arcadius, *would not suffer such a violence against nature to continue in practice; and, inasmuch as the name of grand-child and great-grand-child is undoubtedly common, as well to descendents by females, as to descendents by males, they therefore granted an equal right of succession to descendents from males and descendents from females. But, to the end, that those persons, who have been favored by nature, as well as by the suffrage of antiquity, might enjoy some peculiar privileges, the same emperors have thought it right, that the portions of grand-children, great-grand-children, and other lineal descendents of a female, should be somewhat diminished, and therefore they have not permited such persons to receive so much by a third part, as their mother or grand-mother would have received; or their father or grand-father, paternal or maternal, at the decease of a female; for we now treat concerning inheritances, derived from a female: and, altho' there were only grand children by a female to take an inheritance, yet the emperors did not call the* agnates *to the succession. And as, upon the decease of a son, the law of the twelve tables calls the grand-children, and great grand-children, male and female, to represent their father in respect to the succession of their grand-father, so the imperial ordinance calls them to succession in the place of their mother or grand mother, with the before-regulated diminution of a third part of their share. But, as there still remained matter of dispute between the* agnati *and the above named grand children, the* agnati *claiming the fourth part of the estate of the deceased by virtue of a certain constitution, we have therefore not permited it to be inserted into* our *code from that of* Theodosius *And we have farther taken care to alter the old law by our ordinance, having enacted, that* agnates *shall not be intituled to any part of the goods of the deceased, whilest grand children born of a daughter, or great-grand-children born of a grand-daughter, or any other descendents from a female in the right line, are living, lest those, who proceed from the transverse line, should be prefered to lineal descendents And we now decree, that this our ordinance shall obtain according to it's full tenor. But as the old law ordered, that every inheritance should be divided in* stirpes, *and not in* capita, *between the son of the deceased and his grandsons by a son, so we also ordain, that distribution shall be made in the same manner between sons and grandsons by a daughter, and between all grandsons and grand daughters, great-grandsons and great grand-daughters, and all other descendents in a right line, so that the issue either of a mother or a father, or of a grand mother or a grand-father, may obtain their portions without any diminution, and, if on the one part there should be only one or two claimants, and on the other part three or four, that the greater number shall be intituled only to one half, and the less number to the other half of the inheritance*

Sed ut amplius aliquid.] Nam, si quis decedat relicto filio, et ex filia nepote nepteve, vel pronepote pronepteve, filius quidem octo uncias habebit, nepos vero neptisve, aut pronepos proneptisve, ex filia præmortua, quatuor, hoc est, tertia parte minus quam mater eorum, vel avia, si superesset, haberet Quod si mortua sit fœmina relicto filio, filiave, relicto item nepote aut

aut pronepote ex filio filiave, jam ante defunctis, filius ille, aut filia, octo uncias habebit, nepos vero aut pronepos, sive ex filio, sive ex filia, jam ante defunctis, quatuor hoc est, tertia parte minus quam pater eorum, aut mater, vel avus aviave, sive paterni, sive materni, accepturi essent. *Theophilus.*

Portionem nepotum vel neptum] Descendents by a female were afterwards exempted by *Novel* 18 from suffering any defalcation, when they concurred with descendents from a male.

Unum ordinem *in omnibus ponimus nepotibus et pronepotibus, non ferentes, fœminam a masculo in talibus minui neque enim masculus ipse in se, neque fœmina solum ad nativitatis propagationem sufficiens est, sed sicut utrumque eorum coaptavit Deus ad generationis opus, ita etiam nos eandem utrisque servamus æquitatem.* Novel 18. c. 4. See also *Nov.* 118

Ex cujusdam constitutionis auctoritate] *Cod.* Theod. *de legit. hæred l* 4.

Nostra autem constitutione] *vid Cod.* 6 *de suis et legitimis liberis t.* 55. *l.* 12 by which the *agnati* are prohibited for the future to claim the fourth, which was before due to them, in consequence of a law made by *Theodosius. vid Cod.* Theod *de legit hæred* l. 4

Sine ulla diminutione] " Quartæ scilicet " agnatorum, tertiæ enim deductionem tribu- " tam iis, qui etiam juris veteris suffragatione " nituntur, intactam reliquit sed jure novissi- " mo par est omnium liberorum, in successione " ab intestato, conditio *Vinn* Nov. 118 c 1.

TITULUS SECUNDUS.

De legitima agnatorum successione.

D. xxxviii. T. 16. C. vi. T. 58.

Secundus ordo hæredum legitimorum.

SI nemo suus hæres, vel eorum, quos inter suos hæredes prætor vel constitutiones vocant, existat, qui successionem quoquo modo amplectatur, tunc ex lege duodecim tabularum ad agnatum proximum pertinet hæreditas.

When it happens, that there are no proper heirs to succeed the deceased, nor any of those persons, whom the prætor or the constitutions would call to inherit with proper heirs, then the inheritance, by a law of the twelve tables, appertains to the nearest agnate

Ad agnatum proximum] " Quanquam in " recta linea gradus non curetur, in his tamen, " qui ex transverso conjunguntur, gradus præ- " rogativa omnino attenditur, sic ut proximi " remotioribus anteponantur, quare ULPIANUS, *Hæreditas* (inquit) *proximo agnato,* i e " ei, quem nemo antecedit, defertur *Mynsingerus*

De agnatis naturalibus.

§ I. Sunt autem agnati (ut primo quoque libro tradidimus) cognati per virilis sexus personas cognatione conjuncti, quasi à patre connati. Itaque ex eodem patre nati fratres, agnati sibi sunt; qui et consanguinei vocantur: nec requiritur, an etiam eandem matrem habuerint. Item patruus fratris filio, et invicem is illi, agnatus est. Eodem numero sunt fratres patrueles, id est, qui ex duobus fratribus procreati sunt, qui etiam consobrini vocantur. Qua ratione etiam ad plures gradus agnationis pervenire poterimus. Ii etiam, qui post mortem patris nascuntur, jura consanguisanguinitatis nanciscuntur. Non tamen omnibus simul agnatis dat lex hæreditatem: sed iis, qui tunc proximiore gradu sunt, cum certum esse cœperit, aliquem intestatum decessisse.

§ 1. Agnates, *as we have observed in the first book, are those, who are related or cognated by males,* (quasi à patre cognati) *and therefore brothers, who are the sons of the same father, are* agnates *in regard to each other, they are also called* consanguinei, *being of the same blood; but it is not required, that they should have the same mother. An uncle is also agnated to his brother's son, and* vice versa *the brother's son to his paternal uncle. and* brothers patruel, *that is, the children of brothers, who are also called* consobrini, *are likewise reckoned* agnates *In this manner we may enumerate many degrees of agnation, and even those, who are born, after the decease of their parents, obtain the rights of consanguinity: the law nevertheless does not grant the right of inheritance to all the* agnati, *but to those only, who are in the nearest degree, when it becomes certain, that the deceased hath died intestate.*

" A patre connati.] Cognatio est nomen generale, sed non tantum *generale*, plerumque " autem speciale est, et proprium eorum, qui " vel per fœminei sexus personas conjunguntur, " vel capitis diminutione jura agnationis amiserunt *Vinn h t*

Consobrini] " Per abusionem sic dicti, consobrini enim propriè sunt, qui ex duabus sororibus nati sunt, ita dicti, quasi consororini. *Theoph.*

De adoptivis.

§ II. Per adoptionem quoque agnationis jus consistit, veluti inter filios naturales et eos, quos pater eorum adoptavit: nec dubium est, quin ii impropriè consanguinei appellentur. Item, si quis ex cæteris agnatis tuis, veluti frater aut patruus, aut denique is, qui longiore gradu est, adoptaverit aliquem, agnatus inter tuos esse non dubitatur.

§ 2. *The right of agnation arises also from adoption, thus the natural and adopted sons of the same father are* agnates, *but such persons are without doubt improperly called* consanguinei. *Also if a brother, a paternal uncle, or any other, who is agnated to you in a more remote degree, should adopt any person into his family, then such adopted person is undoubtedly to be reckoned in the number of your* agnati.

De masculis et fœminis.

§ III. Cæterum inter masculos quidem agnationis jure hæreditas, etiamsi longissimo gradu sint, ultro citroque capitur. Quod ad fœminas vero attinet, ita placebat, ut ipsæ, consanguinitatis jure tantum, capiant hæreditatem, si sorores sint; ulterius non capiant. Masculi autem ad earum hæreditates, (etiamsi longissimo gradu sint,) admittantur. Qua de causa fratris tui, aut patrui tui filiæ, vel amitæ tuæ, hæreditas ad te pertinebat: tua vero ad illas non pertinebat. Quod ideo ita constitutum erat, quia commodius videbatur, ita jura constitui, ut plerumque hæreditates ad masculos confluerent. Sed, quia sane iniquum erat, in universum eas quasi extraneas repelli, prætor eas ad bonorum possessionem admittit ea parte qua proximitatis nomine bonorum possessionem pollicetur: ex qua parte ita scilicet admittuntur, si neque agnatus ullus, neque proximior cognatus

tus, interveniat. Et hæc quidem lex duodecim tabularum nullo modo introduxit: sed, simplicitatem legibus amicam amplexa, simili modo omnes agnatos, sive masculos sive fœminas, cujuscunque gradus, ad similitudinem suorum, invicem ad successionem vocabat. Media autem jurisprudentia, quæ erat quidem lege duodecim tabularum junior, imperiali autem dispositione anterior, subtilitate quadam excogitata, præfatam differentiam inducebat, et penitus eas à successione agnatorum repellebat, omni alia successione incognita, donec prætores, paulatim asperitatem juris civilis corrigentes, sive, quod deerat, implentes, humano proposito alium ordinem suis edictis addiderunt; et cognationis linea, proximitatis nomine introducta, per bonorum possessionem eas adjuvabant, et pollicebantur his bonorum possessionem, quæ *unde cognati* appellatur. Nos vero, legem duodecim tabularum sequentes, et ejus vestigia hac in parte conservantes, laudamus quidem prætores suæ humanitatis, non tamen eos in plenum huic causæ mederi invenimus. Quare etenim, uno eodemque gradu naturali concurrente, et agnationis titulis tam in masculis quam in fœminis æqua lance constitutis, masculis quidem dabatur ad successionem venire omnium agnatorum, ex agnatis autem mulieribus nulli penitus, nisi soli sorori, agnatorum successionem patebat aditus? Ideo nos, in plenum omnia reducentes, et ad jus duodecim tabularum eandem dispositionem exæquantes, nostra constitutione sancimus, omnes legitimas personas, id est, per virilem sexum descendentes (sive masculini generis sive fœminini sint) simili modo ad jura successionis legitimæ ab intestato vocari, secundum sui gradus prærogativam; nec ideo excludendas, quia consanguinitatis jura, sicut germanæ, non habent.

§ 3 *Succession among males proceeds according to the right of agnation, altho' they are in the most distant degree. But it hath pleased the antient lawyers, that females should only inherit by consanguinity, if they are sisters; and not in a more remote degree; tho' males might be admited in the most distant degree to inherit females: thus, in case of death, the inheritance of your brother's daughter, or of the daughter of your paternal uncle or aunt, would appertain to you, but your inheritance would not appertain to them. And this was so determined, because it seemed expedient for the benefit of society, that inheritances should for the most part fall into the possession of males. But, inasmuch as it was extremely unjust, that females should be thus almost wholly excluded as strangers, the prætor admited them to the possession of goods in that part of his edict, in which he gives the possession of goods on account of proximity. yet they are only admited upon condition, that there is no* agnate, *or nearer* cognate *But the law of the twelve tables did not introduce these dispositions, for that law, according to the plainness and simplicity, which are agreeable to all laws, called the* agnates *of either sex, or any degree, to succession, in the same manner as it admited* proper *heirs But the middle law, which was posterior to the law of the twelve tables, and prior to the imperial constitutions, subtilly introduced the before mentioned distinction, and intirely repelled females from the succession of* agnates, *no other method of succession being known, till the prætors, correcting by degrees the asperity of the civil law, or supplying what was deficient, added in their edicts a new order of succession, being induced to it by a motive of humanity, and, by introducing the line of cognation on account*

account of proximity, they thus assisted the females, and gave them the possession of goods, which is called unde cognati. *But we, altho' we have adhered to the law of the twelve tables, and strictly maintained it in regard to females, must yet commend the humanity of the prætors, tho' they have not afforded a full remedy in the present case. But, since the same natural degree of relation, and the same title of agnation appertains as well to females as to males, what reason can be assigned, that males should be permited to succeed all their* agnati, *and that no means of succession should be open to any female* agnate, *except a sister? We therefore, reducing all things to an equality, and making our disposition conformable to the laws of the twelve tables, have by our constitution ordained, that all legitime persons, that is, descendents from males, whether male or female, shall be equally called to the rights of succession* ab intestato *according to the prerogative of their degree, and be by no means excluded, altho' they possess not the rights of consanguinity in so near a degree as sisters.*

Nostra constitutione sancimus] *vid. Cod* 6. *t.* 58 *l pen de legit. hæredibus.*

De filiis sororum.

§ IV. Hoc etiam addendum nostræ constitutioni existimavimus, ut transferatur unus tantummodo gradus à jure cognationis in legitimam successionem; ut non solum fratris filius et filia (secundum quod jam definivimus) ad successionem patrui sui vocentur, sed etiam germanæ consanguineæ vel sororis uterinæ filius et filia soli, et non deinceps personæ, una cum his ad jura avunculi sui perveniant: et, mortuo eo, qui patruus quidem est sui fratris filiis, avunculus autem sororis suæ soboli, simili modo ab utroque latere succedant, tanquam si omnes ex masculis descendentes legitimo jure veniant, scilicet ubi frater et soror superstites non sunt. His etenim personis præcedentibus et successionem admittentibus, cæteri gradus remanent penitus semoti, videlicet hæreditate non in stirpes, sed in capita, dividenda.

§ 4 *We have farther thought it necessary to add a clause to our constitution, by which one degree is transfered from the line of cognation to the line of legitime succession, i. e. of* agnation *so that not only the son and daughter of a brother (according to our former definition of* agnates) *shall be called to the succession of their paternal uncle, but the son or daughter of a sister, who is either by the same father or by the same mother, may also be admited with* agnates *to the succession of their maternal uncle, but no one of the descendents of the son or daughter of a sister is by any means to be admited And, when a person dies, who at his decease was both a paternal and maternal uncle, that is, who had nephews or neices living both by a brother and by a sister, then such children succeed in the same manner, as if they were all descendents from males, when the deceased leaves no brother, or sisters: but, if there are brothers or sisters, and they accept the succession, all others of a more remote degree are excluded But it must be observed in relation to the children of brothers and sisters, that inheritances are not to be divided among them* in stirpes, *but in* capita.

Non in stirpes sed in capita] It appears from this section, that as yet brother's children were not allowed to represent their parents. for instance, if *Sempronius* had died intestate, leaving a brother, and children by two other brothers deceased, then, if the surviving brother had

had accepted the succession, the children of the deceased brothers, (*i e* the nephews of *Sempronius*,) would have been intirely ousted; but, if the surviving brother of *Sempronius* had declined the inheritance, the children of the two deceased brothers would have been intituled to a distributive share of their uncle's estate *per capita*, that is, by poll, because they would then take *suo quisque jure* each in his own right and not by representation. But by *Nov* 118 *cap* 3. and *Nov* 127 *cap.* 1. brothers and sisters children are allowed to represent their parents, and yet this representation is only permited by the civil law to prevent exclusion, when the party deceased leaves a brother, and nephews by another brother, and then the uncle and nephews take *per stirpes*, for, when there are only nephews, there is no representation, and the distribution of the estate is consequently made *per capita*, each person taking in his own right. This is also the certain rule of distribution in *England* in the case of collaterals *vid.* 22, 23 *Car.* 2 Bacon's *abr verb.* executors *and* administrators *Abridgment of cas in eq pag.* 249. *Walch v Walch.*

De proximis vel remotis.

§ V. Si plures sint gradus agnatorum, aperte lex duodecim tabularum proximum vocat. Itaque, si (verbi gratia) sint defuncti frater, et alterius fratris filius, aut patruus, frater potior habetur. Et, quamvis singulari numero usa, lex duodecim tabularum proximum vocet, tamen dubium non est, quin, si plures sint ejusdem gradus, omnes admittuntur. Nam et proprie proximus ex pluribus gradibus intelligitur: et tamen non dubium est, quin, licet unus sit gradus agnatorum, pertineat ad eos hæreditas.

§ 5. *When there are many degrees of* agnates, *the law of the twelve tables calls those, who are in the nearest degree. if therefore, for example, there is a brother of the deceased, and a son of another brother, or a paternal uncle, the brother is prefered. But, altho' the law of the twelve tables calls the nearest* agnate *in the singular number, yet it is not to be doubted, but that, if there are many, in the same degree, they ought all to be admited. And, altho' properly the nearest degree must be understood to denote the nearest degree of many, yet, if there is but one degree of* agnates, *the inheritance must undoubtedly appertain to those, who are in that degree*

Quo tempore proximitas spectatur.

§ VI. Proximus autem, si quidem nullo testamento facto quisquam decesserit, per hoc tempus requiritur, quo mortuus est is, cujus de hæreditate quæritur · quod si facto testamento quisquam decesserit, per hoc tempus requiritur, quo certum esse cœperit, nullum ex testamento hæredem extiturum: tunc enim proprie quisque intestatus decessisse intelligitur. quod quidem aliquando longo tempore declaratur. In quo spatio temporis sæpe accidit, ut, proximiore mortuo, proximus esse incipiat, qui moriente testatore non erat proximus

§ 6 *When a man dies and leaves no testament, then that person is esteemed his proximate kinsman, who was the nearest of kin at the decease of the intestate But, when the deceased hath actually made a testament, then that person is esteemed his nearest of kin, who was so at the time, when it became certain, that the testamentary heir had accepted the inheritance, for, till then, a man, who hath made a testament, can not be said to have died intestate and thus an intestacy does not sometimes become evident, till after a long time; in which space, the proximate kinsman being dead,*

dead, it often happens, that he becomes the nearest of kin, who was not so at the death of the testator.

De successorio edicto.

§ VII. Placebat autem, in eo genere percipiendarum hæreditatum successionem non esse: id est, ut quamvis proximus, qui secundum ea, quæ diximus, vocatur ad hæreditatem, aut spreverit hæreditatem, aut, antequam adeat, decesserit, nihilo magis legitimo jure sequentes admittantur. Quod iterum prætores, imperfecto jure corrigentes, non in totum sine adminiculo relinquebant, sed ex cognatorum ordine eos vocabant, utpote agnationis jure eis recluso. Sed nos, nihil perfectissimo juri deesse cupientes, nostra constitutione, quam de jure patronatus humanitate suggerente protulimus, sancimus, successionem in agnatorum hæreditatibus non esse eis denegandam: cum satis absurdum erat, quod cognatis à prætore apertum est, hoc agnatis esse reclusum; maxime cum in onere quidem tutelarum et primo gradu deficiente sequens succedit; et, quod in onere obtinebat, non erat in lucro permissum.

§ 7. *But it hath obtained as law, that there should be no succession among* agnates, *so that, if the nearest* agnate *is called to an inheritance, and hath either refused the heirship, or been prevented by death from entering upon it, his own legitime heir would not be admited to succeed him. But this the prætors have in some measure corrected, and have not left the* agnates *of a deceased person wholly without assistence, but have ordered, that they should be called to the inheritance as* cognates, *because they were debared from the rights of agnation. But we, being earnestly desirous to render our law as perfect and complete as possible, have ordained by our constitution, which, induced by humanity, we published concerning the right of patronage, "that legitime succession should not be denied to* agnates *in the inheritances of* agnates*" for it was sufficiently absurd, that a right, which by means of the prætor was open to* cognates, *should be shut up and denied to* agnates: *but it was more abundantly absurd, that in tutelages the second degree of* agnates *should succeed upon failure of the first, and that the same law, which obtained in that, which was onerous, should not also obtain in that, which was lucrative.*

Successionem non esse.] *Veluti, decessit aliquis intestatus, extante fratre, extante et patruo, frater vocabatur, nimirum ut proximus, si igitur contingat, ut frater, aut, antequam adeat, decedat, aut hæreditatem repudiet, patruus aut agnatus venire non poterit, propterea quod lex duodecim tabularum successionem nesciat, hæreditas igitur ad fiscum deferebatur.* Theoph. *h. l.*

Nostra constitutione.] This constitution is not to be found, nor would it be of use, if it was still extant, since the 118th *Novel* hath destroyed all distinction between *agnates* and *cognates*, and put them upon an equality.

De legitima parentum successione.

§ VIII. Ad legitimam successionem nihilominus vocatur etiam parens, qui contracta fiducia filium vel filiam, nepotem vel neptem, ac deinceps, emancipat. Quod ex nostra constitutione omnino inducitur, ut emancipationes liberorum semper videantur, quasi contracta fiducia, fieri: cum apud veteres non aliter hoc obtinebat, nisi specialiter contracta fiducia parens manumisisset.

§ 8. *A parent, who hath emancipated a ſon or a daughter, a grandſon or a grand-daughter, or any other of his lineal deſcendents under a fiduciary contract, is admited to their legitime ſucceſſion But it is now effected by our conſtitution, that every emancipation ſhall for the future be always regarded, as if it had been made under ſuch a contract : altho' among the antients the parent was never called to the legitime ſucceſſion of his children, unleſs he had actually emancipated them under a fiduciary contract.*

Ex noſtra conſtitutione.] *Cod* 8. *t*. 49. *l* 6. *de emancipationibus liberorum.* See alſo *Book* the 1ſt, *t* 12 *l* 6. But *Heineccius* is of opinion, that the compilers of the inſtitutes refer in this place to ſome other conſtitution, which is not now extant *Videntur compoſitores hoc loco ad aliam reſpexiſſe conſtitutionem, quæ cum codice Juſtinianeo intercidit, qua imperator ſanxerat, ut pactum fiduciæ ſemper interpoſitum eſſe fingeretur, etiamſi expreſſe interpoſitum non eſſet. Sed hac conſtitutione poſt legem ultimam Cod de emanc lib. non amplius opus fuit; unde et omiſſa fuit in codice repetitæ prælectionis Cæterum omnino eatenus excuſari nequeunt compoſitores, quod, immemores novæ iſtius conſtitutionis, vetuſtioris et abolitæ fecerunt mentionem.* Hein. *h. l.*

TITULUS TERTIUS.

De ſenatus-conſulto Tertulliano.

D. xxxviii. T. 17. C. vi. T. 56.

De lege duodecim tabularum et jure prætorio.

LEX duodecim tabularum ita ſtricto jure utebatur, et præponebat maſculorum progeniem, et eos, qui per fœminini ſexus neceſſitudinem ſibi junguntur, adeo expellebat, ut ne quidem inter matrem et filium filiamve ultro citroque hæreditatis capiendæ jus daret: niſi quod prætores ex proximitate cognatorum eas perſonas ad ſucceſſionem bonorum, poſſeſſione *unde cognati* accommodata, vocabant.

Such was the rigor of the law of the twelve tables, that it prefered the iſſue by males, and excluded thoſe, who were related by the female line, ſo that the right of ſucceſſion was not permited to take place reciprocally between a mother and her ſon, or a mother and her daughter. But the pretors, on account of the proximity of cognation, admited thoſe, who were related by the female line, to the ſucceſſion, giving them the poſſeſſion of goods, called unde cognati.

De conſtitutione Divi Claudii.

§ I. Sed hæ juris anguſtiæ poſtea emendatæ ſunt. Et primus quidem Divus Claudius matri ad ſolatium liberorum amiſſorum legitimam eorum detulit hæreditatem.

§ 1. *But theſe narrow limits of the law were afterwards inlarged by the emperor* Claudius, *who firſt gave the legitime inheritance of deceaſed children to their mothers, in aſſuaſion of their grief for ſo great a loſs.*

Liberorum amiſſorum] It is probable, that this indulgence extended only to thoſe mothers, whoſe children died in battle, or fell by the hand of the enemy ' *Procul dubio autem*, (ſays " *Heineccius*) *hoc privilegium a Claudio non tam* " *omnibus fœminis, quam quibuſdam ſpeciali beneficio, conceſſum eſt*

Ad

Ad Senatus-consultum Tertullianum. De jure liberorum.

§ II. Postea autem senatus-consulto Tertulliano, quod Divi Adriani temporibus factum est, plenissime de tristi successione matri, non etiam aviæ, deferenda cautum est: ut mater ingenua trium liberorum jus habens, libertina quatuor, ad bona filiorum filiarumve admittatur intestato mortuorum, licet in potestate parentis sit: ut scilicet, cum alieno juri subjecta est, jussu ejus adeat hæreditatem, cujus juri subjecta est.

§ 2. *But afterwards by the* Tertullian senatus-consultum, *made in the reign of* Adrian, *the emperor, the fullest care was taken, that the succession of children should pass to their mother, though not to their grand-mother: so that a mother, who is born of free parents, and has the right of three children, and also a* libertine *or freed-woman, who has the right of four children, may be admited, altho' they are under the power of a parent, to the goods of their sons or daughters, dying intestate. But, when a mother is under power, it is required, that she should not enter upon the inheritance of her children, but at the command of him, to whom she is subject.*

Divi Adriani temporibus] *i. e.* about an hundred years after the constitution of *Claudius*. for *Tiberius Claudius Cæsar* began to reign in the year of *Christ* 16, and *Adrian* did not begin his reign 'till the year of *Christ* 120 *Mynsinger.*

Non etiam aviæ.] The *Tertullian* decree probably stopped here out of reverence to the old law, but *Justinian* proceded farther, by admiting the grandmother and other ascendents to the succession *vid. Nov* 118 *cap* 2.

Qui præferuntur matri, vel cum ea admittuntur.

§ III. Præferuntur autem matri liberi defuncti, qui sui sunt, quive suorum loco sunt, sive primi gradus, sive ulterioris. Sed et filiæ suæ mortuæ filius vel filia præponitur ex constitutionibus matri defunctæ, id est, aviæ suæ. Pater vero utriusque, non etiam avus et proavus, matri anteponitur; scilicet cum inter eos solos de hæreditate agitur. Frater autem consanguineus tam filii, quam filiæ, excludebat matrem; soror autem consanguinea pariter cum matre admittebatur. Sed, si fuerant frater et soror consanguinei, et mater liberis onerata, frater quidem matrem excludebat, communis autem erat hæreditas ex æquis partibus fratribus et sororibus

§ 3 *But, when a deceased son leaves children, who are proper heirs, or in the place of proper heirs, either in the first or an inferior degree, they are prefered to the mother of such deceased son And the son, or daughter, of a deceased daughter is also prefered by the constitutions to the mother of the deceased daughter, i. e. to their grand mother Also the father of a son, or daughter, is prefered to the mother, but a grand-father or great-grand-father is not prefered to the mother, when the inheritance is contended for by these only without the father. Also the consanguine brother either of a son or a daughter excluded the mother, but a consanguine sister was admited equally with her mother But, if there had been both a brother and a sister of the same blood with the deceased, the brother of the deceased excluded his mother, altho' she was honored with the privilege of those, who have children: But the inheritance, in this case, was always divided in equal parts between brothers and sisters.*

Suorum loco sunt] Emancipated children by the prætorian law, and by the constitutions grand-children and great-grand-children by a daughter, are numbered *in loco suorum*, i.e in the place of proper heirs. *vide t.* 1. *sect* 15 *of this book*

Ex constitutionibus] *Si, matre superstite, filius vel filia, qui quæve moritur, filios dereliquerit, omnimodo patri suo, matri e suæ, ipso jure succedant, quod sine dubio et de pronepotibus observandum esse censemus.* *Cod.* 6. *t.* 54 *l* 11. *Cod.* 6. *t.* 57. *l* 4. ad senatus-consultum Orficianum

Frater autem consanguineus] "Porro, cum fratres duntaxat et sorores hoc loco matri objiciantur, existimandum est, cæteris à latere venientibus, sive *agnatis* sive *cognatis*, matrem præferri Sed et, quia consanguineorum tantum mentio fit, credibile est, fratres et sorores uterinos senatus consulto fuisse exclusos · cæterum *Justinianus* hos etiam cum matre admisit. *vid sect* 5 Novella autem 118 totum hoc jus mutatum est." *Vinn.*

Jus novum de jure liberorum sublato.

§ IV. Sed nos constitutione, quam in codice, nostro nomine decorato, posuimus, matri subveniendum esse existimavimus, respicientes ad naturam, et puerperium, et periculum, et sæpe mortem ex hoc casu matribus illatam. Ideoque impium esse credidimus, casum fortuitum in ejus admitti detrimentum. Si enim ingenua ter, vel libertina quater, non pepererit, immerito defraudabatur successione suorum liberorum. Quid enim peccavit, si non plures, sed paucos, peperit? Et dedimus jus legitimum plenum matribus, sive ingenuis sive libertinis, etsi non ter enixæ fuerint vel quater, sed eum tantum vel eam, qui quæve morte intercepti sunt, ut sic vocentur in liberorum suorum legitimam successionem.

§ 4 *But by a constitution, which we have inserted in the code, and honored with our name, we have thought proper, that mothers should be favored in regard to the law of nature, on account of their pains in child-bearing, their great danger, and death itself, which they often suffer, we therefore have esteemed it to be highly unjust, that the law should make that detrimental, which is in it's nature merely fortuitous; for, if a married woman, who is free-born, does not bring forth three children, or if a freed woman does not become the mother of four children, can such persons, for that reason only, be with justice deprived of the succession of their children? for how can a failure of this nature be imputed to them, as a crime? We therefore, not regarding any fixed number of children, have given a full right to every mother, whether ingenuous or a freed-woman, of being called to the legitime succession of her child or children deceased, whether male or female.*

Sed nos constitutione] *Cod* 8. *de jure liberorum. t.* 59. *l* 2

Quibus mater præponitur, et quibuscum admittitur.

§ V. Sed, cum antea constitutiones, jura legitimæ successionis perscrutantes, partim matrem adjuvabant, partim eam prægravabant, nec in solidum eam vocabant, sed, in quibusdam casibus tertiam ei partem abstrahentes, certis legitimis dabant personis, in aliis autem contrarium faciebant, nobis visum est, recta et simplici via matrem omnibus personis legitimis anteponi, et sine ulla diminutione filiorum suorum successionem accipere: excepta fratris et sororis persona, (sive consanguinei sint, sive sola cognationis jura habentes,) ut, quemadmodum eam toti alii ordini legitimo præposuimus, ita omnes fratres et sorores, (sive legitimi sint, sive non,) ad ad capiendas hæreditates simul vocemus: ita tamen ut, siquidem solæ sorores agnatæ vel cognatæ et mater defuncti vel defunctæ supersint, dimidiam quidem mater, alteram vero dimidiam partem omnes sorores habeant. Si vero, matre superstite, et fratre vel fratribus solis, vel etiam cum sororibus, sive legitima sive sola cognationis jura habentibus, intestatus quis vel intestata moriatur, in capita ejus distribuatur hæreditas.

§ 5 *But, in examining the constitutions of former emperors, relating to the right of succession, we observed, that these constitutions were partly favorable to mothers and partly grievous; not always calling them to the intire inheritance of their children, but in some cases depriving them of a third, which was given to certain legitime persons, and in other cases, doing the contrary, i. e. allowing the mother a third only It hath therefore seemed right to us, that mothers should receive the succession of their children without any diminution, and that they should be exclusively prefered before all legitime persons, except the brothers and sisters of the deceased, whether they are* consanguine, *or only* cognate *But, as we have prefered the mother to all other legitime persons, we are willing to call all brothers and sisters, legitime or otherwise, to the inheritance together with the mother: yet in such manner, that, if only the sisters,* agnate *or* cognate, *and the mother of the deceased survive, the mother shall have one half of the effects, and the sisters the other But, if a mother survives, and also a brother or brothers, or brothers and sisters, whether* legitime *or* cognate, *then the inheritance of the intestate son or daughter must be distributed* in capita, *i. e. must be divided into equal shares.*

Cum antea constitutiones] *vid ll* 1, 2, *et penult Cod* Theod *de leg t. hæred*

Partim matrem] Exempli gratia, " si contigisset, ut quis decederet relinquens matrem, " jure liberorum cohonestatam, superesset autem et patruus, qui est legitimus, aut patrui " filius, mater octo capiebat uncias, sive bessem " hæreditatis, patruus autem aut ejus filius trientem, hoc est, quatuor uncias Quod si ex " contrario jus liberorum mater non habuisset, " tunc patruus aut filius ejus bessem hæreditatis " capiebat, at mater trientem solum " *Theoph. h t.*

Ita tamen, &c] " Quæ sequuntur pertinent ad " modum succedendi, sive rationem distribuendæ hæreditatis inter matrem defuncti, ejusque " fratres et sorores Constituit autem imperator, ut, si cum matre concurrant sorores solæ, sive consanguineæ sive uterinæ, duo semisses fiant, quorum unum mater, alterum " sorores capiant, sin fratres, sive soli, sive " etiam cum sororibus, in capita hæreditas dividatur, totque partes fiant, quot sunt personæ succedentium *Cod* 6. *t* 56 *l*. 7 Hæc " iterum mutata sunt *Novel* 118 qua fratres et " sorores omnes, ex uno tantum latere defuncto " conjuncti, tam à matre, quam a fratribus " utrinque conjunctis, excluduntur, mater cum " his ex æquis partibus succedit " *Vinn h l*

But in *England* the civil law takes place almost in the same manner, as it prevailed before the novel constitution for brothers and sisters by the half blood take equally with brothers and sisters by the whole blood, so that, if a man, whose father is dead, dies intestate, and is survived by a mother and by brothers and sisters, or by brothers only, or sisters only, then the mother and the brothers and sisters will all be intituled to take an equal share, *per capita*, whether such brothers and sisters were related to the deceased by the whole blood, or by the half blood only 1 *Mod*. 209. 1 *Jac* 2 *cap* 17

De tutore liberis petendo.

§ VI. Sed, quemadmodum nos matribus prospeximus, ita eas oportet suæ soboli consulere, scituris eis, quod, si tutores liberis non petierint, vel in locum remoti vel excusati intra annum petere neglexerint, ab eorum impuberum morientium successione merito repellentur.

§ 6.

§ 6. *As we have taken a particular care of the interest of mothers, it behoves them in return, to consult the welfare of their children. Be it known therefore, that, if a mother shall neglect, during the space of a whole year, to demand a tutor for her children, or shall neglect to require a new tutor in the place of a former, who hath either been removed, or excused, she will be deservedly repelled from the succession of such children, if they die within puberty.*

De vulgo quæsitis.

§ VII. Licet autem vulgo quæsitus sit filius filiave, potest tamen ad bona ejus mater ex Tertulliano senatus-consulto admitti.

§ 7. *Altho' a son or a daughter is of spurious birth, yet the mother, by the* Tertullian senatus-consultum, *may be admited to succeed to the goods of either.*

TITULUS QUARTUS.

De senatus-consulto Orficiano.

D. xxxviii. T. 17. C. vi. T. 57.

Origo et summa senatus-consulti.

PER contrarium autem liberi ad bona matrum intestatarum admittuntur ex senatus-consulto Orficiano, quod, Orficio et Rufo consulibus, effectum est Divi Marci temporibus: et data est tam filio, quam filiæ, legitima hæreditas, etiamsi alieno juri subjecti sint, et præferuntur consanguineis et agnatis defunctæ matris.

On the contrary children are reciprocally admited to the goods of their intestate mothers, by the Orfician senatus-consultum, *which was enacted in the consulate of* Orficius *and* Rufus, *in the time of the emperor* Marcus Antoninus, *and, by this decree, the legitime inheritance is given both to sons and daughters, altho' they are under power, and they are also prefered to the consanguine brothers, and to the* agnates, *of their deceased mother.*

Per contrarium] "Lege duodecim tabularum, nec mater liberis nec liberi matri ab intestato succedebant, nam duo duntaxat genera lex agnoscebat, suos hæredes et agnatos, cujusmodi nec mater liberis, nec illi matri sunt Cæterum, cum placitum esset hoc dare naturali conjunctioni, ut mater vocaretur ad legitimam successionem filii et filiæ, æquum erat, ut retro tantundem etiam concederetur liberis, ut scilicet et hi vicissim jus legitimæ successionis consequerentur in bonis matris cum adeo liberorum conditio in causa successionis etiam potior esse debeat, propter naturæ simul et parentum commune votum Id vero effectum est senatus consulto Orficiano viginti ferme annis postea, quam matri legitima hæreditas delata fuerat senatus-consulto Tertulliano, ut ex Fastis colligitur. Cur matri tanto tempore ante consultum fuerit, quam liberis, causam ignorare me fateor. *Vinn.* Maxime autem probabilis est ratio, quam reddit *Schultingius*, quod mater, si vellet, petatus officio per testamentum posset satisfacere, id quod per ætatem liberis sæpe haud licuerit"

Orficio et Rufo Coss] Anno ab urbe condita 930, qui vigesimus annus est à consulatu *Flavii Tertulli*, à quo senatus-consultum Tertullianum

Præferuntur consanguineis] Pleniore jure vocantur filius et filia ad hæreditatem matris ex Orficiano, quam mater ad illorum hæreditatem ex Tertulliano. *vide sect 3. supra tit. prox*

§ 1

De nepote et nepte.

§ I. Sed, cum ex hoc ſenatus-conſulto nepotes et neptes ad aviæ ſucceſſionem legitimo jure non vocarentur, poſtea hoc conſtitutionibus principalibus emendatum eſt, ut, ad ſimilitudinem filiorum filiarumque, et nepotes et neptes vocentur.

§ 1. *But, ſince grandſons and grand-daughters were not called by the* ſenatus-conſultum *to the legitime ſucceſſion of their grand-mother, the omiſſion was afterwards ſupplied, by the imperial conſtitutions, ſo that grandſons and grand-daughters were called to inherit, as well as ſons and daughters.*

Conſtitutionibus principalibus] The *Tertullian* decree confered upon mothers the right of legitime ſucceſſion to their children, and the *Orfician* decree gave children the ſame right in regard to their mothers but neither of theſe decrees went farther out of reverence to the old law, ſo that hitherto grand-mothers were called to the ſucceſſion of their grand-children, and grand-children to the ſucceſſion of their grand-mothers, by the indulgence of the prætor only, i e. *per bonorum poſſeſſionem* UNDE COGNATI, and in default of *agnates.* ff 38. t 8. But the emperors, *Valentinian, Theodoſius,* and *Arcadius,* called grandſons and grand-daughters to the ſucceſſion of their grand mothers, prohibiting them nevertheleſs to take more than two thirds of that ſum, to which their father or mother would have been intituled *l 4 Cod Theod de legit hæred.* But the emperor *Juſtinian*, by his 118th *Novel, cap* 1, makes the condition of all children equal, when they ſucceed their parents upon an inteſtacy And, by the 2d chapter of the ſame *Novel,* the emperor calls alſo the grand-mother to the ſucceſſion of her grand-children

De capitis diminutione.

§ II. Sciendum autem eſt, hujuſmodi ſucceſſiones, quæ ex Tertulliano et Orficiano ſenatus-conſultis deferuntur, capitis diminutione non perimi, propter illam regulam, qua novæ hæreditates legitimæ capitis diminutione non pereunt; ſed illæ ſolæ, quæ ex lege duodecim tabularum deferuntur.

§ 2. *But it muſt be obſerved, that thoſe ſucceſſions, which proceed from the* Tertullian *and* Orfician ſenatus-conſulta, *are not extinguiſhed by diminution For it is an eſtabliſhed rule, that new legitime inheritances are not deſtroyed by diminution, but that it affects only thoſe inheritances, which proceed from the law of the twelve tables.*

De vulgo quæſitis.

§ III. Noviſſime ſciendum eſt, etiam illos liberos, qui vulgo quæſiti ſunt, ad matris hæreditatem ex ſenatus-conſulto admitti.

§ 3 *It is laſtly to be noted, that even illegitimate children are admited by the* Orfician ſenatus-conſultum *to the inheritance of their mother*

Qui vulgo quæſiti ſunt] The *vulgo quæſiti* are thoſe, whom the law emphatically calls *ſpurious*, their father being incertain and not known, but the mother, who is always certain, is allowed to ſucceed even her *ſpurious* iſſue, which is not permited in *England*, where a baſtard is reckoned as a *terminus a quo*, and the firſt of his family, he can therefore have no heir but of his body, and is deemed in law to have no conſanguine relations, except his children, yet this muſt be underſtood, as to civil purpoſes, for, as to moral purpoſes, his natural relation to aſcendents and collaterals is regarded by the law, which will not ſuffer ſuch a perſon to marry his mother, or his baſe ſiſter 3 *Salk* 66, 67

Ad matris hæreditatem] The *vulgo quæſiti*, or *ſpurious* children, are allowed to ſucceed their mother, unleſs ſhe is a perſon of illuſtrious birth, having lawful children, for, if ſhe has no lawful children, her illegitimate iſſue will ſucceed her

her *Cod.* 6. *t.* 57 *l.* 5 And in general *spurious* children will succeed their mother equally with those, who are legitimate and, even if *spurious* children are prætermited in the testament of their mother, they may by the civil law complain of that testament as inofficious and undutiful. *De inofficioso testamento matris spurii quoque filii dicere possunt.* ff. 5. t 2 *l.* 29. Yet spurious children are not in like manner intituled to succeed to the possessions of their father, whom the law does not regard, but supposes to be unknown. Children nevertheless, who are born of a concubine, when their father is certain, and dies without a wife or lawful issue, are intituled, together with their mother, to the sixth part of their father's inheritance, which is to be divided among them *per capita*, or by poll *Nov* 18 *t* 5 *cap* 5 But bastards, begotten in adultery or incest, are wholly incapable of succeeding to their father's or mother's estate. *Nov* 89 *cap* 15 But in *England* bastards are not distinguished into species, being all regarded in the same light, and esteemed equally incapable of succeeding to the personal estate of their intestate parents, being feigned to be *nullius filii*, so that no illegitimate child can take any part either of his father's or mother's estate upon an intestacy; neither can an ordinary or ecclesiastical judge grant the administration of an intestate's estate to the base-born issue of that intestate. *Swinb* 373 Yet any person, altho' he hath legitimate children, may, by the law of *England*, bequeath any part, or the whole of his estate without controul, and may consequently benefit his illegitimate children, or their mother, in what manner he pleases, for such persons are not incapable of taking by purchase, gift, or testament. and in this respect the law of *England* is more favorable to natural children, than the civil law; for, by that law, a man, who had lawful children, could not bequeath more than a 12th part of his possessions to his illegitimate issue. *Nov* 89. *cap.* 12 It is also observable, that, tho' the law of *England* pays no regard immediately to bastards, yet it favors their issue under particular circumstances, in respect to *real* estates; insomuch that the issue of a bastard *eigne*, who died seized, shall bar the right of a *mulier puisne* For example, if a man dies seized of certain lands in fee, leaving two sons, by the same woman, and his eldest son is a bastard, being born before his father's marriage, and the younger is a *mulier*, (that is, legitimate,) in this case, if the bastard enters upon the land, claiming as heir to his father, and occupieth it all his life without any interruption or entry made upon him by the *mulier*, and the bastard hath issue and dies seized of such estate in fee, and the land descends to that issue, then the *mulier* will be without remedy. For he may not enter, nor have any action to recover the land, because there is an antient law in this case used, namely, *Justum non est aliquem post mortem facere bastardum, qui toto tempore vitæ suæ pro legitimo habebatur.* See *Coke*'s first inst. sect. 399, &c. *Bridal*'s lex spuriorum, *pag* 100. Here note, that the term *mulier* is used, by the writers upon the common law, to denote either a son or a daughter lawfully begotten, but, how they came to apply the word *mulier* so very fancifully or rather perversely, it is hard to say, and immaterial to inquire, the most probable conjecture seems to be, that *mulier* is a corruption of *melior* or the French word *meilleur*. vide *Termes de la ley*, and Godolphin's *repertorium*.

De jure accrescendi inter legitimos hæredes.

§ IV. Si ex pluribus legitimis hæredibus quidam omiserint hæreditatem, vel morte, vel alia causa, impediti fuerint, quominus adeant, reliquis, qui adierint, accrescit illorum portio: et, licet ante decesserint, ad hæredes tamen eorum pertinet.

§ 4 *When there are many legitime heirs, and some renounce the inheritance, or are hindered from entering upon it by death, or any other cause, then the shares or portions of such persons fall by the right of accretion to those, who have accepted the inheritance, and, altho' the acceptors happen to die even before the refusal or the failure of their coheirs, yet the portions of such coheirs will appertain to the heirs of the acceptors of the inheritance.*

TITU-

TITULUS QUINTUS.

De successione cognatorum.

Tertius ordo succedentium ab intestato.

POST suos hæredes, eosque, quos inter suos hæredes prætor et constitutiones vocant, et post legitimos, (quorum numero sunt agnati, et hi, quos in locum agnatorum tam supradicta senatus-consulta, quam nostra erexit constitutio,) proximos cognatos prætor vocat.

After the proper heirs and those, whom the prætor and the constitutions call to inherit with the proper heirs, and after the legitime heirs (among whom are the agnati, *and those, whom the above mentioned* senatus consulta *and our constitution have numbered with the* agnati) *the prætor calls the nearest* cognates, *observing the proximity of relation.*

Post suos hæredes] " Lex antiqua duodecim " tabularum duos tantum hæredum ab intestato " ordines fecit, suorum et agnatorum. Novæ " leges et senatus-consulta non addiderunt qui- " dem ordinem novum, sed personas quasdam, " quæ nec sui hæredes, nec agnati, revera sunt, " suorum hæredum et agnatorum numero " esse voluerunt, atque in ordine suorum vel " agnatorum, una cum vere suis hæredibus aut " agnatis, ad hæreditatem intestati admitti Inter " suos hæredes novæ leges numerant, suisque " per omnia exæquant, liberos legitima- " tos inter eosdem quoque, et simul cum iis, " vocant nepotes et pronepotes ex sexu femi- " neo in agnatorum ordinem senatus consul- " ta transtulerunt matrem et liberos Justinia- " nus fratres et sorores uterinos, eorumque et " sororum consanguinearum filios et filias Ana- " stasius fratres et sorores emancipatos Prætor " vero tres succedentium ab intestato ordines " fecit, primum *liberorum*, (non dixit *suorum*, " quia ex liberis vocat etiam non suos,) alte- " rum *legitimorum*, in quo vocantur agnati et " jura agnationis habentes, ex posterioribus legi " bus aut ex senatus-consultis, tertium *cognato-* " *rum*, in quo admisit omnes, quos sola san- " guinis ratio vocat ad hæreditatem, licet jure " civili deficiant, item eos, qui, quod prioribus " ordinibus exclusi essent, ex nullo alio capite " venire poterant Tandem Justinianus cogna- " tos omnes etiam hæredes legitimos fecit, ad- " empta agnatis omni prærogativa. *Nov.* 118. *Vinn.*

Qui vocantur in hoc ordine. De agnatis capite minutis.

§ I. Qua parte naturalis cognatio spectatur. Nam agnati capite diminuti, quique ex his progeniti sunt, ex lege duodecim tabularum inter legitimos non habentur, sed à prætore tertio ordine vocantur, exceptis solis tantummodo fratre et sorore emancipatis, non etiam liberis eorum: quos lex Anastasiana cum fratribus integri juris constitutis vocat quidem ad legitimam fratris hæreditatem, sive sororis; non æquis tamen partibus sed cum aliqua diminutione, quam facile est ex ipsius constitutionis verbis intelligere. Aliis vero agnatis inferioris gradus, licet capitis diminutionem passi non sunt, tamen anteponit eos, et procul dubio cognatis.

§ 1. *By the law of the twelve tables, neither the* agnates, *who have suffered diminution, nor their issue, are esteemed legitime heirs, but they are called by the prætor in the third order of succession: we must nevertheless except a brother and sister, altho' they are emancipated, but not their children, for the constitution of* Anastasius *calls an emancipated brother or sister to the succession of a brother or sister,*

sister, together with those, who have not been emancipated, and are therefore integri juris. *But it does not call them to an equal share of the succession, as may easily be collected from the very words of the constitution. But this constitution prefers an emancipated brother or sister to other* agnates *of an inferior degree, altho' unemancipated; and consequently to all* cognates *in general.*

Quos lex Anastasiana] This constitution is not now extant, it was nevertheless without doubt inserted in the first edition of the code, because it is here refered to, but it was probably omited in the *codex repetitæ prælectionis*, on account of the last law in *Cod* 6. *t* 58 de legit hæred *Qua plenius fratribus et sororibus emancipatis consulitur, et eorum quoque filiis ac filiabus jus legitimæ successionis datur*

Non æquis tamen partibus.] Hoc est, si fides sit *Theophilo*, ut capite diminutus habeat quatuor uncias, et frater integri juris duplum, *i. e.* octo uncias.

Alius vero agnatis.] Ergo, qui decedit, emancipato fratre et patruo superstitibus, fratrem solum hæredem excluso patruo habebit.

De conjunctis per fœminas.

§ II. Eos etiam, qui per fœminini sexus personas ex transverso cognatione junguntur, tertio gradu proximitatis nomine prætor ad successionem vocat.

§ 2 *Those also, who are collaterally related by the female line, are called by the prætor in the third order of succession, according to their proximity.*

Eos etiam.] The 118th *Novel* of *Justinian* hath rendered the learning in this paragraph intirely useless, by taking away all the distinctions of the antient law between *agnation* and *cognation*.

De liberis datis in adoptionem.

§ III. Liberi quoque, qui in adoptiva familia sunt, ad naturalium parentum hæreditatem hoc eodem gradu vocantur.

§ 3 *Children, who are in an adoptive family, are likewise called in the third order of succession to the inheritance of their natural parents.*

De vulgo quæsitis.

§ IV. Vulgo quæsitos nullos habere agnatos, manifestum est: cum agnatio à patre sit, cognatio à matre; hi autem nullum patrem habere intelligantur. Eadem ratione nè inter se quidem possunt videri consanguinei esse. quia consanguinitatis jus species est agnationis. Tantum ergo cognati sunt sibi, sicut et matri cognati sunt. Itaque omnibus istis ex ea parte competit bonorum possessio, qua proximitatis nomine cognati vocantur.

§ 4. *It is manifest, that base born children have no* agnates, *in as much as* agnation *proceeds from the father,* cognation *from the mother, and such children are looked upon as having no father. And, for the same reason, consanguinity can not be said to subsist between the bastard children of the same woman, because consanguinity is a species of* agnation *They can therefore only be allied to each other as they are related to their mother, that is, by* cognation; *and it is for this reason, that all such children are called to the possession of goods by that part of the prætorian edict, by which* cognates *are called by the right of their proximity.*

§ V.

Ex quoto gradu vel agnati vel cognati succedunt.

§ V. Hoc loco et illud necessario admonendi sumus, agnationis quidem jure admitti aliquem ad hæreditatem, etsi decimo gradu sit, sive de lege duodecim tabularum quæramus, sive de edicto, quo prætor legitimis hæredibus daturum se bonorum possessionem pollicetur. Proximitatis vero nomine iis solis prætor promittit bonorum possessionem, qui usque ad sextum gradum cognationis sunt, et ex septimo à sobrino sobrinaque nato natave.

§ 5. *In this place it will be necessary to observe, that any person may, by the right of* agnation, *be admited to inherit, altho' he is in the tenth degree, and this is allowed both by the law of the twelve tables, and the edict, by which the prætor promises, that he will give the possession of goods to the legitime heirs But the prætor promises the possession of goods to* cognates, *only as far as the sixth degree of* cognation, *according to their right of proximity; and, in the seventh degree, to those* cognates *only, who are the descendents of a cousin german*

Usque ad sextum gradum cognationis] It is not easy to determine what should induce the prætor to fix upon the sixth rather than the fifth or any other degree; and, concerning this, the writers have differed much in their opinions. But all, except *Hoffman*, agree, that the difference in the limits of succession between *agnates* and *cognates* hath ceased, since the distinction between *agnation* and *cognation* was abolished by *Novel* 118 Taking it then for granted, that *cognates* can be called in as distant a degree as *agnates*, tne next question will be, whether *agnates* can succeed in a more distant degree, than the tenth, which some deny, and urge, that *Justinian* would not have named the 10th degree, if *agnates* could have been admited in a degree beyond it—— and that, unless some period had been put to the succession of *agnates*, the third and the fourth order of succession, in which are husband and wife, could never or very rarely be admited, and from hence they conclude, that, tho' in consequence of the 118th *Novel*, both *agnates* and *cognates* must now be admited without distinction, according to their proximity, yet this must be in the tenth degree, and not beyond it, and of this opinion are *Mynsinger*, *Faber*, *Wesembecius*, and others But the words of *Justinian*, in the 3d sect of the 2d title of this book, very strongly evince the contrary. v g *Inter masculos quidem agnationis jure hæreditas, etiamsi* longissimo *gradu sint, ultro citroque capitur*, &c And again, in paragraph the 1st, tit 7 of this book, the emperor writes thus—— *Amotis suis hæredibus*, agnatus, *etiamsi* longissimo *gradu, plerumque potior habetur, quam proximior* cognatus *tit* 7 *de servili cognatione* This is also the doctrine of the law of the *twelve tables*, which declares generally, without specifying any limits, that upon a failure of proper heirs, the nearest *agnate* shall succeed And, as to the before-mentioned arguments, they may be answered without much difficulty; for we may safely pronounce, that the words *decimo gradu* are not here used determinately, but merely for the sake of giving an example *Non enim* (says *Vinny*) *eodem modo de* agnatis *et* cognatis *imperator loquitur*, *de* agnatis *non loquitur determinative, sed ait, eos succedere, etsi decimo gradu sint, utens rotundo et certo numero pro incerto. De* cognatis *contra loquitur determinative, ait enim, eos succedere usque ad sextum gradum.* And, to the second argument, it may be answered, that a deceased person may leave no *agnates* by means of emancipation, or that his *agnates*, as such, may be ousted of their succession, by the death or refusal of the nearest *agnate* See *sect* 7 *t* 7. *lib* 3. So that there is no great reason to fear, that the third and fourth order of succession would have been always excluded by allowing *agnates* to succeed in the most distant degree It therefore follows upon the whole, that *cognates* and *agnates* are now called to succeed equally, according to their proximity, and without any limitation.

TITULUS SEXTUS.

De gradibus cognationum.

D. xxxviii. T. 10.

Continuatio, et cognationis diviſio.

HOC loco neceſſarium eſt exponere, quemadmodum gradus cognationis numerentur. Quare in primis admonendi ſumus, cognationem aliam ſupra numerari, aliam infra, aliam ex tranſverſo, quæ etiam à latere dicitur. Superior cognatio eſt parentum: inferior liberorum: ex tranſverſo fratrum ſororumve, et eorum, qui quæve ex his generantur; et convenienter patrui, amitæ, avunculi, materteræ. Et ſuperior quidem et inferior cognatio à primo gradu incipit: at ea, quæ ex tranſverſo numeratur, à ſecundo.

It is neceſſary in this place to ſhew how the degrees of cognation *are to be computed: and firſt we muſt obſerve, that there is one ſpecies of* cognation, *which relates to aſcendents, another to deſcendents, and a third to collaterals. The firſt and ſuperior* cognation *is that relation, which a man bears to his parents —— the ſecond, or inferior, is that, which he bears to his children —— and the third is that relation, which he bears to his brothers and ſiſters, and their iſſue; and alſo to his uncles and aunts, whether paternal or maternal. The ſuperior and inferior* cognation *commence at the firſt degree; but the tranverſe or collateral* cognation *commences at the ſecond.*

De primo, ſecundo, et tertio gradu.

§ I. Primo gradu eſt ſupra pater, mater: infra filius, filia. Secundo gradu ſupra avus, avia: infra nepos, neptis: ex tranſverſo frater, ſoror. Tertio gradu ſupra proavus, proavia: infra pronepos, proneptis: ex tranſverſo fratris ſororiſque filius, filia: et convenienter patruus, amita, avunculus, matertera. Patruus eſt patris frater, qui Græcis πατραδελφος appellatur. Avunculus eſt frater matris, qui græcè μητραδελφος dicitur: et uterque promiſcue θειος appellatur. Amita eſt patris ſoror, quæ græcè πατραδελφη appellatur; matertera vero matris ſoror, quæ græcè μητραδελφη dicitur: et utraque promiſcue θεια appellatur.

§ I. *A father, or a mother, is in the firſt degree in the right line aſcending: and a ſon, or a daughter, is alſo in the firſt degree in the right line deſcending. A grand-father, or a grand-mother, is in the ſecond degree in the right line aſcending: and a grandſon, or grand-daughter, is in the ſecond degree in the right line deſcending: and a brother, or a ſiſter, is alſo in the ſecond degree in the collateral line. A great-grand-father, or a great grand mother, is in the third degree in the right line aſcending, and a great grandſon, or great-grand-daughter, is in the third degree in the right line deſcending: and the ſon or daughter of a brother or ſiſter is alſo in the third degree in the collateral line, and by a parity of reaſoning an uncle, or an aunt, whether paternal or maternal, is alſo in the third degree. A paternal*

nal uncle, called patruus, *is a father's brother*; —— *a maternal uncle, called* avunculus, *is a mother's brother*; —— *a paternal aunt, called* amita, *is a father's sister*, —— *and a maternal aunt, called* matertera, *is a mother's sister. And each of these persons is called in Greek* θεῖος *or* θεία *promiscuously.*

Primo gradu est supra pater.] In *England* all relationship, as far as personal estate only is concerned, is measured according to the computation of degrees by the civil law.

Θεῖοι] The Greeks called their parents θεοὺς, (i. e. *divinities*,) and applied the term θεῖοι (i. e. *divine*,) even to those, who held the place of parents See Dr *Taylor*'s Elem. 325.

Quartus gradus.

§ II. Quarto gradu supra abavus, abavia: infra abnepos, abneptis: ex transverso fratris sororisque nepos neptisve: et convenienter patruus magnus, amita magna, id est, avi frater et soror: item avunculus magnus et matertera magna, id est, aviæ frater et soror: consobrinus, consobrina, id est, qui quæve ex sororibus aut fratribus procreantur. Sed quidam recte consobrinos eos proprie dici putant, qui ex duabus sororibus progenerantur, quasi consororinos: eos vero, qui ex duobus fratribus progenerantur, proprie fratres patrueles vocari: si autem ex duobus fratribus filiæ nascuntur, sorores patrueles appellari. At eos, qui ex fratre et sorore progenerantur, amitinos proprie dici putant. Amitæ tuæ filii consobrinum te appellant, tu illos amitinos.

§ 2 *A great-great-grand-father, or a great great-grand mother, is in the fourth degree in the right line ascending, and a great-great-grandson, or a great great-grand daughter, is in the fourth degree in the right line descending. Also, in the transverse or collateral line, the grandson, or the grand-daughter, of a brother or a sister, is in the fourth degree; and consequently a great uncle, or great aunt, paternal or maternal, is in the fourth degree and also cousins german, who are called* consobrini. *But some have been rightly of opinion, that the children of sisters are only properly called* consobrini, *quasi* consororini, —— *that the children of brothers are properly called* fratres patrueles, *or brothers* patruel, *if males; and* sorores patrueles, *or sisters* patruel, *if females,* —— *and that, when there are children of a brother, and children of a sister, they are properly called* amitini, *but the sons of your aunt by the father's side call you* consobrinus, *and you call them* amitini

Consobrinus consobrina] It will be necessary to explain the following terms of relation before [illegible] ceed —— *Consobrini* and *consobrinæ* denote cousins german in *general*, i e. brother's and sister's children —— *Fratres patrueles* and *sorores patrueles* signify cousins german, when they are the sons or daughters of brothers —— *Consobrini* and *consobrinæ* in a *limited* and strict sense denote cousins german, who are the children of two sisters, *quasi consororini.* —— *Amitini* and *amitinæ* are cousins german, who are the children of a brother on the one side and a sister on the other —— *Sobrini* and *sobrinæ* denote the children of cousins german in general —— *Propior sobrino* and *propior sobrina* denote the son or daughter of a great-uncle or great-aunt, paternal or maternal.

Quintus gradus.

§ III. Quinto gradu supra atavus, atavia: infra atnepos, atneptis: ex transverso fratris sororisque pronepos, proneptis: et convenienter propatruus, proamita, id est, proavi frater et soror et proavunculus et promatertera, id est, proaviæ frater et soror: item fratris patruelis, vel sororis

ris patruelis, consobrini et consobrinæ, amitini et amitinæ filius, filia: propior sobrino, propior sobrina: hi sunt patrui magni, amitæ magnæ, avunculi magni, materteræ magnæ filius, filia.

§ 3. *A great-grand father's grand-father, or a great-grand-father's grand mother, is in the fifth degree in the line ascending, and a great-grandson, or a great-grand-daughter, of a grandson or grand-daughter is in the fifth degree in the line descending. And, in the transverse or collateral line, a great-grandson, or great grand-daughter, of a brother or sister, is also in the fifth degree: and consequently a great-grand father's brother or sister, or a great-grand-mother's brother or sister, is in the fifth degree. The son or daughter also of a cousin german is in the fifth degree; and so is the son or daughter of a great uncle or great aunt, paternal or maternal, and such son, or daughter, is called* propior sobrino *and* propior sobrina.

Sextus gradus.

§ IV. Sexto gradu supra tritavus, tritavia: infra trinepos, trineptis: ex transverso fratris sororisque abnepos, abneptis: et convenienter abpatruus, abamita, id est, abavi frater et soror: abavunculus, abmatertera, id est, abaviæ frater et soror: item propatrui, proamitæ, proavunculi, promaterteræ filius, filia: item propius sobrino sobrinave filius, filia: item consobrini consobrinæ nepos, neptis: item sobrini, sobrinæ; id est, qui quæve ex fratribus vel sororibus patruelibus, vel consobrinis, vel amitinis, progenerantur.

§ 4. *A great-grand-father's great-grand-father, or a great grand-father's great-grand mother, is in the sixth degree in the line ascending, and the great grandson, or great-grand daughter of a great-grandson, or a great-grand daughter, is likewise in the sixth degree in the line descending. And, in the transverse or collateral line, a great-great-grandson, or a great-great-grand-daughter, of a brother or sister, is also in the sixth degree: and consequently a great-great-grand-father's brother or sister, and a great-great grand mother's brother or sister, is in the sixth degree. And the son or daughter of a great-great-uncle, or great great aunt, paternal or maternal, is also in the sixth degree, and so also is the son or daughter of the son or daughter of a great-uncle or great-aunt, paternal or maternal. The grandson also, or the grand-daughter, of a cousin german is in the sixth degree, and, in the same degrees between themselves, we reckon the* sobrini *and the* sobrinæ, *that is, the sons and daughters of cousins german in general, whether such cousins german are so related by two brothers, or by two sisters, or by a brother and a sister.*

De reliquis gradibus.

§ V. Hactenus ostendisse sufficiat, quemadmodum gradus cognationis numerentur. Namque ex his palam est intelligere, quemadmodum ulteriores quoque gradus numerare debeamus: quippe semper generata persona gradum adjicit: ut longe facilius sit respondere, quoto quisque gradu sit, quam proprie cognationis appellatione quemquam denotare.

§ 5. *It is sufficient to have shewed thus far, how the degrees of* cognation *are enumerated: and, from the examples given, it is evident in what manner we ought to compute the more remote degrees, for every person generated always adds one degree, so that it is much easier to determine, in what degree any person is related to another, than to denote such person by a proper term of* cognation.

§ VI

Lib. 3 ent. p. 30 et 31

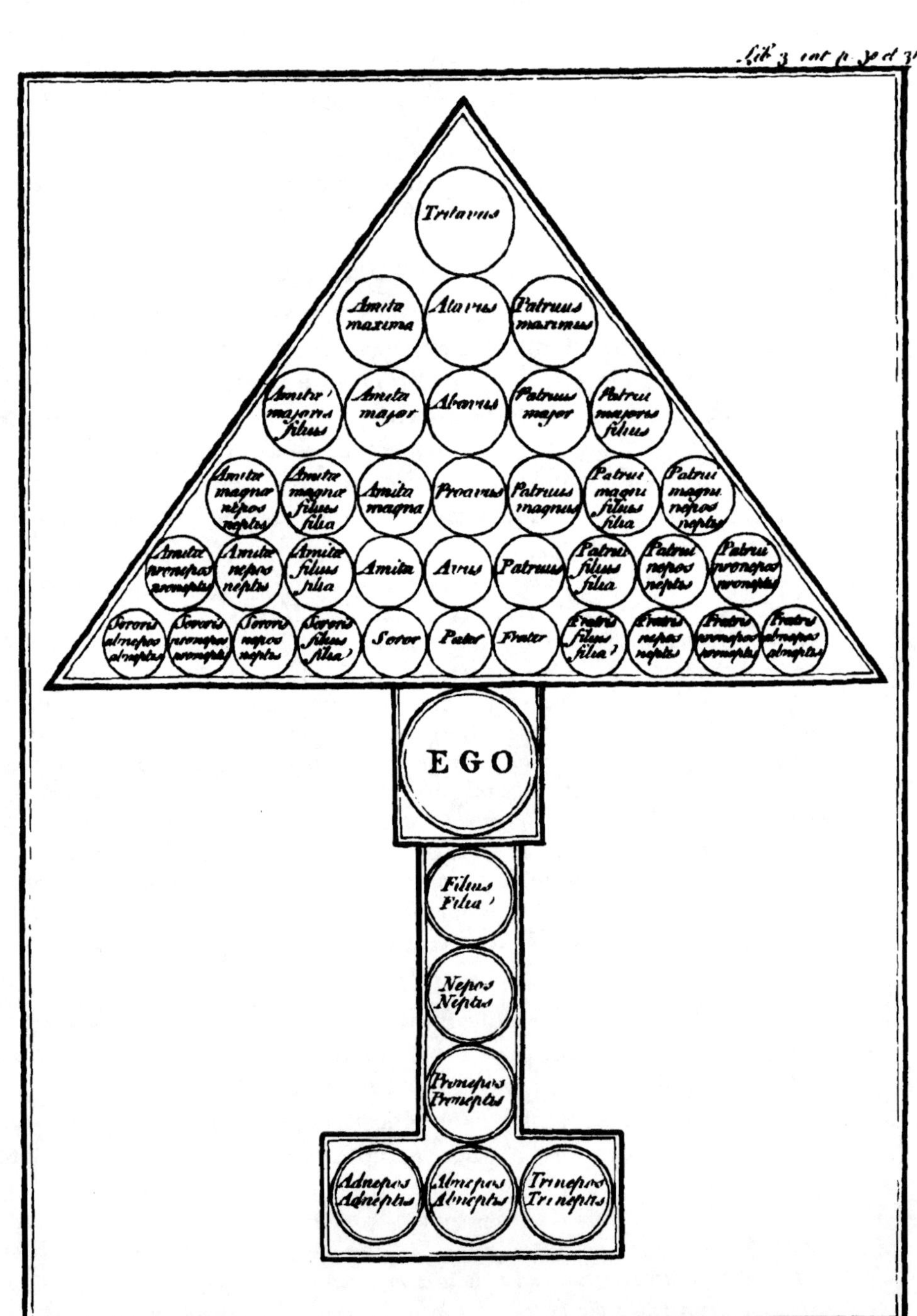

De gradibus agnationis.

§ VI. Agnationis quoque gradus eodem modo numerantur.

§ 6. *The degrees of* agnation *are enumerated in the same manner, as the degrees of* cognation.

De graduum descriptione.

§ VII. Sed, cum magis veritas oculata fide, quam per aures animis hominum, infigatur, ideo necessarium duximus, post narrationem graduum, eos etiam præsenti libro inscribi, quatenus possint et auribus et oculorum inspectione adolescentes perfectissimam graduum doctrinam adipisci.

§ 7. *But as truth is fixed in the mind much better by the eye, than by the ear, we have therefore thought it necessary, to subjoin to the account already given, a tablet with the degrees of* cognation *inscribed upon it, that the student, both by hearing and seeing, may attain a most perfect knowledge of them.*

TITULUS SEPTIMUS.

De servili cognatione.

D. xxxviii. T. 2. C. vi. T. 4.

ILLUD certum est, ad serviles cognationes illam partem edicti, qua proximitatis nomine bonorum possessio promittitur, non pertinere: nam nec ulla antiqua lege talis cognatio computabatur. Sed nostra constitutione, quam pro jure patronatus fecimus, (quod jus usque ad nostra tempora satis obscurum atque nube plenum, et undique confusum fuerat,) et hoc humanitate suggerente concessimus, ut, si quis, in servili constitutus consortio, liberum vel liberos habuerit, sive ex libera sive ex servilis conditionis muliere, vel contra serva mulier ex libero vel servo habuerit liberos cujuscunque sexus, et, ad libertatem his pervenientibus, ii, qui ex servili ventre nati sunt, libertatem meruerint, vel, dum mulieres liberæ erant, ipsi in servitute eos habuerint, et postea ad libertatem pervenerint, ut hi omnes ad successionem patris vel matris veniant, patronatus jure in hac parte sopito. Hos etenim liberos non solum in suorum parentum successionem, sed etiam alterum in alterius successionem mutuam, vocavimus; ex illa lege specialiter eos vocantes, sive soli inveniantur, qui in servitute nati et postea manumissi sunt; sive una cum aliis, qui post libertatem parentum concepti sunt, sive ex eodem patre, sive ex eadem matre, sive ex aliis nuptiis, ad similitudinem eorum, qui ex justis nuptiis procreati sunt.

It

It is certain, that the part of the edict, in which the possession of goods is promised, according to the right of proximity, does not relate to servile cognation, *neither hath such* cognation *been regarded by any antient law. But, by our own constitution, concerning the right of patronage, which right was heretofore obscure, and every way confused, we have ordained (humanity so suggesting) that, if a slave shall have a child, or children, either by a free-woman, or by a bond woman, with whom he lives* in contubernio, *and, on the contrary, that, if a bond woman shall have a child, or children, of either sex by a freeman, or by a slave, with whom she lives* in contubernio, *and such father and mother are afterwards infranchised, the children shall succeed to their father or mother, no regard being paid to the right of patronage. And we have not only called these children to the succession of their parents, but also to succeed each other mutually, whether they are sole in succession, having all been born in servitude and afterwards manumitted, or whether they succeed with others, who were conceived after the infranchisement of their parents, and whether they are all by the same father and mother, or by a different father, or a different mother. And, in brief, we have been willing, that children born in slavery, and afterwards manumitted, should succeed in the same manner, as those, who are the issue of parents legally married.*

Sed nostra constitutione] This constitution is not extant

Collatio ordinum et graduum.

§ I. Repetitis itaque omnibus, quæ jam tradidimus, apparet non semper eos, qui parem gradum cognationis obtinent, pariter vocari: eoque amplius, ne eum quidem, qui proximior sit cognatus, semper potiorem esse. Cum enim prima causa sit suorum hæredum, et eorum, quos inter suos hæredes enumeravimus, apparet, pronepotem vel abnepotem defuncti potiorem esse, quam fratrem, aut patrem, aut matrem defuncti: cum alioqui pater quidem et mater (ut supra quoque tradidimus) primum gradum cognationis obtineant, frater vero secundum, pronepos autem tertio gradu sit cognationis, et abnepos quarto. nec interest, in potestate morientis fuerit, an non, quod vel emancipatus, vel ex emancipato, aut fœmineo sexu, propagatus est. Amotis quoque suis hæredibus, et quos inter suos hæredes vocari diximus, agnatus, qui integrum jus habet agnationis, etiamsi longissimo gradu sit, plerumque potior habetur, quam proximior cognatus. nam patrui nepos vel pronepos avunculo vel materteræ præfertur. Toties igitur dicimus, aut potiorem haberi eum, qui proximiorem gradum cognationis obtinet, aut pariter vocari eos, qui cognati sunt; quoties neque suorum hæredum, quique inter suos hæredes sunt, neque agnationis jure aliquis præferri debeat, secundum ea, quæ tradidimus: exceptis fratre et sorore emancipatis, qui ad successionem fratrum vel sororum vocantur. qui, etsi capite diminuti sunt, tamen præferuntur cæteris ulterioris gradus agnatis.

§ 1 *By what we have already said, it appears, that those, who are in an equal degree of* cognation, *are not always called equally to the succession; and farther, that even he, who is the nearest of kin, is not constantly to be prefered For, inasmuch as the first place is given to* proper heirs, *and to those, who are numbered with proper heirs,*

heirs, it is apparent, that the great-grandson, or great-great-grandson, is prefered to the brother or even the father or mother of the deceased: altho' a father and mother, (as we have before observed,) obtain the first degree of relation, a brother the second, a great-grandson the third, and a great great-grandson the fourth: neither does it make any difference, whether such grand-children were under the power of the deceased, at the time of his death, or out of his power, either by being emancipated, or by being the children of those, who were emancipated. neither can it be objected, that they are descended by the female line. But, when there are no proper heirs, nor any of those, who are permited to rank with them, then an agnate, *who hath the full right of* agnation *in him, altho' he is in the* most distant *degree, is generally prefered to a* cognate, *who is in the nearest degree, thus the grandson or great-grandson of a paternal uncle is prefered to an uncle or aunt, who is maternal. We therefore observe, that, when there are no proper heirs, nor any, who are numbered with them, nor any, who ought to be prefered by the right of* agnation, *(as we have before noted) then he, who is in the nearest degree of* cognation, *is called to the succession, and that, if there are many in the same degree, they are all called equally But a brother and sister, altho' emancipated, are yet called to the succession of brothers and sisters; for, altho' they have suffered diminution, they are nevertheless prefered to all* agnates *of a more remote degree.*

TITULUS OCTAVUS.

De successione libertorum.

D. xxxviii. T. 2.

Qui succedunt. De lege duodecim tabularum.

NUNC de libertorum bonis videamus. Olim itaque licebat liberto patronum suum impune testamento præterire: nam ita demum lex duodecim tabularum ad hæreditatem liberti vocabat patronum, si intestatus mortuus esset libertus, hærede suo nullo relicto. Itaque, intestato mortuo liberto, si is suum hæredem reliquisset, patrono nihil in bonis ejus juris erat. Et, siquidem ex naturalibus liberis aliquem suum hæredem reliquisset, nulla videbatur querela: si vero adoptivus filius fuisset, aperte iniquum erat, nihil juris patrono superesse.

Let us now treat of the succession of freed-men. A freed-man had it formerly in his power, without being subject to any penalty, wholly to omit in his testament any mention of his patron: for the law of the twelve tables called the patron to the inheritance, only when the freed man died intestate and without proper heirs, *and therefore, tho' a freed man had died intestate, yet, if he had left a proper heir, the patron would have received no benefit · and indeed, when the natural and legitimate children of the deceased became his heirs, there seemed no cause of complaint, but, when the freed man left only an adopted son, it was manifestly injurious, that the patron should have no claim.*

De jure prætorio.

§ I. Qua de causa postea prætoris edicto hæc juris iniquitas emendata est. Sive enim faciebat testamentum libertus, jubebatur ita testari, ut patrono partem dimidiam bonorum suorum relinqueret; et, si aut nihil aut minus parte dimidia reliquerat, dabatur patrono contra tabulas testamenti partis dimidiæ bonorum possessio: sive intestatus moriebatur, suo hærede relicto filio adoptivo, dabatur æque patrono contra hunc suum hæredem partis dimidiæ bonorum possessio. Prodesse autem liberto solebant, ad excludendum patronum, naturales liberi, non solum quos in potestate mortis tempore habebat, sed etiam emancipati, et in adoptionem dati, si modo ex aliqua parte scripti hæredes erant, aut præteriti contra tabulas bonorum possessionem ex edicto prætorio petierant. Nam exhæredati nullo modo repellebant patronum.

§ 1. *The law was therefore afterwards amended by the edict of the prætor: for every freed-man, who made his testament, was commanded so to dispose of his effects, as to leave a moity to his patron. and, if the testator left nothing, or less than a moity, then the possession of half was given to the patron* contra tabulas, *i. e contrary to the disposition of the testament. And, if a freed-man died intestate, leaving an adopted son his heir, the possession of a moity of the effects was in this case also given to the patron notwithstanding such heir: yet not only the natural and lawful children of a freed-man, whom he had under his power at the time of his death, excluded the patron, but those children also, who were emancipated, and given in adoption, if they were writen heirs for any part, or even, altho' they were omited, if they had requested the* possession CONTRA TABULAS, *by virtue of the* prætorian edict. *But disinherited children by no means repelled the patron.*

De lege Papia.

§ II. Postea vero lege Papia adaucta sunt jura patronorum, qui locupletiores libertos habebant. Cautum enim est, ut ex bonis ejus, qui sestertium centum millium patrimonium reliquerat, et pauciores quam tres liberos habebat, sive is testamento facto, sive intestatus mortuus erat, virilis pars patrono deberetur. Itaque, cum unum quidem filium filiamve hæredem reliquerat libertus, perinde pars dimidia debebatur patrono, ac si is sine ullo filio filiave intestatus decessisset: cum vero duos duasve hæredes reliquerat, tertia pars debebatur patrono. si tres reliquerat, repellebatur patronus.

§ 2. *But afterwards the rights of those patrons, who had wealthy freed-men, were inlarged by the* Papian *law: by which it is provided, that an equal share shall be due to the patron out of the effects of his freed-man, whether dying testate or intestate, who hath left a patrimony of an hundred thousand* sestertii *and fewer than three children so that, when a freed-man hath left only one son or daughter, then a moity of the effects is due to the patron, as if the deceased had died testate without either son or daughter. But, when there are two heirs male or female, a third part only is due to the patron, and, when there are three, the patron is wholly excluded.*

Lege

Lege Papia] This law was made in the consulate of *M Papius Mutilus* and *Q Poppæus secundus*, in the year of *Rome* 761. *Vinn.*

De constitutione Justiniani.

§ III. Sed nostra constitutio, (quam pro omni natione græca lingua compendioso tractatu habito composuimus,) ita hujusmodi causam definivit: ut, siquidem libertus vel liberta minores centenariis sint, id est, minus centum aureis habeant substantiam, (sic enim legis Papiæ summam interpretati sumus, ut pro mille sestertiis unus aureus computetur,) nullum locum habeat patronus in eorum successione, si tamen testamentum fecerint: sin autem intestati decesserint, nullo liberorum relicto, tunc patronatus jus, quod erat ex lege duodecim tabularum, integrum reservavit. Cum vero majores centenariis sint, si hæredes vel bonorum possessores liberos habeant, sive unum, sive plures, cujuscunque sexus vel gradus, ad eos successiones parentum deduximus, patronis omnibus modis cum sua progenie semotis. Sin autem sine liberis decesserint, siquidem intestati, ad omnem hæreditatem patronos patronasque vocavimus. Si vero testamentum quidem fecerint, patronos autem aut patronas præterierint, cum nullos liberos haberent, vel habentes eos exhæredaverint, vel mater sive avus maternus eos præterierint, ita quod non possint argui inofficiosa eorum testamenta, tunc ex nostra constitutione per bonorum possessionem contra tabulas, non dimidiam, ut antea, sed tertiam partem bonorum liberti consequantur; vel quod deest eis, ex constitutione nostra repleatur, si quando minus tertia parte bonorum suorum libertus vel liberta eis reliquerit: ita sine onere, ut nec liberis liberti libertæve ex ea parte legata vel fideicommissa præstentur, sed ad cohæredes eorum hoc onus redundet: multis aliis casibus à nobis in præfata constitutione congregatis, quos necessarios esse ad hujusmodi dispositionem juris perspeximus: ut tam patroni patronæque quam liberi eorum, nec non qui ex transverso latere veniunt usque ad quintum gradum, ad successionem libertorum libertarumve vocentur, sicut ex ea constitutione intelligendum est Et, si ejusdem patroni vel patronæ vel duorum duarumque pluriumve liberi sint, qui proximior est, ad liberti vel libertæ vocetur successionem: et in capita, non in stirpes, dividatur successio: eodem modo et in iis, qui ex transverso latere veniunt, servando Pene enim consonantia jura ingenuitatis et libertinitatis in successionibus fecimus.

§ 3. *But by our imperial constitution, (which we have caused to be promulged in the Greek language, for the benefit of all nations,) we have ordained, that, if a freed-man, or freed-woman, dies possessed of less than an hundred* aurei, *(for thus have we interpreted the sum mentioned in the* Papian law, *counting one* aureus *for a thousand* sestertii,*) the patron shall not be intituled to any share in the succession, where there is a will. But, if either a freed-man, or freed-woman, dies intestate, and without children, we have in this case reserved the right of patronage intire, as it formerly was, according to the law of the twelve tables But, if a freed person dies with more than an hundred* aurei, *and leaves one child, or many, of* *either sex or any degree, as the heirs and possessors of his goods, we have permited, that such child or children shall succeed their parent to the intire exclusion of the patron and his heirs: and, if any freed-persons die without children and intestate, we have called their patrons or patronesses to their whole inheritances. And if any freed-person, worth more than an hundred* aurei, *hath made a testament, omited his patron, and left no children, or hath disinherited them; or if a mother, or maternal grand-father, being freed-persons, have omited to mention their children in their wills, so that such wills can not be proved to be inofficious, then, by virtue of our constitution, the patron shall succeed, not to a moity as formerly, but to the third part of the estate of the deceased, by the possession of the goods, called* contra tabulas: *and, when freed-persons, men or women, leave less than the third part of their effects to their patrons, our constitution ordains, that the deficiency shall be supplied; and that this third part, due to patrons, shall not be subject to the burden of* trusts, *or legacies, even for the benefit of the children of the deceased, for the co-heirs only of the patron shall be loaded with this burden. In the before-mentioned constitution, we have collected many more cases, which we have thought necessary in relation to the right of patronage, that patrons and patronesses, their children and collateral relations, as far as the fifth degree, might be called to the succession of their freed-men and freed-women; as will appear more fully from our ordinance itself. And, if there are many children of one patron or patroness, or of two or more patrons or patronesses, he, who is nearest in degree, is called to the succession of his freed-man or freed-woman, and, when there are many in equal degree, the estate must be divided* in capita *and not* in stirpes, *and the same order is decreed to be observed among the collaterals of patrons and patronesses. for we have rendered the laws of succession almost the same in regard to the* ingenui *and* libertini.

Sed nostra constitutio] This constitution is not extant

Ex constitutione nostra repleatur] "Intelligit "haud dubie constitutionem, 1 *omnimodo. Cod* "3 *t.* 28 *de inofficioso testamento.*" *Vinn.*

Quibus libertinis succeditur.

§ IV. Sed hæc de iis libertinis hodie dicenda sunt, qui in civitatem Romanam pervenerunt, cum nec sint alii liberti, simul et Dedititiis et Latinis sublatis, cum Latinorum successiones nullæ penitus erant. quia licet ut liberi vitam suam peragebant, attamen ipso ultimo spiritu simul animam atque libertatem amittebant. et, quasi servorum, ita bona eorum jure quodammodo peculii ex lege Junia Norbana manumissores detinebant. Postea vero senatus-consulto Largiano cautum fuerat, ut liberi manumissoris, non nominatim exhæredati facti, extraneis hæredibus eorum in bonis Latinorum præponerentur. Quibus etiam supervenit Divi Trajani edictum, quod eundem hominem, si, invito vel ignorante patrono, ad civitatem Romanam venire ex beneficio principis festinarat, faciebat quidem vivum civem, Latinum vero morientem. Sed nostra constitutione, propter hujusmodi conditionum vices et alias difficultates, cum ipsis Latinis etiam legem Juniam, et senatus-consultum Largianum, et edictum Divi Trajani, in perpetuum deleri censuimus, ut omnes liberi civitate Romana fruantur, et mirabili modo quibusdam adjectionibus ipsas vias, quæ

in

in Latinitatem ducebant, ad civitatem Romanam capiendam tranſpoſuimus.

§ 4. *But what we have ſaid relates to the* libertini *of the preſent time, who are all citizens of* Rome, *for there is now no other ſpecies of freed-men, that of the* Dedititii *and* Latini *being aboliſhed: the latter of whom never enjoyed any right of ſucceſſion, for altho' they led the lives of freed men, yet, with their laſt breath, they loſt both their lives and liberties. for their poſſeſſions, like the goods of ſlaves, were detained by their manumitor, who poſſeſſed them, as a* peculium, *by virtue of the law* Junia Norbana. *It was afterwards provided by the* ſenatus-conſultum Largianum, *that the children of a manumitor, who were not nominally diſinherited, ſhould be prefered to any ſtrangers, whom a manumitor might conſtitute his heirs: then followed the edict of* Trajan, *which ordained, that, if a ſlave either againſt the will or without the knowledge of his patron ſhould obtain the freedom of* Rome *by the favor of the emperor, ſuch ſlave ſhould continue free, whileſt living, but, at his death, ſhould be regarded only as a* Latin. *But we, being averſe to theſe changes of condition and diſſatisfied with the difficulties attending them, have thought proper, by virtue of our conſtitution, for ever to aboliſh, together with the* Latins, *the law* Junia, *the* ſenatus-conſultum Largianum, *and the edict of* Trajan, *to the intent, that all freed-men may become freed-men of* Rome. *And we have happily contrived by ſome additions, that the manner of confering the freedom of* Latins *ſhould now become the manner of confering the freedom of* Rome.

Noſtra conſtitutione] *vid Cod* 7. *t.*6 *de latina libertate tollenda*

TITULUS NONUS.

De aſſignatione libertorum.

D. xxxviii. T. 4.

An aſſignari poſſit, et quis aſſignationis effectus.

IN ſumma, (quod ad bona libertorum attinet,) admonendi ſumus, cenſuiſſe ſenatum, ut quamvis ad omnes patroni liberos, qui ejuſdem gradus ſunt, æqualiter bona libertorum pertineant, tamen licere parenti, uni ex liberis aſſignare libertum, ut poſt mortem ejus ſolus is patronus habeatur, cui aſſignatus eſt; et cæteri liberi, qui ipſi quoque ad eadem bona, nulla aſſignatione interveniente, pariter admitterentur, nihil juris in his bonis habeant, ſed ita demum priſtinum jus recipiant, ſi is, cui aſſignatus eſt, deceſſerit nullis liberis relictis.

In regard to the poſſeſſion of freed-men it muſt be remembered, that the ſenate hath decreed, that, altho' the goods of freed men belong equally to all the children of the patron, who are in the ſame degree, yet it is lawful for a parent to aſſign a freed man to any one of his children, ſo that, after the death of the parent the child, to whom the freed man was aſſigned, is ſolely to be eſteemed his patron and the other children, who would have been equally admitted to [illegible]

[illegible]

vidend of the goods of the freed-man, had he not been assigned, are wholly excluded; but, if the assignèe happens to die without issue, the excluded children regain their former right

Censuisse senatum] This decree was in the reign of CLAUDIAN, *anno urb cond.* 798.

De sexu assignati, et de sexu graduque ejus, cui assignatur.

§ I. Nec tantum libertum, sed etiam libertam, et non tantum filio nepotive, sed etiam filiæ neptive, assignare permittitur.

§ 1. *Every freed-person is assignable, whether man or woman: and an assignment may be made not only to a son or grandson, but to a daughter or granddaughter.*

De liberis in potestate vel emancipatis.

§ II. Datur autem hæc assignandi facultas ei, qui duos pluresve liberos in potestate habebit, ut eis, quos in potestate habet, assignare libertum libertamve liceat. Unde quærebatur, si eum, cui assignavit, postea emancipaverit, num evanescat assignatio? Sed placuit evanescere. quod et Juliano et aliis plerisque visum est

§ 2 *The power of assigning freed-persons is given to him, who hath two or more children unemancipated, so that a father may assign a freed-man or freed woman to those children, whom he retains under his power. and hence it became a question, if a father should assign a freed-man to his son and afterwards emancipate that son, whether the assignment would, or would not be null? and the decision hath been in the affirmative; which hath been approved of by* Julian *and many others.*

Quibus modis aut verbis assignatio fit: et de senatusconsulto.

§ III Nec interest, an testamento quis assignet, an sine testamento; sed etiam quibuscunque verbis patronis hoc permittitur facere, ex ipso SC. quod Claudianis temporibus factum est, Sabellio Rufo et Asterio Scapula Consulibus.

§ 3. *But it makes no difference, whether the assignment of a freed-man is made by testament, or not by testament, for patrons may assign even by word of mouth, which was permitted by the* senatus-consultum, *made in the reign of* Claudian *in the consulate of* Sabellius Rufus *and* Asterius Scapula.

TITU-

TITULUS DECIMUS.

De bonorum possessionibus.

D. xxxvii. T. 1.

Cur introductæ bonorum possessiones; et quis sit earum effectus.

JUS bonorum possessionis introductum est à prætore emendandi veteris juris gratia. Nec solum in intestatorum hæreditatibus vetus jus eo modo prætor emendavit, sicut supra dictum est; sed in eorum quoque, qui testamento facto decesserint. Nam, si alienus posthumus hæres fuerit institutus, quamvis hæreditatem jure civili adire non poterat, cum institutio non valebat, honorario tamen jure bonorum possessor efficiebatur; videlicet cum à prætore adjuvabatur. Sed et is à nostra constitutione hodie recte hæres instituitur, quasi et jure civili non incognitus. Aliquando tamen neque emendandi neque impugnandi veteris juris, sed magis confirmandi gratia, prætor pollicetur bonorum possessionem. Nam illis quoque, qui, recte testamento facto, hæredes instituti sunt, dat secundum tabulas bonorum possessionem. Item ab intestato suos hæredes, et agnatos, ad bonorum possessionem vocat. Sed et remota quoque bonorum possessione ad eos pertinet hæreditas jure civili. Quos autem solus prætor vocat ad hæreditatem, hæredes quidem ipso jure non fiunt: nam prætor hæredem facere non potest: per legem enim tantum, vel similem juris constitutionem, hæredes fiunt, vel per senatus-consulta et constitutiones principales: sed, cum eis prætor dat bonorum possessionem, loco hæredum constituuntur, et vocantur bonorum possessores. Adhuc autem et alios complures gradus prætor fecit in bonorum possessionibus dandis, dum id agebat, ne quis sine successore moreretur. Nam, angustissimis finibus constitutum per legem duodecim tabularum, jus percipiendarum hæreditatum prætor ex bono et æquo dilatavit.

The right of succeeding by the possession of goods was introduced by the prætor, in amendment of the antient law, which he corrected, not only in regard to the inheritances of intestates, (as we have before observed;) but in regard also to the inheritances of those, who die testate: for, if a posthumous stranger was instituted an heir, altho' he could not enter upon the inheritance by the civil law, inasmuch as his institution as heir would not be valid, yet by the prætorian or honorary law he might be made the possessor of the goods, when he had received the assistence of the prætor. *But such stranger may at this time, by virtue of our constitution, be legally instituted an heir, being no longer regarded as a person unknown to the civil law. But the prætor sometimes bestows the possession of goods,* in-

intending neither to amend nor impugn the old law, but only to confirm it: for he gives the possession of goods secundum tabulas *to those, who are appointed the heirs of the deceased by a regular testament. He also calls* proper heirs *and* agnates *to the possession of the goods of intestates, and yet the inheritance would be their own by the* civil law, *altho' the prætor did not interpose his authority. But those, whom the prætor calls to an inheritance merely by virtue of his office, do not become legal heirs, inasmuch as the prætor can not make an heir; for heirs are made only by law, or by what has the effect of a law, as a decree of the senate, or an imperial constitution. But, when the prætor gives any persons the possession of goods, they stand in the place of heirs, and are called the possessors of the goods. But the prætor hath also devised many other orders of persons, to whom the possession of goods can be granted, to the intent, that no man may die without a successor: and, by the rules of justice and equity, he hath greatly inlarged the right of taking inheritances, which was bounded within the most narrow limits by the laws of the twelve tables.*

Jus bonorum possessionis] The *bonorum possessio* is not now in use even in those countries, where the civil law prevails for, succession by testament, or by law, comprehends every case "Jus civile et prætorium hodie in unam consonantiam redactum est, ideoque hujus tituli nullus amplius est usus etenim, qui alius ex testamento et ab intestato succedunt, in universum hæredes appellari solent." *Groenewegen, de leg.bus abrogatis h t.* In *England*, estates in general may be divided into two sorts, *real* and *personal*, and successions to these two different kinds of estates are governed by different rules of law But it is necessary to premise, that by *real* estate is most commonly meant an estate in land in fee, *i e* descendible from a man to his heirs for ever and that by *personal* estate are meant estates in land, determinable upon years, money in the funds or upon mortgages, plate, jewel, *&c.* and that such *personal* estate is generally comprehended, in technical and artificial language, under the terms *goods* and *chattels* Now in *real* estates there is no room for the *bonorum possessio* of the *Roman* law to take place in *England*, for all such estates vest in and descend instantly to the heir, at the death of his ancestor, but in regard to *goods* and *chattels* the office of the ordinary or ecclesiastical judge seems to be similar to that of the *Roman* prætor in granting the possession of goods. For, when a man dies, who has disposed of his personal estate by testament, the heirs or executors, appointed by that testament, must prove it before an ecclesiastical judge, who by granting probate gives the possession of goods to the executors *secundum tabulas*, according to the will, or at least confirms them in the possession already taken *Cowel, h l* And, when any person dies intestate, the ordinary (by virtue of 31 *Edw* 3 chap 11, and 21 *Henry* 8 chap 5) grants the possession and administration of the intestate's goods to the widow or next of kin to such intestate, or to both, at his discretion. And by the 22d and 23d of *Charles the second*, cap 10. it is enacted, "that all ordinaries and "ecclesiastical judges may call administrators to an account and order DISTRIBUTION, "after debts and funeral expenses are paid, to "wit, one third to the widow of the intestate, "and the residue among his children and those "who legally represent them, if any of them "are dead that, if there are no children, or "legal representatives of them, one half of the "intestate's estate shall be allotted to the widow, "and the residue to the next of kindred to the "intestate in equal degree, and those, who re-"present them that no representation shall be "admitted among collaterals after brothers and "sisters children, and that, if there is no wife, "all shall be distributed among the children, "and, if no child, to the next of kin to the in-"testate in equal degree and their representa-"tives" And by 1 *Jac.* 2. cap. 3d it is enacted, "that, if a brother or sister dies, each "brother and sister, and their representatives, "shall have an equal share with the mother" From all which the analogy, between the *civil* law and the law of *England*, is very observable

A nostra constitutione] This constitution is not extant

Confirmandi gratia] "Ob id certe, ut justius "possidere viderentur, qui autore prætore ad "successionem pervenissent, justior enim habe-"tur possessio, quam quis prætore nanciscitur "Præterea non potest non esse commodum plu-"res habere vias consequendæ hæreditatis; quo-"niam, una repudiata, superest tamen altera, "ex quo facile colligitur, hanc prætoriam con-"firmationem, etsi necessaria non sit, sua tamen "utilitate non carere." *Mynsinger, h. l*

Et alios complures gradus] "Complures "gradus fecit prætor in bonorum possessionibus, "non eos solum, qui supra memorati sunt, *unde*

"*liberi*,

"*liberi, unde legitimi, unde cognati, secundum tabulas* his enim addidit, *contra tabulas, unde decem personæ, tanquam ex familia, unde vir et uxor*, nunc confirmans, nunc supplens, nunc corrigens et impugnans jus civile." *Mynsingerus, h. l*

De speciebus ordinariis. Jus vetus.

§ I. Sunt autem bonorum possessiones ex testamento quidem hæ. prima, quæ præteritis liberis datur, vocaturque *contra tabulas*: secunda, quam omnibus jure scriptis hæredibus prætor pollicetur; ideoque vocatur *secundum tabulas*. Et, cum de testatis prius locutus est, ad intestatos transitum fecit. Et primo loco suis hæredibus, et iis, qui ex edicto prætoris inter suos hæredes connumerantur, dat bonorum possessionem, quæ vocatur *unde liberi*. Secundo, legitimis hæredibus. Tertio, decem personis, quas extraneo manumissori præferebat. Sunt autem decem personæ hæ; pater, mater, avus, avia, tam paterni quam materni, item filius, filia, nepos, neptis, tam ex filio, quam ex filia; frater sororve, consanguinei vel uterini Quarto, cognatis proximis. Quinto, *tanquam ex familia*. Sexto, patrono patronæque, liberisque eorum et parentibus. Septimo, viro et uxori. Octavo, cognatis manumissoris.

§ 1. *The kinds or species of the possessions of goods or prætorian successions, when there is a testament, are the following The first is that possession, which is given to children, of whom no mention is made in the testament*; *and this is called* possessio contra tabulas; *i. e.* a possession contrary to the testament *The second is that, which the prætor promises to all written heirs, and it is therefore called* secundum tabulas; *i e.* a possession according to the testament *These being fixed, the prætor proceeded to the possession of goods in regard to intestates*, —— *and first he gives the possession of goods, called* unde liberi, *to the* proper heirs, *or to those, who by the* prætorian edict *are numbered among the* proper heirs: —— *secondly, to the legitime heirs.* —— *thirdly, to ten persons, in preference to a stranger, who was the* manumittor, *viz to a father, a mother, or a grandfather or grand mother, paternal or maternal, to a son, a daughter, or to a grandson or grand daughter, as well by a daughter as by a son, to a brother or sister, either consanguine or uterine* —— *fourthly, to the nearest* cognates · —— *fifthly, to those, who are*, as it were, *of the family*, tanquam ex familia · —— *sixthly, to the patron or patroness, and to their children, and their parents.* —— *seventhly, to an husband and wife*: —— *eighthly, to the* cognates *of a* manumittor *or patron*

Extraneo manumissori] "Extraneus manumissor erat, qui non contracta fiducia emancipasset." *Mynsinger. h. l*

Tanquam ex familia] "Puto familiam significari *patronum, i e* hac bonorum possessio. vocari *patroni cognatos*." *Vinn.*

Jus novum.

§ II. Sed eas quidem prætoria introduxit jurisdictio: a nobis tamen nihil incuriosum prætermissum est: sed, nostris constitutionibus omnia corrigentes, *contra tabulas* quidem *et secundum tabulas* bonorum possessiones admisimus, utpote necessarias constitutas: nec non ab intestato, *unde liberi, et unde legitimi*, bonorum possessiones. Quæ autem in prætoris edicto quinto loco posita fuerat, id est, *unde decem personæ*, eam pio proposito

posito et compendioso sermone supervacuam ostendimus. Cum enim privata bonorum possessio decem personas præponebat extraneo manumissori, nostra constitutio, quam de emancipatione liberorum fecimus, omnibus parentibus eisdemque manumissoribus, contracta fiducia, manumissionem facere dedit; ut ipsa manumissio eorum hoc in se habeat privilegium, et supervacua fiat supradicta bonorum possessio. Sublata igitur prædicta quinta bonorum possessione in gradum ejus sextam antea bonorum possessionem induximus, et quintam fecimus, quam prætor proximis cognatis pollicetur. Cumque antea fuerat septimo loco bonorum possessio, *tanquam ex familia*, et octavo, *unde patroni patronæque, liberi et parentes eorum*, utramque per constitutionem nostram, quam de jure patronatus fecimus, penitus evacuavimus. Cum enim ad similitudinem successionis ingenuorum libertinorum successiones posuerimus, quas usque ad quintum gradum tantummodo coarctavimus, ut sit aliqua inter ingenuos et libertinos differentia, sufficit eis tam *contra tabulas* bonorum possessio, quam *unde legitimi*, et *unde cognati*, ex quibus possunt sua jura vindicare, omni scrupulositate et inextricabili errore istarum duarum bonorum possessionum resoluto. Aliam vero bonorum possessionem, quæ *unde vir et uxor* appellatur, et nono loco inter veteres bonorum possessiones posita fuerat, et in suo vigore servavimus, et altiore loco, id est, sexto, eam posuimus: decima quoque veteri bonorum possessione, quæ erat *unde cognati manumissoris*, propter causas enumeratas merito sublata, ut sex tantummodo bonorum possessiones ordinariæ permaneant, suo vigore pollentes.

§ 2. *The prætor's authority hath introduced these successions, but we, not suffering any useless institution to continue in the law, have nevertheless admited by our constitutions the possession of goods* contra tabulas *and* secundum tabulas, *as necessary, and also the possessions of goods* ab intestato, *called* unde liberi *and* unde legitimi. *but we have briefly shewed, that the possession, called* unde decem personæ, *which was ranked by the prætor's edict in the fifth order, was unnecessary for, whereas that possession prefered ten kinds of persons to a stranger, who was the manumittor at emancipation, our constitution, which regards emancipation, hath permited all parents to manumit their children, a* fiduciary *contract being presumed, so that the possession* unde decem personæ *is now useless. The afore mentioned fifth possession being thus abrogated, we have now made that the fifth, which was formerly the sixth, by which the prætor gives the succession to the nearest* cognates *And, whereas formerly the possession of goods, called* tanquam ex familia, *was in the seventh place, and the possession of goods called* unde patroni patronæque, liberi et parentes eorum, *was in the eighth, we have now annulled them both by our* ordinance *concerning the right of patronage. And having brought the successions of the* libertini *to a similitude with those of the* ingenui, *(except, that we have limited the former to the fifth degree, so that there may still remain some difference between them) we think, that the possessions* contra tabulas— unde legitimi— *and* unde cognati *may suffice, by which all persons may vindicate their rights, the niceties and inextricable errors of those two kinds of possessions,* tanquam ex familia *and* unde patroni, *being removed. The other possession of goods, called* vir et uxor, *which held the ninth place among the antient possessions, we have preserved in full force and have placed in an higher*

higher degree, namely, the sixth. The tenth of the antient possessions, called unde cognati manumissoris, *being deservedly abrogated for causes already enumerated, there now remain only in force six ordinary possessions of goods.*

Nostra constitutio] *Cod* 8 *t* 49. *l ult.* " Hæc " constitutio, quam de emancipationibus con- " scripsit imperator, omnibus parentibus et ma- " numissoribus præsumptionem contractæ fidu- " ciæ admisit, ut ipsa emancipatio tacite id in " se habeat, merito igitur præfata bonorum " possessio pro supervacua habenda est, cum " extraneus posthac manumissor nullus invenia- " tur *Theoph.*

Per constitutionem nostram] " Hæc est ea " dem græca constitutio, cujus superius quoque " aliquoties meminit imperator, et qua totam " se causam successionis libertorum plene defini " visse testatur : non extat hæc constitutio, sed " epitomen ejus nobis ex *Basilicis* repræsenta- " *Cujacius.*" lib. 20. obs 34

Species extraordinaria.

§ III. Septima eas secuta, quam optima ratione prætores introduxerunt. Novissime enim promittitur edicto iis etiam bonorum possessio, quibus, ut detur, lege vel senatus-consulto vel constitutione comprehensum est : quam neque bonorum possessionibus, quæ ab intestato veniunt, neque iis, quæ ex testamento sunt, prætor stabili jure connumeraverit : sed quasi ultimum et extraordinarium auxilium (prout res exigit) accommodavit, scilicet iis, qui ex legibus, senatus-consultis, constitutionibusve principum, ex novo jure, vel ex testamento, vel ab intestato veniunt.

§ 3 *But to these a seventh possession hath been added, which the prætors have introduced with the greatest reason : for, by edict, this possession of goods is promised to all those, to whom it is appointed to be given by any law, senatus-consultum, or constitution: and the prætor hath not positively numbered this possession of goods either with the possessions of the goods of intestate or testate persons, but hath given it, according to the exigence of the case, as the last and extraordinary resource of those, who are called to the successions of testates or intestates, by any particular law, any decree of the senate, or any new constitution.*

De successorio edicto.

§ IV. Cum igitur plures species successionum prætor introduxisset, easque per ordinem disposuisset, et in unaquaque specie successionis sæpe plures extent dispari gradu personæ, ne actiones creditorum differentur, sed haberent, quos convenirent, et ne facile in possessionem bonorum defuncti mitterentur, et eo modo sibi consulerent, ideo petendæ bonorum possessioni certum tempus præfinivit. Liberis itaque et parentibus, tam naturalibus quam adoptivis, in petenda bonorum possessione anni spatium, cæteris autem (agnatis vel cognatis) centum dierum, dedit.

§ 4. *The prætor, having introduced many kinds of successions and ranked them in order, hath thought proper, inasmuch as many persons of different degrees are ofte found in one species of succession, to limit a certain time for demanding the possession of goods, to the intent, that the actions of creditors may not be delayed for want of a proper person, against whom to bring them, and that the creditors themselves may not obtain the possession of the effects of the deceased too easily, and so consult solely their own advantage : therefore to parents and children, whether natural or adopted, the prætor hath given the space of one year, in which they may either accept or refuse the*

the possession of goods. But to all other persons, agnates *or* cognates, *he allows only an hundred days.*

Certum tempus] See *Digest.* 38. title 9 *de successorio edicto* ULPIAN.

De jure accrescendi et iterum de successorio edicto.

§ V. Et, si intra hoc tempus aliquis bonorum possessionem non petierit, ejusdem gradus personis accrescit, vel, si nullus sit, deinceps cæteris bonorum possessionem perinde ex successorio edicto pollicetur, ac si is, qui præcedebat, ex eo numero non esset. Si quis itaque delatam sibi bonorum possessionem repudiaverit, non, quousque tempus bonorum possessioni præfinitum excesserit, expectatur; sed statim cæteri ex eodem edicto admittuntur.

§ 5. *And, if any person intituled does not claim the possession of goods within the time limited, his right of possession accrues first to those in the same degree with himself; and, in default of persons in the same degree, then the prætor by the* successory edict *bestows the possession of goods upon those in the next degree, as if he, who preceded, had no right. And, if any man refuses the possession of goods, when it is open to him, there is no necessity to wait, 'till the time limited is expired, but those, who are the next in succession, may be instantly admited by virtue of the before-mentioned* edict.

Ex successorio edicto] *vid.* ff 38. t. 9

Explicatio dicti temporis.

§ VI. In petenda autem bonorum possessione dies utiles singuli considerantur.

§ 6. *It is here to be observed, that in regard to the time prescribed for demanding the possession of goods, we count all the days, which are* utiles; *i. e those days, on which the party, having knowledge that the inheritance is open to him, might apply to the judge.*

Dies utiles] "Dies in jure nostro alii sunt " continui, alii utiles. Continui, qui sine interruptione, nullisque exceptis, currunt utiles sunt illi duntaxat, quibus experiundi sui " juris potestas est, et hi neque ignoranti, neque agere non valenti, currunt *ff* 44. *t* 3 *l.* 1. *Vinn Theoph h t.*

Quomodo peti debet.

§ VII. Sed bene anteriores principes et huic causæ providerunt, ne quis pro petenda bonorum possessione curet; sed, quocunque modo admittentis eam indicium ostenderit, intra statuta tamen tempora, plenum habeat earum beneficium.

§ 7. *The emperors, our predecessors, have wisely provided in this case, that no person need be solicitous to demand the possession of goods in solemn form · for, if by any act it manifestly appears, that a man has in any manner consented to accept the* prætorian succession *within the prescribed time, he shall enjoy the full benefit of it.*

TITU-

TITULUS UNDECIMUS.

De acquiſitione per arrogationem.

Continuatio.

EST et alterius generis per univerſitatem ſucceſſio: quæ neque lege duodecim tabularum, neque prætoris edicto, ſed eo jure, quod conſenſu receptum eſt, introducta eſt.

There is alſo an univerſal ſucceſſion of another kind, which was introduced neither by the laws of the twelve tables, nor by the edict of the prætor, but by that law, which takes it's riſe from general conſent and uſage

Quæ hoc modo acquiruntur. Jus vetus.

§ I. Ecce enim, cum pater-familias ſeſe in arrogationem dat, omnes res ejus corporales et incorporales, quæque ei debitæ ſunt, arrogatori antea quidem pleno jure acquirebantur, exceptis iis, quæ per capitis diminutionem pereunt; quales ſunt operarum obligationes et jus agnationis. uſus etenim et uſusfructus licet his antea connumerabantur, attamen capitis diminutione minima eos tolli prohibuit noſtra conſtitutio

§ 1 *For example, if the father of a family gave himſelf in arrogation, all things, which appertained to him, whether corporeal or incorporeal, and whatever was due to him, became antiently the property of the* arrogator, *thoſe things only excepted, which periſhed by* diminution *or change of ſtate, as the duties of freed-men to their patrons and the rights of* agnation. *But, altho' uſe and uſufruct were heretofore numbered among thoſe rights, which periſhed by diminution, yet our conſtitution hath prohibited, that the uſe and uſufruct of things ſhould be taken away by the* leaſt diminution *or change of ſtate.*

Prohibuit noſtra conſtitutio] *vid Cod.* 3 *t* 33 *l* 16 *de uſuf. act.*

Jus novum.

§ II. Nunc autem nos eandem acquiſitionem, quæ per arrogationem fiebat, coarctavimus ad ſimilitudinem naturalium parentum. Nihil enim aliud, niſi tantummodo uſusfructus, tam naturalibus parentibus quam adoptivis, per filios-familias acquiritur in iis rebus, quæ extrinſecus filiis obveniunt, dominio eis integro ſervato. Mortuo autem filio arrogato in adoptiva familia, etiam dominium rerum ejus ad arrogatorem pertranſit niſi ſuperſint aliæ perſonæ, quæ ex conſtitutione noſtra patrem in iis, quæ acquiri non poſſunt, antecedant.

§ 2 *But we have now limited the acquiſitions obtained by arrogation, in ſimilitude of what is gained by natural parents. for nothing is now acquired either by natural or adoptive parents, but the bare uſufruct of thoſe things, which their children poſſeſs adventitiouſly and extrinſically in their own right, the property ſtill re-*

maining intire in the adopted or natural child. But, if an arrogated son dies under the power of his arrogator, then even the property *of the effects of such son will pass to the* arrogator *in default of those persons, whom we have by our constitution prefered to the father in the succession of those things, which could not be acquired for him.*

Quæ ex constitutione nostra.] *vid. Cod.* 6. *t.* 59. *l. ult. Communia de successionibus.*

Effectus hujus acquisitionis.

§ III. Sed ex diverso pro eo, quod is debuit, qui se in adoptionem dedit, ipso quidem jure arrogator non tenetur, sed nomine filii convenitur: et, si noluerit eum defendere, permittitur creditoribus, per competentes nostros magistratus, bona, quæ ejus cum usufructu futura fuissent, si se alieno juri non subjecisset, possidere, et legitimo modo ea disponere.

§ 3. *On the contrary an* arrogator *is not bound at law to satisfy the debts of his adopted son in consequence of a direct action; but yet he may be convened in his son's name, and, if he refuses to defend his son, then the creditors, by order of the proper magistrate, may seize upon and legally sell all those goods, of which the usufruct, as well as the property, would both have been in the debtor, if he had not made himself subject to the power of another.*

TITULUS DUODECIMUS.

De eo, cui libertatis causa bona addicuntur.

Continuatio.

ACCESSIT novus casus successionis ex constitutione Divi Marci. Nam, si ii, qui libertatem acceperunt a domino in testamento, ex quo non aditur hæreditas, velint bona sibi addici libertatum conservandarum causa, audiuntur.

A new species of succession hath taken it's rise from the constitution of Marcus Aurelius *For, if those slaves, to whom freedom hath been bequeathed, are desirous, for the sake of obtaining it, that the inheritance, which hath not been accepted by the writen heir, should be adjudged to them, they shall obtain their request.*

Rescriptum D. Marci.

§ I. Et ita Divi Marci rescripto ad Pompilium Rufum continetur: verba rescripti ita se habent. *Si Virginio Valenti, qui testamento suo libertatem quibusdam adscripsit, nemine successore ab intestato existente, in ea causa bona ejus esse cœperunt, ut vænire debeant, is, cujus de ea re notio est,*

aditus

aditus rationem deſiderii tui habebit, ut libertatum, tam earum, quæ directo, quam earum, quæ per ſpeciem fideicommiſſi relictæ ſunt, tuendarum gratia addicantur tibi, ſi idonee creditoribus caveris de ſolido, quod cuique debetur, ſolvendo. Et ii quidem, quibus directa libertas data eſt, perinde liberi erunt, ac ſi hæreditas adita eſſet: ii autem, quos hæres manumittere rogatus eſt, a te libertatem conſequentur; ita autem ut ſi non alia conditione velis tibi bona addici, quam ut ii etiam, qui directo libertatem acceperunt, tui liberti fiant: nam huic etiam voluntati tuæ, ſi ii, quorum de ſtatu agitur, conſentiant, auctoritatem noſtram accommodamus. Et, ne hujus reſcriptionis noſtræ emolumentum alia ratione irritum fiat, ſi fiſcus bona agnoſcere voluerit, et ii, qui bonis noſtris attendunt, ſciant, commodo pecuniario præferendam eſſe libertatis cauſam, et ita bona cogenda, ut libertas eis ſalva ſit, qui eam adipiſci potuerunt, ac ſi hæreditas ex teſtamento adita eſſet.

§ 1. *And to the ſame effect is the reſcript of the* emperor Marcus *to* Pompilius Rufus; *the words of which are theſe.* "If the eſtate of *Virginius Valens*, who "by teſtament hath bequeathed to certain perſons their freedom, muſt neceſſa-"rily be ſold, and there is no ſucceſſor *ab inteſtato*, then the *magiſtrate*, who "has the cognizance of theſe affairs, ſhall upon application hear the merits "of your cauſe, that, for the ſake of preſerving the liberty of thoſe, to whom "it was given, either directly or in truſt, the eſtate of the deceaſed may be ad-"judged to you, on condition, that you give good ſecurity to the creditors, "to pay them the whole of their juſt demands. And all thoſe, to whom free-"dom was *directly* given, ſhall then become free, as if the inheritance had been "entered upon by the writen heir, but thoſe, whom the heir was ordered to "manumit, ſhall obtain their freedom from you only. And, if you are not "willing, that the goods of the deceaſed ſhould be adjudged to you on any "other condition, than that even they, who received their liberty *directly* by "teſtament, ſhall alſo become your freed-men, we then order, that your will "ſhall be complied with, if the perſons agree to it, who are to receive their "freedom And, leſt the uſe and emolument of this our *reſcript* ſhould be "fruſtrated by any other means, be it known to the officers of our revenue, "that, whenever our exchequer lays claim to the eſtate of a deceaſed perſon, "the cauſe of liberty is to be prefered to any pecuniary advantage, and that "the eſtate ſhall be ſo ſeized, as to preſerve the freedom of thoſe, who could "otherwiſe have obtained it: and this in as full a manner, as if the inheritance "had been entered upon by the teſtamentary heir."

Utilitas reſcripti.

§ II. Hoc reſcripto ſubventum eſt et libertatibus et defunctis, ne bona eorum a creditoribus poſſideantur et væneant. Certe, ſi fuerint hac de cauſa bona addicta, ceſſat bonorum venditio: exiſtit enim defuncti defenſor, et quidem idoneus, qui de ſolido creditoribus cavet.

§ 2. *The contents of this* reſcript *are calculated not only in favor of liberty, but alſo for the benefit of deceaſed perſons, leſt their effects ſhould be ſeized and ſold by their creditors: for it is certain, that, when goods are adjudged to a particular man for the preſervation of liberty, a ſale by creditors can never take*

effect

effect. For he, to whom the goods are adjudged, is the protector of the deceased, and must always be a person, who can give security for the full payment of creditors.

Ubi locum habeat.

§ III. In primis hoc rescriptum toties locum habet, quoties testamento libertates datæ sunt. Quid ergo si quis intestatus decedens codicillis libertates dederit, neque adita sit ab intestato hæreditas? Favor constitutionis debebit locum habere: certe, si testatus decesserit et codicillis dederit libertatem, competere eam, nemini dubium est.

§ 3. *This* rescript *takes place, whenever freedom is confered by testament. But, when a master dies intestate, having bequeathed freedom to his slaves by codicil, and his inheritance is not entered upon, what will then be the consequence? We answer, that the favor of the* rescript *shall extend to this case; but it is most certainly not to be doubted, that, if a master dies testate and by codicil bequeaths freedom, the* rescript *shall be of full force.*

§ IV. Tunc enim constitutioni locum esse verba ostendunt, cum nemo successor ab intestato existat. Ergo, quamdiu incertum erit, utrum existat, an non, cessabit constitutio. Si vero certum esse cœperit, neminem existere; tunc erit constitutioni locus.

§ 4. *The words of the* rescript *shew, that it is then in force, when there is absolutely no successor* ab intestato. *It therefore follows, that, as long as it remains doubtful, whether there is or is not a successor, the constitution shall not take place: but, when once it is certain, that no one will enter upon the succession, the* ordinance *shall then have it's effect.*

§ V. Si is, qui in integrum restitui potest, abstinuerit hæreditate, an quamvis potest in integrum restitui, potest admitti constitutio, et bonorum addictio fieri? Quid ergo, si post addictionem, libertatum conservandarum causa factam, in integrum sit restitutus? Utique non erit dicendum, revocari libertates: quia semel competierunt.

§ 5. *But, if he, who has a right to be restored* in integrum *(as a minor for example) should delay to take upon him the inheritance of his father, it may then be asked, whether, notwithstanding this right of being restored, the constitution shall take place, and an adjudication of the goods pass to a stranger, or one of the slaves? And again, it may be demanded, what will be the consequence, if, after an adjudication has been made for the sake of liberty, the heir should be restored* in integrum? *We answer, that freedom, when once obtained, shall not afterwards be revoked*

Si libertates datæ non sunt.

§ VI Hæc constitutio libertatum tuendarum causa introducta est. Ergo, si libertates nullæ sint datæ, cessat constitutio. Quid ergo, si vivus dederit libertates vel mortis causa, et, ne de hoc quæratur, utrum in fraudem creditorum, an non, factum sit, idcirco velint sibi bona addici, an audiendi sunt? Et magis est, ut audiri debeant, etsi deficiant verba constitutionis.

§ 6.

§ 6. This constitution was made for the protection of liberty; and therefore, when freedom is not given, the constitution has no effect. Suppose then, that a master hath given freedom to his slaves either inter vivos, *or* mortis causa, *and that they, to prevent the creditors from complaining, that this was done to defraud them, should petition, that the estate of the deceased may be adjudged to them; are these persons to be heared? we answer, that we incline to grant their request, altho' in this case, the letter of the constitution is deficient.*

De speciebus additis a Justiniano.

§ VII. Sed, cum multas divisiones ejusmodi constitutioni deesse perspeximus, lata est a nobis plenissima constitutio, in qua multæ species collatæ sunt, quibus jus hujusmodi successionis plenissimum est effectum; quas ex ipsius lectione constitutionis potest quis cognoscere.

§ 7. But perceiving, that the rescript *was deficient in many respects, we enacted a most express constitution, containing many cases, which explain the rights of succession in the fullest manner, of which every person, who reads that constitution, will be sensible.*

Plenissima constitutio] *vid. Cod* 7. *t* 2. *l.* 15.

TITULUS DECIMUS-TERTIUS.

De successionibus sublatis, quæ fiebant per bonorum venditiones, et ex senatus-consulto Claudiano.

C. vii. T. 24.

ERANT ante prædictam successionem olim et aliæ per universitatem successiones: qualis fuerat bonorum emptio, quæ de bonis debitoris vendendis per multas ambages fuerat introducta; et tunc locum habebat, quando judicia ordinaria in usu fuerant: sed, cum extraordinariis judiciis posteritas usa est, ideo cum ipsis ordinariis judiciis etiam bonorum venditiones expiraverunt: et tantummodo creditoribus datur officio judicis bona possidere, et, prout utile eis visum est, ea disponere: quod ex latioribus digestorum libris perfectius apparebit. Erat et ex senatus-consulto Claudiano miserabilis per universitatem acquisitio, cum libera mulier, servili amore bacchata, ipsam libertatem per senatus-consultum amittebat, et cum libertate substantiam. Quod indignum nostris temporibus esse existimantes et a nostra civitate deleri, et non inseri nostris digestis concessimus.

There were many other kinds of universal successions before that, which we treated of in the foregoing title: as the bonorum emptio, *which was first introduced, that the*

the estates of debtors might be sold; but this was accompanied by many intricate and tedious proceedings; it continued nevertheless as long as the ordinary judgments were in practice; but, as soon as the extraordinary judgments were made use of, the solemn emptio bonorum *ceased at the same time with the ordinary judgments. And creditors can now possess themselves of the goods of their debtors and dispose of them, as they think most proper, by the decree of a judge. But these points are treated of more perfectly and at large in the books of our digests. There was also, by virtue of the* Claudian *decree, another universal acquisition called* miserabilis: *for example, if a free-woman had debased herself by being enamoured of a slave, she lost her freedom by the before named decree, and, together with her freedom, her estate and substance. But, it being our opinion, that this part of the decree was unworthy of our reign, and ought therefore to be expunged from our laws, we have not permitted it to be inserted in the digests.*

Qualis fuerat bonorum emptio.] "Bona debitoris, postquam aliquandiu celeberrimis in "locis proscripta pependissent, ex edicto possideri jubebantur, deinde magister postulabatur "et creabatur, per quem distrahebantur et "emptori addicebantur, qui omnibus in solidum satisfaciebat aut, antequam emeret, "cum creditoribus de certa parte decidebat" *vid.* Theophilum *in hunc locum, et* Heineccii *antiq. Rom jur. lib* 2 *tit.* 17. This exact species of sale is not in use in *England*; but there is a sale not very unlike it in the case of bankrupts, whose estates and goods are sold and divided among their creditors by commissioners, appointed for that purpose *vid* 13 *Eliz. cap* 7. 1 *Jac.* 1. *cap.* 15 21 *Jac* 1. *cap.* 19. 10 *Ann. cap.* 15 7 *Geo.* 1 *cap.* 31 5 *Geo* 2 *cap.* 20

Ex lationibus digestorum libris.] D 42 *t.* 5. *De rebus auctoritate judicis possidendis.* D 42 *t.* 4. *Quibus ex causis in possessionem eatur.*

Quod indignum nostris temporibus] *vid* Cod. 7. *t.* 24. *De senatus-consulto* Claudiano *tollendo*

TITULUS DECIMUS-QUARTUS.

De obligationibus.

D. xliv. T. 7. C. iv. T. 10.

Continuatio et definitio.

NUNC transeamus ad obligationes. Obligatio est juris vinculum, quo necessitate adstringimur alicujus rei solvendæ secundum nostræ civitatis jura.

Let us now pass to obligations. An obligation is the chain of the law, by which we are necessarily bound to make some payment, according to the laws of our country.

Divisio prior.

§ I. Omnium autem obligationum summa divisio in duo genera deducitur: namque aut civiles sunt aut prætoriæ. Civiles sunt, quæ aut legibus constitutæ aut certo jure civili comprobatæ sunt. Prætoriæ sunt, quas prætor ex sua jurisdictione constituit; quæ etiam honorariæ vocantur.

§ 1. *Obligations are primarily divided into two kinds,* civil *and* prætorian Civil *obligations are those, which are constituted by the laws, or by any species of the*

the civil law. Prætorian *obligations are those, which the prætor hath appointed by his authority; and these are also called* honorary.

Divisio posterior.

§ II. Sequens divisio in quatuor species dividitur. Aut enim ex contractu sunt, aut quasi ex contractu, aut ex maleficio, aut quasi ex maleficio. Prius est, ut de iis, quæ ex contractu sunt, dispiciamus. Harum æque quatuor sunt species. Aut enim re contrahuntur, aut verbis, aut literis, aut consensu: de quibus singulis dispiciamus.

§ 2. *The second or subsequent division of obligations contains four species: for some obligations arise by* contract, *others by* quasi-contract; *some by* malefeasance, *and others by* quasi-malefeasance. *We must first treat of those obligations, which arise from a* contract; *and of these there are also four kinds: for obligations are contracted by the thing itself, by word of mouth, by writing, or by the mere consent of parties. Let us now take a separate view of each of these methods of contracting.*

TITULUS DECIMUS-QUINTUS.

Quibus modis re contrahitur obligatio.

D. xii. T. 1. D. xiii. T. 6. 7. C. iv. T. 1. 23. 24. 34.

De mutuo.

RE contrahitur obligatio, veluti mutui datione. Mutui autem datio in iis rebus consistit, quæ pondere, numero, mensurave, constant, veluti vino, oleo, frumento, pecunia numerata, ære, argento, auro, quas res, aut numerando, aut metiendo, aut appendendo, in hoc damus, ut accipientium fiant. Et, quoniam nobis non eædem res sed aliæ ejusdem naturæ et qualitatis redduntur, inde etiam mutuum appellatum est: quia ita a me tibi datur, ut ex meo tuum fiat: & ex eo contractu nascitur actio, quæ vocatur *certi condictio.*

An obligation is contracted by the thing itself; that is, by the delivery of it, as a loan or mutuum: *and any particular thing, which consists of weight, number, or measure, as wine, oil, corn, coin, brass, silver, gold, may be delivered as a* mutuum; *and these substances, when so delivered, become in specie the absolute property of the receiver: and, since the very identical things lent cannot be restored, but others of the same nature and quality must be paid in lieu of them, this loan is therefore called a* mutuum, *for in this case* I so give, that what is mine may become yours: ut ex MEO TUUM fiat. *From this contract arises that action, which is called* certi condictio.

De indebito ſoluto.

§ I. Is quoque, qui non debitum accepit ab eo, qui per errorem ſolvit, re obligatur, daturque agenti contra eum propter repetitionem condictitia actio: nam perinde ei condici poteſt, *ſi apparet, eum dare oportere,* ac ſi mutuum accepiſſet. Unde pupillus, ſi ei ſine tutoris auctoritate indebitum per errorem datum eſt, non tenebitur indebiti condictione, non magis quam mutui datione. Sed hæc ſpecies obligationis non videtur ex contractu conſiſtere; cum is, qui ſolvendi animo dat, magis voluerit negotium diſtrahere, quam contrahere.

§ 1 *He alſo, who hath received what was not due to him, it being paid or delivered by miſtake, is bound by the thing received, ſo that an action of condition lies againſt him for the recovery of the thing, at the ſuit of him, who paid or delivered it erroneouſly. And this action may be brought againſt the receiver in theſe words,* ſi apparet, eum dare opportere, *in the ſame manner, as if he had accepted the thing delivered, as a* mutuum *And hence it is, that a pupil, when a payment of any thing not due hath been made to him without the authority of his* tutor, *is not ſubject to the action called* condictio indebiti, *becauſe he is not ſubject to an action on account of the delivery of a thing, as a* mutuum *And yet this ſpecies of obligation does not ſeem to proceed from a contract; ſince he, who pays with an intention to ſatisfy his debts, appears more willing to diſſolve, than to make, a contract.*

De commodato.

§. II. Item is, cui res aliqua utenda datur, id eſt, commodatur, re obligatur, & tenetur commodati actione. Sed is ab eo, qui mutuum accepit, longe diſtat: namque non ita res datur, ut ejus fiat; & ob id de ea re ipſa reſtituenda tenetur. Et is quidem, qui mutuum accepit, ſi quolibet fortuito caſu amiſerit, quod accepit, veluti incendio, ruina, naufragio, aut latronum hoſtiumve incurſu, nihilominus obligatus manet. At is, qui utendum accepit, ſane quidem exactam diligentiam cuſtodiendæ rei præſtare tenetur: nec ſufficit ei, tantam diligentiam adhibuiſſe, quantam ſuis rebus adhibere ſolitus eſt, ſi modo alius diligentior poterat eam rem cuſtodire. Sed propter majorem vim, majoreſve caſus, non tenetur, ſi modo non ipſius culpa is caſus intervenerit: alioqui ſi id, quod tibi commodatum eſt domi, peregre tecum ferre malueris, & vel incurſu hoſtium prædonumve, vel naufragio, amiſeris, dubium non eſt, quin de reſtituenda ea re tenearis. Commodata autem res tunc proprie intelligitur, ſi, nulla mercede accepta vel conſtituta, res tibi utenda data eſt: alioqui, mercede interveniente, locatus tibi uſus rei videtur: gratuitum enim debet eſſe commodatum.

§. 2. *He alſo, to whom the uſe of any particular thing is granted or* commodated, *is bound by the delivery of the thing, and is ſubject to an action called* commodataria. *But ſuch perſon widely differs from him, who hath received a* mutuum *for a* commodatum, *or thing lent, is not delivered, to the intent that it ſhould become the property of the receiver, and therefore he is bound to reſtore the identical*

identical thing, which he hath received. There is also another difference; for he, who hath accepted a mutuum, *is not freed from his obligation, if even by any accident, as by the fall of an edifice, fire, shipwreck, thieves, or the incursions of an enemy, he hath lost what he hath received: but he, who hath received a* commodatum, *or a thing lent for his use only, is indeed commanded to employ his utmost diligence in keeping and preserving it; (and it will not suffice, that he hath taken the same care of it, which he was accustomed to take of his own property, if it appears, that a more diligent man might have preserved it,) yet, if it is evident, that the loss of it was occasioned by a superior force, or some extraordinary accident, and not by any fault, he is then not obliged to make good the loss, but, if a man by choice will travel with what he has received as a* commodatum *or loan, and should lose it by shipwreck, or by the incursion of enemies, or robbers, it is not to be doubted, but that he is bound to make restitution, or to pay an equivalent A thing is properly said to be lent or* commodated, *when one man permits another to enjoy the use of it, and receives nothing by way of hire · but, if a price for hire is paid, the thing is* let, *and not* lent; *for a* commodatum, *or loan, must be gratuitous.*

De deposito.

§. III. Præterea & is, apud quem res aliqua deponitur, re obligatur, teneturque actione depositi: quia & ipse de ea re, quam accepit, restituenda tenetur. Sed is ex eo solo tenetur, si quid dolo commiserit: culpæ autem nomine, id est, desidiæ ac negligentiæ, non tenetur. Itaque securus est, qui parum diligenter custoditam rem furto amiserit: quia, qui negligenti amico rem custodiendam tradit, non ei, sed suæ facilitati, id imputare debet.

§ 3. *Any person, who is intrusted with a deposite, is bound by the delivery of the thing, and is subject to an action of deposite, because he is under an obligation of making restitution of that very thing, which he received. But a depositary is only thus answerable on account of fraud, for where a fault only can be proved against him, such as negligence, he is under no obligation; and he is therefore secure, if the thing deposited is stolen from him, even altho' it was carelesly kept. For he, who commits his goods to the care of a negligent friend, should impute the loss of them, not to his friend, but to his own facility and want of caution.*

De pignore.

§. IV. Creditor quoque, qui pignus accepit, re obligatur: quia & ipse, de ea re, quam accepit, restituenda, tenetur actione pignoratitia. Sed, quia pignus utriusque gratia datur, & debitoris, quo magis pecunia ei credatur, & creditoris, quo magis ei in tuto sit creditum, placuit sufficere, si, ad eam rem custodiendam, exactam diligentiam adhibeat, quam si præstiterit, & aliquo fortuito casu rem amiserit, securum esse, nec impediri creditum petere.

§ 4. *A creditor also, who hath received a pledge, is bound by the delivery of it, for he is obliged to restore the very thing, which he hath received, by the action called* pignoratitia. *But, inasmuch as a pledge is given for the mutual*

service

service of both debtor and creditor, (of the debtor, that he may obtain the money the more easily, and of the creditor, that the repayment may be the better secured,) it will suffice, if the creditor shall appear to have used an exact diligence in keeping the thing pledged: for, if such diligence appears to have been used, and the pledge was lost by mere accident, the law secures the creditor, as to the loss of the thing pledged, and he is by no means impeded to sue his debt.

TITULUS DECIMUS-SEXTUS.

De verborum obligationibus.

D. xlv. T. 1. C. viii. T. 38.

Summa.

VERBIS obligatio contrahitur ex interrogatione et responsione, cum quid dari fierive nobis stipulamur: ex qua duæ proficiscuntur actiones, tam condictio certi, si certa sit stipulatio, quam ex stipulatu, si incerta sit: quæ hoc nomine inde utitur, quod stipulum apud veteres firmum appellabatur, forte a stipite descendens.

An obligation in words is made by question and answer, when we stipulate, that any thing shall be given or done; and from hence arise two actions, viz the action called condictio certi, *when the stipulation is certain, and the action called* condictio ex stipulatu, *when the stipulation is incertain. This obligation is called a stipulation, because whatever was firm was termed* stipulum *by the antients; the word* stipulum *being probably derived from* stipes, *denoting the trunk of a tree.*

De verbis stipulationum.

§. I. In hac olim talia verba tradita fuerunt; *Spondes? Spondeo. Promittis? Promitto. Fidepromittis? Fidepromitto. Fidejubes? Fidejubeo. Dabis? Dabo. Facies? Faciam.* Utrum autem Latina an Græca, vel qualibet alia, lingua stipulatio concipiatur, nihil interest: scilicet, si uterque stipulantium intellectum ejus linguæ habeat: nec necesse est eadem lingua utrumque uti, sed sufficit congruenter ad interrogata respondere. Quinetiam duo Græci Latina lingua contrahere obligationem possunt. Sed hæc solemnia verba olim quidem in usu fuerunt: postea autem Leonina constitutio lata est, quæ, solemnitate verborum sublata, sensum et consonantem intellectum ab utraque parte solum desiderat, quibuscumque tandem verbis expressum est.

§ 1 *The following words were formerly used in all verbal obligations.*

Spondes? Spondeo.
Promittis? Promitto.
Fide-promittis? Fide-promitto.
Fide-jubes? Fide-jubeo.

Dabis?

Dabis? Dabo.
Facies? Faciam.

And it is not material, whether the stipulation is conceived in Latin, Greek, or any other language, if the stipulating parties understand it: neither is it necessary, that the same language should be used by each person; for it is sufficient, if a congruent pertinent answer is made to each question. It is moreover certain, that two Greeks may contract in Latin. Antiently indeed it was necessary to use those solemn words before recited; but the constitution of the Emperor Leo *was afterwards enacted, which takes away this verbal solemnity, and requires only the apprehension and consent of each party, expressed in any form of words.*

Leonina constitutio] *Omnes stipulationes, etiamsi non solennibus, vel directis, sed quibuscunque verbis, consensu contrahentium compositæ sunt, vel legibus cognitæ, suam habeant firmitatem. Cod.* 8 *t.* 38. *l* 10

Quibus modis stipulatio fit. De stipulatione pura vel in diem.

§ II. Omnis stipulatio aut pure, aut in diem, aut sub conditione fit. Pure, veluti *quinque* AUREOS *dare spondes?* Idque confestim peti potest. In diem, cum adjecto die, quo pecunia solvatur, stipulatio fit; veluti, *decem* AUREOS *primis calendis Martiis dare spondes?* Id autem, quod in diem stipulamur, statim quidem debetur: sed peti prius, quam dies venerit, non potest: ac ne eo quidem ipso die, in quem stipulatio facta est, peti potest: quia totus is dies arbitrio solventis tribui debet; neque enim certum est, eo die, in quem promissum est, datum non esse, priusquam is dies præterierit.

§ 2. *Every stipulation is made to be performed* simply, *or at a* day certain, *or* conditionally. *A stipulation is made to be performed* simply, *when a man says,* do you promise to pay me five AUREI? *And, in this case, the money may be instantly demanded. A stipulation is made to be performed* at a day certain, *when the day is added, on which the money is to be paid. as when a man says,* do you promise to pay me ten AUREI on the first of March? *but note, that what we stipulate to pay at a* day certain, *tho' it becomes immediately due, yet it cannot be demanded before the day comes, nor can it even* then *be sued, for the whole day must be allowed for payment, because it can never be certain, that there hath been a failure of payment on the day promised, until that day is quite expired.*

De die adjecto perimendæ obligationis causa.

§ III. At, si ita stipuleris, *decem* AUREOS *annuos, quoad vivam, dare spondes?* et pure facta obligatio intelligitur, et perpetuatur: quia ad tempus non potest deberi: sed hæres petendo pacti exceptione submovebitur.

§ 3 *But, if a man thus stipulates; viz.* do you promise to give me ten AUREI annually, as long as I live? *the obligation is understood to be made purely or simply, and becomes perpetual so as to bind the heirs of the obligor; for an obligation cannot continue due for a time certain only. yet, if the heir of the stipulator demands payment, he shall be barred by an exception of agreement.*

Quia

Quia ad tempus.] " Quod alicui deberi cœpit, id certis modis deberi desinit, puta " solutione, acceptilatione, novatione, &c " ff 44 t 7 l 44. *Ulp.* Sed tempus non est " modus tollendæ obligationis, cum tempus sit " quidpiam naturale, et obligatio civile quiddam; naturalia autem non possunt tollere " civilia, sed sunt alii modi a legibus præscripti, quibus extinguitur obligatio. Cum " ergo tempus non possit tollere civilem obligationem, sequitur te hæredi meo remanere " obligatum civiliter, etiam me mortuo, idque " textus sentit in verbo, *perpetuatur* Hac " quidem subtili summoque jure procedunt; " et, quia iniquum videbatur, ultra id, quam " conventum est, te cogi, eliditur hæc civilis " obligatio per exceptionem *pacti conventi*: " et sic, quamvis hæres meus, rigore juris " inspecto, possit abs te illos decem aureos " annuos petere, tamen submovebitur per exceptionem *pacti conventi* de non petendo: " quasi videaris tacite pactum fecisse, quod ego " stipulator possem quidem annuos decem abs " te petere, quamdiu viverem, hæres autem " meus non posset. *Myns.*

De conditione.

§ IV. Sub conditione stipulatio fit, cum in aliquem casum differtur obligatio, ut, si aliquid factum fuerit, vel non fuerit, committatur stipulatio: veluti, *si Titius consul fuerit factus, quinque* AUREOS *dare spondes?* Si quis ita stipuletur, *si in capitolium non ascendero, dare spondes?* Perinde erit, ac si stipulatus esset, cum moreretur, sibi dari. Ex conditionali stipulatione tantum spes est debitum iri; eamque ipsam spem in hæredem transmittimus, si prius, quam conditio extet, mors nobis contigerit.

§ 4 *A stipulation is conditional, when an obligation is refered to an accident, and depends upon some thing to be done or not done, to happen or not to happen, before the stipulation can take effect: for instance, if a man stipulates thus*; do you promise to pay me five AUREI, if TITIUS is made a consul? *or thus,* do you promise to pay me five AUREI, if I do not ascend the capitol? *which last stipulation is in effect the same, as if he had stipulated that five* AUREI *should be paid to him at the time of his death. It is to be observed, that, in every conditional stipulation, there is only an hope, that the thing stipulated will become due*; *and this hope a man transmits to his heirs, if he dies before the event of the condition.*

De loco.

§ V. Loca etiam inseri stipulationi solent; veluti, *Carthagini dare spondes?* quæ stipulatio, licet pure fieri videatur, tamen re ipsa habet tempus adjectum, quo promissor utatur ad pecuniam Carthagini dandam. Et ideo, si quis Romæ ita stipuletur, *hodie Carthagini dare spondes?* inutilis erit stipulatio, cum impossibilis sit repromissio.

§ 5 *Even places are often inserted in a stipulation, as for example,* do you promise to give me such a particular thing at CARTHAGE? *And this stipulation, tho' it appears to be made simply, yet in reality carries with it a space of time, which the obligor may make use of to inable himself to pay the money promised at* Carthage. *And therefore, if a man at* Rome *should stipulate in these words,* do you promise to pay me a sum of money this day at Carthage? *the stipulation would be null, because the performance of it would be impossible.*

De conditione ad tempus præſens vel præteritum relata.

§ VI. Conditiones, quæ ad præſens vel præteritum tempus referuntur, aut ſtatim infirmant obligationem, aut omnino non differunt: veluti, *ſi Titius conſul fuit*, vel, *ſi Mævius vivit, dare ſpondes?* nam, ſi ea ita non ſunt, nihil valet ſtipulatio: ſin autem ita ſe habent, ſtatim valet. Quæ enim per rerum naturam ſunt certa, non morantur obligationem, licet apud nos incerta ſint.

§ 6. *Conditions, which relate to the time preſent or paſt, either inſtantly annul an obligation, or inſtantly inforce it: for example, if a man ſhould thus ſtipulate,* do you promiſe me the payment of a ſum of money, if TITIUS hath ever been a conſul? *or thus,* if MÆVIUS is now living? *If theſe things are not ſo, that is, if* Titius *hath never been a conſul, and* Mævius *is not now living, the ſtipulation is void: and if they are ſo, that is, if* Titius *hath been a conſul, and* Mævius *is actually living, then the ſtipulation is good and may be inforced: for events, which in themſelves are certain, delay not the performance of an obligation, altho' to us they are not certain.*

Quæ in ſtipulatum deducuntur.

§. VII. Non ſolum res in ſtipulatum deduci poſſunt, ſed etiam facta; ut ſi ſtipulemur aliquid fieri, vel non fieri. Et in hujuſmodi ſtipulationibus optimum erit pœnam ſubjicere, ne quantitas ſtipulationis in incerto ſit, ac neceſſe ſit actori probare, quod ejus interſit. Itaque, ſi quis, ut fiat aliquid, ſtipuletur, ita adjici pœna debet, *ſi ita factum non erit, pœnæ nomine decem aureos dare ſpondes?* Sed ſi, quædam fieri quædam non fieri, una eademque conceptione ſtipuletur quis, clauſula hujuſmodi erit adjicienda, *ſi adverſus ea factum erit, ſive quid ita factum non fuerit, tunc pœnæ nomine decem aureos dare ſpondes?*

§ 7. *Not only things, as a field, a ſlave, or a book, but alſo acts, may be the ſubject of ſtipulations; as when we ſtipulate, that ſomething ſhall or ſhall not be done. And, in theſe ſtipulations, it will be right to ſubjoin a penalty, leſt the value of the ſtipulation ſhould be incertain, and the demandant ſhould therefore be forced to prove how far he is intereſted in it. And therefore, if a man ſtipulates, that ſomething ſhall be done, a penalty ought to be thus added,* do you not promiſe to pay me ten AUREI, as a penalty, if the act ſtipulated is not performed? *But, if it is agreed in the ſame obligation, that ſome things ſhall be done, and that others ſhall not be done, then ought ſome ſuch clauſe, as the following, to be added,* do you promiſe to pay me ten AUREI, as a penalty, if any thing is done contrary to agreement; or if any thing is not done according to our agreement?

TITULUS DECIMUS-SEPTIMUS.

De duobus reis ſtipulandi et promittendi.

D.xlv.T.2. C.viii.T.40. Nov.99.

Quibus modis duo rei fieri poſſunt.

ET ſtipulandi et promittendi duo pluresve rei fieri poſſunt. Stipulandi ita, ſi poſt omnium interrogationem promiſſor reſpondeat, *Spondeo*; ut puta, cum duobus ſeparatim ſtipulantibus ita promiſſor reſpondeat, *utrique veſtrum dare ſpondeo.* Nam, ſi prius Titio ſpoponderit, deinde alio interrogante ſpondeat, alia atque alia erit obligatio, nec creduntur duo rei ſtipulandi eſſe. Duo pluresve rei promittendi ita fiunt: *Mævi, decem aureos dare ſpondes? et, Sei, eoſdem decem aureos dare ſpondes?* ſi reſpondeant ſinguli ſeparatim, *Spondeo.*

Two or more perſons may ſtipulate, and two or more may become obligors. The ſtipulating parties are bound, if, after all queſtions have been aſked, the obligor anſwers, I promiſe, *as when, for example, the obligor thus anſwers two perſons ſeparately ſtipulating,* I promiſe to pay each of you. *For, if he firſt promiſes* Titius, *and afterwards promiſes another, who interrogates him, there will then be two obligations, and not two ſtipulators to one obligation. Two or more become obligors, if, after they have been thus interrogated,* MÆVIUS, do you promiſe to pay us ten AUREI? and, SEIUS, do you promiſe to pay us the ſame ten AUREI? *they each of them anſwer ſeparately,* I do promiſe.

De effectu hujusmodi ſtipulationum.

§ I. Ex hujuſmodi obligationibus et ſtipulationibus ſolidum ſingulis debetur, et promittentes ſinguli in ſolidum tenentur. In utraque tamen obligatione una res vertitur: et vel alter debitum accipiendo vel alter ſolvendo omnium perimit obligationem, et omnes liberat.

§ 1. *By theſe ſtipulations and obligations the whole ſum ſtipulated becomes due to every perſon ſtipulating, and every obligor is bound for the payment of the whole. But, as one and the ſame thing is due by each obligation, therefore any one of the ſtipulators by receiving the debt, and any one of the obligors by paying it, diſcharges the obligation of the reſt, and frees all parties.*

De ſtipulatione pura, et de die et conditione.

§ II. Ex duobus reis promittendi, alius pure, alius in diem, vel ſub conditione, obligari poteſt: nec impedimento erit dies aut conditio, quo minus ab eo, qui pure obligatus eſt, petatur.

§ 2. *Where there are two obligors, the one may bind himſelf purely and ſimply, and the other may oblige himſelf only to make payment on a day certain, or upon condition.*

condition. But neither the day certain, nor the condition, will secure the person, who is simply bound, from being sued for the payment of the whole.

TITULUS DECIMUS-OCTAVUS.

De stipulationibus servorum.

D. xlv. T. 3.

An servus stipulari possit.

SERVUS ex persona domini jus stipulandi habet: sed et hæreditas in plerisque personæ defuncti vicem sustinet. ideoque, quod servus hæreditarius ante aditam hæreditatem stipulatur, acquirit hæreditati, ac per hoc etiam hæredi postea facto acquiritur.

A slave obtains the liberty of stipulating from the person of his master; but in many instances the inheritance represents the person of a master deceased: and therefore whatever an hereditary slave stipulates for, before the inheritance is entered upon, he acquires it for the inheritance, and of course for him, who afterwards becomes the heir.

Cui acquirat. De persona, cui stipulatur. De stipulatione impersonali.

§ I. Sive autem domino, sive sibi, sive conservo suo, sive impersonaliter servus stipuletur, domino acquirit. Idem juris est et in liberis, qui in potestate patris sunt, ex quibus causis acquirere possunt.

§ 1. *A slave, let him stipulate how he will, for his master, for himself, for a fellow slave, or generally without naming any person, always acquires for his master. And the same obtains among children, who are under the power of their father, in regard to those things, which they can acquire for him.*

De stipulatione facti.

§ II. Sed, cum factum in stipulatione continebitur, omnimodo persona stipulantis continetur, veluti, si servus stipuletur, ut sibi ire agere liceat: ipse enim tantum prohiberi non debet, non etiam dominus ejus.

§ 2. *But, when a fact or thing to be done is contained in a stipulation, the person of the stipulator is solely regarded; so that, if even a slave stipulates, that he shall be permited to pass thro' a field, and to drive beasts or a carriage thro' it, it is not the master, but the slave only, who is to be permited to pass.*

De servo communi.

§ III. Servus communis stipulando unicuique dominorum pro portione dominii acquirit: nisi jussu unius eorum, aut nominatim alicui eorum, ſtipulatus eſt: tunc enim ſoli ei acquiritur. Quod ſervus communis ſtipulatur, ſi alteri ex dominis acquiri non poteſt, ſolidum alteri acquiritur: veluti ſi res, quam dari ſtipulatus eſt, unius domini ſit.

§ 3. *If a ſlave, who is in common to ſeveral maſters, ſtipulates, he acquires a ſhare for each maſter according to the proportion, which each has in the property of him. But, if ſuch ſlave ſhould ſtipulate at the command of any particular maſter, or in his name, the thing ſtipulated will be acquired ſolely for that maſter. And, whatever a ſlave in common to two maſters ſtipulates for, if part cannot be acquired for one maſter, the whole ſhall be acquired for the other. as when the thing ſtipulated already belongs to one of the two.*

TITULUS DECIMUS-NONUS.

De diviſione ſtipulationum.

Diviſio.

STIPULATIONUM aliæ ſunt judiciales, aliæ prætoriæ, aliæ conventionales, aliæ communes, tam prætoriæ quam judiciales.

Some ſtipulations are judicial, *others* prætorian, *others* conventional, *and others* common; *that is, both* prætorian *and* judicial.

De judicialibus ſtipulationibus.

§ I. Judiciales ſunt duntaxat, quæ a mero judicis officio proficiſcuntur: veluti de dolo cautio, vel de perſequendo ſervo, qui in fuga eſt, reſtituendove pretio.

§ 1. *The* judicial *are thoſe, which proceed merely from the office of the judge; as when ſecurity is ordered to be given againſt fraud, or for perſuing a ſlave, who hath fled, and for paying the price of him.*

De prætoriis.

§ II. Prætoria ſunt, quæ a mero prætoris officio proficiſcuntur; veluti damni infecti vel legatorum. Prætorias autem ſtipulationes ſic audiri oportet, ut in iis etiam contineantur ædilitiæ; nam et hæ a juriſdictione prætoris veniunt.

§ 2. *The* prætorian *ſtipulations are thoſe, which proceed from the mere office of the prætor, as when ſecurity is ordered to be given,* pro damno infecto, *that is, on account of damage not yet done, but likely to happen; and for the payment of legacies. And note, that under* prætorian *ſtipulations we comprehend the* edilitian; *for theſe proceed from the juriſdiction of the prætor.*

Ut in iis contineantur Ædilitiæ] "Ædilitiæ "ſtipulationes ſunt quibus venditor cavet de "morbis et vitiis rerum venalium, puta, *rem* "*morboſam non eſſe, ſervum fugitivum non eſſe*, et "de cæteris, quæ edicto ædilium promittuntur. *ff* 21. *t.* 1. *De ædilitio edicto*

"Prætoris ergo vocabulum hic in ſenſu latiſſimo accipi videtur pro quovis magiſtratu, "cui eſt juriſdictio. *Hein.*

De

De conventionalibus.

§ III. Conventionales sunt, quæ ex conventione utriusque partis concipiuntur; hoc est, neque jussu judicis, neque jussu prætoris, sed ex conventione contrahentium: quarum totidem sunt genera, quot, (pene dixerim,) rerum contrahendarum.

§ 3. Conventional *stipulations are those, which are made by the agreement of parties, that is, neither by order of a judge or prætor, but by the consent of the persons contracting: and of these stipulations there are as many kinds, as of things to be contracted for.*

De communibus.

§ IV. Communes sunt, veluti rem salvam fore pupillo, (nam et prætor jubet rem salvam fore pupillo caveri, et interdum judex, si aliter hæc res expediri non potest,) vel de rato stipulatio.

§ 4. Common *stipulations are those, which are ordered for the security of the effects of a pupil, (for the prætor ordains a caution to be given on this account, and sometimes a judge commands it, when it cannot otherways be avoided,) or for the ratification of a thing done in another's name.*

Nam et prætor jubet] " Hæc stipulatio, rem " salvam fore pupillo, regulariter jussu prætoris " interponitur, nullo interveniente judicio aut " causæ cognitione, et, nisi caveat tutor, pig- " noribus captis et mulcta indicta coercetur, " quorum nihil est *judicis*, qui nudam duntaxat " causæ notionem habet. Sed finge, debitorem " pupilli conventum a tutore post litem con- " testatam demum, inter moras judicii, cogno- " visse non satis dedisse tutorem, atque ad hanc " exceptionem confugere, utique audiendus erit, " et in hoc casu officio *judicis* injungitur stipu- " latio *Vinn*

And, according to the laws of England, whoever is appointed a tutor or guardian by an ordinary, is bound to give security; and he must, before his admission, take an oath to administer all the affairs of his ward to his profit and benefit, and to give a true and faithful inventary of all his goods, and to exhibit it by a certain time assigned by the judge; and also to render an exact and true account of his office, when required And besides this he must find fit and able sureties, who must be bound jointly and severally for his true and faithful administration *Cowel* 1 *inst* t 24

But in practice, (says Dr *Strahan* in his notes upon *Domat*) this law is not now observed, to the very great detriment of minors.

TITULUS VIGESIMUS.

De inutilibus stipulationibus.

C. viii. T. 39.

De his, quæ sunt in commercio.

OMNIS res, quæ dominio nostro subjicitur, in stipulationem deduci potest, sive ea mobilis sit, sive soli.

Every thing, of which we have the property, may be brought into stipulation, whether it is moveable or immoveable.

De

De his, quæ non exiſtunt.

§ I. At, ſi quis rem, quæ in rerum natura non eſt, aut eſſe non poteſt, dari ſtipulatus fuerit, veluti Stichum, qui mortuus ſit, quem vivere credebat, aut Hippocentaurum, qui eſſe non poſſit, inutilis erit ſtipulatio.

§ 1. *But, if a man hath ſtipulated, that a thing ſhall be given, which does not, or can not exiſt, as for inſtance, that* Stichus, *the ſlave, who is dead, but is thought to be living, or that a centaur, who cannot exiſt, ſhould be given to him, the ſtipulation is of no force.*

De his, quæ non ſunt in commercio.

§ II. Idem juris eſt, ſi rem ſacram aut religioſam, quam humani juris eſſe credebat, vel publicam, quæ uſibus populi perpetuo expoſita ſit, ut forum, vel theatrum, vel liberum hominem, quem ſervum eſſe credebat, vel cujus commercium non habuerit, vel rem ſuam dari, quis ſtipuletur. Nec in pendenti erit ſtipulatio ob id, quod publica in privatam deduci, et ex libero ſervus fieri poteſt, et commercium adipiſci ſtipulator poteſt : ſed protinus inutilis eſt. Item contra, licet initio utiliter res in ſtipulatum deducta ſit, ſi tamen poſtea in aliquam eorum cauſam, de quibus ſupra dictum eſt, ſine facto promiſſoris devenerit, extinguitur ſtipulatio. At nec ſtatim ab initio talis ſtipulatio valebit, *Lucium Titium, cum ſervus erit, dare ſpondes?* et ſimilia. Quæ enim natura ſui dominio noſtro exempta ſunt, in obligationem deduci nullo modo poſſunt.

§ 2. *And the law is the ſame, if a thing ſacred, which was thought to be not ſo, is brought into ſtipulation; or if a man ſtipulates for a thing of conſtant public uſe, as a forum or a theatre; or for a free perſon, who was thought to be bond; or for a thing, which he cannot acquire, or for ſome thing, which is already his own: nor ſhall any ſuch ſtipulation continue in ſuſpenſe, becauſe a thing public may become private, a freeman may turn ſlave, a ſtipulator may become capable of acquiring, or becauſe what now belongs to the ſtipulator may ceaſe to be his: but every ſuch ſtipulation ſhall be inſtantly void. And, on the contrary, altho' a thing may properly be brought into ſtipulation at firſt, yet if it afterwards falls under the claſs of any of the things before mentioned without the fault of the obligor, the ſtipulation is extinguiſhed. And ſuch a ſtipulation, as the following ſhall never be valid —for inſtance,* do you promiſe to give me Lucius Titius, when he ſhall become a ſlave? *for thoſe things, which in their natures are exempt from our dominion, are by no means to be brought into obligation.*

De facto vel donatione alterius.

§ III. Si quis alium daturum facturumve quid promiſerit, non obligabitur, veluti ſi ſpondeat Titium quinque aureos daturum. Quod ſi effecturum ſe, ut Titius daret, ſpoponderit, obligatur.

§ 3. *If a man promiſes, that another ſhall give or do ſomething, ſuch promiſſor ſhall not be bound, as if a man ſhould promiſe,* that Titius ſhall pay five

AUREI.

AUREI. *But, if he promises, that he will* cause TITIUS *to pay five* AUREI, *his promise shall be binding.*

De eo, in quem confertur obligatio, vel solutio.

§ IV. Si quis alii, quam ei, cujus juri subjectus est, stipuletur, nihil agit. Plane solutio etiam in extraneam personam conferri potest: veluti, si quis ita stipuletur, *mihi aut* SEIO *dare spondes?* ut obligatio quidem stipulatori acquiratur, solvi tamen Seio, etiam invito eo, recte possit, ut liberatio ipso jure contingat: sed ille adversus Seium habeat mandati actionem. Quod si quis sibi et alii, cujus juri subjectus non sit, dari decem AUREOS stipulatus est, valet quidem stipulatio. Sed utrum totum debeatur stipulatori, quod in stipulationem deductum est, an vero pars dimidia, dubitatum est. Sed placuit, non plus, quam dimidiam partem, ei acquiri Ei vero, qui juri tuo subjectus est, si stipulatus sis, tibi acquiris; quia vox tua tanquam filii intelligitur in his rebus, quæ tibi acquiri possunt.

§ 4 *If a man stipulates for any other, than for him, to whom he is subject, such stipulation is a void act. but nevertheless a payment of a thing promised may be made to a stranger; as if a man should thus stipulate,* do you promise to make payment to me, or to SEIUS? *for, when the obligation is to the stipulator, the payment may well be made to* Seius *tho' against his will, and this is allowed in favor of the debtor, that he may be legally freed from his debt · and the stipulator, if there is occasion, may have an action of mandate against* Seius *And, if a man should stipulate, that ten* AUREI *shall be paid to him, and to another, not under his power, the stipulation would be good · yet it hath been a doubt, whether the whole sum due would be due to the stipulator, or only a moity, and it hath been resolved, that the stipulator in this case acquires a moity only. But, if you stipulate for another, who is subject to your power, you acquire for yourself for your own words are reputed your son's, and your son's words are reputed yours, in regard to all those things, which you can possibly acquire.*

De interrogatione et responsione.

§ V. Præterea inutilis est stipulatio, si quis ad ea, quæ interrogatus fuerit, non respondeat, veluti si quis decem aureos a te dari sibi stipuletur, tu quinque promittas, vel contra: aut si ille pure stipuletur, tu sub conditione promittas, vel contra: si modo scilicet id exprimas, id est, si cui sub conditione vel in diem stipulanti tu respondeas, *præsenti die spondeo.* Nam, si hoc solum respondeas, *Promitto,* breviter videris in eandem diem vel conditionem spopondisse. Neque enim necesse est in respondendo, eadem omnia repeti, quæ stipulator expresserit.

§ 5. *A stipulation is void, if the party interrogated does not answer pertinently to the demand made, as when a person stipulates, that ten* aurei *shall be paid him, and you answer five, or, vice versa, if he stipulates for five, and you answer,* I promise ten. *Also if a man stipulates simply, and you promise conditionally, or, on the contrary, if he stipulates conditionally, and you answer purely, and in express terms, that is, if, when a man is stipulating conditionally or at a day certain, you answer him*

him thus: I promise you payment on this present day. *But, if you answer only,* I promise, *you seem in brief speech to agree to his* day *or* condition. *For it is not necessary, that in the answer every word should be repeated, which the stipulator expressed.*

De his, qui sunt, vel habent, in potestate.

§ VI. Item inutilis est stipulatio, si vel ab eo stipuleris, qui tuo juri subjectus est, vel si is a te stipuletur. Sed servus quidem non solum domino suo obligari non potest, sed ne quidem ulli alii: filii vero familiarum aliis obligari possunt.

§ 6. *A stipulation is also void, if you stipulate with him, who is in subjection to your power, or if he stipulates with you. For a slave is not only incapable of entering into an obligation with his master, but is also incapable of binding himself to any other person. But the son of a family can enter into an obligation with any other person, except his father.*

Filii vero familiarum] " Inter servum et filium familias hoc interest, quod servus non " tantum domino, sed nec ulli alii ex contractu civiliter obligari potest; quia, quod ad " jus civile attinet, servi pro nullis habentur, " filii autem familias, ext.a patrem et causam " mutui, ut reliqui cives, obligantur *Vinn.*

De muto et surdo.

§ VII. Mutum neque stipulari neque promittere posse, palam est; quod et in surdo receptum est: quia et is, qui stipulatur, verba promittentis, et is, qui promittit, verba stipulantis, audire debet. Unde apparet, non de eo nos loqui, qui tardius exaudit, sed de eo, qui omnino non audit.

§ 7. *It is evident, that a dumb man can neither stipulate, nor promise: and the same law is received in regard to deaf persons, for he, who stipulates, ought to hear the words of the obligor; and he, who promises, the words of the stipulator But we speak not of him, who hears with difficulty, but of him, who has no hearing.*

De furioso.

§ VIII. Furiosus nullum negotium gerere potest, quia non intelligit, quod agit.

§ 8. *A madman can transact no business, because he understands not what he does.*

De impubere.

§ IX. Pupillus omne negotium recte gerit, ita tamen ut, ubi tutoris auctoritas necessaria sit, adhibeatur tutor: veluti, si ipse obligetur: nam alium sibi obligare etiam sine tutoris auctoritate potest. Sed quod diximus de pupillis, utique de iis verum est, qui jam habent aliquem intellectum. Nam infans, et qui infantiæ proximus est, non multum a furioso distant: quia hujusmodi ætatis pupilli nullum habent intellectum.

lectum. Sed in proximis infantiæ propter utilitatem eorum benignior juris interpretatio facta est, ut idem juris habeant, quod pubertati proximi. Sed, qui in potestate parentis est impubes, ne auctore quidem patre obligatur.

§ 9. *A pupil is capable of transacting any business, if his tutor consents, where his authority is necessary, as it certainly is, when the pupil would bind himself but a pupil can stipulate or cause others to be bound to him, without the authority of his tutor What we have said of pupils must be understood of those, who have some understanding, for an infant, or one next to an infant, differs but little from a person out of his senses: for pupils of such an age have no understanding · but a more favorable interpretation is given to the law in regard to those, who are but little removed from infancy, whenever their own utility is concerned, so that they are then allowed the same rights, as those, who are near the age of puberty But a son, who is under the power of his father, and within the age of puberty, cannot bind himself, even altho his father consents, and authorises the transaction*

Ne auctore quidem patre.] " Pupillus non " tutori sed sibi acquirit, placetque, eum etiam " sine tutoris auctoritate contrahendo alios sibi " obligare, quo fit, ut ad utilitatem pupilli " pertineat, ut et ipse invicem saltem, tutore " auctore, obligari possit, cum alioqui nemo " facile cum eo contracturus sit, at, qui in po- " testate patris est, non sibi, sed patri acquirit, " non ad suam, sed ad patris, utilitatem con- " trahit, ut proinde nunquam e re impuberi, " in potestate constituti, esse possit, invicem " obligari. *Vinn* h l

De conditione impossibili.

§ X. Si impossibilis conditio stipulationibus adjiciatur, nihil valet stipulatio. Impossibilis autem conditio habetur, cui natura impedimento est, quominus existat, veluti si quis ita dixerit; *si digito cælum attigero, dare spondes?* at, si ita stipuletur, *si digito cælum non attigero, dare spondes?* pure facta obligatio intelligitur, ideoque statim peti potest.

§ 10. *If an impossible condition is added to an obligation, the stipulation is null, and that condition is reckoned impossible, of which nature forbids the event as, for example, if a man should say,* do you promise me ten AUREI, if I touch the heavens with my finger? *but suppose a stipulation to be thus made*; do you promise me payment, if I do not touch the sky with my finger? *such a stipulation would be understood to cause a simple obligation, the performance of which might be instantly demanded.*

Si impossibilis conditio] In *England*, if the condition of a bond is impossible at the time of making, as for instance, if it be, *that the obligor shall arrive at Rome the next day*, such a bond is not regarded as null, but as single, and the same, as if no condition was annexed to it But, if the condition of a bond is possible at the time of making, and, before such condition can be performed, it becomes impossible by the act of God, by the act of the law, or by the act of the obligee, the obligation in such case is saved *Co Lit* 206 *a*

De absentia.

§ XI. Item verborum obligatio, inter absentes concepta, inutilis est. Sed, cum hoc materiam litium contentiosis hominibus præstabat, forte post tempus tales allegationes opponentibus, et non præsentes fuisse vel se vel adversarios suos contendentibus, ideo nostra constitutio propter celeritatem dirimendarum litium introducta est, quam ad Cæsarienses advocatos scripsimus; per quam disposuimus, tales scripturas, quæ præsto esse partes indicant, omnino esse credendas, nisi is, qui talibus utitur improbis allegationibus, manifestissimis probationibus, vel per scripturam, vel per testes idoneos, approbaverit, toto eo die, quo conficiebatur instrumentum, sese vel adversarium suum in aliis locis fuisse.

§ 11. *A verbal obligation, made between absent persons, is also void. But, when this doctrine afforded matter of strife to contentious men, alleging after some time past, that either they or their adversaries were not present, we issued our constitution, addressed as a rescript to the advocates of* Cæsarea, *which effectually provided for the speedy determination of such suits: and by this we have ordained, that full credit shall be given to those written acts, or instruments, which declare, that the contracting parties were present, unless the party, who alleges absence, makes it evident by the most manifest proofs either in writing or by witnesses, that either he, or his adversary, was in some other place, during the whole day, in which the instrument was said to be made*

Ideo nostra constitutione] *vid Cod* 8 *de contrahenda stipulatione t* 38 *l* 14.

De stipulatione post mortem, vel pridie quam alter contrahentium moriatur.

§ XII. Post mortem suam dari sibi nemo stipulari poterat, non magis quam post mortem ejus, a quo stipulabatur. Ac nec is, qui in alicujus potestate est, post mortem ejus stipulari poterat, quia patris vel domini voce loqui videretur. Sed et, si quis ita stipuletur, *pridie quam moriar*, vel, *pridie quam morieris, dare spondes?* inutilis erat stipulatio. Sed, cum, ut jam dictum est, ex consensu contrahentium stipulationes valeant, placuit nobis, etiam in hunc juris articulum necessariam inducere emendationem, ut, sive post mortem, sive pridie quam moriatur stipulator, sive promissor, stipulatio concepta sit, stipulatio valeat.

§ 12. *A man could formerly no more stipulate, that a thing should be given him after his own death, than he could stipulate, that a thing should be given him, after the death of the obligor. Neither could any person under the power of another stipulate, that any thing should be given him after his death, because such person would appear to speak the words of his father or master And, if a man had stipulated in this manner,* do you promise to give me five AUREI the day before I die? *or* the day before you die? *the stipulation was also invalid. But, since all stipulations, as we have already said, take their rise and force from the consent of the contracting parties, we have thought it proper to introduce a necessary emendation in this respect, so that, whether it is stipulated, that a thing shall be given after, or immediately before, the death either of the stipulator, or the obligor, the stipulation shall be good.*

Inducere emendationem] " Justinianus scru- " pulosam hanc veteris juris subtilitatem sustu- " lit constitutionibus suis, quæ extant, in *Cod* " 8 *t* 38 *l* 11 *et Cod* 4 *t* 11 *l un*

" In qua juris mutatione ait, se respexisse non " ad conceptionem verborum, sed ad sententiam " et mentem contrahentium, quasi qui stipu- " latur, *post mortem suam sibi dari*, non debeat " existimari tam stultus, ut sibi ipsi in id tempus " stipuletur, sed hoc perinde sic accipiendum, " ac si post mortem suam stipulatus esset hæredi " suo, in cujus persona quodammodo adhuc " vivere videatur *Vinn.*

De ſtipulatione præpoſtera.

§ XIII. Item, ſi quis ita ſtipulatus erat, *ſi navis cras ex Aſia venerit, hodie dare ſpondes?* inutilis erat ſtipulatio, quia præpoſtere concepta eſt. Sed, cum Leo inclytæ recordationis in dotibus eandem ſtipulationem, quæ præpoſtera nuncupatur, non eſſe rejiciendam exiſtimaverit, nobis placuit et huic perfectum robur accommodare, ut non ſolum in dotibus, ſed etiam in omnibus, valeat hujuſmodi conceptio ſtipulationis.

§ 13 *Alſo, if a man had ſtipulated in theſe words,* do you promiſe me a ſum of money to-day, if a certain ſhip arrives to-morrow from ASIA? *the ſtipulation would have been invalid, becauſe prepoſterouſly conceived But, ſince the emperor* Leo, *of renowned memory, was of opinion, that ſuch ſtipulations ought not to be rejected in regard to marriage portions, it hath pleaſed* us *alſo to give a fuller force to this doctrine by ordaining, that every ſtipulation of like import ſhall hold good not only in marriage portions, but likewiſe in all other contracts.*

Nobis placuit] *vid Cod* 6 *t* 23 *l* 25 *præpoſteri reprehenſionem,* &c

De ſtipulatione collata in tempus mortis.

§ XIV. Ita autem ſtipulatio concepta, veluti ſi Titius dicat, *cum moriar, dare ſpondes?* vel *cum morieris?* et apud veteres utilis erat, et nunc valet.

§ 14. *If a ſtipulation had been conceived in the following words,* do you promiſe to give me ten AUREI, at the time, when I ſhall die? *or thus,* at the time, when you ſhall die? *it was good by the antient law, and is now valid.*

§ XV. Item poſt mortem alterius recte ſtipulamur.

§ 15. *We may alſo legally ſtipulate, that a thing ſhall be given, after the death of a third perſon.*

De promiſſione ſcripta in inſtrumento.

§ XVI. Si ſcriptum in inſtrumento fuerit, promiſiſſe aliquem, perinde habetur, atque ſi interrogatione præcedente reſponſum ſit.

§ 16 *If it is written in an act or inſtrument, properly atteſted, that a man hath entered into an obligation by promiſe, it will be always preſumed, that the promiſe was in anſwer to a precedent interrogation, and that every thing was done regularly.*

De pluribus rebus.

§ XVII. Quoties plures res una ſtipulatione comprehenduntur, ſiquidem promiſſor ſimpliciter reſpondeat, *dare ſpondeo,* propter omnes tenetur. Si vero unam ex his, vel quaſdam, daturum ſe ſpoponderit, obligatio in iis, pro quibus ſpoponderit, contrahitur. Ex pluribus enim ſtipulationibus una vel quædam videntur eſſe perfectæ, ſingulas enim res ſtipulari, et ad ſingulas reſpondere, debemus.

§ 17. *When many things are comprehended in one stipulation, a man binds himself to give them all, if he answers simply* I promise. *But, if he promises to give one or some of the things stipulated, an obligation is contracted only in respect to those things, which he promised to give For, where there are many stipulations, it may happen, that only one, or some of them may be made perfect by a separate answer, and strictly we ought to stipulate for every thing severally, and to answer severally.*

De pœna adjecta stipulationi, alii dari.

§ XVIII. Alteri stipulari (ut supra dictum est) nemo potest. Inventæ enim sunt hujusmodi stipulationes vel obligationes ad hoc, ut unusquisque acquirat sibi, quod sua interest: cæterum, si alii detur, nihil interest stipulatoris. Plane, si quis velit hoc facere, pœnam stipulari conveniet, ut, nisi ita factum sit, ut est comprehensum, committatur pœnæ stipulatio etiam ei, cujus nihil interest. Pœnam enim cum stipulatur quis, non illud inspicitur, quod intersit ejus, sed quæ sit quantitas in conditione stipulationis. Ergo, si quis ita stipuletur, *Titio dari*, nihil agit. Sed, si adjecerit pœnam, *nisi dederis, tot aureos dare spondes?* tunc committitur stipulatio.

§ 18 *No man can stipulate for another, as we have already observed, for stipulations and obligations have been invented, that every person may acquire for himself whatever may be of advantage to him, and, if this is given to another, the stipulator has no interest But, if a man would effectually contract for another, he should stipulate, that unless the covenants of his stipulation are performed, the obligor shall be subject to a penalty, payable to him, who otherwise would receive no advantage from the obligation. for, when a penalty is stipulated, the advantage or interest of the stipulator is not regarded, but the quantity of the penalty is the only thing considered. And therefore, if a man should stipulate,* that a certain thing shall be given to TITIUS, *it will not avail, but, if to the stipulation he adds a penalty as thus,* do you promise to give me ten AUREI, if you do not give the thing stipulated to TITIUS? *the stipulation of the penalty will take place, if the obligation is not performed*

Si intersit ejus, qui alii stipulatur.

§ XIX. Sed et, si quis stipuletur alii, cum ejus interesset, placuit stipulationem valere Nam, si is, qui pupilli tutelam administrare cœperat, cesserit administrationem contutori suo, et stipuletur rem pupilli salvam fore, quoniam interest stipulatoris fieri, quod stipulatus est, cum obligatus futurus sit pupillo, si male res gesserit, tenet obligatio. Ergo, et si quis procuratori suo dari stipulatus sit, habebit vires stipulatio. Et, si creditori suo quis stipulatus sit quod sua interest, ne forte vel pœna committatur, vel prædia distrahantur, quæ pignori data erant, valet stipulatio.

§ 19 *But, if any man stipulates for the benefit of another, when he himself also receives an advantage from it, the stipulation is valid. Thus if he, who hath begun to administer the tutelage of a pupil, should afterwards cede or give up the administration to his co-tutor, and stipulate for the security of the estate of his pupil, in this*

this case, (inasmuch as such a stipulation is for the interest of the stipulator, who would be obliged to answer all damages to the pupil, if the co-tutor did not justly administer the pupillary trust,) the obligation would bind. And upon the same principle, if a man stipulates, that a thing shall be given to his proctor or attorney, the stipulation shall prevail And a stipulation is also good, which is made by a debtor for the use of his creditor, because it is the interest of the debtor, either that the penalty, upon which he borrowed money of his creditor, should not be exacted from him, or that his goods, which are hypothecated with his creditor, should not be sold.

De pœna adjecta promissioni facti alieni.

§ XX. Vice versa, qui alium facturum promisit, videtur in ea esse causa, ut non teneatur, nisi pœnam ipse promiserit.

§ 20. *On the contrary, he, who promises, that another, namely* TITIUS, *shall perform some particular act, is not bound by such promise, unless he makes himself subject to a penalty, if the act is not performed by* TITIUS.

De re stipulantis futura.

§ XXI. Item nemo rem suam futuram, in eum casum, quo sua sit, utiliter stipulatur.

§ 21. *No man can legally stipulate, that a thing shall be given him, when it shall become his own.*

Item nemo] The decision in this paragraph is founded upon the following rule of law *quæ ad eum casum pervenerunt, a quo non potuissent incipere, nullatenus valeat* Ferriere

De dissensu.

§ XXII. Si de alia re stipulator senserit, de alia promissor, perinde nulla contrahitur obligatio, ac si ad interrogatum responsum non esset: veluti si hominem Stichum a te quis stipulatus fuerit, tu de Pamphilo senseris, quem Stichum vocari credideris.

§ 22. *If the stipulator stipulates in regard to one thing, and the obligor promises in relation to another, no obligation is contracted, and the parties are as much at liberty, as if no answer had been made to the interrogation · and this would be the case, if a man should stipulate, that* Stichus *should be given to him, and the obligor should intend to give* Pamphilus, *upon a thorough persuasion, that* Pamphilus *is called* Stichus.

De turpi causa.

§ XXIII. Quod turpi ex causa promissum est, veluti si quis homicidium vel sacrilegium se facturum promittat, non valet.

§ 23. *A promise made for a dishonest purpose, as, for example, to commit homicide or sacrilege, is not binding*

De morte contrahentium.

§ XXIV. Cum quis sub aliqua conditione stipulatus fuerit, licet ante conditionem decesserit, postea existente conditione hæres ejus agere potest Idem est et ex promissoris parte.

§ 24.

§ 24. *If a stipulation hath been entered into upon condition, and the stipulator should die pending the event of it, his heir will be intituled to an action against the obligor, if the event afterwards happens. And, if the obligor should die before the condition happens, his heir may be sued by the* stipulator.

Quando agi potest ex stipulatione.

§ XXV. Qui hoc anno aut hoc mense dari stipulatus est, nisi omnibus partibus anni vel mensis præteritis, non recte petet. Si fundum dari stipuleris, vel hominem, non poteris continuo agere, nisi tantum spatium præterierit, quo traditio fieri possit.

§ 25. *Whoever stipulates, that a thing shall be given to him this year or this month, cannot legally sue the obligor, till the whole year or month is elapsed. And, if a man stipulates, that a piece of ground, or slave, shall be given to him, he cannot instantly sue the obligor, but must wait, till such a space of time hath past, in which a delivery might reasonably have been made.*

TITULUS VIGESIMUS-PRIMUS.

De fidejussoribus.

D. xlvi. T. 1. C. viii. T. 41. Nov. 4.

Cur accipiuntur fidejussores.

PRO eo, qui promittit, solent alii obligari, qui fidejussores appellantur: quos homines accipere solent, dum curant, ut diligentius sibi cautum sit.

It frequently happens, that others bind themselves for him, who promises. These bondsmen or sureties are called fide-jussors, *and are generally required by creditors for their greater security.*

In quibus obligationibus.

§ I. In omnibus autem obligationibus adsumi possunt, id est, sive re, sive verbis, sive literis, sive consensu, contractæ fuerint. Ac nec illud quidem interest, utrum civilis, an naturalis sit obligatio, cui adjicitur fidejussor: adeo quidem, ut pro servo quoque obligetur, sive extraneus sit, qui fidejussorem a servo accipiat, sive ipse dominus, in id, quod sibi naturaliter debetur.

§ 1. Fide-jussors *may be received in all obligations, whether contracted by the delivery of the thing itself, by words, by writing, or the mere consent of parties: nor is it material, whether the obligation is civil or natural, for a man may intervene, and oblige himself, as a* fide-jussor *or surety, even on the behalf of a slave, and this may be done, whether the person, who accepts the* fide-jussor, *is a stranger*

stranger or the master of the slave, when the thing due is a natural debt or obligation.

De hærede.

§ II. Fidejussor non tantum ipse obligatur, sed etiam hæredem relinquit obligatum.

§ 2. *A* fide-jussor *is not only bound himself, but by his death transmits the obligation to his heir.*

Si fidejussor præcedat vel sequatur obligationem.

§ III. Fidejussor et præcedere obligationem et sequi potest.

§ 3 *A* fide-jussor *may be accepted either before or after an obligation is entered into.*

De pluribus fidejussoribus.

§ IV. Si plures sint fidejussores, quotquot erunt numero, singuli in solidum tenentur. Itaque liberum est creditori, a quo velit, solidum petere. Sed ex epistola Divi Hadriani compellitur creditor a singulis, qui modo solvendo sunt litis contestatæ tempore, partes petere. Ideoque, si quis ex fidejussoribus eo tempore solvendo non sit, hoc cæteros onerat. Sed, si ab uno fidejussore creditor totum consecutus fuerit, hujus solius detrimentum erit, si is, pro quo fidejussit, solvendo non sit: et sibi imputare debet, cum potuerit juvari ex epistola Divi Hadriani, et desiderare, ut pro parte in se detur actio.

§ 4. *Where there are* fide jussors *or sureties, let them be ever so numerous, they are each bound by law* in solidum, *i e. for the whole debt, and the creditor is at liberty to chuse from whom he will demand it. But, by a rescript of the emperor* Adrian, *a creditor may be obliged to demand separately from every* fide-jussor, *who is solvent at the Time of contestation of suit, his share of the debt* pro rata; *and, if any of the* fide-jussors, *at the time of the contestation of the suit, is not solvent, the burden falls upon the rest. But, if a creditor obtains his whole demand from one of the* fide-jussors, *the whole loss shall be his, if the party principal, for whom he was bound, is insolvent for such* fide-jussor *can impute this loss only to himself, since he might have called to his aid the rescript of the emperor* Adrian, *and have prayed, that an action should not have been given against him, obliging him to the payment of more than his share of the debt, as a surety.*

Si plures sint fidejussores] In *England*, when two or more are bound, without specifying whether they are bound jointly, or jointly and severally, nothing is more certain, than that each may be sued by the obligee for his whole debt but the party, who was sued, may have his remedy over against the obligor or his fellow surety But, when persons are bound jointly, they must be sued jointly, and, when they are bound jointly and severally, the obligee may sue them jointly or severally at his election See *Bacon*'s abridgement, *verb* obligations D.

In quam summam obligatur fide-jussor.

§ V. Fidejussores ita obligari non possunt, ut plus debeant, quam debet is, pro quo obligantur. Nam eorum obligatio accessio est princi-

pal's

palis obligationis: nec plus in accessione potest esse, quam in principali re: at ex diverso, ut minus debeant, obligari possunt. Itaque, si reus decem aureos promiserit, fidejussor in quinque recte obligatur: contra vero obligari non potest. Item, si ille pure promiserit, fidejussor sub conditione promittere potest; contra vero non potest. Non solum autem in quantitate, sed etiam in tempore, minus aut plus intelligitur. Plus enim est statim aliquid dare, minus est post tempus dare.

§ 5. Fide-jussors *ought not to be bound in a greater sum, than the debtor owes, for whom they are bound; for their obligation is an accession to the principal obligation, and an accessary debt cannot be greater, than the principal, tho' it may be less. Therefore, if the principal obligor promises ten* aurei, *the* fide-jussor *may be bound in five, but the* fide-jussor *cannot be bound in* ten aurei, *when the principal obligor is bound only in five. Also, when the obligor promises simply, the surety may promise conditionally. but, if the surety is bound simply, when the principal debtor is bound only conditionally, the obligation is void. And the terms* greater *and* less *take place not only in quantity but also in time; for an obligation to give or deliver a thing instantly is greater, than an obligation to give or deliver it after a time.*

De actione fidejussoris.

§ VI. Si quid autem fidejussor pro reo solverit, ejus recuperandi causa habet cum eo mandati judicium.

§ 6. *If a* fide jussor *hath been obliged to pay money for the person, for whom he was bound, the* fide-jussor *may have an action of mandate against him for the recovery of the sum paid.*

Si fidejussor græce accipiatur.

§ VII. Græce etiam fidejussor ita accipitur, τῃ ἐμῃ πιστει κελευω λεγω. Sed et si dixerit, θελω, sive βουλομαι, sed et, φημι, pro eo erit, ac si dixerit, λεγω.

§ 7 *A* fide-jussor *may thus bind himself even in greek*; τῃ ἐμῃ πιστει κελευω, λεγω. *that is,* I answer or speak solemnly upon my faith. *But, if a man should use the words* θελω *or* βουλομαι, *I am willing, or* φημι, *I promise, any of these would serve the same purpose, as* κελευω *or* λεγω.

Si scriptum sit, aliquem fidejussisse.

§ VIII In stipulationibus fidejussorum sciendum est, hoc generaliter accipi, ut, quodcumque scriptum sit quasi actum, videatur etiam actum. Ideoque constat, si quis scripserit se fidejussisse, videri omnia solemniter acta.

§ 8. *We must here observe, that it is a general rule in all fide-jussorial stipulations, that whatever is alleged in writing to have been done, is to be presumed to have been actually done· and therefore, if a man in writing confesses, that he hath made himself a* fide jussor, *it is also presumed, that all the necessary forms were observed.*

TITU-

TITULUS VIGESIMUS-SECUNDUS.

De literarum obligationibus.

Cod. iv. T. 30.

OLIM ſcriptura fiebat obligatio, quæ nominibus fieri dicebatur. quæ nomina hodie non ſunt in uſu. Plane, ſi quis debere ſe ſcripſerit, quod ſibi numeratum non eſt, de pecunia minime numerata, poſt multum temporis, exceptionem opponere non poteſt. Hoc enim ſæpiſſime conſtitutum eſt Sic fit, ut et hodie, dum queri non poteſt, ſcriptura obligetur, et ex ea naſcatur condictio, ceſſante ſcilicet verborum obligatione. Multum autem tempus in hac exceptione antea quidem ex principalibus conſtitutionibus uſque ad quinquennium procedebat: ſed, ne creditores diutius poſſint ſuis pecuniis forſitan defraudari, per conſtitutionem noſtram tempus coarctatum eſt, ut ultra biennii metas hujuſmodi exceptio minime extendatur.

A ſpecies of writen obligation antiently prevailed, which was effected by regiſtering the names of the contractors; but theſe contracts, which were called nomina, *are not now in uſe. But, if a man confeſſes in writing, that he owes, what in reality he never received, he cannot, when an action is brought againſt him for this confeſſed debt, oppoſe an exception to it, ſetting forth,* that the money was never paid, *if much time has elapſed after the date of the obligation: and the limitation of this time has frequently been preſcribed by the conſtitutions Hence it is, at this day, that a man muſt be bound by his writen note, if he cannot legally bring an exception, and from this writen contract ariſes an action called a* condiction, *when no ſtipulation or verbal obligation can be proved And formerly the imperial conſtitutions gave a large ſpace of time, not leſs than five years, in which any man was allowed to bring an exception,* pecuniæ non numeratæ, *i e an exception of money not paid But we, for the ſafety of creditors in general, have greatly contracted this allowance of time, by our imperial conſtitution, which ordains, that an exception ſhall not be brought after the expiration of two years.*

Ex principalibus conſtitutionibus] "Qui deſiderat cognoſcere tempora, olim omnibus "cautionibus præſtituta, legat conſtitutionem "Imppp Honorii, Theodoſii, et Conſtantii, "quam reperiet libro 2do Cod Theod tit "*ſi certum Mvnſ*

Per noſtram conſtitutionem] *vid Cod* 4 *t* 30 *l* 14.

TITULUS VIGESIMUS-TERTIUS.

De obligationibus ex consensu.

Continuatio.

CONSENSU fiunt obligationes in emptionibus, venditionibus, locationibus, conductionibus, societatibus, mandatis: ideo autem istis modis obligatio dicitur consensu contrahi, quia neque scriptura, neque præsentia, omnimodo opus est: ac nec dari quicquam necesse est, ut substantiam capiat obligatio, sed sufficit, eos, qui negotia gerunt, consentire: unde inter absentes quoque talia negotia contrahuntur, veluti per epistolam vel per nuntium. Item in his contractibus alter alteri obligatur in id, quod alterum alteri ex bono et æquo præstare oportet, cum alioqui in verborum obligationibus alius stipuletur, alius promittat.

Obligations are made by consent in buying, selling, letting, hireing, societies *or* partenerships, *and* mandates. *And an obligation, entered into by any of those means, is said to be contracted by consent; because neither writing nor the presence of parties is absolutely requisite. Neither is it necessary, that any thing should be given or delivered, to the intent, that the obligation should take effect; for it suffices, that the contractors consent, and, for this reason, these contracts may be entered into by absent parties, either by letters or messengers. And note also, that, in these contracts by consent, the parties are bound to each other mutually to do what is just and right, but in verbal obligations one party stipulates and the other promises.*

TITULUS VIGESIMUS-QUARTUS.

De emptione et venditione.

D. xviii. & xix. T. I. C. iv. T. 38. & 40.

De emptione pura. De pretii conventione, arrhis, et scriptura.

EMPTIO et venditio contrahitur, simul atque de pretio convenerit, quamvis nondum pretium numeratum sit, ac ne arrha quidem data fuerit. nam, quod arrhæ nomine datur, argumentum est emptionis et venditionis contractæ Sed hoc quidem de emptionibus et venditionibus, quæ sine scriptura consistunt, obtinere oportet: nam nihil a nobis in hujusmodi emptionibus et venditionibus innovatum est. In iis autem, quæ scriptura conficiuntur, non aliter perfectam esse venditionem et emptionem

nem constituimus, nisi et instrumenta emptionis fuerint conscripta, vel manu propria contrahentium, vel ab alio quidem scripta, a contrahentibus autem subscripta: et si per tabellionem fiunt, nisi et completiones acceperint, et fuerint partibus absoluta. Donec enim aliquid deest ex his, et pœnitentiæ locus est, et potest emptor vel venditor sine pœna recedere ab emptione et venditione. Ita tamen impune recedere concedimus, nisi jam arrharum nomine aliquid fuerit datum: hoc enim subsecuto, sive in scriptis, sive sine scriptis, venditio celebrata est, is, qui recusat adimplere contractum, si quidem est emptor, perdit quod dedit; si vero venditor, duplum restituere compellitur; licet super arrhis nihil expressum sit. Pretium autem constitui oportet; nam nulla emptio sine pretio esse potest.

The contract of buying and selling is made perfect, as soon as the price of the thing to be sold is agreed upon, altho' it is not paid, nor even an earnest of it given, for whatever is taken, as earnest, does not constitute a contract, but serves only for a proof of it And this is the law in regard to those bargains and sales, which are not in writing, for in such we have made no innovation But, where there is a writen contract, we have ordained, that a bargain and sale shall not become absolute, unless the instruments of sale are written by the contracting parties or at least signed by them, if written by others. And, when the instruments of sale are drawn by a public notary, the contract is not binding, if any formality hath been omitted, or if the instruments are not complete in all their parts. for, if any thing is omitted, either the buyer or seller may recede from his agreement without penalty, if nothing has been given in the name of earnest. But, if earnest has once been given, then the buyer, whether the contract was writen or unwriten, if he refuses to fullfill it, loses his earnest, and the seller, if he refuses, is compellable to restore double the value of the earnest, altho' no agreement of this kind was expresly made But it is always necessary, that the price of the thing to be sold shou'd be fixed, for, till then, there can be no emptio-venditio, *i e. buying and selling*

In iis autem] *vid Cod.* 4 *t* 21 *De fide instrumentorum*

By the civil law all covenants of sale were good, whether writen or unwriten, to whatever value they extended But in *England*, it hath been enacted by 29 *Car cap* 3 *Jul.* 17 "That "no contract for the sale of any goods, wares, "and merchandizes for the price of ten pounds "sterling or upwards, shall be allowed to be "good, except the buyer shall accept part of "the goods so sold, and actually receive the "same, or give something in earnest to bind "the bargain, or in part of payment, or unless "some note, or memorandum, in writing of "the said bargain be made and signed by the "parties to be charged by such a contract, or "their agents thereunto lawfully authorized" 29 *Car.* 2

De pretio certo, vel incerto, vel in arbitrium alienum collato.

§ I. Sed et certum esse pretium debet: alioqui, si inter aliquos ita convenerit, ut, quanti Titius rem æstimaverit, tanti sit empta, inter veteres satis abundeque hoc dubitabatur, constaretne venditio, an non Sed nostra decisio ita hoc constituit, ut, quoties sic composita sit venditio, *quanti ille æstimaverit*, sub hac conditione staret contractus, ut siquidem ille, qui nominatus est, pretium definierit, tunc omnimodo secundum ejus æstimationem et pretium persolvatur, et res tradatur, et venditio ad

effectum

effectum perducatur; emptore quidem ex empto actione, venditore ex vendito agente. Sin autem ille, qui nominatus est, vel noluerit, vel non potuerit, pretium definire, tunc pro nihilo esse venditionem, quasi nullo pretio statuto. Quod jus, cum in venditionibus nobis placuerit, non est absurdum et in locationibus et in conductionibus tradere.

§ 1 *The price, as we have before observed, ought to be certain. And formerly, when it was covenanted, that a thing should be sold,* at whatever price TITIUS should value it, *the antient lawyers much doubted, whether such a sale was good, or not good But we have ordained by our decision, that as often as it is agreed, that a thing shall be sold,* at a price to be fixed by a third person, *such contract shall be valid under that condition; so that, if the nominee, or arbitrator, determines the price, it ought instantly to be paid according to the determination, and the thing* [illegible] *to be delivered, and the sale perfected, for otherwise the buyer may have an action* ex empto, *i. e. on account of the thing bought; and the seller may have an action* ex vendito, *i e on account of the thing sold. But, if the arbitrator either refuses, or is unable to determine the price, the sale is null. And, as it has been our pleasure, that this shall be the law in relation to sales, it is but right, that the same law should prevail, in* locations *and* conductions, *i. e. in letting and hireing*

Sed nostra decisio] *Cod* 4. *t* 38 *l* 15

In quibus pretium consistat. Differentia emptionis et permutationis.

§ II. Item pretium in numerata pecunia consistere debet. Nam in cæteris rebus, an pretium esse posset, valde quærebatur; veluti, an homo, aut fundus, aut toga, alterius rei pretium esse possit? Et Sabinus et Cassius etiam in alia re putabant pretium posse consistere: unde illud, quod vulgo dicebatur, permutatione rerum emptionem et venditionem contrahi: eamque speciem emptionis et venditionis vetustissimam esse. Argumentoque utebantur Græco poeta Homero, qui aliquam partem exercitus Achivorum vinum sibi comparasse ait, permutatis quibusdam rebus, his verbis.

Νηες δ' εκ Λημνοιο παρεστασαν οινον αγουσαι.
Ενθεν αρ οινιζοντο καρηκομοωντες Αχαιοι,
Αλλοι μεν χαλκω, αλλοι δ' αιθωνι σιδηρω,
Αλλοι δε ρινοις, αλλοι δ' αυτοισι βοεσσιν,
Αλλοι δ' ανδραποδεσσι.

Hoc est.

Naves autem e Lemno appulerunt vinum vehentes:
Illinc vinum emebant *Achivi comantes caput,*
Alii quidem ære, alii autem ferro nigro,
Alii pellibus, alii ipsis bobus,
Alii etiam mancipiis. Iliad. VII.

Diversæ

Diversæ scholæ auctores contra sentiebant, aliudque esse existimabant permutationem rerum, aliud emptionem et venditionem: alioqui non posse rem expediri, permutatis rebus, quæ videatur res vænisse, et quæ pretii nomine data esse; nam, utramque videri et vænisse et pretii nomine datam esse, rationem non pati. Sed Proculi sententia, dicentis, permutationem propriam esse speciem contractus a venditione separatam, merito prævaluit: cum et aliis Homericis versibus adjuvabatur, et validioribus rationibus argumentabatur. Quod et anteriores Divi Principes admiserunt, et in nostris Digestis latius significatur.

§ 2. *The price of any thing bought should consist of money told for it hath been much doubted, whether the price of goods can be said to be paid, if any other thing is given for them than money, as, for instance, whether a slave, a piece of ground, or a robe, can be paid, as the price of a thing. The lawyers* Sabinus *and* Cassius *thought, that a price might consist of any thing, and from hence it has been commonly said, that* emptio-venditio, *or buying and selling, is contracted by commutation, and that this species of buying and selling is the most antient The advocates for this side of the question quote* Homer, *who relates in the following lines, that a part of the Grecian army* bought *wine by giving other things in exchange for it.*

Wine the rest *purchased* at their proper cost,
And well the plenteous freight supplied the host
Each in exchange proportioned treasures gave,
Some brass or iron, some an ox or slave *Pope*

But the lawyers of another sect maintained the contrary, and decreed, that commutation was one thing, and emptio-venditio *another, for otherwise said they, in the commutation of any two things it can never appear, which has been sold, and which has been given, as the price of the thing sold, and it is contrary to reason, that each should appear to have been sold, and that each also should appear to have been given, as the price of the other. And the opinion of* Proculus, *who maintained, that commutation is a species of contract, separate from vendition, hath deservedly prevailed for he is supported by other verses from* Homer, *and has inforced his opinion with the strongest arguments, and this is the doctrine, which our predecessors, the emperors* Dioclesian *and* Maximian, *have admitted, as it appears also at large in our Digests.*

Sabinus et Cassius] These lawyers were of opinion, that emption and vendition might be contracted by an exchange of property, without the intervention of money, and in support of their opinion they used this argument · that, if there was such a contract as buying and selling, before any coin was made use of, it is plain that money, or coin, is not essential to buying and selling And to prove the antiquity of emption and vendition they urge the authority of Homer, who says, that the Greeks bought wine at *Lemnos* by giving brass, iron, oxen, and slaves in exchange for it. And it is observable, that Homer in this place uses the word *οινιζοντο*, which is but an ambiguous expression But there is a passage in the *Odyssy*, urged by *Paul* which is much more apposite.

Την ποτε Λαέρτης πρίατο κτεάτεσσιν ἑοῖσιν
i e the slave *Euryclea*, whom *Laertes* bought with his possessions *Odys lib* 1 *sub fin*

In this verse there can be no doubt of the sense of *πρίατο*, and, as to *κτεάτεσσιν*, the poet in the next line ascertains the meaning of it by informing us, that twenty oxen were given for her

But those, who hold a contrary opinion to that of *Cassius* and *Sabinus*, quote *Homer* also in their turn, particularly that passage in the six *Iliad*, where *Diomed* and *Glaucus* exchange their armour.

C,

Ος προς Τυδειδην Διομηδεα τευχε' αμειβε,
Χρυσεα χαλκειων, ἑκατομβοι εννεαβοιων.
For Diomed's brass arms exchanged his own,
Tho wrought with gold and worth an hundred beeves.

But, (says *Vinny*,) if the poets only were to be regarded in this dispute, little could be collected from them, *quippe, dum metro serviunt, verborum proprietatem sæpe negligere coguntur*. And, if we attend to the suggestions of truth and right reason, we must soon be convinced, that the contracts of buying and selling can never be strictly said to exist, without the intervention of money, which was undoubtedly in use long before the Trojan war. *Vinn.*

In nostris Digestis.] *ff.* 18. *t.* 1. *De contrahenda emptione.*

De periculo et commodo rei venditæ.

§ III. Cum autem emptio et venditio contracta sit, (quod effici diximus simul atque de pretio convenerit, cum sine scriptura res agitur,) periculum rei venditæ statim ad emptorem pertinet, tametsi adhuc ea res emptori tradita non sit. Itaque, si homo mortuus sit, vel aliqua parte corporis læsus fuerit, aut ædes totæ, vel aliqua ex parte, incendio consumptæ fuerint, aut fundus vi fluminis totus vel aliqua ex parte ablatus sit, sive etiam inundatione aquæ, aut arboribus turbine dejectis, longe minor aut deterior esse cœperit, emptoris damnum est, cui necesse est, licet rem non fuerit nactus, pretium solvere. Quicquid enim sine dolo et culpa venditoris accidit, in eo venditor securus est. Sed et, si post emptionem fundo aliquid per alluvionem accesserit, ad emptoris commodum pertinet: nam et commodum ejus esse debet, cujus periculum est. Quod si fugerit homo, qui vænit, aut surreptus fuerit, ita ut neque dolus, neque culpa venditoris, intervenerit, animadvertendum erit, an custodiam ejus usque ad traditionem venditor susceperit. Sane enim si susceperit, ad ipsius periculum is casus pertinet: si non susceperit, securus est. Idem et in cæteris animalibus cæterisque rebus intelligimus. Utique tamen vindicationem rei et condictionem exhibere debebit emptori: quia sane, qui nondum rem emptori tradidit, adhuc ipse dominus est. Idem etiam est de furti et de damni injuriæ actione.

§ 3. *When emption and vendition are once contracted, (and this, as we have observed, is effected, as soon as the price is agreed upon, when there is no covenant in writing,) then the buyer is liable to the risque of the loss of the thing sold, or of the damage, which may happen to it, altho' it hath not been delivered to him. And therefore, if a slave, thus sold, should die, or receive any hurt, or if a building, or part of it, should be consumed by fire, or if lands sold, or any portion of them, should be washed away by a torrent, or be made worse by an inundation, or a storm, which may destroy the trees, the loss in all these cases must be sustained by the buyer, who is obliged to pay the price agreed upon, altho' he never had possession of the thing: for whatever the accident is, if it happens neither by the fraud, nor fault of the seller, he is secure. But on the other hand, if, after the sale, any accession is made to the lands by alluvion or otherwise, this increase becomes the gain of the buyer; for it is just, that he should receive the profit, who must have sustained the loss. But, if a slave, who is sold, either runs away or is stolen, and neither fraud nor negligence can be imputed to the seller, it must be inquired, whether the seller undertook the safe custody of the slave, till delivery should be made; if he did, he is answerable for the accident; if he did not, he is secure. The same law takes place in regard to all other animals and things. But, when these accidents happen, and the buyer is to sustain the loss, the seller is obliged to make over his right of vindication and condiction; that is, he must transfer to the buyer all right of action, whether real or personal, if necessary; for he, who has not delivered the thing sold, is still considered as the proprietor of it. Actions also of theft, or damage done, must be transfered by the seller to the buyer, when the Thing sold is stolen, or damaged, before delivery.*

De emptione conditionali.

§ IV. Emptio tam ſub conditione quam pure contrahi poteſt. ſub conditione, veluti, *ſi Stichus intra certum diem tibi placuerit, erit tibi emptus aureis tot.*

§ 4. *A ſale may be contracted conditionally, as well as purely: for inſtance, when the perſon, who is inclined to ſell, ſpeaks thus;* if within a certain time you ſhall approve of the ſlave STICHUS, he ſhall be yours for ſo many AUREI.

De emptione rei, quæ non eſt in commercio.

§ V. Loca ſacra, vel religioſa, item publica, (veluti forum, baſilicam,) fruſtra quis ſciens emit: quæ tamen ſi pro profanis vel privatis deceptus a venditore quis emerit, habebit actionem ex empto, quod non habere ei liceat, ut conſequatur, quod ſua intereſt, eum deceptum non eſſe. Idem juris eſt, ſi hominem liberum pro ſervo emerit.

§ 5. *Whoever knowingly purchaſes a place ſacred, or religious, or a public place, ſuch as a* Forum *or court of juſtice, he makes a void purchaſe. But, if a man ſhould purchaſe any of the before-mentioned places, having taken them for profane or private, being impoſed upon by the ſeller, then ſuch purchaſer, not being able to enjoy the poſſeſſion of what he has bought, may have an action* ex empto *againſt the ſeller, and recover the damage ſuffered by the deceit. The ſame law alſo obtains, if any perſon, thro' error, ſhould buy a freeman inſtead of a ſlave.*

TITULUS VIGESIMUS-QUINTUS.

De locatione et conductione.

D. xix. T. 2. C. iv. T. 65. C. ii. T. 70

Collatio emptionis, et locationis. De mercedis conventione.

LOCATIO et conductio proxima eſt emptioni et venditioni, iiſdemque juris regulis conſiſtit. Nam ut emptio et venditio ita contrahitur, ſi de pretio convenerit, ſic et locatio et conductio ita contrahi intelligitur, ſi merces conſtituta ſit. Et competit locatori quidem locati actio, conductori vero conducti.

Loc.

Location *and* conduction, *i. e. letting and hireing, are nearly allied to* emption *and* vendition, *i. e, to buying and selling; and are governed by the same rules, for as emption and vendition are contracted as soon as the price of the thing is agreed upon, so location and conduction are contracted, when the hire is once fixed by the parties. The* locator, *or person who lets, is intituled to an action, called* actio locati, *if he is aggreived by the* conductor *or hirer, and the conductor may have an action called* actio conducti, *against the* locator.

De mercede collata in arbitrium alienum.

§ I. Et, quæ supra diximus, si alieno arbitrio pretium permissum fuerit, eadem et de locatione et de conductione dicta esse intelligimus, si alieno arbitrio merces permissa fuerit. Qua de causa, si fulloni polienda curandave, aut sarcinatori sarcienda, vestimenta quis dederit, nulla statim mercede constituta, sed postea tantum daturus, quantum inter eos convenerit, non proprie locatio et conductio contrahi intelligitur; sed eo nomine actio *præscriptis verbis* datur

§ 1 *We are willing, that what we have before observed in regard to the sale of a thing, when the price is refered to a third person, should also be understood to have been said of* location *and* conduction, *when the quantity of the hire is not agreed upon between the parties, but left to arbitration. And therefore, if a man sends his cloaths to a fuller to be scoured, or to a taylor to be mended, and does not previously agree upon any price, in this case* location *and* conduction *are not understood to be properly contracted, but an action may be brought by either party,* præscriptis verbis, *i. e. in words prescribed and adapted to the circumstances of the case.*

Actio præscriptis verbis] " Dicta est actio " quoque causam hæc actio dicitur *in factum*, " *præscriptis verbis*, ex eo, quod præscriptis verbis rem gestam demonstret. Ob eandem " et interdum plena oratione *actio utilis præscriptis verbis in factum*" *Vinn.*

In quibus rebus merces consistat.

§ II. Præterea, sicut vulgo quærebatur, an permutatis rebus emptio et venditio contraheretur, ita quæri solebat de locatione et conductione, si forte rem aliquam utendam sive fruendam tibi aliquis dederit, et invicem à te utendam sive fruendam aliam rem acceperit. Et placuit, non esse locationem et conductionem, sed proprium genus contractus: veluti, si, cum unum bovem quis haberet, et vicinus ejus item unum, placuerit inter eos, ut per denos dies invicem boves commodarent, ut opus facerent, et apud alterum alterius bos perierit, neque locati, neque conducti, neque commodati competit actio, quia non fuit commodatum gratuitum verum præscriptis verbis agendum est.

§ 2 *As it was formerly a question, whether* emption *and* vendition *could be contracted by an exchange of things, so it hath also been doubted, whether* location *and* conduction *can be said to exist, when one man lends another a particular thing for his use, and receives in return some other thing, of which he is also permitted to have the use, and it has been determined, that this exchange does not constitute* location *and* conduction, *but is a distinct species of contract for example, if two neighbours have each of them an ox, and each agrees to lend his ox to the other*

other alternately for ten days, to do the labors of the field, and the ox of the one dies in the possession of the other, in this case, he, who has lost his ox, can neither bring the action locati, *nor* conducti, *nor even the action* commodati ; *for the ox was not lent gratuitously ; but he may sue by virtue of an action called* præscriptis verbis , *i. e by an action upon the case.*

De Emphyteusi.

§ III. Adeo autem aliquam familiaritatem inter se videntur habere emptio et venditio, item locatio et conductio, ut in quibusdam causis quæri soleat, utrum emptio et venditio contrahatur, an locatio et conductio: ut ecce de prædiis, quæ perpetuo quibusdam fruenda traduntur, id est, ut, quamdiu pensio sive reditus pro his domino præstetur, neque ipsi conductori, neque hæredi ejus, cuive conductor hæresve ejus id prædium vendiderit, aut donaverit, aut dotis nomine dederit, aliove quocunque modo alienaverit, auferre liceat. Sed talis contractus, quia inter veteres dubitabatur, et a quibusdam locatio, a quibusdam venditio existimabatur, lex Zenoniana lata est, quæ emphyteuseos contractus propriam statuit naturam, neque ad locationem, neque ad venditionem inclinantem, sed suis pactionibus fulciendam: et, si quidem aliquid pactum fuerit, hoc ita obtinere, ac si naturalis esset contractus: sin autem nihil de periculo rei fuerit pactum, tunc, siquidem totius rei interitus accesserit, ad dominum super hoc redundare periculum: sin autem particularis, ad emphyteuticarium hujusmodi damnum venire ; quo jure utimur.

§ 3. *The contract of buying and selling, and that of letting and hiring, are so nearly connected, that, in some cases, it has been difficult to distinguish the one from the other. as when lands have been demised to be enjoyed for ever, upon condition, that, if a certain yearly pension, or rent, is constantly paid to the proprietor, it shall not be in his power to take these lands from the tenent or his heirs, or from any other person, to whom such tenent or his heirs shall have sold them, given them gratuitously, or as a marriage portion, or otherwise disposed of them. But, when this contract, concerning which the antient lawyers had great doubts, was by some thought to be an emption and vendition, and by others a location and conduction, the* Zenonian *law was enacted, which settled the proper nature of an* emphyteusis, *making it to be neither the one nor the other of the before mentioned contracts, but declaring it to be supported by it's own peculiar covenants, and ordaining, that whatever is agreed upon by the parties shall obtain and take place, as a contract and when there is no covenant, which declares, upon whom the loss of the lands shall fall, that then, if the whole estate happens to be destroyed by a torrent, an earthquake, or any other means, the proprietor must be the sufferer ; but, if a part only is destroyed, that the loss shall then be borne by the tenent , and this is the law in use.*

Emphyteuseos contractus] An *emphyteusis* (from ἐμφυτεύειν to plant) is a contract made by consent, by which houses or lands are given to be possessed for ever, or at least for a long term, upon condition, that the lands shall be improved, and that a small yearly rent or pension shall be paid to the proprietor And this pension, rent, or canon, may be paid in money, grain, or any other thing The perpetuity, or long term, granted, distinguishes this contract from letting and hireing for an *emphyteusis* was originally made on account of barren lands, which no person would take for a short time, thro' a fear of the charge of cultivation, but afterwards the

built

best lands were often granted out upon this emphyteutical contract, the nature of which was first fixed by the emperor *Zeno*, who determined it to be a distinct contract from buying and selling, letting and hireing *vid Cod* 4. *t* 66 *De jure emphyteutico* For some thought it to be the contract of hireing, when they considered, that a rent was paid for it to the proprietor and others imagined it to be the contract of buying, when they saw the tenent had a perpetuity, or at least a very long time, and a sort of property in it but the tenent had only *utile dominium*, not a direct dominion; and therefore the contract was distinct from buying and selling.

The tenent is called *emphyteuta*, being under an obligation to plant and improve the land, and he has such an interest, that he may sell the profits of his right in the estate to another, with the consent of the proprietor, to whom two months must be allowed to determine whether he will himself become the purchaser. But, when there is a new tenent, a *laudimium*, (which is almost the same as a relief, and generally amounts to the value of the 50th part of the estate,) must be paid to the proprietor by the new tenent, as an acknowledgment for being put into possession. *Cod*. 4 *t*. 66. *l* 3.

There is also a pension or rent called a *canon*, which must be paid annually, as an acknowledgment of a superior title, and this *canon* is always due every year, whether the tenent receives any profits or not. for it is not paid, in consideration of profits received, but as an acknowledgment of the tenure.

The *emphyteusis* of the Roman law seems to have given rise to our fee-farm and copyhold estates in *England*

Wood's Com. Law Page 339.

De forma alicui facienda ab artifice.

§ IV. Item quæritur, si cum aurifice Titius convenerit, ut is ex auro suo certi ponderis certæque formæ annulos ei faceret, et acciperet, verbi gratia, decem aureos, utrum emptio et venditio, an locatio et conductio contrahi videatur? Cassius ait, materiæ quidem emptionem et venditionem contrahi, operæ autem locationem et conductionem. Sed placuit, tantum emptionem et venditionem contrahi. Quod si suum aurum Titius dederit, mercede pro opera constituta, dubium non est, quin locatio et conductio sit.

§ 4. *Also, if* Titius, *for example, should agree with a goldsmith to make a certain number of rings, of a particular size and weight, and to furnish the gold, for which* Titius *should promise him ten* aurei, *as the value both of the workmanship and the gold, it hath been a question, whether such a contract would be a buying and selling, or a letting and hireing.* Cassius *was of opinion, that it would be a buying and selling in regard to the matter, and a letting and hireing in regard to the work: but it is now settled, that, in this case, an emption and vendition would only be contracted. But, on the other hand, it is not to be doubted, that, if* Titius *should give his own gold, and agree to pay only for the workmanship, this contract would be a location and conduction.*

Quid præstare debet conductor.

§ V. Conductor omnia secundum legem conductionis facere debet: et, si quid in lege prætermissum fuerit, id ex bono et æquo præstare. Qui pro usu aut vestimentorum, aut argenti, aut jumenti, mercedem aut dedit aut promisit, ab eo custodia talis desideratur, qualem diligentissimus pater familias suis rebus adhibet; quam si præstiterit, et aliquo casu fortuito eam rem amiserit, de restituenda ea non tenebitur.

§ 5. *The conductor, or hirer, is not only obliged to observe strictly the covenants of the conduction, but is also bound in equity to perform whatever hath been omited to be inserted And whoever has given or promised hire for the use of cloaths, silver, horses,*

horses, &c. is bound to take the same care of them, as the most diligent master of a family would take of his own property. But, if the hirer does this, and yet loses the things hired by some fortuitous event, he shall not be answerable for the loss.

De morte conductoris.

§. VI. Mortuo conductore intra tempora conductionis, hæres ejus eodem jure in conductione succedit.

§ 6. *If the conductor, or hirer, dies before the time of the conduction is expired, his heir succedes to his right, and is intituled to the thing hired, for the remainder of the term.*

TITULUS VIGESIMUS-SEXTUS.

De societate.

D.xvii. T. 2. C.iv. T. 37.

Divisio a materia.

SOCIETATEM coire solemus aut totorum bonorum, quam Græci specialiter κοινωνιαν appellant; aut unius alicujus negotiationis, veluti mancipiorum vendendorum emendorumque, aut olei, aut vini, aut frumenti emendi vendendique.

It is common for persons to enter either into a general partenership or society of all their goods, and this the greeks emphatically call κοινωνιαν, *i. e communion; or into a particular partenership, which regards only some single species of commerce, as that of buying and selling slaves, oil, wine, or corn.*

De partibus lucri et damni.

§ I. Et quidem, si nihil de partibus lucri et damni nominatim convenerit, æquales scilicet partes et in lucro et in damno spectantur: quod si expressæ fuerint partes, hæ servari debent. Nec enim unquam dubium fuit, quin valeat conventio, si duo inter se pacti sint, ut ad unum quidem duæ partes et lucri et damni pertineant, ad alterum tertia.

§ 1. *If no express agreement has been made by the parteners concerning their shares of profit and loss; the loss must be equally borne, and the profit must be equally divided. But, if any particular agreement has been made, it must be observed; for it was never yet doubted, but that the covenant would be binding, if two persons should agree, that two shares of the profit and loss should belong to one partener, and that only the third part of both should belong to the other.*

De partibus inæqualibus.

§ 2. De illa ſane conventione quæſitum eſt, ſi Titius et Seius inter ſe pacti ſint, ut ad Titium lucri duæ partes pertineant, damni tertia, ad Seium duæ partes damni, lucri tertia, an rata debeat haberi conventio? Quintus Mucius contra naturam ſocietatis talem pactionem eſſe exiſtimavit, et ob id non eſſe ratam habendam: Servius Sulpitius (cujus ſententia prævaluit) contra ſenſit; quia ſæpe quorundam ita pretioſa eſt opera in ſocietate, ut eos juſtum ſit conditione meliore in ſocietatem admitti. Nam et ita poſſe coiri ſocietatem non dubitatur, ut alter pecuniam conferat, alter non conferat, et tamen lucrum inter eos commune ſit: quia ſæpe opera alicujus pro pecunia valet. Et adeo contra Quinti Mucii ſententiam obtinuit, ut illud quoque conſtiterit poſſe convenire, ut quis lucri partem ferat, de damno non teneatur: quod et ipſum Servius convenienter ſibi fieri exiſtimavit. Quod tamen ita intelligi oportet, ut, ſi in alia re lucrum, in alia damnum illatum ſit, compenſatione facta, ſolum quod ſupereſt, intelligatur lucro eſſe.

§ 2. *But, it has been queſtioned, if* Titius *and* Seius *ſhould covenant between themſelves, that* Titius *ſhould receive two parts of the profit and bear but a third of the loſs, and that* Seius *ſhould bear two parts of the loſs, and receive but a third ſhare of the profit, whether ſuch an agreement would be binding?* Quintus Mucius *was of opinion, that ſuch a covenant was contrary to the nature of partenerſhip, and ought not therefore to be ratified; but* Servius Sulpitius *whoſe opinion hath prevailed, thought otherwiſe, and for this reaſon; becauſe the labor of ſome is ſo highly valuable, that it is but juſt, that they ſhould be admitted into ſociety upon the moſt advantageous conditions, for no man doubts, but that partenerſhip may be entered into by two perſons, when one of them only finds money, inaſmuch as the work, and labor of the other, amounts to the value of it, and ſupplies it's place. And alſo, contrary to the opinion of* Mucius, *it hath obtained as law, that a partener may by agreement take a ſhare of the profit, and not be accountable for any part of the loſs, for* Servius *thought, that this likewiſe might be done equitably: but it muſt be ſo underſtood, that, if profit accrues from one ſpecies of things and loſs from another, only what remains, after the loſs is compenſated, ſhall be looked upon as profit.*

De partibus expreſſis in una cauſa.

§ III. Illud expeditum eſt, ſi in una cauſa pars fuerit expreſſa, (veluti in ſolo lucro, vel in ſolo damno,) in altera vero omiſſa, in eo quoque, quod prætermiſſum eſt, eandem partem ſervari.

§ 3. *It is alſo a ſettled point, that, if parteners expreſly mention their ſhares in one reſpect only, either ſolely in regard to gain, or ſolely in regard to loſs, their ſhares of that, which is omited, ſhall be the ſame as of that, which is mentioned.*

Qui-

Quibus modis ſocietas ſolvitur. De renuntiatione.

§ IV. Manet autem ſocietas eo uſque, donec in eodem conſenſu perſeveraverint. At, cum aliquis renuntiaverit ſocietati, ſolvitur ſocietas. Sed plane, ſi quis callide in hoc renuntiaverit ſocietati, ut obveniens aliquod lucrum ſolus habeat; veluti, ſi totorum bonorum ſocius, cum ab aliquo hæres eſſet relictus, in hoc renuntiaverit ſocietati, ut hæreditatem ſolus lucri faceret, cogitur hoc lucrum communicare. Si quid vero aliud lucri faciat, quod non captaverit, ad ipſum ſolum pertinet. Ei vero, cui renuntiatum eſt, quicquid omnino poſt renuntiatam ſocietatem acquiritur, ſoli conceditur.

§ 4. *A partenerſhip laſts as long as the parteners perſevere in their conſent to continue ſuch; and, if one of them renounces the partenerſhip, the ſociety is diſſolved. But, if a man renounces with a fraudulent intent, and for no other end, but that he may enjoy the ſole benefit of ſome future fortune, which he expects, his renunciation will not avail: for, if a partener in common, as ſoon as he finds, that he has been appointed an heir, ſhould renounce his partenerſhip, that he may poſſeſs the inheritance excluſive of all others, he would nevertheleſs be compelled to divide the inheritance equally with his former parteners: yet, if an inheritance, which he did not expect, ſhould by accident fall to him after renunciation, the whole would be his own. But thoſe, from whom a partener hath ſeparated himſelf by renouncing, poſſeſs ſolely for themſelves whatever they acquire, after the renunciation of that partener.*

De morte.

§ V. Solvitur adhuc ſocietas etiam morte ſocii: quia, qui ſocietatem contrahit, certam perſonam ſibi eligit. Sed et, ſi conſenſu plurium ſocietas contracta ſit, morte unius ſocii ſolvitur, etſi plures ſuperſint: niſi in coeunda ſocietate aliter convenerit.

§ 5. *A partenerſhip is alſo diſſolved by the death of one of the parteners; for he, who enters into partenerſhip always chuſes ſome certain known perſon to be his partener, upon whom he can depend. And, altho a partenerſhip is entered into by the conſent of many, it is nevertheleſs diſſolved by the death of one, altho' the reſt ſurvive, and this is the law, unleſs ſpecial covenants are made to the contrary at the time of forming the ſociety.*

De fine negotii.

§ VI. Item, ſi alicujus rei contracta ſocietas ſit, et finis negotio impoſitus eſt, finitur ſocietas.

§ 6 *Alſo, if a partenerſhip is entered into on account of ſome particular commerce, and an end is put to that commerce, the partenerſhip is of courſe ended.*

De publicatione.

§ VII. Publicatione quoque diſtrahi ſocietatem, manifeſtum eſt, ſcilicet ſi univerſa bona ſocii publicentur: nam, cum in ejus locum alius ſuccedat, pro mortuo habetur.

§ 7.

§ 7. It is likewise manifest, that a partenership is dissolved by confiscation; to wit, if all the goods of a partener are confiscated; for when another [for example, the treasurer of the exchequer] succedes in his place, he is reputed as civilly dead.

De cessione bonorum.

§ VIII. Item, si quis ex sociis mole debiti prægravatus bonis suis cesserit, et ideo propter publica et privata debita substantia ejus væneat, solvitur societas. Sed hoc casu, si adhuc consentiant in societatem, nova videtur incipere societas.

§ 8. Also, if a man in partenership, being pressed by his debts, makes a cession or a surrender of his goods, and they are sold to satisfie either public or private demands, the partenership is dissolved. But, if the rest of the coparteners should still desire to be in society either with or without this man, the first partenership would not continue, but a new one would commence.

Bonis suis cesserit] In *England* the benefit of cession, or bankruptcy, is allowed only to persons concerned in trade, who may be discharged from their debts, if they surrender themselves, and make a full discovery of their goods, books, papers, &c. for the benefit of their creditors, and also conform themselves in all other respects to certain statutes of the realm, by which all possible care has been taken to prevent fraudulent bankruptcies, by making it felony without benefit of the clergy, to be guilty of any willful omission in their discoveries *Hawk pl cap* 57. 4. *Ann. cap* 17. *Inst.* 4. *tit* 6.

De dolo et culpa a socio præstandis.

§. IX. Socius socio utrum eo nomine tantum teneatur pro socio actione, si quid dolo commiserit, sicut is, qui deponi apud se passus est, an etiam culpæ, id est, desidiæ atque negligentiæ nomine, quæsitum est? Prævaluit tamen, etiam culpæ nomine teneri eum. Culpa autem non ad exactissimam diligentiam dirigenda est: sufficit enim talem diligentiam communibus rebus adhibere socium, qualem suis rebus adhibere solet. Nam, qui parum diligentem socium sibi adsumit, de se queri, sibique hoc imputare, debet

§ 9. It has been a question, whether a partener, like a depositary, is accountable for fraud only, or whether he is also accountable for his negligence? And it now prevails, that he is answerable for all the damages, which happen through his fault. And, if a man fails in having used the most exact diligence, such a failure is not comprehended under the term culpa, *or fault: for a partener is not liable to answer damages, if, in regard to the goods of the community, it appears, that he has used the same care and diligence towards them, which he has usually observed in keeping his own private property. And it is certain, that whoever chuses a negligent man for his partener, can lay the blame upon himself only and impute his misfortune to his own ill choice.*

TITULUS VIGESIMUS-SEPTIMUS.

De mandato.

D. xvii. T. 1. C. iv. T. 35.

Divisio a fine.

MANDATUM contrahitur quinque modis, sive sua tantum gratia aliquis tibi mandet, sive sua et tua, sive aliena tantum, sive sua et aliena, sive tua et aliena. At, si tua tantum gratia tibi mandatum sit, supervacuum est mandatum; et ob id nulla ex eo obligatio, nec mandati inter vos actio nascitur.

A mandate is framed five ways: either when it is given solely for the benefit of the mandator, or partly for his benefit, and partly for that of the mandatary, or solely for the service of some third person; or partly for the profit of the mandator and partly for the service of a third person, or for the benefit of the mandator, and partly for the use of a third person. But, if a mandate is given solely for the sake of the mandatary, the mandate is useless; for no obligation can arise from it, nor of course any action.

Si mandantis gratia mandetur.

§ I. Mandantis tantum gratia intervenit mandatum, veluti si quis tibi mandet, ut negotia ejus gereres, vel ut fundum ei emeres, vel ut pro eo sponderes.

§ 1. *A mandate is given solely for the benefit of the mandator, when he requires the mandatary to transact his business, to buy lands, or to become a surety for him.*

Si mandantis et mandatarii.

§ II. Tua gratia et mandantis; veluti si mandet tibi, ut pecuniam sub usuris crederes ei, qui in rem ipsius mutuaretur: aut si, volente te agere cum eo ex fidejussoria causa, mandet tibi, ut cum reo agas periculo mandantis; vel ut ipsius periculo stipuleris ab eo, quem tibi deleget in id, quod tibi debuerat.

§ 2. *A mandate is given partly for the benefit of the mandator, and partly for the benefit of the mandatary, if the mandator requires you to lend money upon interest to Titius, who would borrow it for the use of the mandator, or if, when you are upon the point of suing a man on account of a fide-jussory caution, or a suretyship, he should authorise you at his own risque to sue the principal debtor: or if he should impower you at his own hazard to stipulate for the sum, which he owes you, from some other person, whom he appoints.*

Ut

Ut pecuniam sub usuris] "Nam mandatario prodest id, quod agitur, propter usurarum "præstationem, et mandatori, in cujus rem pe-"cunia vertenda est" *Theoph*

Aut si volente te] "Commodum hic fide-"jussoris in eo, quod judicio liberatur, cum a-"lioqui agi cum eo ex causa fide-jussionis po-"tuisset, reo principali neglecto si quidem jure "veteri fide-jussor ante reum principalem con-"veniri potuit" *Vinn.*

Vel ut ipsius periculo] "Hoc etiam man-"datum in rem utriusque interponi intelligitur: "in rem debitoris mandantis, quia ea delega-"tione fit novatio, atque ex priore causa debitor "liberatur. in rem creditoris mandatarii, quo-"niam novus debitor ita substituitur, ut nihilo-"minus ex sequenti mandato cum priore agi "possit" *Vinn.*

Si aliena gratia.

§ III. Aliena tantum causa intervenit mandatum; veluti si tibi aliquis mandet, ut Titii negotia gereres, vel ut Titio fundum emeres, vel ut pro Titio sponderes.

§ 3. *A mandate is interposed only for the sake of a third person, when the mandator requires the mandatary to perform some office for* Titius, *to buy lands for him, or to become his bail.*

Si mandantis et aliena.

§ IV. Sua et aliena, veluti si de communibus suis et Titii negotiis gerendis tibi mandet, vel ut sibi et Titio fundam emeres, vel ut pro eo et Titio sponderes.

§ 4. *A mandate tends to the benefit of the mandator, and also of a third person, when the mandator requires you, who are the mandatary, to transact some affair for the common benefit of both him and* Titius, *or to buy lands for them both, or to be bound for them.*

Si mandatarii et aliena.

§ V. Tua et aliena; veluti si tibi mandet, ut Titio sub usuris crederes; quia, si sine usuris pecuniam crederes, aliena tantum gratia intercedit mandatum.

§ 5. *A mandate is given in favor of the mandatary and of a third person, when the mandator requires you to lend money to* Titius, *upon interest; but, if you are required to lend money without interest, the mandate can only be in favor of him, to whom it is lent.*

Si mandatarii.

§. VI. Tua tantum gratia intervenit mandatum; veluti si tibi mandet, ut pecunias tuas in emptiones potius prædiorum colloces, quam fœneres: vel ex diverso, ut pecunias tuas fœneres potius, quam in emptiones prædiorum colloces. Cujus generis mandatum magis consilium, quam mandatum est, et ob id non est obligatorium; quia nemo ex consilio mandati obligatur, etiam si non expediat ei, cui mandabatur, cum liberum cuique sit apud se explorare, an sibi expediat consilium. Itaque, si otiosam pecuniam domi te habentem hortatus fuerit aliquis, ut rem aliquam emeres vel eam crederes, quamvis non expediat eam tibi emisse, vel credidisse, non tamen

tamen tibi mandati tenetur. Et adeo hæc ita sunt, ut quæsitum sit, an mandati teneatur, qui mandavit tibi, ut pecuniam Titio fœnerares. Sed obtinuit Sabini sententia, obligatorium esse in hoc casu mandatum: quia non aliter Titio credidisses, quam si tibi mandatum esset.

§ 6. *A mandate is given solely for your own benefit, if the mandator requires you rather to make a purchase of lands, than to lend your money upon interest, or on the contrary rather to lend your money upon interest, than to buy lands. But a mandate of this species seems rather to be good advice, than a mandate, and is therefore not obligatory; for an action of mandate cannot be brought against a man on account of the advice, which he has given, altho it has not proved beneficial to him, to whom it was given, inasmuch as every one is at full liberty to consult his own reason, whether the counsil given to him is expedient or not And therefore, if you should be advised to employ your money, which now lies dead, either by lending it out at interest, or in making a purchase, and you should become a loser by following this advice, the adviser would not be liable to an action And this is so true, that it has even been a question, whether an action of mandate will lie against him, who hath required you by mandate to lend money to* Titius, *who is insolvent But the opinion of* Sabinus *hath obtained, and a mandate in this case is now judged to be obligatory, for you would never have trusted* Titius, *but in obedience to the mandate.*

De mandato contra bonos mores.

§ VII. Illud quoque mandatum non est obligatorium, quod contra bonos mores est: veluti si Titius de furto, aut de damno faciendo, aut de injuria facienda, mandet tibi: licet enim pœnam istius facti nomine præstiteris, non tamen ullam habes adversus Titium actionem

§ 7. *A mandate contrary to good manners is not obligatory, as if* Titius *should command* Sempronius *to commit theft, or to do some act to the damage or injury of a third person; for, altho'* Sempronius *should suffer a penalty or punishment in consequence of his obedience to such a mandate, he will not be intituled to any action against* Titius

Veluti si Titius] " Si Sempronius ex Titii " mandato aliquem occidit, aut vulneravit, aut " contumelia affecit, etsi hic nulla ex contractu " inter eos obligatio oritur, uterque tamen obligatur ex delicto, neque Titium, qui mandavit, excusat, quod Sempronius facinus perpetravit, neque Sempronium, quod Titius " mandaverit *Vinn*

De executione mandati.

§ VIII. Is, qui exequitur mandatum, non debet excedere fines mandati: ut ecce, si quis usque ad centum aureos mandaverit tibi, ut fundum emeres, vel ut pro Titio sponderes, neque pluris emere debes, neque in ampliorem pecuniam fidejubere; alioqui non habebis cum eo mandati actionem: adeo quidem, ut Sabino et Cassio placuerit, etiamsi usque ad centum aureos cum eo agere volueris, inutiliter te acturum Sed diversæ scholæ auctores recte usque ad centum aureos te acturum existimant: quæ sententia sane benignior est. Quod si minoris emeris, habebis scilicet cum eo mandati actionem: quoniam, qui mandat, ut sibi

centum aureorum fundus emeretur, is utique mandasse intelligitur, ut minoris, si possit, emeretur.

§ 8. *He, who executes a mandate ought not to exceed the bounds of it: for example, if a mandator should require you to purchase lands, or to be bound for* TITIUS, *to the amount of an hundred* aurei; *you ought not to buy the lands at an higher price, or be bound for* TITIUS *in a greater sum: for, if you exceed the mandate, you will not be intituled to an action for the recovery of the excess And* CASSIUS *and* SABINUS *were even of opinion, that, altho' you were willing to bring an action of mandate for no more than the hundred* aurei, *you could not recover them But it was held by the lawyers of a different school, that the mandatary might sue the mandator for the hundred* aurei; *and this appears to be the more equitable opinion But, if you buy certain lands at a less price than that, which the mandator has allowed, you will undoubtedly be intituled to an action of mandate: for, if he hath ordered, that an hundred* aurei *shall be expended in the purchase of a particular estate, he will certainly be understood to have ordered, that the same estate should, if possible, be purchased at a less price.*

De revocatione mandati.

§ IX. Recte quoque mandatum contractum, si, dum adhuc integra res sit, revocatum fuerit, evanescit.

§ 9. *A mandate, properly contracted, becomes null, if it is revoked whilest* intire, *that is, before any act has been done in consequence of it.*

De morte.

§ X. Item, si adhuc integro mandato mors alterius interveniat, id est, vel ejus, qui mandaverit, vel illius, qui mandatum susceperit, solvitur mandatum. Sed utilitatis causa receptum est, si eo mortuo, qui tibi mandaverat, tu, ignorans eum decessisse, executus fueris mandatum, posse te agere mandati actione: alioqui justa et probabilis ignorantia tibi damnum afferet. Et huic simile est, quod placuit, si debitores, manumisso dispensatore Titii, per ignorantiam liberto solverint, liberari eos; cum alioqui stricta juris ratione non possent liberari. quia alii solvissent, quam cui solvere debuerint.

§ 10 *A mandate also becomes null, if either the* mandator, *or the mandatary, dies, whilest it continues intire. But it is allowed for the benefit of society, that, if a mandator dies, and the mandatary, not knowing of his death, should afterwards execute the mandate, he may bring his action against the heirs of the* mandator: *for otherwise an unblameable and unavailable want of knowledge would be prejudicial. And, in a similar case, it hath been determined, that, if the debtors of* TITIUS, *whose steward has been manumitted, should, without knowledge of the manumission, pay this freed-man what was due to* TITIUS, *they would be cleared from their debt, and the payment would be good, altho, by the rigor of the law, it would be otherwise, since they had made their payment to another than him, to whom it ought to have been made.*

De renunciatione.

§ XI. Mandatum non suscipere cuilibet liberum est: susceptum autem consummandum est, aut quam primum renuntiandum, ut per semetipsum, aut per alium, eandem rem mandator exequatur. Nam, nisi ita renuntietur, ut integra causa mandatori reservetur eandem rem explicandi, nihilominus mandati actio locum habet; nisi justa causa intercesserit aut non renuntiandi, aut intempestive renuntiandi.

§ 11. *Every man is at liberty to refuse a mandate; but, if it is once accepted, it must be performed, or renounced, as soon as possible, that the mandator may transact the business himself, or by another. But, if the renunciation is made so late, that the mandator can have no opportunity of transacting this business properly, an action will lie against the mandatary, unless he can shew some just cause for his delay in not making a timely renunciation.*

De die et conditione.

§ XII. Mandatum et in diem differri et sub conditione fieri potest.

§ 12. *A mandate may be contracted to transact a particular business at a distant day, or upon condition.*

De mercede.

§ XIII. In summa sciendum est, mandatum, nisi gratuitum sit, in aliam formam negotii cadere: nam, mercede constituta, incipit locatio et conductio esse. Et, (ut generaliter dicamus,) quibus casibus, sine mercede suscepto officio, mandati sive depositi contrahitur negotium, iis casibus interveniente mercede locatio et conductio intelligitur contrahi. Et ideo, si fulloni polienda curandave quis dederit vestimenta, aut sarcinatori sarcienda, nulla mercede constituta, neque promissa, mandati competit actio.

§ 13. *In fine it must be observed, that, if a mandate is not gratuitous, it then becomes another species of contract: for, if a price is agreed upon, the contract of* location *and* conduction *commences. And in general, when a trust or business is undertaken without hire, the contract regards either a* mandate, *or a* deposit; *but, when there is an agreement for hire, it constitutes* location *and* conduction. *And therefore, if a man gives his cloaths to a fuller, that they may be cleaned, or to a taylor, that they may be mended, and there is no agreement or promise made, an action of* mandate *will lie.*

TITULUS VIGESIMUS-OCTAVUS.

De obligationibus, quæ quasi ex contractu nascuntur.

Continuatio.

POST genera contractuum enumerata, dispiciamus etiam de iis obligationibus, quæ quidem non proprie nasci ex contractu intelliguntur: sed tamen, quia non ex maleficio substantiam capiunt, quasi ex contractu nasci videntur.

Having already enumerated the various kinds of direct obligations, we will now treat of those, which can not be said properly to arise from a contract, but yet, inasmuch as they take not their origin from any thing criminal, seem to arise from an implied, or a quasi *contract.*

De negotiorum gestione.

§ I. Igitur, cum quis negotia absentis gesserit, ultro citroque inter eos nascuntur actiones, quæ appellantur negotiorum gestorum. Sed domino quidem rei gestæ adversus eum, qui gessit, directa competit actio; negotiorum autem gestori contraria: quas ex nullo contractu proprie nasci manifestum est: quippe ita nascuntur istæ actiones, si sine mandato quisque alienis negotiis gerendis se obtulerit, ex qua causa ii, quorum negotia gesta fuerint, etiam ignorantes obligantur. Idque utilitatis causa receptum est, ne absentium, qui subita festinatione coacti, nulli demandata negotiorum suorum administratione, peregre profecti essent, desererentur negotia: quæ sane nemo curaturus esset, si de eo, quod quis impendisset, nullam habiturus esset actionem. Sicut autem is, qui utiliter gessit negotia, dominum habet obligatum negotiorum gestorum, ita et contra iste quoque tenetur, ut administrationis reddat rationem: quo casu ad exactissimam quisque diligentiam compellitur reddere rationem: nec sufficit talem diligentiam adhibere, qualem suis rebus adhibere solet: si modo alius, diligentior eo, commodius administraturus esset negotia.

§ 1. *When one person transacts the business of another, who is absent, they reciprocally obtain a right to certain actions, called* actiones negotiorum gestorum, *i. e. actions on account of business done and it is manifest, that these can arise from no proper or regular contract; for they take place only, when one man assumes the care of the affairs of another without a* mandate: *and, in this case, those persons, for whom business is transacted, are always bound without their knowledge, and this is permitted for the public good, because the business of those, who are absent in a foreign country, and have not committed the administration of their affairs to any particular person, would otherwise be totally neglected: for no man would take this*

care

care upon himſelf, if he could not afterwards bring an action to recover what he had expended. But, as the principal is bound to reimburſe the agent, who has negotiated his affairs properly, ſo is the agent bound to render a juſt account of his adminiſtration to his principal. And an agent, in this caſe, is obliged to uſe the moſt exact diligence; for it will not ſuffice, altho' he proves, that he has taken the ſame care of the affairs of his principal, which he uſually took of his own, if it can by any means appear, that a more diligent man could have acted with greater advantage to his principal.

De Tutela.

§ II. Tutores quoque, qui tutelæ judicio tenentur, non proprie ex contractu obligati eſſe intelliguntur: nullum enim negotium inter tutorem et pupillum contrahitur. Sed, quia ſane non ex maleficio tenentur, quaſi ex contractu teneri videntur. Hoc autem caſu mutuæ ſunt actiones. Non tantum enim pupillus cum tutore habet tutelæ actionem; ſed et contra tutor cum pupillo habet contrariam tutelæ, ſi vel impenderit aliquid in rem pupilli, vel pro eo fuerit obligatus, aut rem ſuam creditoribus ejus obligaverit.

§ 2 *A* tutor, *altho' he is ſubject to an action of* tutelage, *is not reckoned to be bound by any pact, or agreement; for between a tutor and his pupil there is no expreſs contract. But, altho' tutors are not ſubject to an action of male-feaſance, they are underſtood to be bound by an implied, or* quaſi-*contract, and thus both tutor and pupil may bring actions reciprocally; the pupil may bring a direct action of tutelage againſt his tutor, and the tutor, if he has expended his own money in the affairs of his pupil, or has been bound for him, or has mortgaged his own poſſeſſions to the creditors, is intituled to the action called* contraria tutelæ.

De rei communione.

§ III. Item, ſi inter aliquos communis res ſit ſine ſocietate; veluti quod pariter eis legata donatave eſſet, et alter eorum alteri ideo teneatur communi dividundo judicio, quod ſolus fructus ex ea re perceperit, aut quod ſocius ejus ſolus in eam rem neceſſarias impenſas fecerit: non intelligitur ex contractu proprie obligatus eſſe, quippe nihil inter ſe contraxerunt: ſed, quia ex maleficio non tenetur, quaſi ex contractu teneri videtur.

§ 3. *When a thing happens to be in common among perſons, who have never entered into a voluntary partenerſhip; as when the ſame field, or part of an inheritance, is deviſed, or given generally, between two; in this caſe the one may be called to anſwer the other by the action* communi dividundo, *either becauſe the one hath taken to his uſe the whole produce of the ground; or becauſe the other hath been at the ſole expence of maintaining it in good order. But neither of theſe perſons can properly be ſaid to be bound by contract, ſince they made no agreement between themſelves, but, inaſmuch as they are exempt from any criminal action, they are accounted as bound by a* quaſi *contract.*

De hæreditatis communione.

§ IV. Idem juris est de eo, qui cohæredi familiæ erciscundæ judicio ex his causis obligatus est.

§ 4. *And the same law prevails in regard to him, who for the same causes is bound to his co-heir and is liable to the action* familiæ erciscundæ, *for the partition of an universal inheritance.*

De aditione hæreditatis.

§ V Hæres quoque legatorum nomine non proprie ex contractu obligatus intelligitur, (neque enim cum hærede, neque cum defuncto ullum negotium legatarius gessisse proprie dici potest,) et tamen, quia ex maleficio non est obligatus, quasi ex contractu debere intelligitur.

§ 5 *An* heir *for the same reason cannot properly be said to be bound by contract to a* legatary; *for the* legatary *can never be supposed to have entered into any compact either with the heir, or with the deceased. But, as the heir cannot be prosecuted by an action of* male-feasance, *he is presumed to be indebted to the legatary by a* quasi *contract.*

De solutione indebiti.

§ VI. Item is, cui quis per errorem non debitum solvit, quasi ex contractu debere videtur: adeo enim non intelligitur proprie ex contractu obligatus esse, ut, si certiorem rationem sequamur, magis, (ut supra diximus,) ex distractu quam ex contractu possit dici obligatus esse. Nam, qui solvendi animo pecuniam dat, in hoc dare videtur, ut distrahat potius negotium, quam contrahat. Sed tamen perinde is, qui accipit, obligatur, ac si mutuum ei daretur; et ideo condictione tenetur.

§ 6. *He, to whom another has paid by mistake what was not due, appears to be indebted by* quasi *contract; for he is certainly not bound by an express agreement: and, strictly speaking, he might rather be said, (as we have before observed,) to be bound by the dissolution than by the making of a contract: for he, who paid the money with an intent to discharge his debts, seemed rather inclined to dissolve an engagement, than to contract one. But neverthelesss, whoever receives money by the mistake of another, is as much bound to repay it, as if it had been lent to him; and he is therefore liable to an action of condiction.*

Quibus ex causis debitum solutum non repetitur.

§ VII. Ex quibusdam tamen causis repeti non potest, quod per errorem non debitum solutum sit; sic namque definierunt veteres, ex quibus causis inficiando lis crescit, ex iis causis non debitum solutum repeti non posse: veluti ex lege Aquilia, item ex legato: quod veteres quidem in iis legatis locum habere voluerunt, quæ certa constituta per damnationem cuique fuerant: nostra autem constitutio, cum unam naturam omnibus legatis et fideicommissis indulsit, hujusmodi augmentum

in

in omnibus legatis et fideicommiſſis extendi voluit: ſed non omnibus legatariis hoc præbuit, ſed tantummodo in iis legatis et fideicommiſſis, quæ ſacroſanctis Eccleſiis, et cæteris venerabilibus locis, quæ vel religionis vel pietatis intuitu honorantur, relicta ſunt, quæ, ſi indebita ſolvantur, non repetuntur.

§ 7. *In ſome caſes money paid by miſtake, when not due, cannot afterwards be demanded. for the antient lawyers have delivered it as a maxim, that where an action for double the value of the debt is given upon the denial of it, (as by the law Aquilia, and in the caſe of legacies) the debtor, who has thro error paid money to him, to whom it was not due, ſhall never recover it. But theſe lawyers would have this rule to take place only in regard to fixed and certain legacies, deviſed* per damnationem. *But our imperial conſtitution, which reduced all legacies and truſts to one common nature, hath cauſed this augmentation in* duplum *after denial to be extended to legacies and truſts in general: yet the privilege of not refunding what is paid by miſtake is by our conſtitution only granted to churches and other holy places, which are honored on account of religion and piety.*

Ex quibuſdam cauſis.] "Cujus rei ratio perobſcura eſt, nec habeo, quod reſpondeam, niſi quod veriſimile eſt, certis in cauſis receptum fuiſſe, ut interrogati in jure, ſi negarent, et mendacii convincerentur, in duplum irent unde poſtea inductum, ut, qui, ex his cauſis conventus, ſolviſſet quantumvis indebitum, non repeteret, quaſi ſimplum ideo ſolverit, ne inficiando periculum dupli ſubiret, et ita, quaſi tranſigendo, hoc periculum a ſe amovere voluerit Oportet vero aliquam cauſam ſubeſſe, verbi gratia, damnum eſſe datum, licet forte non ab eo, qui convenitur, ſed ab alio, legatum aliquod ad pios uſus relictum eſſe, licet forte minus ſolemniter. Nam, ſi nullum damnum datum ſit, aut nihil relictum, puto, locum eſſe repetitioni Excipiuntur et aliæ cauſæ ex quibus indebitum per errorem ſolutum non repetitur, ut cauſa dotis et tranſactionis" *Vinn*

Ex lege Aquilia.] *vid ff* 9 *t* 2 *l* 9 *p* 10

Noſtra autem conſtitutio] *C* 6 *t* 43 *l* 2 *Comm de legat* "qua conſtitutione legatis omnibus et fideicommiſſis eadem natura attributa eſt Illa autem conſtitutio, qua jus, de quo hic agitur, ad legata et fideicommiſſa, religionis aut pietatis cauſa relicta, coarctavit imperator, non extat *Vinn.*

TITULUS VIGESIMUS-NONUS.

Per quas perſonas obligatio acquiritur.

C. iv. T. 27.

De his, qui ſunt in poteſtate.

EXPOSITIS generibus obligationum, quæ ex contractu vel quaſi ex contractu naſcuntur, admonendi ſumus, acquiri nobis non ſolum per noſmetipſos, ſed per eas quoque perſonas, quæ in noſtra poteſtate ſunt, veluti per ſervos et filios noſtros: ut tamen, quod per ſervos noſtros nobis acquiritur, totum noſtrum fiat: quod autem per liberos, quos in poteſtate habemus, ex obligatione fuerit acquiſitum, hoc dividatur ſecundum imaginem rerum, proprietatis, et uſusfructus, quam noſtra decrevit conſtitutio: ut, quod ab actione commodum perveniat, hujus uſumfruc

tum

tum quidem habeat pater, proprietas autem filio ſervetur, ſcilicet patre actionem movente, ſecundum novellæ noſtræ conſtitutionis diviſionem.

Having explained the various kinds of obligation, which ariſe from contracts or quaſi *contracts, we muſt now obſerve, that we acquire obligations not only by means of ourſelves, but alſo by thoſe, who are under our power; as by our ſlaves, and our children. and whatever is acquired by our ſlaves is wholly our own; but that, which is acquired by our children, under our power, by virtue of their contracts, muſt be divided according to the decree of our conſtitution, which gives to the father the uſufruct of the thing gained, but reſerves the property of it to the ſon. But a father, in bringing an action, muſt act in obedience to our novel conſtitution.*

Quam noſtra decrevit conſtitutio] *vide Cod* 6 *t* 61. *l* 6 *cum oportet, &c*
Novellæ conſtitutionis] *Cod* 6 *t*. 61 *l* 8

De bona fide poſſeſſis.

§ I. Item per liberos homines et alienos ſervos, quos bona fide poſſidemus, acquiritur nobis: ſed tantum ex duabus cauſis, id eſt, ſi quid ex operis ſuis, vel ex re noſtra, acquirant.

§ 1. *We may alſo acquire things by means of freemen, and the ſlaves of others, whom we poſſeſs* bona fide. *But this we can only do in two caſes, to wit, when they have gained an acquiſition by their labor, or by virtue of ſomething, which belongs to us.*

De ſervo fructuario, vel uſuario.

§ II. Per eum quoque ſervum, in quo uſumfructum vel uſum habemus, ſimiliter ex duabus iſtis cauſis nobis acquiritur.

§ 2 *We may alſo acquire in either of the above named caſes, by means even of thoſe ſlaves, of whom we have only the uſufruct or uſe.*

De ſervo communi.

§ III. Communem ſervum pro dominica parte dominis acquirere certum eſt, excepto eo, quod nominatim uni ſtipulando, aut per traditionem accipiendo, illi ſoli acquirit; veluti cum ita ſtipulatur, *Titio domino meo dare ſpondes?* Sed, ſi domini unius juſſu ſervus fuerit ſtipulatus, licet antea dubitabatur, tamen poſt noſtram deciſionem res expedita eſt, ut illi tantum acquirat, qui hoc ei facere juſſit, ut ſupra dictum eſt.

§ 3. *It is certain, that a ſlave, who is in common between two or more, acquires for his maſters, in proportion to the property, which each of them has in him; unleſs he ſtipulates, or receives ſomething, in the name of one of them only, as if he had thus ſtipulated;* do you promiſe to give ſuch a particular thing to TITIUS, *my maſter? for altho' it was a doubt in times paſt, whether a ſlave, when commanded, could ſtipulate for the ſole benefit of one of his maſters, yet, ſince our deciſion, it has become a ſettled point, (as we have ſaid before,) that a ſlave, in this caſe, can acquire for him only, who hath ordered the ſtipulation.*

Poſt noſtram deciſionem] *Cod* 4 *t* 27 *l* 3 *ſi duo, &c.*

TITU-

TITULUS TRIGESIMUS.

Quibus modis tollitur obligatio.

D. iv. T. 2, 3, 4. C. viii. T. 42, 43, 44.

De solutione.

TOLLITUR autem omnis obligatio solutione ejus, quod debetur: vel si quis consentiente creditore aliud pro alio solverit. Nec interest, quis solvat, utrum ipse, qui debet, an alius pro eo: liberatur enim et alio solvente, sive sciente, sive ignorante debitore, vel invito eo solutio fiat. Item, si reus solverit, etiam ii, qui pro eo intervenerunt, liberantur. Idem ex contrario contingit, si fide-jussor solverit: non enim ipse solus liberatur, sed etiam reus.

An obligation is dissolved by the payment of what is due; or by the payment of one thing for another, if the creditor consents: neither is it material, by whom payment is made, whether by the debtor himself, or by another for him, for a debtor becomes free from his debt, when another has paid it, either with or without his knowlege, or even against his consent. Also when a principal debtor pays his creditors, then those, who have been bound for him, are freed from their obligation and, on the contrary, when a fide-jussor *or bondsman clears himself from his obligation by payment, he not only becomes free himself, but the principal debtor is also cleared from his debt.*

De acceptilatione.

§ I. Item per acceptilationem tollitur obligatio: est autem acceptilatio imaginaria solutio. Quod enim ex verborum obligatione Titio debetur, id, si velit Titius remittere, poterit sic fieri, ut patiatur hæc verba debitorem dicere: *quod ego tibi promisi, habesne acceptum?* et Titius respondeat, *habeo.* Sed et Græce potest acceptilatio fieri; dummodo sic fiat, ut Latinis verbis solet: εχεις λαβων δηναρια τοσα, εχω λαβων. Quo genere, (ut diximus,) tantum eæ solvuntur obligationes, quæ ex verbis consistunt, non etiam cæteræ. Consentaneum enim visum est, verbis factam obligationem aliis posse verbis dissolvi. Sed et id, quod alia ex causa debetur, potest in stipulationem deduci, et per acceptilationem dissolvi. Sicut etiam quod debetur pro parte recte solvitur, ita in parte debiti acceptilatio fieri potest.

§ 1. *An obligation is also dissolved by* acceptilation; *which is an imaginary payment for, if* TITIUS *is willing to remit what is due to him by a verbal contract, it may be done, if the debtor says,* do you regard what I promised you, as accepted and received? *and* TITIUS *answers,* I do. *An* acceptilation *may also be made in Greek, if it is so worded, as to agree with the Latin form,* εχεις λαβων δηναρια τοσα, εχω λαβων *But the obligations, which are thus dissolved, are verbal contracts, and no other. and it seems to be a just consequence, that an obliga-*

tion

tion, made by words only, may be dissolved by other words of a contrary import. But it is observable, that any species of contract may be deduced to a stipulation, and of course may be dissolved by acceptilation. *And note, that as a debt may be paid in part by money, so may it be paid in part also by* acceptilation.

De Aquiliana stipulatione et acceptilatione.

§ II. Est autem prodita stipulatio, quæ vulgo Aquiliana appellatur, per quam contingit, ut omnium rerum obligatio in stipulatum deducatur, et ea per acceptilationem tollatur. Stipulatio enim Aquiliana renovat omnes obligationes, et a Gallo Aquilio ita composita est; *quicquid te mihi ex quacunque causa dare facere oportet oportebitve, præsens in diemve, aut sub conditione; quarumcunque rerum mihi tecum actio est, quæque adversus te petitio, vel adversus te persecutio, est eritve; quodve tu meum habes, tenes, possides, dolove malo fecisti, quo minus possideas; quanti quæque earum rerum res erit, tantam pecuniam dari stipulatus est Aulus Agerius, spospondit Numerius Nigidius. Quod Numerius Nigidius Aulo Agerio spospondit, id haberetne a se acceptum Numerius Nigidius Aulum Agerium rogavit: Aulus Agerius Numerio Nigidio acceptum fecit.*

§ 2. *There is another species of stipulation, called commonly the* Aquilian *stipulation, by virtue of which every other kind of obligation may be reduced to a stipulation, and may afterwards be dissolved by* acceptilation. *For the* Aquilian *stipulation changes all obligations, and was constituted by* GALLUS AQUILIUS *in the following manner*; do you promise, said AULUS AGERIUS to NUMERIUS NIGIDIUS, to pay me a sum of money, in lieu of what you was, or shall be, obliged to give me or to perform for my benefit, either simply, at a day to come, or upon condition; and in lieu of those things, which, being my property, you HAVE, DETAIN, OR POSSESS, or of which you have fraudulently quitted the possession, and for which I may, or shall be, intituled to any species of action, plaint, or prosecution? NUMERIUS NIGIDIUS *answered* I do *and, when this was said,* NUMERIUS NIGIDIUS asked AULUS AGERIUS, if he regarded the money as accepted and received, which he (NUMERIUS) had promised? *to which* AULUS AGERIUS *answered,* that he did regard it as accepted and received.

De novatione.

§ III. Præterea novatione tollitur obligatio; veluti si id, quod tibi Seius debebat, a Titio stipulatus sis. Nam interventu novæ personæ nova nascitur obligatio, et prima tollitur, translata in posteriorem: adeo ut interdum, licet posterior stipulatio inutilis sit, tamen prima novationis jure tollatur: veluti si id, quod tu Titio debes, a pupillo sine tutoris auctoritate stipulatus fuerit; quo casu res amittitur: nam et prior debitor liberatur, et posterior obligatio nulla est. Non idem juris est, si a servo quis fuerit stipulatus: nam tunc prior perinde obligatus manet, ac si postea nullus stipulatus fuisset. Sed, si eadem persona sit, a qua postea stipuleris, ita demum novatio fit, si quid in posteriore stipulatione novi sit, forte si conditio

ditio aut dies aut fide-jussor adjiciatur aut detrahatur. Quod autem diximus, si conditio adjiciatur, novationem fieri, sic intelligi oportet, ut ita dicamus factam novationem, si conditio extiterit: alioqui, si defecerit, durat prior obligatio. Sed, cum hoc quidem inter veteres constabat, tunc fieri novationem, cum novandi animo in secundam obligationem itum fuerat, per hoc autem dubium erat, quando novandi animo videtur hoc fieri, et quasdam de hoc præsumptiones alii in aliis casibus introducebant, ideo nostra processit constitutio, quæ apertissime definivit, tunc solum novationem prioris obligationis fieri, quoties hoc ipsum inter contrahentes expressum fuerit, quod propter novationem prioris obligationis convenerunt: alioquì et manere pristinam obligationem, et secundam ei accedere, ut maneat ex utraque causa obligatio, secundum nostræ constitutionis definitionem, quam licet ex ipsius lectione apertius cognoscere.

§ 3. *An obligation is also dissolved by* novation*: as when you stipulate with* TITIUS *to receive from him what is due to you from* SEIUS *For, by the intervention of a new debtor, a fresh obligation arises, by which the prior obligation is discharged, and transfered to the latter. And sometimes, altho the latter stipulation is of no force, yet the prior contract is discharged by the mere act of* novation *as if* TITIUS *should stipulate to receive a debt, which I owe him, from a pupil without the authority of his tutor; for in this case the debt is lost, because the first debtor is freed from his debt, and the second obligation is null. but it is not the same, if a man stipulates from a slave, with a design to make a* novation*; for then the first debtor remains bound, as if there had been no second stipulation. And, if you stipulate from the same person a second time, a* novation *arises, if any thing new is covenanted in the latter stipulation, as when a condition, a day, or a bondsman is added, or taken away. But note, that, when a condition only is added,* novation *does not take place, till the event happens, and, till then, the prior obligation continues. It was observed as a rule among the antient lawyers, that a* novation *arose, when a second contract was entered into with an intent to dissolve the former; but it was always a matter of great difficulty to know with what intent the second obligation was made, and the judges, having no positive proof before them, were forced to form their opinions upon presumptions, and according to the circumstances of every particular case. This incertainty of judging gave rise to our constitution, which enacts, that a* novation *of a former contract shall only take place, when it is expressed by the contractors, that they covenanted with an intent to make a* novation, *and that, when this is not expressed, the prior contract shall continue valid; and the second be regarded as an accession to it: so that an obligation shall remain by virtue of both contracts, according to the determination of our before named constitution, which may be better known by perusal.*

Nostra processit constitutio] *vid Cod.* 8 *t* 42. *l.* 8 *De novationibus*

De contrario consensu.

§ IV. Hoc amplius, eæ obligationes, quæ consensu contrahuntur, contraria voluntate dissolvuntur. Nam, si Titius et Seius inter se consenserint, ut fundum Tusculanum emptum Seius haberet centum aureis; deinde, re nondum secuta, (id est, neque pretio soluto, neque fundo tradito,) placuerint cuerit inter eos, ut discederetur ab ea emptione et venditione, invicem liberantur. Idem est in conductione et locatione, et in omnibus contractibus, qui ex consensu descendunt, sicut jam dictum est.

§ 4. *We must observe farther, that those obligations, which are contracted by consent, may be dissolved by dissent. For, if* TITIUS *and* SEIUS *have agreed by compact between themselves, that* SEIUS *shall have a certain estate for an hundred* aurei, *and afterwards before execution, that is, before the price is paid, or livery is made of the lands, if the parties dissent from their agreement, they are mutually discharged from it. And the same may be said of* location *and* conduction, *and of all other contracts, which arise from consent.*

FINIS LIBRI TERTII.

DIVI

DIVI JUSTINIANI INSTITUTIONUM LIBER QUARTUS.

TITULUS PRIMUS.

De obligationibus, quæ ex delicto naſcuntur.

D. xlvii. T. 2. C. vi. T. 2.

Continuatio et diviſio obligationum ex delicto.

CUM ſit expoſitum ſuperiore libro de obligationibus ex contractu & quaſi ex contractu, ſequitur, ut de obligationibus ex maleficio & quaſi ex maleficio diſpiciamus. Sed illæ quidem, ut ſuo loco tradidimus, in quatuor genera dividuntur: hæ vero unius generis ſunt. nam omnes ex re naſcuntur, id eſt, ex ipſo maleficio, veluti ex furto, rapina, damno, injuria.

Having explained in the preceding book the nature of obligations, which ariſe from contracts and quaſi-*contracts, it follows, that we ſhould here treat of thoſe, which ariſe from male-feazance and* quaſi-*male-feazance. The former, as we have ſhewed in the proper place, are divided into four ſpecies, but the latter are of one kind only; for they all ariſe* ex re, *that is, from the crime or male-feazance itſelf; as from theft, rapine, damage, injury.*

Definitio furti.

§ I. Furtum eſt contrectatio fraudulosa, lucri faciendi gratia, vel ipſius rei, vel etiam uſus ejus, poſſeſſioniſve: quod lege naturali prohibitum eſt admittere.

§ 1. *Theft is a fraudulent ſubſtraction of the thing itſelf, the uſe of it, or the poſſeſſion, for the ſake of gain. And this is prohibited by the law of nature.*

Poſſeſſionis.] In *England* theft is commited of the poſſeſſion when goods are ſtolen from a carrier, or a pledge from a creditor, and, if [illegible] the owner of ſuch goods or pledge ſhould take them away fraudulently, he would be guilty of larciny in regard to the poſſeſſion, for though the property is in him, yet the right of poſſeſſion is veſted in another. 3 *Co. Inſt.* 110.

Etymologia.

§ II. Furtum autem vel à furvo, id eſt, nigro, dictum eſt, quod clam & obſcure fiat, vel plerumque nocte: vel à fraude. vel à ferendo, id eſt, auferendo: vel à Græco ſermone, qui φωρας appellant fures. Imo & Græci, ἀπο τȣ φερειν, φωρας dixerint.

§ 2. *The word* furtum [*theft*] *is derived from* furvum [*black or dark*] *because theft is committed privately, and generally in the night* ——*or from* fraus [*fraud*]. ——*or from* ferendo, *which is of the ſame import with* auferendo, *and denotes a ſubſtraction, or taking away. Or perhaps* furtum *is derived from the* Greek, *for the* Greeks *call* fures, φωρας, *and* φωρας *is derived from* φερειν, *which ſignifies* to take away.

Diviſio.

§ III. Furtorum autem duo ſunt genera; manifeſtum et nec manifeſtum. Nam conceptum & oblatum ſpecies potius actionis ſunt furto cohærentes, quam genera furtorum, ſicut inferius apparebit. Manifeſtus fur eſt, quem Græci ἐπ' ἀυτοφωρῳ appellant: nec ſolum is, qui in ipſo furto deprehenditur, ſed etiam is, qui eo loco deprehenditur, quo furtum fit: veluti qui in domo furtum fecit, &, nondum egreſſus januam, deprehenſus fuerit: & qui in oliveto olivarum, aut in vineto uvarum, furtum fecit, quamdiu in eo oliveto aut vineto deprehenſus fuerit. Imo ulterius furtum manifeſtum eſt extendendum, quamdiu eam rem fur tenens viſus vel deprehenſus fuerit, ſive in publico, ſive in privato, vel à domino, vel ab alio, antequam eo pervenerit, quo deferre vel deponere deſtinaſſet. Sed, ſi pertulit, quo deſtinavit, tametſi deprehendatur cum re furtiva, non eſt manifeſtus fur. Nec manifeſtum furtum quid ſit, ex iis, quæ diximus, intelligitur. nam quod manifeſtum non eſt, id ſcilicet nec manifeſtum eſt.

§ 3. *Of theft there are two ſpecies,* manifeſt *and not* manifeſt: *for the thefts, called* conceptum *and* oblatum, *rather denote the ſpecies of action ariſing on account of theft, than the ſpecies of theft, as will appear in the next paragraph. A manifeſt thief, whom the* Greeks *call* ἐπ' ἀυτοφωρῳ, *is he, who is taken in the act of thieving, or in the place, where he committed* [illegible] *as if a man, having committed a theft within an houſe, ſhould be apprehended before he had paſſed through the outward gate of it: or, having ſtolen grapes or olives, ſhould be taken in the vineyard or the orchard. Manifeſt theft is alſo farther extended. for, if the thief is apprehended, whilſt he is ſeen to have poſſeſſion of the things ſtolen, or if he is taken in public or in private, by the owner or by a ſtranger, at any time before his arrival at the place, to which he propoſed to carry it, he is guilty of a manifeſt theft. But if he actually arrives, before apprehenſion, at the place propoſed, then, altho' the things ſtolen are found upon him, he is yet not reputed in law to be a manifeſt thief. By this deſcription, which we have given of* manifeſt *theft, it may be clearly underſtood what is meant by theft* not manifeſt.

De furto concepto, oblato, prohibito, non exhibito.

§ IV. Conceptum furtum dicitur, cum apud aliquem testibus præsentibus furtiva res quæsita, et inventa sit. nam in eum propria actio constituta est, quamvis fur non sit; quæ appellatur concepti. Oblatum furtum dicitur, cum res furtiva ab aliquo tibi oblata sit, eaque apud te concepta sit, utique si ea mente tibi data fuerit, ut apud te potius, quam apud eum, qui dedit, conciperetur. Nam tibi, apud quem concepta sit, propria adversus eum, qui obtulit, quamvis fur non sit, constituta est actio, quæ appellatur oblati. Est etiam prohibiti furti actio adversus eum, qui furtum quærere testibus præsentibus volentem prohibuerit. Præterea pœna constituitur edicto prætoris per actionem furti non exhibiti adversus eum, qui furtivam rem apud se quæsitam & inventam non exhibuit. Sed hæ actiones, scilicet concepti, & oblati, & furti prohibiti, nec non furti non exhibiti, in desuetudinem abierunt. Cum enim requisitio rei furtivæ hodie secundum veterem observationem non fiat, merito ex consequentia etiam præfatæ actiones ab usu communi recesserunt. cum manifestum sit, quod omnes, qui scientes rem furtivam susceperint, & celaverint, furti nec manifesti obnoxii sunt.

§ 4. *A theft is called* conceptum [*i. e. found*] *when a thing stolen is searched for and found in the possession of some person in the presence of witnesses, and a particular action, called* actio concepti, *lies against such possessor, altho' he did not commit the theft. A theft is called* oblatum [*i. e. offered*] *when a thing stolen is offered for reference to* Titius, *and found upon him, it having been given to him by* Seius, *to the intent that it might rather be found upon* Titius *than upon himself. and in this case a special action, called* actio oblati, *may be brought by* Titius *against* Seius, *altho'* Seius *was not guilty of the theft. There is also an action, called* prohibiti furti, *which lies against him, who hinders another to inquire of theft in the presence of witnesses. And farther, a penalty was constituted, by the edict of the prætor, to be [illegible] by the action* furti non exhibiti *against any [illegible] for not having exhibited things stolen, which upon a search were found to have been in his possession. But these four actions are become quite obsolete, for, since a search after things stolen is not [illegible] according to the antient formalities, these actions [illegible] of course [illegible] to be in use. for it is a settled point, that all, who knowingly have [illegible] and concealed a thing stolen, are subject to the penalty of theft* not manifest.

Re[illegible] rei fur[illegible]] This inquiry after things stolen was made [illegible], and is at least as antient as the law of the twelve tables, in which it is mentioned [illegible] *Cul* [illegible] But the commentators are not [illegible] the *lanx* [illegible] the [illegible]

[illegible] intrabat, hancumque ante oculos tenebat propter matrum-familiarum et virginum [illegible] Ma[illegible] putat, [illegible] L[illegible] agnoscer[illegible] H[illegible] esse [illegible] ab institutis Atheniensium [illegible] P[illegible], lib. [illegible] de legibus, [illegible] "[illegible] quæ [illegible]" "[illegible] et d[illegible]"

[illegible]

vocant, ne quid forte vestibus conditum inferrent, dominoque ædium falsum crimen objectare possent

Hanc autem furti investigandi rationem, jam suo tempore sublatam fuisse, refert Gellius, *ut verisimile est, in locum ejus successisse, quod hic scribit* Justinianus, *ut, testibus adhibitis, furtum in domo aliena quæreretur, quod tamen et ipsum, ut durum atque inhumanum, quoniam hoc modo secreta cujusque hominum nimiæ curiositati panduntur, postea exoleverit* Vinn

Qui ſcientes rem furtivam] Before the 3d and 4th of *W* and *M* the receiving of ſtolen goods was only a treſpaſs or miſdemeanor by the law of *England*, and the receivers were puniſhable by fine and impriſonment, and not as acceſſaries But by the 3d. and 4th of *W* and *M cap* 9 "Receivers of ſtolen goods, knowing them to be ſtolen, are to be deemed acceſſaries after the fact, and to ſuffer as ſuch" But becauſe theſe receivers often concealed the principal felons, and thus eſcaped puniſhment as acceſſaries, inaſmuch as an acceſſary cannot be convicted, 'till after the conviction of the principal, it was therefore enacted, by 1 *Ann cap* 9 "That whoever ſhall buy, or receive, ſtolen goods, knowing them to be ſtolen, may be proſecuted for a miſdemeanor, and puniſhed by fine and impriſonment, altho' the principal felon be not convicted"

And by 5 *Ann cap* 31 "if any Perſon ſhall receive or buy knowingly any ſtolen goods, or knowingly harbour or conceal any felon, he ſhall be taken as acceſſary to the felon, and ſuffer as a felon" ——— But, becauſe it was difficult to prove the receipt of ſtolen goods, the confederates of thieves frequently diſpoſing of them to the owners for a reward, it is provided by 4 *Geo* 1 *cap.* 11. "that whoever ſhall take a reward under the pretenſe of helping any one to ſtolen goods, ſhall ſuffer, as if he himſelf had ſtolen them, unleſs he cauſe the thief to be apprehended and brought to trial, and give evidence againſt him"

Upon this clauſe the famous *Jonathan Wild* was convicted and executed, 10 G 1. *Hiſt. pl cor* 620

Pœna.

§ V. Pœna manifeſti furti quadrupli eſt, tam ex ſervi, quam ex liberi perſona: nec manifeſti, dupli.

§ 5. *The penalty of commiting a manifeſt theſt is quadruple, whether the thief is free or bond and the penalty of commiting a theft* not manifeſt *is double the value of the thing ſtolen.*

Pœna manifeſti] The puniſhment of manifeſt theft was not always the ſame among the *Romans*, for, at different times, it hath been a pecuniary mulct, whipping, the loſs of eyes, the cutting off the offending member, and even death The emperor *Juſtinian* indeed abſolutely forbad, that any member ſhould be cut off, or limb diſlocated on account of theft, ordering only a pecuniary mulct, or baniſhment, to be the puniſhment of thoſe, who were guilty of it [illegible] 134 *cap* 13 *de pœnarum moderati*[illegible]

But ſucceeding emperors ordered ſeverer puniſhments, [illegible] for the firſt offenſe, whipping, for the ſecond, ſtigmatizing on the back, or cutting off a member, and, for the third, hanging, yet theſe puniſhments were often varied, and ſometimes a theft was wholly forgiven, if it had been committed, through abſolute neceſſit[illegible] But altho' a criminal ſhould undergo a corporal puniſhment, as whipping, yet by the *Roman* law the perſon injured might, notwithſtanding this, maintain a civil action againſt the offender for reſtitution

[illegible] or larceny is, by the law of *England*, [illegible] into ſimple and mixed larceny Simple [illegible] is divided into grand and petit Grand larceny is committed, when the thing ſtolen is above the value of twelve pence, petit larceny is committed, when the thing ſtolen is of the value of twelve pence only, or under The nature of the offenſe is the ſame in both, but the puniſhment of the firſt is death and loſs of goods, and the puniſhment of the latter is loſs of goods and whipping, but not death But in grand larceny the jury may find the goods ſtolen of leſs value than twelve pence, and ſo convict the priſoner of petty larceny only *Hal*. 66 And this is often done

Mixed larceny, or robbery, is a violent taking away of money or goods from the perſon of a man, putting him in fear, be the value of the thing taken above or under the value of one ſhilling the puniſhment is death and forfeiture of all his eſtate A felonious entering into a man's houſe in the night time, with an intent to commit felony, as to ſteal ſomething, whether ſuch intention is executed or not, is termed burglary, from the *Saxon* word *burgh*, a houſe, and *lar*[illegible], a theft

And if ſuch offenſe is committed in the daytime it is called houſe breaking [illegible] 3 *Co* [illegible] 64 and *Hale's* [illegible] *of the pl of the crown* In regard to caſes of neceſſity, ſome authors, and particularly [illegible] [illegible]

[illegible]

rap rest p. 473. and *Grotius de jur. bell & pac lib.* 2. *cap* 2 write, that in cases of extreme necessity, either of hunger or cloathing, the civil distributions of property cease, and that by a kind of tacit condition the first community doth return, and upon this those common assertions are grounded. *Quicquid necessitas cogit, defendit* ——— *necessitas est lex temporis et loci* ——— *in casu extremæ necessitatis omnia sunt communia* And therefore it follows, that, in these cases, theft is no theft, or at least not punishable as such, and even some of our own lawyers have asserted the same *Brit cap* 10 *Ploud* 18 *b* 19 *a* But it is the opinion of Sir *Matthew Hale*, that, where persons live under the same civil government, it is a bold and dangerous assertion to say, that necessity can excuse theft, at least by the laws of *England*, and therefore, if a person being under necessity for want of sustenance, or cloathes, shall clandestinely, and *animo furandi*, steal another man s goods, it is felony, and a crime by the laws of *England* punishable with death altho' the judge, before whom the trial is, in this case [as in other cases of extremity] is by the law of *England* intrusted with a power to reprieve the offender, before or after judgment in order to the obtaining the king s mercy *Hale's hist P C vol* 1 *p* 54

As to the restitution of stolen goods there are three ways of obtaining it, *viz* By appeal of robbery or larciny —— By the Statute of 21 *Hen* VIII *cap* 11 —— And by the course of common law

Upon an appeal, if the party appealed against was convicted, a restitution of the goods contained in the appeal was of course made to the appellant, and hence it is, that goods, omited in an appeal, are regarded as forfeited to the king

But the Statute of 21 *Hen* VIII *cap* 11 introduced a new law for the restitution of stolen goods, — ordaining, " that, if any person do " rob or take away the goods of any of the " king's subjects within the realm, and be in- " dicted, and found guilty by the evidence of " the party so robbed, or owner of the goods, " or by the evidence of any other by their " procurement, then the party robbed shall " be restored to his money, or goods, and the " justices, before whom the felon is found " guilty, shall have power to award writs of " restitution in like manner, as tho' the felon " was attainted at the suit of the party in an " appeal "

For before this statute there was no restitution upon an indictment, but only upon an appeal.

Restitution by course of law, is either by taking the goods stolen, or by action As to retaking them, if A steals the goods of B, and B takes his goods again, with intent to favor the thief, this is punishable by fine and imprisonment; but, if he takes them without such intent, the taking is justifiable

The party robbed may also proceed by action for the recovery of his money or goods, if he hath prosecuted the law against the offender —— For example, if A steals the goods of B, *viz* 50 *l* in money, and is convicted and hath his clergy upon the prosecution of B, and B afterwards brings a trover and conversion for this 50 *l* and, upon not guilty pleaded, the special matter is found, restitution will be adjudged to the plaintiff, who hath already done his duty in prosecuting the law against the robber, so that the commonwealth can receive no injury, but it hath been held, that if a man feloniously steals goods, and, before prosecution by indictment, the party robbed brings an action of trover, it will not lie, for by such practice felonies might be compounded *H hist of the pleas of the crown, p* 546

Quomodo furtum fit; de contrectatione.

§ VI Furtum autem fit, non solum cum quis intercipiendi causa rem alienam amovet: sed generaliter, cum quis alienam rem, invito domino, contrectat. Itaque sive creditor pignore, sive is, apud quem res deposita est, ea re utatur; sive is, qui rem utendam accepit, in alium usum eam transferat, quam cujus gratia ei data est, furtum committit · veluti, si quis argentum utendum acceperit, quasi amicos ad cœnam invitaturus, & id peregre secum tulerit. aut si quis equum, gestandi causa commodatum sibi, longius aliquo duxerit. quod veteres scripserunt de eo, qui in aciem equum perduxisset.

§ 6 *Theft is committed not only, when one man takes the property of another for the sake of appropriating it to himself, but also in a more general sense, when one man uses the property of another against the will of the proprietor: thus, if a creditor makes use of a pledge, or a depository of the deposit left with him, or if a man, who hath only the use of a thing for a special purpose, converts it to other uses, a theft is committed. And if any one borrows plate under pretence of using it, at an entertainment of his friends, and then carries it with him into a foreign country,—— or if a man borrows an horse, and rides it farther than he ought; theft is also committed and the antients have held this to be law, in regard to him, who rides a borrowed horse into a field of battle.*

Furtum autem fit] The law of *England*, where theft is more severely punished than it was formerly at *Rome*, is more sparing than the civil law in ranking certain offenses under the appellation of theft, for with us the malfeazances, mentioned in the text, are not reckoned thefts, and the persons guilty of them are only liable to a civil action

De affectu furandi.

§ VII Placuit tamen, eos, qui rebus commodatis aliter uterentur, quam utendas acceperint, ita furtum committere, si se intelligant id, invito domino, facere; eumque, si intellexisset, non permissurum at si permissurum credant, extra crimen videri, optima sane distinctione; quia furtum sine affectu furandi non committitur.

§ 7 *But it hath nevertheless been adjudged, that whoever applies a thing borrowed to other uses than those, for which he borrowed it, is not guilty of theft, unless the borrower knew, that he so applied it, contrary to the will of the owner, who would not have permitted such application, if he had been apprized of it. But it has also been held, that the borrower in this case is not guilty of theft, if it appears, that he thought, that the owner would have given his consent And this is a good distinction, for a theft can never be committed, unless there appears to have been a design or intention of stealing*

De voluntate domini.

§ VIII Sed et, si credat aliquis, invito domino, se rem commodatam sibi contrectare, domino autem volente id fiat, dicitur furtum non fieri. Unde illud quæsitum est, cum Titius servum Mævii solicitaverit, ut quasdam res domino surriperet, et ad eum perferret, et servus id ad dominum pertulerit: Mævius autem, dum vult Titium in ipso delicto deprehendere, permiserit servo quasdam res ad eum perferre, utrum furti, an servi corrupti, judicio teneatur Titius, an neutro? Et cum nobis super hac dubitatione suggestum est, et antiquorum prudentium super hoc altercationes perspeximus, quibusdam neque furti, neque servi corrupti, actionem præstantibus, quibusdam furti tantummodo: nos, hujusmodi calliditati obviam euntes, per nostram constitutionem sancimus, non solum furti actionem, sed et servi corrupti contra eum dari Licet enim is servus deterior à solicitatore minime factus est, et ideo non concurrunt regulæ, quæ servi corrupti actionem introducunt, tamen consilium corruptoris ad perniciem probitatis servi introductum est, ut sit ei pœnalis actio imposita, tanquam si re ipsa fuisset servus corruptus. ne

ex

ex hujuſmodi impunitate et in alium ſervum, qui facile poſſit corrumpi, tale facinus à quibuſdam perpetretur.

§ 8. *But, if a man imagines, that he uſes a thing borrowed in ſome manner contrary to the intention and will of the proprietor, when in reality the proprietor conſents, that it ſhould be ſo uſed, theſt is not commited: and from hence ariſes a queſtion upon the following caſe.* Titius *ſolicited the ſlave of* Mævius *to rob his maſter, and to bring him the things ſtolen; of this the ſlave informed his maſter, who, being willing to diſcover* Titius *in the fact, permitted the ſlave to carry certain things to* Titius, *as ſtolen, would* Titius, *in this caſe, be ſubject to an action of theft, or to an action for having corrupted a ſlave, or to neither? When this was propoſed to us as a matter of doubt, and we perceived the altercations, which had formerly ſubſiſted among the antient lawyers upon the ſame point, ſome of them allowing of neither of the before-named actions, and others allowing an action of theft only, we therefore, being willing to obviate all ſubtilties, decreed by our conſtitution, that not only an action of theft might be brought, but alſo the action* ſervi corrupti, *which lies for having corrupted a ſlave. For altho' the ſlave became not the worſe for the ſolicitation, and therefore the cauſes, which introduce the action* ſervi corrupti, *do not concur, yet inaſmuch as ſuch ſolicitation was intended to corrupt, it hath therefore pleaſed us, that a penal action ſhall lie againſt the party ſoliciting, in the ſame manner as if he had actually ſucceeded by corrupting the ſlave: and this we have ordained, leſt impunity might incourage any evil-diſpoſed perſons to make the ſame attempt upon other ſlaves, who have leſs ſtrength of mind, and may be more eaſily corrupted.*

Per noſtram conſtitutionem.] *Vid. Cod.* 6. *t.* 2. *l.* 20.

Quarum rerum furtum fit. De liberis hominibus.

§ IX. Interdum etiam liberorum hominum furtum fit, veluti ſi quis liberorum noſtrorum, qui in poteſtate noſtra ſunt, ſubreptus fuerit.

§ 9. *A theft may be committed even of free perſons, as, for inſtance, when children, who are under power, are ſurreptitiouſly taken from their parents.*

Liberorum hominum furtum fit.] This crime in *England* is called *Kidnapping*, which is ſtealing away a man, woman, or child: it is an offenſe at common law, and puniſhable by fine, pillory, &c. *Raym.* 474. *Wood's Inſt.* 426.

By the 11 and 12 *W.* 3. cap. 7. if the maſter of a merchant ſhip ſhall during his being abroad force any man on ſhore, or wilfully leave him behind, ſuch maſter ſhall [illegible] months impriſonment.

De re propria.

§ X. Aliquando etiam ſuæ rei furtum quis committit, veluti ſi debitor rem, quam creditori pignoris cauſa dedit, ſubtraxerit.

§ 10. *A man may alſo poſſibly commit a theft even of his own property, as when a debtor hath taken away any particular thing, which he had left in pledge with his creditor.*

Qui tenentur furti. De eo cujus ope, conſilio, furtum factum eſt.

§ XI. Interdum quoque furti tenetur, qui ipſe furtum non fecit: qualis eſt is, cujus ope & conſilio furtum factum eſt. In quo numero est, qui tibi nummos excussit, ut alius eos raperet; aut tibi obstiterit, ut alius rem tuam exciperet; aut oves tuas, vel boves fugaverit, ut alius eas acciperet. Et hoc veteres scripserunt de eo, qui panno rubro fugavit armentum. Sed, si quid eorum per lasciviam, & non data opera, ut furtum admitteretur, factum est, in factum actio dari debet. At ubi ope Mævii Titius furtum fecerit, ambo furti tenentur. Ope & consilio ejus quoque furtum admitti videtur, qui scalas forte fenestris supponit, aut ipsas fenestras vel ostium effringit, ut alius furtum faceret; quive ferramenta ad effringendum, aut scalas, ut fenestris supponerentur, commodaverit, sciens, cujus rei gratia commodaverit. Certe qui nullam opem ad furtum faciendum adhibuit, sed tantum consilium dedit, atque hortatus est ad furtum faciendum, non tenetur furti.

§ 11. *An action of theft will, in some cases, lie against persons, who did not actually commit the theft it will lie, for example, against those, by whose aid and advice the theft was commited, and whoever strikes money out of your hand, to the intent that another may pick it up, or whoever so obstructs you, as to give an opportunity to his accomplice to take your sheep, oxen, or any part of your property, must be reckoned in the number of aiders and advisers. The antient lawyers also included him in this number, who frightened away a herd from its pasture with a red cloth. But, if a man should do any of these acts wantonly, and without an intention of commiting theft, then an action can lie only* in factum, *i e. upon the case, or the fact done. but when* Titius *commits theft by the aid of* Mævius, *they are both subject to an action of theft Theft seems to be commited both by aid and advice, when a man puts a ladder to a window, or breaks open a door or window, to the intent, that another may commit theft; or when one man lends another iron bars, or ladders, knowing the bad purposes, to which they are to be applied. but it is certain, that he, who hath afforded no actual assistence, but hath only given his council by advising the crime, is not liable to an action of theft.*

Non tenetur furti] By the law of *England* a man, who only advises another to commit grand larciny, is an accessary before the fact, but, in petit larciny, there can be no accessary, for altho' petit larciny is felony, yet the smallness of the offense, inasmuch as it is not capital, excludeth accessaries both before and after. *Hal pl cor vol* 1 616

De his qui sunt in potestate. Et de ope ac consilio extranei.

§ XII Hi, qui in parentum vel dominorum potestate sunt, si rem eis surripiunt, furtum quidem faciunt, & res in furtivam causam cadit, nec ob id ab ullo usucapi potest, antequam in domini potestatem revertitur: sed furti actio non nascitur, quia nec ex ulla causa potest inter eos actio nasci. Si vero ope & consilio alterius furtum factum fuerit, quia utique furtum committitur, convenienter ille furti tenetur: quia verum est, ope et consilio ejus furtum factum esse.

§ 12 *When persons under the power of parents or masters take any thing surreptitiously from such parents or masters, a theft is committed, and the thing is looked upon as stolen, so that it cannot be prescribed to by any one, until it hath first returned into the power of the proprietor, and yet an action of theft will not lie, for between parents and their children, or masters and slaves, no action can arise. But*

if a

if the fact was done by the aid and advice of any other, inasmuch as a theft is commited, an action of theft will lie against the aider.

Sed furti actio non nascitur.] No action was allowed in this case on account of the power, which parents and masters had over their children and slaves by the *Roman* law; *servi & filii nostri furtum quidem nobis faciunt, ipsi autem furti non tenentur: neque enim, qui potest in furem statuere, necesse habet adversus furem litigare; idcirco nec actio ei a veteribus prodita est.* ff. 47 t. 2 l. 17. Ulpian.

Quibus datur actio furti.

§ XIII. Furti autem actio ei competit, cujus interest rem salvam esse, licet dominus non sit. Itaque nec domino aliter competit, quam si ejus intersit, rem non perire.

§ 13. *An action of theft may be brought by any man, who has an interest in the safety of the thing stolen, altho he is not the proprietor of it: and the proprietor himself can have no action, unless he has an interest.*

Cujus interest rem salvam] By the law of *England* every person is deemed to have a sufficient interest to prosecute another for the commission of a public crime, such as treason, robbery, theft, &c by an indictment, which is defined to be a brief narrative of an offense, commited by any person, who ought to be punished for the good of the public, and it is therefore said to be a prosecution at the suit of the king, for which reason the party, who prosecutes, is always admited as a good witness to prove the fact

And, tho' an indictment for theft should be of the goods of an unknown person, it would yet be good, for otherwise, in many cases, felons would escape unpunished *Hist pl cor.* 512. *Bacon's abridgment* indictment.

De pignore surrepto creditori.

§ XIV Unde constat creditorem de pignore surrepto furti actione agere posse, etiamsi idoneum debitorem habeat: quia expedit ei pignori potius incumbere, quam in personam agere: adeo quidem ut, quamvis ipse debitor eam rem surripuerit, nihilominus creditori competat actio furti.

§ 14. *From hence it follows, that a creditor may bring an action of theft, on account of a pledge stolen, altho' his debtor is solvent; because it may be more expedient for him to rely upon his pledge, than to bring an action against the person of his debtor, and, altho' the debtor himself should have been the taker of the pledge, yet an action of theft will lie against him*

De re fulloni, vel sarcinatori, vel bonæ fidei emptori, surrepta.

§ XV. Item si fullo polienda curandave, aut sarcinator sarcienda, vestimenta mercede certa constituta acceperit, eaque furto amiserit, ipse furti habet actionem, non dominus, quia domini nihil interest, eam rem non perire; cum judicio locati à fullone, aut sarcinatore, rem suam persequi possit. Sed et bonæ fidei emptori surreptare, quam emerit, quamvis dominus non sit, omnino competit furti actio, quemadmodum & creditori. Fulloni vero & sarcinatori non aliter furti actionem competere placuit, quam si solvendo fuerint, hoc est, si domino rei æstimationem solvere possint. Nam si solvendo non sint, tunc, quia ab eis suum consequi non possit, ipsi domino furti competit

actio:

actio: quia hoc casu ipsius interest, rem salvam esse. Idem est, etsi in parte solvendo fuerit fullo aut sarcinator.

§ 15 *If a fuller receives cloaths to clean, and they are afterwards stolen from him, the fuller may bring an action of theft, but not the owner; for the owner is reputed to have no interest in their safety, because he has a right of action, called* locati, *against the fuller. But, if a thing is stolen from a* bona fide *purchaser, he is intituled, like a creditor, to an action of theft, altho' he is not the proprietor. But an action of theft is not maintainable by the fuller, or any tradesman in similar circumstances, unless he is solvent, that is, unless he is able to pay the owner the full value of the thing lost; for, if the fuller is insolvent, then the owner, who cannot recover from the fuller, is allowed to bring an action of theft, having in this case an interest. And note, that whoever is unable to pay the whole of what is due, such person is esteemed insolvent, let the deficiency be ever so small.*

De re commodata.

XVI. Quæ de fullone et sarcinatore diximus, eadem et ad eum, cui commodata res est, transferenda, veteres existimabant. Nam ut ille fullo, mercedem accipiendo, custodiam præstat, ita is quoque, qui commodatum utendi causa accepit, similiter necesse habet custodiam præstare. Sed nostra providentia etiam hoc in nostris decisionibus emendavit, ut in domini voluntate sit, sive commodati actionem adversus eum, qui rem commodatam accepit, movere desiderat, sive furti adversus eum, qui rem surripuit, et, alterutra earum electa, dominum non posse ex pœnitentia ad alteram venire actionem, sed, siquidem furem elegerit, illum, qui rem utendam accepit, penitus liberari. sin autem commodator veniat adversus eum, qui rem utendam accepit, ipsi quidem nullo modo competere posse adversus furem furti actionem: eum autem, qui pro re commodata convenitur, posse adversus furem furti habere actionem: ita tamen, si dominus, sciens rem esse surreptam, adversus eum, cui res commodata fuerit, pervenit. Sin autem nescius et dubitans, rem esse surreptam, apud eum commodati actionem instituerit: postea autem, re comperta, voluerit remittere quidem commodati actionem, ad furti autem actionem pervenire, tunc licentia ei concedatur et adversus furem venire, obstaculo nullo ei opponendo: quoniam incertus constitutus movit adversus eum, qui rem utendam accepit, commodati actionem; nisi domino ab eo satisfactum fuerit: tunc etenim omnimodo furem a domino quidem furti actione liberari; suppositum autem esse ei, qui pro re sibi commodata domino satisfecit. cum manifestissimum sit, etiamsi ab initio dominus actionem commodati instituerit, ignarus rem esse surreptam, postea autem, hoc ei cognito, adversus furem transierit, omnimodo liberari eum, qui rem commodatam acceperit, quemcunque causæ exitum dominus adversus furem habuerit. eadem definitione obtinente, sive in parte, sive in solidum solvendo sit is, qui rem commodatam acceperit.

§ 16

§ 16. *The antients were of opinion, that what we have said of a fuller is equally applicable to him, to whom something is lent. For as the fuller, by agreeing for a certain price, is obliged to make good the cloathes commited to his custody, so is he also, who receives a loan for the sake of using it, under the like necessity of preserving it. But we have amended the law in this point by our decisions, so that it is now at the will of the owner either to bring an action of theft against the thief, or an action, on account of the thing lent, against the borrower. But, if the owner once makes an election of the one, he can never afterwards have recourse to the other; and, if he chuses to prosecute the thief, the borrower is altogether free from any action; and if the owner, or lender, brings a suit against the borrower, he can by no means bring an action against the thief. But the borrower, who is convened on account of the thing lent, may bring an action of theft against the thief, if the owner, who convened him, was apprized, that the thing was stolen; but if the owner, either not knowing or doubting of the theft, institutes an action of loan against the borrower, and afterwards upon information is willing to withdraw it, and recur to an action of theft, he shall have liberty, in consideration of his incertainty, to prosecute the thief without obstacle, if the borrower has not satisfied his demand; but, if the borrower has given the owner satisfaction, then the thief is freed from any action of theft, which can be brought by the owner, but he is nevertheless subject to the prosecution of the borrower, who hath satisfied the owner. But it is most manifest, that, if the owner of any particular thing, not knowing, that it is stolen, should at first institute an action of loan against the borrower, but should afterwards, upon better information, chuse to persue the thief by an action of theft, the borrower is secure, whatever may be the issue of the cause brought against the thief. And this obtains as law, whether the borrower is able to answer the whole, or a part only, of the value of the thing.*

De re deposita.

§ XVII. Sed is, apud quem res deposita est, custodiam non præstat, sed tantum in eo obnoxius est, si quid ipse dolo malo fecerit. qua de causa, si res ei surrepta fuerit, quia restituendæ ejus rei, nomine depositi, non tenetur, nec ob id ejus interest rem salvam esse, furti agere non potest: sed furti actio domino competit.

§ 17. *A depositary is not obliged to make good the thing deposited, unless he is himself guilty of some fraud, or malefeazance: and therefore, as a depositary is not obliged to make restitution, when the deposit is stolen, and as he has consequently no interest in the conservation of the deposit, he is not allowed to bring an action of theft, which in this case can only be maintained by the owner.*

An impubes furti teneatur.

§ XVIII. In summa sciendum est, quæsitum esse, an impubes rem alienam amovendo furtum faciat? Et placuit, quia furtum ex affectu furandi consistit, ita demum obligari eo crimine impuberem, si proximus pubertati sit, et ob id intelligat se delinquere.

§ 18. *It hath been a question, whether a [illegible] carry the property of another, can be guilty of theft? [illegible] that, inasmuch as theft consists in the intention of defrauding, a person under puberty*

may

may be charged with theft, if he is near the age of puberty, and can be proved to have been sensible, that what he did was criminal.

Quæsitum est an impubes] It is clear, that, in *England*, a minor above fourteen is subject to capital punishment, as well as persons of full age, for it is a presumption of law, that minors after fourteen are *doli capaces*, and able to discern between good and evil But an infant, under fourteen, and above twelve, is not presumed to be capable of fraud, yet, if it appears to the court, that he could discern between good and evil at the time of the offense committed, he may be convicted, and undergo judgement and execution of death, tho' he hath not completed his fourteenth year, but it is at the discretion of the judge to reprieve him before or after judgement, in order to obtain the king's pardon

And farther, if an infant, even under twelve, and above seven, commits felony, tho' he is *prima facie* to be judged not guilty, because he is supposed not sensible of the nature of the crime; yet, if in this case it should appear by pregnant evidence and circumstances, that he had discernment to judge between good and evil, judgement of death may be given against him *Hist. pl cor.* 26. 27. *vol.* 1.

Quid veniat in hanc actionem: et de affinibus actionibus.

§ XIX. Furti actio, sive dupli, sive quadrupli, tantum ad pœnæ persecutionem pertinet. Nam ipsius rei persecutionem extrinsecus habet dominus, quam aut vindicando aut condicendo potest auferre. Sed rei vindicatio quidem adversus possessorem est, sive fur ipse possidet, sive alius quilibet. Condictio autem adversus furem ipsum, hæredemve ejus, licet non possideat, competit.

§ 19. *An action of theft can only be brought for the penalty, whether double or quadruple: for the owner of the thing stolen may recover the thing itself either by vindication or condiction. An action of vindication may be brought against him, who hath possession, whether he is the thief or any other; but condiction is maintainable only against the thief himself, or his heir; yet it will lie against either of them, whether he is or is not in possession of the thing stolen.*

TITULUS SECUNDUS.

De vi bonorum raptorum.

D. xlvii. T. 8. C. ix. T. 33.

Origo hujus actionis, et quid in eam veniat.

QUI vi res alienas rapit, tenetur quidem etiam furti; (quis enim magis alienam rem, invito domino, contrectat, quam qui vi rapit? ideoque recte dictum est, eum improbum furem esse,) sed tamen propriam actionem ejus delicti nomine prætor introduxit, quæ appellatur *vi bonorum raptorum*; et est intra annum quadrupli, post annum simpli; quæ actio utilis est, etiamsi quis unam rem, licet minimam, rapuerit. Quadruplum autem non totum pœna est, sicut in actione furti manifesti

festi diximus; sed in quadruplo inest et rei persecutio; ut pœna tripli sit, sive comprehendatur raptor in ipso delicto, sive non. Ridiculum enim esset, levioris conditionis esse eum, qui vi rapit, quam qui clam amovet.

He, who takes the property of another by force, is liable to an action of theft; [for who can be said to take the property of another more against his will, than he, who takes it by force? and it hath therefore been rightly observed, that such a thief is one of the worst kind] but the prætor hath nevertheless introduced a peculiar action in this case, called vi bonorum raptorum; *which, if brought within a year after the robbery, inforces the payment of the quadruple value of the thing taken; but, if it is brought after the expiration of a year, then the single value only is claimable, and this action is of such a nature, that it may be brought for any single thing, tho' it was of the least value imaginable, if it was taken by force. But the whole quadruple value is not exacted merely for the penalty, as in an action of* manifest theft; *for, in this quadruple value, the thing itself is included, so that, strictly, the penalty is only threefold; but then it is inflicted without distinguishing whether the robber was, or was not taken in the actual commission of the fact. For it would be ridiculous, that a robber, who uses force, should be in a better condition, than he, who is only guilty of a clandestine theft.*

Licet minimam rapuerit] Robbery is defined, by the *English* lawyers, to be a felonious and violent taking of money or goods from the person of another, putting him in fear, let the value of the thing, or things taken, be what it will, above or under one shilling *Hist of the pleas of the crown*, p 532

Adversus quos datur.

§ I. Ita tamen competit hæc actio, si dolo malo quis rapuerit: nam, qui aliquo errore ductus, rem suam esse existimans, et imprudens juris, eo animo rapuerit, quasi domino liceat etiam per vim rem suam auferre à possessoribus, absolvi debet: cui scilicet conveniens est, nec furti teneri eum, qui eodem hoc animo rapuit. Sed, ne, dum talia excogitantur, inveniatur via, per quam raptores impunè suam exerceant avaritiam, melius divalibus constitutionibus pro hac parte prospectum est, ut nemini liceat vi rapere vel rem mobilem, vel se moventem, licet suam eandem rem existimet. Sed, si quis contra statuta principum fecerit, rei quidem suæ dominio cadere: sin autem aliena res sit, post restitutionem ejus, etiam æstimationem ejusdem rei præstare. Quod non solum in mobilibus rebus, quæ rapi possunt, constitutiones obtinere censuerunt, sed etiam in invasionibus, quæ circa res soli fiunt: ut, ex hac causa, ab omni rapina homines abstineant.

§ 1. *The action* de vi bonorum raptorum *is only maintainable, when there is fraud used, as well as force: for, if a man, being ignorant of the law and erroneously thinking any particular thing to be his own, should take it away by force from the possessor, upon a full persuasion, that he, as proprietor, could justify such a proceeding, he ought to be acquitted upon this action. neither is he subject, under the before-mentioned circumstances, to an action of theft. But, lest robbers should from hence find out a way of practising their villanies with impunity, it is provided by the imperial constitu-*

tions,

tions, that no man shall be at liberty to take by force any moveable thing, or living creature, out of the possession of another, altho' he believes it to be his own, and that, whoever offends, by forcibly seizing his property, shall forfeit it, and that, whoever takes the property of another, imagining it to be his own, shall be obliged not only to restore the thing itself, but also to pay the value of it as a penalty. And the emperors have thought proper, that this should obtain, not only in regard to things moveable and moving, which may be carried away, but also in regard to invasions, or forcible entries, made upon things immoveable, as lands or houses, to the intent, that mankind may be detered from commiting any species of rapin.

Sit ab omni rapina] *vid. ff.* 4. *t.* 2. *l.* 13. *cod.* 8. *t.* 4. *l.* 7. It seems, that, by the common law of *England*, a man disseised of lands or tenements, is permited to regain the possession by force: but this indulgence having been found by experience to be prejudicial to the public peace, by giving an opportunity to powerful men, under the pretence of feigned titles, forcibly to eject their weaker neighbours, and to retain their wrongful possessions, it hath been thought necessary to restrain all persons, by many severe acts of parliament, from the use of such violent methods of doing themselves justice. *Vid.* 5 *Ric.* 2. *stat.* 1. *cap.* 8. 15 *Ric.* 2. *cap.* 2. 8 *Hen.* 6. *cap.* 9. 31 *Eliz. cap.* 11. 21 *Jac.* 1. *cap.* 15. *Hawk. pleas of the crown b.* 1. *chap.* 64.

Quibus datur.

§ II. Sane in hac actione non utique expectatur rem in bonis actoris esse: nam, sive in bonis sit, sive non, si tamen ex bonis sit, locum hæc actio habebit. Quare sive locata, sive commodata, sive etiam pignorata, sive deposita, sit res apud Titium sic, ut intersit ejus, eam rem per vim non auferri, (veluti si in deposita re culpam quoque promisit,) sive bona fide possideat, sive usumfructum quis habeat in ea, vel quid aliud juris, ut intersit ejus non rapi, dicendum est, ei competere hanc actionem, non ut dominium accipiat, sed illud solum, quod ex bonis ejus, qui rapinam passus est, id est, quod ex substantia ejus ablatum esse proponatur. Et generaliter dicendum est, ex quibus causis furti actio competit in re clam facta, ex iisdem causis omnes hanc habere actionem.

§ 2. *In this action, it is not considered, whether the thing, taken by force, is, or is not, the property of the complainant; for, if he has an interest in it, the action is maintainable: and therefore, if a thing is let, lent, or pledged to* Titius, *or deposited with him, so that he becomes interested in the preservation of it, as he may be, even in the case of a deposit, if he hath promised to be answerable for its safe custody; or, if Titius is a* bona fide *possessor, or intituled to the usufruct, or has any other right, which gives him an interest, he may then bring this action, not for the recovery of the absolute property, but of that only, to which his interest extends. And we may in general affirm, that the same causes, which intitule a man to institute an action of theft, when any thing hath been privately stolen from him, will also intitule him to bring the action* vi bonorum raptorum, *when force has been used.*

TITULUS

TITULUS TERTIUS.

De lege Aquilia.

D. ix. T. 2. C. iii. T. 35.

Summa. Caput primum.

DAMNI injuriæ actio constituitur per legem Aquiliam; cujus primo capite cautum est, ut, si quis alienum hominem, alienamve quadrupedem, quæ pecudum numero sit, injuria occiderit, quanti ea res in eo anno plurimi fuerit, tantum domino dare damnetur.

The action for injurious damage is given by the law Aquilia; *which enacts, in the first chapter, that, if any man injuriously kills the slave, or four-footed beast of another, which may be reckoned in the number of his cattle, he shall be condemned to pay the owner the greatest price, which the slave or beast might have been sold for, at any time within a year, computing backward from the day, when the wound was given.*

Damni injuria actio] Almost all the suits, which may be instituted according to the civil law, under the law *Aquilia*, may be commenced in *England* by means of an action of trespass upon the case. *Cow. inst. h. t.* The law *Aquilia* is supposed to have been *a plebiscite*, made by *Aquilius*, tribune of the people, *ann. U. C.* 572. *Vid. Hein. Syntag. lib.* 4. *t.* 3.

Injuria occiderit] It is enacted by 23 *Car.* 2. *cap.* 7. that, if any person shall maliciously maim or hurt any cattle, or destroy any plantation of trees, or throw down inclosures, he shall forfeit treble damages in an action of trespass.

In eo anno] see the ninth section of the third title of this book.

De quadrupede, quæ pecudum numero est.

§ I. Quod autem non præcise de quadrupede, sed de ea tantum, quæ pecudum numero est, cavetur, eo pertinet, ut neque de feris bestiis, neque de canibus, cautum esse intelligamus, sed de iis tantum, quæ gregatim proprie pasci dicuntur, quales sunt equi, muli, asini, oves, boves, capræ. De suibus quoque idem placuit. Nam et sues quoque pecudum appellatione continentur: quia et hi gregatim pascuntur. Sic denique et Homerus in Odyssea ait, (sicut Ælius Marcianus in suis institutionibus refert.)

Δηεις τονγε συεσσι παρημενον, αἱ δε νεμονται
Παρ Κορακος πετρῃ, επι τε κρηνῃ Ἀρεθουσῃ.

Hoc est,

Apud eas subus, quorum grex magnus in agris
Pascitur, ad Coracis saxum, fontemque Arethusam.

§ I. *As the law does not speak of four-footed beasts in general, but of those only, which may be reckoned cattle, we may collect, that wild beasts and dogs do not come within the intention of the law, which can be understood to include only those animals, which feed in herds, as horses, mules, asses, sheep, oxen, goats, &c.—It hath also been determined*

determined, that swine are comprized under the term cattle, because they feed in herds; and this Homer *testifies in the Odyssy, for which he is quoted by* Ælius Marcian *in his institutes:*— you will find him taking care of the swine, which feed in herds at the *Corasian* rock, *&c. Odys. b.* 13.

Ut neque de feris bestiis] The law of *England* allows an action of trespass to be brought on account of mastiffs, spaniels, grayhounds, and also on account of some things wild by nature, if they are reclaimed by art and industry, as bears, foxes, ferrets, &c. or their whelps *Hale's hist pl cor* 5 12 And, when beasts, wild by nature, are fit for food, and reduced to tameness, it is agreed, that whoever takes any of these from the possessor commits theft, and it appears to be the better opinion, that it is felony to take wild pidgeons from a dove-house, or hares, or deer, in an house, or even a park, inclosed in such a manner, that the owner may take them whenever he pleases, without any danger of their escaping; in which cases, they are as much in his power as fish in a pond, or young pidgeons, or hawks in a nest, in taking of which it is agreed, that felony may be committed *Hawk. pl. of the cr b* 1 *ch.* 34.

De injuria.

§ II. Injuria autem occidere intelligitur, qui nullo jure occidit. Itaque, qui latronem insidiatorem occidit, non tenetur: utique si aliter periculum effugere non potest.

§ 2. *A man, who kills another without having a right or authority so to do, is understood to kill him injuriously: but, when there is a right, there can be no punishment, and therefore he is not subject to the law, who kills a robber, or an assassin, if there was no other way of avoiding the danger threatened.*

Itaque qui latronem] At common law, if a thief had assaulted a man, with an intention to rob him, and he had killed the assaulter, it had been *se defendendo*, but yet he would, according to some opinions, have forfeited his goods. 11 *Co rep* 82 *b* tho' other books hold the contrary 26 *Assiz* 32

But it is now provided by 24 *H* 8 *c.* 10 " that, if any person is indicted, or appealed for " the death of any evil-disposed persons at- " tempting to murder, rob, or break mansion- " houses, the person so indicted or appealed, " and by verdict so found, shall not forfeit any " lands or goods, but shall be thereof acquited, " in like manner as if he had been acquited of " the death of the said evil-disposed persons "

But this statute extends not to indemnify the killing a felon, when the felony is not accompanied with force; for it speaks of robbery, therefore the killing a man, who only attempts to pick a pocket, is not within the act, because there can, in such a case, be no necessity to kill. *Hale's hist of the pl of the crown vol* 1 *p* 488

De casu, dolo, et culpa.

§ III. Ac ne is quidem hac lege tenetur, qui casu occidit, si modo culpa ejus nulla inveniatur. Nam alioqui non minus ex dolo, quam ex culpa, quisque hac lege tenetur.

§ 3 *Neither is he subject to the* Aquilian *law, who hath killed another by accident; if no fault can be found in him But the law does not punish a man less for damage, done by his fault or negligence, than for damage done by fraud or design.*

De jaculatione.

§ IV. Itaque, si quis, dum jaculis ludit vel exercitatur, transeuntem servum tuum trajecerit, distinguitur. Nam, si id à milite in eo campo, ubi solitum est exercitari, admissum est, nulla culpa ejus intelligitur, si alius tale quid admiserit, culpæ reus est. Idem juris est de milite, si in in alio loco, quam qui ad exercitandum militibus destinatus est, id admiserit.

§ 4. *But, if a man, by throwing a javelin, for his diversion or exercise, happens to kill a slave, who is passing, we must, in this case, make a distinction: for, if the slave is killed by a soldier, whilest he is exercising in a place appointed for that purpose, the soldier is guilty of no fault; but if any other person should accidentally kill a slave by throwing a javelin, he is guilty of a fault; and even, if a soldier should kill a slave accidentally by throwing a javelin in any other place, than that appointed for soldiers to exercise in, he also is guilty of a fault.*

De putatione.

§ V. Item si putator, ex arbore ramo dejecto, servum tuum transeuntem occiderit, si prope viam publicam aut vicinalem id factum est, neque proclamavit, ut casus evitari posset, culpæ reus est; sed, si proclamavit, nec ille curavit præcavere, extra culpam est putator. Æque extra culpam esse intelligitur, si seorsum à via forte, vel in medio fundo cædebat, licet not proclamavit: quia in eo loco nulli extraneo jus fuerat versandi.

§ 5. *If a man is lopping a tree, and happens to kill a slave, who is passing, the lopper is guilty of a fault, if he worked near a public road, or in a way leading to a village, without giving a proper warning by proclamation; but, if he made due proclamation, and the other did not take care of himself, the lopper is exempt from fault and he is equally exempt from fault, altho' he did not make proclamation, if he worked apart from the high road, or in the middle of a field; for a stranger has no right of passage thro' such places.*

De curatione relicta.

§ VI. Præterea, si medicus, qui servum tuum secuit, dereliquerit curationem ejus, et ob id mortuus fuerit servus, culpæ reus erit.

Also, if a physician, or chirurgeon, who has made an incision in the body of a slave, should afterwards neglect or forsake the cure, by which the death of the slave is occasioned, he is guilty of a fault.

De imperitia medici.

§ VII. Imperitia quoque culpæ adnumeratur; veluti si medicus ideo servum tuum occiderit, quia male eum secuerit, aut perperam ei medicamentum dederit.

§ 7. *The want of skill in a profession is also regarded as a fault; thus a physician, for instance, is culpable, and of course subject to an action, who occasions the death of a slave by an unskillful incision, or a rash administration of medicines.*

De imperitia et infirmitate mulionis, aut equo vecti.

§ VIII. Impetu quoque mularum, quas mulio propter imperitiam retinere non potuit, si servus tuus oppressus fuerit, culpæ reus est mulio.

lio. Sed et, si propter infirmitatem eas retinere non potuerit, cum alius firmior eas retinere potuisset, æque culpæ tenetur. Eadem placuerunt de eo quoque, qui cum equo veheretur, impetum ejus, aut propter infirmitatem, aut propter imperitiam suam, retinere non potuerit.

§ 8. *If a mule-driver, by reason of unskilfulness, is unable to manage his mules, and a slave is run over by them, the mule-driver is in fault; and, if he wants strength to rein them in, when another man is able to do it, he is then equally culpable: and the same may be said of a rider, who, thro' want either of strength or skill, is not able to manage his horse.*

Quanti damnum æstimetur, et de hæredibus.

§ IX. His autem verbis legis, *quanti id eo in anno plurimi fuerit*, illa sententia exprimitur, ut si quis hominem tuum, qui hodie claudus, aut mancus, aut luscus erit, occiderit, qui in eo anno integer aut pretiosus fuerit, non tanti teneatur, quanti hodie erit, sed quanti in eo anno plurimi fuerit: qua ratione creditum est pœnalem esse hujus legis actionem, quia non solum tanti quisque obligatur, quantum damni dederit, sed aliquando longe pluris. Ideoque constat, in hæredem eam actionem non transire, quæ transitura fuisset, si ultra damnum nunquam lis æstimaretur.

§ 9. *These words of the law* Aquilia, let him, who kills a slave, or beast of another, forfeit the greatest price, which either could have been sold for in that year, *are to be understood in the following sense, as thus, if* Titius *accidentally kills a slave, who was then lame, or wanted a limb, or an eye, but had been within the space of a year perfect in all his parts, and very valuable, then* Titius *shall be obliged to pay, not what the slave was worth on the day, when he was killed, but what he was worth at any time within a year preceding his death, when he was in the fullest vigor. An action therefore, upon the law* Aquilia, *has always been regarded as penal; for it obliges a man to pay not only the full value of the damage done, but often much more than the full value, and of consequence can by no means pass against the heir of the offender but it might legally have been transfered against the heir, if the condemnation had never exceeded the quantum of the damage.*

Quid æstimatur.

§ X. Illud non ex verbis legis, sed ex interpretatione, placuit, non solum perempti corporis æstimationem habendam esse secundum ea, quæ diximus, sed, eo amplius, quicquid præterea, perempto eo corpore, damni nobis illatum fuerit, veluti si servum tuum hæredem ab aliquo institutum ante quis occiderit, quam is jussu tuo hæreditatem adierit: nam hæreditatis quoque amissæ rationem esse habendam constat. Item, si ex pari mularum unam, vel ex quadrigis equorum unum, quis occiderit, vel ex comœdis unus servus occisus fuerit, non solum occisi fit æstimatio,

æſtimatio, ſed eo amplius id quoque computatur, quanti depretiati ſunt, qui ſuperſunt.

§ 10. *It hath prevailed by conſtruction, tho' not by virtue of the expreſs words of the law, that not only the value of a ſlave is to be computed, as we have already mentioned, but that an eſtimation muſt be made of whatever farther damage is occaſioned by his death, as if* Titius, *for example, ſhould kill a ſlave at the time, when he was inſtituted an heir, and before he had actually entered upon the heirſhip at the command of his maſter; for, in this caſe, the loſs of the inheritance muſt be brought into the computation. Alſo if an horſe, or mule is killed, by which a pair, or ſet, is broken, or if a ſlave is ſlain, who made one of a company of comedians, an eſtimation muſt be made not only according to the value of that ſlave or animal, but according to the value of thoſe, which remain, for, if they are damaged, the diminution of their value is alſo taken into the account.*

De concurſu hujus actionis et capitalis.

§ XI. Liberum autem eſt ei, cujus ſervus occiſus fuerit, et ex judicio privato legis Aquiliæ damnum perſequi, et capitalis criminis eum reum facere.

§ 11. *The maſter of a ſlave, who is killed, is at liberty to ſue for damages by a private action, founded upon the law* Aquilia, *and at the ſame time to proſecute the offender publicly, for a capital crime.*

Liberum autem eſt ei] It ſeems to be the better opinion, that a perſon in *England*, who is guilty of felony, and pardoned, or burned in the hand, may be proceeded againſt in a civil action at the ſuit of the party injured, for, when the offender hath been pardoned, or proſecuted, there can be no inconvenience in allowing the action, and the previous criminal proſecution ought to be no bar to it; for why ſhould not the criminal anſwer in damages to the party injured, as well as be made an example for the ſake of the public, whom he hath offended? *Bacon's abridgment, vol.* 1. *p.* 64.

But no action can be brought, whileſt the felon is under indictment for the crime, for, if that were allowed, it might hinder an exemplary puniſhment. *Styl.* 346.

Caput ſecundum.

§ XII. Caput ſecundum legis Aquiliæ in uſu non eſt.

§ 12. *The ſecond chapter of the law* Aquilia *is not in uſe.*

Caput tertium, quod damnum vindicatur.

§ XIII. Capite tertio de omni cætero damno cavetur, itaque, ſi quis ſervum, vel eam quadrupedem, quæ in pecudum numero eſt, vulneraverit, ſive eam quadrupedem, quæ in pecudum numero non eſt, veluti canem, aut feram beſtiam, vulneraverit aut occiderit, hoc capite actio conſtituitur. In cæteris quoque omnibus animalibus, item in omnibus rebus, quæ anima carent, damnum per injuriam datum hac parte vindicatur. Si quid enim uſtum, aut ruptum, aut fractum fuerit, actio ex hoc capite conſtituitur, quanquam poterat ſola rupti appellatio in omnes iſtas cauſas ſufficere: ruptum enim intelligitur, quod quoquo modo corruptum eſt, unde non ſolum fracta, aut uſta, ſed

etiam

etiam ſciſſa, et colliſa, et effuſa, et quoquo modo perempta atque deteriora facta, hoc verbo continentur. Denique reſponſum eſt, ſi quis in alienum vinum aut oleum id miſcuerit, quo naturalis bonitas vini aut olei corrumperetur, ex hac parte legis Aquiliæ eum teneri.

§ 13. *By the third chapter of this law, a remedy is given for every other kind of damage; and therefore, if a man wounds a ſlave, or four-footed animal, which is ranked among cattle, or which is not ranked among cattle, as a dog or wild beaſt, an action will lie againſt him by virtue of this third part of the law. A reparation may alſo be obtained, under this chapter, for all damage injuriouſly done to animals in general, or to things inanimate, and the ſame chapter appoints an action for the recovery of the value of whatever is burned, ſpoiled, or broken; but the term* ruptum *would alone be ſufficient in any of theſe caſes; for in whatever manner a thing is damaged, or corrupted, it is underſtood to be* ruptum, *or ſpoiled, in ſome degree; ſo that whenever a thing is broken, burned, or even torn, bruiſed, ſpilled, or in any manner made worſe, it may be ſaid to be* ruptum. *It hath alſo been determined, that, if a man intermixes any thing, with the wine or oil of another, ſo as to corrupt or impair it's natural goodneſs, he is liable to an action founded upon this chapter of the law* Aquilia.

De dolo et culpa.

§ XIV. Illud palam eſt, ſicut ex primo capite demum quiſque tenetur, ſi dolo aut culpa ejus homo aut quadrupes occiſus occiſave fuerit, ita ex hoc capite, de dolo aut culpa, et de cætero damno, quemque teneri: ex hoc tamen capite, non quanti in eo anno, ſed quanti in diebus triginta proximis res fuerit, obligatur is, qui damnum dederit.

§ 14. *It is evident, that the firſt part or chapter of the law ſubjects every man to an action, who kills the ſlave or beaſt of another, and that the third part gives a remedy for any other damage, occaſioned either by a fraud or a fault. But by this third chapter the perſon, who did the damage, is not obliged to pay the higheſt price, which the thing damaged might have been ſold for, at any time within the year, but only the value of it at any time within thirty days, previous to the damage.*

Quanti damnum æſtimetur.

§ XV. Ac nec *plurimi* quidem verbum adjicitur. Sed Sabino recte placuit, perinde habendam æſtimationem, ac ſi etiam hac parte *plurimi* verbum adjectum fuiſſet; nam plebem Romanam, quæ, Aquilio tribuno rogante, hanc legem tulit, contentam fuiſſe, quod prima parte eo verbo uſa eſſet.

§ 15 *But it is not ſaid in the third part of the law, that the* higheſt *value of the thing damaged ſhall be recovered by action But, in the opinion of* Sabinus, *the valuation ought to be made, as if the word higheſt had not been omited, for, when* Aquilius, *the tribune, propoſed this law, the commonalty of* Rome *thought it ſufficient to inſert the word* higheſt *in the firſt chapter.*

De

De actione directa, utili, et in factum.

§ XVI. Cæterum placuit, ita demum directam ex hac lege actionem esse, si quis præcipue corpore suo damnum dederit. Ideoque in eum, qui alio modo damnum dederit, utiles actiones dari solent; veluti si quis hominem alienum, aut pecus, ita incluserit, ut fame necaretur: aut jumentum ita vehementer egerit, ut rumperetur: aut pecus in tantum exagitaverit, ut præcipitaretur: aut si quis alieno servo persuaserit, ut in arborem ascenderet, vel in puteum descenderet, et is ascendendo, vel descendendo, aut mortuus, aut aliqua parte corporis læsus fuerit; utilis actio in eum datur: sed, si quis alienum servum aut de ponte, aut de ripa, in flumen dejecerit, et is suffocatus fuerit, eo quod projecit, corpore suo damnum dedisse non difficulter intelligi potest: ideoque ipsa lege Aquilia tenetur. Sed, si non corpore damnum fuerit datum, neque corpus læsum fuerit, sed alio modo alicui damnum contigerit, cum non sufficiat neque directa, neque utilis legis Aquiliæ actio, placuit, eum, qui obnoxius fuerit, in factum actione teneri: veluti si quis misericordia ductus alienum servum compeditum solverit, ut fugeret.

§ 16. *It has been determined, that, if a man hath, with his own hand or body, done damage to another, a direct action will lie by virtue of this law. But when damage is done by any other means, as by imprisoning a slave, or impounding the cattle of another, till they die with hunger, by driving a beast of burden so vehemently as to spoil him, by chasing an herd of cattle, till they leap down a precipice, or by persuading a slave to climb a tree, or go down into a well, by which he is killed or maimed, then the action, called* utilis, *is given, by which reparation may be obtained. And note, that, if* Titius *thrusts the slave of another into the water from the top of a bridge or bank, and the slave is drowned, in consequence of the fall, it is plain that* Titius *occasioned this damage with his own hands, and he is therefore subject to a direct action. But if the damage received was not done by the hand or body of another, and is not corporal, so that neither a direct nor beneficial action can be brought by virtue of the* Aquilian *law, then in these circumstances an action upon the case, or fact, will lie against the causer of the damage. and therefore, if any man thro compassion should unchain the slave of another, and so promote his escape, a reparation may be obtained against him by an action upon the fact.*

Utiles actiones dari.] The actions, termed *utiles*, may, in general, be defined to be actions introduced by equity in all cases, where the strict law is deficient, and does not supply the necessary remedies.

Thus these beneficial, or equitable actions, called *utiles*, bear some similitude to those actions, which in *England* are called actions upon the case.

In factum actione.] It may be proper here to observe in general, that for every right, and every injury, done to a man in person, reputation, or property, the law of *England* allows a remedy, but this remedy must, in general, be taken according to the writs and settled actions prescribed by law, as debt upon contract, trespass on a manifest and open invasion, &c. but where the law has made no provision, or rather, where no general action could well be framed before-hand, the ways of injuring, and methods of deceiving, being so various, every person is allowed to bring a special action on his own case. *Bacon's abridg. vol.* 1. *p.* 44.

TITULUS

TITULUS QUARTUS.

De Injuriis.

D. xlvii. T. 10. C. ix. T. 35. et 36.

Verbum injuria quot modis accipitur.

GEneraliter injuria dicitur omne, quod non jure fit: specialiter, alias contumelia, quæ à contemnendo dicta est, quam Græci ὕβριν appellant: alias culpa, quam Græci ἀδίκημα dicunt, sicut in lege Aquilia damnum injuria datum accipitur: alias iniquitas et injustitia, quam Græci ἀνομίαν καὶ ἀδικίαν vocant: cum enim prætor vel judex non jure contra quem pronunciat, injuriam accepisse dicitur.

The Word Injuria *in a general sense denotes every act, which is unjust: but, when specially used, it is of the same import with* contumelia, *which takes it's derivation from* contemno, *and is in* greek *termed* ὕβρις. *sometimes it signifies a fault, called by the* greeks ἀδίκημα, *in which acceptation it is used in the law* Aquilia, *when damage, injuriously given, is spoken of: at other times it signifies iniquity or injustice, which the* greeks *call* ἀνομίαν *and* ἀδικίαν. *thus, when the prætor or judge pronounces sentence unjustly against any person, such person is said to have suffered an injury.*

Quibus modis injuria fit.

§ I. Injuria autem committitur, non solum cum quis pugno pulsatus, aut fustibus cæsus, vel etiam verberatus erit; sed et si cui convitium factum fuerit, sive cujus bona quasi debitoris, qui nihil debebat, possessa fuerint ab eo, qui intelligebat, nihil eum sibi debere: vel si quis ad infamiam alicujus libellum aut carmen (aut historiam) scripserit, composuerit, ediderit, dolove malo fecerit, quo quid eorum fieret. sive quis matremfamilias, aut prætextatum prætextatamve, adsectatus fuerit: sive cujus pudicitia attentata esse dicetur: et denique, aliis plurimis modis admitti injuriam, manifestum est.

§ I *An injury may be done not only by beating and wounding, but also by contumelious language, or by seizing the goods of a man, as if he were a debtor, when the person, who seized them, well knew, that nothing was due to him. It is also manifest, that an injury may be committed by writing a defamatory libel, poem, or history, or by maliciously causing another so to do, also by continually soliciting the chastity of a boy, girl, or woman of reputation; and by various other means, which are too numerous to be specified.*

Libellum aut carmen] A libel, according to the definition given of it in the law of *England*, is a malicious defamation, expressed either in words or writing, or by signs, pictures, &c. tending either to blacken the memory of one, who is dead, or the reputation of one, who is living. 5 *Co. rep. de libellis famosis*, p. 125.

By the *Roman* law the punishment of the author or publisher of an infamous libel, if it contained a capital crime, was [illegible]

But

But, if it brought no man's life into danger, and affected only reputation, the offender was rendered incapable of giving testimony, and of making a will *ff* 47 *t* 10 *l* 5 In *England* the punishment may be by fine, pillory, or whiping, when the offender is proceeded against by indictment, or information, but in a civil action the punishment sounds only in costs and damages. But as to mere words of defamation, they are at common law not actionable, except when they have been of real damage and injury to the person spoken against, for mere contumely is of but little consideration, and the ecclesiastical courts may be prohibited by the temporal courts from proceeding in a cause of defamation, when the suit is not wholly of a spiritual nature as for calling a man an heretic, schismatic, adulterer, fornicator, &c 4 *Co rep p* 20 *Palmer v. Thorpe*

Qui et per quos injuriam patiuntur. De parente et liberis, viro et uxore, socero et nuru.

§ II. Patitur autem quis injuriam non solum per semetipsum, sed etiam per liberos suos, quos in potestate habet, item per uxorem suam; id enim magis prævaluit. Itaque, si filiæ alicujus, quæ Titio nupta est, injuriam feceris, non solum filiæ nomine tecum injuriarum agi potest, sed etiam patris quoque et mariti nomine. Contra autem, si viro injuria facta sit, uxor injuriarum agere non potest. Defendi enim uxores à viris, non viros ab uxoribus, æquum est. Sed et socer nurus nomine, cujus vir in ejus potestate est, injuriarum agere potest.

§ 2. *A man may receive an injury not only in his own person, but in that of his children under his power, and also in the person of his wife, for this is now the more prevalent opinion, and therefore, if an injury is done to Seius's daughter, who is married to* Titius, *an action may be brought not only in the name of the daughter, but in the name either of her father or her husband, but, if the husband receives an injury, the wife is not allowed to institute a suit in his defense, for it is a maxim, that wives may be defended by their husbands, but not husbands by their wives And note, that a father-in-law may also commence a suit in the name of his son's wife, on account of an injury done to her, if her husband is under the power of his father*

De servo.

§ III. Servis autem ipsis quidem nulla injuria fieri intelligitur, sed domino per eos fieri videtur: non tamen iisdem modis, quibus etiam per liberos et uxores, sed ita, cum quid atrocius commissum fuerit et quod aperte ad contumeliam domini respicit; veluti si quis alienum servum atrociter verberaverit; et in hunc casum actio proponitur. At, si quis servo convitium fecerit, vel pugno eum percusserit, nulla in eum actio domino competit.

§ 3. *An injury is never understood to be done to a slave, but is reputed to be done to the master, thro' the person of his slave but what amounts to an injury in regard to a wife or child, does not amount to an injury, suffered thro' the person of a slave and therefore to constitute an injury, by means of the person of a slave, some considerable damage must be done to him, and something which openly affects his master, as if a stranger should beat the slave of another in a cruel manner for in this case an action would lie, but, if a man should only give ill language to a slave, or strike him with his fist, the master can bring no action upon that account.*

De servo communi.

§ IV. Si communi servo injuria facta sit, æquum est, non pro ea parte, qua dominus quisque est, æstimationem injuriæ fieri, sed ex dominorum persona, quia ipsis fit injuria.

§ 4. *If an injury is done to the common slave of many masters, the estimation of the injury received is not to be made according to their several proportions of property in the slave, but according to the quality of each master; for it is to them, to whom the injury is done.*

De servo fructuario.

§ V. Quod si ususfructus in servo Titii est, proprietas Mævii, magis Mævio injuria fieri intelligitur.

§ 5. *If* Titius *has the usufruct of a slave, and* Mævius *the property, then any injury, which is done to that slave, is understood to be done to* Mævius *the proprietor.*

De eo, qui bona fide servit.

§ VI Sed, si libero homini, qui tibi bona fide servit, injuria facta sit, nulla tibi actio dabitur, sed suo nomine is experiri poterit, nisi in contumeliam tuam pulsatus sit; tunc enim competit et tibi injuriarum actio. Idem ergo est et in servo alieno bona fide tibi serviente, ut toties admittatur injuriarum actio, quoties in tuam contumeliam injuria ei facta est.

§ 6 *But, if an injury is done to a free person, who is in the service of* Titius, Titius *can bring no action of injury, but the servant must commence a suit in his own name, unless the person, who beat him, did it principally for the sake of affronting his master, and, in this case,* Titius *may also bring an action of injury. The same law likewise obtains, if your servant is the slave of another, for as often as he receives an injury, which was intended to affront you, you may yourself bring an action of injury.*

Pœna injuriarum ex l. 12. tabb. et ex jure prætorio.

§ VII Pœna autem injuriarum ex lege 12. tabularum propter membrum quidem ruptum talio erat: propter os vero fractum nummariæ pœnæ erant constitutæ, quasi in magna veterum paupertate. Sed postea prætores permittebant ipsis, qui injuriam passi sunt, eam æstimare, ut judex vel tanti reum condemnet, quanti injuriam passus æstimaverit, vel minoris, prout ei visum fuerit. Sed pæna quidem injuriæ, quæ ex lege 12. tabularum introducta est, in desuetudinem abiit: quam autem prætores introduxerunt, (quæ etiam honoraria appellatur,) in judiciis frequentatur. Nam, secundum gradum dignitatis vitæque honestatem, crescit aut minuitur æstimatio injuriæ. Qui gradus condemnationis

demnationis et in servili persona non immerito servatur, ut aliud in servo actore, aliud in medii actus homine, aliud in vilissimo vel compedito, jus æstimationis constituatur.

§ 7 *The punishment of an injury, according to the 12 tables, was a return of the like injury, if any limb was broken; but, if a blow only was given, or a single bone broken, then the punishment was pecuniary, which was not without effect among the antients, who lived in great poverty. The prætors afterwards permited the parties injured to fix their damages at a certain sum, which might serve as a guide to the judge, but not preclude him from lessening the estimate at his discretion. The species of pecuniary punishment, which was introduced by the law of the 12 tables, fell by degrees into desuetude, and that, which the prætors gave rise to, is now solely in use, and is termed honorary; for the estimation of an injury is either increased or diminished according to the degree and quality of the person injured, and this distinction of degree is not improperly observed even in regard to slaves; so that the same injury may be variously estimated, according to the state and condition of him, who suffered it; at an higher rate, if he had acted as steward or agent to his master, and at a lower estimation, if he was a slave of an inferior sort.*

Pœna autem injuriarum] *Aulus Gellius* is of opinion, that retaliation was never executed even among the antient *Romans*, unless the party offending consented, for he asserts, that the offender was always at liberty to commute his punishment on paying a certain sum of money in proportion to his circumstances *vid Aul Gell lib* 20 *cap* 1 And it were to be wished, for the honor of antient *Rome*, that this opinion was rightly founded, for the law of retaliation, altho' it has the appearance of great equity, is certainly full of absurdity and injustice upon various accounts And, to obviate any objection, which may be made from the law of *Moses*, the best commentators upon the pentateuch have always looked upon such expressions, *as an eye for an eye, and a tooth for a tooth*, to be only proverbial *vid Mr. Le Clerc on Exod* 21. *v* 24 *Deut* 19. *v* 21

Sed postea prætores] The law of the 12 tables, as given by *Gellius*, is in these words *Si injuriam faxit alteri viginti quinque æris pænæ sunto* To which he adds, *quis enim tam inops, quem ab injuriæ faciendæ lubidine viginti quinque asse deterreat? itaque cum ad eam legem Q Labeo in libris, quos ad duodecim tabulas conscripsit, non probaret, quidam, inquit, Lucius Veratius fuit, egregie homo improbus atque immani vecordia, is pro delectamento habebat os hominis liberi manus suæ palma verberare Eum servus sequebatur crumenam plenam assium portitans et, quemcunque depalmaverat, numerari statim secundum duodecim tabulas viginti et quinque asses jubebat Propterea, inquit, prætores postea hanc abolescere et relinqui censuerunt, injuriisque æstimandis recuperatores se daturos edixerunt* Noct att lib 20 cap 1.

De lege Cornelia.

§ VIII Sed et lex Cornelia de injuriis loquitur, et injuriarum actionem introduxit, quæ competit ob eam rem, quod se pulsatum quis, verberatumve, vel domum suam vi introitam esse, dicat. Domum autem accipimus, sive in propria domo quis habitet, sive in conducta, sive gratis, sive hospitio receptus sit.

§ 8 *The law* Cornelia *speaks also of injuries, and hath introduced an action, which lies, when a man alleges, that he hath been struck or beaten, or that another hath entered forcibly into his house, and any man is allowed in this case to allege an house to be his own, whether it is in reality his, or whether he only hires or borrows it, or even lives in it as a guest.*

Sed et lex Cornelia] " Tres sunt causæ, ex " quibus etiam lex Cornelia actionem injuriarum dedit, quod quis pulsatus, verberatusve, " domusve cujus vi introita sit *ff* 47 *t* 10 *l* 5 " Nam etsi actio prætoria ad omnes injurias " pertinebat tam quæ manu quam quæ verbis "fiunt, eam tamen non nisi civiliter instituere "licebat: cum itaque prætoria illa actio civilis "impar cohibendæ hominum petulantiæ videretur, Cornelius Sulla dictator novam tulit "legem *Corneliam de injuriis*, qua et criminale "judicium constitutum est ob certas injurias, "ob quas alias etiam civiliter agere licebat." *Vinn. h. l. Hein. syn l.* 4 *t* 4.

De æstimatione atrocis injuriæ.

§ IX. Atrox injuria æstimatur vel ex facto, veluti si quis ab alio vulneratus sit, vel fustibus cæsus; vel ex loco, veluti si cui in theatro, vel in foro, vel in conspectu prætoris, injuria facta sit; vel ex persona, veluti si magistratus injuriam passus fuerit, vel si senatori ab humili persona injuria facta sit, aut parenti patronove fiat à liberis vel libertis. Aliter enim senatoris et parentis patronique, aliter extranei et humilis personæ injuria æstimatur. Nonnunquam & locus vulneris atrocem injuriam facit, veluti si in oculo quis percussus fuerit. Parvi autem refert, utrum patri-familias, an filio-familias, talis injuria facta sit: nam et hæc atrox injuria æstimabitur.

§ 9. *An injury is esteemed atrocious, sometimes from the nature of the fact, as when a man is wounded by another, or beaten with a club ——sometimes from the place, as when an injury is done in a public theater, in an open market, or in the presence of the prætor —— and sometimes by reason of the rank of the person, as when a magistrate, or a senator, receives an injury from one of mean condition; or when a parent is injured by his child, or a patron by his freed-man, for an injury, done to a senator, or to a parent by his child, or to a patron by his freed-man, must be attoned for by an heavier punishment, than an injury done to a stranger, or a person of low degree Also the part, in which a wound is given, may constitute an injury atrocious; as if a man should be wounded in his eye; but it makes no manner of alteration, whether such an injury is done to the father of a family, or to the son of a family; for the injury will neither be the more nor the less atrocious upon this account.*

De judicio civili et criminali.

§ X. In summa sciendum est, de omni injuria eum, qui passus est, posse vel criminaliter agere, vel civiliter. Et, si quidem civiliter agatur, æstimatione facta, secundum quod dictum est, pœna reo imponitur; sin autem criminaliter, officio judicis extraordinaria pœna reo irrogatur. Hoc videlicet observando, quod Zenoniana constitutio introduxit, ut viri illustres, quique super eos sunt, et per procuratores possint actionem injuriarum criminaliter vel persequi vel suscipere, secundum ejus tenorem, qui ex ipsa manifestius apparet.

§ 10 *In fine, it must be observed concerning every injury, that the party injured may sue the offending party either criminally or civilly If the party injured sues civilly, the damage occasioned by the injury must be estimated, and the penalty injoined accordingly, as we have before noticed but, if he sues criminally, it is the duty of the judge to inflict an extraordinary punishment upon the offender; observing the constitution of* Zeno, *which permits all persons, who have a right to be called* illustrious, *and of consequence all, who enjoy a superior title, either to persue or defend criminally any*

any action of injury by their proctors; but the tenor of this law will more fully appear by a perusal of the ordinance itself.

Zenoniana constitutio.] *vid. Cod* 9 *t.* 35 *l* 11. *Cod* 12. *t.* 8. *l.* 2. *ut dignitatum ordo servetur.*

Qui tenentur injuriarum.

§ XI. Non solum autem is injuriarum tenetur, qui fecit injuriam, id est, qui percussit; verum ille quoque tenetur, qui dolo fecit injuriam, vel qui procuravit, ut cui mala pugno percuteretur.

§ 11. *An action of injury does not only lie against him, who hath done an injury, by giving a blow,* &c. *but also against him, who by his craft and persuasion hath caused the injury to be done.*

Quomodo tollitur hæc actio.

§ XII. Hæc actio dissimulatione aboletur; et ideo, si quis injuriam dereliquerit, hoc est, statim passus ad animum suum non revocaverit, postea ex pœnitentia remissam injuriam non poterit recolere.

§ 12. *All right to an action of injury may be lost by dissimulation; and therefore, if a man takes no notice of an injury at the time, in which he receives it, he cannot afterwards, altho' he repents of his former behavior, commence a suit on account of that injury.*

TITULUS QUINTUS.

De obligationibus, quæ quasi ex delicto nascuntur.

D. xlvii. T. 5. C. ix. T. 3.

Si judex litem suam fecerit.

SI judex litem suam fecerit, non proprie ex maleficio obligatus videtur: sed quia neque ex maleficio, neque ex contractu obligatus est, et utique peccasse aliquid intelligitur, licet per imprudentiam, ideo videtur quasi ex maleficio teneri, et, in quantum de ea re æquum religioni judicantis videbitur, pœnam sustinebit.

If a judge makes a suit his own, by giving an unjust determination, an action of male-feazance will not properly lie against him but, altho' he is not subject to an action of male-feazance, or of contract, yet, as he hath certainly committed a fault, altho' it was not by design, but thro' imprudence and want of skill, he may be sued by an action of quasi-*male-feazance; and must suffer such a penalty, which seems equitable to the conscience of a superior judge.*

Litem suam fecerit] i. e. litem in seipsum convertit. *Theoph.*

De dejectis vel effusis, et positis aut suspensis.

§ I. Item is, cujus ex cœnaculo, vel proprio ipsius, vel conducto, vel in quo gratis habitat, dejectum effusumve aliquid est, ita ut alicui noceret, quasi ex maleficio obligatus intelligitur. Ideo autem non proprie ex maleficio obligatus intelligitur, quia plerumque ob alterius culpam tenetur, aut servi aut liberi. Cui similis est is, qui ea parte, qua vulgo iter fieri solet, id positum aut suspensum habet, quod potest, si ceciderit, alicui nocere: quo casu pœna decem aureorum constituta est. De eo vero, quod dejectum effusumve est, dupli, quantum damni datum sit, constituta est actio. Ob hominem vero liberum occisum, quinquaginta aureorum pœna constituitur. Si vero vivat, nocitumque ei esse dicatur, quantum ob eam rem æquum judici videtur, actio datur. Judex enim computare debet mercedes medicis præstitas, cæteraque impendia, quæ in curatione facta sunt; præterea operas, quibus caruit aut cariturus est, ob id quod inutilis est factus.

§ 1 *Whoever occupies a chamber, from whence any thing hath been either thrown or spilt, by which damage is done, he is liable to an action of* quasi-*male-feazance; and it is not material, whether the chamber is the property of the occupier; whether he pays rent for it, or whether he inhabits it* gratis *and the reason, why such occupier is not suable for strict male-feazance, is, because he is generally sued for the fault of another. Any man is also subject to the same action, who hath hung or placed any thing in a public road, so as to endanger passengers by the fall of it, in which case, a penalty of ten* aurei *is appointed; but, when any thing hath been thrown or spilt, the action is always for the double of what the damage amounts to. If a freeman is killed by accident, the penalty is fifty* aurei; *but, if he only receives some hurt, the quantum of the damage is left to the discretion of the judge, who ought to take the fees of the physician into the account, and all other expenses, attendent upon the cure, over and above the time, which the patient hath lost in his illness, or may lose by being unable to persue his business.*

De filiofam, seorsum habitante à patre.

§ II. Si filius-familias seorsum à patre habitaverit, et quid ex cœnaculo ejus dejectum effusumve fuerit, sive quid positum suspensumve habuerit, cujus casus periculosus est, Juliano placuit, in patrem nullam esse actionem, sed cum ipso filio agendum esse. Quod et in filio-familias judice observandum est, qui litem suam fecerit.

§ 2 *If the son of a family lives separate from his father, and any thing is either thrown, or spilt, from his apartment, or so hung, or placed, that the fall of it may do damage, it is the opinion of* Julian, *that no action will lie against the father, and that the son only can be sued. The same rule of law is also to be observed, in regard to the son of a family, who hath acted as a judge, and given an unjust determination.*

De damno aut furto, quod in navi, aut caupona, aut ſtabulo, factum eſt.

§ III. Item exercitor navis, aut cauponæ, aut ſtabuli, de damno aut furto, quod in navi, aut caupona, aut ſtabulo, factum erit, quaſi ex maleficio teneri videtur; ſi modo ipſius nullum eſt maleficium, ſed alicujus eorum, quorum opera navem, aut cauponam, aut ſtabulum, exercet. Cum enim neque ex maleficio, neque ex contractu, ſit adverſus eum conſtituta hic actio, et aliquatenus culpæ reus eſt, quod opera malorum hominum uteretur, ideo quaſi ex maleficio teneri videtur. In his autem caſibus in factum actio competit; quæ hæredi quidem datur, adverſus hæredem autem non competit.

§ 3. *The maſter of a ſhip, tavern, or inn, is liable to be ſued for a* quaſi-*male-feazance, on account of every damage, or theft, done or commited in any of theſe places, by himſelf or his ſervants. for altho' no action, either of direct male-feazance, or of contract, can be brought againſt the maſter, yet, as he has, in ſome meaſure, been guilty of a fault in imploying diſhoneſt perſons as his ſervants, he is therefore ſubject to a ſuit for a* quaſi-*male-feazance. But, in all theſe caſes, the action given is an action upon the fact, which may be brought in favor of an heir, but not againſt him.*

Item exercitor] By the law of *England* an inn keeper ſhall be charged, if there is any default in him or his ſervants in keeping the goods of a gueſt, for an innholder is bound by law to keep them ſafe, and it is no excuſe to ſay, that he delivered the gueſt the key of the chamber-door, and that the gueſt left it open And altho' the gueſt does not deliver his goods to the innholder to keep, yet, if they are ſtolen, even by perſons unknown, the innholder is chargeable, for, in this caſe, either the innholder, or his ſervants, are in fault for their neglect 8 *rep.* 32 *Calye's caſe.*

TITULUS SEXTUS.

De actionibus.

D. xliv. T. 7. C. iv. T. 10.

Definitio.

SUpereſt, ut de actionibus loquamur. Actio nihil aliud eſt, quam jus perſequendi in judicio, quod ſibi debetur.

It now remains, that we ſhould treat of actions An action is nothing more, than the right, which every man has, of bringing an action at law for whatever is due to him.

Divisio prima.

§ I Omnium autem actionum, quibus inter aliquos apud judices arbitrosve de quacunque re quæritur, summa divisio in duo genera deducitur: aut enim in rem sunt, aut in personam: namque agit unusquisque aut cum eo, qui ei obligatus est, vel ex contractu, vel ex maleficio; quo casu proditæ sunt actiones in personam, per quas intendit, adversarium ei dare aut facere oportere, et aliis quibusdam modis: aut cum eo agit, qui nullo jure ei obligatus est, movet tamen alicui de aliqua re controversiam: quo casu proditæ actiones in rem sunt: veluti si rem corporalem possideat quis, quam Titius suam esse affirmet, possessor autem dominium ejus se esse dicat: nam, si Titius suam esse intenderit, in rem actio est

§ 1 *All actions in general, whether they are determinable before judges or arbitrators, [illegible] divided into two kinds, real and personal; for the plaintiff must sue [illegible], either because the defendent is obligated to him by contract, or hath [illegible] of some m[illegible] and, in this case, the action must be personal, in [illegible] the plaintiff alleges, that his adversary is bound to give, or to do something for [illegible], or some other matter, as the occasion requires or otherwise, the plaintiff [illegible] sue the defendent, on account of some corporeal thing, when there is no obligation, in which case the action must be real as for example, if* Sempronius *possesses land, which* Titius *affirms to be his property, the other denying it,* Titius *must bring a real action against* Sempronius *for the recovery.*

Judices, arbitrosve] " Judicium nomin[illegible] in[illegible] actionibus stricti juris [illegible] addictis judicis bonæ fidei [illegible]

In rem sunt, aut in personam] Actions, by the [illegible] are divided into real, personal, [illegible] Actions real, or relating to lands, [illegible] or [illegible], if they [illegible] derived from an ancestor, and [illegible] complain of the violation of [illegible] we were possessed But the [illegible] distinguished between a right of en[illegible] and therefore gave differ[illegible] each case [illegible], in order to recover [illegible] right, the law only allowed a [illegible] action, the defen[illegible], might either be tried by a [illegible] but when the person dis[illegible] of entry [illegible] was presumed, [illegible] was fresh and recent and there[illegible] were men But, if the [illegible] till the heir of the dis[illegible] and had paid [illegible], then the entry of [illegible] and his trial be [illegible] the judges appealed [illegible], so that, if any, [illegible] defend the [illegible] was obliged [illegible] for him

But the antient way of recovering the right of possession was by a writ of entry, and then the issue, [illegible], or not *disseised*, was always tried by a jury, for, when the disseisin was recent, our ancestors made no appeal to providence, reserving that remedy for those cases only, in which the long possession had rendered the right doubtful. *Bac abr vol* 1 *p* 27

But it is here proper to observe, " that, in a " writ of right, neither the tenent, nor the " demandant, shall fight for themselves, but " must find a champion to fight for them, be- " cause, if either tenent, or demandant, should " be slain, no judgement could be given for " the lands or tenements in question yet, in " an appeal for murder the defendent shall fight " for himself, and so shall the plaintiff, for, if " the defendent is slain, the plaintiff hath the " effect of his suit, *i e* the death of the de- " fendent *Co Litt* 295" As to the order and solemnity of a trial by battel, see the *year-books*, 29 *Ed* 3 *p* 12 30 *Edw* 3 *p* 20 1 *H* 6 *p* 7 *Spel gloss* campus *Origines judicial* *p* 65

But trial by combat, being thought by some to be unchristian, king *Hen* the second refered it to the choice of the person challenged [*viz* the supposed wrongdoer, or defendent] whether he would defend his title to the land in question by by battel, or put it upon trial by a jury of twelve good and lawfull men, which trial was then, and hath ever since been called the trial by great assise *vid Glan. l 2 cap 2 Orig jud* 71 And combat continues to be even now a method of trial in consequence of a real action, if the defending party is so disposed But, proceedings upon real actions being dilatory and expensive, and, in many cases, concluding the party upon one trial, a more commodious method was contrived of disputing a title to lands, which began in the reign of *Hen* 7 by bringing a mixed action, called an ejectment and it is probable, that the last real action, in which battel was waged, was in the 13th year of *Eliz* in the case of *Lowe* and *Kime* against *Paramour*, which is very fully reported by *Dyer*, p 301 But trial by battel, on a criminal accusation, was last admited in the 6th year of king *Charles* the first, between *Donnold* lord *Rey*, appellant, and *David Ramsey*, defendent, in the painted chamber at *Westminster*, before *Robert* earl of *Lindsey*, lord high constable, and *Thomas* earl of *Arundel*, earl-marshal, with other lords, where, after the court had met several times, it was at last determined, that the matter should be referred to the king's will and pleasure *See Blount's* [illegible] *combat*

The oath of each of the combatants was, upon these occasions, to the very great disgrace of our ancestors, in the following most ridiculous terms *viz Hoc audite o justiciarii, quod ego nec comedi, nec bibi, nec aliquis per me* [illegible], *propter quod lex Dei deprimi debeat et lex diaboli exaltari Bract de corona lib* 3 *cap* 21 "Hear this, O ye judges, that I have neither eat nor drank any thing, nor any other by my procurement, or for me, by which the law of God may be depressed, or the law of the devil exalted"

A personal action is that, which one man hath against another, by reason of any contract for money or goods, or for offense done by him, or some other person, for whose fact he is by law answerable

And a mixed action is that, which lies indifferently against the thing detained, or against the person of the detainer, and is so called, because it hath a mixed respect, both to the thing and the person, or, as others define it, [illegible] suit given by law, to recover the thing demanded, and damages also for the wrong done, [illegible] in an assise of novel disseisin, which [illegible], [illegible] the disseisor makes a feofment to another, the disseisee shall be intituled to against the disseisor, and the feoffee, or other ter tenent, to recover not only the land, but damages [illegible]

Actions of wast, [illegible], ejectment, &c are also mixed *Bac abr* [illegible] *p* 28. *Blount's dict* &c

De actione confessoria, et negatoria.

§ II. Æque, si agat quis, jus sibi esse fundo forte, vel ædibus utendi fruendi, vel per fundum vicini eundi agendi, vel ex fundo vicini aquam ducendi, in rem actio est. Ejusdem generis est actio de iure prædiorum urbanorum, veluti, si quis agat, jus sibi esse altius ædes suas tollendi, prospiciendive, vel projiciendi aliquid, vel immittendi tignum in vicini ædes. Contra quoque de usufructu, et de servitutibus prædiorum rusticorum, item prædiorum urbanorum, invicem quoque prodite sunt actiones: ut si quis intendat, jus non esse adversario utendi fruendi, eundi agendi, aquamve ducendi, item altius tollendi, prospiciendive, vel projiciendi, immittendive, istæ quoque actiones in rem sunt, sed negativæ: quod genus actionis in controversiis rerum corporalium proditum non est; nam in his is agit, qui non possidet; ei vero, qui possidet, non est actio prodita, per quam neget rem actoris esse. Sane non uno casu, qui possidet, nihilhominus is actoris partes obtinet; sicut in latioribus digestorum libris opportunius apparebit.

§ 2 *Also, if any man brings an action, alleging, that he has a right to the fruct of a field, or house, or a right of driving* [illegible] *the land of his neighbour, such action is denominated real* [illegible] *the rights of houses or city estates, which* [illegible] *same kind, as when a man commences a suit,* [illegible] *prospect, a right to raise the height of his house, a right of making a part of it to project, or a right of laying the beams of his building upon his neighbour's walls. There are also contrary actions to these, which relate to usu-fructs, and the rights of country and city estates, as when the complainant alleges, that his adversary is* not *intituled to the usufruct of a particular ground, or to the right of passage,* &c. &c. *these actions are also real, but are negative in their nature, and cannot therefore be used in regard to things corporeal, for, in respect to things corporeal, the agent, or plaintiff, is the person out of possession; for a possessor can bring no action · there are however, many cases, in which a possessor may be obliged to act the part of a plaintiff, but we refer the reader to the books of the digests.*

Sane non uno casu] Others read, *sane uno casu*, but the insertion of *non* seems most conformable to the words of *Justinian*, in the latter part of this section, for the emperor does not say, that the possessor of a corporeal thing can ever become plaintiff, by commencing a suit, but that he may perform the part of a plaintiff, *partes actoris*, which is only saying, that he may be obliged to take the proof upon himself, which often happens *Vinn.*

De actionibus prætoriis realibus.

§ III. Sed istæ quidem actiones, quarum mentionem habuimus, et si quæ sunt similes, ex legitimis et civilibus causis descendunt Aliæ autem sunt, quas prætor ex sua jurisdictione comparatas habet tam in rem, quam in personam: quas et ipsas necessarium est exemplis ostendere: ut ecce, plerumque ita permittit prætor in rem agere, ut vel actor dicat se quasi usucepisse, quod non usuceperit, vel ex diverso possessor dicat, adversarium suum non usucepisse, quod usuceperit.

§ 3 *The actions, of which we have made mention, and all actions of a similar nature, are derived from the civil law. but the prætor, by virtue of his jurisdiction, hath introduced other actions, both real and personal, of which it will be necessary to give some examples for he often permits a real action to be brought, either by allowing the demandant to allege, that he hath acquired, by prescription, what he hath not so acquired; or, on the contrary, by permiting a former possessor to allege, that his adversary hath not acquired by prescription, what, in reality, he hath so acquired*

De Publiciana.

§ IV. Namque, si cui ex justa causa res aliqua tradita fuerit, (veluti ex causa emptionis, aut donationis, aut dotis, aut legatorum,) et necdum ejus rei dominus effectus est, si is ejus rei possessionem casu amiserit, nullam habet in rem directam actionem ad eam persequendam: quippe ita proditæ sunt jure civili actiones, ut quis dominium suum vindicet Sed, quia sane durum erat, eo casu deficere actionem, inventa est à prætore actio, in qua dicit is, qui possessionem amisit, eam rem se usucepisse, quam usu non cepit, et ita vindicat suam esse: quæ actio Publiciana appellatur, quoniam primum à Publicio prætore in edicto proposita est.

§ 3 *If any particular thing, belonging to one man, should be delivered in trust to another, that it might be deposited with him upon some just account, as by reason of a purchase, a gift, a marriage, or a bequest, and it should so happen, that such trustee*

should

should lose the possession, before he hath gained a property in the thing possessed, he could have no direct action for the recovery of it, inasmuch as real actions are given by the law for the re-vindication of those things only, in which a man hath a vested property or dominion But, it being hard, that an action should be wanting in such a case, the prætor hath supplied one, in which the person, who hath lost his possession, is allowed to aver, that he hath a prescriptive right to the thing in question, altho' he hath not obtained it; and he may thus recover the possession This action is called actio Publiciana, *because it was first instituted by the edict of* Publicius *the prætor.*

De rescissoria.

§ V. Rursus ex diverso, si quis, cum reipublicæ causa abesset, vel in hostium potestate esset, rem ejus, qui in civitate esset, usuceperit, permittitur domino, si possessor reipublicæ causa abesse desierit, tunc intra annum rescissa usucapione eam rem petere, id est, ita petere, ut dicat, possessorem usu non cepisse, et ob id suam rem esse. Quod genus actionis quibusdam et aliis simili æquitate motus prætor accommodat, sicut ex latiore digestorum seu pandectarum volumine intelligere licet

§ 5. *On the contrary, if any man, whilest he is abroad in the service of his country, or a prisoner in the hands of the enemy, should gain a prescriptive title to a thing, which belongs to another, who was not abroad, then the former proprietor is permitted at any time, within a year after the return of the possessor, to bring an action against him, the prescriptive title being rescinded, and the proprietor being allowed to allege, that the possessor hath not effectually prescribed, and that therefore the thing in litigation is his own. The same motive of equity hath also induced the prætor to allow the use of this species of action to certain other persons, as we may learn more at large from the digests*

Quibusdam et aliis] That is, to persons (for example) who had been absent upon a just account, for every man, who had been necessarily abroad, was also allowed to take the benefit of this action to recover his right of possession against those, who had resided at home *Cod* [illegible] *t* 51 *l* 18 [illegible]

And to this we have something similar in the law of *England*, for, if any person is dispossessed of his estate, whilest he is in durance, and, if the lands even descend to the heir of the disseisor, the disseisee his liberty, by his own proper act, to re enter, and, if judgment is given against him, he may reverse it afterwards by a writ of error, because his absence was not contumacious And there is the same law for those, who are in the king's service, or are beyond the seas on any business, which concerns the commonwealth, and some affirm, that, if a man is abroad upon his own business, and is disseised, he may, at his return, re enter upon the heir of the disseisor, even without bringing an [illegible] *Co I* [illegible] 4,5 439 440 *continual claim* Any invasion of the right of persons in prison, or beyond sea is also guarded against by [illegible] acts of parliament [illegible] 5 *H* 4 [illegible] 4 *H* [illegible] 24 [illegible]

De Pauliana.

§ VI. Item, si quis in fraudem creditorum rem suam alicui tradiderit, bonis ejus a creditoribus possessis ex sententia præsidis, permittitur ipsis creditoribus rescissa traditione eam rem petere, id est, dicere eam rem traditam non esse, et ob id in bonis debitoris mansisse

§ 6 *If a debtor disposes of any thing, by delivering it to some person in order to defraud his creditors, the creditors are then permitted, notwithstanding the delivery, to bring an action for the thing, if they have previously obtained the sentence of the proper magistrate, for putting themselves into possession, that is, they are allowed to plead, that the thing was not delivered, and of course, that it continues to be a part of their debtor's goods.*

Si quis in fraudem] In *England*, the effect of the action *Pauliana*, is fully answered by the 13th of *Eliz. cap* 5. which renders void every alienation of lands or goods, made to defraud creditors, and inflicts a penalty upon all, who are parties to such fraudulent alienations *Cowel h. t.*

De Serviana et quasi-Serviana, seu hypothecaria.

§ VII. Item Serviana, et quasi Serviana, (quæ etiam hypothecaria vocatur,) ex ipsius prætoris jurisdictione substantiam capiunt. Serviana autem experitur quis de rebus coloni, quæ pignoris jure pro mercedibus fundi ei tenentur. Quasi Serviana autem est, qua creditores pignora hypothecasve persequuntur. Inter pignus autem & hypothecam, (quantum ad actionem hypothecariam attinet,) nihil interest: nam de qua re inter creditorem et debitorem convenerit, ut sit pro debito obligata, utraque hac appellatione continetur: sed in aliis differentia est. Nam pignoris appellatione eam proprie rem contineri dicimus, quæ simul etiam traditur creditori, maxime si mobilis sit, at eam, quæ sine traditione nuda conventione tenetur, proprie hypothecæ appellatione contineri dicimus.

§ 7. *Also the action* Serviana, *and the action* quasi Serviana, *(which is also called hypothecary,) both take their rise from the prætor's jurisdiction. By the action* Serviana, *a suit may be commenced for the stock and cattle of a farmer, which are obligated as a pledge for the rent of the ground, which he farms of his landlord. The action* quasi-Serviana *is that, by which a* creditor *may sue for a thing pledged or hypothecated to him, and, in regard to this action, there is no difference between a pledge and an hypotheque, tho' in other respects they differ, for, by the term pledge, is meant that, which hath actually been delivered to a creditor, especially if the thing was a moveable, and, by the word hypotheque, we comprehend what is obligated to a creditor by a mere agreement only, without a delivery.*

Item Serviana.] The law of *England* seems to go farther in this than the *Roman* law, for a lessor in *England* may, of proper right, distrain the effects and cattle, which are brought upon his fee, and detain them, till his rent is satisfied, for they are regarded as a gage or pledge: and even the cattle of a stranger, escaping into his neighbour's grounds, and being there *levant* and *couchant*, may be distreined by the lessor, for it shall be imputed to the owner's folly that he did not provide against this mischief, by proper bounds and fences. *Pro.* 1 . 57 . 6, *Bacon's Abr.* 108. 109. *vol* 2. distress.

De actionibus prætoriis personalibus.

§ VIII. In personam quoque actiones ex sua jurisdictione propositas habet prætor, veluti de pecunia constituta: cui similis videbatur receptitia. Sed ex nostra constitutione, (cum, et si quid plenius habebat, hoc in actionem pecuniæ constitutæ transfusum est,) et ea quasi supervacua jussa est cum sua auctoritate a nostris legibus recedere. Item prætor proposuit actionem de peculio servorum, filiorumque familiarum; et eam, ex qua quæritur, an actor juraverit; et alias complures.

§ 8. *Personal actions have also been introduced by the prætors, in consequence of their authority; such is the action* de pecunia constituta; *which much resembles that called* receptitia; *which we have now taken away by our constitution, as unnecessary, and whatever advantageous matter it contained, we have added it to the action* de pecunia constituta. *The prætors have likewise introduced the action concerning the* peculium *of slaves, and the sons of families; and also the actions, in which the only question is, whether the plaintiff hath made oath of his debt, they have likewise introduced many others*

Receptitia] " Hæc actio tantum ad trapezitas sive mensarios aut argentarios pertinebat, apud quos, ut tum moris erat, pecuniæ et res civium Romanorum deponebantur Itaque, si mensarius citra stipulationem recepisset, se certo die soluturum, quod hic vel ille apud se deposuisset, hoc conventionis genus *receptum* dicebatur, et actio, quæ ex ea re competebat, *receptitia*, sive pecuniæ receptæ " *Vinn*

Ex nostra constitutione] *C* 4 *t* 18 *l* 2. *de constituta pecunia.*

De constituta pecunia.

§ IX. De constituta autem pecunia cum omnibus agitur, quicunque vel pro se, vel pro alio, soluturos se constituerint, nulla scilicet stipulatione interposita. Nam alioqui, si stipulanti promiserint, jure civili tenentur.

§ 9. *A suit may be commenced by the action* de pecunia constituta, *against any person, who hath ingaged to pay money, either for himself or another, without stipulation, but, when there is a stipulation, the prætorian action is not wanted, for the performance of the promise may be inforced by the civil law.*

De peculio.

§ X. Actiones autem de peculio ideo adversus patrem dominumve comparavit prætor, quia licet ex contractu filiorum servorumve ipso jure non teneantur, æquum tamen est, peculio tenus, (quod veluti patrimonium est filiorum filiarumque, item servorum,) condemnari eos.

§ 10. *The prætor hath also given actions* de peculio *against fathers and masters, inasmuch as they are not legally bound by the contracts of their children and slaves: it is therefore but equity, that parents and masters should be condemned to pay to the extent of a* peculium, *which is, as it were, the patrimony, and separate estate of a son, a daughter, or a slave*

De actione in factum ex jurejurando.

§ XI. Item, si quis postulante adversario juraverit, deberi sibi pecuniam, quam peteret, neque ei solvatur, justissime accommodat ei talem actionem, per quam non illud quæritur, an ei pecunia debeatur, sed an juraverit.

§ 11. *Also if any man, at the prayer or request of the adverse party, makes oath, that the debt, which he sues for, is owing and due to him, he then becomes intitled to an action upon the fact; in which no inquiry is made, whether the debt is due, but whether the oath hath been taken.*

De actionibus pœnalibus.

§ XII. Pœnales quoque actiones prætor pene multas ex ſua juriſdictione introduxit: veluti adverſus eum, qui quid ex albo ejus corrupiſſet: et in eum, qui patronum vel parentem in jus vocaſſet, cum id non impetraſſet: item adverſus eum, qui vi exemerit eum, qui in jus vocaretur, cujuſve dolo alius exemerit: et alias innumerabiles.

§ 12. *The prætors have alſo introduced a great number of penal actions, by virtue of their authority. But, to mention ſome only out of many, they have provided for instance an action againſt him, who hath wilfully damaged or eraſed an edict, againſt an emancipated ſon, or a freed-man, who hath commenced a ſuit againſt his parent or patron, without a previous permiſſion from the proper magiſtrate; and alſo againſt any perſon, who by force or fraud hath hindered another from appearing to the proceſs of a court of juſtice. But theſe are only ſome inſtances out of a great number, which might be produced.*

De præjudicialibus actionibus.

§ XIII. Præjudiciales actiones in rem eſſe videntur: quales ſunt, per quas quæritur, an aliquis liber, an libertus ſit, vel ſervus, vel de partu agnoſcendo. Ex quibus fere una illa legitimam cauſam habet, per quam quæritur, an aliquis liber ſit? cæteræ ex ipſius prætoris juriſdictione ſubſtantiam capiunt.

§ 13. *Prejudicial actions are alſo real; ſuch are theſe, by which it is inquired, whether a man is born free, or made free; whether he is a ſlave, or a baſtard? but of theſe actions, that only proceeds from the civil law, by which it is inquired, whether a man is free born? the reſt all take their riſe from the prætor's juriſdiction.*

Præjudiciales actiones] *Bracton* gives the following account of prejudicial actions. *Præjudiciales ſunt, quæ oriuntur ex incidentibus quæſtionibus, vel emergentibus, in quibus quæritur, utrum aliquis ſit ingenuus vel libertinus, liber vel ſervus, filius an non, et, ſi filius, utrum legitimus vel baſtardus, et hujuſmodi, et dicuntur præjudiciales actiones, quia prius judicantur, quam actio principalis. Angl.* "Thoſe actions are called prejudicial, "which ariſe from incident queſtions, in which "it is inquired, whether a man is born free, or "not? and, if not born free, whether he is a freed-"man, or a ſlave? Alſo, whether a man is the "ſon of another, or not? and, if he is the ſon, "whether he is the legitimate ſon, or a baſ-"tard?"

"All theſe, and the like actions, or iſſues, are "termed prejudicial, becauſe they muſt be ad-"judged and determined before the principal "action." *Brac. lib. 3. cap. 4. n. 9.*

An res ſua condici poſſit.

§ XIV. Sic itaque diſcretis actionibus, certum eſt, non poſſe actorem ſuam rem ita ab aliquo petere, *ſi paret, eum dare oportere.* Nec enim, quod actoris eſt, id ei dari oportet. ſcilicet, quia dari cuiquam id intelligitur, quod ita datur, ut ejus fiat: nec res, quæ jam actoris eſt, magis ejus fieri poteſt. Plane odio furum, quo magis pluribus actionibus

nibus teneantur, effectum est, ut, extra pœnam dupli aut quadrupli, rei recipiendæ nomine, fures etiam hac actione teneantur, *si appareat, eos dare oportere:* quamvis sit adversus eos etiam hæc in rem actio, per quam rem suam quis esse petit.

§ 14. *Actions being thus divided into real and personal, it is certain, that a man cannot sue for his own property by a condiction, or a personal action in the following form,* viz. if it appears, that the defendent ought to GIVE it me: *for the act of* giving *implies the confering of property, and therefore that, which is the property of the plaintiff, can never be understood to be given to him, or to become more his own, than it already is But, notwithstanding this, in order to shew a detestation for thieves and robbers, and to increase the number of actions, which may be brought against them, it hath been determined, that, besides the double and quadruple penalty, to which they are liable, they may be persued by a condiction for the thing taken, in the very form before recited,* if it appears that they ought to GIVE it. *And this is allowed, altho' the party injured may also bring a real action against them, by which he may demand the thing taken, as his own.*

De nominibus actionum.

§ 15. Appellamus autem in rem quidem actiones vindicationes: in personam vero actiones, quibus dare aut facere oportere intenditur, condictiones. Condicere enim est denuntiare, prisca lingua Nunc vero abusive dicimus, condictionem actionem in personam esse, qua actor intendit dari sibi oportere. Nulla enim hoc tempore eo nomine denuntiatio fit.

§ 15 *Real actions are called vindications; and personal actions, in which it is intended, that something ought to be done or given, are called condictions for the word* condicere *was in our old language of the same import with* denuntiare *to denounce, but the term condiction is now improperly used to denote a personal action, by which the plaintiff contends, that something ought to be given to him, for denunciations are not in use.*

Condicere enim est] " Condicere priscâ lingua significat denunciare, nam, qui olim cum " aliquo litem habebat, denuntiabat ei, *ut illo* " *die ad judicium accipiendum adesset* Hodie vero " per abusionem condictio dicitur actio, quam " actor intentans dicit, *si paret hunc dare oportere* Nulla enim hoc tempore adversario fit " denuntiatio *Theoph. h t*

Divisio secunda.

§ XVI. Sequens illa divisio est, quod quædam actiones rei persequendæ gratia comparatæ sunt, quædam pœnæ persequendæ, quædam mistæ sunt.

§ 16. *Actions are also farther divided into those, which are given, for the sake of obtaining the very thing in dispute, into those, which are given, for the penalty only; and lastly into mixed actions, which are given for the recovery both of the thing and the penalty.*

De actionibus rei persecutoriis.

§ XVII. Rei persequendæ causa comparatæ sunt omnes in rem actiones. Earum vero actionum, quæ in personam sunt, eæ quidem, quæ ex contractu nascuntur, fere omnes rei persequendæ causa comparatæ videntur: veluti quibus mutuam pecuniam, vel in stipulatum deductam, petit actor: item commodati, depositi, mandati, pro socio, ex empto, vendito, locato, conducto. Plane, si depositi agatur eo nomine, quod tumultus, incendii, ruinæ, naufragii causa depositum sit, in duplum actionem prætor reddit, si modo cum ipso, apud quem depositum sit, aut cum hærede ejus, de dolo ipsius agitur: quo casu mista est actio.

§ 17. *All real actions are given for the recovery of the thing in litigation; and almost all the personal actions, which arise from a contract, are also given for the recovery of the thing itself; as the action for a* mutuum, *a* commodatum, *or on account of a stipulation, also the action on account of a deposit, a mandate, partenership, buying and selling, letting and hiring. But, when a suit is commenced for a thing deposited by reason of a riot, a fire, or any other calamity, the prætor always gives an action for a double penalty, besides the thing deposited, if the suit is brought against the depositary himself, or against his heir, for fraud, in which case the action is mixed.*

De actionibus pœnæ persecutoriis.

§ XVIII. Ex maleficiis vero proditæ actiones, aliæ tantum pœnæ persequendæ causa comparatæ sunt: aliæ tam pœnæ, quam rei persequendæ; et ob id mistæ sunt. Pœnam tantum persequitur quis actione furti: sive enim manifesti agatur, quadrupli, sive non manifesti, dupli, de sola pœna agitur: nam ipsam rem propria actione persequitur quis, id est, suum esse petens, sive fur ipse eam rem possideat, sive alius quilibet. Eo amplius adversus furem etiam condictio est rei.

§ 18 *In cases of male-feazance, some actions are given for the penalty only, and some both for the thing and the penalty; and these are therefore called mixed actions. But, in an action of theft, whether manifest or not manifest, nothing more is sued for than the penalty, which, in manifest theft is quadruple, and, in theft not manifest, double for the owner may recover by a separate action whatever hath been stolen from him, if he alleges, that the thing stolen is his own; and he is intituled to this action, not only against the thief, but against any other person, who is in possession of his property. The thief may also be sued by a condiction, or personal action, for the recovery of the thing stolen.*

De mixtis, hoc est, rei et pœnæ persecutoriis.

§ XIX. Vi autem bonorum raptorum actio mista est, quia in quadruplo rei persecutio continetur: pœna autem tripli est. Sed et legis Aquiliæ actio de damno injuria dato mista est: non solum si adversus infi-

inficiantem in duplum agatur, sed interdum etsi in simplum quisque agat, veluti si quis hominem claudum aut luscum occiderit, qui in eo anno integer et magni pretii fuerit: tanti enim damnatur, quanti is homo eo in anno plurimi fuerit, secundum jam traditam divisionem. Item mista est actio contra eos, qui relicta sacrosanctis Ecclesiis, vel aliis venerabilibus locis, legati vel fidei-commissi nomine, dare distulerint, usque adeo ut etiam in judicium vocarentur. Tunc enim et ipsam rem vel pecuniam, quæ relicta est, dare compelluntur, et aliud tantum pro pœna: et ideo in duplum ejus fit condemnatio.

§ 19 *An action for goods taken by force is a mixed action, because the value of whatever is taken is included under the quadruple value to be recovered by the action, and thus the penalty is but triple. The action, introduced by the law* Aquilia, *on account of damage injuriously done, is also a mixed action, not only when it is given for double value against a man denying the fact, but sometimes, when the action is only for single value, as when a man hath killed a slave, who at the time of his death was lame, or wanted an eye, but had within the year, previous to his decease, been free from any defect, and of great price, for in this case the defendent is obliged to pay as much as the slave was worth at any time within the year preceding his death, according to what has already been observed. B. 4. t. 3. A mixed action may also be brought against those, who have delayed to deliver a legacy, or gift in trust, given for the benefit of a church, or any other holy place, till they have been called before a magistrate for that purpose, and then they are compelled to deliver up the thing, or to pay the money bequeathed, and also the value of as much more, by way of penalty, and thus they are condemned to pay the double of what was due.*

De mixtis, id est, tam in rem, quam in personam.

§ XX. Quædam actiones mixtam causam obtinere videntur, tam in rem, quam in personam. qualis est familiæ erciscundæ actio, quæ competit cohæredibus de dividenda hæreditate: item communi dividundo, quæ inter eos redditur, inter quos aliquid commune est, ut id dividatur. item finium regundorum actio, quæ inter eos agitur, qui confines agros habent. In quibus tribus judiciis permittitur judici rem alicui ex litigatoribus ex bono et æquo adjudicare, et, si unius pars prægravari videbitur, eum invicem certa pecunia alteri condemnare.

§ 20 *There are also some actions, which are of a mixed nature, by being, in effect, as well real as personal. Of this sort is the action* familiæ erciscundæ, *which may be brought by coheirs for the partition of their inheritance. So also is the action* de communi dividundo, *given for the division of any particular thing or things, which, exclusive of coinheritance, are in common* [illegible] *the action* finium regundorum, *which* [illegible] *contiguous. And, in these three actions, it is lawful in the judge* [illegible] *to give the ground or thing in dispute, to either of the parties* [illegible] *if necessity so requires, to recompense his adversary* [illegible] *him a just* [illegible] *quality in the* [illegible]

Familiæ erciscundæ [illegible] The word [illegible] Hein Syntag [illegible] made [illegible] or [illegible] used in England, divide, which is derived from [illegible] all the purposes of the three actions mentioned

mentioned in the text, *viz* the writs *de partitione facienda — de rationabili divisis — de perambulatione facienda — de curia claudenda — de reparatione facienda*.

For a particular account of these writs, the reader is refered to *Fitzherbert's natura brevium* in 4to p 142 300 309 297 295

Divisio tertia.

§ XXI. Omnes autem actiones vel in simplum conceptæ sunt, vel in duplum, vel in triplum, vel in quadruplum: ulterius autem nulla actio extenditur.

§ 21 *All actions are for the single, double, triple, or quadruple value of the thing in litigation, for no action extends farther.*

Ulterius autem] On some actions, nothing more is given by the law of *England*, than the bare damages sustained, as in actions of trespass, — but double and triple damages are given in many cases, and even ten-fold damages are recoverable against a juror, who receives a bribe for bringing a verdict 38 *Edw* 3 *cap* 12 *Cowel h l*

De actionibus in simplum.

§ XXII. In simplum agitur, veluti ex stipulatione, ex mutui datione, ex empto, vendito, locato, conducto, mandato, et denique ex aliis quam plurimis causis

§ 22 *The single value is sued for, when an action is given upon a stipulation a loan, a mandate, the contract of buying and selling, letting and hiring, and also upon other very numerous accounts.*

In duplum.

§ XXIII In duplum agimus, veluti furti nec manifesti, damni injuriæ ex lege Aquilia, depositi ex quibusdam causis. item servi corrupti, quæ competit in eum, cujus hortatu consiliove servus alienus fugerit, aut contumax adversus dominum factus est, aut luxuriose vivere cœperit, aut denique quolibet modo deterior factus sit: in qua actione earum etiam rerum, quas fugiendo servus abstulerit, æstimatio deducitur. item ex legato, quod venerabilibus locis relictum est, secundum ea, quæ supra diximus.

§ 23 *The double value is sued for, in an action of theft* not manifest, *of injury, by virtue of the law* Aquilia, *and sometimes in an action of deposite. The double value is likewise sued for, in an action brought, on account of a slave corrupted, against him, by whose advice such a slave hath fled from his master, grown disobedient, luxurious, or become in any manner the worse; and, in this action, an estimation is to be made of whatever things the slave hath stolen from his master, before his flight. An action for the detention of a legacy, left to an holy place, is also given for double the value, as we have before remarked*

In triplum.

§ XXIV. Tripli vero agimus, cum quidam majorem vera æstimatione quantitatem in libello conventionis inserunt, ut ex hac causa viatores, id est, executores litium, ampliorem summam sportularum nomine

nomine exigerent: tunc enim id, quod propter eorum causam damnum passus fuerit reus, in triplum ab actore consequetur; ut in hoc triplo etiam simplum, in quo damnum passus est, connumeretur. Quod nostra constitutio introduxit, quæ in nostro codice fulget, ex qua procul dubio certum est, ex lege condictitiam emanare.

§ 24. *A suit may be brought for triple value, when any person inserts a greater sum, than is due to him, in the libel of convention, to the intent, that the officers of any court may exact a larger fee, or sportule, from the defendent in which case the defendent may obtain the triple value of the extraordinary fee from the plaintiff, including the fee in the triple value. The fees of officers are regulated by our constitution, and it is not to be doubted, but that the action, called* condictio ex lege, *may be given by virtue of that ordinance*

Nostra constitutio] not extant. *vid Theoph in hunc locum.*

In quadruplum.

§ XXV. Quadrupli autem agitur; veluti furti manifesti, item de eo, quod metus causa factum sit; deque ea pecunia, quæ in hoc data sit, ut is, cui datur, calumniæ causa negotium alicui faceret, vel non faceret. Item ex lege condictitia, nostra ex constitutione, oritur, in quadruplum condemnationem imponens iis executoribus litium, qui contra nostræ constitutionis normam à reis quicquam exegerint.

§ 25 *A suit may be commenced for quadruple or fourfold value, by an action for theft manifest, by an action for putting a man in fear, and by an action on account of money, given to bring on a litigious suit against some third person, or on account of money given to desist from it A condiction* ex lege, *for the quadruple value, arises also from our constitution against all officers of courts of justice, who demand any thing from the party defendent, contrary to the regulations of the said constitution.*

Subdivisio actionum in duplum.

§ XXVI. Sed furti quidem nec manifesti actio et servi corrupti à cæteris, de quibus simul locuti sumus, eo differunt, quod hæ actiones omnimodo dupli sunt: at istæ, (id est, damni injuriæ ex lege Aquilia et interdum depositi,) inficiatione duplicantur: in confitentem autem in simplum dantur. Sed illa, quæ de iis competit, quæ relicta venerabilibus locis sunt, non solum inficiatione duplicatur, sed etiamsi distulerit relicti solutionem, usque quo jussu magistratuum conveniatur. In confitentem vero, antequam jussu magistratuum conveniatur, solventem, simpli redditur.

§ 26. *But an action of theft* not manifest, *and an action on account of a* slave corrupted, *differ from the others, of which we have spoken, in that they always inforce a condemnation in double the value but in an action, given by the law* Aquilia *for an injury done, and sometimes in an action of deposite, the double value may be exacted in case of a denial, yet whenever the party defendent makes a confession, then the single value is all, which can be recovered. But, when a demand is made by an action for a legacy to pious uses, due to any holy place or society, the penalty is not only doubled by the denial of the defendent, but also by any delay of payment, which may be adjudged to have given a just cause for citing the defendent before a magistrate. but, if the legacy is confessed and paid, before any citation issues at the command of the judge, the party complainant must rest satisfied with the single value.*

Subdivisio actionum in quadruplum.

§ XXVII. Item actio de eo, quod metus causa factum sit, à cæteris, de quibus simul locuti sumus, eo differt, quod ejus natura tacite continetur, ut, qui judicis jussu ipsam rem actori restituat, absolvatur: quod in cæteris casibus non est ita, sed omnimodo quisque in quadruplum condemnatur: quod est et in furti manifesti actione.

§ 27. *An action for putting a man in fear differs also from other actions* in quadruplum, *because it is tacitly implied in the nature of this action, that the party, who hath obeyed the command of the judge or magistrate, in restoring the things taken, may be dismissed, for, in all other actions for the fourfold value, every man must be condemned to pay the full penalty, as in the action of theft manifest.*

Absolvatur.] The commentators give no satisfaction, in regard to the reason of this practice.

Divisio quarta de actionibus bonæ fidei.

§ XXVIII. Actionum autem quædam bonæ fidei sunt, quædam stricti juris. Bonæ fidei sunt hæ: ex empto, vendito; locato, conducto, negotiorùm gestorum; mandati; depositi; pro socio; tutelæ; commodati, pignoratitia; familiæ eriscundæ, communi dividundo; præscriptis verbis, quæ de æstimato proponitur; et ea, quæ ex permutatione competit; et hæreditatis petitio. Quamvis enim usque adhuc incertum erat, inter bonæ fidei judicia connumeranda hæreditatis petitio esset, an non: nostra tamen constitutio aperte, eam esse bonæ fidei, disposuit.

§ 28. *The fourth division of actions is into those of good faith, and those of strict right Those of good faith are the following,* viz. *actions of buying and selling, letting and hiring; of affairs transacted, of mandate, deposit, partenership, tutelage, loan, mortgage, of the partition of an inheritance, and of the division of any particular thing or things, which belong in common to diverse persons; also actions in prescribed words, which are either estimatory, or derived from commutation; and lastly that action, by virtue of which we demand an inheritance; for altho' it hath long been doubtful to what class this action belonged; yet it is now clearly determined by our constitution, that the demand of an inheritance is to be numbered among the actions of good faith*

Actionum autem] Altho' no such distinction is made by *English* lawyers in their writings, yet they make it in practice — for the damages, which are received from contracts and trespasses, are always remited to the equity of jurors, and judgment is given according to their estimation. *Cowel h l*

Nostra tamen constitutio] *C* 3 *t* 31. *l.* 3.

De

De rei uxoriæ actione in ex stipulatu actionem transfusa.

§ XXIX. Fuerat antea et rei uxoriæ actio una ex bonæ fidei judiciis: sed cum, pleniorem esse ex stipulatu actionem invenientes, omne jus, quod res uxoria antea habebat, cum multis divisionibus in actionem ex stipulatu, quæ de dotibus exigendis proponitur, transtulerimus, merito rei uxoriæ actione sublata, ex stipulatu actio, quæ pro ea introducta est, naturam bonæ fidei judicii tantum in exactione dotis meruit, ut bonæ fidei sit: sed et tacitam ei dedimus hypothecam. Præferri autem aliis creditoribus in hypothecis tunc censuimus, cum ipsa mulier de dote sua experiatur, cujus solius providentia hoc induximus.

§ 29. *The action, called* rei uxoriæ, *which was given for the recovery of a marriage portion, was formerly numbered among the actions of good faith; but when, upon finding the action of stipulation to be more full and advantageous, we abrogated the action* rei uxoriæ, *and transfered all it's effects, with the addition of many other powers, to the action of stipulation, which is given on account of marriage portions, we then not only thought, that this action of stipulation, as far as it related to marriage portions, deserved to be numbered with actions of good faith, but we also added to it, by implication, the full powers of an action of hypotheque, and we have likewise judged it proper, that women, in whose sole behalf we enacted our constitution, should be prefered to all other creditors by mortgage, whenever they themselves sue for their marriage portions.*

Rei uxoriæ] Soluto matrimonio dabatur uxori adversus maritum rei uxoria actio ad repetendas res dotales. *Theoph.*

Hoc induximus] Scilicet, constitutione, *Cod.* 5 *t* 13

De potestate judicis in judicio bonæ fidei, et de compensationibus.

§ XXX. In bonæ fidei judiciis libera potestas permitti videtur judici ex bono et æquo æstimandi, quantum actori restitui debeat. In quo et illud continetur, ut, si quid invicem præstare actorem oporteat, eo compensato, in reliquum is, cum quo actum est, debeat condemnari. Sed et in stricti juris judiciis ex rescripto divi Marci, opposita doli mali exceptione, compensatio inducebatur. Sed nostra constitutio easdem compensationes, quæ jure aperto nituntur, latius introduxit, ut actiones ipso jure minuant, sive in rem, sive in personam, sive alias quascunque, excepta sola depositi actione, cui, aliquid compensationis nomine opponi, sane iniquum esse credimus: ne, sub prætextu compensationis, depositarum rerum quis ex actione defraudetur.

§ 30. *In all actions of good faith a full power is given to the judge of calculating, according to the rules of justice and equity, how much ought to be restored to the plaintiff, and of course, when the plaintiff is found to be indebted to the defendant in any sum, it is in the power of the judge to allow a compensation, and to condemn the defendant in the payment of the difference: and even in actions of strict right, the emperor* Marcus *introduced a compensation by opposing an exception of fraud. But we have extended compensations much farther by our constitution, which*

we

the debt of the defendent is evident; so that actions of strict right, whether real, personal, or of whatever kind they are, may be diminished by compensation; except only an action of deposit, against which we have not judged it proper to permit any compensation to be alleged, lest the pretence of compensation should give a color and incouragement to fraud.

Sed nostra constitutio] The constitution mentioned in this section may be found in the fourth book of the code, *t* 31 *l* 14.

In the court of *Chancery*, where it is an established rule, that he, who would have equity, must do equity, the plaintiff, in a bill of account, has always been obliged to discount as much of his demand, as the defendent can prove to be due to him. But the common law does not allow of any stopage, or compensation, from whence there arose great inconveniences, which at length gave rise to the statutes of the 2d and 8th of *George* the second. By the 1st of which, it is enacted, "that " where there are mutual debts between the " plaintiff and defendent, or, if either party " sue, or be sued, as executor or administrator, " where there are mutual debts between the " testator or intestate and either party, one " debt may be set against the other, and such " matter may be given in evidence upon the " general issue, or pleaded in bar, as the case " shall require, if, at the time of pleading the " general issue, notice be given of the particu- " lar sum or debt intended to be insisted upon. " 2 *Geo* 2 *cap.* 22" And, by the second of these statutes, it is declared, " that mutual " debts may be set against each other, either " by being pleaded, or on the general issue, " notwithstanding such debts are of a different " nature, unless where either of the debts shall " accrue by a penalty contained in a bond or " specialty. And in all such cases the debt in- " tended to be set off shall be pleaded in bar, " in which plea shall be shewn how much is " justly due on either side, and in case the " plaintiff recovers, then judgment shall be " entered for no more, than shall appear to be " justly due, after one debt is set against an- " other." 8 *Geo.* 2. *cap* 24. § 5.

De actionibus arbitrariis.

§ XXXI. Præterea actiones quasdam arbitrarias, id est, ex arbitrio judicis pendentes, appellamus: in quibus nisi arbitrio judicis is, cum quo agitur, actori satisfaciat, veluti rem restituat, vel exhibeat, vel solvat, vel ex noxali causa servum dedat, condemnari debeat. Sed istæ actiones tam in rem, quam in personam, inveniuntur. In rem; veluti Publiciana, Serviana de rebus coloni, quasi Serviana, quæ etiam hypothecaria vocatur. in personam; veluti quibus de eo agitur, quod vi aut metus causa, aut dolo malo, factum est. Item cum id, quod certo loco promissum est, petitur. Ad exhibendum quoque actio ex arbitrio judicis pendet. In his enim actionibus, et cæteris similibus, permittitur judici ex bono et æquo, secundum cujusque rei, de qua actum est, naturam, æstimare, quemadmodum actori satisfieri oporteat.

§ 31 *There are also some actions, which we call arbitrary, because they depend intirely upon the arbitration of the judge, for, in these, if the party does not obey the legal commands of the court, by exhibiting whatever is required, by restoring the thing in litigation, or by paying the value of it, or by giving up a slave in consequence of an action of male-feazance, the judge ought immediately to proceed to condemnation by his definitive sentence. Of these arbitrary actions some are real and some personal. Some are real, as the action* Publiciana, Serviana, *and* quasi-Serviana, *which is likewise called hypothecary: others are personal, as those, by which a suit is commenced on account of something done by force, fear, or fraud or on account of something, which was promised to be paid or restored in a certain place · and the action* ad exhibendum, *which was given to the intent, that something particular should be exhibited, is also of of the same kind: and, in all these and the like actions, the judge has full power to determine, according to equity and the nature of the thing sued for, in what manner and proportion the plaintiff ought to receive satisfaction*

Actiones arbitrarias] The laws of *England* take no notice of arbitrary actions, or actions of good faith, but the Lord Chancellor, to whose equity every one, who is without remedy at common law, may appeal, is not bound down or circumscribed by any rules of strict law, but may decide a cause, properly brought before him, *juxta boni viri arbitrium*, i e according to the judgment and conscience of a good man And he may incarcerate any party, who is contumacious, or refractory to his decrees, and detain him in durance, till he submits himself to the orders of the court.

Quinta divisio, de incertæ quantitatis petitione.

§ XXXII. Curare autem debet judex, ut omnino, quantum possibile ei sit, certæ pecuniæ vel rei sententiam ferat, etiamsi de incerta quantitate apud eum actum est.

§ 32. *A judge ought always to take as much care as possible so to frame his sentence, that it may be given for a thing or sum certain; altho' the claim, upon which the sentence is founded, may be for an incertain sum or quantity.*

De pluris petitione.

§ XXXIII. Si quis agens intentione sua plus complexus fuerit, quam ad eum pertineat, causa cadebat, id est, rem amittebat, nec facile in integrum restituebatur à prætore, nisi minor erat 25 annis: huic enim, sicut in aliis causis, causa cognita succurrebatur, si lapsus juventute fuerat: ita et in hac causa succurri solitum erat. Sane, si tam magna causa justi erroris interveniebat, ut etiam constantissimus quisque labi posset, etiam majori 25 annis succurrebatur; veluti si quis totum legatum petierit, post deinde prolati fuerint codicilli, quibus aut pars legati adempta sit, aut quibusdam aliis legata data sint, quæ efficiebant, ut plus petiisse videretur petitor, quam dodrantem; atque ideo lege Falcidia legata minuebantur. Plus autem quatuor modis petitur, re, tempore, loco, et causa. Re, veluti si quis pro decem aureis, quæ ei debebantur, viginti petierit, aut si is, cujus ex parte res est, totam eam, vel majorem partem, suam esse intenderit. Tempore, veluti si quis ante diem vel ante conditionem petierit. Qua enim ratione qui tardius solvit, quam solvere deberet, minus solvere intelligitur, eadem ratione, qui præmature petit, plus petere videtur. Loco plus petitur, veluti cum quis id, quod certo loco sibi dari stipulatus est, alio loco petit sine commemoratione illius loci, in quo sibi dari stipulatus est: verbi gratia, si is, qui ita stipulatus fuerit, *Ephesi dari spondes?* Romæ pure intendat, sibi dari oportere. Ideo autem plus petere intelligitur, quia utilitatem, quam haberet promissor, si Ephesi solveret, adimit ei pura intentione: propter quam causam alio loco petenti arbitraria actio proponitur; in qua scilicet ratio habetur utilitatis, quæ promissori competitura fuisset, si illo loco solveret, quo se soluturum spospondit. Quæ utilitas

utilitas plerumque in mercibus maxima invenitur; veluti vino, oleo, frumento, quæ per singulas regiones diversa habent pretia. Sed et pecuniæ numeratæ non in omnibus regionibus sub iisdem usuris fœnerantur. Si quis tamen Ephesi petat, id est, eo loco petat, in quo, ut sibi detur, stipulatus est, pura actione recte agit: idque etiam prætor demonstrat, scilicet quia utilitas solvendi salva est promissori. Huic autem, qui loco plus petere intelligitur, proximus est, qui causa plus petit: ut ecce, si quis ita à te stipuletur, *hominem Stichum, aut decem aureos, dare spondes?* deinde alterum petat, veluti hominem tantum, aut decem aureos tantum. Ideo autem plus petere intelligitur, quia in eo genere stipulationis promissoris est electio, utrum pecuniam, an hominem, solvere malit: qui igitur pecuniam tantum, vel hominem tantum, sibi dari oportere intendit, eripit electionem adversario, et eo modo suam quidem conditionem meliorem facit, adversarii vero sui deteriorem. Qua de causa talis in ea re prodita est actio, ut quis intendat hominem Stichum aut aureos decem sibi dare oportere, id est, ut eodem modo peteret, quo stipulatus est. Præterea, si quis generaliter hominem stipulatus sit, et specialiter Stichum petat; aut generaliter vinum stipulatus sit, et specialiter campanum petat; aut generaliter purpuram stipulatus sit, deinde specialiter Tyriam petat; plus petere intelligitur, quia electionem adversario tollit, cui stipulationis jure liberum fuit, aliud solvere, quam quod peteretur. Quinetiam licet vilissimum sit, quod quis petat; nihilhominus plus petere intelligitur: quia sæpe accidit, ut promissori facilius sit illud solvere, quod majoris pretii est. Sed hæc quidem antea in usu fuerant; postea vero lex Zenoniana, et nostra, rem coarctavit. Et, si quidem tempore plus fuerit petitum, quid statui oporteat, Zenonis divæ memoriæ loquitur constitutio. Sin autem quantitate, vel alio modo, plus fuerit petitum, id omne, si quod forte damnum ex hac causa accideret ei, contra quem plus petitum fuerit, commissa tripli condemnatione, sicut supra diximus, puniatur.

§ 33 *Formerly, if a plaintiff claimed more in his libel, than was due or belonged to him, he failed in his cause, that is, he even lost that, which really did belong to him: nor was it easy for him to be restored to it by the prætor, unless he was under the age of 25 years: for in this, as well as in other cases, it was usual to aid minors, if it appeared upon examination, that the error was owing to their youth; and whenever an error was such, that one of the most knowing of men might have been deceived [illegible], then even persons of full age might have been aided by the magistrate: as for example, if a legatee had demanded his whole legacy, and codicils were afterwards produced, by which a part of it was revoked, or new legacies bequeathed to other persons, so that the plaintiff appeared to have demanded more than three fourths of his legacy, [illegible] it was subject to a diminution by the [illegible]; in such a case, the legatee would be relieved, notwithstanding the excess of his demand. It is here necessary to be observed, that a man may demand more than what is due to him four several ways, viz. in respect to the thing itself, to time, to place, and to [illegible] the cauſe. In reſpect to the thing itſelf, as when the plaintiff, inſtead of ten* aurei, *which are due to him, demands twenty: or if, when he is, in reality, the owner but of part of ſome particular thing, he claims the whole as his own, or a greater ſhare of it than he is intituled to. In reſpect to time, as when the plaintiff makes his demand before the day of payment, or before the time of the performance of a condition, for, as he, who does not pay ſo ſoon as he ought, is always underſtood to pay leſs than he ought, ſo, by a parity of reaſoning, whoever commences a ſuit prematurely, demands more than his due. In reſpect to place, as when any perſon requires, that what was ſtipulated to be given, or delivered to him at a certain place, ſhould be given or delivered to him at ſome other place, without taking any notice in his libel of the place ſpecified in the ſtipulation; as if* Titius, *for example, ſhould ſtipulate in theſe words* do you promiſe to give ſuch a particular thing at *Epheſus? and ſhould afterwards declare ſimply in his libel, that the ſame thing ought to be given to him at* Rome: *for* Titius *would thus be underſtood to demand more than his due, by endeavoring to deprive his debtor of the advantage, which he might have had in paying his creditor at* Epheſus. *And, it is upon this account, that an arbitrary action is given to him, who would demand payment in another place than that, which was agreed upon; for, in that action, the advantage, which might have accrued to the debtor, by paying his debt in the place ſtipulated, is always taken into conſideration at the diſcretion of the judge. This advantage is generally found the greateſt in merchandiſe. as in wine, oil, corn, &c. which, in different places, bear different prices; and, indeed, money itſelf is not lent every where at the ſame intereſt. But, if a man would ſue the performance of a ſtipulation at* Epheſus, *or at any other place, where it was agreed, that the ſtipulation ſhould be performed, he may legally commence his ſuit by a pure action, that is, without mentioning the place; and this the prætor allows of, inaſmuch as the debtor does not loſe any advantage Next to him, who demands more than his due, in regard to place, is he, who demands more than his due, in regard to the cauſe: as for inſtance, if* Titius *ſtipulates thus with* Sempronius, --- do you promiſe to give either your ſlave *Stichus* or ten aurei? *and then demands from* Sempronius, *either the ſlave ſpecially, or the money ſpecially, for in this caſe* Titius *would be adjudged to have demanded more than his due, the right of election being in* Sempronius, *by whom the promiſe was made, and therefore, when* Titius *ſues either for the money ſpecially, or for the ſlave, he deprives the adverſe party of the power of election, and betters his own condition, by making that of his adverſary the worſe: and it is upon this account, that an action has been given, by which the party agent may make his demand conformable to the ſtipulation, and claim either the ſlave, or the money. And farther, if a man ſhould ſtipulate generally, that wine, purple, or a ſlave, ſhould be given him, and ſhould afterwards ſue for the wine of* Campania, *the purple of* Tyre, *or the ſlave* Stichus *in particular, he would then be adjudged to have demanded more than his due; for the power of election would thus be taken from the adverſe party, who was not bound by the ſtipulation to pay the thing demanded, and altho', in any of theſe caſes, the thing ſued for ſhould be of little or no value, yet the demandant would be thought to claim more than his due, becauſe it is often eaſier for the debtor to pay the thing ſtipulated, altho' it may be of greater value than the thing demanded.——Such was the law according to the antient practice, in regard to an over-demand,* viz. *that the demandant ſhould loſe even that, which was really due to him. But this law has been greatly reſtrained by the conſtitution of* Zeno *the emperor, and by our own, for, if more than is due is demanded in regard to time, the judge muſt be directed in his proceeding by the conſtitution of*

the

that emperor of glorious memory, but, if more is demanded, in respect to quantity, or on any other account, then the loss suffered by him, upon whom the demand is made, must be recompensed, as we have before declared, by the condemnation of the party agent in triple damages.

Lege Falcidia] See book the second, title the twenty-second

Lex Zenoniana et nostra] The constitutions of *Zeno* and *Justinian*, refered to in the text, are not extant,

De minoris summæ petitione.

§ XXXIV. Si minus intentione sua complexus fuerit actor, quam ad eum pertineat; veluti si, cum ei decem aurei deberentur, quinque sibi dare oportere intenderit; aut si, cum totus fundus ejus esset, partem dimidiam suam esse petierit; sine periculo agit: in reliquum enim nihilominus judex adversarium eodem judicio ei condemnat, ex constitutione divæ memoriæ Zenonis.

§ 34 *If a plaintiff sues for less, than what he has a claim to, demanding, for instance, only 5* aurei, *when ten are due, or the moiety of an estate, when the whole belongs to him, he acts safely by this method, for the judge, in consequence of* Zeno's *constitution, may nevertheless condemn the adverse party, under the same process, to the payment or delivery of all, which appears of right to belong to the plaintiff*

Si aliud pro alio petatur.

§ XXXV. Si quis aliud pro alio intenderit, nihil eum periclitari placet, sed in eodem judicio, cognita veritate, errorem suum corrigere ei permittitur, veluti si is, qui hominem stichum petere deberet, Erotem petierit: aut si quis ex testamento dari sibi oportere intenderit, quod ex stipulatu debetur.

§ 35 *When a plaintiff demands one thing instead of another, he risks nothing by the mistake, which he is allowed to correct under one and the same process: as if a litigant should demand the slave* Erotes, *instead of the slave* Stichus, *or should claim, as due by testament, what is found to be due upon a stipulation.*

Divisio sexta. De peculio.

§ XXXVI. Sunt præterea quædam actiones, quibus non semper solidum, quod nobis debetur, persequimur, sed modo solidum persequimur, modo minus. ut ecce, si in peculium filii servive agamus: nam, si non minus in peculio sit, quam persequimur, in solidum dominus paterve condemnatur: si vero minus inveniatur, eatenus condemnat judex, quatenus in peculio sit. Quemadmodum autem peculium intelligi debeat, suo ordine proponemus.

§ 36 *There are also some actions, by which we do not always sue for the whole, which is due to us, but for the whole, or less, than the whole, as it proves to be most expedient, thus, when a suit is brought against the* peculium *of a son or a slave, if the* peculium *is sufficient to answer the demand, the father or master must be condemned to pay the whole debt, but, if the* peculium *is not sufficient, the judge*

can

can condemn the defendents only to the extent of its value. We will hereafter explain, in it's proper place, what we mean by the term peculium.

De repetitione dotis.

§ XXXVII. Item, si de dote in judicio mulier agat, placet, eatenus maritum condemnari debere, quatenus facere possit, id est, quatenus facultates ejus patiuntur. Itaque, si dotis quantitati concurrant facultates ejus, in solidum damnatur, sin minus, in tantum, quantum facere potest. Propter retentionem quoque dotis repetitio minuitur: nam ob impensas, in res dotales factas, marito quasi retentio concessa est; quia ipso jure necessariis sumptibus dos minuitur, sicut ex latioribus digestorum libris cognoscere licet.

§ 37. *Also, if a woman commences a suit for the restitution of her marriage portion, the man must be condemned to pay as far as he is able, i. e. as far as his income or faculties will permit: and therefore, if the portion demanded and the faculties of the man are equal, he must be adjudged to satisfy the whole demand; but, if his faculties are less than the claim, he must nevertheless be condemned to pay as much as he is able. But the claim of a woman may in this case be lessened by a retention; for the husband is permitted to retain an equivalent for whatever he hath necessarily expended upon the estate given with his wife, as a marriage portion; but this will fully appear by a perusal of the digests, to which the reader is refered.*

De actione adversus parentem, patronum, socium, et donatorem.

§ XXXVIII. Sed et, si quis cum parente suo patronove agat, item si socius cum socio judicio societatis agat, non plus actor consequitur, quam adversarius ejus facere potest. Idem est, si quis ex donatione sua conveniatur.

§ 38. *And, if any person commences a suit against his parent or patron, or if one partner sues another, the plaintiff can by no means obtain sentence for a greater sum, than his adversary is able to pay: and the same is to be observed, when a donor is* [illegible] *of his donation.*

De compensationibus.

§ XXXIX. Compensationes quoque oppositæ plerumque efficiunt, ut minus quisque consequatur, quam ei debeatur. Nam ex bono et æquo habita ratione ejus, quod invicem actorem ex eadem causa præstare oportet, potest judex in reliquum eum, cum quo actum est, condemnare, sicut jam dictum est.

§ 39. *When a compensation is alleged by the defendent, it generally happens, that the plaintiff recovers less than his demand; for it is in the power of the judge,* [illegible]*, to make an equitable deduction from the demand of the plaintiff of* [illegible] *he owes to the defendant, and to condemn the defendant to the payment only of the remainder.*

De eo, qui bonis cessit.

§ XL. Cum eo quoque, qui creditoribus suis bonis cessit, si postea aliquid acquisierit, quod idoneum emolumentum habeat, ex integro in id, quod facere potest, creditores experiuntur. Inhumanum enim erat, spoliatum fortunis suis in solidum damnari.

§ 40. *Creditors also, to whom a debtor hath made a cession of his goods, may afterwards, if he hath gained any considerable acquisition, bring a fresh suit against him, for as much as he is able to pay, but not more, for it would be inhuman to condemn a man* in solidum, *who hath already been deprived of his whole fortune.*

Si postea aliquid acquisierit] The statute law of *England* in regard to bankrupts and insolvent debtors, who have been discharged, is much of the same tenor with the *Roman* law for it is enacted, by the 5th of *Geo* 2d, "that "in case any commission of bankruptcy shall "issue against any person, who after *June* "1732 shall have been discharged by virtue "of this act, or shall have compounded with "his creditors, or delivered to them his effects, "and been released by them, or been discharged by any act for the relief of insolvent debtors, then the *body only* of such person conforming shall be free from arrest, but "his future estate shall be liable to his creditors [the tools of trade, necessary houshold-goods, and necessary wearing apparel of "such bankrupt and his wife and children "excepted] unless the estate of such person "shall produce clear fifteen shillings in the "pound 5 *Geo* 2 *cap* 3 § 9.

TITULUS SEPTIMUS.

Quod cum eo, qui in aliena potestate est, negotium gestum esse dicitur.

D. xiv. T. 5. C. iv. T. 16.

Scopus et nexus.

QUIA tamen superius mentionem habuimus de actione, qua in peculium filiorum servorumque agitur, opus est, ut de hac actione et de ceteris, quae eorundem nomine in parentes dominosve dari solent, diligentius admoneamus. Et quia, sive cum servis negotium gestum sit, sive cum iis, qui in potestate parentum sunt, eadem fere iura servantur, ne verbosa fiat disputatio, dirigamus sermonem in personam servi dominique, idem intellecturi de liberis quoque et parentibus, quorum in potestate sunt. Nam, si quid in his proprie servetur, separatim ostendemus.

We have already made mention of the action, by which a suit may be brought against the peculium, *or separate estate of a son or a slave, but it is now necessary to speak of it more fully, and also of some other actions, which are given on account of children*

children and slaves against their parents and masters But, inasmuch as the law is almost the same, whether an affair is transacted with a slave, or with him, who is under the power of his parent, we will therefore, to avoid being prolix, treat only of slaves and their masters, leaving what we say of them to be understood also of parents and children under power; for, whenever there is any thing peculiar to be observed, in regard to children and parents, we intend to point it out separately.

De actione quod jussu.

§ I. Si igitur jussu domini cum servo negotium gestum erit, in solidum prætor adversus dominum actionem pollicetur: scilicet quia is, qui ita contrahit, fidem domini sequi videtur

§ 1 *If any business is negotiated by a slave, who acts by the command of his master, the prætor will give an action against the master for the whole value of the transaction, for whoever makes a contract with a slave, is presumed to have done it upon a confidence in the master.*

Si igitur jussu domini] In general by the law of *England*, if a servant borrows money in his master's name, the master shall not be charged with it, unless it comes to his use, and that by his assent And the law is the same, if a servant makes a contract in his master's name, for the contract shall not bind his master, unless it were by his master's command, or came to his master's use by his assent *Doctor and Student, dial 2 cap* 42 But in some cases the law will presume the consent of the master, altho' it is not particularly expressed, as in those contracts, which are made by servants, whom merchants place in their shops or warehouses, as their factors *Cowel's inst. lib* 4 *t* 7

De exercitoria et institoria actione.

§ II. Eadem ratione prætor duas alias in solidum actiones pollicetur; quarum altera exercitoria, altera institoria, appellatur. Exercitoria tunc habet locum, cum quis servum suum magistrum navi præposuerit, et quid cum eo, ejus rei gratia, cui præpositus erit, contractum fuerit Ideo autem exercitoria vocatur, quia exercitor is appellatur, ad quem quotidianus navis quæstus pertinet. Institoria tunc locum habet, cum quis tabernæ forte, aut cuilibet negotiationi, servum suum præposuerit, et quid cum eo, ejus rei gratia, cui præpositus erit, contractum fuerit. Ideo autem institoria appellatur, quia, qui negotiationibus præponuntur, institores vocantur. Istas tamen duas actiones prætor reddit, et si liberum quis hominem, aut alienum servum, navi aut tabernæ aut cuilibet negotiationi præposuerit, scilicet quia eadem æquitatis ratio etiam eo casu interveniat.

§ 2 *The prætor also gives two other actions* in solidum *upon the same motive; the one of which is called* exercitoria, *the other* institoria *The action* exercitoria *takes place, when a master hath constituted his slave to be the commander of a vessel, and hath contracted with such slave touching that concern, [illegible] exercitoria, because he, to whom the profits of a ship or [illegible] is called* exercitor. *The action* institoria *is made use of, when a [illegible] the slave the management of a shop, or committed any particular [illegible] to his care; [illegible] with such slave: and this action is called* institoria, *because all persons, to whom a negotiation is commited, are denominated* institores. *The prætor hath likewise been induced, by the same equity, to give these two actions against any man, who imploys a free person, or the slave of another, in the management of a ship, a warehouse, or any particular affair.*

De tributoria.

§ III. Introduxit et aliam actionem prætor, quæ tributoria vocatur: namque si servus in peculiari merce, sciente domino, negotietur, et quid cum eo ejus rei causa contractum erit, ita prætor jus dicit, ut, quicquid in his mercibus erit, quodque inde receptum erit, id inter dominum, si quid ei debebitur, et cæteros creditores, pro rata portione distribuatur. Et ideo tributoria vocatur, quia ipsi domino distributionem prætor permittit. Nam, si quis ex creditoribus queratur, quasi minus ei tributum sit, quam oportuerit, hanc ei actionem accommodat, quæ tributoria appellatur.

§ 3 *The prætor hath also introduced another action called* tributoria, *or tributory; for, if a slave, without the command, but with the knowledge of his master, trafics with the product of his* peculium, *and persons are thus induced to contract with him, the prætor ordains, that the merchandize, or money, arising from his traffic, shall be distributed between the master, (if he has any just claim,) and the rest of the creditors in a ratable proportion, and the master himself is always permited to make the distribution but, if any creditor complains, that too small a share hath been apportioned to him, the prætor will allow him to use the before-named action, which is called* tributoria, *on account of the distribution.*

De peculio, et de in rem verso.

§ IV. Præterea introducta est actio de peculio, deque eo, quod in rem domini versum erit; ut quamvis sine voluntate domini negotium gestum erit, tamen sive quid in rem ejus versum fuerit, id totum præstare debeat, sive quid non sit in rem ejus versum, id eatenus præstare debeat, quatenus peculium patitur. In rem autem domini versum intelligitur, quicquid necessario in rem ejus impenderit servus, veluti si mutuatus pecuniam creditoribus ejus solverit, aut ædificia ruentia fulserit, aut familiæ frumentum emerit, vel etiam fundum aut quamlibet aliam rem necessariam mercatus erit. Itaque, si ex decem puta aureis, quos servus tuus à Titio mutuo accepit, creditori tuo quinque aureos solverit, reliquos vero quinque quolibet modo consumpserit, pro quinque quidem in solidum damnari debes; pro cæteris vero quinque eatenus, quatenus in peculio sit. Ex quo scilicet apparet, si toti decem aurei in rem tuam versi fuerint, totos decem aureos Titium consequi posse. Licet enim una sit actio, qua de peculio, deque eo, quod in rem domini versum sit, agitur; tamen duas habet condemnationes. Itaque judex, apud quem de ea actione agitur, ante dispicere solet, an in rem domini versum

sit·

sit: nec aliter ad peculii æstimationem transit, quam aut nihil in rem domini versum intelligatur, aut non totum. Cum autem quæritur, quantum in peculio sit, ante deducitur, quicquid servus domino eive, qui in potestate ejus sit, debet; et, quod superest, id solum peculium intelligitur. Aliquando tamen id, quod ei debet servus, qui in potestate domini sit, non deducitur ex peculio, veluti si is in ipsius peculio sit: quod eo pertinet, ut, si quid vicario suo servus debeat, id ex peculio ejus non deducatur.

§ 4 *The action concerning a* peculium, *and things converted to the profit of the master of a slave, hath likewise been introduced by the prætor; for altho' a contract hath been entered into by a slave, without the consent of his master, yet, where the money arising from it is converted to the benefit of such master, the master ought to be answerable for the performance of it; and, even altho' the master should receive no emolument from the transaction, yet it is right, that he should be answerable for as much as the* peculium *of his slave is found to be worth. But, to be more explicit, we understand, that whenever money, or any other thing, is necessarily used or expended by a slave upon his master's affairs, it is a conversion of it to his benefit; as for example, if a slave, who hath borrowed money, should pay the debts of his master, repair his buildings, purchase an estate, provision, or any other thing, which is useful. and therefore, if out of ten* aurei, *borrowed by a slave, he should pay only five to his master's creditors, and squander the rest, the master would nevertheless be condemned to the payment* in solidum *of the five* aurei, *which had been expended for his use; but, as to the other five, he could be obliged to pay only so much as the* peculium *could answer; and from hence it will appear, that, if all the ten* aurei, *which were borrowed, had been converted by the slave to his master's emolument, the lender might have recovered the whole ten from the master; for altho' it is one and the same action, by which a suit is commenced against a* peculium, *and for the recovery of what a slave hath converted to his master's use, yet this action comes with it two different condemnations; and it is for this reason, that the judge does not begin to make an estimate of the value of the* peculium, *till he has previously examined, whether the whole, or any part of the money, arising from the slave's contract, hath been expended for the service of the master: but, when the judge proceeds to the valuation of the* peculium, *a deduction is made of whatever the slave owes to his master, or to any other under the power of his master, and the remainder only is understood to be strictly the* peculium, *and chargeable with debts due to strangers. But it sometimes happens, that what one slave owes to another under the power of the same master, is not deducted; as when the slave, who is the creditor, composes a part of his debtor's* peculium; *for, if a slave is indebted to his vicarial slave, this debt cannot be deducted from the* peculium.

Aliquando tamen.] When an action *de peculio* is brought for the full value of a *peculium*, which is worth, for example, an hundred *aurei*, and the slave, to whom the *peculium* belongs, owes 50 *aurei* to the son of his master, or to some other slave under the power of the same master, the judge must then deduct these fifty *aurei*, so that the plaintiff can can only receive the remaining fifty: but, when a suit is commenced for 100 *aurei* against a *peculium*, which is worth but 100 *aurei*, and the slave, to whom this *peculium*, or separate estate belongs, is indebted in 50 *aurei* to another slave, who is under the same master, but makes a part or parcel of the *peculium*, as being appendent to it, in this case the judge is not authorized to order the 50 *aurei* due to the vicarial or subordinate slave, to be deducted, but must cause the payment of the 100 *aurei*, [illegible] the whole value of the *peculium*, to be made [illegible] the plaintiff: and the reason, assigned for this by [illegible] is the following, *et, cum ita se res ha-* [illegible] *non potest* [illegible] *æstimatione peculium* [illegible] *minuere, eo nomine, quod sibi aliquid debeatur, ne eadem persona duas contrar*[illegible] *habere functiones videatur, ut simul et augeat* [illegible] *minuat peculium.* [illegible]

De concursu dictarum actionum.

§ V. Cæterum dubium non est, quin is quoque, qui jussu domini contraxerit, cuique institoria vel exercitoria actio competit, de peculio deque eo, quod in rem domini versum est, agere possit. Sed erit stultissimus, si, omissa actione, qua facillime solidum ex contractu consequi possit, se ad difficultatem perducat probandi, in rem domini versum esse, vel habere servum peculium, et tantum habere, ut solidum sibi solvi possit. Is quoque, cui tributoria actio competit, æque de peculio et de in rem verso agere potest. Sed sane huic modo tributoria expedit agere, modo de peculio, et de in rem verso. Tributoria ideo expedit agere, quia in ea domini conditio præcipua non est, id est, quod domino debetur, non deducitur, sed ejusdem juris est dominus, cujus et ceteri creditores: at, in actione de peculio, ante deducitur, quod domino debetur: et in id, quod reliquum est, creditori dominus condemnatur. Rursus de peculio ideo expedit agere, quod in hac actione totius peculii ratio habetur: at in tributoria ejus tantum, quo negotiatur. et potest quisque tertia forte parte peculii, aut quarta, vel etiam minima, negotiari, majorem autem partem in prædiis aut fœnebri pecunia habere. Prout ergo expedit, ita quisque vel hanc actionem, vel illam, eligere debet. Certe, qui potest probare, in rem domini versum esse, de in rem verso agere debet.

§ 5. *It is nevertheless not to be doubted, but that he, who hath made a contract with a slave at the command of the master of that slave, and is intitled either to the action* institoria *or* exercitoria, *is also intitled to the action* de peculio *and* de in rem verso: *but it would be highly imprudent in any person to relinquish an action, by which he could most easily recover his whole demand, and, by recurring to another, subject himself to the difficulty of proving, that the money he lent to the slave was turned to the use of the master, or that the slave is possessed of a* peculium *sufficient to answer the whole debt. He also, to whom the action* tributoria *is given, is equally intitled to the action* de peculio, *and* de in rem verso; *but it is expedient, in some cases, to use the one, and in some cases the other: yet it is frequently most expedient to use the action* tributoria, *because, in this, the condition of the master is not principally regarded, i. e. there is no previous deduction made of what is due to him, his title being esteemed in the same light with that of other creditors: but, in the action* de peculio, *the debt due to the master is first deducted, and he is condemned only to distribute the remainder among the creditors. Again, in some cases, it may be more convenient to commence a suit by the action* de peculio, *because it affects the whole* peculium, *whereas the action* tributoria *regards only so much of it as hath been made use of in traffic; and it is possible, that a slave may have trafficked only with a third, a fourth, or some very small part, and that the rest, consisting of lands, slaves or money,* [illegible] *therefore it greatly behoves every man to chuse* [illegible] *to him; but, if the creditor of a slave can prove*

prove a conversion to the use of the master of that slave, he ought most certainly to commence his suit by the action de in rem verso

De filiis familiarum.

§ VI. Quæ diximus de servo et de domino, eadem intelligimus et de filio et filia, et nepote et nepte, et patre avove, cujus in potestate sunt

We understand what we have said, concerning a slave and his master, to take place equally in regard to children under power, and their parents

De senatus-consulto Macedoniano.

§ VII. Illud proprie servatur in eorum persona, quod senatus-consultum Macedonianum prohibuit mutuas pecunias dari eis, qui in potestate parentis sunt, et ei, qui crediderit, denegatur actio tam adversus ipsum filium filiamve, nepotem neptemve, (sive adhuc in potestate sint, sive morte parentis vel emancipatione suæ potestatis esse cœperint,) quam adversus patrem avumve, sive eos habeat adhuc in potestate, sive emancipaverit. Quæ ideo senatus prospexit, quia sæpe onerati ære alieno creditarum pecuniarum, quas in luxuriam consumebant, vitæ parentum insidiabantur.

§ 7 *But children are, in some respects, particularly regarded by the* Macedonian *decree of the senate, which prohibits money to be lent them, whilest they are under the power of their parents, for creditors are not suffered to bring any action, either against the children, even after they are emancipated, or against their parents, who emancipated them This was a caution, which the senate thought proper to take, because young men, who were loaded with their debts, contracted for the support of luxury, have often endeavored, by private methods, to take away the lives of their parents*

Senatus consultum Macedonianum] This decree was called Macedonian from *Macedo*, the name of the person, who gave rise to it but, whether this *Macedo* was a young patrician under the power of his father, or an old usurer, the learned commentators are in very great doubt, and they are even far from being unanimous, as to the time when this decree was first made [illegible] certain, that the [illegible] *Claudius* [illegible] published a law, by which, to use the words of [illegible], he [illegible] the cruelty of creditors, [illegible] And this law is conjectured to have been the *Macedonian Senatus-consultum*, which, in order to reconcile the two historians *Tacitus* and *Suetonius*, is supposed by some to have grown obsolete in the reign of *Nero*, and afterwards to have been revived by *Vespasian* for *Suetonius* writes as follows in the life of that emperor, [illegible] Those, who have time and inclination to read more upon this subject, are refered to the *Syntagma* of *Heineccius*, lib 4 tit 7 but particularly to [illegible], lib 1 cap 25

De actione directa in patrem vel dominum.

§ VIII Illud in summa admonendi sumus, id, quod jussu patris dominive contractum fuerit, quodque in rem ejus versum erit, directo quoque posse à patre dominove condici, tanquam si principaliter cum ipso negotium gestum esset. Ei quoque, qui exercitoria vel institoria actione

tenetur

tenetur, directo posse condici placet, quia hujus quoque jussu contractum intelligitur.

But, in fine, we must observe, that whatever hath been contracted for at the command of a parent or master, and converted to their use, may be recovered by a direct action against the father or master in the same manner, as if the contract had been originally made with them. And it is likewise certain, that he, who is liable to the action institoria *or* exhibitoria, *may also be sued by a direct action, inasmuch as the contract is presumed to have been made at his command.*

TITULUS OCTAVUS.

De noxalibus actionibus.

D. ix. T. 4. C. iii. T. 41.

De servis. Summa.

EX maleficiis servorum, veluti si furtum fecerint, aut bona rapuerint, aut damnum dederint, aut injuriam commiserint, noxales actiones proditæ sunt, quibus domino damnato permittitur aut litis æstimationem sufferre, aut ipsum hominem noxæ dedere

Noxal actions are given on account of the offenses of slaves, as when a slave commits a theft or robbery, or does any other damage or injury And, when the master or owner of a slave is condemned upon this account, it is in his option either to pay the estimation of the damage done, or to deliver up his slave as a recompense

Ex maleficiis servorum] The action *noxalis*, which lies against masters for the crimes of their servants, was always unknown in *England*, for even villeins, before the tenures in villenage were abolished, might have been convened for their own crimes *Cow. inst. l 4 t 8* But there is something in the law of *England* similar to a noxal action, in regard to animals and things inanimate, by which the death of a man was occasioned for, if a vitious horse, or bull, or a cart drawn by horses or oxen, occasions the death of any person, the thing, or animal, which did the mischief, becomes, as it were, forfeited, and is called a *Deodand*, [*i e* a thing given to God,] because it was sold in antient times by the king's almoner, who distributed the money to pious uses But, in regard to *Deodands*, the law makes many distinctions, *e g* if a ship or boat is laden with merchandise, and a man is killed, or drowned by the motion, yet the merchandise are no *Deodand*, tho' the accident happened in fresh water but, if any particular merchandise falls upon a man, and kills him, that merchandise shall be *Deodand*, but not the ship —— See *Hale's Hist of the pl of the Crown Vol 1 p 422 Hawk pl of the crown lib 1 cap 26*

Quid sit noxa et noxia.

§ I. Noxa autem est ipsum corpus, quod nocuit, id est, servus: noxia ipsum maleficium, veluti furtum, rapina, damnum, injuria.

The

The term noxa *denotes the slave, by whom the male-feazance was done; and, by the word* noxia, *we understand the male-feasance itself, be it of what kind it will, theft, damage, rapin, or injury.*

Ratio harum actionum.

§ II. Summa autem ratione permissum est noxæ deditione fungi: namque erat iniquum, nequitiam eorum ultra ipsorum corpora dominis damnosam esse.

§ 2. *It is with the utmost reason allowable, that a master should deliver the slave, who is culpable, as a full compensation to the party injured, for it was unjust, that that it should be in the power of slaves to cause their master to suffer any greater damage, than the value of their own bodies would amount to.*

Effectus noxæ deditionis.

§ III. Dominus, noxali judicio servi sui nomine conventus, servum actori noxæ dedendo liberatur: nec minus in perpetuum ejus servi dominium à domino transfertur. Sin autem damnum ei, cui deditus est servus, resarcierit quæsita pecunia, auxilio prætoris, invito domino, manumittetur.

§ 3. *If a noxal action is given against a master, he may free himself from it by delivering his slave into the possession of the plaintiff, in whom the property in such slave will become absolutely vested, but, if the slave can pay his new master in money the value of the damage, the slave may be manumited by the assistence of the prætor, altho' his new master is ever so unwilling.*

De origine harum actionum.

§ IV. Sunt autem constitutæ noxales actiones aut legibus, aut edicto prætoris: legibus, veluti furti ex lege 12 tabularum, damni injuriæ ex lege Aquilia: edicto prætoris, veluti injuriarum, et vi bonorum raptorum.

§ 4 *Noxal actions are constituted either by the laws, or by the edict of the prætor. They are constituted on account of theft by the laws of the* 12 tables, *and, on account of damage injuriously done, by virtue of the law* Aquilia *But, on account of injuries and goods taken by force, they are constituted by the edict of the prætor*

Qui conveniuntur noxali actione.

§ V. Omnis autem noxalis actio caput sequitur: nam, si servus tuus noxam commiserit quamdiu in tua potestate sit, tecum actio est. Si autem in alterius potestatem pervenerit, cum illo incipit actio esse. At, si manumissus fuerit, directo ipse tenetur, et extinguitur noxæ deditio. Ex diverso quoque directa actio noxalis esse incipit: nam, si liber homo noxiam commiserit, et is servus tuus esse cœperit, (quod quibusdam

casibus effici primo libro tradidimus,) incipit tecum esse noxalis actio, quæ ante directa fuisset.

§ 5. Every noxal action follows the person of the slave, by whom the male-feazance was commited, but, as long as he continues under the power of his master, his master only is liable to an action, and, if he becomes subject to a new master, then the new master becomes liable. but, if the slave is manumited, he may be prosecuted by a direct action, for then the noxæ deditio *is extinguished; because no surrender can then be made of him, by whom the male-feazance was commited. But, on the contrary, an action, which was at first direct, may afterwards become noxal: for if a man, who is free, does any male-feazance, and afterwards becomes a slave, [and we have, in our first book declared in what cases this may happen,] then the action, which was before direct, begins to be a noxal action against his master.*

Si servus Domino noxiam commiserit, vel contra.

§ VI. Si servus domino noxiam commiserit, actio nulla nascitur: namque inter dominum et eum, qui in potestate ejus est, nulla obligatio nasci potest. Ideoque, si in alienam potestatem servus pervenerit, aut manumissus fuerit, neque cum ipso, neque cum eo, cujus nunc in potestate sit, agi potest: unde, si alienus servus tibi noxiam commiserit, et is postea in potestate tua esse cœperit, interdicitur actio: quia in ea casum deducta sit, in quo consistere non potuit. Ideoque, licet exierit de tua potestate, agere non potes: quemadmodum si dominus in servum suum aliquid commiserit, nec, si manumissus aut alienatus fuerit servus, ullam actionem contra dominum habere potest.

§ 6 Altho' a slave commits a male-feazance against his master, yet no action is given; for no obligation can arise between a master and his slave; and therefore, if that slave passes under the power of another master, or is manumited, no action can be brought either against him in his own person, or against his new master, from whence it follows, that, if the slave of another should commit any male-feazance, for example, against Titius, *and should afterwards become the slave of the same* Titius, *the action is extinguished, for it is a maxim, that an action becomes extinct, whenever it is brought into a state, in which it could not have had a commencement, and hence it is, that altho' a slave, from whom a master hath received damage, should cease to be under the power of that master, yet no action can afterwards be given against such slave, neither can a slave, who hath been aliened or manumited, bring any action against his late master, by whom he hath been ill treated.*

De filiis-familiarum.

§ VII. Sed veteres quidem hoc in filiis-familiarum masculis et fœminis admisere: nova autem hominum conversatio hujusmodi asperitatem recte respuendam esse existimavit, et ab usu communi hoc penitus recessit. Quis enim patiatur, filium suum, et maxime filiam, in noxam alii dari? ut pene per filii corpus pater magis quam filius periclitetur; cum in filiabus etiam pudicitiæ favor hoc bene excludat. Et ideo placuit, in servos tantummodo noxales actiones esse proponendas, cum, apud

apud veteres legum commentatores, invenerimus sæpius dictum, ipsos filios-familiarum pro suis delictis posse conveniri.

§ 7. The antients indeed admited this law of the forfeiture of the person to take place, even in cases, in which their children were concerned, whether male or female: but the later ages have rightly thought that such a rigorous proceeding ought, by all means, to be exploded; and it hath therefore passed wholly into disuse: for who could suffer a son, and more especially a daughter, to be delivered up as a forfeiture to a stranger? for, in the case of a son, the punishment of the father would be greater, than that of the son; and, in the case of a daughter, the rules of modesty forbid such a practice. It hath therefore prevailed, that noxal actions should only take place in regard to slaves; and, in the books of the antient commentators of the law, we find it often repeated, that the sons of a family may themselves be convened for their own misdeeds.

TITULUS NONUS.

Si quadrupes pauperiem fecisse dicatur.

D. ix. T. 1.

De actione, si quadrupes ex l. 12 tab.

ANimalium nomine, quæ ratione carent, si qua lascivia, aut pavore, aut feritate, pauperiem fecerint, noxalis actio lege 12 tab. prodita est: quæ animalia, si noxæ dedantur, proficiunt reo ad liberationem: quia ita lex tabularum scripta est, ut puta, si equus calcitrosus calce percusserit, aut bos, cornu petere solitus, cornu petierit. Hæc autem actio in iis, quæ contra naturam moventur, locum habet. Ceterum, si genitalis sit feritas, cessat actio. Denique, si ursus fugerit à domino, et sic nocuerit, non potest quondam dominus conveniri, quia desiit dominus esse, ubi fera evasit. Pauperies autem est damnum sine injuria facientis datum. Nec enim potest animal injuriam fecisse dici, quod sensu caret. Hæc quidem ad noxalem pertinent actionem.

A noxal action is given by the law of the 12 tables, *whenever any damage is done by brute animals, thro' wantonness, fright, or furiousness; but, if they are delivered up in atonement for the damage done, the defendent must be discharged from the action; for it is thus written in the law of the* 12 tables, *if* an horse, apt to kick, should strike with his foot, or if an ox, accustomed to gore, should wound any man with his horns, &c. *But a noxal action takes place only in regard to those animals, which act contrary to their nature, for, when the ferocity of a beast is innate, no action can be given, so that, if a bear breaks loose from his master, and mischief is done, the person, to whom this animal belonged, cannot be convened; for he ceased to be the master as soon as the beast escaped. But it is here to be noted, that the word* pauperies *denotes a damage, by which no injury is intended; for an animal, which hath no reason, cannot be said to have commited an injury. This is what relates to noxal actions.*

De actione ædilitia, concurrente cum actione de pauperie.

§ I. Cæterum sciendum est, ædilitio edicto prohiberi nos canem, verrem aprum, ursum, leonem, ibi habere, qua vulgo iter fit: et, si adversus ea factum erit, et nocitum libero homini esse dicatur, quod bonum et æquum judici videtur, tanti dominus condemnetur: cæterarum vero rerum, quanti damnum datum sit, dupli. Præter has autem ædilitias actiones, et de pauperie locum habebit: nunquam enim actiones, præsertim pœnales, de eadem re concurrentes, alia aliam consumet.

§ 1. *It must be observed, that the edict of the Edile prohibits any man to keep a dog, a boar, a bear, or a lion, where there is a public passage or highway: and, if this prohibition is disobeyed, and any freeman receives hurt, the master of the beast may be condemned in whatever sum seems agreeable to equity in the opinion of the judge; yet, in regard to every other damage, the condemnation must be in the double of what the damage amounts to. It is here necessary to inform the student, that not only the* Edilitian *action, but also an action for the damage, called* pauperies, *may both take place against the same person, for, altho' actions, and more especially those, which are penal, concur together on account of the same thing, they are not destructive the one of another.*

De eadem re concurrentes] The same doctrine is delivered by *Ulpian, ff* 44 *t* 7 *l* 60. *ff* 50 *t* 17 *l* 130 which doctrine we must [illegible] to regard penal actions, concurring on account of the same thing, but yet arising from different facts and offenses, as for instance, if a man steals a slave, and afterwards murders him, such a criminal may be doubly prosecuted, for theft and injurious damage, for as the actions of theft and injurious damage would arise in this case from different offenses, the one will not bar the other: but, on the contrary, if two penal actions, concurring on account of the same thing, should arise from the same offense, the one would destroy the other, and therefore the plaintiff must make his election. *vid. Cuj. observ. lib.* 8 *c.* 24. *Hotoman. illust. quæst.* 29.

TITULUS

TITULUS DECIMUS.

De iis, per quos agere poſſumus.

Per quos agere liceat.

NUNC admonendi ſumus, agere poſſe quemlibet hominem aut ſuo nomine aut alieno. Alieno, veluti procuratorio, tutorio, curatorio, cum olim in uſu fuiſſet, alterius nomine agi non poſſe, niſi pro populo, pro libertate, pro tutela. Præterea lege Hoſtilia permiſſum erat furti agere eorum nomine, qui apud hoſtes eſſent, aut reipublicæ cauſa abeſſent, quive in eorum cujus tutela eſſent. Sed, quia hoc non minimam incommoditatem habebat, quod alieno nomine neque agere, neque excipere actionem, licebat, cœperunt homines per procuratores litigare. Nam et morbus et ætas et neceſſaria peregrinatio, itemque aliæ multæ cauſæ ſæpe hominibus impedimento ſunt, quo minus rem ſuam ipſi exequi poſſint.

Any man may commence a ſuit, either in his own name, or in that of another, as in the name of a proctor, a tutor, or a curator, but anciently, one perſon could not ſue in the name of another, unleſs in a cauſe of liberty, tutelage, or where a ſociety was concerned. It was afterwards permitted by the law Hoſtilia, *that an action of theft might be brought in the names of thoſe, who were captives in the hands of the enemy, --- who were abſent upon the affairs of the republic, --- or who were under the care of tutors. But, as it was found in later times to be highly inconvenient, that any man ſhould be prohibited, either from ſuing, or defending in the name of another, it by degrees became a practice to ſue by proctors: for ill health, old age, the neceſſity of voyaging, and many other caſes, continually prevent mankind from being able to proſecute their own affairs in perſon.*

Aut ſuo nomine aut alieno] In *England* the liberty of conſtituting an attorney to proſecute ſuits is given chiefly by the ſtatute law. [illegible] 20 *H.* 3 *cap.* 10. 12 *Edw.* 2 *cap.* 1. 15 *Edw.* 2 *cap.* 1. 7 *Ric.* 2 *cap.* 14. 7 *Hen.* 4 *cap.* 13. 29 *Eliz.* *cap.* 5. For, by the common law, the plaintiff or defendent, demandant or tenent, could not appear by attorney without the king's writ, or letters patent, but ought to follow his ſuit in his own proper perſon. *Abſence* (ſays the author of the Mirror) *a retener attorny ſans breve de la chancery.* Co. Litt. 128. *a.*

Quibus modis procurator conſtituatur.

§ I. Procurator neque certis verbis, neque præſente ſemper adverſario, imo et plerumque eo ignorante, conſtituitur. Cuicunque enim permiſeris rem tuam agere, aut defendere, is tuus procurator intelligitur.

§ 1. *It is not neceſſary to uſe any certain form of words in appointing a proctor, nor to make the appointment in the preſence of the adverſe party, for it is generally done*

even

even without his knowledge: and note, that whoever is imployed either to sue or to defend for another, is understood to be a proctor.

Quibus modis tutores vel curatores constituuntur.

§ II. Tutores et curatores quemadmodum constituantur, primo libro expositum est.

§ 2. *We have already explained in the first book of our institutes, how tutors and curators may be appointed.*

Primo libro] vid. book the 1st, title 13.

TITULUS UNDECIMUS.

De satisdationibus.

D. ii. T. 8. C. ii. T. 57.

De judicio personali.

SAtisdationum modus alius antiquitati placuit, alium novitas per usum amplexa est. Olim enim, si in rem agebatur, satisdare possessor compellebatur, ut, si victus esset, nec rem ipsam restitueret, nec litis æstimationem, potestas esset petitori aut cum eo agendi, aut cum fidejussoribus ejus: quæ satisdatio appellatur *judicatum solvi*: unde autem sic appelletur, facile est intelligere. Namque stipulabatur quis, ut solveretur sibi, quod fuisset judicatum: multo magis is, qui in rem actione conveniebatur, satisdare cogebatur, si alieno nomine judicium accipiebat. Ipse autem, qui in rem agebat, si suo nomine petebat, satisdare non cogebatur. Procurator vero, si in rem agebat, satisdare jubebatur, *rem ratam dominum habiturum*. Periculum enim erat, ne iterum dominus de eadem re experiretur. Tutores vero et curatores eodem modo, quo procuratores, satisdare debere, verba edicti faciebant. Sed aliquando his agentibus satisdatio remittebatur. Hæc ita erant, si in rem agebatur.

In taking security, the antients persued a different method from that, which the moderns have made choice of; for antiently, if a real action was brought, the defendent, or party in possession, was compelled to give security, to the end, that, if he lost his cause, and would neither restore the thing itself, nor pay the estimation of it, the demandant might be inabled either to sue such defendent, or the parties bound for him; and this species of caution is termed judicatum solvi, *nor is it difficult to understand, why it is so called; since every demandant stipulated, that the thing adjudged to him should be paid. We have already observed, that whoever defended his own cause, was obliged to give security, it is therefore with much greater reason, that the proctor in the cause of another should be compelled to give caution. But, if a demandant in a real a real action had sued in his own name, he was under no necessity of giving security; yet, if he sued only as a proctor, he was obliged to give caution, that his acts would be ratified by his principal* rem ratam dominum habiturum, *for the danger was, lest the client or party principal should bring a fresh suit for the same thing: and, by the words of the edict, even tutors and curators were compelable to give caution, as well as proctors, tho' it was sometimes remitted, when tutors, or curators, were demandants, and such was the practice in regard to real actions.*

De judicio personali.

§ I. Si vero in personam, ab actoris quidem parte eadem obtinebant, quæ diximus in actione, qua in rem agitur: ab ejus vero parte, cum quo agitur, siquidem alieno nomine aliquis interveniret, omnimodo satisdaret, quia nemo defensor in aliena re sine satisdatione idoneus esse creditur. Quod si proprio nomine aliquis judicium accipiebat in personam, *judicatum solvi* satisdare non cogebatur.

§ I. *The same rules, which were observed in real, obtained also in personal actions, in regard to the taking security on the part of the plaintiff, and, if the defendent in a personal action proceeded in another's name, he was obliged to give caution, for no one was reputed a competent defendent in the cause of another, unless security was given, but, wherever any man was convened in a personal action to defend his own cause, he was not compeled to give caution, that the thing adjudged should be paid.*

Jus novum. De reo.

§ II. Sed hodie hæc aliter observantur. Sive enim quis in rem actione convenitur, sive personali, suo nomine, nullam satisdationem pro litis æstimatione dare compellitur, sed pro sua tantum persona, quod in judicio permaneat usque ad terminum litis, vel committitur suæ promissioni cum jurejurando, quam juratoriam cautionem vocant, vel nudam promissionem, vel satisdationem, pro qualitate personæ, suæ dare compellitur.

§ 2. *But at present we observe a very different practice; for, if a defendent is now convened either in a real or personal action, in his own cause, he is not compelable to give security for the payment of the estimation of the suit, but only for his own person, to wit, that he will remain in judgment till the cause is determined and this security is sometimes given by sureties, sometimes by a promise upon oath, which is called a juratory caution, and sometimes by a simple promise without an oath, according to the quality of the person of the defendent*

De procuratore actoris.

§ III. Sin autem per procuratorem lis vel infertur vel suscipitur; in actoris quidem persona, si non mandatum actis insinuatum est, vel præsens dominus litis in judicio procuratoris sui personam confirmaverit, ratam rem dominum habiturum, satisdationem procurator dare compellitur.

pellitur. Eodem observando et si tutor vel curator, vel aliæ tales personæ, quæ alienarum rerum gubernationem receperunt, litem quibusdam per alium inferunt.

§ 3. *But, if a suit is commenced or defended by a proctor, the proctor of the plaintiff, if he does not either inrol a mandate of appointment in the acts of court, or cause his client to nominate him publicly, is obliged to give security, that his client will ratify his proceeding. The same rule is also to be observed, if a tutor, curator, or any person, to whom the management of the affairs of others is intrusted, commences a suit by a proctor.*

De procuratore rei præsentis.

§. IV. Si vero aliquis convenitur, siquidem præsens procuratorem dare paratus est, potest vel ipse in judicium venire, et sui procuratoris personam per *judicatum solvi* satisdationem solemni stipulatione firmare, vel extra judicium satisdationem exponere, per quam ipse sui procuratoris fidejussor existat pro omnibus *judicatum solvi* satisdationis clausulis. Ubi et de hypotheca suarum rerum convenire compellitur, sive in judicio promiserit, sive extra judicium caverit, ut tam ipse quam hæredes ejus obligentur. Alia insuper cautela, vel satisdatione propter personam ipsius exponenda, quod tempore sententiæ recitandæ in judicium venerit, vel, si non venerit, omnia dabit fidejussor, quæ in condemnatione continentur, nisi fuerit provocatum.

§ 4. *But, when a party is convened, if he is ready to nominate a proctor, such party may appear in open court, and confirm the nomination by giving the caution* judicatum solvi *under the usual stipulation; or he may appear out of court, and become himself the surety, that his proctor will perform all the covenants in the instrument of caution, and whether the party convened does this in court, or out of court, he is obliged to make his estate chargeable, that his heirs, as well as himself, may be liable to an action. And a farther security must likewise be given, that he will either appear in person at the time of pronouncing sentence, or that his sureties, in case of his non-appearance, shall be bound to pay whatever the sentence exacts, if no appeal is interposed.*

De procuratore rei absentis.

§ V. Si vero reus præsto ex quacunque causa non fuerit, et alius velit defensionem ejus subire, nulla differentia inter actiones in rem vel personales introducenda, potest hoc facere: ita tamen ut satisdationem *judicatum solvi* pro litis æstimatione præstet. Nemo enim secundum veterem regulam (ut jam dictum est) alienæ rei sine satisdatione defensor idoneus intelligitur.

§ 5 *When a defendent does not give an appearance, then any other person, who is willing, may take upon himself the defense for him, and this may be done either in a real or personal action without distinction, if the caution* judicatum solvi *is entered into for the payment of the estimation of the suit, for no man, (according to the antient rule*

rule already mentioned,) can be said to defend the cause of another legally, unless security is given.

Unde hæc forma discenda.

§ VI. Quæ omnia apertius et perfectius quotidiano judiciorum usu in ipsis rerum documentis apparent.

§ 6. *But all such formalities may be more perfectly learned, from the usage and practice of courts.*

Ubi hæc forma observanda.

§ VII. Quam formam non solum in hac regia urbe, sed etiam omnibus nostris provinciis, (etsi propter imperitiam forte aliter celebratur,) obtinere censemus: cum necesse sit, omnes provincias caput omnium nostrarum civitatum, id est, hanc regiam urbem, ejusque observantiam, sequi.

§ 7. *We have judged it expedient, that these forms shall obtain not only in* Constantinople, *but also in all our other provinces, in which a different practice may have hitherto prevailed thro' the want of knowledge; for it is necessary, that all the provinces should be guided by the example of the capitol of our dominions, and follow the practice of our royal city.*

TITULUS DUODECIMUS.

De perpetuis et temporalibus actionibus, et quæ ad hæredes et in hæredes transeunt.

C. iv. T. ii.

De perpetuis et temporalibus actionibus.

HOC loco admonendi sumus, eas quidem actiones, quæ ex lege, senatusve consulto, sive ex sacris constitutionibus, proficiscuntur, perpetuo solere antiquitus competere, donec sacræ constitutiones tam in rem, quam in personam, actionibus certos fines dederunt: eas vero, quæ ex propria prætoris jurisdictione pendent, plerumque intra annum vivere: nam et ipsius prætoris intra annum erat imperium. Aliquando tamen et in perpetuum extenduntur: id est, usque ad finem constitutionibus introductum: quales sunt eæ, quas bonorum possessori,

 cæte-

cæterisque, qui hæredis loco sunt, accommodat. Furti quoque manifesti actio, quamvis ex ipsius prætoris jurisdictione proficiscatur, tamen perpetuo datur. Absurdum enim esse existimavit, anno eam terminari.

All those actions, which took their rise from the law, the decrees of the senate, or the constitutions, were antiently reputed perpetual; but the later emperors have by their ordinances fixed certain limits both to real and personal actions. Actions, given by virtue of the prætor's authority, are generally limited to the space of one year; for such is the duration of his office, but sometimes the prætorian actions are made perpetual; that is, they are extended to the limits introduced by the constitutions; such are those actions, which the prætor gives to the possessors of goods, and to others, who hold the place of heirs. The action of manifest theft is also perpetual, altho' it proceeds from the mere authority of the prætor, for it was thought absurd, that this action should determine within the space of a year.

Perpetuo solere] It is certain, that the time of bringing actions in *England* has been limited by some of our earliest acts of parliament, and from hence it hath become the general opinion, that limitations were unknown to the common law. Till the 20th of *Henry* the 3d's reign, the limitation of a writ of right was from the time of *Henry* the *first*, [*a tempore regis Henrici senioris*] but, by the statute *de merton, editum anno* 20 *Hen.* 3. it is enacted, that the limitation of a writ of right shall commence from the time of *Henry* the 2d, who began his reign in 1154, whereas *Henry* the 1st began his reign in *August* 1100, so that this statute made the limitation shorter by 54 years. Assises of mort-auncester were also by the same statute reduced to commence from the last return of king *John* out of *Ireland*, which was in the 12th year of his reign: and, in regard to assizes of novel disseisin, it is likewise enacted, *ut non excedant primam transfretationem domini regis, qui nunc est* [viz. H. 3.] *in Vasconiam*. The limitation of a writ of right was afterwards reduced to a narrower compass by the stat. of *Westminster*, 3 *Edw.* 1. which limits it to commence only from the time of *Richard* the 1st, *i. e.* from the 1st day of his reign. But these limitations from fixed periods became in process of time too large and extended; so that, as lord *Coke* observes, many suits, troubles, and inconveniences arose, and therefore the makers of the statute of 32 *H.* 8. took another and more direct course, which might indure for ever, and that was, to impose diligence and vigilance in him, who was to bring his action, so that, by one constant law, certain limitations might serve, both for the time present and all future times. *vid. Co. Litt.* 115. *a.* 2 *Co. inst.* 94. 95. The reader is refered to the statutes of 32 *H.* 8. *cap.* 2. and 21 *Jac.* 1. *cap.* 16. in which acts the time of bringing almost every species of action is ascertained within permanent and salutary limits.

Constitutionibus introductum] *vid. Cod.* 7. *t.* 39. *l.* 4. 5. *Cod.* 7. *t.* 40. *ff.* 5. *t.* 5.

De actionibus, quæ in hæredes transeunt vel non.

§ I. Non autem omnes actiones, quæ in aliquem aut ipso jure competunt, aut à prætore dantur, et in hæredem æque competunt, aut dari solent. Est enim certissima juris regula, ex maleficiis pœnales actiones in hæredem rei non competere, veluti furti, vi bonorum raptorum, injuriarum, damni, injuriæ. Sed hæredibus hujusmodi actiones competunt, nec denegantur; excepta injuriarum actione, et si qua alia similis inveniatur. Aliquando tamen etiam ex contractu actio contra hæredem non competit; veluti cum testator dolose versatus sit, et ad hæredem ejus nihil ex eo dolo pervenit. Pœnales autem actiones, quas supra diximus, si ab ipsis principalibus personis fuerint contestatæ, et hæredibus dantur et contra hæredes transeunt.

§ 1. But

§ 1. But all actions in general, which either the law, or the prætor, gives against any man, will not also be given against his heirs, for it is a most certain rule of law, that penal actions, arising from a male-feazance, will not lie against the heir of an offender, as for instance, actions of theft, rapin, injury, or damage injuriously done. but nevertheless these actions will pass to heirs, and are never denied, but in an action of injury, and in other cases of a similar nature; yet sometimes even an action of contract will not lie against an heir, as when a testator acts fraudulently, and nothing comes to the possession of the heir by reason of the fraud, but, if the penal actions, of which we have already spoken, are once contested by the principal parties concerned, they will afterwards pass both to, and against, the heirs of such parties

Non autem omnes actiones.] It is a maxim in the law of *England*, "that personal actions "die with the person, so that, if a tenent for "years commits waste, and dies, an action of "waste will not lie against his executors —— "or if the keeper of a prison permits a man "in execution to escape and afterwards dies, "no action will lie against his executors —— "or if a battery is commited upon a man, "and either the aggressor, or the party aggriev-"ed should die, the action is gone."

Si, pendente judicio, reus actori satisfecerit.

§ II. Superest, ut admoneamus, quod, si ante rem judicatam is, cum quo actum est, satisfaciat actori, officio judicis convenit eum absolvere; licet in ea causa fuisset judicii accipiendi tempore, ut damnari deberet; et hoc est, quod antea vulgo dicebatur, omnia judicia absolutoria esse.

§ 2 It remains to be observed, that, if the defendent before sentence gives full satisfaction to the plaintiff, it is the duty of the judge to dismiss such defendent, altho', at the time of contestation of suit, his cause was so bad, that he deserved to be condemned; and upon this account it was antiently a common saying, that all actions were dismissible.

TITULUS DECIMUS-TERTIUS.

De exceptionibus.

D. xliv. T. 1. C. viii. T. 36.

Continuatio. Ratio exceptionum.

SEquitur, ut de exceptionibus dispiciamus. Comparatæ autem sunt exceptiones defendendorum eorum gratia, cum quibus agitur. Sæpe enim accidit, ut licet ipsa persecutio, qua actor experitur, justa sit, tamen iniqua sit adversus eum, cum quo agitur.

It follows, that we should treat of exceptions Exceptions have been introduced into causes for the defense of the party cited; for it often happens, that a suit, which in itself is just, may yet become unjust, when commenced against a wrong person.

Exempla: quod metus causa, de dolo, in factum.

§ I. Verbi gratia, si metu coactus, aut dolo inductus, aut errore lapsus, stipulanti Titio promisisti, quod non debueras promittere, palam est, jure civili te obligatum esse, et actio, qua intenditur, dare te oportere, efficax est: sed iniquum est, te condemnari. Ideoque datur tibi exceptio, quod metus causa, aut doli mali, aut in factum, composita ad impugnandam actionem.

§ 1 *If a man, who is compelled by fear, or induced by fraud or mistake, makes a promise to* Titius, *for example, by stipulation; yet it is evident, that he is bound by the civil law, and that* Titius *may have an efficacious action; but it would be unjust, that a condemnation should follow, and therefore the party, who made such promise, is permitted to plead exceptive matter in bar to the action, by setting forth, that the promise was extorted by fear or fraud, or otherwise by alleging the peculiar circumstances of the case, whatever they are, and these are called exceptions* in factum composita, *i. e. exceptions on the fact.*

De non numerata pecunia.

§ II Idem juris est, si quis quasi credendi causa pecuniam a te stipulatus fuerit, neque numeraverit. Nam, eam pecuniam à te petere posse eum, certum est. dare enim te oportet, cum ex stipulatione tenearis. Sed, quia iniquum est, eo nomine te condemnari, placet, exceptione pecuniæ non numeratæ te defendi debere: cujus tempora nos (secundum quod jam superioribus libris scriptum est) constitutione nostra coarctavimus.

§ 2 *The* [illegible] *practice prevails, if* Sempronius, *for example, causes* Titius *to* [illegible] *to repay him money, which* Titius *never received from him. It is certain,* [illegible] Sempronius [illegible] *an action, for* Titius *is bound by the stipu-* [illegible]*, but he should be condemned upon that account, he* [illegible] *by an exception* pecuniæ non numeratæ, *i. e. on ac-* [illegible] *But by our express constitution we have shortened the time* [illegible] *this exception, as we have already observed in the former* [illegible]

Constitutione nostra] See Cod. 4. t. 30. l. 14 [illegible] The time allowed for bringing the exception of [illegible] was anciently the space of five years, but *Justinian* restrained it to two years. *See the 22d title of the 3d institute*

De pacto.

§ III Præterea debitor, si pactus fuerit cum creditore, ne à se pecunia peteretur, nihilominus obligatus manet, quia pacto convento obligationes non omnino dissolvuntur: qua de causa efficax est adversus eum actio, quam actor intendit, *si paret, eum dare oportere*: sed, quia iniquum est, contra pactionem eum condemnari, defenditur per exceptionem pacti conventi.

§ 3. *And*

§ 3 And farther, altho' a debtor enters into a compact with his creditor, that his creditor ſhall not ſue him, yet the debtor remains bound, for obligations are not to be wholly diſſolved by a nude agreement; and therefore an action in this form, ſi paret, eum dare oportere, *would be efficacious againſt the debtor, but, as it would be unjuſt, that the debtor ſhould be condemned to make payment, notwithſtanding the agreement, he is therefore permited to defend himſelf by an exception of compact.*

De jurejurando.

§ IV. Æque, ſi debitor creditore deferente juraverit, nihil ſe dare oportere, adhuc obligatus permanet: ſed, quia iniquum eſt de perjurio quæri, defenditur per exceptionem jurisjurandi. In iis quoque actionibus, quibus in rem agitur, æque neceſſariæ ſunt exceptiones; veluti ſi petitore deferente poſſeſſor juraverit, eam rem ſuam eſſe, et nihilo minus petitor eandem rem vindicet. Licet enim verum ſit, quod intendit, id eſt, rem ejus eſſe, iniquum tamen eſt, poſſeſſorem condemnari.

§ 4. If an oath is adminiſtered to a debtor at the inſtance of his creditor, and ſuch debtor ſwears, that nothing is due from him, yet he ſtill remains obligated: but, as it would not be right, that the plaintiff ſhould afterwards complain of perjury, the debtor may defend himſelf by alleging his own oath by way of exception. Exceptions of this ſort are likewiſe equally neceſſary in real actions, as when the party in poſſeſſion takes an oath at the requeſt of the demandant, and ſwears, that the thing in diſpute is his own, and the demandant will nevertheleſs indeavor to recover it: for altho' the demandant's allegation is true, viz that the thing claimed appertains to him, yet it is unjuſt, that the poſſeſſor ſhould be condemned

De re judicata.

§ V. Item, ſi judicio tecum actum fuerit, ſive in rem, ſive in perſonam, nihilominus obligatio durat: et ideo ipſo jure de eadem re poſtea adverſus te agi poteſt: ſed debes per exceptionem rei judicatæ adjuvari.

§ 5 If a man hath been ſued either upon a real or perſonal action, the obligation nevertheleſs remains, and therefore, in ſtrict law, he may again be ſued upon the ſame account, but, in caſe of a ſecond ſuit, he may be relieved, if he alleges by way of exception, that the cauſe hath already been adjudged

De cæteris exceptionibus.

§ VI Hæc exempli cauſa retuliſſe ſufficiat: alioqui, quam ex multis variiſque cauſis exceptiones neceſſariæ ſint, ex latioribus digeſtorum ſeu pandectarum libris intelligi poteſt.

§ 6 It may ſuffice to have given theſe inſtances of exceptions in general, but how many and in what various caſes they are neceſſary, may be more fully learned from the larger book of the digeſts

Ex latioribus digeſtorum libris] vid ff 4 t 1 cum ſeqq

Divisio prima.

§ VII. Quarum quædam ex legibus, vel iis, quæ legis vicem obtinent, vel ex ipsius prætoris jurisdictione, substantiam capiunt.

§ 7 *Some exceptions proceed from the laws themselves, or from those regulations, which hold the place of laws; but others take their rise from the authority of the prætor.*

Divisio secunda.

§ VIII. Appellantur autem exceptiones aliæ perpetuæ et peremptoriæ, aliæ temporales et dilatoriæ.

§ 8. *Some exceptions are called perpetual and peremptory; others are termed temporary and dilatory.*

De peremptoriis.

§ IX. Perpetuæ et peremptoriæ sunt, quæ semper agentibus obstant, et semper rem, de qua agitur, perimunt. qualis est exceptio doli mali, et quod metus causa factum est, et pacti conventi, cum ita convenerit, ne omnino pecunia peteretur.

§ 9 *The perpetual and peremptory are those, which always obstruct the party agent, and destroy the force of the action --- of this sort is the exception of fraud, of fear, and of compact, when it is agreed, that the money shall not be sued for.*

De dilatoriis.

§ X. Temporales atque dilatoriæ sunt, quæ ad tempus nocent, et temporis dilationem tribuunt: qualis est pacti conventi, cum ita convenerit, ne intra certum tempus ageretur, veluti intra quinquennium: nam, finito eo tempore, non impeditur actor rem exequi. Ergo ii, quibus intra certum tempus agere volentibus objicitur exceptio aut pacti conventi, aut alia similis, differre debent actionem, et post tempus agere. Ideo enim dilatoriæ istæ exceptiones appellantur. Alioqui, si intra tempus egerint, objectaque sit exceptio, neque eo judicio quicquam consequebantur propter exceptionem, neque post tempus olim agere poterant, cum temere rem in judicium deducebant et consumebant; qua ratione rem admittebant. Hodie autem non ita stricte hoc procedere volumus; sed eum, qui ante tempus pactionis vel obligationis litem inferre ausus sit, Zenonianæ constitutioni subjacere censemus, quam sacratissimus legislator de iis, qui tempore plus petierint, protulit: et inducias, quas ipse actor sponte indulserit, vel quas natura actionis continet, si contempserit, in duplum habeant ii, qui talem injuriam passi sunt, et, post eas finitas, non aliter litem suscipiant, nisi omnes expensas litis antea acceperint: ut actores, tali pœna perterriti, tempora litium doceantur observare.

§ 10. *Tem-*

§ 10. *Temporary and dilatory exceptions are those, which operate for a time, and create delay: such is the exception of an agreement not to persue a debt within a certain time, as within five years; but at the expiration of that time the creditor may proceed, and therefore those, against whom an exception of agreement, or any other similar exception can be objected, must delay their action, and not sue, till the time agreed upon is expired, and it is for this reason, that those exceptions are termed dilatory. and formerly, if the parties agent had sued within the time, in which it was agreed not to sue, and an exception was interposed, it not only hindered such parties from obtaining in that cause, but it also disabled them from proceeding, even after the expiration of the time agreed on; for they were reputed to have lost their right, by having commenced a temerary suit. But we have been willing to mitigate this rigor, and have decreed, that whoever presumes to commence a suit before the time limited by the agreement, shall be subject to the constitution of* Zeno *concerning those, who demand more than their due · and, if a party agent breaks in upon the time, which he has before spontaneously allowed, or contemns the limits, which the nature of some actions allow, the party defendent, who suffers such injurious treatment, becomes intituled to twice the time before allowed, and, even when that is expired, can not be obliged to give an appearance, till he has been reimbursed the whole of his expenses, and this we have ordained* in terrorem, *that all plaintiffs may be taught to observe the proper time of commencing their suits*

Subjacere censemus] Neither the constitution of *Zeno*, nor that of *Justinian*, is extant

De dilatoriis ex persona.

§ XI. Præterea etiam ex persona sunt dilatoriæ exceptiones, quales sunt procuratoriæ, veluti si per militem, aut mulierem, agere quis velit. Nam militibus nec pro patre, vel matre, vel uxore, nec ex sacro rescripto, procuratorio nomine experiri conceditur. Suis vero negotiis superesse sine offensa militaris disciplinæ possunt. Eas vero exceptiones, quæ olim procuratoribus propter infamiam vel dantis, vel ipsius procuratoris, opponebantur, cum in judiciis frequentari nullo modo perspeximus, conquiescere sancimus; ne, dum de his altercatur, ipsius negotii disceptatio protcletur

§ 11. *Dilatory exceptions may also arise by reason of the person of the party suing, such are those, which are made against proctors, as if a suitor should imploy a soldier or a woman to act for him, for soldiers are not permitted to appear in any cause, even in behalf of a father, a mother, or a wife, altho' they obtain the sanction of an imperial rescript, but they are allowed to act in their own affairs, without offending against military discipline But we have put a stop to the exceptions of infamy, which were formerly made, both against proctors and their constituents, having observed them to be little practised, and fearing, lest by means of such altercations, a disquisition into the merits of causes should be retarded.*

TITULUS DECIMUS-QUARTUS.

De replicationibus.

De replicatione.

INterdum evenit, ut exceptio, quæ prima facie justa videtur, tamen inique noceat: quod cum accidit, alia allegatione opus est, adjuvandi actoris gratia: quæ replicatio vocatur; quia per eam replicatur atque resolvitur jus exceptionis: veluti cum pactus est aliquis cum debitore suo, ne ab eo pecuniam petat, deinde postea in contrarium pacti sunt, id est, ut creditori petere liceat: si creditor agat, et excipiat debitor, ut ita demum condemnetur, si non convenerit, ne eam pecuniam creditor petat, nocet ei exceptio: convenit enim ita. Namque nihilominus hoc verum manet, licet postea in contrarium pacti sint. Sed quia iniquum est, creditorem excludi, replicatio ei dabitur ex posteriore pacto convento.

Sometimes an exception, which appears at the first view to be valid, is nevertheless not so. and, when this happens, there is a necessity for an additional allegation in aid of the plaintiff, and this is called a replication, because the force of the exception is replicated, *that is, unfolded, and destroyed by it · as if a creditor should covenant with his debtor not to sue him, and it should afterwards be agreed between them, that the creditor may sue, in consequence of which agreement the creditor brings an action, to which the debtor excepts, alleging the agreement of his creditor not to sue him; in this case, the exception would be of weight, for, as such an agreement was entered into, it remains good, altho' a subsequent one was afterwards made to a contrary effect: but, as it would be unjust, that a creditor should be concluded by the exception, he is allowed to make a replication, by reason of the subsequent compact.*

De duplicatione.

§ I Rursus interdum evenit, ut replicatio, quæ prima facie justa est, inique noceat: quod cum accidit, alia allegatione opus est, adjuvandi rei gratia; quæ duplicatio vocatur.

§ 1 *It also sometimes happens, that a replication at first appears to be concludent, tho' it is not so in reality, and, when it so happens, then another allegation, called a duplication, must be offered in support of the defendent.*

De triplicatione.

§ II. Et, si rursus ea prima facie justa videatur, sed propter aliquam causam actori inique noceat, rursus alia allegatione opus est, qua actor adjuvetur; quæ dicitur triplicatio.

§ 2. *And*

§ 2. And when a duplication carries with it an appearance of justice, but is, upon some account, injurious to the party agent, he may also, in his turn, give another allegation, which is termed a triplication.

De cæteris exceptionibus.

§ III. Quarum omnium exceptionum usum interdum ulterius, quam diximus, varietas negotiorum introducit, quas omnes apertius ex digestorum latiore volumine facile est cognoscere.

§ 3. But the great variety of business, which continually occurs, often extends the use of all these exceptions, much farther, than we have mentioned, but of those a fuller knowlege may be obtained by a perusal of the larger volumes of the digests.

Quæ exceptiones fidejussoribus prosunt vel non.

§ IV. Exceptiones autem, quibus debitor defenditur, plerumque accommodari solent etiam fidejussoribus ejus; et recte. quia, quod ab iis petitur, id ab ipso debitore peti videtur: quia mandati judicio redditurus est eis, quod ei pro eo solverint. Qua ratione, et si de non petenda pecunia pactus quis cum eo fuerit, placuit, perinde succurrendum esse per exceptionem pacti conventi illis quoque, qui pro eo obligati sunt, ac si etiam cum ipsis pactus esset, ne ab eis pecunia peteretur. Sane quædam exceptiones non solent his accommodari. Ecce enim debitor, si bonis suis cesserit, et cum eo creditor experiatur, defenditur per exceptionem, *si bonis cesserit*. Sed hæc exceptio fidejussoribus non datur: ideo scilicet, quia, qui alios pro debitore obligat, hoc maxime prospicit, ut, cum facultatibus lapsus fuerit debitor, possit ab iis, quos pro eo obligavit, suum consequi.

§ 4. The exceptions, by which a debtor may defend himself, are generally allowed to be used by his bondsmen, and this is a right practice; for a demand, made upon them, is, as it were, a demand upon the debtor himself, who is compelable by an action of mandate to pay over to his sureties whatever they have been obliged to pay upon his account, and therefore, if a creditor hath covenanted with his debtor not to sue him, the bondsmen of such debtor may be aided by an exception of compact, in the same manner, as if the promise had been made expressly to them But there are some exceptions, which can not be made use of in behalf of sureties, for altho', when a debtor hath made a cession of his goods, he may defend himself by alleging that cession, as an exception to a suit brought by a creditor, yet the same exception cannot be alleged by the bondsmen, and the reason is evident, for whoever demands sureties hath always this principally in view, that he may be able to recover his debt from those sureties, in case of failure in the principal debtor.

TITULUS DECIMUS-QUINTUS.

De interdictis.

D. xliii. T. 1. C. viii. T. 1.

Continuatio et definitio.

SEquitur, ut dispiciamus de interdictis, seu actionibus, quæ pro his exercentur. Erant autem interdicta formæ atque conceptiones verborum, quibus prætor aut jubebat aliquid fieri, aut fieri prohibebat; quod tunc maxime fiebat, cum de possessione aut quasi possessione inter aliquos contendebatur.

We are now led to treat of interdicts, or of those actions, which supply their place. Interdicts were certain forms of words, by which the prætor either commanded or prohibited something to be done; and these were chiefly used, when any contention arose concerning possession, or quasi-*possession.*

Seu actionibus, quæ pro his exercentur] Interdicts are wholly out of use among civilians, so that at this day there is no difference between interdicts and actions. See *the last section of this title*. And formerly the Roman prætors used them chiefly to suppress tumultuary and sudden violence, in regard to possessions; but, in these cases, our ancestors were accustomed to delegate justices of *oyer* and *terminer*, or justices of assise; and these, not to determine all causes at set times, as now, but upon every particular emergency, as soon as it first arose; but such affairs are now managed by judicial writs, or by the assistence of the sheriff and justices of peace in every county. vide *Bracton*, *Britton*, and *Fleta*, in their proper places. *Cowel's inst. h. t.*

Divisio prima.

§ I. Summa autem divisio interdictorum hæc est, quod aut prohibitoria sunt, aut restitutoria, aut exhibitoria. Prohibitoria sunt, quibus prætor vetat aliquid fieri, veluti vim sine vitio possidenti, vel mortuum inferenti, quo ei jus erat inferendi; vel in sacro loco ædificari, vel in flumine publico ripave ejus aliquid fieri, quo pejus navigetur. Restitutoria sunt, quibus restitui aliquid jubet: veluti bonorum possessori possessionem eorum, quæ quis pro hærede, aut pro possessore, possidet ex ea hæreditate: aut cum jubet, ei, qui vi de possessione dejectus sit, restitui possessionem. Exhibitoria sunt, per quæ jubet exhiberi, veluti eum, cujus de libertate agitur, aut libertum, cui patronus operas indicere velit, aut parenti liberos, qui in potestate ejus sunt. Sunt tamen, qui putent, interdicta ea proprie vocari, quæ prohibitoria sunt; quia interdicere sit denuntiare et prohibere: restitutoria autem et exhibitoria proprie decreta vocari. Sed tamen obtinuit, omnia interdicta appellari, quia inter duos dicuntur.

§ 1. *The first division of them is into prohibitory, restoratory, and exhibitory interdicts; the prohibitory are those, by which the prætor prohibits something to be done,*

done, as when he forbids force to be used against a lawful possessor, or against a person, who is burying another, where he had a right or when he forbids an edifice to be raised in a sacred place, or hinders a work from being erected in a public river, or on the banks of it, which may render it less navigable The restoratory are those interdicts, by which the prætor orders something to be restored, as the possession of goods to the universal successor, who has been kept out of possession by one, who had no right; or when the prætor commands possession to be restored to him, who hath been forcibly ejected And the exhibitory interdicts are those, by which the prætor commands some exhibit to be made, as of a slave, for example, concerning whose liberty a cause is depending; or of a freed-man, from whom a patron would exact the service due to him; or of children to their parent, under whose power they are Some nevertheless imagine, that interdicts can with propriety be only prohibitory, because the word interdicere *signifies to* denounce *and* prohibit --- *and that the restoratory and exhibitory interdicts might more properly be called decrees; yet it hath obtained by usage, that they should all be termed interdicts, because they are pronounced between two,* [inter duos dicuntur,] *the demandant and the possessor.*

Divisio secunda.

§ II. Sequens divisio interdictorum hæc est, quod quædam adipiscendæ possessionis causa comparata sunt, quædam retinendæ, quædam recuperandæ.

§ 2 *The second division of interdicts is into those, which are given for the acquisition, the retention, or the recovery of a possession.*

De interdictis adipiscendæ.

§ III. Adipiscendæ possessionis causa interdictum accommodatur bonorum possessori, quod appellatur, *Quorum bonorum*, ejusque vis et potestas hæc est, ut, quod ex iis bonis quisque, quorum possessio alicui data est, pro hærede aut pro possessore possideat, id ei, cui bonorum possessio data est, restituere debeat. Pro hærede autem possidere videtur, qui putat se hæredem esse. Pro possessore is possidet, qui nullo jure rem hæreditariam, vel etiam totam hæreditatem, sciens ad se non pertinere, possidet. Ideo autem adipiscendæ possessionis vocatur interdictum, quia ei tantum utile est, qui nunc primum conatur adipisci possessionem Itaque, si quis adeptus possessionem amiserit eam, hoc interdictum ei inutile est. Interdictum quoque Salvianum adipiscendæ possessionis causa comparatum est: eoque utitur dominus fundi de rebus coloni, quas is pro mercedibus fundi pignori futuras pepigisset.

§ 3 *An interdict for the acquisition of possession is given to him, whom the prætor appoints to be the possessor of the goods of a deceased person This interdict is called* quorum bonorum, *and the effect of it is, that it obliges all persons, who retain goods in their hands as heirs or possessors, to restore such goods to him, to whom the possession of them hath been committed by the magistrate and note, that he is reputed to possess, as heir, who thinks and takes himself so to be, and that he is deemed to possess, as possessor, who without authority detains a part, or the whole, of an inhe-*

 ritance,

ritance, knowing that the possession does not belong to him. An interdict of acquisition is so called, because it is useful to him only, who first *indeavors to acquire the possession; and therefore this interdict would be useless to any one, who had once acquired a possession, but afterwards lost it. The interdict, called the* Salvian *interdict, is also appointed for the acquisition of possession; and is used by the proprietors of farms, in order to acquire the goods, which their tenents have pledged and ingaged, as a security for the payment of rent.*

Salvianum] This interdict is so called from *Salvius Julianus*, who drew it up by the order of *Adrian*, the Emperor. *vid. ff.* 43. *t.* 33. *et* Menagii *juris civ. amœnitates p.* 132.

De interdictis retinendæ.

§ IV. Retinendæ possessionis causa comparata sunt interdicta, *uti possidetis, et utrubi*, cum ab utraque parte de proprietate alicujus rei controversia sit, et ante quæratur, uter ex litigatoribus possideat, et uter petere debeat. Namque, nisi ante exploratum fuerit, utrius eorum possessio sit, non potest petitoria actio institui: quia et civilis et naturalis ratio facit, ut alius possideat, et alius à possidente petat. Et, quia longe commodius est et potius possidere, quam petere, ideo plerumque, et fere semper, ingens existit contentio de ipsa possessione. Commodum autem possidenti in eo est, quod, etiam si ejus res non sit, qui possidet, si modo actor non potuerit suum esse probare, remanet in suo loco possessio: propter quam causam, cum obscura sunt utriusque jura, contra petitorem judicari solet. Sed interdicto quidem *uti possidetis* de fundi vel ædium possessione contenditur. *utrubi* vero interdicto de rerum mobilium possessione: quorum vis ac potestas plurimam inter se differentiam apud veteres habebat. nam *uti possidetis* interdicto is vincebat, qui interdicti tempore possidebat; si modo nec vi, nec clam, nec precario, nactus fuerat ab adversario possessionem: etiamsi alium vi expulerat, aut clam arripuerat alienam possessionem, aut precario rogaverat aliquem, ut sibi possidere liceret. *Utrubi* vero interdicto is vincebat, qui majore parte anni nec vi, nec clam, nec precario, ab adversario possidebat. Hodie tamen aliter observatur: nam utriusque interdicti potestas (quantum ad possessionem pertinet) exæquata est, ut ille vincat et in re soli, et in re mobili, qui possessionem nec vi, nec clam, nec precario, ab adversario, litis contestatæ tempore, detinet.

§ 4 *The interdicts* uti possidetis *and* utrubi *have been introduced for the sake of retaining possession; for, when there is a controversy between two parties concerning property, it is necessary to inquire, which of them is in possession, that it may be known, who ought to be the demandant, for, till the possession is ascertained, an action of demand can not be instituted, and natural reason teaches us, that, when one of the parties is in possession, the other must of course be the demandant in the suit. but, as it is by far more advantageous to be the possessor, than the demandant, there is generally great contention for the possession, for altho' the possessor is not in reality the true proprietor, yet the possession will still remain in him, if the plaintiff does not prove the thing in litigation to be his own. and therefore, when the rights of parties are not clear,*

clear, the sentence is always against the demandant By the interdict uti possidetis, *the possession of a farm or house is contended for; and, by the interdict* utrubi, *the possession of things moveable is disputed These interdicts antiently differed much in their force and effects, for, by the interdict* uti possidetis, *that party, who was in possession at the time of bringing the interdict, prevailed, if he had not obtained the possession from his adversary, by force, clandestinely, or precariously, but it was not material in what manner the possessor had obtained the possession from any other person and, by the interdict* utrubi, *that party prevailed, who had been in possession for the greatest part of the year preceeding the contest, if he had not acquired that possession clandestinely, precariously, or by force. But the present practice is nevertheless otherwise, for the power of both interdicts in regard to possession is now made equal, so that in any cause, instituted either for things moveable or immoveable, that party prevails, who was in possession at the time of contesting suit, if it is not made apparent, that he gained such possession by force, by clandestine means, or precariously.*

Uti possidetis] *vid ff.* 43 *t* 17 *Ulp. lib.* 69. Utrubi] *vid ff* 43 *t* 31. De utrubi *ad edictum Cod* 8 *t* 6

De retinenda et acquirenda possessione.

§ V. Possidere autem videtur quisque, non solum si ipse possideat, sed et si ejus nomine aliquis in possessione sit, licet is ejus juri subjectus non sit: qualis est colonus et inquilinus. Per eos quoque, apud quos deposuerit quis, aut quibus commodaverit, ipse possidere videtur: et hoc est, quod dicitur, retinere possessionem posse aliquem per quemlibet, qui ejus nomine sit in possessione. Quinetiam animo quoque solo retineri possessionem placet: id est, ut, quamvis neque ipse sit in possessione, neque ejus nomine alius, tamen si non relinquendæ possessionis animo, sed postea reversurus inde decesserit, retinere possessionem videatur. Adipisci vero possessionem per quos aliquis potest, secundo libro exposuimus. Nec ulla dubitatio est, quin animo solo adipisci possessionem nemo possit.

§ 5. *A man is regarded as a possessor, not only when he is himself in possession, but also when any other, who is not under his power, holds possession in his name, as for instance, a farmer, or a tenant Any person may also possess by means of those to whom he hath committed the thing in [illegible] tion, either as a deposit or a loan, and this is what is meant by saying, that a possession may be retained by any one, by means of another, who possesses in his name. It is moreover held, that a possession may be retained, by the mere intention only, for, altho' a man is neither in possession himself, nor any other for him, but has quited the possession of certain lands with an intent to return to them again, he shall nevertheless be deemed to continue in possession We have already explained, in our second institute, by what persons any man may acquire possession, and, altho' it may be retained* solo animo, *that is, by an intention only, yet it is indubitable, that a mere intention is not sufficient for the acquisition of possession*

De interdicto recuperandæ, et affinibus remediis.

§ VI. Recuperandæ possessionis causa solet interdici, si quis ex possessione fundi vel ædium vi dejectus fuerit. Nam ei proponitur interdictum

dictum *unde vi:* per quod is, qui dejecit, cogitur ei restituere possessionem, licet is ab eo, qui vi dejecit, vi, clam, vel precario, possideat. Sed ex constitutionibus sacris, (ut supra diximus,) si quis rem per vim occupaverit, siquidem in bonis ejus est, dominio ejus privatur: si aliena, post ejus restitutionem, etiam æstimationem rei dare vim passo compellitur. Qui autem aliquem de possessione per vim dejecerit; tenetur lege Julia de vi privata, aut de vi publica. Sed de vi privata, si sine armis vim fecerit; sin autem armis eum de possessione vi expulerit, de vi publica tenetur. Armorum autem appellatione non solum scuta et gladios et galeas, sed et fustes et lapides, significari intelligimus.

§ 6 *The interdict for the recovery of possession is generally made use of, when any person hath been forcibly ousted from the possession of his house or estate; for the party ousted is then intituled to the interdict* unde vi, *by which the intruder is compeled to restore him to possession, altho' he, who had been thus forcibly ousted, was himself in possession by clandestine means, by force, or precariously. But, as we have before observed, it is provided by the imperial constitutions, that, whenever any man seizes a thing by force, if it is his own, he shall lose his property in it, and, if it belongs to another, he shall be compeled not only to make restitution, but also to pay the full value to the party, who suffered the force. But whoever ousts another of possession by force, is likewise subject to the law* Julia, de vi privata, *or* de vi publica: --- *if the seizing or intrusion was effected without weapons, then the offender is only liable to the law* de vi privata, *but, if it was effected by an armed force, he is then subject to the law* de vi publica. *We comprehend not only shields, swords, and helmets under the term arms, but also clubs and stones.*

Sed ex constitutionibus] *vid. Cod* 8 *t* 4 *unde vi.* Tenetur lege Julia] *vid ff.* 43 *t* 16 *ff.* 47 *t* 1

Divisio tertia.

§ VII. Tertia divisio interdictorum est, quod aut simplicia sunt, aut duplicia. Simplicia sunt, veluti in quibus alter actor, alter reus est: qualia sunt omnia restitutoria, aut exhibitoria. Nam actor is est, qui desiderat aut exhiberi aut restitui: reus autem is est, à quo desideratur, ut restituat, aut exhibeat: prohibitoriorum autem interdictorum alia simplicia sunt, alia duplicia. Simplicia sunt, veluti cum prætor prohibet in loco sacro, vel in flumine publico, ripave ejus, aliquid fieri. Nam actor est, qui desiderat, ne quid fiat: reus est, qui aliquid facere conatur. Duplicia sunt, veluti *uti possidetis* interdictum, et *utrubi.* Ideo autem duplicia vocantur, quia par utriusque litigatoris in his conditio est: nec quisquam præcipue reus vel actor intelligitur: sed unusquisque tam rei, quam actoris, partes sustinet.

§ 7 *The third division of interdicts is into simple and double interdicts: the simple are those, in which there is both a plaintiff and a defendent, and of this sort are all restoratory and exhibitory interdicts, for the plaintiff, or demandant, is he, who requires something to be exhibited or restored, and the defendent is he, from whom the exhibition or restitution is required. But of the prohibitory interdicts some are simple, some double,*

double; they are simple, when the prætor forbids something to be done in a sacred place, on a public river, or upon the banks of it; for the demandant is he, who desires, that some act should not be done, and the defendent is he, who indeavors to do it. The interdicts uti possidetis *and* utrubi *are instances of the double interdicts; and they are called double, because in these the condition of either litigant is equal, the one not being understood to be more particularly the plaintiff or the defendent, than the other, inasmuch as each sustains the part of both.*

De ordine et vetere exitu.

§ VIII. De ordine et vetere exitu interdictorum supervacuum est hodie dicere. Nam quoties extra ordinem jus dicitur, (qualia sunt hodie omnia judicia,) non est necesse reddi interdictum: sed perinde judicatur sine interdictis, ac si utilis actio ex causa interdicti reddita fuisset.

§ 8. *It would be superfluous at this day to speak of the order, and antient effect of interdicts for, when judgments are extraordinary, (and at present all judgments are so,) an interdict is rendered unnecessary, and judgments are therefore now delivered without interdicts, in the same manner, as if a beneficial action was given in consequence of an interdict.*

TITULUS DECIMUS-SEXTUS.

De pœna temere litigantium.

De pœnis in genere.

NUNC admonendi sumus, magnam curam egisse eos, qui jura sustinebant, ne facile homines ad litigandum procederent: quod et nobis studio est. Idque eo maxime fieri potest, quod temeritas tam agentium, quam eorum, cum quibus agitur, modo pecuniara pœna, modo jurisjurandi religione, modo infamiæ metu coerceatur.

Our legislators and magistrates have ever been careful to hinder mankind from entering into rash and litigious contentions, and we also are studious to effect the same purpose And, that such suits may be the better prevented, the rashness both of plaintiffs and defendents hath been properly restrained, by pecuniary punishments, the religion of an oath, and the fear of infamy

De jurejurando et pœna pecuniaria.

§ I. Ecce enim jusjurandum omnibus, qui conveniuntur, ex constitutione nostra defertur: nam reus non aliter suis allegationibus utitur, nisi prius juraverit, quod, putans se bona instantia uti, ad contradicendum pervenit. At adversus inficiantes, ex quibusdam causis dupli actio constituitur, veluti si damni injuriæ, aut legatorum locis venerabilibus relictorum, nomine agatur. Statim autem ab initio pluris quam simpli

est

eſt actio; veluti furti manifeſti, quadrupli; nec manifeſti, dupli. Nam ex his, et aliis quibuſdam cauſis, ſive quis neget, ſive fateatur, pluris quam ſimpli eſt actio. Item actoris quoque calumnia coercetur: nam etiam actor pro calumnia jurare cogitur ex noſtra conſtitutione, quod non calumniandi animo litem moviſſet, ſed exiſtimando, ſe bonam cauſam habere. Utriuſque etiam partis advocati jusjurandum ſubeunt, quod alia noſtra conſtitutione comprehenſum eſt. Hæc autem omnia pro veteri calumniæ actione introducta ſunt; quæ in deſuetudinem abiit; quia in partem decimam litis actores multabat; quod nuſquam factum eſſe invenimus: ſed pro his introductum eſt et præfatum jusjurandum, et ut improbus litigator et damnum et impenſas litis inferre adverſario ſuo cogatur.

§ 1. *By virtue of one of our conſtitutions, an oath muſt be adminiſtered to every man, againſt whom an action is brought, for a defendent is not permited to plead, till he hath firſt ſworn, that he proceeds as a contradictor, upon a firm belief, that his cauſe is good. But actions lie, in particular caſes, for double and triple value againſt thoſe, who have given a negative iſſue, as when a ſuit is commenced on account of* [illegible] *damage, or for a legacy, left to a ſacred place, as a church, hoſpital,* &c. *There are alſo actions, upon which more than the ſimple value is recoverable at the time of their commencement, as upon an action of theft* manifeſt, *which is for fourfold the value, and upon an action of theft* not manifeſt, *which lies for double the value, becauſe in theſe, as well as in ſome other caſes, the action is at firſt given for more than the ſimple value, whether the defendent denies or confeſſes the charge brought againſt him. But the calumny of the plaintiff is alſo under reſtraint, for he too is compeled by our conſtitution to ſwear, that he did not commence the ſuit with an intention to calumniate, but upon a thorough confidence, that he had a good cauſe: and, what is more, the advocates on both ſides are likewiſe compelable to take a ſimilar oath, the ſubſtance of which is ſet forth in another of our conſtitutions. This practice hath been introduced in the place of the antient action of calumny, which compeled the plaintiff to pay the tenth part of his demand as a puniſhment; but this action is now diſuſed, and, inſtead of it, we have introduced the before-mentioned oath, and have ordained, that every raſh litigant, who hath failed in his proof, ſhall be compeled to pay his adverſary the damages and coſts of ſuit.*

Ex conſtitutione] The oath of calumny was in uſe long before the reign of *Juſtinian*, as appears from many paſſages in the digeſts, *ff* 12. t. 2. l. 4. — *ff* 12. t. 2. ll. 16. 31. — *ff* 39. t. 2. l. 13. § 3. *Qui damni infecti caveri ſibi poſtulat, prius de calumnia jurare debet.* And in ſection 4. of the ſame book are theſe words — [illegible] *cavere mihi damni infecti poſtulem, jurare debeo,* NON CALUMNIÆ CAUSA ID EUM, CUJUS NOMINE CAUTUM POSTULO, FUISSE POSTULATURUM. *Ulpian.*

But the oath ſeems afterwards to have fallen into deſuetude, and to have been only revived by the conſtitution refered to, part of which is conceived in the following terms. *Actor quidem juret,* NON CALUMNIANDI ANIMO LITEM SE MOVISSE SED ESTIMANDO BONAM CAUSAM HABERE.

Reus autem non aliter ſuis allegationibus utatur, niſi prius et ipſe juraverit, — QUOD, PUTANS SE BONA INSTANTIA UTI, AD RELUCTANDUM PERVENERIT. *Cod.* 2. t. 59. l. 2.

The canon law permits even a proctor to ſwear *in animam domini ſui.* vid. *decret. Greg.* ix. *lib.* 2. t. 7. And this was formerly the practice in all the eccleſiaſtical courts in *England.* vid. *can. judiciorum tit.* 99. *and* 110. — *canon* 132. — But the oath of calumny is now diſuſed not only in *England*, but alſo in thoſe countries, where the canon law is in full force, and where the civil law is the law of the land. *vid. La juriſprudence du code conferée avec les ordonnances royaux*

royaux de France tom. 1. p 296.——*Groenw de ll abr in 4tam inst t 16*—*Philiberti Bugnion ll abr. tractatus lib 1 cap 3*

Alia nostrâ constitutione] *vid Cod 3 t 2. l. 14* et novellam *Patroni autem caesarum, &c.*

De infamia.

§ II. Ex quibusdam judiciis damnati ignominiosi fiunt, veluti furti, vi bonorum raptorum, injuriarum, de dolo; item tutelæ, mandati, depositi, directis, non contrariis actionibus; item pro socio, quæ ab utraque parte directa est: et ob id quilibet ex sociis, eo judicio damnatus, ignominia notatur. Sed furti quidem, aut vi bonorum raptorum, aut injuriarum, aut de dolo, non solum damnati notantur ignominia, sed et pacti: et recte: plurimum enim interest, utrum ex delicto aliquis, an ex contractu, debitor sit.

§ 2. *In some cases the parties condemned become infamous, as in actions of theft, rapin, injury, or fraud. The parties condemned are likewise rendered ignominious, in an action of tutelage, mandate, or deposit, if it is a* direct, *and not a contrary, action. An action of partenership has also the same effect, for it is direct in regard to all the parteners, and therefore any one of them, who is condemned in such action, is branded with infamy But not only those, who have been condemned in an action of theft, rapine, injury, or fraud, are rendered infamous, but those also, who have bargained to prevent a criminal prosecution, and this is a right practice, for there is a wide difference between a debtor, on account of a crime, and a debtor upon contract*

Ignominiosi fiunt] *vid ff 3 t 2 Cod 2 t. 12*

Non contrariis actionibus] " Nam in contrariis judiciis de dolo aut perfidia non agitur, " sed tantum de calculo et supputatione ejus, " quod contrario judicio agenti abest *Vinn*

De in jus vocando.

§ III. Omnium autem actionum instituendarum principium ab ea parte edicti proficiscitur, qua prætor edicit de in jus vocando. Utique enim in primis adversarius in jus vocandus est, id est, ad eum vocandus, qui jus dicturus sit. Qua parte prætor parentibus et patronis, item parentibus liberisque patronorum et patronarum, hunc præstat honorem, ut non aliter liceat liberis libertisque eos in jus vocare, quam si id ab ipso prætore postulaverint et impetraverint. Et, si quis aliter vocaverit, in eum pœnam solidorum quinquaginta constituit.

§ 3. *All actions take their commencement from that part of the prætor's edict, in which he treats* de in jus vocando, *that is, of calling persons into judgment: for the first step to be taken, in all matters of controversy, is to cite or call the adverse party to appear before the judge, who is to determine the cause And, in the same part of the edict, the prætor hath treated parents and patrons, and even the children of patrons and patronesses, with so great a respect, that he does not suffer them to be called into judgment by their children or their freedmen, until application hath been first made to him, and leave obtained and, if any man presumes to cite a parent, a*

patron,

patron, or the children of a patron, without such previous permission, he is subject to a penalty of fifty solidi

De in jus vocando] *vid. ff* 2 *t* 4. *Cod* 2 *t* 2

TITULUS DECIMUS-SEPTIMUS.

De officio judicis.

De officio judicis in genere.

SUpereſt, ut de officio judicis diſpiciamus. Et quidem in primis illud obſervare debet judex, ne aliter judicet, quam legibus, aut conſtitutionibus, aut moribus, proditum eſt.

It now remains, that we should inquire into the office and duty of a judge. And it is certain, that it ought to be his principal care never to determine otherways, than the laws, the constitutions, or the customs and usages, direct.

De judicio noxali.

§ I. Ideoque, ſi noxali judicio aditus eſt, obſervare debet, ut, ſi condemnandus videtur dominus, ita debeat condemnare: *Publium Mævium Lucio Titio in decem aureos condemno; aut noxam dedere.*

§ I *And therefore, if a suit is commenced by a noxal action, the judge ought always to observe the following form of condemnation, if the defendent deserves to be condemned.* e. g. I condemn PUBLIUS MÆVIUS to pay LUCIUS TITIUS ten *aurei*, or to deliver up the ſlave, who did the damage.

De actionibus realibus.

§ II. Et, ſi in rem actum ſit coram judice, ſive contra petitorem judicaverit, abſolvere debet poſſeſſorem: ſive contra poſſeſſorem, jubere ei debet, ut rem ipſam reſtituat cum fructibus. Sed, ſi poſſeſſor neget, in præſenti ſe reſtituere poſſe, et ſine fruſtratione videbitur tempus reſtituendi cauſa petere, indulgendum eſt ei, ut tamen de litis æſtimatione caveat cum fidejuſſore, ſi intra tempus, quod ei datum eſt, non reſtituerit. Et, ſi hæreditas petita ſit, eadem circa fructus interveniunt, quæ diximus intervenire de ſingularum rerum petitione. Illorum autem fructuum, quos culpa ſua poſſeſſor non perceperit, ſive illorum, quos perceperit, in utraque actione eadem ratio pene habetur, ſi prædo fuerit. Si vero bonæ fidei poſſeſſor fuerit, non habetur ratio neque conſumptorum, neque non perceptorum. Poſt inchoatam autem petitionem

petitionem etiam illorum fructuum ratio habetur, qui culpa possessoris percepti non sunt, vel percepti consumpti sunt.

§ 3. *When a cause, commenced upon a real action, is brought before a judge for his determination, and he thinks proper to pronounce against the demandant, the possessor ought then to be acquited, but, if the judge thinks it just to condemn the possessor, the party condemned must be admonished to restore the very thing, which was in dispute, together with all it's produce But, if the possessor alleges, that he is unable to make an immediate restitution, and petitions for a longer time, without any seeming intention to frustrate the sentence, he is to be indulged, provided always, that he gives caution by a sufficient bondsman, for the full payment of the condemnation and costs of suit, if he should fail to make restitution within the time appointed And, if an inheritance is sued for, a judge ought to determine just in the same manner in regard to the profits, as he would in a suit for some particular thing only, for, if the defendent appears to have been a possessor* in mala fide, *then almost the same reasoning prevails in both actions in regard to the profits, whether they were taken by the possessor, or, thro' negligence, not taken by him but, if the defendent was a* bona fide *possessor, then no account is expected, either of fruits consumed, or of fruits not gathered, before the contestation of suit, yet note, that, from the time of contestation, all fruits must be accounted for, whether they were gathered and used, or left ungathered, thro' the negligence of the possessor.*

De actione ad exhibendum.

§ III. Si ad exhibendum actum fuerit, non sufficit, si exhibeat rem is, cum quo actum est; sed opus est, ut etiam rei causam debeat exhibere, id est, ut eam causam habeat actor, quam habiturus esset, si, cum primum ad exhibendum egisset, exhibita res fuisset Ideoque, si inter moras exhibendi usucapta sit res à possessore, nihilominus condemnabitur. Præterea fructuum medii temporis, id est, ejus, quod post acceptum ad exhibendum judicium, ante rem judicatam, intercesserit, rationem habere debet judex. Quod si neget reus, cum quo ad exhibendum actum est, in præsenti se exhibere posse, et tempus exhibendi causa petat, idque sine frustratione postulare videatur, dari ei debet, ut tamen caveat, se restituturum. Quod si neque statim jussu judicis rem exhibeat, neque postea se exhibiturum caveat, condemnandus sit in id, quod actoris intererat, si ab initio res exhibita esset.

§ 3 *If a man proceeds by an action* ad exhibendum, *it is not sufficient, that the defendent should exhibit the thing in question, but he must also be answerable for all profits and emoluments accruing from it, that the plaintiff may be in the same state, as if his property had been restored to him at the time, when he first brought his action. and therefore, if the possessor, during his delay to produce the thing in dispute, shall gain a prescriptive title to it, yet such possessor shall notwithstanding be condemned to restitution, for he shall not be allowed to profit by a delay of his own. And farther, it is the duty of the judge to take an account of the profits of the middle time, that is, of the time between contestation and sentence. But, if the defendant declares, that he is not able instantly to produce the thing required, and prays* [illegible] *then time, without any appearance of affecting a delay, a term ought to be assigned him, upon his giving caution to make restitution. But, if he neither obeys the commands of the magistrate in instantly producing the thing adjudged, nor in giving a sufficient caution for the production of it at a future day, he must then be condemned to pay the full damages, which the demandant hath sustained by not having the thing delivered to him at the commencement of the suit.*

Familiæ erciſcundæ.

§ IV. Si familiæ erciſcundæ judicio actum ſit, ſingulas res ſingulis hæredibus adjudicare debet: et, ſi in alterius perſona prægravare videatur adjudicatio, debet hunc invicem cohæredi certa pecunia (ſicuti jam dictum eſt) condemnare. Eo quoque nomine cohæredi quiſque ſuo condemnandus eſt, quod ſolus fructus hæreditarii fundi perceperit, aut rem hæreditariam corruperit, aut conſumpſerit. Quæ quidem ſimiliter inter plures quoque quam duos cohæredes ſubſequuntur.

§ 4 *When a suit is commenced by the action* familiæ erciſcundæ, *for the partition of an inheritance, it is the duty of the judge to decree to each heir his respective portion: and, if the partition, when made, is more advantageous to the one than to the other, then ought the judge, as we have before observed, to oblige him, who has the largest part to make a full recompense in money to his coheir. it therefore follows, that every coheir, who hath taken the profits of an inheritance to his sole use, and consumed them, is liable to be compeled to make a restitution. And this is the law not only when there are two heirs, but also when there are many.*

Si familiæ erciſcundæ] That, which the Romans called *judicium familiæ erciſcundæ*, is termed in the law of *England* the partition of an inheritance, and this is made either by conſent of co-heirs, or by the authority of the law. A partition by conſent requires but little explanation: it may be made by reference to friends, by lot, or by any other way, which the parties can agree upon. But partition by law is, when one, or more, of the parceners would have partition, and the reſt will not agree to it, for then he, or they, who deſire, that the inheritance ſhould be divided, muſt bring the writ *de partitione facienda*, by virtue of which thoſe, who refuſe to agree, may be compelled to ſee their lands or inheritance portioned out by twelve jurors, and aſſigned to each coheir by the ſheriff. *Vid. Co. Litt. lib. 3. cap. 1. — Terms de la ley* v. partition. *Bract. lib. 3. cap. 33. 34. de acquirendo rerum dominio.* Note, that joint-tenents, and tenents in common, could not be obliged at common law to ſuffer partition, but they are now compellable by act of parliament. *See 31 H. 8. cap. 1. and 32 H. 8. cap. 32. Co. Litt. 109. 187. 198. b.*

Communi dividundo.

§ V. Eadem interveniunt, etſi communi dividundo de pluribus rebus actum ſit. quod ſi de una re, veluti de fundo: ſiquidem iſte fundus commode regionibus diviſionem recipiat, partes ejus ſingulis adjudicare debet, et, ſi unius pars prægravare videtur, is invicem certa pecunia alteri condemnandus eſt. Quod ſi commode dividi non poſſit, vel ſi homo forte, aut mulus erit, de quo actum ſit, tunc totus uni adjudicandus eſt, et is invicem alteri certa pecunia condemnandus eſt.

§ 5 *The same law is also observed, when a suit is brought upon the action* communi dividendo, *for one particular thing only, it being but a part or parcel of an inheritance, as for example, a field, or any piece of ground, which, if it can be conveniently*

veniently divided, ought to be adjudged to each claimant in equal portions, and, if the share of one is larger than the share of another, the party, possessing such large portion, must be condemned to make a recompense in money. But, if the thing sued for is of such a nature, that it can not be divided, as a slave, or an horse for example, it must be given intirely to one of the coparceners, who must be ordered to make a satisfaction in money to the other.

Finium regundorum.

§ VI. Si finium regundorum actum fuerit, dispicere debet judex, an necessaria sit adjudicatio: quæ sane uno casu necessaria est, si evidentioribus finibus distingui agros commodius sit, quam olim fuissent distincti. Nam tunc necesse est, ex alterius agro partem aliquam alterius agri domino adjudicari. Quo casu conveniens est, ut is alteri certa pecunia debeat condemnari. Eo quoque nomine condemnandus est quisque hoc judicio, quod forte circa fines aliquid malitiose commisit, verbi gratia, quia lapides finales furatus est, vel arbores finales excidit. Contumaciæ quoque nomine quisque eo judicio condemnatur, veluti si quis jubente judice metiri agros passus non fuerit.

§ 6. *When the action* finium regundorum *is brought for the determination of boundaries, the judge ought first to examine, whether it is absolutely requisite to proceed to an adjudication: but it is, in one case, undoubtedly necessary, and this happens, whenever it becomes expedient, that any grounds should be divided by more conspicuous boundaries than they formerly were, and then necessity sometimes requires, that a part of one man's ground should be adjudged to another, in which case it is incumbent upon a judge to condemn him, whose estate is inlarged, to pay an equivalent to the other, whose estate is diminished. It is also by virtue of this action, that any one may be prosecuted, who hath committed any fraud in relation to boundaries, by either removing stones, or cutting down trees, which supplied the place of landmarks. The same action will also subject any man to condemnation on account of contumacy, if he refuses to suffer his lands to be measured at the command of a judge.*

Si finium regundorum.] The writs *de perambulatione facienda*, and *de rationabilibus divisis*, are of the same use in the law of *England*, as the *judicium finium regundorum* in the *Roman* law.

The writ *de perambulatione* lies, when two lordships are near each other, and some incroachment hath been made; for then, by assent of both lords, the sheriff shall take with him the parties and their neighbours, and shall make perambulation, and fix the bounds, as they were before. But, if one lord incroaches upon another, and will not agree to a perambulation, the party aggrieved shall have the writ *rationabilibus divisis* against the other. *Vid. Termes de la ley, and Fitzherbert's nat. brev. p.* 303. 309.

De adjudicatione.

§ VII. Quod autem istis judiciis alicui adjudicatum fuerit, id statim ejus fit, cui adjudicatum est.

§ 7. *And note, that whatever is adjudged by virtue of a sentence proceeding from any of these actions, the same instantly becomes the property of him, to whom it was so adjudged.*

TITULUS DECIMUS-OCTAVUS.

De publicis judiciis.

D. xlviii. T. 1.

De differentia a privatis.

PUBLICA judicia neque per actiones ordinantur, neque omnino quicquam ſimile habent cum cæteris judiciis, de quibus locuti ſumus: magnaque diverſitas eorum eſt et in inſtituendo et in exercendo.

Public judgments are not introduced by actions; nor are they in any thing ſimilar to the other judgments, of which we have been treating. They alſo differ greatly from one another in the manner of being inſtituted and proſecuted.

Etymologia.

§ I. Publica autem dicta ſunt, quod cuivis ex populo executio eorum pleriumque datur.

§ 1 *Theſe judgments are denominated public, or popular, becauſe, in general, they may be ſued to execution by any of the people.*

Diviſio.

§ II. Publicorum judiciorum quædam capitalia ſunt, quædam non capitalia. Capitalia dicimus, quæ ultimo ſupplicio afficiunt homines, vel etiam aquæ et ignis interdictione, vel deportatione, vel metallo. Cætera, ſi quam infamiam irrogant cum damno pecuniario, hæc publica quidem ſunt, ſed non capitalia.

§ 2 *Of theſe judgments ſome are capital, and others not capital. Thoſe, we term capital, by which a criminal is prohibited from fire and water, or condemned to death, to deportation, or to the mines. The other judgments, by which men are fined and rendered infamous, are public indeed, but yet not capital.*

Exempla; de læſa majeſtate.

§ III. Publica autem judicia hæc ſunt. Lex Julia majeſtatis, quæ in eos, qui contra imperatorem vel rempublicam aliquid moliti ſunt, ſuum vigorem extendit. Cujus pœna animæ amiſſionem ſuſtinet, et memoria rei etiam poſt mortem damnatur.

§ 3 *The following laws denounce public judgments. The law* Julia majeſtatis *extends it's force againſt thoſe, who have been hardy enough to undertake any enterprize againſt the*

the emperor or the republic. The penalty of this law is the loss of life, and the very memory of the offendor becomes infamous after his death.

Lex Julia majestatis] *vid ff* 48. *t* 4 and *Calvin's lexicon juridicum*

In *England* the stated judgment for high-treason, in all cases except counterfeiting the coin, is, that the offendor shall be drawn to the place of execution, and there hanged by the neck and cut down alive, — that his intrails shall be taken out and burned, his head cut off, his body quartered, and his head and quarters put up, where the king shall direct. — The judgment in the case of a woman is, — " that " she shall be drawn and burned "

In this judgment is implied the forfeiture of all the offendor's manors, lands tenements, and hereditaments his wife loses her dower his children become base and ignoble he loses his posterity, for his blood is stained and corrupted All his goods and chattels are likewise forfeited 3 *Co inst* 210 211 *Strahan's Domat supp* *Hale's pl of the crown*, 268

De adulteriis.

§ IV. Item lex Julia de adulteriis coercendis, quæ non solum temeratores alienarum nuptiarum gladio punit, sed et eos, qui cum masculis nefandam libidinem exercere audent. Sed eadem lege etiam stupri flagitium punitur, cum quis sine vi vel virginem vel viduam honeste viventem stupraverit. Pœnam autem eadem lex irrogat stupratoribus, si honesti sunt, publicationem partis dimidiæ bonorum, si humiles, corporis coercitionem cum relegatione.

§ 4 *The law* Julia, *which was made for the suppression of adulteries, not only punishes those men with death, who violate the marriage bed of others, but also those, who commit acts of detestable lewdness with persons of their own sex The same law also inflicts a punishment upon all, who are guilty of the crime called* stuprum, *which is that of debauching a virgin, or a widow of honest fame, without using force. The punishment of this crime in persons of condition is the confiscation of a moiety of their possessions, but offendors of low degree undergo a corporal chastisement with relegation.*

Lex julia] *vid ff* 48 *t* 5 *ad legem Juliam de adulteriis coercendis*

Gladio punit] In *England*, and most other countries at this day, adulterers are punished by fine

Cum masculis nefandam libidinem] The crime here meant is buggery or sodomy, under which words all unnatural carnal copulations are to be understood The antient English lawyers all agree, that it ought to be punished with death, *ultimo supplicio*, though [illegible], as to the manner of inflicting it *Britton* says, that *Sodomites* and miscreants shall be burned — *Fleta* writes, that they shall be buried alive, [illegible] *rantes et sodomitæ in terra* [illegible] — The author of the *mirror* also delivers himself much to the same purpose; and adds [illegible] *domie est crime de majestie vers le roy celestre* [illegible] at this day by 25 *Hen* 8 *cap* 6 and 5 *Eliz* [illegible] the committers of this crime, whether male or female, are no otherwise punishable, than as common felons, who are denied the benefit of the clergy 3 *Co inst cap* 10 *Hale's pl of the crown*, *lib* 1 *cap* 4

De sicariis.

§ V. Item lex Cornelia de sicariis, quæ homicidas ultore ferro persequitur, vel eos, qui hominis occidendi causa cum telo ambulant. Telum autem, ut Cajus noster ex interpretatione legum duodecim tabularum scriptum reliquit, vulgo quidem id appellatur, quod arcu mittitur, sed et nunc omne significat, quod manu cujusque jacitur. Sequitur ergo, ut lignum, et lapis, et ferrum, hoc nomine contineantur, dictum ab eo,

quod

quod in longinquum mittitur, à Græca voce τηλȣ figuratum. Et hanc significationem invenire possumus et in Græco nomine: nam, quod nos telum appellamus, illi βελος appellant ἀπο τȣ βαλλεσθαι. Admonet nos Xenophon, nam ita scribit; και τα βελη ὁμȣ ἐφερετο, λογχαι, τοξευματα, σφενδοναι, πλεισοι δὲ και λιθοι. Sicarii autem appellantur à sica, quod significat ferreum cultrum. Eadem lege et venefici capite damnantur, qui artibus odiosis, tam venenis, quam susurris magicis, homines occiderint; vel mala medicamenta publice vendiderint.

§ 5. *The law* Cornelia de sicariis *punishes those, who commit murder, with death, and also those, who carry weapons, called* tela, *with an intent to kill. The term* telum, *according to* Caius's *interpretation, commonly signifies an arrow made to be shot from a bow, but it is now used to denote any missive weapon, or whatever is thrown from the hand: it therefore follows, that a club, a stone, or a piece of iron, may be comprehended under that appellation. The word* telum *is evidently derived from the* Greek *adverb* τηλου, procul, *because thrown from a distance. And we may trace the same analogy in the* Greek *word* βελος; *for what we call* telum, *the* Greeks *term* βελος, *from* βαλεσθαι *to throw*, *and of this we are informed by* Xenophon, *who writes thus* --- Darts also were carried, spears, arrows, slings, and a multitude of stones. *Assassins and murderers are called* sicarii *from* sica, *which signifies a short crooked sword or ponyard. The same law also inflicts a capital punishment upon those, who practise odious arts, or sell pernicious medicaments, occasioning the death of mankind, as well by poison, as by magical incantations.*

Lex Cornelia de sicariis.] [illegible] 48. t. 8. *ad legem Corneliam de sicariis et veneficis.*

[illegible] capite damnantur.] In *England* all persons suspected of conjuration, witchcraft, or inchantment, were anciently cited into the spiritual courts, where, if they were found guilty, sentence was pronounced, upon which the aid of the secular power was commanded by the ecclesiastical judges, and the supposed delinquents were burned as heretics, by virtue of the writ [illegible], which was not taken away till the [illegible] of *Charles* the 2d, *cap.* 9. [illegible]

Thus the ecclesiastical judges had the intire jurisdiction in respect to sorcery and inchantments, which were all ranked under the general term heresy, till the statute of the 33 *H.* 8. which was the first statute, by which any of these offences were made felony; but this act was repealed by the 1st of *Edw.* 6. *cap.* 12.

Conjuration and the invocation of wicked spirits were afterwards made felony by 5 *Eliz.* *cap.* 16. And again, by a statute in the first year of *James* the first, by which the 5th of *Eliz.* was repealed.

The 1st of *Jac.* 1. *cap.* 12. is to the following purport.

"That the act of 5 *Eliz.* against conjurati-
"ons, inchantments, and witchcrafts, be utterly
"repealed. —— That if any person or persons
"shall use, practice or exercise any invocation
"or conjuration of any evil and wicked spirit,
"or shall consult, covenant with, entertain,
"employ, feed, or reward any evil and wicked
"spirit to and for any intent or purpose, ——
"or take up any dead man, woman, or child,
"out of his, her, or their grave, or any other
"place, where the dead body resteth, or the
"skin, bone, or any other part of any dead
"person, to be imployed in any manner of
"witchcraft, inchantment, charm or sorcery,
"whereby any person shall be killed, destroy-
"ed, wasted, consumed, pined or lamed in
"his or her body, or any part thereof, that
"then every such offendor, or offendors, their
"aiders, abettors, and counsellors being of
"any of the said offences duly and lawfully
"convicted, shall suffer pains of death, as a
"felon or felons, and shall lose the benefit of
"clergy and sanctuary.

"And farther, to the intent, that all manner
"of practice, use or exercise of witchcraft, in-
"chantment, charm, or sorcery, should be
"from henceforth utterly abolished, be it en-
"acted, that, if any person, or persons, shall
"from and after the feast of St. *Michael* next
"coming, take upon him or them by witch-
"craft, inchantment, charm, or sorcery, to
"tell or declare in what place any treasure
"might be found, or where goods, or things
"lost or stolen, should be found, or to the
"intent to provoke any person to unlawful
"love,

" love, or whereby any cattel or goods of " any perſon, ſhall be deſtroyed, waſted, or " impaired, or to hurt or deſtroy any per- " ſon in his or her body, altho' the ſame " be not effected, that then all perſons, ſo " offending, and being convicted, ſhall ſuffer " a year's impriſonment, and ſtand in the pil- " lory once every quarter for ſix hours, and " there openly confeſs his, or her error, and " offenſe" The ſecond offenſe is felony 1 *Jac* 1 *cap* 12

Lord *Coke* hath written a learned comment upon this ſtatute, in which he declares, that it would be a very great defect in government to ſuffer ſo great an abomination, as conjuration, witchcraft, and ſorcery, to paſs with impunity 3 *inſt* 44

But the tendency of the ſtatute of the 1ſt of *James* the 1ſt may beſt appear from the cheats, perjuries, and various other miſchiefs, which it produced, to the ruin of many innocent perſons, all which are but too well known to require any particular mention This act nevertheleſs continued to be a ſcandal and reproach to the good ſenſe of the nation, till the 9th year of *George* the 2d, when it was enacted by parliament—" That the ſtatute, made in the firſt " year of king *James* the firſt, intituled, *An* " *act againſt conjuration, witchcraft, and dealing* " *with evil and wicked ſpirits*, ſhall be repealed " and utterly void, except ſo much as repeals " the ſtatute of the 5th of *Elizabeth*, intituled " an act againſt conjuration, *&c &c*—that an " act paſſed in *Scotland*, in the ninth parlia- " ment of queen *Mary*, intituled, *Anentis witch-* " *crafts*, ſhall be repealed—and that from " the 24th of *June* no proſecution, ſuit, or pro- " ceeding, ſhall be carried on againſt any per- " ſon for witchcraft, ſorcery, inchantment, or " conjuration, or for charging another with any " ſuch offenſe, in any court whatſoever in " *Great Britain*—but that any perſon, pre- " tending to exerciſe witchcraft, tell fortunes, " or diſcover ſtolen goods, ſhall ſuffer impri- " ſonment for one whole year, ſtand in the " pillory once every quarter for an hour, and, " if the court ſhall think proper, be obliged to " give ſureties to behave well for the future." 9 *Geo* 2

De parricidiis.

§ VI. Alia deinde lex aſperrimum crimen nova pœna perſequitur, quæ Pompeia de parricidiis vocatur · qua cavetur, ut, ſi quis parentis aut filii, aut omnino affectionis ejus, quæ nuncupatione parentum continetur, fata præparaverit, (ſive clam, ſive palam, id auſus fuerit,) nec non is, cujus dolo malo id factum eſt, vel conſcius criminis exiſtit, licet extraneus ſit, pœna parricidii puniatur : et neque gladio, neque ignibus, neque ulli ſolemni pœnæ ſubjiciatur, ſed inſutus culeo cum cane, et gallo gallinaceo, et vipera, et ſimia, et inter eas ferales anguſtias comprehenſus, (ſecundum quod regionis qualitas tulerit,) vel in vicinum mare, vel in amnem, projiciatur ut omnium elementorum uſu vivus carere incipiat, et ei cœlum ſuperſtiti, et terra mortuo, auferatur Si quis autem alias cognatione vel affinitate perſonas conjunctas necaverit, pœnam legis Corneliæ de ſicariis ſuſtinebit

§ 6 *The law* Pompeia de parricidiis *inflicts a new puniſhment upon those, who commit parricide, which is the moſt execrable of all crimes, and by this law it is ordained, that whoever, either publicly or privately, haſtens the death of a parent or a child, or of any perſon comprized under the title, or denomination, of a parent, ſhall be puniſhed as a commiter of parricide; and that any one, who hath adviſed, or been privy to the death of any of theſe perſons, is alſo guilty of parricide, altho' he is a ſtranger, and not related to their family A criminal, in caſe of parricide, is neither put to death by the ſword, by fire, nor by any other ordinary puniſhment, for the law directs, that he ſhall be ſewed up in a kind of ſack, with a dog, a cock, a viper, and an ape, and, being put up in this horrid incloſure, ſhall be thrown either into the ſea, or an adjacent river, according to the ſituation of the place, where the*

N

puniſh

punishment is inflicted: thus, whilest he is yet alive, he is deprived of the very elements, so that his living body is denied the benefits of the air, and his dead body the use of the earth. But, if a man is guilty of the murder of any other persons, related to him, either by cognation or affinity, he is only subject to the punishment inflicted by the law Cornelia de sicariis.

Pompeia de parricidiis] *vid ff* 48 *t.* 9. *Cod* 9 *t.* 17 *De lege Pompeia de parricidiis*

In *England* parricide and homicide are not distinguished, as to the punishment inflicted upon criminals.

De falsis.

§ VII. Item lex Cornelia de falsis, quæ etiam testamentaria vocatur, pœnam irrogat ei, qui testamentum vel aliud instrumentum falsum scripserit, signaverit recitaverit, subjecerit, vel signum adulterinum fecerit, sculpserit, expresserit, sciens, dolo malo. Ejusque legis pœna in servos ultimum supplicium est; quod etiam in lege Cornelia de sicariis et veneficis servatur: in liberos vero deportatio.

§ 7. *The law* Cornelia de falsis, *which is also called* testamentaria, *punishes any man, who knowingly and with a fraudulent intent, hath writen, signed, dictated, or produced a false will, or any other instrument; it also punishes every one, who hath made, ingraved, or in any manner counterfeited the seal of another. The punishment inflicted by the law upon slaves in these cases is death, but the punishment of free persons is deportation*

Lex Cornelia de falsis] *vid ff* 48 *t* 10. 5 *Eliz cap* 14. 8 *Geo.* 1 *cap* 22 12 *Geo* 1. *cap* 32 2 *Geo* 2 *cap* 25

De vi.

§ VIII. Item lex Julia de vi publica seu privata adversus eos exoritur, qui vim vel armatam, vel sine armis, commiserint. Sed, siquidem armata vis arguatur, deportatio ei ex lege Julia de vi publica irrogatur: si vero sine armis, in tertiam partem bonorum suorum publicatio imponitur. Sin autem per vim raptus virginis, vel viduæ, vel sanctimonialis, vel alterius, fuerit perpetratus, tunc et raptores, et ii, qui opem huic flagitio dederunt, capite puniuntur, secundum nostræ constitutionis definitionem, ex qua hoc apertius possibile est scire.

§ 8 *The law* Julia, *concerning public and private force, takes place against all, who use force, whether they are armed or unarmed, but, if proof is made of an armed force, the punishment is deportation by that law, and, if the force was not accompanied with arms, the penalty to be inflicted is the confiscation of one third part of the offender's goods, nevertheless, if a rape is commited upon a virgin, a widow, a nun, or upon any other person, both the ravishers and their accomplices are all equally subject to a capital punishment, according to the decision of our constitution, in which the student may read more at large of this matter*

Lex Julia de vi] *vid ff* 48 *t* 6 *and* [illegible]

Secundum nostræ const definitionem] *vid.* *Cod* 9 *t* 13

De

De peculatu.

§ IX. Item lex Julia peculatus eos punit, qui publicam pecuniam, vel rem ſacram, vel religioſam, furati fuerint. Sed, ſiquidem ipſi judices tempore adminiſtrationis publicas pecunias ſubtraxerint, capitali animadverſione puniuntur: et non ſolum hi, ſed etiam qui miniſterium eis ad hoc exhibuerint, vel qui ſubtractas ab his ſuſceperint. Alii vero, qui in hanc legem inciderint, pœnæ deportationis ſubjugentur.

§ 9. *The law* Julia de peculatu *puniſhes thoſe, who have been guilty of theft, in regard to public money, or any thing, which is ſacred: and, if judges themſelves, during the time of their acting as ſuch, commit a theft of this kind, their puniſhment is capital, and the puniſhment of all thoſe, who aſſiſt in ſuch a theft, or knowingly receive the things ſtolen, is alſo cap[illegible]al. But all other perſons, who offend againſt this law, are only ſubject to depor[illegible].*

Lex Julia peculatus] By the crime *pe[illegible]* [ſo called *a pecore*, in which antiently all rich[illegible]s conſiſted] is meant the ſtealing, or embezling, of money, which belongs either to the church, or to the public in general. *[illegible] ff* 48 *t* 13

De plagiariis.

§ X. Eſt et inter publica judicia lex Fabia de plagiariis, quæ interdum capitis pœnam ex ſacris conſtitutionibus irrogat, interdum leviorem.

§ 10. *The law* Fabia *againſt plagiaries is alſo numbered among public judgments; but, in conſequence of the imperial conſtitutions, the offenders againſt this law are ſometimes puniſhed with death, and ſometimes by a milder puniſhment.*

Lex Fabia de plagiariis] *vid ff* 48 *t* 15 *Cod* 9 *t* 20

A plagiary in this place denotes a manſtealer, and is ſo called from *plagium*, which ſignifies man ſtealing

The puniſhment of a plagiary is death both by the divine law, and the canon law *Exod* xxi 16 *Deut* xxiv 1. *Decret G ix lib* 5 *t* 18 *de furtis*

But, in *England* the ſtealing of man, woman, or child, [called in the law *kidnapping*] is puniſhed by fine, pillory, [illegible] *Reyn.* [illegible]

De ambitu, repetundis, annona, reſiduis.

§ XI. Sunt præterea publica judicia, lex Julia de ambitu, lex Julia repetundarum, et lex Julia de annona, et lex Julia de reſiduis: quæ de certis capitulis loquuntur, et animæ quidem amiſſionem non irrogant; aliis autem pœnis eos ſubjiciunt, qui præcepta earum neglexerint

§ 11 *There are alſo other public judgments, ſuch are the* Julian *laws* de ambitu, repetund[illegible], de annona, de reſiduis, *which do not puniſh with death, but inflict other puniſhments upon thoſe, who offend*

Lex Julia de ambitu] [illegible] *ff* 48 *t* 14

The [illegible], which the Romans called *ambitus*, [illegible] public offices [illegible] and it ſeems to [illegible] in regard to temporal offices, [illegible] in regard to ſpiritual preferment [illegible] *G*[illegible] 5 *t* 3

[illegible] or the [illegible] and ſelling of offices, ceaſed to be criminal, and became common among the *Romans* ſoon after the demolition of the republic, and the practice continued, till [illegible], becoming [illegible] of its evil tendency [illegible] laws in order to reſtrain [illegible] *cap* [illegible]

In *France* [illegible] offices [illegible] to ſale, and [illegible] and perhaps, as *Vinny* observes, there may be less reason to prohibit this species of commerce in a monarchy than in a democracy

But in *England* the statute of the 5th and 6th of *Edw* 6 restrains "all persons, under pain "of forfeiture and disability for the future, "from buying certain offices, which concern "the king's revenue, and the execution of "justice" And under these offices not only that of the chancellor of a diocese is comprehended, but also that of a commissary and register for it was resolved in the case of doctor *Trevor*, the chancellor of a diocese in *Wales*, that both the offices of chancellor, and register, are within the statute, because they concern the administration of justice 3 *Co inst* 148 12 *Co rep* 78 79 3 *Lev* 289 *Woodward v. Fox*

Lex Julia repetundarum] This law forbids all persons in public offices to take money or presents, either for administering justice, or commiting injustice *Lege Julia repetundarum [pecuniarum] tenetur, qui, cum aliquam potestatem haberet, pecuniam ob judicandum, decernendumve, acceperit* ff 48. t 11

Fortescue, on the laws of *England*, declares "bribery to be a great misprision, which is "commited, when any man in a judicial place "takes any fee or pension, robe or livery, gift, "reward or brocage of any person, who hath "to do before him any way, for doing his "office, or by color of his office, but of the "king only, unless it be of meat and drink, "and that of small value *cap* 51." 3 *Co inst* 145

De annona] The crime *fraudatæ annonæ* is that of abusing the markets, by raising the price of provisions, forestalling, monopolizing, &c

This offense is punishable in *England* by imprisonment and forfeiture of the goods or merchandise forestalled See 25 *Ed.* 3 *cap* 3. 2 *Ric* 2. *cap* 2. 27 *Ed* 3. *cap* 11 5. 6. *Edw* 6 *cap* 14, 3 *Co inst p* 195.

De residuis] *Crimen residui* is commited by retaining the public money, or converting it to other uses than those, to which it was appropriated *Lege Julia de residuis tenetur, qui publicam pecuniam delegatam in usum aliquem retinuit, neque in eum consumpsit.* ff. 48 t. 13.

Conclusio.

§ XII Sed de publicis judiciis hæc exposuimus, ut vobis possibile sit, summo digito, et quasi per indicem ea tetigisse: alioqui diligentior eorum scientia vobis, ex latioribus digestorum seu pandectarum libris, Deo propitio, adventura est.

§ 12 *But it is now time to conclude our institutes; and we declare it to be our intent, that this brief exposition of public judgments should serve only, as an index, to give a general idea of that knowledge, which, thro' the blessing of God, may be most fully and particularly obtained, by perusing the digests with a diligent attention.*

FINIS

LIBRI QUARTI ET ULTIMI

INSTITUTIONUM.

NOV. CXVIII.

ΚΕΦ. Α.

Περι διαδοχης των κατιοντων.

Ει τις τοινυν των κατιοντων ὑπειη τῳ ἀδιαθετῳ τελευτησαντι, οιασδηποτε φυσεως ἢ βαθμου, ἐιτε ἐξ ἀρρενογονιας ἐιτε ἐκ θηλυγονιας καταγομενος, και ἐιτε αὐτεξουσιος ἐιτε ὑπεξουσιος ἐιη, παντων των ἀνιοντων και των ἐκ πλαγιου συγγενων προτιμασθω. Κἀν γαρ ὁ τελευτησας ἑτερου ὑπεξουσιος ἠν, ὁμως τους αὐτου παιδας, οιασδηποτε ἀν ὠσι φυσεως ἢ βαθμου, και αὐτων των γονεων προτιμασθαι κελευομεν, ὠν ὑπεξουσιος ἠν ὁ τελευτησας, ἐπ' ἐκεινοις δηλαδη τοις πραγμασιν, ἁτινα, κατα τους ἀλλους ἡμων νομους, τοις πατρασιν οὐ προσπορίζεται· ἐπι γαρ τῃ χρησει των πραγματων τουτων, ὀφειλουσῃ προσπορίζεσθαι ἢ φυλαττεσθαι, τους περι τουτων ἡμων νομους τοις γονευσι φυλαττομεν· οὐτω μεντοιγε ὡστε, ἐι τινα τουτων των κατιοντων παιδας καταλιποντα τελευτησαι συμβαιη, τους ἐκεινου ὑιους ἢ θυγα-

CAP. I.

De descendentium successione.

SI quis igitur descendentium fuerit ei, qui intestatus moritur, cujuslibet naturæ aut gradus, sive ex masculorum genere sive ex fœminarum descendens, et sive suæ potestatis sive sub potestate sit, omnibus ascendentibus et ex latere cognatis præponatur. Licet enim defunctus sub alterius potestate fuerit, tamen ejus filii, cujuslibet sexus sint aut gradus, etiam ipsis parentibus præponi præcipimus, quorum sub potestate fuerit, qui defunctus est, in illis videlicet rebus, quæ, secundum nostras alias leges, patribus non acquiruntur: nam in usu harum rerum, qui debet acquiri aut servari, nostras de his omnibus leges parentibus custodimus: sic tamen, ut, si quem horum descendentium filios relinquentem mori contigerit, illius τερας ἢ τȣς ἀλλȣς κατιοντας εἰς τον τȣ ἰδιȣ γονεως τοπον ὑπεισιεναι, εἰτε ὑπεξȣσιοι τῳ τελευτησαντι εἰτε αὐτεξȣσιοι εὑρεθειεν, τοσȣτον ἐκ της κληρονομιας τȣ τελευτησαντος λαμβανοντας μερος, ὁσοι δηποτε ἀν ὡσιν, ὁσον ὁ αὐτων γονευς, ει περιην, ἐκομιζετο· ἡν τινα διαδοχην in ſtirpes ἡ ἀρχαιοτης ἐκαλεσεν· ἐπι ταυτης γαρ της ταξεως τον βαθμον ζητεισθαι ȣ̓ βȣλομεθα· ἀλλα μετα των ὑων και των θυγατερων τȣς ἐκ τȣ προτελευτησαντος ὑȣ ἡ θυγατρος ἐγγονȣς καλεισθαι θεσπιζομεν, ȣ̓δεμιας εἰσαγομενης διαφορας, εἰτε ἀρρενες εἰτε θηλειαι ὠσι, και εἰτε ἐξ ἀρρενογονιας εἰτε ἐκ θηλυγονιας καταγωνται, εἰτε ὑπεξȣσιοι εἰτε και αὐτεξȣσιοι εἰησαν. Και ταυτα μεν περι της των κατιοντων διαδοχης ἐτυπωσαμεν.

filios aut filias, aut alios deſcendentes, in proprii parentis locum ſuccedere, ſive ſub poteſtate defuncti ſive ſuæ poteſtatis inveniantur; tantam de hereditate morientis accipientes partem, quanticunque ſint, quantam eorum parens, ſi viveret, habuiſſet: quam ſucceſſionem in ſtirpes vocavit antiquitas: in hoc enim ordine gradum quæri nolumus: ſed cum filiis et filiabus ex præmortuo filio aut filia nepotes vocari ſancimus; nulla introducenda differentia, ſive maſculi ſive fœminæ ſint, et ſeu ex maſculorum ſeu fœminarum prole deſcendant, ſive ſuæ poteſtatis ſive ſub poteſtate ſint conſtituti. Et hæc quidem de ſucceſſionibus deſcendentium diſpoſuimus.

CHAPTER I.

Of the ſucceſſion of deſcendents.

If a man dies inteſtate, leaving a deſcendent of either ſex or any degree, ſuch deſcendent, whether he derives his deſcent from the male or female line, or whether he is under power or not, is to be prefered to all aſcendents and collaterals And, a'tho' the deceaſed was himſelf under parental power, yet we ordain, that his children of either ſex or any degree ſhall be prefered in ſucceſſion to the parents, under whoſe power the inteſtate died, in regard to thoſe things, which children do not acquire for their parents, according to our other laws; for we would maintain the laws in reſpect to the uſufruct, which is allowed to parents ſo that, if any of the deſcendents of the deceaſed ſhould die, leaving ſons or daughters or other deſcendents, they ſhall ſucceed in the place of their own father, whether they are under his power or *ſui juris*, and ſhall be intituled to the ſame ſhare of the inteſtate's eſtate, which their father would have had,

it

if he had lived. And this kind of ſucceſſion has been termed by the antient lawyers a ſucceſſion *in ſtirpes:* for in the ſucceſſion of deſcendents we allow no priority of degree, but admit the grandchildren of any perſon by a deceaſed ſon or daughter to be called to inherit that perſon together with his ſons or daughters, without making any diſtinction between males and females, or the deſcendents of males and females, or between thoſe, who are under power, and thoſe, who are not. Theſe are the rules, which we have eſtabliſhed, concerning the ſucceſſion of deſcendents.

Ει τι, τοινυν Si quis igitur] The three firſt chapters of this novel conſtitution deſerve the attentive conſideration of the reader, not only becauſe they contain the lateſt policy of the civil law in regard to the diſpoſition of the eſtates of inteſtates; but becauſe they are the foundation of our ſtatute law in this reſpect vid *Holt's* caſes, p. 259 *Peere Williams's* rep. p 27 Prec in chan p 593 Sir *Thom Raymond's* rep p 496 And they are ſtill almoſt of continual uſe, by being the general guide of the courts in *England*, which hold cogniſance of diſtributions, in all thoſe caſes, concerning which our own laws have either been ſilent, or not ſufficiently expreſs

Εις τον του ἰδιου γονεως. In proprii parentis locum ſuccedere] Nothing is more clear in the civil law, than that grandchildren, even when alone, (altho' they deſcend from various ſtocks and are unequal in their numbers,) would take the eſtate of their deceaſed grandfather *per Stirpes*, and not *per Capita* Suppoſe therefore, that *Titius* ſhould die leaving grandchildren by three different ſons, already dead; to wit, three by one ſon, ſix by another, and twelve by another, each of theſe claſſes of grandchildren would take a third of the eſtate without any regard to the inequality of the numbers in each claſs. But, as to this point in *England*, the law-reports mention no judicial determination, yet it ſeems probable, that the courts, in which diſtributions are cogniſable, would order the diviſion of an eſtate in ſuch a caſe to be made *per Capita*, and this, partly from a motive of equity, and partly from a conſideration of the intent of the ſtatute, relating to the eſtates of inteſtates, for the ſtatute directs an *equal* and *juſt* diſtribution and, when the act mentions repreſentation, it muſt be underſtood to refer to it, in thoſe caſes only, where repreſentation is neceſſary to prevent excluſion, but not to refer to it in thoſe caſes, where all the claimants are in equal degree, and therefore can take *ſuo quiſque jure*, each in his own right vid 23, 24, Car 2, cap. 10. lib. 3 Inſt pag 4.

ΚΕΦ. Β.

Περι των ανιοντων διαδοχης.

ΕΙ τοινυν ὁ τελευτησας κατιοντας μεν μη καταλιποι κληρονομους, πατηρ δε ἡ μητηρ ἡ ἀλλοι γονεις ἀυτῳ ἐπιζησουσι, παντων των ἐκ πλαγιου συγγενων τουτους προτιμασθαι θεσπιζομεν, ἐξῃρημενων μονων ἀδελφων ἐξ ἑκατερου γονεως συναπτομενων τῳ τελευτησαντι, ὡς δια των ἑξης δηλωθησεται. Ει δε πολλοι των ἀνιον-

CAP. II.

De aſcendentium ſucceſſione.

SI igitur defunctus deſcendentes quidem non relinquat heredes, pater autem aut mater aut alii parentes ei ſuperſint, omnibus ex latere cognatis hos præponi ſancimus, exceptis ſolis fratribus ex utroque parente conjunctis defuncto, ſicut per ſubſequentia declarabitur. Si autem plurimi aſcendentium vivunt,

των περιεισι, τουτους προτιμασθαι κελευομεν, οἱ τινες ἐγγυτεροι τῳ βαθμῳ ἑυρεθειεν, ἀρρενας τε και θηλειας, ἐιτε προς μητρος ἐιτε προς πατρος ἐιεν. Ει δε τον ἀυτον ἐχουσι βαθμον, ἐξ ἰσης ἐις ἀυτους ἡ κληρονομια διαιρεθησεται, ὡστε το μεν ἡμισυ λαμβανειν παντας τους προς πατρος ἀνιοντας, ὁσοι δηποτε ἀν ὠσι· το δε ὑπολοιπον ἡμισυ τους προς μητρος ἀνιοντας, ὁσους δηποτε ἀν αυτους ἑυρεθηναι συμβαιη. Ει δε μετα των ανιοντων ευρεθωσιν ἀδελφοι ἡ ἀδελφαι ἐξ ἑκατερων γονεων συναπτομενοι τῳ τελευτησαντι, μετα των ἐγγυτερων τῳ βαθμῳ ἀνιοντων κληθησονται· ἐι και πατηρ ἡ μητηρ ἐιησαν, διαιρουμενης ἐις ἀυτους δηλαδη της κληρονομιας κατα τον των προσωπων ἀριθμον· ἱνα και των ἀνιοντων και των ἀδελφων ἑκαστος ἰσην ἐχοι μοιραν, ὀυδεμιαν χρησιν ἐκ της των ὑιων ἡ θυγατερων μοιρας ἐν τουτῳ τῳ θεματι δυναμενου του πατρος ἑαυτῳ παντελως ἐκδικειν, ἐπειδη ἀντι ταυτης της χρησεως μερος ἀυτῳ της κληρονομιας και κατα δεσποτειας δικαιον δια του παροντος δεδωκαμεν νομου, ὀυδεμιας φυλαττομενης διαφορας μεταξυ των προσωπων τουτων, ἐιτε θηλειαι ἐιτε ἀρρενες ἐιησαν, οἱ προς την κληρονομιαν κα-

hos præponi jubemus, qui proximi gradu reperiuntur, maſculos et fœminas, ſive paterni ſive materni ſint. Si autem eundem habeant gradum, ex æquo inter eos hereditas dividatur; ut medietatem quidem accipiant omnes a patre aſcendentes, quanticunque fuerint, medietatem vero reliquam a matre aſcendentes, quantoſcunque eos inveniri contigerit. Si vero cum aſcendentibus inveniantur fratres aut ſorores ex utriſque parentibus conjuncti defuncto, cum proximis gradu aſcendentibus vocabuntur, ſi et pater aut mater fuerint, dividenda inter eos quippe hæreditate ſecundum perſonarum numerum, uti et aſcendentium et fratrum ſinguli æqualem habeant portionem, nullum uſum ex filiorum aut filiarum portione in hoc caſu valente patre ſibi penitus vindicare, quoniam pro hac uſus portione hæreditatis jus et ſecundum proprietatem per præſentem dedimus legem, differentia nulla ſervanda inter perſonas iſtas, ſive fœminæ ſive maſculi fuerint, qui ad hæreditatem vocantur, et ſive per maſ-

λουμενοι,

λημενοι, και ειτε δι' αρρενος η θηλεως προσωπε συναπλονται, και ειτε αυτεξεσιος ειτε υπεξεσιος ην, ον διαδεχονται.

culi sive per fœminæ personam copulantur; et sive suæ potestatis sive sub potestate fuerit is, cui succedunt.

CHAPTER II.

Of the succession of ascendents.

But, when the deceased leaves no descendents, if a father, or mother, or any other parents, grand-fathers, great-grand-fathers, &c. survive him, we decree, that they shall be prefered to all collateral relations, except brothers of the whole blood to the deceased, as shall hereafter be more particularly declared. But, if many ascendents are living, we prefer those, who are in the nearest degree, whether they are male or female, paternal or maternal, and, when several ascendents concur in the same degree, the inheritance of the deceased must be so divided, that the ascendents on the part of the father may receive one half, and the ascendents on the part of the mother the other half, without regard to the number of persons on either side. But, if the deceased leaves brothers and sisters of the whole blood together with ascendents, these collaterals of the deceased shall be called with the nearest ascendents; and, altho the surviving parents are a father and mother, the inheritance must be so divided according to the number of persons, that each of the ascendents, and each of the brothers, may have an equal portion; nor shall the father, in this case take to himself any usufruct of the portions belonging to his sons and daughters, because by this law we have given him the absolute property of one portion and we suffer no distinction to be made between those persons, who are called to an inheritance, whether they are males or females, or related by males or females, or whether he, to whom they succeed, was, or was not, under power, at the time of his decease

Ει και πατηρ η μητηρ ... Si et pater aut mater fuerint] By the Law of *England*, when a person dies intestate, leaving a father, the father is solely intituled to the whole personal estate of the intestate, exclusive of all others, and anciently, [i e in the reign of *Henry* the first vid LL Hen prim., *Wilkins* ed ..., p 266] a surviving father, or mother, could have taken even the real estate of their deceased child But this law of succession was altered soon afterwards, for we find by *Glanville*, that, in the time of *Henry* the second, a father or mother could not have taken the real estates of their deceased children, the inheritance being then carried over to the collateral line vid *Glanville*, lib 7 cap 1, 2, &c 1 *Pere Williams* 50 And it has ever since been held as an inviolable maxim, that an inheritance cannot ascend *Co Lit* 11 a But this alteration in the law, made since the reign of *Henry* the first, did not extend to personal estate, so that, before the statute of the first of *James* the second, if a child had died intestate without a wife, child, or father, the mother would have been intituled to the whole personal estate, exclusive of the brothers and sisters of the intestate, but it is enacted by that statute, "that, if, after the death of a father, "any of his children shall die intestate, without "wife or children, in the life time of the mo"ther, every brother and sister, and their re"presentatives, shall have an equal share with "her" 1 *Jac* 2 cap 17 § 6

But should it here be asked, whether the brother of an intestate would exclude the grandfather by the civil law? the novel appears at first sight to answer it very fully in the negative by enacting, "*that, if the deceased leaves brothers and sisters* "*together with ascendents in the right line, these* "*collaterals shall be called with the nearest ascen*"*dents*, &c And indeed the generality of writers, namely, *Gudelin*, *Forster*, *Ferriere*, *Domat*, and others, all understand this passage, as admitting

admitting ascendents and brothers to take jointly, yet a contrary interpretation has been given by some civilians, of whom *Voet* is the principal, whose reasonings in support of it are therefore here copied at large

" Illud non satis expeditum est, an etiam cum " avo aut proavo, ubi alius proximior ascendens " non est, fratres germani ejus, qui defunctus " est, concurrere debeant, an magis avo proavove præferendi sunt, eosque excludant? Concursum enim ascendentium naturaliter gradu " remotiorum, quos nullus intermedius existens " excludit, cum fratribus germanis defuncti tuentur plerique, moti eo, quod cum *proxime* " *ascendentibus* fratres veniunt vid novel. 118 " Proximus autem sit, quem nemo antecedit "

" Sed Juris rationibus convenientius videtur, " avum proavumve defuncti a fratribus ejus " germanis in successione excludi, quia Imperator in dicta novella 118. emphatice dixit, " fratres et sorores cum *proximis gradu ascendentibus* vocari, qualis mentio *proximorum gradu* " inutilis plane ac superflua esset, si non per " *gradu proximos* denotarentur illi, qui in primo " lineæ ascendentis gradu sunt, cum juris certi " atque indubitati sit, nunquam in ascendente " linea locum esse juri repræsentationis, per quod " remotior subintraret in locum proximioris defuncti, atque adeo suffecisset, si generaliter " expressum esset, fratres cum *ascendentibus* vocari Ne dicam hoc ipso, quo in linea ascendente repræsentatio personæ proximioris admissa non est, fieri non posse, ut avus vel proavus defuncti, qui a patre vel matre defuncti " certo certius excluditur, concurreret cum fratribus, qui cum patre matreque defuncti concurrunt Quibus accedit, quod sententia, de " avo defuncti cum germanis ejus fratribus concurrente, ad absurda ducit Si enim verum " est, quod in casu quo fratres et sorores cum " proximis gradu ascendentibus ita concurrant, " ut hereditas inter eos secundum personarum " numerum dividenda sit, ac ascendentium et " fratrum singuli æqualem habeant portionem " secundum d nov 118 eveniret necessario, ut " remotiores ascendentes ob defectum proximiorum cum fratribus defuncti concurrentes plus " fratribus nocituri essent, quam proximiores, " dum, positis duobus fratribus germanis defuncti, pater et mater concurrens duas tantum " partes æquales auferendo efficerent, ut fratres " singuli quartam hereditatis fraternæ partem " capiant, quatuor autem avi aviæque existentes, " viriles totidem partes occupando, non nisi sextam singulis defuncti fratribus relicturi essent, " sicuti tantum partem decimam duo fratres singuli essent habituri, si cum proavis atque proaviabus (quales octo esse possunt) deberent concurrere. Quam autem a ratione id alienum " sit, ut magis alii concursu suo noceant remotiores, quam qui ejusdem lineæ proximiores " sunt, nemo, ut opinor, non sponte satis agnoscit Denique tantum concursum esse fratrum " cum patre et matre, non vero cum aliis ascendentibus remotioribus, ubi pater materque deficit, aperte probant verba novellæ 118 dum " illic diserte cautum, si cum ascendentibus inveniuntur fratres aut sorores ex utrisque parentibus conjuncti defuncto, eos *cum proximis* " *gradu ascendentibus vocari, si aut pater aut mater* " *fuerint* unde sequitur, eos non omni casu, nec " promiscue cum omnibus ascendentibus, venire, " sed *si pater aut mater fuerint*. ideoque mox igitur subjicitur, in hoc casu *patrem nullum usum* " *ex filiorum aut filiarum portione posse sibi penitus* " *vindicare*, nulla *avi* facta mentione; cum tamen id *avo* æque interdicendum fuisset, si et " avus cum defuncti nepotis fratribus succedere " potuisset, dum fratres succedentes æque potuissent in avi quam in patris potestate esse Ut " proinde nihil in contrarium efficiat, quod, in " jure, proximus dicatur, quem nemo antecedit. " cum id tum demum admitti debeat, quando " nulla inde absurditas profluit; prout in hoc " casu futurum, supra monstratum est " vid *Joannis Voet* com. ad Pandectas, tom 2. lib. 38 t 17 § 13

But this question seems now to be settled in *England* in consequence of three determinations; the first of which was given in the Exchequer in the case of *Poole* vers *Wilshaw* on the 9th of July 1708 —— the second in the case of *Norbury* vers *Vicars*, before Mr *Fortescue*, Master of the Rolls in november 1749 —— and the third was delivered on the 14th of Jan 1754, in the case of *Evelin* vers *Evelin*, by the Lord Chancellor, who decreed in favor of the brother in exclusion of the grandfather, having founded his opinion partly in deference to the former determinations, partly in consideration of the *present* common law computation of degrees, relative to *real* estates, and partly upon the benefit, which must accrue to the Public by prefering a younger man to an older, the brother of a deceased person to the grandfather, *propter spem accrescendi*

And it was also declared to be the opinion of the court, that, if the point in question had been *res integra*, and solely determinable by the *Roman* law, the decree would still have been the same, which declaration, from so high an authority, must have great weight in ascertaining the meaning of the Novel, and must incline civilians in general to think more favorably for the future of *Voet's* arguments, which were particularly quoted and much relied upon by the court

ΚΕΦ. Γ.

Περι διαδοχης των ἐκ πλαγιου κατιοντων.

ΕΙ τοινυν ὁ τελευτησας μηδε κατιοντας μηδε ἀνιοντας καταλειψη, πρωτους προς την κληρονομιαν καλουμεν τους ἀδελφους και τας ἀδελφας, τους ἐκ του ἀυτου πατρος και της ἀυτης μητρος τεχθεντας, ὁυς και μετα των πατερων προς την κληρονομιαν ἐκαλεσαμεν. Τουτων δε μη ὑποντων, ἐν δευτερᾳ ταξει ἐκεινους τους ἀδελφους προς την κληρονομιαν καλουμεν, ὁιτινες ἐξ ἑνος γονεως συναπτονται τῳ τελευτησαντι ἐιτε δια του πατρος μονου, ἐιτε δια της μητρος. Ει δε τῳ τελευτησαντι ἀδελφοι ὑπειησαν, και ἑτερου ἀδελφου ἠ ἀδελφης προτελευτησαντων παιδες, κληθησονται προς την κληρονομιαν ὁυτοι μετα των προς πατρος και προς μητρος θειων, ἀρρενων τε και θηλειων· και, ὁσοι δηποτε ἀν ὠσι, τοσουτον ἐκ της κληρονομιας ληψονται μερος, ὁσον ὁ ἀυτων γονευς ἠμελλε λαμβανειν, ἐι ἐπεζησεν. Οθεν ἀκολουθον ἐστιν, ἱνα, ἐι τυχον ὁ προτελευτησας ἀδελφος, ὁυ οι παιδες περιεισι, δι' ἑκατερου γονεως τῳ νυν τελευτησαντι προσ-

CAP. III.

De successione ex latere venientium.

SI igitur defunctus neque descendentes neque ascendentes reliquerit, primos ad hæreditatem vocamus fratres et sorores ex eodem patre et ex eadem matre natos, quos etiam cum patribus ad hæreditatem vocavimus. His autem non existentibus, in secundo ordine illos fratres ad hæreditatem vocamus, qui ex uno parente conjuncti sunt defuncto, sive per patrem solum, sive per matrem. Si autem defuncto fratres fuerint et alterius fratris aut sororis præmortuorum filii, vocabuntur ad hæreditatem isti cum de patre et matre thiis, masculis et fœminis; et, quanticunque fuerint, tantam ex hæreditate percipient portionem quantam eorum parens futurus esset accipere, si superstes esset. Unde consequens est, ut, si forte præmortuus frater, cujus filii vivunt, per utrumque parentem nunc defunctæ

ἀπῳ

ωπῳ συνηπτετο, ὁι δε περιοντες ἀδελφοι δια του πατρος μονου τυχον, ἡ της μητρος, ἀυτῳ συνηπτοντο, προτιμηθωσιν ὁι τουτου παιδες των ἰδιων θειων, ἐι και τριτου ἐισι βαθμου, ἐιτε προς πατρος ἐιτε προς μητρος ἐιησαν ὁι θειοι, και ἐιτε ἀρρενες ἐιτε θηλειαι, ὡσπερ ὁ ἀυτων γονευς προετιματο, ἐι περιην. Και ἐκ των ἐναντιων, ἐι ὁ μεν περιων ἀδελφος ἐξ ἑκατερου γονεως συναπτεται τῳ τελευτησαντι, ὁ δε προτελευτησας δι' ἑνος γονεως συνηπτετο, τους τουτου παιδας ἐκ της κληρονομιας ἀποκλειομεν, ὡσπερ και ἀυτος, ἐι περιην, ἐξεκλειετο. Το δε τοιουτον προνομιον ἐν ταυτῃ τῃ ταξει της συγγενειας μονοις παρεχομεν τοις των ἀδελφων, ἀρρενων ἡ θηλειων, ὑιοις ἡ θυγατρασιν, ἱνα ἐις τα των ἰδιων γονεων δικαια ὑπεισελθωσιν· ὀυδενι δε ἀλλῳ παντελως προσωπῳ, ἐκ ταυτης της ταξεως ἐρχομενῳ, τουτο το δικαιον συγχωρουμεν. Ἀλλα και ἀυτοις τοις των ἀδελφων παισι τοτε ταυτην την ἐυεργεσιαν παρεχομεν, ὁτε μετα των ἰδιων κρινονται θειων, ἀρρενων τε και θηλειων, ἐιτε προς πατρος ἐιτε προς μητρος ἐιεν. Ει δε μετα των ἀδελφων του τελευτησαντος και ἀνιοντες, ὡς ἠδη προειπομεν, προς την κλη-

personæ jungebatur, superstites autem fratres per patrem solum forsan aut matrem ei jungebantur, præponantur istius filii propriis thiis, licet in tertio sint gradu, (sive a patre sive a matre sint thii, et sive masculi sive fœminæ,) sicut eorum parens præponeretur, si viveret. Et ex diverso, siquidem superstes frater ex utroque parente conjungitur defuncto, præmortuus autem per unum parentem jungebatur, hujus filios ab hæreditate excludimus sicut ipse, si viveret, ab hæreditate excludebatur. Hujusmodi vero privilegium in hoc ordine cognationis solis præbemus fratrum masculorum et fœminarum filiis et filiabus, ut in suorum parentum jura succedant: nulli enim alii omnino personæ, ex hoc ordine venienti, hoc jus largimur Sed et ipsis fratrum filiis tunc hoc beneficium conferimus, quando cum propriis judicantur thiis masculis et fœminis, sive paterni sive materni sint. Si autem cum fratribus defuncti etiam ascendentes, sicut jam dixi-

ρονομιαν

ρονομιαν καλουνται, ουδενι τροπῳ προς την ἐξ ἀδιαθετου διαδοχην τους του αδελφου ἡ της ἀδελφης παιδας καλεισθαι συγχωρουμεν· ουδε ἐι ἐξ ἑκατερου γονεως ὁ ἀυτων πατηρ ἡ μητηρ συνηπτετο τῳ τελευτησαντι. Ὁποτε τοινυν τοις του ἀδελφου και της ἀδελφης παισι τοιουτο προνομιον δεδωκαμεν, ἱνα τον των γονεων ὑπεισιοντες τοπον μονοι τριτου ὀντες βαθμου μετα των ἐκ πρωτου και δευτερου βαθμου προς την κληρονομιαν καλωνται· ἐκεινο προδηλον ἐςιν, ὁτι των θειων του τελευτησαντος ἀρρενων τε και θηλειων, ἐιτε προς πατρος ἐιτε προς μητρος ἐιησαν, προτιμωνται, ἐι και ἐκεινοι τριτον ὁμοιως συγγενειας βαθμον ἐχοιεν.

Ει δε μητε ἀδελφους, μητε παιδας ἀδελφων, ὡς ἐιρηκαμεν, ὁ τελευτησας καταλειψει, παντας τους ἐφεξης ἐκ πλαγιου συγγενεις προς την κληρονομιαν καλουμεν, κατα την ἑνος ἑκαςου βαθμου προτιμησιν, ἱνα ὁι ἐγγυτεροι τῳ βαθμῳ ἀυτοι των λοιπων προτιμωνται· ἐι δε πολλοι του ἀυτου βαθμου ἑυρεθωσι, κατα τον των προσωπων ἀριθμον μεταξυ ἀυτων ἡ κληρονομια διαιρεθησεται· ὁπερ in capita ὁι ἡμετεροι λεγουσι νομοι.

mus, ad hæreditatem vocantur; nullo modo ad ſucceſſionem ab inteſtato fratris aut ſororis filios vocari permittimus, neque ſi ex utroque parente eorum pater aut mater defuncto jungebatur. Quandoquidem igitur fratris et ſororis filiis tale privilegium dedimus, ut in propriorum parentum ſuccedentes locum, ſoli in tertio conſtituti gradu, cum iis, qui in ſecundo gradu ſunt, ad hæreditatem vocentur; illud palam eſt, quia thus defuncti maſculis et fœminis, ſive a patre ſive a matre, præponuntur, ſi etiam ille tertium cognationis ſimiliter obtineant gradum. Si vero neque fratres, neque filios fratrum, ſicut diximus, defunctus reliquerit, omnes deinceps a latere cognatos ad hæreditatem vocamus, ſecundum uniuscujuſque gradus prærogativam, ut viciniores gradu ipſi reliquis præponantur Si autem plurimi ejuſdem gradus inveniantur, ſecundum perſonarum numerum inter eos hæreditas dividatur quod *in capita* noſtræ leges appellant.

CHAPTER III.

Of the succession of collaterals.

If a man leaves neither descendents nor ascendents at the time of his death, we first call his brothers and sisters of the whole blood, whom we have also called to inherit with the fathers of deceased persons.

But, when there are no brothers of the whole blood with the deceased, we call those, who are either by the same father only, or by the same mother. And, if the deceased leaves brothers and also nephews by a deceased brother or sister, these nephews shall be called to succeed with their uncles and aunts of the whole blood to the deceased, but, however numerous these nephews are, they shall be intituled only to that share, which their parent would have taken, if alive. From whence it follows, that, if a man dies and is survived by the children of a deceased brother of the whole blood, and also by brothers of the half blood, then his nephews, [that is, the children of his brother, by the whole blood,] are to be prefered to their uncles and aunts, for, altho' such nephews are themselves in the 3d degree, yet they are prefered, as their parent would have been, if living. And on the contrary, if a man dies, and is survived by a brother of the whole blood, and by children of a brother of the half blood deceased, these nephews are excluded, as their father would have been, if he had lived. But among collaterals we allow the Privilege of representation to the sons and daughters of brothers and sisters, and no farther; and we grant it only to brothers and sisters children, when they concur with their uncles or aunts, paternal or maternal for, when ascendents are called to inherit, we by no means permit the children of a deceased brother or sister to share in the succession, altho' the father or mother was of the whole blood with the deceased brother But we have so far allowed the right of Representation to brothers and sisters children, that being only in the 3d degree, they are called to inherit with those, who are in the second and this is evident, because brothers and sisters children are prefered to the uncle and aunts of the deceased, paternal as well as maternal; altho' they are all in the 3d degree of cognation

But, if a deceased person leaves neither brothers nor brothers children, we then call all the other collaterals, according to the prerogative of their respective degrees, prefering the nearer to the more remote; and, if many are found in the same degree, the inheritance must be divided according to the number of persons, and our laws distinguish this manner of dividing an inheritance by calling it a division *in capita*.

Πρώτους πρὸς τὴν κλῆρον καλοῦμεν· Primos ad hæreditatem vocamus] We must here observe in relation to the distinction between the whole blood and the half blood, that in *England* the rules of law are different, according to the nature of the estate, which is to be taken, for, in case of lands the whole blood is always prefered, and *the half blood is no blood inheritable by descent* 1 Co inst 14 a But, in respect to personal estate, the law has not always been fixed and certain; inasmuch as the statute of the 23d of *Car* II [for *the better settlement of the estates of intestates*] takes no notice of this distinction between the whole blood and the half blood, but directs, that distribution shall be made among all those, who are in equal degree of kindred to the intestate But, it being certain, that brothers and sisters of the half blood are in the same degree with brothers

thers and sisters of the whole blood, it hath been the general opinion, that brothers and sisters of the half blood were intituled, by virtue of the statute, to an equal share of the intestate's estate, with the brothers and sisters of the whole blood, altho' there are several precedents of judgments given, since the statute, allowing the half blood to have but an half share But the law in this respect has been fully settled ever since the decree of the house of Lords in the case of *Watt's* and others vers *Crooke*, upon an appeal from a decree in chancery, which had been given in favor of the half blood, and was affirmed by the House. vid *Shower's* Cases in Par. 108. and *Strahan's* Domat 683

Οὐδὲν τρόπῳ. Nullo modo.] "Sancimus, ut, "si quis moriens relinquat ascendentium aliquem "et fratres, qui possint cum parentibus vocari, "et alterius præmortui fratris filios, cum ascen-"dentibus et fratribus vocentur etiam præmortui "fratris filii, et tantam accipiant portionem, "quantam eorum futurus erat pater accipere, si "vixisset." vid. Nov. CXXVII. cap 1.

FINIS.

INDEX RUBRICARUM,

Secundum librorum et titulorum

ORDINEM.

LIBER I

XXIV.

LIBER II.

LIBER III.

VIII.

INDEX RUBRICARUM.

LIBER IV.

XIII.

INDEX RUBRICARUM.

FINIS.

CPSIA information can be obtained at www.ICGtesting.com
Printed in the USA
LVOW11s2212280114

371328LV00018B/430/P